American Hymns Old and New

*Notes on the Hymns
and Biographies
of the Authors and Composers*

CHARLES W. HUGHES

New York   1980

COLUMBIA UNIVERSITY PRESS

Library of Congress Cataloging in Publication Data

Main entry under title:

American hymns old and new.

   With music.
   Bibliography: p.
   Includes index.
   CONTENTS: [v. 1.] The hymns.—[v. 2.] Notes on the
hymns and biographies of authors and composers.
   1. Hymns, English. I. Christ-Janer, Albert, 1910–
1973. II. Hughes, Charles William, 1900–
III. Smith, Carleton Sprague, 1905–
M2117.A573   783.9′52   79-4630
ISBN [v.1] 0-231-03458-X
      [v.2] 0-231-04934-X
      [set] 0-231-05148-4

Columbia University Press
New York   Guildford, Surrey

Contents

THIS BOOK is a companion volume to *American Hymns Old and New,* where will be found a generous selection of hymns with suitable tunes. If that book plays the role of a hymnal, or rather a history of the development of American religious song by examples, the companion volume is the handbook, containing information about the hymns and their authors and the tunes and their composers. The Notes on the hymns are arranged alphabetically by first line. They are followed by brief Biographies of authors and composers in one alphabetical series.

The headings on the left side of the Notes are unusually full, giving the first line of the text, sometimes the title, the numbers of the psalm verses or the stanzas included, and finally the name of the author and the publication date. In the early psalters faithfulness to the Hebrew original was zealously sought and it is quite simple to relate the metric to the prose versions. As these literal versions gave way to freer renditions we simply indicate the chosen stanzas, leaving it to the reader to trace their relation to the prose psalm.

The headings on the right side describe the music. For the tunes the name (where there is one) is followed by the meter, expressed by the usual abbreviations for the more familiar patterns, and by figures for those less frequently employed. Thus S.M. (or short meter) indicates a four line stanza with six syllables to the line except for line three which has eight, C.M. (or common meter) also has four line stanzas but the pattern is 8.6.8.6. In the old books "peculiar meter" was reserved for hymns which fitted none of the usual patterns. To a modern ear this sounds slightly invidious, and we have followed recent practice by using the term "irregular."

If a melody is a chorale or chorale-derived we give a number to facilitate reference to Johannes Zahn's monumental work on the Lutheran chorale, *Die Melodien der deutschen evangelischen Kirchenlieder.* In a similar fashion we give references for tunes included in Maurice Frost's *English & Scottish Psalm & Hymn Tunes c. 1543–1677.* Regrettably there is no equally inclusive work on English and Scottish tunes in the eighteenth century. The name of the composer and the date of publication, or the date of composition followed by the date of publication, complete the music heading. In the case of traditional or folk tunes the given name is that of the collector or arranger. Many of these tunes were sung long before they were notated, printed, or arranged.

That this abundant documentation carries with it a corresponding risk of error is only too true, but it is hoped that it will be useful to the reader. Perhaps a few remarks concerning hymn tune names may illustrate the kinds of problems which had to be solved for each item. The same tune name was often given (unwittingly) to two or more different tunes. For example, only one tune called VERMONT is included in our collection but it is quite simple to point to others. We do include two different tunes, each called CHARITY. There are even cases where a single composer used the same tune name twice, evidently forgetting that he had used it before. And, there are many instances where the same tune has been known by different names. For example, a tune by the American pianist-composer Louis Moreau Gottschalk, is sometimes called by his surname and sometimes MERCY. Variations in hymn titles or first lines also lurk to trip the hymnbook editor. "Happy, Saviour, Would I Be" or "Saviour, Happy I Would Be" and "Weeping Sinner, Dry Your Eyes" or "Weeping Sinner, Dry Your Tears" were among the questions to be settled. Such are our headings.

Since our readers may turn to the Notes seeking information either about the text or the music, it seemed that it would be helpful to establish a regular pattern in each. After the heading there is a brief discussion of the hymn text, then of the tune. At the end are placed details about editorial emendations and for the older tunes a listing of the original clefs, a statement as to which voice sings the principal melody, the original time signature, any reduction of note values and, for all tunes which have been transposed, the original key or the interval of transposition. This portion will not be useful to readers without musical training, but it will help the musician to understand how the music was notated and how it has been edited. We have described any important variants in the text, and in instances where the music is changed we have given the details in the appropriate Note.

Changes in hymns and in their music have often been attempts at improvement, and some of them have been widely accepted as such. Francis Rous' metrical paraphrase of the psalms, for example, was first published under his own name, but before it was approved for use in the Scottish churches, it was repeatedly revised. The form in which it was approved contained lines taken from ten different sources (including Rous himself)! The modern reader is likely to be aghast at such a piecemeal method, yet the result justified the method, even if not all the authors whose lines were appropriated were happy about it. Changes were frequently made to bring a desirable hymn into harmony with the beliefs of a particular editor. Sometimes the attempt was simply to express in a more felicitous fashion what the author had said.

Psalm and hymn tunes were equally variable. The reader who turns to our selections from Henry Ainsworth's version of the psalms will note that the meters which he employs often differ from those in the French psalter, yet he is quite ready to borrow and alter the appropriate French tune. We sometimes think of folk songs as being fixed when they are written down, yet really all that is fixed is that particular performance by a particular singer. If the song continues in use not only that singer, but all the others will continue to produce variants as they sing. This is also true of hymns which, long after their first appearance in print, reappear with variations. Even when the melody remains stable, the harmonization may vary. Such changes are more usually the work of later music editors, but there are instances where the composer reharmonized his own tune. In Lowell Mason's *The Hallelujah* he not only reprints his well-known MISSIONARY HYMN but also offers two other harmonizations of the same tune, which he regards as improvements. American tunes of the last century often seem oversimple if not insipid in harmony to later editors and therefore are likely to be reharmonized. Thus, in returning to the original edition, and this we have tried to do, we do not necessarily claim that it is better, but we do establish a starting point and we give the harmony regarded as appropriate by the composer.

The Biographies which follow the Notes do not constitute a biographical dictionary but, since we concentrate not on hymn writers in general but on American hymn writers, not on composers of religious music but on American composers of hymn tunes, we are able to cover a more limited field with reasonable thoroughness. We have tried to shape our biographies in terms of our special interests. John Wesley is important to us as a missionary in Georgia and as the compiler of the historic Charleston hymnal of 1737. Our justification for including John Quincy Adams is the fact that he wrote a metrical version of the psalms. At the close of a hymn writer's biography, we give those hymns by that author included in *American Hymns Old and New.* For the composers we not only add the names of their tunes, but also the first lines of the texts associated with those tunes. This should facilitate reference to the appropriate entry since the Notes are arranged according to the first line of the hymn.

In the Biographies there have been many occasions when a decision between conflicting dates or facts had to be made. Even John Julian, who might well be called the patron saint of hymnology, occasionally nodded. Thus, in his *Dictionary of Hymnology,* George Richards, an early Universalist preacher and hymn writer, is said to have settled in Portsmouth, New Haven instead of Portsmouth, New Hampshire. Anna Warner was well known in her own period as a writer, yet her year of birth has been variously stated as 1820, c.1822, and 1827. Three respectable sources agree that Harriet Beecher Stowe was born in Litchfield, Conn., in the month of June.

Two state that the year was 1812, one that it was 1811. Two give the day of the month as the fourteenth and the third as the fifteenth. If this can be true of the author of *Uncle Tom's Cabin,* what can we expect for more obscure figures? Yet on the whole American hymn writers and their hymns are better documented than the tunes to which they were sung.

The tune JOYFULLY, JOYFULLY by Abraham Down Merrill was much used in its period. Its date has been given as 1845, a date we have accepted. Is this the date of publication? If so, in what was it published? No one seems to know. Over a long period we sent queries concerning the first appearance of hymn tunes to the late Rev. Charles L. Atkins, whose index of over a thousand American hymnals gave him an incomparable insight into the field. He would send back requested dates with the notation "the earliest I have." As a careful scholar he knew that there might be an earlier hymnal containing that particular hymn which he had not seen.

Where a popular collection of tunes was repeatedly republished, like Lowell Mason's *The Boston Handel and Haydn Society Collection of Church Music,* less popular tunes might be dropped and others added. Thus, even after it was clear that a tune had appeared in this particular collection, it still might be necessary to advance from the front and the rear, pushing back the dates of editions in which it did appear and pushing forward with the editions in which it was missing, until the critical point was reached. This task was not made easier by the fact that no library available to us possessed all eighteen editions.

Here it would be well to insert a word of appreciation to Donna Walsh, who copyedited the manuscript of the present volume and coped with all its challenges. Her searching queries were most helpful in clarifying the text and making it more consistent.

In *American Hymns Old and New* are gathered a selection of the hymns and tunes sung by Americans over a span of four centuries. In the final section of the companion volume are the lives of those who wrote the hymns and composed the tunes, the famous and the obscure, the well remembered and the almost forgotten, learned divines and distinguished authors, gifted composers and noted organists, rural versifiers, country singing masters, wandering camp meeting preachers, and forgotten black singers, people as various as our nation, but each contributing in some way or other to American religious song.

Charles W. Hughes
Thetford Center, Vermont

March 1980

AMERICAN HYMNS OLD AND NEW

Notes on the Hymns
and Biographies
of the Authors and Composers

NOTES ON THE HYMNS

Abide in Me, O Lord, and I   CUBA 10.10.10.10.
  in Thee
St. 1 (new), 2, 3, 5, 6
Harriet Beecher Stowe, 1855   Anon., 1853

The complete form of this hymn, with the first line "That mystic word of thine, O Sovereign Lord," appeared in the *Plymouth Collection* (1855), compiled for Henry Ward Beecher's Brooklyn church. Two shortened versions have come into use: one beginning with the second stanza, "Abide in me; o'er shadow by thy love," and the one given here. Stanza 1 is new, with the first line "Abide in me, O Lord, and I in Thee." Then follow stanzas 2, 3, 5, and 6. This form, with some alterations, has persisted into the twentieth century in the *Pilgrim Hymnal* of 1912 and in at least three other hymnals.

In the *Plymouth Collection* this text is one of a group to be sung to REST ("When Winds Are Raging") (q.v.). We have set it to CUBA, which appeared in George Kingsley's *Templi Carmina* (Northampton, Mass., 1853) and was later reprinted in the *Plymouth Collection*.

Abide Not in the Realm of   EAST HAYES L.M.
  Dreams
St. 1: lines 1, 2; st. 2: lines 3,
  4; st. 4, 6, 7, 10
William Henry Burleigh,   Thomas Comer, 1840
  1871

The complete poem in ten stanzas may be found in William Henry Burleigh's *Poems* (1871) and in Alfred P. Putnam's *Singers and Songs of the Liberal Faith* (1875). As a hymn it consisted of a composite first stanza made of lines 1 and 2 of stanza 1, followed by lines 3 and 4 of stanza 2 and then stanzas 4, 6, 7, and 10. In this form it appeared in the Unitarian *Hymn and Tune Book* of 1877 (except that stanza 6 is omitted) and its successors of 1914, 1937, and 1958.

It has generally been sung to Hatton's fine English tune DUKE STREET. EAST HAYES, the tune used here, was composed by Thomas Comer and was one of a number of original tunes published in *The Boston Musical Institute's Collection of Church Music* (1840), a collection intended for Unitarian use.

Ach Kinder, wollt ihr lieben?   IHR SÜNDER KOMMT GEGAN-
O Children, Would You   GEN 7.6.7.6.6.6.7.6.
   Cherish?
St. 1, 9, 11, 13
Christopher Dock, after 1764   Anon.
Samuel W. Pennypacker,
   trans. 1883

This is the second of the two hymns by Christopher Dock included in the *Geistliches Magazien* with the heading, "Ein ander Geistlich Lied von selbigem Autor" ("Another Spiritual Song by the Same Author"). Both hymns reveal the Mennonite schoolteacher's love for children and his interest in their welfare. The English translation is by Samuel W. Pennypacker, who published an informative essay on Dock in his *Historical and Biographical Sketches* (Philadelphia, 1883).

Dock himself said of the role of music in his teaching: "But the freedom has been given to me, in singing, to sing hymns and psalms. So I have then sung with them both hymns and psalms." Presumably "Ach Kinder, wollt ihr lieben?" was among the songs sung at the little schoolhouse on the Skippack.

Dock printed only the melody in uniform whole notes. Since no contemporary version with continuo has been found, the bass as well as the inner parts are editorial additions. Dock wrote his melody in F major, though the B♭ is missing in the original imprint; transposed up a major sixth.

Again as Evening's Shadow   SELENA L.M.
   Falls
St. 1–4
Samuel Longfellow, 1859   Isaac B. Woodbury, 1850

"Again as Evening Shadows Fall," which Henry Wilder Foote, in *Three Centuries of American Hymnody,* calls one of the most beautiful evening hymns in our language, was published in *Vespers* (1859).

SELENA was first published in Woodbury's *Dulcimer* (1850) without Woodbury's name. Later sources, such as *The Sacred Lute* by T. E. Perkins (1864), attribute it to Woodbury. The tune is intended either for L.M. or L.M. 6 lines depending on whether the first part is repeated.

Ah! Lovely Appearance of STOCKHOLM L.M.D.
  Death!
St. 1–3, 7, 11, 12
Charles Wesley, 1746 Jacob Kimball, 1793

American sources persistently attribute this poem to George Whitefield. The belief that death should be regarded with delight as the gateway to a happier world has hardly been expressed in a more extreme form than here. It cannot be omitted in an anthology that presents the religious songs sung by the American people. Not only was it circulated in the form of broadsides and included in many hymnbooks, but it was also repeatedly set by American composers.

William Billings printed the text in his *The New England Psalm Singer* (1770) and indicated BROOKFIELD, WESTFIELD, and MARSH-FIELD as suitable tunes. He set still another tune, SAVANNAH, to this text in the *Singing Master's Assistant* (1778). Jacob Kimball associated "Ah! Lovely Appearance of Death!" with STOCKHOLM in his *Rural Harmony* of 1793. Taken up by country singers, this poem persisted to the twentieth century. John and Alan Lomax recorded a folk version in 1937 in Clay County, Kentucky (*Our Singing Country*, pp. 38–39).

The first notes in the upper parts, bars 2 and 3, were written as long appoggiaturas in the form of eighth notes. In both instances they are interpreted as notes with half the value of the principal notes. This tune is an attempt to write in the fluent three-voice style of the eighteenth century. From that point of view the setting is marred by parallel and near parallel octaves (bars 4, 10–11, 22). The simplest way of adjusting bar 4 would be to let the medius sing F on the last beat of bar 3 and on the first beat of bar 4. The other passages have been altered.

Alleluia! Christ Is Risen 9.11.9.11.D., with chorus
  Today
St. 1–5
John Henry Hopkins Jr., John Henry Hopkins Jr.,
  1863 1863

Hopkins liked to punctuate or close his carols with joyful exclamations, "Hosannah" or "Alleluia." In the Easter carol, "Alleluia! Christ Is Risen Today," the folklike unison melody begins in E minor, followed by a choral Alleluia. The melody returns, transposed to G major and with a modified close, leading to a recurrence of the refrain in major. The musical plan is simple but well-suited to a song celebrating Christ's resurrection. Music and words appeared without date in Hopkins' collected *Carols, Hymns, and Songs* (1863). It is presented here as a less well-known counterpart to his familiar Christmas carol "We Three Kings of Orient Are" (q.v.).

All-Knowing God, 'Tis Thine To Know LANG L.M.

St. 1–5
Anon., 1783 James Hewitt, 1812

This plea for tolerance appeared in the *Collection of Hymns, more particularly designed for the Use of the West Society in Boston.* (In his *American Unitarian Hymn Writers and Hymns* Henry Wilder Foote gives the date as 1782.) It has been chosen to represent our earliest Unitarian hymnbook. No author is named, and it is presumably among the hymns of local origin included in this volume.

Although Hewitt is better known for his ballad operas and for program music like the *Battle of Trenton,* he published *Harmonia Sacra* in 1812. It included LANG, which combines a vigorous tune with simple tonal harmonies that seem to go astray in bars 2 and 6. These have been altered without changing the tune itself.

All Praise to Thee DEED 10.10.10.4.

St. 1–5
F. Bland Tucker, writ. 1938, Daniel Gregory Mason, comp.
   pub. 1940 1927, pub. 1928

Tucker's hymn is based on a passage from Philippeans (2:5–11) praising Christ for assuming human form.

The tune SINE NOMINE by the late English composer Ralph Vaughan Williams was the model on which the somewhat unusual metric structure of F. Bland Tucker's poem was formed. However, when it was printed in *The Hymnal 1940* the given tune was ENGELBERG by Charles Villiers Stanford. Here the preference has been given to DEED by the American composer and educator Daniel Gregory Mason. Composed for H. Augustine Smith's *American Student Hymnal* of 1928 it appeared there as a setting of John Drinkwater's "Grant Us the Will to Fashion as We Feel."

All That I Am
Verna Arvey, writ. 1955   William Grant Still, comp.
                                       1955

This hymn, which attributes all good gifts to God, was composed
for *American Hymns* by William Grant Still to a text by his wife, Verna
Arvey, who also wrote song lyrics and ballet scenarios for him. The
music exists in two versions: one with piano accompaniment; the
other, printed here, for voices without any accompaniment. It is in
ternary form. The contrasting section begins with the words "You
are the source of light" and the opening phrase returns at the end.
The setting is largely note against note and somewhat chantlike—a
chord to a syllable, with many repeated harmonies. It is well suited
to performance by a vocal quartet or by a choir.

All the Past We Leave Behind   PAUMANOK 7.8.8.8.7.7.
St. 1–4
Walt Whitman, 1882   Philip James, cop. 1964

The buoyant and optimistic lines of Walt Whitman have to only a
limited degree been considered suitable for hymns in the twentieth
century; an English hymnbook set the example. "All the Past We
Leave Behind" is a cento from *Leaves of Grass* (1st ed., 1855; but the
cento was based on the 1882 ed.). The arrangement of lines has
been made with the utmost freedom. The original first line was
"Come my tan-faced children"; the present opening is line 1 of
stanza 5. The first stanza is made of stanza 5, line 1; stanza 4, line 3;
stanza 6, line 3; followed by the refrain "Pioneers! O Pioneers!" This
cento was published in the Anglican *Songs of Praise* with a tune composed for it by Martin Shaw and republished in H. Augustine
Smith's *American Student Hymnal* of 1928. Since then Irving Lowens
and Philip James have written tunes for it. PAUMANOK was copyrighted in 1964 and first published as a single sheet.

Almighty God in Being Was   SOLEMNITY C.M.D.
St. 1, 3, 4–9
Silas Ballou, 1785   Eliakim Doolittle, 1798

Silas Ballou was the earliest of the three members of the Ballou
family who contributed to Universalist hymnology. Indeed, he was
the second American hymn writer of that denomination and the first

to be born in this country. (John Murray, the author of five hymns included in the Portsmouth, N.H., edition of James Relly's *Christian Hymns, Poems, and Sacred Songs,* was a convert of Relly's in England before coming to this country.) "Almighty God in Being Was," a rhymed account of the days of creation as related in Genesis, was first published in *New Hymns on Various Subjects.*

A tune from northern New England seemed appropriate to a poet who lived in Vermont. SOLEMNITY is by Eliakim Doolittle, who spent his later years in Pawlett, Vt. It is given here as printed in Asahel Benham's *Social Harmony* of 1798.

Time signature $\supset$; tune in tenor.

Almighty God, Thy Constant   ROLLAND 8.8.8.8.8.
  Care
St. 1–4
Henry S. Washburn, writ.   William Batchelder Brad-
  1841, pub. 1843   bury, 1851

"Almighty God, Thy Constant Care," written for the dedication of the Harvard Street Baptist Church in Boston (1841), was published in 1843 in *The Psalmist,* edited by Samuel Francis Smith and Baron Stowe. We tend to associate Bradbury with rollicking Sunday-School tunes or with such folklike melodies as SHINING SHORE. ROLLAND is both more severe and more churchlike in style. It is reproduced here from *Psalmista; or, Choir Melodies* (1851), by Bradbury and Thomas Hastings. The rhythmic pattern—|∪∪--|∪∪--|—also characterizes such familiar tunes as old WINDHAM and Lowell Mason's HEBRON.

Almighty Lord, with One   PATTEN C.M.
  Accord
St. 1–4
Melancthon W. Stryker, 1896   Peter C. Lutkin, cop. 1902

Since Stryker was president of Hamilton College and editor of *The College Hymnal* (1896), it is appropriate that his best remembered hymn should have been written for students. "Almighty Lord, with One Accord" was included in the Methodist *Hymnal* (1905) to PATTEN by Peter C. Lutkin. The vigorous unisons which open both halves of the tune are well suited to a hymn for youth.

Almighty Sovereign of the Skies!	PSALM 97
St. 1, 3–5, 8	
Nathan Strong, 1799	William Tuckey, 1761

"Almighty Sovereign of the Skies!" appeared in *The Hartford Selection of Hymns*. Designated as a hymn for national thanksgiving, it has been set to William Tuckey's PSALM 97, a tune popular in the early nineteenth century. This tune was made from the second section of an anthem with the same title published in *Urania* (1761) by James Lyon. The opening of the tune, originally for tenor and bass, has been amplified by the addition of a soprano part in *Village Harmony* (14th ed., 1817), and in the *Bridgewater Collection* (ed. of 1818) it is for four voices. Our version follows that in *Village Harmony*. However the only other differences between the tune and the anthem are a turn for the soprano (over the B♭, bar 7) and a B♮ for the soprano in bar 12.

Th'Almighty Spake, and Gabriel Sped	ABERDEEN 8.6.8.8.6.
St. 1, 3, 4, 6	
George Richards, 1792	Oliver Holden, 1793

Our text by George Richards appeared in *The Universalist Hymn Book: Psalms, Hymns, and Spiritual Songs*. Oliver Holden published it in his *Union Harmony* with the tune ABERDEEN, which is marked "Original" and hence presumably composed by Holden himself. However, the same text had already been set under the name CHRISTMAS in Samuel Holyoke's *Harmonia Americana* of 1791. This earlier setting was a short anthem rather than a hymn tune.

Countertenor, C clef, third line. Time signature Ɔ; tune in tenor; transposed down a minor third.

Almost Persuaded	ALMOST PERSUADED
St. 1–3	9.9.6.6.6.4.
Philip Bliss, 1871	Philip Bliss, 1871

Philip Bliss, at a service in Chicago conducted by an evangelist named Brundage, heard the preacher speak of Paul's trial before Agrippa, using as his text "Almost thou persuadest me to be a Christian" (Acts 26:28). The evangelist concluded, "He who is almost per-

suaded is almost saved, and to be almost saved is to be entirely lost."
"Almost Persuaded," written as a result of this experience, was first
published in *The Charn* in 1871. Simplicity could hardly be carried
further than in this melody. Four notes suffice for the earlier part,
and when the fifth arrives on the word "go" it produces a climax.

Along the Banks	DESOLATION 10.10.10.10.
Ps. 137, st. 1–6	
Joel Barlow, 1785	Stephen Jenks, 1791

Isaac Watts purposely omitted the imprecatory psalms from his
paraphrases. Thus Psalm 137 with its beautiful and moving opening
lines was left for later versifiers like the Connecticut poet Joel Barlow, whose version appeared in 1785. Barlow endeavored to "correct
and enlarge Watts." His attempt was severely criticized in a day
when Watts was regarded as sacrosanct.

"Along the Banks" was set by Asahel Benham as BABYLON (Oliver
Bronson's *Select Harmony,* 1783), by Lewis Edson as CAPTIVITY (*Social
Harmonist,* 2d ed., 1801), by Alexander Gillet as BABYLON (Andrew
Law's *Rudiments of Music,* 1785), and by Samuel Holyoke as MENDON
(*Colombian Repository,* 1802). Jenks's setting, reproduced here, is a
somber plain tune in the Aeolian mode. A later setting of the same
text in the Southern tradition is Elkanah Kelsey Dare's BABYLONIAN
CAPTIVITY.

Countertenor, G clef, second line, an octave too high. Time signature Ɔ ; tune in tenor; transposed down one step.

Als Ik Des Herren Werk	FORTUNE MY FOE 6.6.6.6.D.
When I Admire the Greatness	
St. 1, 4, 8	
Jacob Steendam, 1650	Adrianus Valerius, arr. 1621

Jacob Steendam's *Den Distelfink (The Goldfinch)* is of interest to us
not only for the religious verse it contains but also because suitable
tunes are named to which the poems may be sung. Among the tunes
are at least two of English origin: MALL SIMMS and the English FOR-
TUNE (ENGELESCHE FORTUYN). Not only was the latter used for Steendam's "Als ik des Herren Werk" in the third part of *Den Distelfink,*
but it had also been used for a love song in part one. Its popularity
on the continent was also shown by its use by Samuel Scheidt of
Halle as the theme for a set of organ variations. The version for lute

and voice given here was transcribed from the *Nederlandsche Gedenck-clanck* of Valerius.

Amazing Sight! The Saviour Stands   NEWMARK C.M.
St. 1–4
Henry Alline, 1785   Amos Bull, 1795

At least four editions of Henry Alline's *Hymns and Spiritual Songs* were printed. "Amazing Sight!" was later included in the widely circulated *Village Hymns* (1824) of Asahel Nettleton. In that volume CLARENDON and NEWMARK were assigned to Alline's text. NEWMARK has been preferred here. It appeared first in Amos Bull's *The Responsary,* where it was starred to indicate that it was a new tune. It was reprinted by William Little and William Smith in *The Easy Instructor* (1813, perhaps earlier), where the index named Bull as the composer.

Bull's collection was notable because it marked a break with the older practice of using counters (countertenors) for the second part. Indeed, Bull's title page states that the collection was "Set with Second Trebles, instead of Counters." The treble and countertenor parts are characterized by triplets in quarter notes, a trait which also characterizes Timothy Swan's CHINA (q.v.).

Ancient of Days, Who Sittest Throned in Glory   ANCIENT OF DAYS
                                          11.10.11.10.
St. 1–5
William Croswell Doane, writ.   J. Albert Jeffery, comp. 1886,
  1886, pub. 1892   pub. 1892

This hymn was written by the Protestant Episcopal Bishop of Albany, N.Y., to celebrate the bicentennial of that city in 1886. There is also an altered version beginning "O Holy Father, Who hast led Thy children," which is the first line of the original second stanza. Its marching rhythm was stressed by the amplified accompaniment for organ provided by the composer. The tune was first called ALBANY.

And Canst Thou, Sinner,   STATE STREET S.M.
  Slight
St. 1–4
Abby Bradley Hyde, 1824   Jonathan C. Woodman, 1844

"And Canst Thou, Sinner, Slight" is one of a group of nine hymns by Mrs. Hyde included in Asahel Nettleton's *Village Hymns* of 1824. It was based on Ephesians 4:30, "And grieve not the Holy Spirit of God, whereby ye are sealed unto the day of redemption."

The tunes indicated in Nettleton are SHIRLAND by Samuel Stanley and ST. THOMAS by Aaron Williams. Both are English, although ST. THOMAS was so persistently used here that it may almost be considered as naturalized. Those who wish to sing this tune will find it with Timothy Dwight's "I love thy kingdom, Lord." Here we have preferred one by an American. Jonathan C. Woodman wrote other tunes, but he is best remembered by one, STATE STREET, which appeared in *The Musical Casket* (1858), a collection compiled by the composer.

And Have the Bright   TREGARON C.M.D.
  Immensities
St. 1, 2
Howard Chandler Robbins,   Philip James, 1941
  1931

This hymn, which speaks of the ancient mysteries of the heavens in the language of both science and religion, was published in *The Living Church* in 1931, then in the author's *Way of Light* (1933). In 1937 it was republished in *The New Church Hymnal* of H. Augustine Smith.

In *The Hymnal 1940* this poem was associated with TREGARON by the American composer Philip James. Tregaron is the place where the composer's grandfather was born.

And the Cock Begins to Crow
St. 1–4
Richard K. Avery, cop. 1970   Donald S. Marsh, cop. 1970

This rhymed account of Peter's denial of Christ (Luke 22:31–34 and 54–62) was published in *More, More, More*. Like Joseph Wise's "Glory" (q.v.), it is for voices with a guitar accompaniment indicated by letters above the voice part. It begins with the chorus which includes a passage suggesting the cock crow. The longer verse section that follows is punctuated by the refrain line "Poor, poor, Peter!"

And Truly It Is a Most Glorious Thing	SONG 24 10.10.10.D.
Selected couplets	Frost 360
William Bradford, 1623	Orlando Gibbons, 1623

In spite of the demands of his office as governor of Plymouth, William Bradford found time to write three extended poems: "Some Observations of God's Merciful Dealing," "A Word to New Plymouth," and "A Word to New England." The "Epitaphium Meum," his only published poem, was included in Nathaniel Morton's *New England's Memoriall* (Cambridge, Mass., 1669). Since none of these poems could well be sung as a whole, some of the more lyric lines from "Some Observations of God's Merciful Dealing" have been arranged as a cento and set to SONG 24, one of the sixteen tunes by Orlando Gibbons published with George Wither's *Hymns and Songs of the Church.* The inner parts are editorial additions.

Angel of Peace, Thou Hast Wandered Too Long	AMERICAN HYMN 10.10.10.10.D.
St. 1–3	
Oliver Wendell Holmes, 1869	Matthias Keller, 1866

Oliver Wendell Holmes wrote his poem for AMERICAN HYMN by Matthias Keller, who had composed it for his own text, "Speed Our Republic, O Father on High." Text and music were published together with other choral numbers in *Music To Be Performed at the Grand National Peace Jubilee* (Boston, 1869). The version of AMERICAN HYMN given here is adapted from this publication. It was sung with orchestral accompaniment, omitted here save for an indication of the instrumental figures which bridge the cadences. The final phrase of the hymn was repeated by the orchestra as interlude or postlude.

The Angels Sung a Carol	Song 4 10.10.10.D.
St. 1, 6–9	Frost 352
Edward Taylor, 1712	Orlando Gibbons, 1623

At the beginning of "Meditation One Hundred and Ten" is a quotation from Matthew 26:30: "And when they had sung an hymn, they went out into the Mount of Olives." Taylor expresses the idea of self-surrender to God in musical imagery. He thinks of his heart as a pipe, a golden trumpet, or a cittern to sound forth His praises.

The tune chosen here is Song 4 by Orlando Gibbons, originally published as the setting for George Wither's version of Psalm 21 in *Hymnes and Songs of the Church* (London, 1623). Taylor often leaves the sense incomplete at the end of a line and in these instances the singer must sustain the phrase into the following line.

The original is for melody and bass only; the middle parts are editorial additions.

Arise and See the Glorious Sun	Philadelphia C.M.
St. 1, 3, 7, 9–11	
Francis Hopkinson, 1792	Francis Hopkinson, 1816

Two morning hymns are included in Francis Hopkinson's *Miscellaneous Essays and Occasional Writings* (1792). We have preferred "Arise and See the Glorious Sun" to "Once More the Rising Source of Day." Among the stanzas omitted in this hymn is the fifth, written in a somewhat "Gothic" spirit.

> Loud shrieks the melancholy owl,
> And prowling wolves thro' deserts howl;
> The fancied spectre glides the green,
> And midnight murder walks unseen.

Since Hopkinson was a composer as well as a poet, we have set his verses to Philadelphia, the most popular of his psalm tunes. Our version comes from *A Collection of Chants & Tunes for the Use of the Episcopal Church in the City of Philadelphia*, edited by "B. Carr, Organist of St. Peter's Church." This version is for soprano, tenor, and bass, with organ accompaniment.

The tenor part was originally the top line of the score. We have compressed the score by moving the tenor to its usual location above the bass. The small notes under the soprano part are intended for the organist, who thus needs to play only these parts and the bass.

Arise, My Soul! With Rapture   HEREFORD L.M.D.
   Rise!

St. 1–5

Samuel J. Smith, 1792   Henry Purcell, 1809

This morning hymn by a New Jersey Quaker was No. 46 in *A Selection of Psalms, with Occasional Hymns,* edited by two Episcopal clergymen of Charleston: Robert Smith, Rector of St. Philip's Church, and Henry Purcell, Rector of St. Michael's Church. This rare and historically important volume was reissued in facsimile (1956) by the Dalcho Historical Society of the Diocese of South Carolina.

Purcell was represented in Jacob Eckhard's *Choirmaster's Book,* which contained tunes designed for the 1792 hymnal. HEREFORD has been chosen as the melody for Smith's text. (It was originally intended for a metrical version of Psalm 23.) The florid character of the tune is well suited to the jubilant text. Since the tune is a double one, two stanzas of text are sung to each repetition of the tune.

Original for melody and figured continuo; inner parts added. The first melody notes in bars 4, 8, 20, and 24 were written as long appoggiaturas in the form of quarter notes. They are realized here as half notes in each instance. In bar 12 the appoggiatura is treated as a whole note. The melody in bar 21 originally read C E D F E G in quarter notes, producing octaves with the bass from beat one to beat two. The last bass note in bar 30 was C, the first in bar 31, F, making octaves with the soprano. Both passages have been altered. The fifth stanza may be sung to the second half of the tune or, if it seems desirable to repeat the whole tune, the fifth stanza may be sung to the first part of the tune and stanza one to the second.

Arise, O Glorious Zion   ARISE, O GLORIOUS ZION
                                     7.6.7.6.D.

St. 1–4

William G. Mills, 1851   George Careless, 1889

Many tunes used by the Latter-day Saints were borrowed but the earlier tunes composed for them were largely the work of English converts trained in music. George Careless, one of these converts, was active not only in developing choral singing, but also as editor and tune composer. ARISE, O GLORIOUS ZION, was first published in *Sacred Hymns and Spiritual Songs* (1851). Careless contributed a text, "The Lord Imparted from Above," and several tunes to *The Latter-day Saints' Psalmody* (1889), which he compiled with E. Beesley, J. J. Daynes, E. Stevens, and T. C. Griggs.

Arise, Ye Saints of Latter Days	MERIBAH 8.8.6.8.8.6.
St. 1–5	
Anon., 1845	Lowell Mason, 1839

This text comes from a Mormon hymnal, edited by Charles A. Adams and printed in Bellows Falls, Vt., in 1845. The editor points out that the church "as it were, is still in its infancy," and hopes that the collection "may answer every purpose till more [hymns] are composed." Hymn 103 is in honor of Joseph Smith, the Mormon prophet, who was born in Sharon, Vt. Hymn 104, headed "Written in Prison," is a bitter complaint against Missouri, where the author was imprisoned, and an appeal to the Saints to flee to Illinois where "the eagle's bold wing is stretched o'er a people determined and free."

No tunes are named in this little volume, but the Mormons are known to have used a variety of melodies, secular as well as sacred, for their hymns. We have chosen Lowell Mason's MERIBAH as a suitable tune. Published in the February 1839 issue of *The Seraph,* it was also included in Mason's *The Modern Psalmist,* which appeared in the same year. The same tune has also been set to "Jesus Enthroned and Glorified."

As Down a Lone Valley	MURILLO'S LESSON 11.11.11.11.D.
St. 1, 2	
Timothy Dwight, bet. 1777 and 1783	Morelli, 1820

This strange union of a brisk fifer's tune by an obscure worthy called Morelli and balladlike verses that may be by Timothy Dwight pleased Southern singers. Dwight may have written his poem during the period when he was an army chaplain.

The tune is called "Morelli's Lesson" in Alvan Robinson's *Massachusetts Collection of Martial Musick* but, in the 1850 edition of *The Sacred Harp,* it has become MURILLO'S LESSON. Tune in tenor; transposed down a whole step.

As Flows the Rapid River	PASSAIC 7.6.7.6.D.
St. 1–3	
Samuel Francis Smith, 1833	William Batchelder Bradbury, 1851

This hymn first appeared in the *Christian Psalmody* in 1833 and was reprinted in *Hymns for the Vestry and Fireside* (Boston, 1841), edited by Rev. Sewall S. Cutting. When Smith, with Baron Stowe, edited *The Psalmist: A New Collection of Hymns,* in 1843, "As Flows the Rapid River" was included. The comparison of human life to the course of a river passing finally into the great sea has a certain analogy to the theme of Tennyson's "Crossing the Bar." The artists of the period were also devoted to allegorical paintings in which life was depicted as a voyage.

PASSAIC appeared in *Psalmista, or Choir Melodies* (1851), edited jointly by Thomas Hastings and Bradbury.

As Gentle Dews Distill	WATKINS S.M.
St. 1, 2	
George Rogers, 1845	Thomas Whittemore, 1841

"As Gentle Dews Distill" was one of twenty-six original hymns which Rogers included in his *Universalist Hymn Book* of 1845. Four of these, including the present hymn, were retained in a later Universalist collection, *Church Harmonies: New and Old* (1895). We have associated this text with Thomas Whittemore's WATKIN from *The Gospel Harmonist,* a tune book intended for Universalist use.

As I Went Down to David's Town	THE SHEPHERDS Irregular
St. 1–6	
George Craig Stewart, 1934	Leo Sowerby, comp. 1956

This Christmas song, with the subtitle "A Christmas Ballad," retells the story of the shepherds who went to Bethlehem seeking the newborn Christ-child. The setting by Sowerby has the animation and the festive mood which is suitable to its subject. The composer has taken special pains to adjust his setting to the varying number of syllables in the different stanzas of the poem and the prudent choir director will need to take equal pains to ensure that his singers can follow these indications.

As Shadows Cast by Cloud   Sydney C.M.
  and Sun
St. 1–4
William Cullen Bryant, writ.   Henry Kemble Oliver, comp.
  1874, pub. 1877   1858, pub. 1875

This hymn was written for the Semi-Centennial Celebration of the Church of the Messiah in Boston, March 19, 1875. Published in the *Hymnal* of the Methodist Episcopal Church (1878), as Julian notes, it appeared earlier in the Unitarian *Hymn and Tune Book* of 1877. The date of composition given there is 1874.

Bryant's hymn has been set here to Sydney by Henry Kemble Oliver, composed in 1858 and included in his *Original Hymn Tunes* of 1875. The setting has been transposed down one step.

As Spring the Winter Doth   Psalm 9 L.M.
  Succeed
St. 1–4   Frost 373
Anne Bradstreet, writ. 1657   Henry Lawes, 1638

Anne Bradstreet had a strong feeling for the beauty of nature which was closely associated with her belief in the immanence of God. She believed implicitly in His grace and wrote on one occasion: "I have had great experience of God's hearing my Prayers, and returning comfortable Answers to me, either in granting ye Thing I prayed for, or else in satisfying my mind without it."

The tune, by Henry Lawes, was first published in 1638 for George Sandys' *Paraphrase upon the Divine Poems.* A later edition appeared in 1676. This simple tune, which was originally used to the text "Thee will I praise with Heart and Voice," is admirably suited for private devotion. The opening phrase of Lawes's tune reappears in William Croft's familiar St. Anne (a tune which is often sung to "Our God, our help in ages past").

Melody, C clef, first line; unfigured bass, F clef, fourth line. Time signature ¢ ; note values reduced by half. The inner parts have been added to the original melody and bass.

As Tranquil Streams   Grace L.M.
St. 1–5
Marion Franklin Ham, writ.   Charles L. Ziegler, 1902
  1933, pub. 1937

Although Ham began writing poetry as early as 1888 and hymns from 1911, his real influence on hymn singing began with the inclusion of four of his hymns in the Unitarian *New Hymn and Tune Book* of 1914. Of this earlier group "O Thou Whose Gracious Presence Shone" and "Touch Thou Mine Eyes" will be found in *American Hymns.* "As Tranquil Streams" was one of a later group of five hymns included in *Hymns of the Spirit* (1937).

Charles L. Ziegler, one of the musical editors of *The Pilgrim Hymnal,* composed GRACE, which was originally sung to another American text, Oliver Wendell Holmes's "O Love Divine, That Stooped to Share."

At Length the Busy Day Is Done	ST. MICHAEL'S L.M.
St. 1–4, 12	
Francis Hopkinson, 1792	Peter Valton, c.1770

Francis Hopkinson's "An Evening Hymn," like his two morning hymns, was published in his *Miscellaneous Essays & Occasional Writings.* It reflects a lively imagination and the capacity to absorb and reflect the style and imagery of his period. The association of evening with thoughts of death and the brevity of life is developed in stanzas devoted to illusory hope, vain ambition, and "av'rice, feeble grey and old."

Hopkinson's poem has been coupled with a minor tune by Peter Valton, ST. MICHAEL'S, named for the church in Charleston, where Valton played the organ for about two years from 1781.

The original, which is for soprano and figured bass, has been realized in four parts. In bar 9, third half note, the A^b indicated in the figuring has been omitted in the realization to avoid the parallel movement of a diminished to a perfect fifth.

At Length There Dawns the Glorious Day	CORWIN 8.6.8.6.6.D.
St. 1–3	
Ozora S. Davis, writ. 1909, pub. 1912	J. W. Lerman, 1908

This hymn of universal brotherhood undivided by "sundering strains of blood, or ancient caste and creed," develops a theme neglected by earlier American hymn writers but one which occupies the hearts and pens of a number of our twentieth-century poets.

CORWIN is a double tune in the movement of a processional march. First published in *Hymns of Worship and Service for the Sunday School* (1908, ed. George Whelpton), it later appeared in H. Augustine Smith's *Hymnal for American Youth* (1919) as the tune for Samuel Longfellow's "God's Trumpet Wakes the Slumbering World."

At the Door of Mercy Sighing   TALMAR 8.7.8.7.
St. 1–4
Thomas Mackellar, 1872   Isaac B. Woodbury, 1850

The text of this hymn comes from *Rhymes Atween Times* (1872), where the first line was "Long of restful peace forsaken." It appeared in *Hymns and Songs of Praise* (1874), edited by Roswell D. Hitchcock, Zachary Eddy, and Philip Schaff, and in Edwin A. Bedell's *The Church Hymnary* (1890) with the first line as given above. In the latter volume the tune was TALMAR by Isaac B. Woodbury, which had appeared in *The Dulcimer* (1850).

The harmonization given here comes from *The Church Hymnary* and it differs slightly from the original edition. There the last three bars were notated in $\frac{2}{2}$. Woodbury composed TALMAR for a text of his own, "Listen to the gentle promptings."

Auf, Ihr Christen   MEINE HOFFNUNG STEHET
Rise, Ye Children   FESTE 8.7.8.7.6.7.
St. 1, 5, 11   Zahn 4870
Justus Falckner, 1697   Christian Gregor, arr. 1784
Emma Frances Bevan, trans.
   1858

Justus Falckner is remembered for this hymn, composed during his student days at Halle. First published in 1697, it was included in Johann Anastasius Freylinghausen's *Geist-reiches Gesang-Buch* (1704). Translated as "Rise, Ye Children" by Emma Frances Bevan, it appeared in her *Songs of Eternal Life* (1858). In the German original the fifth line has six syllables but it is extended to seven in this translation.

The melody MEINE HOFFNUNG STEHET FESTE appears here in the version from the *Choral-Buch* edited by Christian Gregor in 1784. The fermata in bar 5, third beat, has been omitted.

Awake My Soul, Betimes   ST. MARTIN'S C.M.
  Awake
St. 1–5
Isaac Chanler, 1745   William Tans'ur, version of
                            1767

This hymn, like "Thrice Welcome First and Best of Days" (q.v.), was found in the diary of Isaac Chanler. "Awake My Soul, Betimes Awake" appeared with the entry for October 7, 1745.

After another good night's rest, added to a great number which it hath pleased the Lord to give me, I awoke, broke silence, and praised his holy name, and once more wrestled with him for his gracious presence, and withal put up many requests unto the Lord on the account of my dear children; I engaged in family duty; I expounded the third psalm and say a morning hymn of my own composing.

ST. MARTIN'S was one of the most popular of the florid eighteenth-century English tunes. It was credited to Tans'ur and may be found in *The American Harmony or Royal Melody Compleat,* Vol. 1 (8th ed., with additions, 1773).

Counter in C clef, third line. Tune in tenor; transposed up a minor third. The first countertenor note in the last line appears to be B in the original.

Awake, My Soul! In Grateful   HYMN 6 C.M.
  Songs
St. 1–3
Andrew Fowler, 1793   John C. Bechler, c.1813

This hymn, like "O Gracious Jesus, Blessed Lord!" appeared in the collection which Andrew Fowler published in 1793 in the hope that the proceeds might contribute to the support of a free school erected by the trustees of his church.

Although John Bechler was a Moravian, the eight hymns which he published were set to texts *Selected from the Common Prayer Book of the Episcopal Church,* possibly at the request of Miss R. C. Bininger, to whom the collection is dedicated. HYMN 6, which we have chosen, was set to a portion of Psalm 14 beginning "Thee I'll extoll, my God and king." It is marked "solo or chorus."

The melody and bass are in larger notes, the inner parts in smaller, to help the organist.

Away in a Manger   MUELLER 6.5.6.5.D.
St. 1, 2
Anon. Lutheran, 1885   James R. Murray, 1887

   This familiar Christmas text has been attributed to Martin Luther
and the tune to Carl Mueller. Neither attribution is correct. The
poem appeared in the *Little Children's Book for Schools and Family,* published in Philadelphia in 1885 under the auspices of the Evangelical
Lutheran Church. The familiar tune was published in Cincinnati
two years later in *Dainty Songs for Little Lads and Lasses* with the heading "Luther's Cradle Hymn." The music was marked "J.R.M.," the
initials of the editor, James R. Murray. Later editors gave him no
credit for his own tune. However, in *Worship and Song* (1921) the
name of Carl Mueller was given as the composer. Since no other
proof of the existence of Carl Mueller has been found, the prior
claim of Murray seems justified. This favorite text has also been
sung to J. E. Spilman's melody for "Flow Gently Sweet Afton."

Behold, the Shade of Night Is   DEVOTION 11.11.11.5.
   Now Receding
Ecce Iam Noctis
St. 1–3
Gregory the Great, 6th cent.   John Knowles Paine, comp.
                                   1873, pub. 1874
Ray Palmer, trans. 1869

   Although translations by Americans are in general excluded from
American Hymns, the work of such a figure as Ray Palmer could be
adequately represented only if certain of his free renderings from
the Latin were included. Indeed, four of the seven best-loved hymns
by Palmer are translations. "Behold, the Shade of Night" is a rendering of Gregory's *Ecce iam noctis,* which appeared in the Dutch Reformed *Hymns of the Church* (1869).
   Perhaps because of the unusual meter a special setting was composed for this poem by John Knowles Paine, which may be found in
Hymns and Songs of Praise (1874), edited by Roswell D. Hitchcock,
Zachary Eddy, and Philip Schaff.

Behold with Joy   Paris L.M.
St. 1, 2, 4, 6, 7
Elhanan Winchester, 1776 William Billings, 1781

Elhanan Winchester's hymn expresses his hopes for an America "where each free liberty enjoys." It was published in his collection of *Thirteen Hymns Suited to the Present Times* "Dedicated to the Thirteen United Colonies." It is Hymn VIII of the collection with the heading "The Happiness of a free Government."

Paris appeared in Billings' *Music in Miniature* and was reprinted in *The Chorister's Companion* by Simeon Jocelyn and Amos Doolittle (New Haven, Conn., 1782).

Soprano, G clef, second line (clef like a manuscript G); countertenor, C clef, third line; tenor, modern G clef, second line; bass, F clef, fourth line. Time signature ₵ ; transposed down one step. Billings begins with whole rests in each part which are omitted here.

Be Strong! We Are Not Here Fortitude Irregular
 To Play
St. 1–3
Maltbie Davenport Babcock, David S. Smith, 1905
 1901

This text, first published in Babcock's posthumous volume of verse in 1901, is very American in its advocacy of the strenuous Christian life. From a metrical point of view it is unusual; the opening words, "Be strong," are followed by three long decasyllabic lines.

The musical setting is designed to match the form of the poem and was published with it in *The Methodist Hymnal* of 1905. The words of command at the opening move on in rapid progressions which only broaden at the cadence. The composer has extended the last line to four bars by repeating the injunction "Be strong" at the end.

Blessed Assurance, Jesus Is 9.10.9.9., with chorus
 Mine
St. 1–3
Fanny J. Crosby, 1873 Mrs. Joseph F. Knapp, 1873

Fanny J. Crosby was undoubtedly one of the most prolific writers of hymns during a period in which volume after volume of gospel hymns poured from the presses. Most have been forgotten, but those that survive have become part of the experience of everyone who has attended services of an evangelical type. "Blessed Assurance" belongs to this group of remembered songs.

It gains added interest because the tune was written by a woman composer who was a friend of the writer. Indeed the tune preceded the text according to Fanny Crosby's own statement. "My friend, Mrs. Knapp composed a melody, and played it over to me two or three times on the piano. She then asked me what it said, and I immediately replied 'Blessed Assurance.'" The key phrase suggested the remainder of the poem. Published in 1873, it passed into *Gospel Hymns, No. 5,* in 1887 which brought it to the attention of a multitude of singers.

Blessed Comforter Divine	LOUDON 6.6.8.6.6.
St. 1–4	
Lydia Sigourney, 1824	Timothy Olmstead, 1805

"Blessed Comforter Divine" was contributed by Mrs. Sigourney to Asahel Nettleton's *Village Hymns* (1824), where it was marked only with the letter "H" as were her three other contributions. "H" evidently stood for Huntley, Mrs. Sigourney's maiden name. The diction of this early poem has a directness and simplicity which is in contrast with the florid diction of others of her poems.

Timothy Olmstead's own collection, the *Musical Olio,* appeared in Northampton in 1805. A few of his tunes were sufficiently popular to be repeated in other collections. LOUDON, for example, was reprinted in Nathaniel D. Gould's *National Church Harmony* of 1832. It is a dignified tune developed with complete simplicity.

Tune in tenor; transposed from C to B♭ major. The following adjustments have been made to soften unnecessary dissonance: alto, bar 16, last quarter, F instead of E♭; bar 17, original was dotted half on E♭, quarter on C. Olmstead endeavored to accommodate himself both to older and more recent practice by making "some [settings] with counters, and some with second trebles. Part of the airs are placed for the tenor voice, and part for the female voice." He might have added that where the C clef on the third line is used the part is sometimes marked alto, sometimes counter. LOUDON is unmarked, but the use of the C clef and the range suggest an alto part.

Blessed Is Everyone	OLD 148TH H.M.
Ps. 128: 1–6	Frost 174
Anon., 1640	George Kirbye, arr. 1621

This psalm, with its promise of a fruitful increase for those who fear Jehovah, must have comforted many an early settler. There is a kind of joyful vigor about hallelujah meter which may be due to the way in which the four lines of six feet are followed by four lines of four. The "Admonition to the Reader" in the *Bay Psalm Book* says there are "about five" psalms in this meter. Actually there are six: Psalms 97, 99, 128, 133, 147, and 148.

The tune, known as the OLD 148TH, first appeared in the Anglo-Genevan psalter of 1558. Published in England in 1560, it has long been a favorite. It was also one of the thirty-nine tunes in Henry Ainsworth. Harmonized versions are found in William Daman, Richard Allison, William Barley, Thomas Ravenscroft (from which the Kirbye setting is taken), and John Playford.

The striking boldness of the opening skips gives this tune a very marked character. It is mentioned in the "Admonition to the Reader" in the *Bay Psalm Book*, from which this metrical version of Psalm 128 is taken.

Cantus, C clef, first line; medius, C clef, third line; tenor or plainsong, C clef, fourth line; bassus, F clef, fourth line. Time signature C ; note values halved. In line four, second note, the tenor has B♭ but the bass lacks the flat in Ravenscroft. The penultimate note in the medius has a sharp indicating B♮, but this is superfluous.

Blest Be the Wondrous Grace	ST. LOUIS 6.6.8.6.6.8.
St. 1–3	
George Barrell Cheever, 1851	Joseph Emerson Sweetser, 1849

"Blest Be the Wondrous Grace" appeared in Cheever's *Christian Melodies.* The musical editor of the volume was Joseph Emerson Sweetser, who also composed ROSEHILL ("O Life That Maketh All Things New") (q.v.). ST. LOUIS comes from *A Collection of Church Music* (1849), edited jointly by Sweetser and George F. Root. It should be distinguished from Lewis H. Redner's familiar tune for "O Little Town of Bethlehem," which is also called ST. LOUIS.

Blest Is the Man Whose	NEW JERSEY L.M.
Tender Breast	
Ps. 41: 1–4	
Abijah Davis, 1813	Ishmael Spicer, 1788

Among the attempts at a metrical paraphrase of the Psalms, that of Abijah Davis takes a modest place. George Hood, in his *History of Music in New England* (Boston, 1846), has censured Davis for his dependence on Isaac Watts and, more particularly, for not admitting this indebtedness. On the other hand, it must be confessed that his "Blest Is the Man" reads more pleasantly to the modern reader than the corresponding lines in Watts: "Blest is the man, whose bowels move,/And melt with pity to the poor."

We have chosen NEW JERSEY from Andrew Adgate's *Rudiments of Music* (1788) as a tune well suited to a poet who resided in that state. The original begins with an empty bar omitted here. Time signature ᴐ.

The Bounty of Jehovah	PSALM 10 8.8.4.4.8.6.6.
Praise	
Ps. 136: 1–3	Frost 374
George Sandys, 1636	Henry Lawes, 1638

These verses come from George Sandys's *Paraphrase upon the Psalmes of David*. The rhymes follow the pattern a a b b a c c and the final couplet "For from the King of kings/Eternal mercy springs" returns at the end of each stanza. Sandys translated part of Ovid's *Metamorphoses* (1626) during the years he was in Virginia, and in the preface he speaks of these verses as "sprung from the Stocke of the ancient Romans; but bred in the New-World, of the rudeness whereof it cannot but participate; especially having Warres and Tumults to bring it to light instead of the Muses." His psalm paraphrases were published after he had returned to England, although it is possible that some may have been written during his stay here.

Henry Lawes provided a group of tunes which were published with Sandys's psalm paraphrases. The tune selected here was intended for Psalm 10. Since Lawes speaks of his lower part as a "thorow base" we have added inner parts. Time signature ₵ ; note values halved.

Bow Down, Mountain
St. 1, 2
Norma Farber, writ. 1955   Daniel Pinkham, comp. 1955

This unusual Christmas song calls on all nature to pay tribute to the newborn child.

The tune has something of the energetic earnestness of certain early New England tunes. Its distinctive characteristic is its rhythm. The poet has written a short line followed by longer ones, and the musician has matched this pattern by one in which a vigorous initial four-note rhythm is punctuated by a rest, followed by a phrase which flows without pause to the end of the poetic idea.

Braving the Wilds All   MARCUS WHITMAN
    Unexplored   8.8.8.10.8.8.
St. 1–4
Robert Freeman, writ. 1927,   William Pierson Merrill,
    pub. 1928   comp. 1927, pub. 1928

This hymn honoring pioneer missionaries was written in 1927 by one Presbyterian minister and the tune was composed by another. Robert Freeman wrote the text to celebrate the 125th anniversary of the founding of the Board of National Missions.

William Pierson Merrill has left an account of the genesis of the tune. It was requested only three days in advance of the anniversary and he had indicated that he did not feel he could compose a suitable melody under such circumstances. Nevertheless the text was sent to him. "Busy all that morning, I did not look at it until I was walking home at noon. At once it captivated me by its fine swing, rhythm, and highly religious tone. By the time I had reached my door, a walk of less than ten minutes from the church, the tune had found itself in my mind, at least the main part of the melody. I recall that the last two lines came first. I worked at it that afternoon, mailed it . . . that night, and it was used at the celebration."

The tune is named for a pioneer missionary and physician who went to Oregon as agent of the Board of National Missions. Copyrighted in 1928, both text and tune were included in the Presbyterian *Hymnal* of 1933.

Break Thou the Bread of Life	BREAD OF LIFE 6.4.6.4.D.
St. 1–3	
Mary Artemisia Lathbury, writ. 1877	William Fiske Sherwin, comp. 1877

The opening line "Break thou the bread of life" comes from John 6:33. Widely sung and loved, this hymn was written at the Chautauqua Assembly in the summer of 1877 and set to music in the same summer by William Fiske Sherwin. The tune, quiet and meditative in character, rises to a climax at the beginning of the last line, "My spirit pants for thee, O living Word."

The favorite "Day Is Dying in the West" (q.v.), written and composed during the same summer, has also been very widely used. In both cases, tune and words have retained their original associations.

Broad Is the Road	WINDHAM L.M.
St. 1–4	
Isaac Watts, 1707–09	Daniel Read, 1785

In a sense all of Isaac Watts's hymns were naturalized here. Our own sampling has been restricted to a few which were associated with particular American tunes, including "Broad Is the Road," often sung to Daniel Read's WINDHAM. Watts's text appeared in his *Horae Lyricae* (1707–09).

Read's WINDHAM first appeared in his *American Singing Book* and then in such later volumes as Oliver Holden's *Union Harmony* (1793).

It is interesting to note how each cadence except the last is extended by sustained notes in treble and bass after the countertenor and tenor have stopped singing.

Brother, Hast Thou Wandered Far	MARTYN 7.7.7.7.D.
St. 1–4	
James Freeman Clarke, 1844	Simeon B. Marsh, 1834

"Brother, Hast Thou Wandered Far," based on the parable of the prodigal son, was written for the first edition of *The Disciples' Hymn Book* (1844; 2d. ed. with additions, 1852). In a shortened form as "Hast thou wasted all thy powers" (the opening of stanza 2), it was repeated in both the 1853 *Hymns for the Church of Christ* and the well-known *Plymouth Collection* (1855).

Marsh is one of the tune writers who produced only one enduring composition. MARTYN is of the utmost simplicity, and Frank J. Metcalf, in *American Writers and Compilers of Sacred Music,* remarked that it was "one of the first pieces of sacred music that the amateur tries to learn." Composed in 1834, it was frequently sung to Wesley's "Jesus, Lover of My Soul."

Brother, Though from Yonder Sky	FULTON 7.7.7.7.
St. 1–5	
James Henry Bancroft, writ. 1842, pub. 1843	William Batchelder Bradbury, 1847

Written while James Henry Bancroft was a student at Andover as a funeral hymn for Dudley Leavitt, a member of his class, this poem was widely used in its period. Although Bancroft was studying for the Congregational ministry, his hymn was first printed in *The Psalmist* (1843), the most important Baptist hymnal of its period.

FULTON by the Baptist convention leader and composer, William Batchelder Bradbury, appeared in *Flora's Festival* (1847) and was repeated with the Bancroft text in *Psalmista, or Choir Melodies* (1851), which Bradbury edited with Thomas Hastings.

By Babel's Streams	PSALM 46 8.8.8.D
Ps. 137, st. 1–4	
Philip Freneau, writ. bet. 1768 and 1794	Amos Bull, 1793

Perhaps best known as a satirist and as a poet with a strong feeling for nature, Freneau also wrote religious verse. The present spirited "Paraphrase of Psalm 137—The Jewish Lamentation at Euphrates" takes on a special interest when we remember that Freneau himself had been held on a British prison ship during the Revolution and had tasted the bitterness of captivity at first hand.

The earliest appearance of PSALM 46 is in *The American Harmony* (1793) by Nehemiah Shumway. It is not included in Bull's own collection *The Responsary* (1795). There is a version in $\frac{6}{4}$ in *The Bridgewater Collection* (6th ed., 1818). PSALM 46, MIDDLETOWN, and NEWMARK, were more widely used than Bull's other tunes. Although we retain the original barring, it does not express the true movement of the music which might be more accurately expressed as follows: $\frac{2}{2}$—| $\frac{3}{2}$∪∪—— | ∪∪— | $\frac{2}{2}$—— | $\frac{3}{2}$∪∪—— | $\frac{2}{2}$∪∪———.

Countertenor, C clef, third line. Original key F major; time signature $\mathbb{C}$. The harmony has been slightly altered in bars 10, 11, 14, 15, 18, 22, and 23. The empty bar at the beginning has been omitted. The A♮ in bar 6 is not in the original but it does appear in later editions such as *The Baltimore Collection* (1819).

By Vows of Love Together Bound	IRA C.M.
St. 1–5	
Eleazar Thompson Fitch, 1845	Charles Zeuner, 1845

American marriage hymns are not numerous and these simple and touching verses by Eleazar Thompson Fitch form the only wedding hymn in the Connecticut Congregational collection of 1845, *Psalms and Hymns for Christian Use and Worship.*

IRA, evidently composed for *The Psaltery* (1845) of Lowell Mason and George J. Webb, was one of the new tunes which distinguished that volume. This unassuming but melodious tune is a good match for Fitch's text. The sixth step of the scale is used frequently enough in it to give it a slightly plaintive character in spite of the fact that it is in major. "Treble and Tenor may change parts" is printed above the tune. The tune would thus be transferred to the tenor, an arrangement usual with early American tune writers.

Calm, on the Listening Ear of Night	GOULD C.M.
St. 1–6	
Edmund Hamilton Sears, 1834	John E. Gould, 1846

Sears is perhaps the only American hymn writer to have written two Christmas hymns of the finest quality, lyrics which are still performed in the Christmas season after over a century of use. "Calm, on the Listening Ear of Night" is less frequently performed than "It Came upon the Midnight Clear." Perhaps it still has not found its ideal musical setting. Oliver Wendell Holmes considered it "one of the finest and most beautiful hymns ever written." The accounts of the origin of this hymn in Julian and in Henry Wilder Foote's *American Unitarian Hymn Writers and Hymns* do not agree. Julian states that it appeared in the *Boston Observer* in 1834 and in the following year in the *Christian Register*. It was revised by the author and in this form appeared in the *Monthly Magazine* and in Alfred P. Putnam's *Singers and Songs of the Liberal Faith* (1875). Foote states that it was written in 1839 and published anonymously in *The Christian Psalter* in 1841. It was subsequently included in two Unitarian hymnals: *The New Hymn and Tune Book* of 1914 and *Hymns of the Spirit* of 1937.

Among the many settings of this text are: Leonard Marshall's SEARS (*Fountain of Sacred Song*, 1871), W. O. Perkins' JUDEA (*The Chorister*, 1870), and John E. Gould's anthem setting, later adapted as a hymn tune under the name GOULD.

Calvary   Anon.
St. 1–4
Traditional, 1940   John W. Work, arr. 1940

The heart-rending cry on the word "Calvary" gives this spiritual its touching and dramatic character. The melody is distinguished by its persistent alternation of ascending passages using the raised seventh step with descending passages using the lowered seventh step. The sixth step is not used at all. The ascending formula may also be found in "Tryin' to Get Home" (see Work's *American Negro Songs*, p. 55).

Cast Thy Bread upon the   AGAWAM 8.7.8.7.
    Waters
St. 1–4
Phoebe A. Hanaford, 1852   Thomas Whittemore, 1841

Only one of Mrs. Hanaford's hymns, "Cast Thy Bread upon the Waters," was widely used. It was based on Ecclesiastes 11:1, a passage which seems especially appropriate for a woman born on Nantucket. Her hymn was included in Isaac B. Woodbury's *New Lute of Zion* (1856), William Batchelder Bradbury's *Cottage Melodies* (1860), the Universalist *Church Harmonies* (1873), and the *Hymns and Songs of Praise*, edited by Roswell D. Hitchcock, Zachary Eddy, and Philip Schaff (1874).

AGAWAM appeared in 1841 in a collection intended for Universalist use, *The Gospel Harmonist* of Thomas Whittemore.

Chilled by the Blasts of   HYMN ON THE EXCELLENCY OF
   Adverse Fate   THE BIBLE   C.M.
St. 1–4
Jacob Duché, c.1785   Thomas Spence Duché, 1801

Jacob Duché's loyalist views caused him to seek refuge in England, where he became the chaplain of the Asylum or House of Refuge for Female Orphans in London. "Chilled by the Blasts of Adverse Fate," written for *Hymns and Psalms Used at the Asylum,* was to be sung by the girls sheltered there. Duché himself is said to have edited the editions of 1785 and 1789.

The music for this text (presumably by François Hippolyte Barthélémon, the musical editor) has the character of a miniature cantata and thus falls outside the scope of this collection. We have substituted a HYMN ON THE EXCELLENCY OF THE BIBLE by Thomas Spence Duché, the son of our poet, recognized in England as "an artist of some ability." Though musical as well as artistic, he was not sufficiently learned to furnish his melody with a bass, which was supplied by his friend Barthélémon. The inner parts are editorial additions.

In the original the bass was designed for the organ, since it descends to low D. For those who may wish to sing this tune in four parts, we have added the first half note for tenor and bass. Where the bass part is in octaves, the upper note is for voices, the lower, the original instrumental bass line.

The Chosen Three, on   TAMAR C.M.
   Mountain Height
St. 1–4
David H. Ela, 1878   Isaac B. Woodbury, 1850

This account of the transfiguration of Christ (Matthew 17:1) was written at the suggestion of the committee entrusted with the revision of *The Methodist Hymnal* and was published in that volume in 1878 and in its successor in 1905. In the former volume the tune was Lowell Mason's NOEL. Woodbury's TAMAR, which was also included in the hymnal of 1878, has been substituted here. It appeared without attribution in Woodbury's *Dulcimer* (New York, 1850).

Christ for the World! We   MACEDON 6.6.4.6.6.6.4.
  Sing
St. 1–4
Samuel Wolcott, 1869   Frederick Field Bullard, 1904

At a meeting held by the YMCA of Ohio, the slogan "Christ for the World, and the World for Christ" was outlined in evergreen letters above the pulpit. As Samuel Wolcott left the meeting, the stanzas of his hymn took shape. The hymn's meter is the same as that of the familiar ITALIAN HYMN of Giardini, and this is the tune set in Charles Robinson's *Laudes Domini* (1884) for Wolcott's text.

Some texts have to wait beyond their period for a suitable American tune. This was such a text. In MACEDON Bullard has written a simple vigorous tune largely free of his Victorian mannerisms. He has found musical equivalents both for the exultant motto lines at the opening of the hymn and the more reflective lines that follow. For other words that can be sung to this music, see "My Country, to Thy Shore." MACEDON was written for *The Pilgrim Hymnal* (Boston, 1904), of which Bullard was a musical editor. A more nearly contemporary tune, CUTTING, by William Fiske Sherwin (q.v.), has also been sung to Wolcott's text.

Christian, Be Up   10.10.10.6.
St. 1–4
Robert Nathan, 1940   Everett Helm, comp. 1959

Everett Helm is among the composers who have utilized hymn tunes in their instrumental works, as in his *Three Gospel Hymns for Orchestra* (1955). The tunes developed in these compositions are COME AND TASTE, JACOB'S LADDER, and WHEN THE ROLL IS CALLED. His vigorous and dissonant unison hymn with keyboard accompaniment moves freely in measures of varying length. First published in *A Winter Tale*, Nathan's poem bears the title "Epistle."

Christ's Life Our Code   COPELAND L.M.
St. 1–5
Benjamin Copeland, 1900   Karl P. Harrington, 1905

Harrington's tune, composed for the Copeland text and named for its author, belongs stylistically with the hymn tunes by Henry M. Dunham and Peter C. Lutkin included in this volume. The poem begins with its most striking idea, "Christ's life our code, his cross our creed," an idea which is literally repeated in the last line of the last stanza. The last line in each stanza has an importance which the musician has stressed by the emphatic character of his final phrase. Copeland's hymn was published in two periodicals in 1900: the *Northern Christian Advocate* (Syracuse, N.Y.) and the *Daily Christian Advocate.* It was associated with Harrington's setting in *The Methodist Hymnal* of 1905.

The City, Lord, Where Thy Dear Life	Brooklyn C.M.
St. 1–5	
William E. Dudley, 1929	Frank Kasschau, 1929

William E. Dudley wrote "The City, Lord, Where Thy Dear Life" while he was pastor of the Flatbush Congregational Church in Brooklyn, N.Y. The musical setting was composed by Frank Kasschau, organist and choirmaster of the church. In spite of the number of urban congregations, very few hymns reflect an awareness of the problems that such an environment poses for the Christian conscience.

Columbia, Trust the Lord	Columbia 10.10.10.D.
Anon., 1801	Abraham Maxim, 1804

The author of this patriotic hymn has not been identified, but his text must have enjoyed a certain popularity, since, in addition to the setting by the Maine composer Abraham Maxim, there was another less attractive treatment with the same name by Timothy Swan. Maxim's Columbia appeared in his *Northern Harmony* and is a plain, vigorous minor tune which nevertheless is of some harmonic interest. Most psalm tunes of the period were based largely on fundamental triads and this quality contributed to their straightforward sturdy character. Maxim, however, at two points uses transitional chromatic harmonies, which were, of course, commonplace in contemporary European music but rare in American psalmody. The first example is in bar 11, last quarter, where the tenor passes through $D^\sharp$ in going from D to E, producing a chord of the augmented sixth. The second is in bar 22, beat 4, where the bass takes $G^\sharp$ on its way from G to A. Here a momentary diminished seventh chord is formed. It was a foreshadowing of a style which in its full development was to be the antithesis of the plain psalm tune.

Countertenor, C clef, third line. Time signature in the original Ɔ; tune in tenor.

Come All Ye Mourning Pilgrims	PILGRIM 8.6.8.6.7.6.8.6.
St. 1, 3, 5, 6	
John A. Granade, writ. c. 1801	William Hauser, arr. 1878

This setting of a popular hymn by the Western poet John A. Granade comes from the *Olive Leaf,* compiled by William Hauser. The text may be found in earlier tune books like Allen D. Carden's *Missouri Harmony* (1820), John B. Jackson's *Knoxville Harmony* (1838), and Hauser's own *Hesperian Harp* (1848). There is a variant to a different tune in Jeremiah Ingalls' *Christian Harmony* (1805).

The musical settings in the *Olive Leaf* differ from those in Hauser's earlier *Hesperian Harp* and, indeed, from those in most of the Southern books, since the tune is in the soprano, not the tenor, and the harmony is more conventional.

Come, All Ye People	FESTAL DAY L.M.
St. 1–6	
George R. Seltzer, comp. 1956, pub. 1958	Ralph P. Lewars, comp. 1956, pub. 1958

Lewars' jubilant tune FESTAL DAY, together with Seltzer's text, made its first appearance in print in the *Service Book and Hymnal of the Lutheran Church in America* (1958).

Come, Every Soul	STOCKTON C.M., with chorus
St. 1–4	
John H. Stockton, 1868	John H. Stockton, 1868

This hymn first appeared in Joseph Hillman's *Revivalist* (Troy, N.Y., 1868). *The Revivalist* was not only important for the folk hymns which it contained, but also included early examples of the gospel hymn with chorus, like this one. In *My Life and the Story of the Gospel Hymns* Ira D. Sankey wrote that he came upon the title of the hymn in a list in his scrapbook in 1873. Later, feeling that the words in the refrain had lost their appeal through too frequent repetition, he altered the original "Come to Jesus" to "Only trust him" as they appear in this volume. The hymn was published in the *Gospel Hymns and Sacred Songs* of Sankey and Philip Bliss in 1875.

Come, Friends and Neighbors, Come St. 1–5 Lewis Hartsough, 1868	THE PASTOR'S APPEAL 6.4.6.4.6.6.6.4. Lewis Hartsough, arr. 1868

In "Let Me Go Where Saints Are Going" (q.v.), Lewis Hartsough wrote the text and composed the music in the style of the gospel hymn. In "Come, Friends and Neighbors, Come," he wrote his text to a tune which he adapted to his purpose, according to the heading, "Words and arr. by Rev. L. Hartsough" in *The Revivalist.*

That the tune was derived from folk sources is evident both from its scale structure and from its interesting rhythm. The melody is plagal, cadencing on G but with a range from D to D. Both the fourth and seventh steps are missing. The free movement of the melody coupled with the regular and unsatisfactory barring suggest that Hartsough wrote the tune down as he remembered it.

The regular barring accents such words as "and" and "from" and stresses the first syllable of words which are normally accented on the second syllable like "salvation" and "arouse." Actually, if barring is to be employed, an alternation of measures containing two and three quarter notes is satisfactory. The melody only is given in *The Revivalist,* and the hymn may be sung in unison if desired.

Come, Happy Children
 	
St. 1, 2
Anon., 1864
	CANAAN 8.7.8.7.D., with
	    chorus
	
	Traditional, used here from
	    c.1820

This song in praise of cold water appeared in Edwin Thompson's *Band of Hope Melodies consisting of Temperance Songs, Duets, and Glees, especially adapted to Bands of Hope, and other Juvenile Temperance Associations* (Boston, 1864). Although no music is included, the tune is named at the beginning of each song. Many are popular songs of the day like "Lily Dale," "Prairie Flower," and "O Susanna."

"Come, Happy Children" is to be sung to CANAAN. The tune is of English origin, although it was naturalized here. It was first introduced by Rev. John N. Maffitt, an Englishman who conducted revival services in New England around 1820. In the English Baptist *Sunday School Hymnary* it was designated as "English traditional." However, in *Fellowship Hymns* and in several later books it was called "Swiss traditional." This attribution was adopted in the Pilgrim hymnal of 1958 where it is called THE STAFF OF FAITH. The arrangement used here was taken from D. H. Mansfield's *American Vocalist* of 1849 where it is in G major.

Come Harken unto Me	YORK C. M.
Ps. 66, third part: 16–20	Frost 205
Anon., 1640	Version from *Bay Psalm Book*, 1698

Our text is a metrical version of Psalm 66 from the *Bay Psalm Book* of 1640. YORK, long a favorite tune on both sides of the Atlantic, first appeared in the Scottish psalter of 1615 where it was called the STILT. Thomas Ravenscroft was so fond of this "Northerne" tune that he used it for five different psalms and "A Prayer to the Holy Ghost." John Hawkins calls attention to YORK in his *History of Music:* "The tenor part [i.e., the air] of this tune is so well-known, that within memory half of the nurses in England were used to sing it by way of lullaby: and the chimes of many country churches have played it six or eight times four and twenty hours from time immemorial." The tune is one of the "near forty" common meter tunes in Ravenscroft mentioned in the "Admonition to the Reader" in the *Bay Psalm Book*.

Our setting comes from the 1698 edition, the earliest surviving edition with music. The music was derived from either the 1674 or the 1679 edition of John Playford's *Breefe Introduction to the Skill of Musicke*. Both there and in the *Bay Psalm Book* the music is for melody and bass. We have added a middle voice for those who prefer to sing in three parts. This has been adapted from the medius in John Playford's *The Whole Book of Psalms* by altering the note values where they differ from those in the *Bay Psalm Book*.

Come, Holy Spirit, Dove Divine	BENEVOLENT STREET L.M.
St. 1–4	
Adoniram Judson, 1832	Oliver Shaw, 1815

This hymn by Adoniram Judson, pioneer missionary to Burma, stresses the Baptist belief in baptism by immersion.

We die to sin, and seek a grave
With thee, beneath the yielding wave.

In its earlier form the poem began "Our Saviour bowed beneath the wave" and consisted of seven stanzas. In later hymnals this form is commonly presented in an abbreviated form consisting of stanzas 1–3, while another hymn, "Come Holy Spirit, Dove Divine," was made by rearranging the remaining four, beginning with the seventh. Julian traces this form to the 1832 edition of James M. Winchell's *An Arrangement of the Psalms, Hymns, and Spiritual Songs of the Rev. Isaac Watts D.D. to which Is Added a Supplement* (or, more conveniently, *Winchell's Watts*).

We have matched this hymn by a famous Baptist missionary with a tune by a blind Baptist singing master. Oliver Shaw liked to name his tunes for streets in Providence, R.I., where he lived, and this is true of BENEVOLENT STREET. It is simpler than most of the composer's tunes, but even here the trills in the final cadence might well be omitted. It was taken from the composer's *Providence Selection* (Dedham, Mass., 1815).

Come, Let Us Tune Our   WHITEFIELD L.M.
   Loftiest Song
St. 1–4
Robert A. West, 1849   R. N., 1849

Robert West's "Come, Let Us Tune Our Loftiest Song" has appeared in Methodist hymnals from 1849 to the present. In the hymnal of 1878 DUKE STREET was the tune. However, in *The Devotional Harmonist* of 1849 the tune WHITEFIELD was assigned to this text. The music was signed only by the initials "R. N."

Come, O Sabbath Day   7.7.7.7.6.
St. 1–3
Gustav Gottheil, 1887   Abraham W. Binder, 1932

This hymn for the Sabbath appeared in Gottheil's *Music to Hymns and Anthems for Jewish Worship* (1887). The first edition of the *Union Hymnal* (1897) was largely based on Gottheil's hymnal. Binder's tune for "Come, O Sabbath Day," however, was composed for the third edition (1932), of which he was the musical editor.

Come, Precious Soul

St. 1, 2, 10, 13
Anon., version of 1868

CALVARY or GETHSEMANE
Irregular

Anon., melody pub. 1868

The text is in the form of a dialogue. The first stanza invites the soul to "take a walk becoming you and me." In the second the doubting soul protests that this is "much too hard a task for me." The lines are extremely variable in length. The arrangement presented here is to be sung as a solo or in unison, and the melody has been reprinted for the four selected stanzas. An earlier arrangement of this hymn appeared in 1849 in D. H. Mansfield's *The American Vocalist*.

The fine melody given here was published in Joseph Hillman's *The Revivalist* (1868) as sung by G. C. Wells. J. Baker is given credit as arranger. He may have written the tune down as it was sung. The F's in the melody are sharped in bars 1 and 6, and B's made natural in bar 3 and in the last bar. These accidentals have been omitted here, and the melody thus appears in the Aeolian mode.

Come unto Me, When
     Shadows Darkly Gather
St. 1–3
Catherine H. Watterman,
     1839

HENLEY 11.10.11.10.

Lowell Mason, 1854

In 1840 Catherine H. Watterman became Mrs. Esling, and the brief account in Julian is under her married name. Her best-known poem was first published in one of the gift anthologies popular in her day, the *Christian Keepsake* (1839). She was an Episcopalian, but "Come unto Me" was not included in the hymnals of that denomination, though it was widely used elsewhere. This prayer for help "when shadows darkly gather" has a certain similarity to Henry F. Lyte's famous "Abide with Me, Fast Falls the Eventide." As a hymn it was generally sung in a shortened version. The stanzas given here are stanzas 3, 8, and 9 of the complete poem.

Lowell Mason set HENLEY to this text in *The Hallelujah* of 1854. The association persisted, for we find HENLEY with the same text twenty years later in *Hymns and Songs of Praise*, edited by Roswell D. Hitchcock, Zachary Eddy, and Philip Schaff.

Complete in Thee, No Work   WARE L.M.
  of Mine
St. 1–5
Aaron R. Wolfe, 1850/1851   George Kingsley, 1838

Although less familiar in our own day than Wolfe's "A Parting
Hymn We Sing" (q.v.), Julian (*A Dictionary of Hymnology*, 1892) considered it one of the author's most widely used hymns. Seven of
Wolfe's hymns were included in Thomas Hastings' *Church Melodies*
(1859), and the present example had previously appeared in "1850
or 51" in the *New York Evangelist*.

WARE is one of the tunes, popular at mid-century, in which the
third line is set as a duet, in this instance for alto and soprano. It is
designated as a chant in Kingsley's *The Sacred Choir* (1838). Transposed from B$\flat$ to A major. Last chord printed as a whole note in
Kingsley. The accompanying part in bars 6 and 7 was A (whole
note), A (half), E (quarter note).

Confess We All, Before the   LORD THOMAS AND FAIR
  Lord   ELLINOR C.M.
Lines 197–208, 217–228
John Wilson, 1626   Anon., 1650

This passage from John Wilson's *Song of Deliverance* is a hymn of
rejoicing which follows his account of the plague of 1625 in England. The "works of the Lord" which he described may be summed
up in his own lines:

> Thou Lord which from the Spanish yoke,
> And from the powder blast,
> And from that former sickness stroak
> And from this newly past
> Hast saved us and ours and thine,
> So many as survive,
> Oh do not of thy grace divine
> Our feeble souls deprive.

The final couplet in our hymn, with the phrase "the infectious dart,"
is a direct reference to the plague. The whole passage is a kind of
Protestant *Te Deum* written in the popular ballad meter which Wilson
used for all of his poem save the introduction. The poem was written and first published in England, before Wilson came to the New
World. After his death his poem was reprinted in Boston (1680) as a
memorial to him and "for the sake of several who have much desired to see and read this work."

In the sixteenth and seventeenth centuries religious texts were often sung to folk tunes. Even George Wither, who protested against the practice, suggested secular tunes for some of his own devotional poems. In accordance with this practice we have adapted ballad tunes to a number of our religious texts.

Although the verses for LORD THOMAS AND FAIR ELLINOR were published in Percy's *Reliques of Ancient Poetry,* the tune appeared as late as 1833 in William Sandys's *Christmas Carols Ancient and Modern.* A variant of this tune associated with "Who List To Lead a Soldier's Life" was included in the *English Dancing Master* in 1650. The tune there is major. Sandys prints it with raised fourth step (Lydian mode). Another peculiarity of the melody is the short measure at the mid-point. The comparable measure in the *English Dancing Master* is of normal length. No contemporary harmonization of this melody has been located. See "Whoso Would See This Song of Heavenly Choice" for another lyric passage from the *Song of Deliverance.*

Creation's Lord, We Give   SEABURY L.M.
  Thee Thanks
St. 1–4
William deWitt Hyde, 1903   Claude Means, 1941

The first publication of Hyde's poem was in the May 1903 issue of the *Outlook.* It passed into usage as a hymn through its inclusion in the Unitarian *Unity Hymns and Carols* of 1911, reduced to four stanzas by the omission of the original third stanza. At the same time the following stanza (now stanza 3) was slightly altered. Hyde had written:

> What though its coming long delay!
> With haughty foes it still must cope!

Although the present association of tune and text was made in the Episcopal *Hymnal 1940,* SEABURY, which bears the name of the first Episcopal bishop in America, was composed in 1941 but not copyrighted until 1943. ETERNAL LIGHT, SURSUM CORDA, TREGARON, and VERMONT, all of which were published in *The Hymnal 1940,* were also composed or submitted for publication in 1941.

Creator of Infinities   L.M.
St. 1–3
Chadwick Hansen, writ. 1958   Howard Hanson, comp.
                               1956

Most of Howard Hanson's many compositions are in the larger
forms, opera, symphony, and choral works of substantial length like
the *Hymn of the Cherubim*. Yet the psalm singing of the Puritans in his
opera *Merrymount* revealed his ability to suggest the rude strength
and fervor of the congregation.

The present hymn was composed at the request of the editors of
American Hymns and was later revised slightly by the composer. Originally it was set to a translation from Saint Ambrose beginning "O
trinity of blessed light." A search was made for a suitable contemporary poem by an American, a search which ended when Chadwick
Hansen wrote his hymn of praise. In this instance the writing of the
text followed rather than preceded the composition of the tune.

Day Is Dying in the West   CHAUTAUQUA 7.7.7.7.4., with
                                    chorus
St. 1, 2
Mary Artemisia Lathbury,   William Fiske Sherwin, 1877
    writ. 1877

Written, as was "Break Thou the Bread of Life," for the Chautauqua Assembly of 1877, this evening hymn has been very widely
sung. W. Garrett Horder went so far as to say that "it is one of the
finest and most distinctive hymns of modern time. It deserves to
rank with 'Lead, Kindly Light' of Cardinal Newman . . ."
William Fiske Sherwin composed the familiar musical setting, calling it CHAUTAUQUA for the place where both text and tune originated.

The Day Is Past and Gone   EVENING SHADE S.M.
St. 1–5
John Leland, 1792   Stephen Jenks, 1805

This hymn is one of the most attractive of those written in this
country in the eighteenth century. The Rev. S. W. Duffield wrote
that "there is an Ambrosian simplicity about this hymn which
suggests at once a pure and unaffected piety, like that of the early
church. The piece is really classic in its unpretending beauty." F. M.

Bird states that the first known publication of this hymn was in *Philomela, or A Selection of Spiritual Songs* by George Roberts (Petersburg, 1792). Its popularity dates from 1799 when it was included in the *Hartford Selection of Hymns* and it is this text which we reproduce. It will be noted that it was written in the first person as an individual prayer, although later editors have altered this feature of the text.

Among the early settings was a fuguing tune by Stephen Jenks published in 1805 which later gained a place in the Southern tune books and was retained in the *Original Sacred Harp* of 1936. However Jenks's EVENING SHADE was only a shortened version of his own MOUNT VERNON, which appeared in 1800 in his *New England Harmonist*. The earlier version is in the Aeolian mode. In the later arrangement the seventh step is sharped in the tune in the third and in the penultimate bars suggesting a trend to minor. The traditional form printed by Annabel Morris Buchanan in her *Folk Hymns of America* is also modal. Jeremiah Ingalls includes a setting of this text in his *Christian Harmony* (1805).

Time signature Ɔ ; transposed down one step.

Day of God! Thou Blessed Day	BERLIN 7.7.7.7.
St. 1–4	
Hannah Flagg Gould, 1841	Josiah Osgood, 1867

This hymn appeared in the last edition of Hannah Flagg Gould's *Poems*. From this volume a number of poems, including "Day of God," were selected for use in various hymnbooks. Three American tunes were printed in Philip Phillips' *New Hymn and Tune Book* (New York, 1867) for a group of texts in long meter: ST. LOUIS and VALDIVIA by Isaac B. Woodbury and BERLIN by Osgood. The last named was printed with the opening stanza of "Day of God! Thou Blessed Day." In the alto, bar 6, the second eighth has been changed from F to A♭ to avoid parallel octaves with the bass.

Dear Brethren, Are Your Harps in Tune?	NEWTON C.M.D.
St. 1–4, 10, 13	
Eunice Smith, 1798	Samuel Babcock, 1807

This is one of the poems added to the religious discourse which Eunice Smith published in Greenfield, Mass. It is matched here with NEWTON, a tune in marching rhythm which was first published in

Samuel Babcock's *Middlesex Harmony* (1795). However, the version reproduced here comes from Elisha West's *Musical Concert* of 1807. The harmonies move in a uniform beat broken only by the long chords at the cadential points and the "gathering chord" at the beginning. The chord at the end of the first section appears to be too long. It is really a written-out hold. The conflict between soprano and tenor on the last beat of bar 5 has been resolved by letting the soprano sing D C instead of C B♭ on the last beat. The first soprano note in the second section was printed a step too high in the original.

Countertenor C clef, third line. Time signature ℈; tune in tenor; transposed down one step.

Dear Friend, Whose Presence   Downs C.M.
   in the House
St. 1–5
James Freeman Clarke, 1852   Lowell Mason, 1835

This hymn is a warm and tender application of the story of the miracle at Cana (John 2) to daily living.

> Revive our souls and make us see
> Life's water glow as wine.

Clarke's poem appeared in his own *Disciples' Hymn Book* and was reprinted in Henry Ward Beecher's *Plymouth Collection* (1855) and in Charles Dexter Cleveland's *Lyra Sacra Americana* (1868).

In the *Plymouth Collection* an English tune, Chesterfield, by Dr. Haweis was used. Downs, which is preferred here, appeared in *The Choir; or, Union Collection* (1832), edited by Lowell Mason. It is given here as it appears in the *Boston Academy's Collection of Church Music* (1835). The second ending may be reserved for the final stanza or it may be omitted.

Dear Happy Souls   Rich Provision C.M.D.
St. 1, 3, 6, 8
Eunice Smith, 1798   Jeremiah Ingalls, 1805

This hymn, which exhorts the convert to "ever run the blessèd Christian race," is one of the poems included in Eunice Smith's volume entitled *Some Motives to engage those who have professed the name of the Lord Jesus*.

Rich Provision is set by Ingalls in his *Christian Harmony* (1805) to a text by Isaac Watts beginning "Jesus thy blessings are not few."

The tenor melody has the character of a country dance adapted to sacred uses. In bars 14 and 15 Ingalls has consecutive octaves and fifths in his lower two parts. We print the passage as it appears in Ingalls and offer also an alternative version.

Dear Lord and Father of Mankind WOODLAND 8.6.8.8.6.
St. 1–5
John Greenleaf Whittier, writ. 1872 Nathaniel D. Gould, 1832

This hymn is part of a longer poem, "The Brewing of Soma," which Whittier wrote in 1872. It begins with stanza 12, and includes stanzas 13, 14, 16, and 17. In the older hymnbooks the pattern 8.6.8.8.6. was called C.P.M. (Common Peculiar or Particular Meter).

In the Unitarian *Hymn and Tune Book* of 1877 Whittier's hymn is set to WOODLAND by Nathaniel D. Gould. WOODLAND first appeared in *National Church Harmony,* compiled by the composer. He also provided a version in minor. The soprano is printed above the bass in the original edition and the harmonies are filled in in smaller notes for the benefit of organists who had difficulty in reading from an open score.

Dear Lord, Behold Thy Servants BLUE HILL L.M.
St. 1–5
Hosea Ballou I, 1808 Daniel Belknap, 1800

Richard Evans, in his volume on the Unitarians and Universalists (*The American Church History Series,* Vol. 10), praised "Dear Lord, Behold Thy Servants," stating that it "would fill a high place in any collection of hymns." It was written to be sung at an annual convention. Included in the *Hymns Composed by Different Authors* (Walpole, Mass., 1808), it was also printed in *A Collection of Psalms and Hymns for the Use of Universalist Societies and Families* (1839), edited by his grandnephew Hosea Ballou II. The Universalists shared with the Unitarians a reputation for freely altering the hymns they used. In this instance the younger Ballou found it desirable to alter this hymn, and he marked it with an asterisk to show that this was the case. It was one of five hymns by Hosea Ballou I to be included in *Church Harmonies New and Old* (1895)

BLUE HILL, a fuguing tune, was one of the most popular compositions of Daniel Belknap. Included in his *Evangelical Harmony* of 1800, it was repeated in such retrospective anthologies as *Ancient Harmony Revived* (1847) and Father Robert Kemp's *Old Folks' Concert Tunes.*

Dear Saviour, If These   Woodworth L.M.
  Lambs Should Stray
St. 1–4
Abby Bradley Hyde, 1824   William Batchelder Brad-
                                  bury, 1849

Mrs. Hyde's "Prayer on Behalf of Children" was published in Asahel Nettleton's *Village Hymns* of 1824. It became associated with Woodworth in the latter half of the last century. Woodworth was published in *The Mendelssohn Collection* (1849), edited jointly by Thomas Hastings and Bradbury. The text there was "The God of Love Will Sure Indulge" by Elizabeth Scott (q.v.). Woodworth became a favorite tune for Charlotte Elliot's "Just As I Am Without One Plea," to which it is still sung; see also "Just As Thou Art," which is also set to Woodworth.

Defend Us, Lord, from Every   Joshua L.M.
  Ill
St. 1–3
John Hay, writ. 1896   Peter C. Lutkin, 1905

John Hay's prayer for strength and vision was printed in *The Methodist Hymnal* of 1905 with a melody composed for it by Peter C. Lutkin. Both the tune name, Joshua, and the second stanza of the poem refer to the conquest of the Promised Land by the Israelites. Horeb or Sinai was the holy mountain where Moses received the promise of land for his people, and Joshua was the leader who conquered and took possession of it. This tune, which, as the composer indicates, is to be sung in unison, begins with minor harmonies but finally cadences in major. Possibly the composer wished to suggest spiritual triumph after struggle in musical terms.

Didn't My Lord Deliver
  Daniel
St. 1–4
Traditional, version from *Ju-
  bilee Songs,* 1872

This song of deliverance could be interpreted in various ways, depending on what the singer had in mind. The lion's den from which the Lord delivered Daniel might be sin or unbelief, or it might be the bondage of slavery. The improvised character of the version given in *Jubilee Songs* is shown by the fact that the "verse" sections vary so much that the music is written out for each one. Moreover, the relationship of the sections is extremely loose. Verse 4, for example, "I set my foot on the Gospel ship," is more related to "The Old Ship of Zion" theme than to the story of Daniel. On the question of improvised harmony in Negro singing, it is interesting to note that the chorus sections here were marked "Sung in Unison." The syncopations in the chorus may be claimed as a characteristic figure of many spirituals. Two elaborations of this melody may be noted, one by S. Coleridge-Taylor in his *Twenty-Four Negro Melodies Transcribed for the Piano* (1904) and in the fifth of Henry F. B. Gilbert's *Negro Dances* (1914).

Dies Irae, Dies Illa   L.M.
That Day of Wrath, That
  Direful Day
St. 1–3, 8
Thomas of Celano, 13th cent.   Benjamin Carr, 1805
Anon. trans.

Carr composed and published music for both Catholic and Protestant Episcopal services. His *Masses, Vespers, Litanies, Hymns, Psalms, Anthems and Motets,* from which this setting of a translation of the "Dies Irae" was taken, was "composed, selected, and arranged for the use of the Catholic Churches in the United States of America." Although this music is for the choir, not the congregation, it is inserted here as an early American composition for Catholic use. The brief prelude and postlude for organ should be noted. We do not know who made this translation of Thomas of Celano's famous Latin poem, but it was familiar to American Catholics from its inclusion in early American hymnals.

Don't You Be Like the
  Foolish Virgin
St. 1, 3, 4, 7
Traditional, 1942

This song is presented here in the form in which it was printed in Lydia Parrish's *Slave Songs of the Georgia Sea Islands* (1942). Based on the parable of the wise and foolish virgins (Matthew 25:1–13), the reference to the coming of the bridegroom made it suitable for a wedding hymn. Although Lydia Parrish noted that most Negro wedding ceremonies did not involve music, she described one such occasion on which this song was both sung and acted out:

Two ushers walked from the altar with lighted lamps in their hands and met the bridal party at the door. Two little girls headed the procession and strewed flowers in its path . . . To the music of "O Zion—When the Bridegroom Comes," sung by the guests who filled the church, the participants moved to the altar, where the ushers put down their lamps . . .

We are told that the rhythm of this song led to its use by the Negro boatmen of Butler Island as a rowing song.

Down to the Sacred Wave   FERGUSON S.M.
St. 1–3
Samuel Francis Smith, 1832   George Kingsley, 1843

This baptismal hymn appeared in the *Additional Hymns* (1832) which served as a supplement to James M. Winchell's collection of 1817. It was retained in *The Psalmist* (1843), but because of its specifically Baptist teaching in regard to baptism it has remained within that denomination.

The tranquil movement of FERGUSON seemed well suited to this text. It was included in Kingsley's *The Harp of David* (1843), the title page of which notes that the collection contains "a number of Original Pieces of Music by the Editor." In the *Baptist Hymnal for Use in the Church and Home* (1883) Kingsley is given as the composer of this tune.

Ein von Gott Geborner Christ   CHRISTI WAHRES SEELENLICHT
Every Christian Born of God   7.6.7.6.D.
St. 1–2, 8, 10
Anon., 1829   Johann A. Freylinghausen,
                                    arr. 1704

This poem by an anonymous American Mennonite, included in John Joseph Stoudt's *Pennsylvania German Poetry,* was first published in 1829 in Lancaster, Pa., as part of the second supplement to the Mennonite *Unpartheyisches Gesang-Buch.*

The tune selected here comes from the *Geist-reiches Gesang-Buch* of Johann A. Freylinghausen. The original is for figured bass and melody. The figuring indicates not only chords but also suspensions (for example at the cadence of the first section) and ornamental passages (as in bar 10, second beat). In this bar the sopranos sing the simple melody, leaving the sixteenths to the organ. In bar 5, the last two quarters were originally figured $^6_5$.

Eternal God, How They're   WORCESTER C.M.
    Increased
Ps. 3: 1–3, 5, 8   Frost 46
Cotton Mather, 1718   John Playford, arr. 1671

This version of Psalm 3 in blank verse comes from Cotton Mather's *Psalterium Americanum,* where each psalm was provided with notes. "Every Psalm is here satellited with illustrations which are not fetched from vulgar annotations, but are the more fine, deep and uncommon thoughts, which in a course of long reading and thinking have been brought in the way of the collector. They are the golden keys to immense treasures of truth." Mather's notes for stanza one show his eagerness (which he shared with Watts) to interpret the Old Testament in terms of the New. "Singer, Now meditate on the sufferings of the Saviour. The fifth verse evidently mentions his death and resurrection." The fifth verse begins "I laid me down, and took my sleep, / And then I did awake . . ."

WORCESTER first appeared in Playford's *Psalms and Hymns in Solemn Musick of four parts* for Psalm 36. In the *Whole Book of Psalms,* under the name LITCHFIELD, he used it for Psalms 31 and 53.

Altus, C clef, third line; countertenor, C clef, third line; tenor, C clef, fourth line; bassus, F clef, fourth line. Time signature ₵ ; note values reduced by half. Playford intended his arrangement for male voices. We have adapted it for mixed voices by moving the tenor up an octave, thus placing the given melody in a register suitable for the soprano.

Eternal God, Whose Power   Eternal God C.M.D.
   Upholds
St. 1–5
Henry Hallam Tweedy, 1929   Douglas Moore, comp. 1957

In 1929, this hymn won a prize offered by the Hymn Society for a new missionary hymn.

Modern hymnals often provide alternate tunes for especially noteworthy texts. We follow this practice by printing two settings of Henry Hallam Tweedy's hymn, one by Douglas Moore and one by Quincy Porter. The Moore setting remains completely within the accepted conventions of the hymn tune and provides a fine straightforward setting of the text. The composer felicitously characterized his setting as "simple, but with strength."

Eternal God, Whose Power   Power C.M.D.
   Upholds
St. 1–5
Henry Hallam Tweedy, 1929   Quincy Porter, comp. 1956

Professor Tweedy was a friend of Quincy Porter's father when both were members of the Yale faculty. Young Porter was a student at Yale when Tweedy wrote his hymn and he composed and submitted a tune for it. It was not accepted and the composer asked himself why. When Dr. Carleton Sprague Smith asked him to compose new tunes for *American Hymns,* a mature Quincy Porter thought of his early composition. "On looking at the hymn yesterday, I could see a good many reasons why . . . so I completely rewrote it saving only the first measure." It is this almost completely new composition which is printed here. See also Quincy Porter's setting of William Vaughan Moody's "I stood within the heart of God."

Eternal Spirit, Source of   Psalm 104   8.8.8.D.
   Light
St. 1–4
Samuel Davies, 1769   James Lyon, 1761

This hymn, like others of Davies', is a prayer for a revival. His favorite device, the final refrain couplet, is freely treated. Added to a quatrain it produces a six-line stanza. Appearing first in Thomas Gibbons' *Hymns Adapted to Divine Worship* (London, 1769), the hymn was included in such widely circulated collections as *A Selection of Hymns from the Best Authors* by John Rippon (1787), the *Hartford Selection,* edited by Nathan Strong, Joseph Steward, and Abel Flint (1799), Asahel Nettleton's *Village Hymns* (1824), and others as late as the third quarter of the ◆neteenth century.

The tune, from Lyon's *Urania,* is here set to Isaac Watts's version of Psalm 104. Lyon has treated the text as a solo followed by a chorus for four voices. Oscar Sonneck, who published a detailed study on James Lyon, dates *Urania* 1762, relying on an advertisement which appeared in June of that year. However, this advertisement implies that some subscribers had already received their copies, and the example preserved at the Research Library for the Performing Arts is inscribed "Hetty Chambers . . . 1761."

Except the Lord that He for Us Had Been	FRENCH TUNE: PSALM 124 10.10.10.10.10.
Ps. 124: 1, 3, 4, 7–9	Frost 139
Henry Ainsworth, 1612	Giles Farnaby, arr. 1592

Psalm 124 is notable for the lines comparing the soul of man to a bird saved from the "entangling fowler's snare." Ainsworth himself used the FRENCH TUNE for PSALM 124 for his rendering of Psalm 8. It was one of the militant tunes of its period, sung by Protestants in 1602 when the Savoyards had been beaten back after attempting to capture Geneva by scaling the walls, the famous "escalade." It was also one of the few tunes of its period to remain in use to the present as TOULON or OLD 124 with the five lines reduced to four by omitting the third line of the original. It first appeared to a text by Théodore de Bèze in 1551 and passed into English usage by way of the Anglo-Genevan psalter of 1561. From that time it was included in a long series of English and Scottish psalters. The setting given here, from Thomas East's psalter of 1592, is by Giles Farnaby. See also the treatment of the same tune by William Daman ("Now Israel May Say, and That Truly").

Faint Falls the Gentle Voice St. 1–3	BETTEVER'S CHANT L.M.
Henry Timrod, writ. 1864	Benjamin H. Everett, 1871

This poem was written for music since it was "sung at a sacred concert at Columbia, S.C." A prayer for peace in the tragic period of the Civil War, it is in marked contrast to Timrod's partisan poems such as "Carolina" or "A Cry to Arms."

Asa Brooks Everett of Virginia was editor of *The Sceptre* with Benjamin H. Everett, who appears to claim BETTEVER'S CHANT. A number of tunes in *The Sceptre* were credited to Bettever. Perhaps this tune was named for him as a compliment. Possibly he composed the tune and Everett harmonized it. (Joan McQuary has suggested that Bettever is an anagram on B. Everett. Compilers of this period sometimes liked to disguise the fact that many of the tunes included were of their own composition.)

Far from Our Friends ST. SEPULCHRE C.M.
Ps. 137, st. 1–6
Jeremy Belknap, 1795 William Selby, 1762

Although Belknap's paraphrase portrays the fate of the Israelites deprived of liberty and far from their own land, it does so in general terms which deprive the psalm of much of its local color. "Far from our friends and country dear" replaces "By the rivers of Babylon." Omitted are the harps hung on the willow trees and the poignant rejoinder of the captives, "How shall we sing the Lord's song in a strange land?"

Both ALHALLOWS TUNE and ST. SEPULCHRE were composed by William Selby before he came to this country.

Father, Hear the Prayer We STOCKWELL 8.7.8.7.
  Offer
St. 1–4
Love Maria Willis, pub. 1859, Darius Eliot Jones, 1851
  alt. 1864

This hymn is one more example of the reshaping that many poems undergo before they assume the form with which we are familiar. The poem appeared in its original form in *Tiffany's Monthly* in 1859. It was extensively revised for publication in Samuel Johnson and Samuel Longfellow, *Hymns of the Spirit* (1864), possibly by Longfellow. The revised version was taken into a number of hymnbooks in England as well as in this country.

STOCKWELL is the tune by which Darius Eliot Jones is chiefly remembered. In *Temple Melodies,* edited by the composer, STOCKWELL was printed in B♭ major.

Father, in Thy Mysterious   WHITE 11.10.11.10.
    Presence Kneeling
St. 1–4
Samuel Johnson, 1846   T. B. White, 1877

"Father, in Thy Mysterious Presence Kneeling" first appeared in *A Book of Hymns for Public and Private Devotion*. This appeal for inner peace is one of Johnson's finest hymns. The coupling of Johnson's text and WHITE, named for its composer, T. B. White, is found in the Unitarian *Hymn and Tune Book* of 1877. Johnson's hymn has remained in use to the present day and is included in the *Hymns of the Spirit* of 1937.

Father! I Own Thy Voice   ASPIRATION 6.6.8.6.6.
St. 1–5
Samuel Wolcott, writ. 1868,   Luther O. Emerson, 1869
    pub. 1869

Samuel Wolcott, best remembered for his "Christ for the World! We Sing" (q.v.), has left an interesting account of the composition of "Father! I Own Thy Voice," his first hymn. "I was then in my fifty-sixth year, had never put two rhymes together, and had taken it for granted that I was as incompetent to write a hymn, or even a stanza, as to work a miracle. However, I resolved that I would try to write a hymn of five stanzas, and proceeded to plan it precisely as I would plan a sermon. I said, the first stanza shall be a recognition of God, the Father; the second, a recognition of Christ the Redeemer; the third a prayer to God the Father; the fourth a prayer to Christ the Redeemer, and the fifth shall blend the two in one address . . . I sent the hymn to Mr. [Darius Eliot] Jones who was so much pleased with it that he composed a tune for it, and inserted both in his *Songs for the New Life* (Chicago, 1869)."

ASPIRATION, a setting of Wolcott's poem by Luther O. Emerson, appeared in *The Choral Tribute* in the same year. A later setting of the same text by the same composer is WALCOTT (*sic*), which may be found in Emerson's *Choral Worship* (1884).

Father, Who Mak'st Thy
  Suff'ring Sons
St. 1–4
Arthur C. Coxe, writ. 1883
	HOSPITAL SUNDAY HYMN
	  8.8.8.D.
	
	George W. Warren, comp.
	  1883, pub. 1888

This text, written for the Hospital Saturday and Sunday Association of New York by Arthur C. Coxe, was set to music in 1883 by George W. Warren and published in *Warren's Hymns and Tunes, as Sung at St. Thomas's Church* in 1888. Designed for the choir, rather than the congregation, as indicated by the detailed directions for dynamic shading and articulation, it is also noteworthy for its freedom and variety of phrasing. Although the poem is composed of six lines of eight syllables each, the composer moves without pausing through two lines of the text to a cadential point in the fifth bar. In the next two musical sections the poetic line corresponds to rhythmically uniform two-bar groups. Beginning with line 5 an expressive prolongation of the words "Oh teach" expands the section to three bars of music, and the final line is similarly extended. Thus we have a poem with uniform lines rendered by a musical version containing varied and unsymmetrical groupings.

Fear Not, Poor Weary One St. 1–4 Thomas Cogswell Upham, writ. 1872, pub. 1874	DANVERS S.M. William Oscar Perkins, 1867

Like "O Thou Great Ruler of the Sky," this hymn was first published in *Hymns and Songs of Praise,* edited by Roswell D. Hitchcock, Zachary Eddy, and Philip Schaff.

A poem of consolation requires a tune of a gentle character. DANVERS, by William Oscar Perkins, was published in 1867 in *The Church Bell,* edited by Perkins and his brother Henry Southwick Perkins. It also appeared in his *The Choral Choir* (1882) with the upbeat and first measure altered. It is this version which we reproduce here.

Fire in My Meditation Burned	BENEDICTUS C.M.D.
Ps. 39: 3–9, last part of 12, 13	Frost 3
Henry Ainsworth, 1612	Richard Allison, arr. 1599

"A pilgrim as my fathers all" wrote Ainsworth in his version of Psalm 39, a line which the settlers in Plymouth could hardly have sung without thinking of their own wanderings.

The melody of this psalm, which first appeared in the 1560 edition of the Old Version, is known as the SONG OF ZACHARIAS or BENEDICTUS. The setting given here, by Richard Allison, places the melody in the soprano. A copy of Allison came to this country in the Mayflower as part of the library of William Brewster. The melody as given by Ainsworth, which differs slightly in rhythm from the form used by Allison, is printed after the polyphonic setting.

Not only the inclusion of optional accompanying parts for lute and the wire-strung cittern (omitted here) but the very layout of the original page show that this volume was intended for domestic recreation. If we open the book we find the cantus and lute at the bottom of the left page. The tenor was at the bottom of the right page. At the top of the pages, bottom side up to make them readable by performers seated on the other side of the table, were the cittern (left page) and altus part (right page). The bass sat at the right end of the table between tenor and altus and his part is in the middle of the right page and printed at right angles to the other parts.

Cantus, G clef, second line; altus, C clef, second line; tenor, C clef, third line; bassus, F clef, third line. Time signature ¢; note values halved. Tenor, last note, line 5, was D, corrected to C; cantus, line 8, fourth note, was E♮, corrected to E♭.

Five Were Foolish	THE DOOR WAS SHUT L.M., with chorus
St. 1–4	
Arthur J. Hodge, 1880	Robert Lowry, 1880

This hymn is a charming and almost playful treatment of the parable of the wise and foolish virgins as related in Matthew 25:1–13. Three times within the first stanza the poet contrasts the five wise with the five foolish virgins ending:

> Five were ready and five were not,
> Five remembered, and five forgot.

The tune by Robert Lowry matches the text naturally and with complete simplicity. Text and tune appeared in *Good as Gold* (1880), one of the many small oblong Sunday-School song books which poured forth from the presses in the latter half of the nineteenth century.

Fling Out the Banner!	BANNER L.M.D.
St. 1–6	
George Washington Doane, writ. 1848, pub. 1860	G. B. Lissart, 1894

Doane's missionary hymn was written in 1848 for a flag-raising ceremony at St. Mary's School in Burlington, N.J. First published in 1860 in *Hymns for Church and Home. Compiled by Members of the Protestant Episcopal Church*, it was republished in the authorized *Additional Hymns* (1865). It has been closely associated with the tune CAMDEN which the English composer Jean-Baptiste Calkin wrote in 1872.

The tune BANNER by G. B. Lissart, which appeared in Charles L. Hutchins' *The Church Hymnal Revised and Enlarged* (1894), was composed for "Fling Out the Banner!"

Floods Swell Around Me, Angry, Appalling	SCHELL 10.10.11.12.
St. 1–4	
Zachary Eddy, 1869	Uzziah C. Burnap, 1869

While minister of the Reformed Dutch Church in Brooklyn (1867–71), Eddy took a leading part in compiling *Hymns of the Church with Tunes* (1869). Three of his own hymns were included, among them "Jesus, Enthroned and Glorified" (q.v.) and the present hymn, a free paraphrase of Psalm 42, the "De Profundis."

The tune was SCHELL, composed by Uzziah C. Burnap, editor of the 1869 hymnal. Many of Burnap's tunes now seem sentimental because of his cloying chromatic alterations, but SCHELL has an admirable directness and simplicity.

For Just Men Light Is Sown	PSALM 71 S.M.D.
St. 2, 5, 7, 9, 10	Frost 88
Michael Wigglesworth, 1670	Anon., arr. 1635

The text printed here consists of stanzas from Michael Wigglesworth's *Meat out of the Eater* . . . . Could he have recalled the famous

Latin hymn known in English as "O Mother Dear, Jerusalem," when he penned the fourth stanza of our selection?

The tune given here was set to Psalm 71 in the Scottish psalter of 1635. The melody had appeared earlier in the English psalter of 1560, the Anglo-Genevan psalter of 1561, and in Scottish psalters from 1564/65. It has something of the sturdy vigor which characterizes the text. Since the third line of stanza 5 is one syllable short, the first syllable of the word "mansions" should be sung to two notes. (Possibly Wigglesworth pronounced the word in three syllables.)

Soprano, C clef, first line; countertenor, C clef, third line; tenor, C clef, fourth line; bass, F clef, fourth line. Time signature lacking; note values halved; transposed up one step.

For Lo! My Jonah How He   CANTERBURY C.M.
  Slumped
Anagram 2, St. 1–4, 6, 8
John Wilson, copied bet. 1712   John Playford, arr. 1677
  and 1723

This poem by John Wilson has interest for us from several points of view. It was preserved in the manuscript journal of Joseph Tompson of Billerica, Mass., together with eleven other poems written as "memorialls and epitaphs upon my Deare." Of these, six dealt with William Tompson, father of Joseph and also of Benjamin, the latter remembered as one of our early poets. William Tompson, who came to Boston in 1637, was called as minister to Braintree in 1639. John Wilson's poem developed a parallel between the trials of Jonah and the "black melancholy" which, as Cotton Mather said, "for divers Years almost wholly disabled him for the Exercise of his Ministry." As Jonah was delivered from the whale, so William Tompson was given strength to conquer his black moods and to die in peace. "For Lo! My Jonah How He Slumped" is an anagram on William Tompson. The anagram was a favorite device with this early New England divine and writer of verse. This is the second of two anagrams on William Tompson included in Joseph Tompson's journal. The text has a balladlike quality which is well suited to singing. Our excerpt closes with line 32, although the poet continues, reinforcing his point by considering the afflictions of Job:

> If Paul and Jonah will not serve
>   To satisfie your mind,
> Concider Job, and be not like
>   To his unfriendly friends.

CANTERBURY is presented here as arranged by John Playford in *The Whole Book of Psalms: With the Usual Hymns and Spiritual Songs* (London, 1677).

Time signature ¢. Playford uses two sharps in his key signature and does not have a G♯ for the bass in bar 2. In stanza 1, line 3, "commandment" must be given three syllables.

From Age to Age They Gather	HOSMER	Irregular
St. 1–4		
Frederick Lucian Hosmer, writ. 1891, pub. 1894	Frederick Field Bullard, 1902	

This poem, with its marching stride, follows the rhythmic pattern of the BATTLE HYMN OF THE REPUBLIC and may be sung to that tune. Indeed that was the tune used for it in H. Augustine Smith's *Hymnal for American Youth* (1926).

The tune HOSMER used here was composed by Frederick Field Bullard for *The Pilgrim Hymnal* of which he was associate musical editor. Vigorous in rhythm, the tune is sequential in construction. The same melodic pattern serves for three lines, rising a third each time and then concluding with sustained chords. "From Age to Age They Gather," a vigorous affirmation of the ultimate triumph of right and truth, was an occasional poem intended for the dedication of Unity Church, Decorah, Iowa. In 1894 it was published in *The Thought of God, 2nd Series.*

From Countless Hearts (A Prayer for Peace)	8.8.7.10.
St. 1–3	
Gail Brook Burket, submitted 1955	Paul Nordoff, comp. 1955

The refrain of this poem becomes more inclusive with each stanza (We pray for peace to bless our lives, our lands, the world). Paul Nordoff's setting follows the pattern of the poem by providing a musical refrain, marked "Slower." For the third stanza the refrain is altered, forming the climax of the composition. This is a unison hymn with keyboard accompaniment. The varied dynamic scheme, the changes in tempo, and the high climax notes make it more suitable for choir, or junior choir, than for congregational performance.

From Heart to Heart   Clovelly C.M.
St. 1–4
William Channing Gannett,   Horatio Parker, 1903
    writ. 1875, pub. 1885

"From Heart to Heart," one of the most widely used of the author's hymns, was written to celebrate the 150th anniversary of the First Religious Society of Newburyport. First published in *The Thought of God* (1st series, 1885), it was also included in the Unitarian *New Hymn and Tune Book* (1914), the *Hymns of the Spirit* (1937), and *Hymns for the Celebration of Life* (1964). Horatio Parker's Clovelly was one of a number of original tunes which he composed for the *Hymnal* (1903) of which he was the editor.

From Whence Doth This   Savannah L.M.
    Union Arise?
St. 1–3, 6
Thomas Baldwin, writ. c.   William Billings, 1778
    1780

"From Whence Doth This Union Arise?" was written about 1780. The lines of the hymn came into Thomas Baldwin's mind when he was returning to Canaan from Newport, N.H., where he had gone to resolve differences that were threatening to split the church there. It was first published in J. Asplund, *New Collection* (Baltimore, Md., 1793).

A number of musicians made settings for the hymn, including Samuel Holyoke and Jeremiah Ingalls. Savannah appeared in Billings' *The Singing Master's Asssistant* to Charles Wesley's "Ah! Lovely Appearance of Death" (q.v.), although Billings himself attributes the text to "G.W.," i.e., George Whitefield. The coupling of Baldwin's hymn and Billings' tune seems to have been made in the South. At any rate it is found in William Walker's *Southern Harmony* (1835), but with the setting slightly altered and the tune name changed from Savannah to Union. Billings himself used Union as the name of a different tune in *The New England Psalm Singer*.

Soprano, G clef, second line; countertenor, C clef, third line; tenor, G clef, second line; bass, F clef, fourth line. In *The Singing Master's Assistant* Billings consistently uses the old form of the clef, written like a manuscript G, for the soprano and the modern form for the tenor. Time signature ₵ ; tune in tenor.

Gebenedyt Sey Allzeit	ALLEIN GOTT IN DER HÖHE
Be Glorified Eternally	8.7.8.7.8.8.7.
St. 1, 2, 5, 8	Zahn 4457
Balthasar Hoffman, 1762	Balthasar Schmid, arr. 1748
Sheema Z. Buehne, trans.	
1965	

Thirty-nine hymns by Balthasar Hoffman, including the example here, appear in the first printed hymnal of the Schwenkfelder sect. It was doubly important because, in Silesia, the Schwenkfelders were not allowed to print their hymns but had to circulate them in manuscript.

The melody, designated only by name in the 1762 hymnal, is supplied here from the choral book of Balthasar Schmid. Since the original is for melody and figured bass only, the middle parts are realized here in accordance with these indications. The figure 6 in bar 2 would usually be rendered as $\frac{6}{5}$. Schmid assumes that the organist has both melody and bass before him and figures only the notes that appear in neither. The figure $\natural$ in bar 9 means that the sixth above the bass is sharped.

Give Ear, O God, to My Loud Cry	HACKNEY C.M.
Ps. 61: 1–6	Frost 333a
Thomas Prince, 1758	Version from John Tufts, 1726

The congregation at the Old South Church, Boston, where Thomas Prince was pastor, refused to give up the *Bay Psalm Book*, but did sanction a revision to remove the "flatness in diverse places" which Prince had criticized. This revision appeared in 1858 under the title *The Psalms, Hymns, and Spiritual Songs of the Old and New Testaments, Faithfully translated into English metre, Being the New England Psalm-Book Revised and Improved.* The congregation at the Old South Church used this book for thirty years. Elsewhere the dominant trend was toward a freer and more literary treatment of the Psalms and a more general use of hymns in religious worship.

HACKNEY, like SOUTHWELL, has been taken from a musical supplement which was bound with Prince's revision of the *Bay Psalm Book*. Ultimately both were derived from John Playford's *Whole Book of Psalms* of 1677.

Time signature $\math₵$; bar lines omitted except at the end of each line; note values halved; transposed down a whole step.

Give Ear, O Heavens, to That Which I Declare	FRENCH TUNE: PSALM 120 10.10.10.10.D.
Deut. 32: 1–3, 6, 7	Frost 328
Henry Ainsworth, 1619	Claude Goudimel, arr. 1565

This metrical version of Moses' Song comes from *Annotations upon the Fifth Book of Moses Called Deuteronomie* by Henry Ainsworth (Amsterdam, 1619, republished 1627). The melody appeared first in the French Genevan psalter of 1551 for Psalm 120. The original version is 9.9.9.9.9.9.8.8. Ainsworth lengthened all the lines to ten syllables. He adapted the tune by repeating one note of the original in lines 1 to 6 and by repeating two notes in line 7. In line 8 he adds a new note (B♭) between A and its repetition. We print Ainsworth's form of the melody after the Goudimel setting. Ainsworth also used this melody for his versions of Psalms 49, 78, 80, 91, and 94.

Superius, C clef, first line; countertenor, C clef, third line; tenor, C clef, fourth line; bassus, F clef, fourth line. Note values halved. In the Jaqui edition of Goudimel the bass has E♮ in line 2, third note; line 4, seventh note; and line 8, third note. We suggest E♭ in each case to correct the diminished fifth.

Give Peace in These Our Days, O Lord	DA PACEM or HIGH DUTCH TUNE 8.7.8.7.D.
St. 1–3	Frost, 183; Zahn 7556
Edmund Grindal, 1561	Thomas Ravenscroft, arr. 1621

Wolfgang Köpfel's "Gib Fried zu unser Zeit," which appeared in the Strassburg *Gesangbuch* of 1533, was translated as "Give Peace in These Our Days" by the English exile Edmund Grindal when he was living in that city. It was published in the English psalter of 1561. Both text and tune closely followed the German originals. Harmonizations may be found in John Day (1563), in William Damon's publications of 1579 and 1591, in Giles Farnaby (1592), Richard Allison (1599), and Ravenscroft (1621). Ravenscroft's setting is reproduced here.

Cantus, C clef, second line; medius, C clef, third line; "tenor or faburden," C clef, fourth line; bassus, F clef, fourth line. Time signature C ; note values halved. Tenor, line 3, next to last note altered from A to F in conformity with line 1. The consecutive fifths, line 6, medius and tenor, notes 5 and 6, are in the original. In stanza 1, line 4, and in stanza 3, lines 4 and 8, have six syllables. In stanzas 2 and 3 the third line has an added syllable. The music has been edited to compensate for these irregularities.

Give Peace, O God, the   VERMONT C.M.
   Nations Cry
St. 1–5
John W. Norris, 1940   Anne Langdon Miller, 1941

This hymn for peace speaks for itself; the year it was submitted (1939) marked the outbreak of World War II. The tune followed it by two years. Anne Langdon Miller named her tune for Vermont, where she had played in the state symphony orchestra for several years. Both text and music were intended for inclusion in *The Hymnal 1940* and were first published in that volume. In the opening phrase the soprano melody is doubled by the tenor. Only in the second part of the tune is four-part harmony employed.

The Gloomy Night of   GEORGE 7.6.7.6.D.
   Sadness
St. 1–4
Anon., 1834   Abraham Down Merrill, 1834

This sprightly melody is taken from *The Wesleyan Harp* of which Merrill was an editor. The preface is a forthright defense of simplicity and ease of comprehension as the cardinal qualities in good revival hymn tunes. "Our plan has been to take *good* tunes wherever we could find them," said the editors, and the borrowings from Joshua Leavitt's *The Christian Lyre* (1831) show the direction taken. "Scots Who Hae with Wallace Bled," "Home Sweet Home," and "Blow the Wind Southerly" are found here with spiritual texts. The claim that some tunes in general use were written down and here published for the first time is to be particularly noted. GEORGE, claimed by Merrill, has something of "As I Went to Sandgate" about it and is altogether in the movement of a lively folk dance. The anonymous text is a joyful description of Christ's second coming.

Glory
St. 1–4
Joseph Wise, cop. 1967   Joseph Wise, cop. 1967

A literature of devotional songs has developed in recent years, accompanied by the guitar and expressed in an idiom derived from the folk song and the popular song. Joseph Wise's "Glory" and Richard Avery's "And the Cock Began to Crow" illustrate this trend. Structurally "Glory" resembles certain spirituals. The refrain precedes the verse section and the short verse lines alternate with "Glory, sing to the Lord." This, however, is no liturgical Gloria and the short lines tell in colloquial language of the coming of Christ, of his love for children, and compare the rising of the sun to the rising of Christ.

The composer calls this melody a "walking blues" and the blue note (the lowered sixth step) appears near the end of the refrain and the verse melody. The chords for guitar are indicated by letters: G, for example, symbolizes the G major chord: G, B, D. Copyright © 1967, this song was included in the Catholic *People's Mass Book* (Cincinnati, 1970).

Glückselger ist uns Doch
   keine Nacht
For Us No Night Can Be
   Happier
St. 1, 6, 9
Nicolaus L. Zinzendorf, im-
   provised 1742, pub. 1743
John Gambold (?), trans.
   1754

Nun Bitten Wir

Zahn 2029a
Christian Gregor, 1784

This hymn had the heading "In der Christ-Nacht zu Bethlehem 1742." It was the second Christmas which Count Zinzendorf had passed in Bethlehem, Pa. In the previous year he had given the new settlement its name from the phrase "not Jerusalem but Bethlehem" in the second stanza of Adam Drese's "Jesu rufe mich." In 1742, says the record, "Brother Ludwig [Zinzendorf] sung extemporaneously for this occasion the hymn 'Glückselger ist uns doch keine Nacht' . . . We spent these blessed Christmas Eve hours in reverent singing and prayer until one o'clock of the midnight."

The text was first printed in Appendix xi (1743) of the *Herrnhuter Gesangbuch* in thirty-seven stanzas. It was translated into English, perhaps by John Gambold, the editor of *A Collection of Hymns of the Children of God in All Ages,* where it appeared in Part ii, which was devoted to Moravian hymns of the eighteenth century. A recent American translation of the complete Zinzendorf text is the work of Bishop Kenneth G. Hamilton.

The tune Nun Bitten Wir utilizes the melody and figured bass as printed in the *Choral-Buch* of Christian Gregor.

"Go, Bring Me," Said the   THE DYING BACKSLIDER
  Dying Fair   C.M.D.
St. 1–4
William Hunter, 1854   Samuel Wakefield, 1854

" 'Go, Bring Me,' Said the Dying Fair" may more properly be
called a religious ballad than a hymn. Like "The Backslider" from
the same volume, *The Minstrel of Zion* of Hunter and Wakefield, it
presents the experience of one who has fallen from grace. In this instance the sinner is a girl tempted by jewels and "robes of princely
cost" to satisfy her pride and that of her father. To the modern
reader her sad fate is likely to seem a drastic atonement for wearing
a pretty dress. However, the plain garb of such groups as the
Quakers and the Amish shows how closely they linked simplicity of
dress with religious belief. "Miss Hataway's Experience," in William
Hauser's *Hesperian Harp,* is a similar religious ballad, although Miss
Hataway's weakness was dancing rather than fine clothes.

The original setting was for soprano and unfigured bass. The
inner parts printed here are editorial additions. Although we have
preferred Wakefield's tune this text was usually sung to a Scottish
air, THE ROSE OF ALLENDALE.

God Be with You Till We   GOD BE WITH YOU 9.8.8.9.,
  Meet Again   with chorus
St. 1–4
Jeremiah E. Rankin, writ.   William G. Tomer, comp.
  1882   1882

"God Be with You Till We Meet Again" is the accepted song of
farewell in the tradition of the gospel hymn. It was a successor to the
hymns sung on the final morning of a camp meeting before people
dispersed to their homes. PARTING HAND in the *Original Sacred Harp*
illustrates the type. Rankin stated that his hymn was "written in 1882
as a Christian good-bye, it was called forth by no person or occasion,
but was deliberately composed as a Christian hymn on the basis of
the etymology of 'good-bye,' which means 'God be with you.' " It was
first published with the setting by Tomer in *Gospel Bells* (1883).

God from His Throne with   Russia L.M.
   Piercing Eye
St. 1–6
Joseph Steward, 1799   Daniel Read, 1793

In 1833, a writer, summing up the effect of *The Hartford Selection* (1799), noted that "it has been printed in greater numbers, has been diffused more exclusively, and has imparted more alarm to the sinner, and more consolation to the saint, than any other compilation of religious odes in this country." The hymns of Joseph Steward seem admirably adapted to produce alarm. This is especially true of the present hymn, which is headed by the word "Depravity." First printed in *The Hartford Selection,* it was repeated with the writer's name in Asahel Nettleton's *Village Hymns* (1824), where the tunes suggested were Bath, Leyden, and Truro.

Russia, one of the best-known compositions of Daniel Read, is not in his *American Singing Book* (1785) or his *Columbian Harmonist,* No. 1 (1793), but it does appear in Jacob French's *Psalmodist's Companion* (1793).

Countertenor, C clef, third line. Time signature Ɔ ; tune in tenor.

The God of Bethel Heard Her New Britain C.M.
   Cries
St. 1–3
Richard Allen, 1793   Anon., version of 1859

Two hymns appear in Richard Allen's printed works, "The God of Bethel Heard Her Cries," from *Life, Experience, and Labors* (1793), and "Ye Ministers that Are Called to Preaching," from *A Short Address to the Friend of Him that Hath No Helper.* They appear to be the earliest hymns published by a Negro in the United States. More important is *A Collection of Hymns & Spiritual Songs* (Philadelphia, 1801), which contains unidentified hymns that may have been written by the compiler.

Since Allen for a time attended a church in Philadelphia with a predominantly white congregation, he must have been acquainted with the psalm tunes sung there. The earliest collection of Negro spirituals would not be published for nearly three quarters of a century.

The tune chosen here is New Britain, better known as Amazing Grace. It was printed in many of the Southern tune books, and has been sung to the present. Our score is based on *The Sacred Harp* (1859). Original key E major.

God of My Life!   STANDISH C.M.
St. 1–3, 6
Benjamin Colman, 1711   Version from John Tufts,
                                        1726

Benjamin Colman, a correspondent of Isaac Watts, was also an occasional writer of verses in a similar manner. In a letter to Cotton Mather, Colman praised Watts as a "great Master in Poetry, and a burning Light and Ornament of the Age." He went on to write: "You will forgive that I emulate, and have dared to imitate his Metre in the Inclosed; its flame, brevity and Metre. Be candid, and think not that I name 'em with the least of His. Yet I have succeeded better, I confess, than I expected." Colman's poem has the subtitle "On a recovery from sickness" and stanzas 2 and 3 tell of his ills until his "Saviour came, bid me revive, take up my bed and go."

STANDISH, English in origin, was among the tunes in the 1726 edition of John Tufts's *Art of Singing Psalm Tunes,* but the staff ruled for the medius was blank. The version given here follows this edition of Tufts with certain changes noted below.

The medius is supplied from the musical supplement to the 1742 edition of the *Bay Psalm Book.* The following changes have been made: cantus, line 2, Tufts has D$^\sharp$; medius, line 1, note 6, *Bay* has G$^\sharp$; medius, line 3, note 4, *Bay* has B; bassus, line 2, notes 4 and 5, Tufts has E, D.

God of Our Fathers   ITHACA 9.9.9.9.
St. 1–3
Melancthon W. Stryker, 1889   William Piutti, 1884

Stryker, a Presbyterian minister and educator, contributed to American hymnology as an editor of hymnbooks and as a hymn writer. Among the volumes which he edited was *The College Hymnal* (1896). "God of Our Fathers" is one of several original poems included in that volume. Written in 1889, it was abbreviated by the author to three stanzas. The tune ITHACA to which Stryker's verses were set in *The College Hymnal* is retained here.

God of Our Fathers, Bless This Our Land	5.4.5.4.5.4.5.4.5.5.5.5.
St. 1–4	
John Henry Hopkins Jr., 1882	Dudley Buck, 1894

Although Dudley Buck's compositions may be largely forgotten today, his prestige in his own time as a brilliant organist and composer of anthems and other choral works for the church service was very great. His influence on the hymn tune was most directly felt through *The Hymnal Revised and Enlarged* (1894, edited by J. Ireland Tucker and William Rousseau), for which he composed four tunes. Most were set to English texts in special meters. His setting of John Henry Hopkins' "God of Our Fathers, Bless This Our Land" was a vigorous treatment of a national hymn in stanzas of twelve lines. Hopkins published this hymn together with his own tune in his *Carols, Hymns, and Songs.*

God of Our Fathers, Whose Almighty Hand	NATIONAL HYMN 10.10.10.10.
St. 1–4	
Daniel C. Roberts, writ. 1876, pub. 1892	George W. Warren, 1892

This hymn was written for the centennial Fourth of July celebration at Brandon, Vt., in 1876.

The author had originally thought of the Russian national anthem by Alexis F. Lvoff as a tune for his text, but Dr. J. Ireland Tucker asked George W. Warren, organist of St. Thomas' Church, New York, to write a more suitable tune. Entitled NATIONAL HYMN, his majestic melody was published in *The Hymnal Revised and Enlarged* of the Protestant Episcopal Church, 1892.

God of Peace, in Peace Preserve Us	PAX 8.7.8.7.7.7.
St. 1–3	
Ernst W. Olson, 1958	Clive Harold Kilgore, 1958

"God of Peace, in Peace Preserve Us" was printed in *The Service Book and Hymnal of the Lutheran Church in America* (1958). It was provided with a tune composed for it by Clive Harold Kilgore, to which the appropriate name PAX was given. This vigorous setting in conservative church style is in a diminutive three-part song form, with the return modified to reach a climax to form a more emphatic cadence.

God of the Nations	PRO PATRIA 10.10.10.10.
St. 1–4	
Walter Russell Bowie, writ.	Horatio Parker, 1894
1913, pub. 1914	

"God of the Nations" is a plea for growth in brotherhood among the peoples of the earth. First published by the Survey Associates in *Social Hymns of Brotherhood and Aspiration* (1914) it was included in a number of hymnals edited by H. Augustine Smith (the earliest, *Hymns for the Living Age,* 1923, where it is dated 1913). The first line of this hymn must be distinguished from the similar line by John Haynes Holmes "God of the Nations, near and far" (q.v.).

Horatio Parker's PRO PATRIA appeared in Charles L. Hutchin's *The Church Hymnal Revised and Enlarged* (1894) as a setting for Daniel C. Roberts' well-known "God of Our Fathers, Whose Almighty Hand" (q.v.). We have preferred the contemporary American tune by George W. Warren for Roberts' hymn and have matched Parker's tune with Bowie's twentieth-century national hymn of freedom and brotherhood. See also "Heralds of Christ."

God of the Nations, Near and	HOLMES C.M.
Far	
St. 1–6	
John Haynes Holmes, writ.	Edward Shippen Barnes,
1911, pub. 1914	writ. 1936, pub. 1937

This prayer for peace strikes a characteristic note in its emphasis on the longing for peace on the part of scientists, labor, and the common people. Holmes wrote "God of the Nations" in 1911 for use on Peace Sunday and submitted it in a competition sponsored by the Federal Council of Churches of Christ in America. It has been widely used and was included in the Unitarian *New Hymn and Tune Book* of 1914 and in *Hymns of the Spirit* (1937) where the second stanza was altered.

HOLMES, named for the author of the text, is a unison hymn by the American organist-composer Edward Shippen Barnes. Composed in 1936, it was published in H. Augustine Smith's *The New Church Hymnal* in 1937.

God of the Prophets! Bless the Prophets' Sons	ASSURANCE 10.10.10.10.
St. 1–6	
Denis Wortman, 1884	William Fiske Sherwin, 1878

This hymn was written for, and was originally used to celebrate, the hundredth year of service of the New Brunswick Theological Seminary where Wortman himself had been a student. It has found a wider application as a hymn stating in poetic terms the ideals of a Christian ministry.

Sherwin, the composer of ASSURANCE, is best remembered for his settings of two poems by Mary Artemisia Lathbury, "Break Thou the Bread of Life" (q.v.) and "Day Is Dying in the West" (q.v.). ASSURANCE was first published in Charles S. Robinson's *Spiritual Songs* (1878).

God of the Strong, God of the Weak	GODWIN L.M.
St. 1–4	
Richard W. Gilder, writ. 1903, pub. 1910	William G. Blanchard, comp. 1934, pub. 1935

"God of the Strong, God of the Weak" by Richard W. Gilder was written for and first used at a service in memory of Dr. J. L. M. Curry which took place in Richmond, Va., April 26, 1903, under the auspices of the Southern Educational Conference. It was chosen for inclusion in *The Methodist Hymnal* of 1932, where it was shortened by omitting the last two of the original six stanzas.

The tune GODWIN was especially composed for Gilder's text in 1934. Our version is based on that in *The Methodist Hymnal*.

God of the World, Thy Glories Shine	SUCCOTH L.M.
St. 1–4	
Sewall Sylvester Cutting, 1843	Anon., 1835

Although this hymn of praise to God was published in the *Select Hymns* of James H. Linsley and Gustavus F. Davis beginning "Creator, God! thy glories blaze," we have preferred the version with an altered first line as printed in *The Psalmist* (1843). An expanded variant of the hymn with the first line changed to "Great God, Thy glories blaze" appeared in *The Service of Song for Baptist Churches* (1871).

Possibly the most influential collection of tunes of the 1830s was Lowell Mason's *The Boston Academy's Collection*. SUCCOTH, with its vigorous unisons, seemed well suited to this hymn of praise, although MENDON from the same collection will be found to be a satisfactory substitute. Henry L. Mason lists SUCCOTH among the original hymn tunes of Lowell Mason, although he gives 1840 as the date of composition. There is no attribution in *The Boston Academy's Collection*.

God Stelt Ons Hier   FRENCH TUNE: PSALM 116
God Set Us Here   10.10.10.10.
St. 1–3, 5   Frost 329; Zahn 859
Nicasius de Sille, writ. after   *Thysius Lute Book*, arr. c.1610
  1657

This "Song in the Manner of the 116th Psalm" comes from the third part of a poem describing the pleasures of life in New Utrecht (now part of Brooklyn), where the author lived. Our translation has been slightly modified from the version given in Murphy's *Poets of the New Netherlands*. The prayer for deliverance from the Indians was written at a time when the devastating attacks on the Dutch settlers were a matter of recent history.

The Dutch settlers sang psalms, perhaps in the translation by Dathenius, to Calvinist tunes. The tune to Psalm 116 passed into Lutheran use and was used by Henry Ainsworth for his version of Psalm 97. The Dutch organist Antony van Noordt used it as the theme for an interesting set of variations. Our own setting is adapted from a manuscript version in the *Thysius Lute Book*.

The *Livre de luth de Thysius*, a manuscript owned by the Thysius Library in Leyden, contains precious transcriptions of vocal compositions, both religious and secular, and dances of the seventeenth century. Its probable compiler and first owner was a pastor in Rotterdam named Adriaan Joriszoon Smout. The collection was presumably made in Leyden about 1600. Its later owner, Johann Thysius, first a reader, later a preacher in Rotterdam, gave his name to the manuscript collection.

The *Thysius Lute Book* contains settings of forty-four tunes from the Genevan psalter, many of them appearing in different versions, some of them taken from the psalm settings of Claude Goudimel (q.v.), Claude Le Jeune (q.v.), and Sweelinck. Occasionally the French texts of Clément Marot or the Dutch texts of Dathenius and Smout are given.

The tune is diatonic and in major, but the arrangement alters it by sharpening the C in bars 1, 8, and 13.

God Supreme! To Thee We   7.7.7.7.7.
  Pray
St. 1–4
Penina Moise, 1840, st. 1, 2   Joseph Achron, 1932
Edward N. Calisch, st. 3, 4

Penina Moise wrote the first hymnbook in English intended for the synagogue to be published in the United States (Charleston, S.C., 1840). Fourteen of her hymns were chosen for inclusion in the *Union Hymnal* of 1914, including the present example. "God Supreme! To Thee We Pray" had six stanzas in the 1840 hymnal. "We" was substituted for "I" in the opening line and the original refrain was "Hallelujah, be it so."

The setting, by the Russian-American violinist Joseph Achron, appeared in the *Union Hymnal* of 1932.

God, To Thee We Humbly   IMPERIAL 7.7.7.7.D.
  Bow
St. 1, 2, 4, 5
George H. Boker, 1864   C. M. Wyman, 1868

During the Civil War George H. Boker turned from drama to the writing of verses on patriotic themes. His battle hymn, "God, To Thee We Humbly Bow," survives as an expression of a critical and tragic period in our history as viewed by a Northern poet. His poem was hardly written with the usual meters of the hymnbook in mind, since few if any contemporary tune books provide music for poems with seven lines of seven syllables each. Nevertheless it was included in the *Voice of Praise* (1871) as the only hymn under the heading "In Time of War, in the Field."

IMPERIAL was composed by C. M. Wyman, then of Keene, N.H., who was one of the contributors to George F. Root's *The Triumph* of 1868. In singing Boker's text to this tune the last line of each stanza must be repeated.

Gracious Saviour, We Adore   FENWICK 8.7.8.7.4.7.
  Thee
St. 1, 2
Sewall Sylvester Cutting, 1832   Anon., 1845

The unusual meter of this simple and appropriate baptismal hymn sets it apart from other contemporary Baptist poems on the same subject: Adoniram Judson's "Come Holy Spirit, Dove Divine" and Samuel F. Smith's "Down to the Sacred Wave" (q.v.). The use of the word "wave," which seems too dramatic a term for a quiet stream or lake, is common to all three. In Cutting's poem the word appears in stanza 2, "Thou wast laid beneath the wave." This text was included in two of the important Baptist books of the period: James N. Winchell's *Additional Hymns* of 1832 and Samuel F. Smith's *The Psalmist* (1843).

The composer, presented with a rhyme scheme with a short line, was likely to expand it to the length of the longer lines. This was the course followed by George B. Loomis in his AMELIA which appeared in George F. Root's *The Diapason* (1860). Perhaps because the modern ear is pleased with variety of musical phrasings we have preferred FENWICK which was printed without attribution in *The Psaltery* (1845) of Lowell Mason and George J. Webb. Here the short line is represented as a two-bar unit while lines of seven and eight syllables correspond to normal four-bar phrases.

The Gray Hills Taught Me Patience	MANCHESTER 7.6.7.6.
St. 1–3	
Allen Eastman Cross, 1926	G. Waring Stebbins, 1927

In his *Three Centuries of American Hymnody* Henry Wilder Foote has characterized "The Gray Hills Taught Me Patience" as "not quite a hymn in form" but "a lovely little poem of meditation." It has been used as a hymn, however, and may be found in H. Augustine Smith's *American Student Hymnal* (1928) with a tune by G. Waring Stebbins.

The tune name MANCHESTER suggests that the composer may have associated Cross's "gray hills" with Mount Equinox, which towers behind that Vermont town. Stebbins' setting with its accompaniment in organ style is intended as a unison hymn.

Great God, How Frail a Thing Is Man	THOMAS-TOWN C.M.D.
St. 1, 2	
Mather Byles, 1744	William Billings, 1781

This poem on the brief span of man's life by the learned and witty divine Mather Byles appeared in the author's *Poems on Several Occasions*. THOMAS-TOWN was included both in *The Psalm Singers Amusement* (1781) and in *The Continental Harmony* (1794) of William Billings.

The hymn is not a fuguing tune of the type commonly associated with Billings, but is of a simple and serious character in keeping with the message of the text. Although the musical phrases are symmetrical throughout, each begins with a preliminary half rest and half note, and each ends with a whole note. Thus each phrase is extended beyond the normal length of four bars. The effect may represent the performance practice of a country choir of the eighteenth century: a solidly sustained chord at the end of each phrase, a half rest to give time for a big breath, a half note to get ready, and then off on the new phrase.

Countertenor, C clef on the third line. Original time signature $\mathcal{C}$; tune in tenor.

Great God, Preserver of All
  Things
St. 1–3, 4 (selected lines)
Francis Daniel Pastorius

DIE HELLE SONNE IST DAHIN
  C.M.
Zahn 206
Laurentius Erhardi, arr. 1659

A fine Latinist and a writer of verses both German and English, Pastorius was distinguished by a gently ingratiating spirit. Even when he wrote against slavery he did so with a quiet reasonableness which was not less effective because of that characteristic. In the present poem the figure of the Lord as the "good husbandman" pruning the branches to make them more fruitful in this "wild and woody land" is both vivid and picturesque.

We do not know that Pastorius intended his verses to be sung. Although the present poem was written in alternate lines of eight and six syllables, perhaps the most usual hymn meter, the difficulty of dividing it into stanzas of uniform length seems to show that the poet did not consider the demands of music. Yet his is a voice that would be missed among our early poets. His verses have been associated here with a chorale tune of a type which he might have heard either in the land of his birth or among the German settlers in Pennsylvania.

DIE HELLE SONNE IST DAHIN is reproduced after the arrangement in Erhardi's *Harmonisches Chor und Figural Gesang-Buch* with the note values reduced by half. The music in this chorale book was printed in score for four voices and the inner parts as well as the bass are therefore by Erhardi.

Great God, the Followers of Thy Son	WOODSTOWN L.M.
St. 1–4	
Henry Ware Jr., writ. 1819, pub. 1868	Benjamin Holt, 1822

This ordination hymn, written in 1819, finally appeared in two anthologies of religious verse: Charles Dexter Cleveland's *Lyra Sacra Americana* (1868) and Alfred Putnam's *Singers and Songs of the Liberal Faith* (1875). The Unitarian *Hymn and Tune Book* (1877) included it, as did its successors of 1914 and 1937, setting it to Hatton's DUKE STREET.

In accordance with our practice of choosing American tunes of the same period as the text, we have selected WOODSTOWN, from Lowell Mason's *The Boston Handel and Haydn Society Collection* (1822), composed by one of its early conductors, Benjamin Holt.

In bar 12, the first notes in soprano and alto were written as long appoggiaturas.

Great God, Thy Works (Hymn at Sea)	ARNHEIM L.M.
St. 1–5	
Mather Byles, writ. 1732, pub. 1744	Samuel Holyoke, 1791

Governor Belcher of Massachusetts invited Mather Byles to accompany him on a voyage to the coast of Maine. The latter declined, but consented to conduct the service on the governor's ship, which was anchored for the Sabbath. Tea followed the service, but when Byles finally went on deck he found that the ship was already under way. On the following Sunday Byles, still an involuntary passenger, wrote his "Hymn at Sea" for the service on that day, since no hymn-book could be found.

This was not the end of the episode. On Byles's return Joseph Green (q.v.) wrote a most unclerical parody of his hymn beginning:

> With vast amazement we survey
> The can so broad, so deep,
> Where punch succeeds to strong sangree,
> Both to delightful flip.

Byles parodied the parody in similar vein:

> In Byles's works an oversight,
> Green spy'd as once he smok'd his chunk;

Alas! that Byles should never write
A song to sing when folks are drunk.

Byles's hymn was later published in his *Poems on Several Occasions.*

The tune chosen here for Byles's text is ARNHEIM, the most famous composition of Samuel Holyoke, which appeared in the latter's *Harmonia Americana.* This version in three voices has been preferred to the later arrangement in four parts in Holyoke's *Columbian Repository.*

Time signature Ɔ; tune in tenor; transposed down a minor third.

Great Lord of All, Whose   HYMN FOR WHITSUNDAY L.M.
  Work of Love
St. 1, 2, 4–6
Jacob Duché, c.1785   Thomas Spence Duché, 1801

"Great Lord of All," like "Chilled by the Blasts of Adverse Fate," was to be sung by the orphans in the Asylum or House of Refuge in London where Duché was the chaplain as a hymn of thanksgiving: "Blest guardian whose fraternal care/ With bounteous hand our want supplies."

This poem appeared as the text for a brief cantata for girls' voices in *Hymns and Psalms Used at the Asylum* with music by François Hippolyte Barthélémon, the music editor. Since Barthélémon's setting is too extended for inclusion here, we have substituted the HYMN FOR WHITSUNDAY from the same collection. The melody is by Thomas Spence Duché, son of the poet, the figured bass by Barthélémon.

Green Plumes of Royal Palms   PALM SUNDAY 10.10.10.10.D.
St. 1, 2
LeRoy V. Brant, 1930   Annabel Morris Buchanan,
                             comp. 1955

Like "Oh, Day of Days" (q.v.), this poem for Palm Sunday was first published in LeRoy V. Brant's volume of poetry entitled *Beauty* (1930). The poem which was in the form of a sonnet has been turned into two uniform stanzas by retaining the octave as written but extending the sestet by repeating the last two lines. The composer suggests that this composition, in the Aeolian mode, is suitable for "processional or other use, on Palm Sunday."

Guter Gott! Dir Ich Befehle

Lord, Dear God! To Thy Attending

St. 1–3, 7, 8

Heinrich Otto, 1785

Sheema Z. Buehne, trans. 1965

Von dem Trost aus Jesu Leiden 8.8.7.7.

Zahn 1376

Christian Gregor, 1784

This poem is folklike in character yet devotional. In addition to the more formal hymns sung as church services there were others, more popular in character, published as broadsides, as was this poem by Heinrich Otto.

The melody of Von dem Trost aus Jesu Leiden comes from a collection of chorales edited by Christian Gregor in 1784.

Hail, Holy Land

St. 1–3

Thomas Tillam, writ. 1638

Song 1   10.10.10.10.D.

Frost 350

Orlando Gibbons, 1623

These lines by Thomas Tillam convey the hope and the sense of dedication which brought some of the noblest souls of the period to the New World, and they do it in terms which still move us more than three centuries later.

The poem is associated here with a tune which Orlando Gibbons composed for George Wither's *Hymnes and Songs of the Church*. Like the settings made by Henry Lawes for the psalm versions of George Sandys, it is for treble and bass only. The inner parts have been added. The meaning of Tillam's verse is often left incomplete at the end of a line. The singer must therefore be prepared to continue without a break into the next line. Stanza 3 contains only six lines and the repeat should not be observed. Those who wish to take the repeat can sing it to the two opening lines of the poem.

Hail, Oh Hail to the King

St. 1–3

Beatrice Quickenden, writ. 1957

Stevenson 12.10.12.4.

John St. Edmunds, comp. 1957

Among the composers enthusiastic at the idea of creating new American hymn tunes was John St. Edmunds, who was at the time in charge of the Americana Collection in the Music Division of the New York Public Library. The result was a group of new tunes including Stevenson, composed to a text written for music by his wife, Beatrice Quickenden. Her poem suggests the atmosphere of the psalms of praise, which is heightened by the references to silver trumpets and shawms in the second stanza. Other tunes by this composer may be found in the *Hymnal of Christian Unity* (Gregorian Institute of America, 1964).

Hail Our Incarnate God!   Tigris S.M.
St. 1–5
William Duke, 1790   Raynor Taylor, version of
                                 1822

This Christmas hymn was published in William Duke's *Hymns and Poems on Various Occasions.* A manuscript copy of this volume in the Diocesan Library of Maryland agrees with the printed text of this hymn. It is associated here with Tigris by Raynor Taylor.

Tigris, which we reproduce from Francis D. Allen's *New York Selection of Sacred Music,* has been transposed down one step. The upper staff was marked "tenor," the middle one "air." Since the tune was immediately above the bass, it was easier for a singer who played his own accompaniment. In our score the voices have been arranged in the order of pitch.

Hail the Glorious Golden City   8.7.8.7.
St. 1–3
Felix Adler, writ. 1878   Jacob Weinberg, 1932

This poem, entitled "The City of Our Hopes," has analogies both in subject matter and treatment with the familiar "Jerusalem the Golden." Written in 1878 by Felix Adler, it was included in *The Pilgrim Hymnal* of 1904.

Jacob Weinberg's tune appeared in the *Union Hymnal* of 1932 where it was associated with Isabella R. Hess's "Hear My Pray'r." It is a unison hymn with accompaniment for organ or piano.

Hail to the Brightness of   Wesley 11.10.11.10.
   Zion's Glad Morning
St. 1–4
Thomas Hastings, 1832   Lowell Mason, 1832

Unlike the other church musicians of his period, Thomas Hastings was a devoted and successful writer both of hymn texts and tunes.

Frederick M. Bird, in a notice published in Julian's *Dictionary of Hymnology* (1892), was able to list over fifty hymns by Hastings then in common use. See also "Jesus, Merciful and Mild," "Now Be the Gospel Banner," and "Now from Labor and from Care" in this collection.

Wesley, which is sometimes called Salvation, first appeared in Hastings and Mason's *Spiritual Songs for Social Worship* (1832). It was associated with Hastings' text in that volume.

Hail to the Joyous Day   Amherst H.M.
St. 1, 3, 4, 7, 10
Royall Tyler, 1793   William Billings, 1770

A rare broadside preserved in the Baker Library, Dartmouth College, reveals Royall Tyler as the author of "A Christmas Hymn . . . sung at Claremont, N.H., 1793." No tune is named.

Amherst, chosen here, was a favorite tune by Billings. It appeared in his first collection, *The New England Psalm Singer*.

Countertenor, C clef, third line. Original key G major; tune in tenor.

Hail to the Queen   Salve Regina L.M.
St. 1–3
Anon.   Anon.

John Aitkin's *A Compilation of the Litanies, Vesper Hymns and Anthems as Sung in the Catholic Church* (Philadelphia, 1787) is an important document since it contains the first music for Catholic services printed in North America. Yet some of the music included is not of Catholic origin and none has been shown to be the work of an American. Aitkin printed the melodies for the mass and those of a number of the ancient hymns of the church. The translation of the hymn "Salve Regina" which Aitkin gives appeared in 1685 in a primer published in Antwerp. A "primer" in this sense was a devotional book addressed to the laity. A general feature of the early primers was the inclusion of translations of vesper hymns such as this.

The tune seems unrelated to the three versions given in the *Vesperale Romanum*. The ornaments are printed in small notes and should be omitted if the melody is sung as a unison hymn. The justification for adding inner parts to the original soprano and bass is the sharp under the third bass note.

Hail to the Sabbath Day	Compton S.M.
St. 1–5	
Stephen Greenleaf Bulfinch, 1832	E. K. Prouty, 1835

Like "Hath Not Thy Heart Within Thee Burned" and "O Suffering Friend of Human Kind," "Hail to the Sabbath Day" was published in the author's *Contemplations of the Saviour*. It served as a conclusion to Section XII, "Walk Through the Corn-Fields." The revised Unitarian *Hymn and Tune Book* of 1877 (and other collections) omit the first stanza and begin with the opening line of the second stanza, "Lord, in this sacred hour."

The tune Compton by E. K. Prouty was included in the *Boston Academy's Collection* of 1835. It has a festive diatonic character in harmony with the text.

Hail, Tranquil Hour of Closing Day	Corinth C.M.
St. 1–5	
Leonard Bacon, 1845	Anon., 1831

This hymn, which was long popular, was written as a substitute for the well-known evening hymn "I Love to Steal Awhile Away" by Phoebe Hinsdale Brown (q.v.). Mrs. Brown's hymn had appeared in Asahel Nettleton's *Village Hymns* (1824). When a request for permission to reprint it in *Psalms & Hymns for Christian Use and Worship* was refused, Bacon wrote "Hail, Tranquil Hour of Closing Day."

Corinth appeared without the name of the composer in Lowell Mason's *Boston Handel and Haydn Society Collection of Church Music* (10th ed., 1831) as a setting of Mrs. Brown's hymn. Another Corinth, which is claimed by Lowell Mason, appeared in 1836 in two different collections: *The Sacred Lyre*, vol. 1, and *The Choir*. Mason evidently forgot that the name was already in use. Considering the number of tunes which he composed this is hardly surprising. Yet another tune with the same name is set to "When God Descends with Men to Dwell" (q.v.).

Hallelujah! Praise the Lord	Hallelujah 7.6.7.6.7.7.7.7.
St. 1–3	
Edwin Francis Hatfield, writ. 1837, pub. 1872	Samuel Prowse Warren, comp. 1871, pub. 1872

Hatfield's scholarly *Church Hymn Book* (1872) includes five of his original hymns. His joyous "Hallelujah! Praise the Lord," if not unique in meter, is certainly very unusual. Poems with eight-line stanzas on the pattern 7.6.7.6.D. are not uncommon, those on 7.7.7.7.D. less so, and variants on these patterns are rare in nineteenth-century hymnals. Warren was the musical editor of the *Church Hymn Book*.

The Happy Day Will Soon Appear St. 1, 2 Anon., early 19th cent.	SWEET MORNING 8.11.8.11., with chorus H. S. Reese, arr. 1859

The singing in early revivals and camp meetings had to be conducted in such a way that the songs could be easily learned by the hearer. One age-old solution was the chorus repeated after each stanza. In "The Happy Day" each line of text is followed by a refrain line, "And we'll all shout together on that morning." The chorus is sung after two such alternations. It is easy to see how a skillful leader could keep such a song going indefinitely by improvising new opening lines, with his audience joining in with a response that is always the same.

Somewhat similar in melodic outline is the secular TROOPER AND THE MAID (Cecil Sharp, *English Folksongs from the Southern Appalachians,* New York, 1917, I, 305). The melody was also taken up by Negro singers (*Slave Songs,* No. 197). This hymn appears in *The Sacred Harp* of 1859 in a three-part arrangement attributed to H. S. Reese. In the *Original Sacred Harp* of 1936 it had been adapted for four-part singing with the addition of an alto part by S. M. Denson. It has been transposed down a step.

Happy, Saviour, Would I Be St. 1–3 Edwin H. Nevin, 1858	TRUST 7.7.7.D. George F. Root, 1880

The first line of this hymn as it appeared in Elias Nason's *Congregational Hymn Book* of 1857 was "Happy, Saviour, would I be." The text was reprinted in Charles Dexter Cleveland's *Lyra Sacra Americana* (1868) with the first line "Saviour, happy should I be." Cleveland stated in a note that the change was his, "with the consent and approbation of the author." We have retained the original form.

Root's tune for Nevin's text, called TRUST, appeared in Rev. Charles H. Richards' *Songs of Christian Praise* (1880). The contour of the melody in the opening bar resembles Stephen Foster's "Massa's in de Cold, Cold Ground," and Charles C. Converse's "What a Friend We Have in Jesus." Root had given the same name to another tune which was published in his *Choir and Congregation: A Collection of Music on a New Plan* (1875).

Hard Heart of Mine   SUNBURY C.M.
St. 1, 2, 4–6
Henry Alline, 1785   Samuel Holyoke, 1791

This hymn by Henry Alline was published in his *Hymns and Spiritual Songs.* "Hard Heart of Mine" is one of the nine poems by Alline set by Samuel Holyoke in his *Harmonia Americana.* Holyoke opposed the fuguing tune and stressed the importance of an expressive projection of the text. "The music requires a moderate movement, for it is very difficult to follow the exact motion of the pendulum and pronounce with that propriety and elegance which the importance of the subject may demand. It may then be proper here to remark that sentiment and expression ought to be the principal guide in vocal music."

Counter in C clef, third line. Tune evidently in tenor.

Hark, and Hear My Trumpet   THREE O'CLOCK TRUMPET
   Sounding   8.7.8.7.D.
Anon., early 19th cent.   Anon., early 19th cent.

This anonymous rhymed Shaker poem warning the listeners to "tune their hearts" is reproduced from a manuscript in the collection of Edward D. Andrews. Since the Shakers were believers in the second coming of Christ, the symbol of the trumpet sounding a warning was especially appropriate. The melody suits the text with its leaps of a fifth in the manner of a trumpet call. The rather free harmonization presented here may be omitted if it seems desirable to sing this tune in unison as the Shakers did.

Hark! Hark! with Harps of   CATON S.M.D.
   Gold
St. 1–4
Edwin Hubbell Chapin, 1846   Anon., 1846

This Christmas hymn was included in the Universalist *Hymns for Christian Devotion.* No tunes were indicated in the volume and CATON has been chosen as a suitably jubilant tune in the rare S.M.D. meter. CATON appeared in 1846 in *The Modern Harp,* edited by Edward L. White and John E. Gould. Although the editors stated that it was "a collection of entirely new music" with the exception of "a few old tunes," they did not indicate the composers of many of the tunes, including CATON. However, American contributors other than the editors do appear to be identified.

Hark! 'Tis the Saviour of   JORDAN C.M.D.
  Mankind
St. 1, 2, 4, 5
John Murray, 1782   William Billings, 1781

The first hymns written specifically for Universalists were those by James and John Relly, first published in London in 1754 and re-printed in this country in Burlington, N.J., in 1776. Noah Webster, who had been converted to Universalism by John Murray, settled in Portsmouth, N.H., and in 1782 issued a second American reprint of Relly to which he added five "hymns by J. M."

Billings composed tunes for a number of Relly's texts and his JORDAN from *The Psalm Singer's Amusement* is presented here as a set-ting for this hymn by the first American Universalist.

Countertenor, C clef, third line. Time signature $\text$; tune in tenor; transposed down one step. JORDAN is a double tune and therefore requires two stanzas of text for each repetition of the tune. Murray's text has five stanzas. The first stanza might be repeated at the end to extend it to six.

The Harvest Dawn Is Near   LEIGHTON S.M.
St. 1, 2
George Burgess, 1839   Henry Wellington Greatorex,
                                        1849

This short paraphrase of Psalm 126 came into general use in the nineteenth century. Since both the author and the composer were in Hartford for a number of years in the service of the Episcopalian Church, the tune LEIGHTON seems especially suitable for this text. It was originally intended for Tate and Brady's version of Psalm 15. Greatorex contributed several tunes to the *Collection of Church Music* (1849), edited by George F. Root and Joseph Emerson Sweetser. Among them was AHIRA, the tune later called LEIGHTON.

Hast Thou Heard It, O My
    Brother
St. 1–4
Theodore Chickering Wil-
    liams, 1902

PANOPLY OF LIGHT 8.7.8.7.D.
    with chorus

Leonard Parker, 1926

This hymn of youth and aspiration, written by Theodore Chickering Williams in 1902, appeared in the Unitarian *New Hymn and Tune
Book* of 1914 to a tune by the American musician Frank Lynes called
THE ARMOR OF LIGHT. The text reappeared in H. Augustine Smith's
Hymnal for American Youth (1926) to PANOPLY OF LIGHT by Leonard Parker. The tune name was derived from the second stanza of
the poem:

> Set thy forehead to the morning,
> Wear thy panoply of light.

Hear, Hear, O Ye Nations
St. 1–5
Frederick Lucian Hosmer,
    writ. 1909, pub. 1914

GORDON 11.11.11.11.

Adoniram J. Gordon, 1872

This prophetic vision of the nations of the world living in peace
and mutual good will was written by Hosmer, whom Henry Wilder
Foote, in *Three Centuries of American Hymnody,* called "the foremost
American hymn writer of the end of the nineteenth and the beginning of the twentieth century." First published in *The New Hymn and
Tune Book* (1914), it was republished in *Hymns of the Spirit* (1937), and
in *Hymns for the Celebration of Life* (1964).

The rather unusual meter, 11.11.11.11., restricts the choice of
tunes, but GORDON has been selected as appropriate. Named for its
composer, Adoniram J. Gordon, it appeared in *The Methodist Hymnal*
of 1932.

Heaven Is Here
St. 1–4
John G. Adams, 1845

EDEN 8.7.8.7.

Josiah Osgood, 1849

"Heaven Is Here," which first appeared in *Hymns for Christian Devotion* (1845), edited by Adams and Edwin Hubbell Chapin, is still in
use in the twentieth century. Not only was it included in *Church Harmonies* (1873), *Hymns of the Church* (1907), and *Hymns of the Spirit*

(1937), but also in *The Plymouth Hymnal* of 1893 and *The Pilgrim Hymnal* of 1904. In the last three volumes the first line appeared as "Heaven is here where songs of gladness." The Plymouth and Pilgrim hymnals not only introduced changes, but attributed the hymn to John Quincy Adams rather than John Greenleaf Adams.

EDEN appeared in *The Bay State Collection of Church Music,* edited jointly by Artemus N. Johnson, Sumner Hill, and Osgood himself, though without any attribution. It is attributed to Osgood in Johnson's later *Handel Collection* (Boston, 1854). The original time signature is 3 . The figures in the next to last bar have been added by the editor.

Heaven, Heaven, Heaven Is
    the Place
(Children's Hymn)
Langston Hughes, writ. 1955   Paul Nordoff, comp. 1955

This child-like vision of heaven as a place where "happiness is everywhere," by Langston Hughes, has been treated in like spirit by Paul Nordoff. Since the poem is not strophic in form the setting is continuous, following the variations in the text. The music for "Heaven is the place where happiness is everywhere" forms a kind of refrain, appearing with some modification to the words "And the streets of gold so bright" and again at the end as a sort of coda.

The Heavens Do Declare   LONDON S.M.
Ps. 19: 1–6   Frost 45
Anon., 1640   Edmund Hooper, arr. 1592

This metrical version of Psalm 19 comes from the *Bay Psalm Book* of 1640. The attractive short meter tune was first published in William Daman's *The former booke* (1591) to Psalm 25. Thomas East used it to Psalms 1, 67, and 70 in a setting by Hooper which we reproduce. The name LONDON, which it usually bears, was given to the tune by Thomas Ravenscroft. John Playford called it SOUTHWELL.

Cantus, C clef, first line; altus, C clef, third line; tenor, C clef, fourth line; bassus, F clef, fourth line. Time signature ¢ ; note values halved; transposed up one step.

He Hides Within the Lily   RESURRECTION 7.6.7.6.D.
St. 1–4
William Channing Gannett,   Alice Nevin, 1879
  1893

Henry Wilder Foote, in his *Three Centuries of American Hymnody,* compared Frederick Lucian Hosmer (q.v.) and Gannett, two literary Unitarian clergymen of the late nineteenth century, with Samuel Longfellow (q.v.) and Samuel Johnson (q.v.), who contributed so much to Unitarian and American hymnody at the mid-century. "Like that earlier pair Frederick Lucian Hosmer and William Channing Gannett were in Divinity School together (though not in the same class), were lifelong friends, and were both hymn writers and joint editors of a hymnbook." Gannett was able to accept the doctrine of evolution and to give it a spiritual interpretation as the working out of a divine plan. " 'He Hides Within the Lily,' " to quote Foote again, was "certainly one of the earliest, if not the very first to make use of the religious possibilities of the new scientific thought."

Alice Nevin's *Hymns and Carols for Church and Sunday School* (1879) contained RESURRECTION and four other tunes which she had composed.

He Leadeth Me, O Blessed   HE LEADETH ME   L.M., with
  Thought   chorus
St. 1–4
Joseph Henry Gilmore, 1862   William Batchelder Brad-
                                  bury, 1864

This hymn, inspired by Psalm 23, was written after the author had preached a sermon in the First Baptist Church of Philadelphia on "David's Confidence in God's Grace." Mrs. Gilmore sent the poem to the *Watchman and Reflector,* where it was published on December 4, 1862, under the name "Contocook." Stephen Foster appears to have composed the first setting of this text which was published on April 1, 1863, though he gives the author as "W.R." Phil Kerr, in *Music in Evangelism,* states that Bradbury saw the poem in the *Watchman and Reflector* and composed the familiar tune, which he published in the *Golden Censer* in 1864. The Rev. F. M. Bird, who wrote the brief account in Julian, says that Gilmore's hymn was written in 1859.

Help, Lord, Because the Godly Man	BON ACCORD C.M.
Ps. 12: 1, 2, 5, 6	Frost 211
Francis Rous, 1650	Anon., 1625

"Help, Lord, Because the Godly Man" from the Scottish psalter of 1650 has been set to a tune of a more elaborate character than most psalm tune harmonizations used in Scotland. However BON ACCORD, though included in the Scottish psalters of 1625, 1633, and 1635 as well as in John Forbes's *Psalm Tunes to Four Voices* (Aberdeen, 1666), was actually composed by Claude Goudimel. The Scottish psalter of 1635 describes such tunes as "in reports," that is enlivened with imitative passages.

The version of 1625 is followed here. Unfortunately this edition and the later one of 1635 do not show how the text was adjusted to the music. Since there are only five notes in the upper parts for line 2, the notes for these parts have been divided on the word "daily." The bass and tenor have two quarter notes rather than a half note in the second half of the penultimate measure. In system two, bar 2, there are consecutive fifths between treble and counter on the last two quarters. In the edition of 1635 the D in the countertenor is dotted and the following C is sharped thus avoiding this difficulty. This edition also repeats the second section, going back to the tenor lead, bar 4, second quarter.

Treble, G clef, second line; countertenor, C clef, second line; tenor, C clef, third line; bass, F clef, fourth line. No time signature; note values reduced by half; "church part" in treble according to the 1625 and 1633 editions, in tenor according to the 1635 edition.

Help Thy Servant	WARNING VOICE
	7.6.7.6.7.7.7.6., with chorus
St. 1, 2	
Andrew Broaddus, 1828	Anon., 1860

Although Andrew Broaddus was best known as an eloquent preacher, he was also the editor of the *Dover Selection of Spiritual Songs* (1828) and the *Virginia Selection of Psalms, Hymns and Spiritual Songs* (1836). "Help Thy Servant" was included in both of these collections. Perhaps Broaddus had a particular tune in mind when he wrote his hymn. Certainly there are few contemporary tunes to which it can be sung. WARNING VOICE, chosen here, appeared in *Harmonia Sacra* published by Joseph Funk and Sons (10th ed., 1860). Since *Harmonia Sacra* had appeared as early as 1832 under the title of *Genuine Church Music*, WARNING VOICE may be considerably earlier than 1860.

He Raise a Poor Lazarus
St. 1–3
Traditional, 1918

Cabin and Plantation Songs (1874) was the collection that made the songs of the Hampton Institute students generally available, Edited by three Institute teachers, Thomas P. Fenner, Frederick G. Rathburn, and Bessie Cleaveland, its preface was signed by Fenner, who arranged the songs and coached the first "Hampton Student Singers." "He Raise a Poor Lazarus," however, does not appear in the 1874 edition but in that of 1918, and in R. Nathaniel Dett's *Religious Folk-Songs of the Negro* (1927). Although credit for additional songs is given in the 1918 edition, we are not given sources for individual tunes. That for "He Raise a Poor Lazarus" was also selected by the Negro composer Samuel Coleridge-Taylor for inclusion in his *Twenty-Four Negro Melodies Transcribed for the Piano* (pref. 1904). It is a poignant melody of longer and more varied development than most. Here the first two phrases are followed by brief interjections from the basses like the words of approval that interrupt the preacher's periods.

Heralds of Christ   PRO PATRIA 10.10.10.10.
St. 1–4
Laura S. Copenhaver, 1894   Horatio Parker, 1914

This militant hymn, written by a member of the United Lutheran Church, has also been used in hymnals of other denominations. It is most commonly associated with the NATIONAL HYMN of George W. Warren. Since we have preferred to use that tune for the text for which it was composed, "God of Our Fathers, Whose Almighty Hand" (q.v.), we have chosen Horatio Parker's PRO PATRIA for Mrs. Copenhaver's poem. This association of text and tune had already been made in H. Augustine Smith's *Hymnal for American Youth* (New York, 1919). See also "God of the Nations."

Here Is a Song   WEST SUDBURY C.M.D.
(A Poem on Death)
St. 1,2, 8, 9, 14, 15
John Peck, 1773   William Billings, 1794

The two poems of John Peck included here are parts of his longer work *A Description of the Last Judgment*. Like Michael Wigglesworth's (q.v.) *Day of Doom* this poem is a kind of New England "Dies Irae." The "Poem on Death" has the character of a lugubrious folk ballad rather than a hymn.

The poem finds a suitable counterpart in William Billings' WEST SUDBURY, which has both the melancholy and the rhythmic energy which characterize the poem. Since WEST SUDBURY is a double tune, each singing of it will require two stanzas of the text. Another early setting of the same poem is SOLEMN SONG, which appeared in Elisha West's *Musical Concert* (Northampton, Mass., 1802).

Countertenor, C clef, third line. Time signature $\flat$; transposed down one half step.

Here, Lord, Retired, I Bow in Prayer	LAWRENCE L.M.
St. 1–4	
Matthew Bolles, 1836	Deodatus Dutton Jr., 1834

It was appropriate that a poem by Matthew Bolles should be included in a collection published in a state which he served as a Baptist minister and in the city in which he died. "Here, Lord, Retired, I Bow in Prayer" appeared in the *Select Hymns* of James H. Linsley and Gustavus F. Davis (Hartford, Conn.), with the heading "Pastor's prayer in the study."

The tune indicated there is HAMBURG (q.v.). We have selected a tune published in a Hartford collection of 1834 (3d ed.), the *American Psalmody* of Dutton and Elam Ives Jr. Deodatus Dutton's numerous contributions are marked with his initial, "D," and among them is the pensive minor tune LAWRENCE, originally set to a grim text beginning "Shall Life Revisit Dying Worms."

High O'er the Hills	FRENCH BROAD L.M.
St. 1, 2, 4–6, 8	
William Walker, writ. 1831	William Walker, arr. 1831

William Walker, in a footnote to this song in his *Southern Harmony* said, "This song was composed by the AUTHOR, in the fall of 1831, while travelling over the mountains, on French Broad River, in North Carolina and Tennessee." He evidently adapted a variant of an older tune called KEDRON to his verses.

KEDRON is the same as Walker's tune from bar 5 to the end with few and slight variations. Walker himself stated that he "learned the air of this tune from my mother when only five years old." The melody is built on an incomplete scale with the sixth tone missing both in the melody and in the accompanying parts. The ascent of the melody to a climax tone on the words, "Their summits tower toward the skies," has an especial appropriateness.

Text and setting are from Walker's own *Southern Harmony* (1854) transposed down one tone; original time signature $\backsim$. The setting has been rebarred in $\frac{3}{2}$ time without change of note values.

Hills of God, Break Forth in Singing	PACIFIC 8.7.8.7.7.7.7.7.
St. 1–3	
John Wright Buckham, writ. 1898, pub. 1904	Henry J. Storer, comp. 1903, pub. 1904

Henry Storer's tune for this hymn of rejoicing by John Buckham, who in 1903 became professor of theology in the Pacific School of Religion, was named PACIFIC in celebration of that event. The long stanza provided the composer with the opportunity for writing a double tune in vigorous processional style. The association of text and tune is preserved here as in *The Pilgrim Hymnal* (1904).

Hither We Come, Our Dearest Lord	HOLINESS L.M.
St. 1, 2, 4, 6	
Enoch W. Freeman, 1829	David Paine, 1839

"Hither We Come, Our Dearest Lord" was one of the "few originals" included in Enoch W. Freeman's *Selection of Hymns* (1829). Julian noted that it was in common use in his period. It stressed the Baptist belief in baptism by immersion in a characteristic phrase:

> Thou wast immers'd beneath the wave,
> The emblem of thy future grave.

Freeman was born and educated in Maine, and we have matched his hymn with a tune by a Maine musician, David Paine. HOLINESS appeared in his *Portland Sacred Music Society's Collection of Church Music* in 1839.

Holy Father, Great Creator   ABERCROMBIE 8.7.8.7.D.
St. 1–4
Alexander V. Griswold, 1835   C. Hommann, 1844

Written and first published in Griswold's *Family Prayers* of 1835, "Holy Father, Great Creator" was repeated with some changes in *Hymns for Church and Home* (1860), a collection edited by a committee of distinguished Episcopalians "as a Contribution to Any Addition that May be Made to the Hymns Now Attached to the Prayer Book." Not until 1871 was it included in the official hymnal of the Protestant Episcopal Church. In the musical edition of that hymnal, edited by J. Ireland Tucker in 1874, Griswold's text is set to the tune NEELY by W. H. Walter.

A hymn with a very gradual entrance into general use presents a special problem in a historical anthology like *American Hymns.* Over thirty-five years elapsed between the first publication of the poem and its appearance in an authorized hymnal. Obviously the tunes in the several musical editions of the hymnal of 1871 were the first to which it was generally sung. We have preferred a tune available soon after the text appeared. ABERCROMBIE was published in 1844 in *Cantus Ecclesiae,* edited by W. H. W. Darley and J. C. R. Stanbridge.

Holy God, We Praise Thy   7.8.7.8.7.7.
    Name
St. 1–7
Clarence A. Walworth, 1858   Alfred Young, 1884

"Te Deum Laudamus," an ancient hymn of jubilation, has often been translated into English. This version appeared in the *Catholic Psalmist* (Dublin, 1858) according to Julian. It was included in Alfred Young's *Catholic Hymnal* (New York, 1884) with a tune by the editor. The association was natural, since Walworth was a founder and Young a member of the Congregation of St. Paul (Paulist Fathers).

Holy Spirit, Faithful Guide   7.7.7.7.D.
St. 1–3
Marcus Morris Wells, writ.   Marcus Morris Wells, comp.
    1858   1858

This hymn by the upstate New York Baptist Marcus Wells has been widely used. Wells states that "the sentiment of the hymn" came to him in October 1858, "while at work in my cornfield." He sent the finished hymn to Isaac Woodbury. Woodbury died in 1858, but Sylvester Main, who edited *The Dayspring* (1859), found Wells's hymn among the manuscripts left by Woodbury. Wells's tune is called PELTON in *The Dayspring*. PELTON, like MARTYN (q.v.), has the merit of offering no difficulties to the singer. The ability to conceive a musical idea that is completely simple yet characteristic is rarer than might be supposed.

Holy Spirit, Truth Divine St. 1–4	MERCY 7.7.7.7.
Samuel Longfellow, 1864	Louis Moreau Gottschalk, comp. 1840 Edwin Pond Parker, arr. 1867

Literary distinction and devotional hymnody were closely allied among Unitarians of the mid-nineteenth century. In addition to figures whose chief claims to fame lay in other fields, like Emerson and Henry Wadsworth Longfellow, there were writers who attained excellence in both hymn writing and other literary pursuits, such as William Cullen Bryant and Oliver Wendell Holmes. Finally, there were figures chiefly remembered by modern churchgoers as writers of fine hymns. Among these the most distinguished were Samuel Longfellow and Samuel Johnson, joint editors of *Hymns of the Spirit* (1864), the most important collection of Unitarian lyric poems of the period. It was for this volume that Samuel Longfellow wrote "Holy Spirit, Truth Divine." Unitarian in origin it is sufficiently universal in spirit to have been welcomed in hymnals of other Protestant denominations to the present.

In 1867 Edwin Pond Parker, a Congregational minister who was also his own music director, made an arrangement of "The Last Hope" as a hymn tune. "The Last Hope" was a showy and sentimental piano piece by Louis Moreau Gottschalk which every aspiring student of the period longed to play. Parker's arrangement (MERCY) attained a popularity that prolonged the life of the composition which, largely forgotten as a piano piece, still survives as a hymn tune.

How Glorious Are the Morning Stars St. 1–3, 6	ST. DAVID's C.M. Frost 234
Benjamin Keach, 1691	John Playford, arr. 1701

Benjamin Keach's importance to us lies in his advocacy and introduction of "conjoint singing" in his London congregation. It is said that his was the first Baptist church to sing hymns. In *The Breach Repaired* (1691), which he wrote to defend the practice, he stated that a hymn had been sung by his congregation at communion for eighteen years. The treatise was intended to prepare the way for singing at church each Sunday. A bitter controversy followed, but Keach was able to introduce his *Spiritual Melody* (1691) in his own church and in other congregations.

"How Glorious Are the Morning Stars" is based on Job 38:7. It has been set here to John Playford's arrangement of St. David's as found in his *The Whole Book of Psalms* (1677).

Time signature ₵ ; note values halved; tune in top voice; transposed down one step.

How Goodly Is Thy House   L.M.
St. 1–3
Henry S. Jacobs, 1887   Jacob Weinberg, c.1947

"How Goodly Is Thy House," a call to worship, was included in Gustav Gottheil's *Music to Hymns and Anthems for Jewish Worship* (1887) and was retained in the *Union Hymnal* (3d ed., 1932) where it was set to an arrangement from Mozart. Jacob Weinberg also composed a setting for it which was published in his *Original Hymn Tunes* as No. 20. It is this setting that is reproduced here.

How Long, Jehovah?   The Complaint of a Sinner
                                   6.6.6.6.6.6.6.6.
Ps 13: 1–6   Frost 185
Henry Ainsworth, 1612   John Farmer, arr. 1592

This metrical version of Psalm 13 is to be sung to a tune called The Complaint of a Sinner, which was introduced into the Sternhold and Hopkins psalter in 1562. Ainsworth's version is identical in pitch though the note values are slightly changed

There are five settings in John Day (1563) and three in William Damon (one published in 1579 and two in 1591; one of the latter has the melody in the treble). It also finds a place in the psalters of Thomas East, Richard Allison, and Thomas Ravenscroft, as well as in a series of Scottish psalters from 1594 to 1634. Our setting was contributed to East's *Whole Booke of Psalmes* by the English madrigal composer John Farmer.

Cantus, G clef, second line; altus, C clef, third line; tenor, C clef, fourth line; bassus, F clef, third line. Original key signature, one flat; time signature ₵ ; note values halved; tune in tenor.

How Often Have Our AMANDA L.M.
  Restless Foes
Ps. 129: 1–5
Jeremy Belknap, 1795 Justin Morgan, 1790

In Belknap's *Sacred Poetry Consisting of Psalms and Hymns* . . .
Psalm 129 was indicated as a new version, and it seems reasonable to
ascribe it to the editor. It was perhaps natural for a man who had
lived through the stern days of the Revolution to turn to a psalm in
which the Israelites called on the Lord for victory over their enemies. The original text of Morgan's AMANDA was "Death, like an
overflowing stream."

Singers may need to be reminded, especially in instances like this
where the meter changes, that the moods of psalmody indicated def-
inite tempi. Here the first mood had three beats sung in the time of
three seconds. In the second section the original metric signature $\mathfrak{C}$
(altered here to $\frac{2}{2}$) indicated two beats to the bar sung in the time of
two seconds. The beat thus remains constant. AMANDA was first published in Asahel Benham's *Federal Harmony*.

Countertenor, C clef, third line. Melody in tenor; transposed
down one tone. In bar 1 the F in the bass was sharped, while
that in the countertenor was not. (See MAJESTY by William Billings
for a similar conflict.) The next to last note in the tenor was sometimes sharped in later editions, but not in the original.

How Sweet Is the Language SUNCOOK L.M.D.
  of Love
St. 1–4
Oliver Holden, 1806 Samuel Holyoke, 1804

"How Sweet Is the Language of Love," which may have appeared in *The Young Converts Companion* (Boston, 1806), was reprinted in a number of later collections. It is joined here to Holyoke's SUNCOOK, which appeared in the *Christian Harmonist* (Salem,
Mass., 1804).

Time signature $\mathfrak{C}$.

Hurry On, My Weary Soul
St. 1, 3–5
Traditional, version from
  Slave Songs, 1867

Slave Songs was the first publication to present a substantial collection of the songs of Southern Negroes with their melodies and is thus a document of great importance. The preface deals with peculiarities of pronunciation and performance practice. The songs are grouped by region. "Hurry On," for example, is placed with songs of the southeastern slave states. Where we use the word "heard" the Negroes sang "year-de" (with two syllables). The preface states flatly that the Negroes "have no part-singing." The variants noted are merely different ways of singing the same passage. For example, the Negroes sometimes sang D C (dotted quarter, followed by an eighth) in bar 5 instead of the notes we give. Lower parts have been added to the melody for those who prefer to sing it in harmony or with an accompaniment.

Hush Thee, Princeling   Lullaby 10.10.10.9.
  (Lullaby for the Christ
  Child)
St. 1, 2
Anna Elizabeth Bennett, writ.   Norman Dello Joio, comp.
  1940   1956

Anna Elizabeth Bennett's tender poem, at once a Christmas and a slumber song, was sent to us as a poem suitable for music. We sent it to Norman Dello Joio, who set it to music very simply in a rocking six-eight rhythm. It is interesting to note how the opening period is lengthened to bring it to a gentler and more gradual close, how the same period, returning at the end to the words "They are singing," is extended one extra bar to bring the work to a quiet final cadence.

I Am Weary of Straying   Prescott 11.11.11.11.
St. 1–5
Sarah E. York, 1847   George Oates, 1832

This poem, by a member of the Reformed Dutch Church, is similar to the earlier "I Would Not Live Alway," by William Augustus Mühlenberg (q.v.). Both express weariness over the troubles and temptations of this transitory life, and both express a longing for "the far distant land of the pure and the blessed." "I Am Weary of Straying" first appeared in the Reformed Dutch *Psalms and Hymns* of 1847.

Like "I Would Not Live Alway" it was usually sung to George Kingsley's FREDERICK (q.v.). We have preferred George Oates's PRESCOTT, another American tune in the same unusual meter, which first appeared in Lowell Mason's *The Choir; or, Union Collection* (1832).

I Bless Thee, Lord, for Sorrows Sent	ROCKPORT L.M.
St. 1–4	
Samuel Johnson, 1864	August Kreissman, 1854

This hymn headed "Affliction—Perfect through Suffering" was "Written at the request of Dorothea L. Dix for a collection made by her for the use of an asylum." Miss Dix was a pioneer in seeking improved conditions in insane asylums. Johnson's poem was included in the *Hymns of the Spirit* of 1864 and in the Unitarian *New Hymn and Tune Book* of 1914.

It is set here to a gently melodious mid-century tune by the German-American conductor and composer August Kreissman. ROCKPORT may be found in *The Handel Collection of Church Music* (1854), edited by A. N. Johnson.

Ich bin ein Herr	PSALM 4 8.8.7.4.4.7.
I Am the Lord	
St. 1–3	Zahn 4170
Alexander Mack I, 1774	Heinrich Schütz, 1628
Sheema Z. Buehne, trans. 1965	

Alexander Mack's hymn entitled "Der sünden austilgende Jesus" was published after his death in the *Kurze und einfaltige Vorstellung der äussern aber doch heiligen Rechten u. Ordnungen des Hauses Gottes* (Germantown, Pa., 1774). Although in general the tunes selected for *American Hymns* are contemporaneous with the text, we have here chosen PSALM 4 from the *Psalmen Davids* of Heinrich Schütz (Freiburg, 1628), which contained settings of the German psalm paraphrases of Cornelius Becker. The simplicity of treatment is indicated by the phrase "Nach gemeiner Contrapunctus Art," i.e., in simple (as opposed to florid) counterpoint. In fact, the setting of PSALM 4 is note against note throughout. Schütz stated that ninety-two of his melodies were new and eleven were from traditional sources. The tune for PSALM 4 is his own. A flat under a bass note indicates a minor third, a sharp a major third.

Ich liebe Jesus noch allein	THE BEST CHOICE 8.9.8.9.8.9.7.
I Love My Jesus Quite Alone St. 1, 6–8	
Johannes Kelpius, writ. before 1705	Anon., before 1705
Christopher Witt, trans. before 1705	

The German and English texts of "Ich liebe Jesus noch allein" have been selected from a Pennsylvania manuscript entitled *The Lamenting Voice of Hidden Love* (1705). This manuscript contains pietistic poems in German, presumably written by the early mystic Johannes Kelpius, with versified translations into English by Dr. Christopher Witt, and the music to which they were to be sung. Since this is the earliest manuscript containing music from the Pennsylvania area it has attracted scholarly attention. Until recently the music was regarded as having been composed by Kelpius himself, but a careful examination, of the musical settings contained in the manuscript by Albert G. Hess resulted in tracing all but two to German sources, although in some instances to sources dated later than *The Lamenting Voice of Hidden Love*. We reproduce one of the two unidentified tunes.

The music of THE BEST CHOICE has the character of a religious aria or solo sung with keyboard accompaniment. The character of the setting confirms this impression, since it is in keyboard style largely in two parts but with cadential chords filled in with a variable number of parts. It has been amplified as a four-part setting here, and the bass has also been modified slightly. The original has been reproduced in facsimile in *Church Music and Musical Life in Pennsylvania in the Eighteenth Century*, 1, 21–165 (Philadelphia, 1926–38). Dr. Witt has so arranged his text that his second line is interrupted by a rest in the middle of a word. After the rest he simply repeats the opening syllable and completes the word: for example, "With ear-(pause) earnestness apply it."

If Birds That Neither Sow nor Reap	DUMFERMELING C.M.
St. 1–3	Frost 206
Roger Williams, 1643	Thomas Ravenscroft, arr. 1621

At the ends of the chapters of his *A Key into the Language of America* Roger Williams added verses which were always picturesque, sometimes poetic, and which always deduced a moral. "If Birds That Neither Sow nor Reap" is based on Matthew 10:29-31, "Are not two sparrows sold for a farthing? and one of them shall not fall on the ground without your father."

We have ventured to associate this poem with DUMFERMELING, one of the Scottish common meter tunes that appeared in psalters from 1615 to 1635. Ravenscroft included it in his psalter of 1621 in his own arrangement for Psalms 35 and 89.

Cantus, C clef, second line; medius, C clef, third line; tenor, C clef, fourth line; bassus, F clef, fourth line. Time signature **C**; note values reduced by half.

If I Can Stop One Heart from Breaking	CHARITY IRREGULAR
St. 1, 2	
Emily Dickinson, 1890	Peter C. Lutkin, comp. 1927, pub. 1928

This poem by Emily Dickinson, with its setting by Peter C. Lutkin, appeared in two hymnals edited by H. Augustine Smith, *The American Student Hymnal* (1928) and *The New Hymnal for American Youth* (1930). It may be compared with the Roy Harris setting of "How Others Strove" (q.v.).

Lutkin's setting is intended for congregational singing and is the first setting of a poem by Emily Dickinson to appear in an American hymnal as far as we can ascertain. It raises questions about the suitability of so personal a poem for group singing and about the suitability of the hymn tune as a setting for such a poem. The hymn tune by its very nature must be broad and simple in character and can attain only a general suitability of style and mood with its text. In a somewhat similar fashion the hymn text should present aspirations and beliefs common to those who are to sing it.

If Thou Wilt Hear	MARTYRS C.M.
Selected lines	Frost 209
John Grave, 1662	Simeon Stubbs, arr. 1621

In 1662 John Grave published a long poem beginning "If thou wilt hear." Our text is a cento from that poem. Written in the popular ballad meter, it might appropriately be sung to either a folk song or a psalm tune.

Although MARTYRS is a psalm tune, it is somewhat folklike in character. Found in Scottish psalters as early as 1615, it was included in Thomas Ravenscroft's psalter in an arrangement by Simeon Stubbs, which was used for six psalms.

Cantus, C clef, first line; medius, C clef, second line; tenor, C clef, third line; bassus, F clef, fourth line. Note values reduced by half.

I Have Fought the Good Fight	THE DEATH SONG
St. 1–6	12.12.12.12.
Jared B. Waterbury, 1831	Anon., 1831

Headed "The Martyr's Death Song," this poem by Jared B. Waterbury appeared in Volume II of Joshua Leavitt's *The Christian Lyre* (1831). The tune, unlike most in *The Christian Lyre,* is arranged in three parts and has the character of a rousing march. Among advocates of a more sober style of church music, *The Christian Lyre* and, indeed, revival and camp-meeting songs in general were much criticized. It is easy to see that a hearty performance of a tune of this kind would jar on the ear of a conservative church musician, much as the songs of Dwight Moody and Ira Sankey or the Salvation Army might distress an organist devoted to the English Victorian tradition.

I Have Some Friends Before Me Gone	A HOME UP YONDER 8.8.6.D. with chorus
St. 1, 4–6	
Anon., 1868	Anon., version sung by Rev. B. I. Ives, 1868

This hymn is reprinted from *The Revivalist,* collected and edited by Joseph Hillman of Troy, N.Y. (1868), with Lewis Hartsough (q.v.) as music editor. *The Revivalist* was designed to furnish hymns for revivals and other informal religious meetings. Some of the material was written down from the performances of singers. It is thus a valuable record of the folk and revival hymns actually sung in the North in the mid-nineteenth century at a time when the music of Lowell Mason (q.v.) and his followers was established in formal church services. The hymn, a rousing revival song, was recorded from the singing of a Methodist preacher. Only the melody is printed in *The Revivalist.* It is harmonized here in four parts.

I Heard the Bells on Christmas Day	CHRISTMAS BELLS L.M.
St. 1–3, 6, 7	
Henry Wadsworth Longfellow, 1864	J. T., 1910

Longfellow wrote his familiar carol for the children of the Sunday School of the Unitarian Church of the Disciples in Boston. The version which passed into hymnbooks consisted of stanzas 1, 2, 6, and 7 or 1, 2, 3, 6, and 7 of the original seven-stanza poem. Written while the Civil War was still in progress, stanzas 4 and 5 refer to that tragic struggle. It is included, to the tune MANN, in *Unity Hymns and Carols* (1880), edited by Frederick Lucian Hosmer, William Channing Gannett, and J. V. Blake. In 1910 it was published in *Heart and Voice,* edited by Rev. Charles W. Wendté. It may also be found in *The New Hymn and Tune Book* (1914), *Hymns of the Spirit* (1937), and *The Pilgrim Hymnal* (1912–31). We reproduce it with the tune by J. T. from Wendté's hymnal.

I Know a Flower So Fair and Fine	FLOWERS OF LOVE 8.7.8.4.7.
St. 1–3	
Nicolai F. S. Grundtvig	F. Melius Christiansen, 1919
Olav Lee, trans. 1919	

Both the translation by Olav Lee and the musical setting by F. Melius Christiansen were made for the *Concordia Hymnal* which served the needs of Norwegian-Americans of the Lutheran faith. The text has a folk quality which is well matched in the musical setting. Particularly happy is the appearance of the short phrase which corresponds with the short line of four syllables in the poem.

I Know Not How That Bethlehem's Babe	Our Christ C.M.
St. 1–3	
Harry Webb Farrington, writ. 1910, pub. 1921	Oscar R. Overby, comp. 1926, pub. 1933

This Christmas hymn stresses the mystery inherent in the Christian view of the birth, crucifixion, and resurrection of Christ. The poem has been included in a number of hymnbooks including the Lutheran *Concordia Hymnal* (1933) where it is sung to the simple and folklike music of Oscar R. Overby. It was first published in the author's *Rough and Brown* (spirituals) in 1921. In the Episcopal *Hymnal 1940* it is associated with the tune Bouwerie, composed by William A. Goldsworthy and named for St. Mark's-in-the-Bouwerie, the New York City church where he was organist-choirmaster.

I Know Not Where the Road Will Lead	Laramie C.M.D.
St. 1–6	
Evelyn Atwater Cummins, writ. 1922, pub. 1940	Arnold G. H. Bode, comp. 1941

The refrain of this hymn, "I walk the King's highway," came from the title of a broadcast by Dr. Samuel Parkes Cadman which Mrs. Cummins heard over an early radio set with earphones. The hymn was printed in *The Hymnal of the Protestant Episcopal Church* (New York, 1940) with the tune Laramie by the Australian-American clergyman and musician Arnold G. H. Bode.

Named for Laramie, Wyo., Laramie is a double tune in which the last phrase begins like the first.

I Lift My Eyes Up To the Hills	Ixworth C.M.
Ps. 121: 1–8	
Cotton Mather, 1718	Version of 1767

This version of Psalm 121 appeared in the *Psalterium Americanum* of Cotton Mather. It was written in blank verse because, as he complained, "other translators leave out a vast heap of those rich things, which the Holy Spirit of God speaks in the Original Hebrew, and that they *put in* as Large an heap of poor things, which are entirely *their own.* All this has been merely for the sake of preserving the *Clink* of the Rhime: Which after all, is of small consequence unto a generous *Poem;* and of none at all unto the Melody of *Singing."* Psalm 121 is in common meter. For some of the other psalms Mather provided optional syllables printed in "black letter," allowing a line to be lengthened from six to eight syllables or shortened from eight to six. An example from Psalm 23 illustrates this feature (syllables originally in black letter are in parentheses).

> My shepherd is th'eternal God;
> I shall not be in (any) want;
> In pastures of a tender grass
> He (ever) makes me to lie down.

Without the optional words this is in common meter, with them it is in long meter.

In 1845 Lowell Mason and George J. Webb included Mather's version of Psalm 121 in *The Psaltery* to the tune KULER from Thomas Ravenscroft's psalter of 1621. It was a graceful tribute to one of our early sacred poets. Although of English origin IXWORTH was available to American singers from 1767 in Daniel Bayley's reprint of William Tans'ur's *Royal Melody Compleat.*

I Lift My Heart to Thee | PSALM 25 S.M.D.
Ps. 25: 1, 4–9 | Frost 44
Thomas Sternhold, before | William Daman, arr. 1579
1549

This metrical version of Psalm 25 by Thomas Sternhold was among the nineteen psalms which appeared in the undated first edition of his *Certayne Psalmes chose out of The Psalter of David and drawe into Englishe metre.* The second edition was dated 1549. This little volume was of great historical importance as the beginning of an important English psalter, the so-called "Old Version." Sternhold's verses are among the tenderest he wrote.

The tune with which it has long been associated came out in the Anglo-Genevan psalter of 1558. Two years later it was taken into the English psalter where it enjoyed great popularity until the end of the seventeenth century. This melody was harmonized in John Day's psalter, in the three volumes by Daman (the plainsong being in the superius in one of the versions), in Thomas East's psalter in 1592, and in that of Richard Allison in 1599. There are only four short meter double tunes in the Old Version psalters.

No time signature; note values reduced by half; tune in tenor; transposed up a minor third. The conventional whole rests between lines are retained here since they show that the lines were grouped in pairs.

I Love the Lord   Windsor C.M.
Ps. 116: 1–7   Frost 129
Anon., 1640   Version from Bay Psalm
                                   Book, 1698

This metrical version of Psalm 116 from the *Bay Psalm Book* of 1640 is set to a melody first found in William Damon's *The former booke* (London, 1591) to Psalm 116. Christopher Tye used it for "Peter and John They Took Their Way" in *The Actes of the Apostles translated into Englysche Metre wyth notes to eche Chapter, to synge and also to play upon the Lute* (1553). In 1592 Thomas East called it Suffolk Tune and in 1615 Hart's Scottish psalter called it Dundie, the name by which it is still known in Scotland. In 1621 Thomas Ravenscroft called it Windsor or Eaton and the former name has continued in general use. Samuel Sewall mentions the tune frequently in his diary. On August 13, 1695, for example, he writes, "Sung the 27 Ps. 7–10, & set Windsor Tune and burst so into Tears that I could scarce continue singing." The tune is given here as it appeared in the 1698 edition of the *Bay Psalm Book,* the earliest surviving edition with music notation. It had been copied from John Playford's *Breefe Introduction to the Skill of Musicke* (edition of 1674 or 1769). The middle part, which is missing in the *Bay Psalm Book,* has been adapted from that in John Playford's *Whole Book of Psalms*. The note values have been altered where they differed from those in the *Bay Psalm Book* and the sixth note in line 3 (B$\flat$) has been added.

I Love Thy Kingdom, Lord   St. Thomas S.M.
Ps. 137: third part, st. 1, 2,
   5–8
Timothy Dwight, 1800   Aaron Williams, 1770

"I Love Thy Kingdom, Lord" is perhaps the earliest poem by an American which is in general use in American churches today. It is the third part of Psalm 137 given in Dwight's own edition of *The Psalms of David . . . By I. Watts, D.D., a New Edition in which the Psalms omitted by Dr. Watts are versified, local passages are altered, and a number of Psalms are versified anew in proper metres*. Originally in eight stanzas, it has generally been shortened by recent editors to five or six.

St. Thomas has been closely associated with this text, especially in the South, *The Baptist Hymnal* of 1956, edited by Walter Hines Sims, still uses this tune for Dwight's text. Composed by Aaron Williams it appeared in the 1770 (fifth) edition of his *New Universal Psalmodist,* the original title of which was *The Universal Psalmodist.* It was made available to American singers at an early date in a reprint made by Daniel Bayley in Newburyport in 1771. Time signature ɔ ; tune in tenor.

The hymn may also be sung to Howard Boatwright's setting of "O Day of God, Draw Nigh") (q.v.). Indeed, the composer originally intended his music to be sung to Dwight's hymn.

I Love To Steal Awhile Away   Monson C.M.
St. 1–5
Phoebe Hinsdale Brown, writ.   Samuel R. Brown, 1842
    1818, pub. 1824

While living in a small, crowded house in Ellington, Conn., Mrs. Brown liked to walk and meditate at twilight near a garden which belonged to a prosperous neighbor. Her poem was written to explain her presence to the neighbor who had seen her there. The original poem of nine stanzas was headed: "An Apology for my Twilight Rambles, addressed to a Lady." It was altered and abbreviated to five stanzas (2, 4, 5, 7, 9) for publication in Asahel Nettleton's *Village Hymns* (1824), and the original second stanza thus became the first. We reproduce this version.

Among the tunes written for this very popular text were Brown, by William Batchelder Bradbury and Monson, by Mrs. Brown's son, the Rev. Samuel Brown. Monson was the town in Massachusetts where Mrs. Brown had lived and where most of her hymns were written.

I'm Agoing to Lay Down My
    Sword
St. 1–3
Traditional, pub. 1940   John W. Work, arr. 1940

This poignant vision of a world at peace is presented in the version published by John W. Work. The verse section consists of a solo entry with choral response, then a brief duet for soprano and tenor which is again answered by the chorus. The refrain follows the verse section. The plaintive opening of this melody has a resemblance to that of "Nobody Knows de Trouble I've Seen" (q.v.) with the leap from 3 down to 5 of the scale, ascending to 6 and then to 1.

I Minded God	FRENCH TUNE: PSALMS 28, 109 10.10.10.10.10.
Ps. 77: 3–9, 12–14	Frost 323
Henry Ainsworth, 1612	Melody from Henry Ainsworth, 1612

Such lines from Ainsworth's rendering of Psalm 77 as "I minded in the night my melodie" are both pithy and concise if compared with the smoother but longer "I call to remembrance my song in the night" of the King James version.

Our melody was used for Psalms 28 and 109 in the French psalter of 1551. The meter there was 9.9.9.9.8.8., which Ainsworth adapted to 10.10.10.10.10. The music was adapted to Ainsworth's longer line by repeating notes. In addition the note G was added at the end of line 5 to make a final cadence. The music for the original sixth line was omitted. Since Ainsworth's text is incompatible with the French form of the tune and with the polyphonic treatments composed for it, only Ainsworth's adapted melody is reproduced with his text.

It was originally written with the C clef on the first line. Time signature ¢ ; note values halved.

Immortal Love, Forever Full St. 1–6	ABBY C.M.
John Greenleaf Whittier, 1856	S. Allen, 1845

"Immortal Love, Forever Full" is a cento consisting of stanzas 1, 5, 13, 14, 15, and 16 selected from the long poem "Our Master," which appeared in *The Panorama and other Poems* in 1856.

Among the American tunes in *The Psaltery* of Lowell Mason and George J. Webb was ABBY. It was there associated with Anne Steele's "In Vain I Trace Creation O'er." The editors note the use of "directing terms and dynamic marks" in prefatory remarks, and it is evident that ABBY was intended to be sung in a markedly expressive and varied style.

I'm on My Way to Canaan St. 1–4	WAY TO CANAAN C.M.D.
Anon., version of 1866	Anon., version of 1866

The text, together with a tune and its bass, comes from the Advent Christian *Jubilee Harp.* This version is abbreviated but otherwise well preserved. A version in eight stanzas, in Peter D. Myers' *Zion Songster* of 1836, does not have the stanza that begins " 'But stop,' says Patience, 'wait awhile' " with which our version closes. However, this stanza may be found in M. Springer's *Songs of Zion* (1853). Two tunes have been associated with this text: one that George Pullen Jackson found in the *Southern and Western Pocket Harmonist* of 1846 (see his *Down-East Spirituals,* No. 7) and the melody given here. Eventually this extended hymn was reduced to a chorus. In the *Original Sacred Harp* (1936), p. 82, nothing is left but the first line, which appears three times followed by "To the New Jerusalem," and this chorus is attached to John Leland's well-known "O When Shall I See Jesus."

In All the Magic of Christmas-Tide
St. 1–3
John Jacob Niles, 1955

Magic Night L.M.
John Jacob Niles, 1955

John Jacob Niles, best-known as a collector, singer, and arranger of the folk music of the Southern Appalachians, is represented in this Christmas carol both as poet and composer. The folklike aeolian melody is harmonized only with the tones of that scale. Although the pitch chosen by the composer is more brilliant, the carol would be more practical for congregational use if transposed down a third.

"In All the Magic of Christmas-Tide" was especially composed for *American Hymns.*

In God's Eternity
St. 1–4
Hosea Ballou I, 1821

Thornton S.M.
John G. Adams, 1841

John G. Adams, Universalist minister, writer of hymns, and editor, wrote Thornton, a hymn tune published in Thomas Whittemore's (q.v.) *The Gospel Harmonist* (1841). We have associated it with "In God's Eternity" by the elder Hosea Ballou, who was to a very large degree the founder of the Universalist Church in America. This hymn, which appeared in *The Universalist Hymn-Book: A New Collection* (1821), compiled by Ballou and Edward Turner, was retained in the 1895 *Church Harmonies New and Old.*

In Heaven Soaring Up	SONG OF THE THREE
	CHILDREN 10.8.10.8.8.8.
St. 1–4	Frost 363
Edward Taylor, late 17th cent.	Orlando Gibbons, c.1660

This poem of the blessed saints "that sang for joy" as they rode "Christ's Coach" to glory is an example of the musical imagery which is so frequent with Taylor. The final couplet forms a refrain which reappears at the close of each stanza. The figure of the coach is also used in the Negro spiritual "Swing Low, Sweet Chariot," not to mention the more modern "Gospel Train."

The melody by Orlando Gibbons seems well adapted to the character of the poem. However, since no available tune of the period has precisely the meter of the Taylor poem, the first and third lines of the Gibbons tune have been extended from eight to ten syllables, in the first instance by repeating each of the two Cs, in the latter by repeating the F and E of the melody. Since the original is for treble and unfigured bass, the middle parts here are editorial additions. Frost obtained this setting from Christ Church, Gibbons MS., No. 365, folio 38.

Time signature ¢; note values halved.

In Mercy, Lord, Incline Thine Ear	C.M.
St. 1–4	
Isaac M. Wise, 1897	Abraham W. Binder, 1932

The preface of the *Union Hymnal* says that "some original compositions are frankly in the style of traditional Jewish music," a remark that applies to Binder's setting of this hymn and to Joseph Aehron's music for "God Supreme! to Thee We Pray." There is an opening imitation between soprano and bass. The text is suitable for the dedication of a synagogue:

> To truth be laid this cornerstone,
> Be reared these massive walls.
> To Thee, Most High, and only One,
> Be arched these sacred halls.

In Pilgrim Life Our Rest	PSALM 90
	6.6.8.6.6.8.6.6.6.8.6.
Ps. 90: selected lines	Frost 417
Edwin Sandys, 1615	Robert Tailour, 1615

The *Sacred Hymns* of Edwin Sandys contained psalms to be sung in five parts or optionally by one voice to the viol, and lute or orpharion. Sandys' collection was published in 1615 "for the use of such as delight in the exercise of music in his original honor." PSALM 90 is preceded by a long explanation: "Moses . . . beseecheth God to have particular compassion upon his chosen people, sore wasted with the punishments which their sins had called doun upon them; to make them wise by his grace; to comfort them with his returning favour, and Lastly so to frame the coorse of their Labours, that his promise continuing clear and helpful to them, might at length yet in their children have a glorious accomplishment."

The interesting but complex setting is barred as in the cantus part of the original. These bars separated the lines of the text. To assist the eye of the singer additional bars at intervals equivalent to four or six half notes have been added between the staves. Tailour prints the text for the treble part only. It is possible to sing this part only and play the remaining parts on instruments or on the organ. For those who wish to sing all the parts slurs and dotted ties have been added.

Treble, G clef, second line; countertenor, C clef, third line; tenor, C clef, fourth line; bass, F clef, fourth line. In stanza 3 we have ventured to read "ill" where the original reads "evil" to avoid an extra syllable in the line.

In Pleasant Lands Have Fallen the Lines	WALLINGFORD L.M.
St. 1–4	
James Flint, writ. 1840, pub. 1845	Benjamin F. Baker, 1854

The bicentenary of Quincy, Mass., May 25, 1840, furnished the occasion for the composition of this hymn which was later included in the author's *A Collection of Hymns* in 1845. Headed "Remembrance of Our Fathers," it dealt with a theme similar to that of Leonard Bacon's "O God! Beneath Thy Guiding Hand" (q.v.). Its continued use is shown by its inclusion in *The New Hymn and Tune Book* (1914) and the *Hymns of the Spirit* (1937).

WALLINGFORD by Benjamin F. Baker was included in Artemas N. Johnson's *The Handel Collection* (1854).

Baker wrote E–C$^\sharp$ for the bass in the second bar. We read A–C$^\sharp$ to avoid a second inversion at the beginning of the bar. In bar 12 we read A, not C$^\sharp$ for the second tenor note to avoid octaves with the soprano.

In Some Way or Other
  the Lord Will Provide   THE LORD WILL PROVIDE
St. 1–4   11.6.6.6.5., with chorus
Mrs. M. A. W. Cook, 1873   Philip Phillips, 1875

One of the most amazing musical phenomena of the period following the Civil War was the enormous success gained by Philip Bliss, Philip Phillips, Ira Sankey, and by others in lesser degree through the solo performance of evangelical songs set to innocent little melodies hardly more complicated than a nursery tune. Philip Phillips' *The Singing Pilgrim* typified a period during which evangelical meetings centered rather in halls and tabernacles than in wilderness clearings and the audience was urban rather than rural. The songs were gentler and had lost much of the earthy directness and the folk quality of camp-meeting examples. THE LORD WILL PROVIDE, written by Phillips to a text by an obscure American writer of verse, is typical in its expression of hope and confidence. The spinning out of the second phrase beginning "It may not be *my* way" to six bars, followed by the emphatic 2-bar "The Lord will provide" provides a vigorous and varied plan which is well in advance of most examples of the type. It will be found in the *Gospel Hymns and Sacred Songs* (1875) of Philip Bliss and Ira D. Sankey. A reference there indicates that it was taken from "Hallowed Songs by per." It has not been located in available editions of *Hallowed Songs*. In Phillips' *Descriptive Songs and Gem Solos* (1887) the author refers this hymn to *Singing Annual No. 4* (1877).

In the Distress upon Me   FRENCH TUNE: PSALM 23
                              10.10.10.D.
Ps. 18: 7, 8, 11–13, 27–29   Frost 320; Zahn 3190
Henry Ainsworth, 1612   Claude Goudimel, arr. 1565

This tune was associated with a poem by Clément Marot when it was published in 1544. Ainsworth used it in 1612 for Psalms 18 and 69, but in doing so he shortened each of the lines from eleven to ten feet. In the following year it passed into Lutheran usage. The Goudimel version is given first to show a polyphonic setting of this fine tune. It is followed by the melody as adapted by Ainsworth. Stanza

2, which describes Jehovah riding on the storm, will have a familiar ring to those who have sung MAJESTY, the famous tune by William Billings, since Billings has set this passage as it appears in the Old Version. However, the most touching lines are those which Ainsworth renders: "For thou dost make my candle to be light; Jehovah, my God, makes my darkness bright."

Superius, C clef, first line; countertenor, C clef, third line; tenor, C clef, fourth line; bassus, F clef, fourth line. Key signature one flat B♭ ; time signature ₵ ; note values halved; melody in tenor. There is an additional syllable in stanza 2, line 6. One way of adjusting the text to the music is to sing " 'fore his eyes" instead of "before his eyes." Another is to sing two syllables on the seventh note.

In the Morning I Will Pray   BENSON 7.7.7.7.
St. 2–6
William Henry Furness, 1840   Lowell Mason, 1830

This morning hymn deals with a theme used earlier by Isaac Watts in his "Lord, In the Morning Thou Shalt Hear." Furness develops his poem with touching simplicity. The poem originally had six stanzas, beginning "In the morning I will raise." In the *Book of Hymns* (1846) of Samuel Longfellow and Samuel Johnson, the first stanza is omitted and the poem begins as above with the opening line of stanza two.

Mason's BENSON was first included in the ninth edition of *The Boston Handel and Haydn Society Collection of Church Music* (1830). The earlier signature, ₵ , was later altered to $\frac{2}{2}$.

In the Silent Midnight   8.5.8.5.D.
   Watches
St. 1–3
Arthur Cleveland Coxe, 1842   Hubert P. Main 1877

The well-known painting "The Light of the World" by the English artist Holman Hunt, Mrs. Stowe's poem "Knocking, Knocking, Who Is There," and the poem under discussion here all portray Christ as knocking for entrance at the closed door of the soul. Arthur Cleveland Coxe's poem, which was formerly much sung in this country, first appeared in an early volume of poetry, *Athanasion* (1842). It was associated in the 1878 *Hymnal of the Methodist Episcopal Church* with a tune written for it by Hubert P. Main, an associate of William Batchelder Bradbury, a collector of old hymnals, and a most prolific writer of tunes, most of them of the gospel hymn type. His singable and appealing melodies gained a wide vogue.

In the present example he reduced the uneven lines of his original to uniform sections of two bars each by representing the lines of eight syllables by eight notes, the lines of five syllables by four notes followed by a long one which brought it to the same length. The plan was followed throughout the piece and the only element of rhythmic variety depended on dotting alternately the first note or the third note of the sections corresponding with the short lines of the poem. Such uniformity made for easy comprehension and a quick response from singers and congregations. Main's tune appears in *Life-Time Hymns* (H. R. Palmer, 1896), where it is dated 1877.

Into the Woods My Master Went	LANIER IRREGULAR
(A Ballad of Trees and the Master)	
St. 1, 2	
Sidney Lanier, writ. 1880	Peter C. Lutkin, 1905

This poignant and poetic treatment of Christ's spiritual crisis in the olive groves of Gethsemane stresses the solace to be found in a close contact with nature. The poem was apparently not used as a hymn until it appeared in *The Methodist Hymnal* of 1905.

Peter Lutkin's setting admirably reflects the pathos of the poem with a touch of the folk atmosphere that Lanier evidently had in mind when he called his poem a ballad.

I Shall Not Want: In Deserts Wild	LOWRY L.M.
St. 1–4	
Charles F. Deems, writ. 1872, pub. 1874	Anon., 1849

This hymn, included in Eben Tourjée's *Tribute of Praise* (1874), was written at a time when the author was the minister of the Church of the Strangers. The opening phrase comes from Psalm 23:1. The hymn was conceived one night when the author was discouraged by the problems and demands imposed on him by his church. He began to recall appropriate lines from the Bible and in particular the phrase "I shall not want." His meditations began to take metrical form, and when he woke the following morning the hymn was so clearly in his mind that he had only to transcribe it.

LOWRY is interesting for its five-bar phrases. The manner in which the opening rhythm passes into longer note values at the climax points is well adapted to the movement and meaning of the poem. It first appeared in the *Collection of Church Music* (New York, 1849) by George F. Root and Joseph Emerson Sweetser without the name of the composer. The second beat of bar 3 was figured $5^\natural$, which has been corrected here to $6^\natural$.

I Spread Out unto Thee My Hands	DE PROFUNDIS C.M.D.
Ps. 143: 6, beginning of 7, 8	Frost 149; Zahn 5352
Henry Ainsworth, 1612	Orlando di Lasso, arr. 1564

DE PROFUNDIS, the melody associated with Psalm 130, was sung by the Lutherans as well as the Calvinists. It is used here for lines from Ainsworth's version of Psalm 143, which is also a psalm of supplication. Loys Bourgeois made the earliest setting.

Lasso's version appeared in *Le Premier Livre de chansons à quatre parties* (Anvers, 1564) and was republished in 1570, 1576, 1578, 1592, and 1595. More elaborate than Bourgeois, it shows Lasso in an unusual role, treating a text and a melody which had been associated with French Protestant worship since 1539. Lasso composed his setting for the beginning of Clément Marot's French version of Psalm 130.

Since Marot's verse alternates lines of seven and six syllables while Ainsworth wrote in common meter, some slight modifications of the score were necessary. Our musical score is based on Lasso's *Works,* vol. 16, p. 159. Note values halved; transposed down one step.

Is There No Balm in Christian Lands?	ON THE DEATH OF A CHILD C.M.
St. 1–4	
Anon., 1834	Anon., 1849

This antislavery song was one sung by the Hutchinsons, a New Hampshire singing family, at many abolitionist meetings. It has survived in the form of a broadside. No tune is indicated nor is it among the Hutchinson songs which appeared as sheet music. It has been matched here with a plaintive melody ON THE DEATH OF A CHILD from D. H. Mansfield's *American Vocalist* of 1849 to a text beginning "Thy life I read, my gracious Lord." Since the original is for melody and bass only, the inner parts are editorial additions. Transposed from E minor to D minor.

I Stood Within the Heart of God	8.8.8.6.D.
St. 1–6	
William Vaughn Moody	Quincy Porter, comp. 1956

This hymn of union with God has been fittingly set by Quincy Porter in a double tune that embraces two stanzas of the Moody poem. In style and modulatory trend this setting develops in the tradition of the Anglican hymn but with a freedom in the use of diatonic dissonance that goes far beyond anything the composers of that school envisaged.

The poem comes from the third act of Moody's poetic drama, *The Fire Bringer,* where it is sung by Pandora. She is interrupted after the second stanza, then continues to the end.

It Came Upon the Midnight Clear	CAROL C.M.D.
St. 1–3	
Edmund Hamilton Sears, writ. 1849, pub. 1850	Richard S. Willis, 1850

The text of this celebrated carol was written the year before it was published in the *Christian Register* (Boston, 1850). It has become one of the most loved songs on the Nativity in our language and the association of the story of the Christ child with concern for social justice is moving and ever pertinent.

Richard S. Willis' STUDY NO. 23 was originally published in his *Church Chorals and Choir Studies* (New York, 1850) to Philip Doddridge's "See Israel's Gentle Shepherd Stand." Sometime afterwards, as a vestryman in the Church of the Transfiguration (the "Little Church around the Corner"), he expanded it and adapted the revised melody to Nahum Tate's "While Shepherds Watched Their Flocks by Night." "Later," as we learn from a letter written to Hubert P. Main dated Detroit, 25 Oct. '87, "Dr. (later Bishop) Potter requested a copy of the manuscript for Grace Church, which I gave him. On my return from Europe in '76, I found that it had been incorporated into various church collections apparently to Edmund Sears' text: 'It Came Upon the Midnight Clear.' "

I to the Hills Will Lift Mine Eyes	PSALM 18 C.M.D.
Ps. 121: 1–8	Frost 36
Francis Rous, 1650	Anon., arr. 1635

This metrical version of Psalm 121 first appeared in 1650 in *The Psalms of David in English Meeter*. It is generally attributed to Francis Rous, although his text has been so extensively revised that few of his lines survived. The result is a composite and among the sources used was our own *Bay Psalm Book* from which 269 lines were taken. This psalter was retained by Presbyterians for a hundred years and was used in the New World as well as in Scotland.

The four consecutive fifths on the last four notes of line 3 appear thus in the edition of 1635. The tenor leaps a diminished fourth from the last note of line 3 to the first of line 4, and from the last note of line 6 to the first of line 7. The sixth note of the bass in line 7 was G. We have altered it to F.

Treble, C clef, first line; countertenor, C clef, third line; tenor, C clef, fourth line; bassus, F clef, fourth line. No time signature; note values reduced by half; tune in tenor.

I to the Lord from My Distress	PSALM 69 C.M.D.
Jonah 2: 2–6, last part of 9	Frost 86
Anon., 1651	John Playford, arr. 1671

The story of Jonah must have had a particular appeal for New England fishermen and sailors. This metrical version of "The Prayer of Jonah to the Lord his God out of the Fish's belly" was added to the 1651 edition of the *Bay Psalm Book*. Samuel Sewall records in his diary on October 23, 1686, "Sung the Prayer of Jonah." Although out tune was named for its association with Psalm 69, Playford in his *Psalms and Hymns of solemn musick* (1671) set it to Psalm 71.

Altus, C clef, third line; countertenor, C clef, third line; tenor or common tune, C clef, fourth line; bassus, F clef, fourth line. Time signature ₵; note values halved. In line 3, notes 3, 4, and 5, the countertenor moves up and down a diminished fourth.

It Seems That God Bestowed   C.M.
  Somehow
(Song for the Stable)
St. 1–5
Amanda Benjamin Hall, 1938   Virgil Thomson, comp. 1955

Virgil Thomson's interest in the hymn as part of the American scene has been shown in such larger works as his *Symphony on a Hymn Tune* and in passages from *Mother of Us All.* His setting of Amanda Benjamin Hall's Christmas song has the artful simplicity and folk atmosphere which is a characteristic element of his musical personality.

Amanda Benjamin Hall's Christmas poem, which was published in her *Honey Out of Heaven,* deals not with the shepherds or the magi who came from afar but rather with the barnyard animals who were present at Christ's birth.

I've Reached the Land of   BEULAH LAND L.M., with
  Corn and Wine   chorus
St. 1–4
Edgar P. Stites, writ. c.1875   John R. Sweney, comp. c.
                                  1875

The title BEULAH LAND was derived from Isaiah 62:4. In Bunyan's *Pilgrim's Progress* Beulah was a place of rest for pilgrims. The poem is said to have been written at a Methodist camp meeting in Ocean Grove, N.J. John R. Sweney, who was the musical director there, provided a setting for the poem. The pattern set by the opening measure (a dotted eighth and sixteenth followed by two quarter notes) pursues an inexorable course through the entire piece. In spite of this lack of rhythmic variety BEULAH LAND has remained a favorite gospel hymn. It appeared in *The Garner,* edited by Sweney and published in 1878. This was evidently not a first publication since it is credited there to *Goodly Pearls.* Ira D. Sankey, the famous singer of gospel hymns, sang BEULAH LAND at Sweney's funeral.

I Worship Thee, O Holy   COOLING C.M.
  Ghost
St. 1–4
William F. Warren, writ.   Alonzo J. Abbey, 1858
  1877, pub. 1878

William F. Warren wrote "I Worship Thee, O Holy Ghost" because, as he told a friend, "many Christians are unintentionally thinking too little about the Holy Spirit or the Infinite."

Alonzo J. Abbey's Cooling first appeared in *The American Choir* in 1858.

I Would Not Live Alway	Frederick 11.11.11.11.
St. 1–4	
William Augustus Mühlenberg, writ. 1824, pub. 1826	George Kingsley, 1838

This hymn first appeared anonymously in six double stanzas, June 3, 1826, in the *Episcopal Recorder* of Philadelphia. Abridged by the Rev. Henry Ustic Onderdonk of Philadelphia, it was incorporated into the *New Selection of Hymns* adopted by the General Convention of the Episcopal Church of that year. During the nineteenth century it was extremely popular.

In *Music of the Church,* which Mühlenberg published with Jonathan Mayhew Wainwright in 1828, the text is set to Mühlenberg by P. K. Moran, organist of St. John's in New York City. Ten years later George Kingsley set it to a tune entitled Frederick in *The Sacred Choir*. This melody, sometimes called Kingsley, became very popular and was often reprinted.

Jehovah, God, Who Dwelt of Old	Temple C.M.
St. 1–6	
Lewis R. Amis, writ. 1904, pub. 1905	Maro L. Bartlett, 1905

This hymn was written by request for *The Methodist Hymnal* of 1905 at a time when the author was the minister of the Arlington Methodist Episcopal Church, South, of Nashville, Tenn. The final stanza was added at the request of the Joint Commission to provide a more stirring conclusion.

The tune associated with this poem in *The Methodist Hymnal* is Temple, by the American composer Maro L. Bartlett. In its straightforward movement in quarter notes relieved and lightened by eighth notes, it possesses something of the character of the Lutheran chorale. Its name suggests the suitability of the hymn for services dedicating a new church.

Jehovah, Herr und Majestät

Jehovah, Lord and Majesty
St. 1, 2, 12, 13
Conrad Weiser, writ. 1753
Sheema Z. Buehne, trans.
   1964

Nun Freut Euch, Lieben
   Christen Gmein
   8.7.8.7.8.8.7.

Zahn 4427
Balthasar Schmid, arr. 1748

When a Lutheran church in Reading, Pa., was dedicated on June 17, 1753, Conrad Weiser wrote "Jehovah, Herr und Majestät" for the ceremony. It was later printed in the *Halle'sche Nachrichten.*

The joyful choral melody Nun Freut Euch, Lieben Christen Gmein seemed suitable for Weiser's poem. Though Johann Sebastian Bach was one of the musicians who made a setting of this melody, we have preferred a simpler setting for soprano and continuo by Balthasar Schmid as closer in date to Weiser's poem.

Jesous Ahatonhia

Hommes, Prenez Courage,
   Jésus Est Né
Let Christian Hearts Rejoice
   Today
St. 1, 3, 6
Jean de Brebeuf, S.J., writ.
   1641
Paul Picard, Fr. trans. 1913
Francis X. Curley, S.J., Eng.
   version 1953

Une Jeune Pucelle 8.6.8.6.
      8.8.6.4.7.

Anon., 16th cent.

The Huron Indians at Lorette claimed that this carol had been taught to their ancestors by the Jesuit missionary Jean de Brebeuf. The text was transcribed in 1750 by Father Girault de Villeneuve, S.J., and was translated from Huron into French by Paul Picard, one of the last Indians to understand and speak Huron. It was published in 1913 in *Noëls anciens de la Nouvelle France,* edited by the Rev. Ernest Myrand. There are several English translations. The one given here is by Francis X. Curley, S.J., and was published in *America,* 90 (Dec. 19, 1953):320. The tune is an ancient Breton noël, "Une Jeune Pucelle."

Jesu, Komm Herein

Jesu, Come on Board
(Hymn of the Second Sea
   Congregation)
St. 1, 4, 12, 19
Johann C. Pyrlaeus, writ.
   1743
Sheema Z. Buehne, trans.
   1965

Seelenbräutigam, Jesu
   Gottes Lamm 5.5.8.8.5.5.

Zahn 3255b
Johann D. Mueller, arr. 1754

Pyrlaeus came to this country as the pastor and leader of the Second Sea Congregation, thirty married couples from the Moravian churches at Herrnhaag and Marienborn. For them he wrote this hymn about their voyage to the New World. It may have been sung on the ship *Irene,* which reached Staten Island in 1743. Three years later he wrote another poem, "The Great Wedding," celebrating the anniversary of the mass wedding that had preceded the voyage. The poem cited many names, with a bit of news about each one.

The tune originally associated with this text is given here in the version printed by Johann D. Mueller in 1754. Since the original was for melody (C clef, first line) and figured bass, the inner parts are editorial additions.

Jesus a Child His Course
   Begun
St. 1–5
Margaret Fuller, 1859

Ernan L.M.

Lowell Mason, 1850

This poem for children by one of the gifted Unitarian writers of the mid-nineteenth century first appeared in the author's *Life Without and Life Within* (1859). It was reprinted in T. C. Moulton's *Christian Hymn Book* (1863), in George T. Ryder's *Lyra Americana* (1865), and later in Joseph P. Holbrook's *Baptist Praise Book* (1871) and Charles H. Richards' *Songs of Christian Praise* of 1880.

In Holbrook the tune Gratitude arranged by Thomas Hastings was used, in Richards, Lowell Mason's Ernan. The latter has been preferred here as a contemporary tune to which "Jesus a Child" was sung. It first appeared in the composer's *New Carmina Sacra* of 1850.

Jesus, Enthroned and Glorified	MERIBAH 8.8.6.8.8.6.
St. 1–4	
Zachary Eddy, 1869	Lowell Mason, 1839

This hymn, like "Floods Swell Around Me, Angry, Appalling," was written for the Dutch Reformed *Hymns of the Church with Tunes* (1869), of which Eddy was an editor. It was there set to Lowell Mason's MERIBAH, the tune retained here. The six-line stanza with two lines of eight syllables followed by one of six was a variant of common meter which, in some of the older books, was marked "C.P.M.," i.e., common peculiar meter. Henry Mason includes MERIBAH among the original hymn tunes of Lowell Mason. In February 1839 it appeared in *The Seraph,* a monthly music periodical and in the same year in Mason's *The Modern Psalmist.* MERIBAH has also been chosen as the tune for "Arise, Ye Saints of Latter Days."

Jesus, I Come to Thee	LUTHER 6.6.8.6.6.
St. 1–6	
Nathan S. S. Beman, 1832	Thomas Hastings, 1836

"Jesus, I Come to Thee" first appeared in the author's own *Sacred Lyrics* (1832). It passed into Presbyterian usage when an augmented edition (1841) with the same title was adopted and reissued in 1847 as the New School Presbyterian *Church Psalmist.* It also appeared in the Dutch Reformed *Hymns of the Church* (1869). It is set here to LUTHER, which may be found in the *Manhattan Collection,* edited by the composer, Thomas Hastings.

Jesus, I Live to Thee	LAKE ENON S.M.
St. 1–4	
Henry Harbaugh, writ. c. 1860, pub. 1861	Isaac B. Woodbury, 1854

This hymn, which stresses a mystical union with Christ, was written either at Lancaster or Lebanon, Pa., about 1860 and was first published in the author's *Hymns and Chants for Sunday Schools* (1861). However, Julian states that the hymn was dated 1850 and gives a later date of publication (1869). The account given here is based on Armin Haeussler's *The Story of Our Hymns* (1952). The hymn, sung at every service in the church of the Mercersburg Academy, was regarded as the Academy hymn. Harbaugh may have been inspired by the German hymn "Jesu, Dir leb' Ich."

LAKE ENON (MERCERSBURG), one of Woodbury's most popular tunes, first appeared in *The Cythera* (1854). It was to this tune that Harbaugh sang his hymn.

Jesus, in Sickness and in Pain PITT C.M.
St. 1–4
Thomas H. Gallaudet, 1845   Anon., 1845

Since much of Thomas Gallaudet's career was devoted to the unfortunate, it seems appropriate that his one hymn dealt with Jesus as "a help and comfort" in time of trial. It appeared in 1845 in the Connecticut Congregational *Psalms and Hymns for Christian Use and Worship*.

A minor tune seemed appropriate for such a text. PITT, published in *The Psaltery* by Lowell Mason and George J. Webb, has been selected.

Jesus, Keep Me Near the   NEAR THE CROSS 7.6.7.6., with
    Cross   chorus
St. 1–4
Fanny J. Crosby, 1869   William Howard Doane, 1869

This celebrated hymn was written by Mrs. Alexander Van Alstyne, more generally known as Fanny Crosby, one of the most prolific hymn writers of her period. Since many of her songs were taken up by gospel singers, thousands of people sang her verses.

NEAR THE CROSS was first published in *Bright Jewels* (ed., Robert Lowry with W. F. Sherwin and C. G. Allen, Bigelow & Main, 1869). Doane's tune resembles Lowell Mason's popular BETHANY (q.v.) as well as "Oft in the Stilly Night."

Jesus Loves Me, This I Know   JESUS LOVES ME 7.7.7.7., with
                                    chorus
St. 1–4
Anna B. Warner, 1859   William Batchelder Brad-
                                    bury, 1862

"Jesus Loves Me, This I Know" was first printed in Anna Warner's novel *Say and Seal* (1859) and was subsequently included in many

Sunday-School songbooks and in the children's section of church hymnals. Its selection by Maria Leiper and Henry Simon for their anthology *A Treasury of Hymns* demonstrates its continued popularity.

Anna Warner's poem early became associated with the tune which Bradbury provided for it in one of his "Golden" collections, the *Golden Shower* (1862). Both tune and text retain a certain childlike simplicity which has saved them from the fate of untold quantities of contemporary Sunday-School songs.

Jesus, Master, O Discover	HELMSLEY 8.7.8.7., with
	chorus
St. 1, 2, 5, 6	
Anon., before 1770	Thomas Olivers, 1765

The text of this baptismal hymn was recorded in the first volume of Morgan Edwards' *Materials Toward a History of the American Baptists,* which also included a quaint engraving of the rural spot on the Schuylkill River used for baptisms. The engraving pictured one preacher standing on a flat stone addressing the gathering, while another, together with a candidate for baptism, was waist-deep in the stream which is labeled SCHUYLKILL in large letters. Saddle horses were tethered to trees in the grove, while others, harnessed to shays, were hitched to a post and rail fence.

George Pullen Jackson, in *White and Negro Spirituals* (p. 36), speaks of HELMSLEY as the tune to which this hymn was sung. However, Edwards says that his text was printed "with some additions to accommodate it to Helmsley-tune; if it be sung to the old tune the additions must be omitted, and two verses put together." Thus there was an older tune to which this hymn was sung, but we are given no further clue to its identity.

The trills in our score should be attempted by trained solo voices only. The figuring under the bass has been reproduced here. The 5 with a line through it indicates a diminished fifth.

Jesus, Merciful and Mild!	ALSEN 7.7.7.7.
St. 1–5	
Thomas Hastings, 1858	Frederick L. Abel, 1822

Frederick L. Abel, one of the many German musicians who contributed to the musical life of this country, was in Savannah, Ga., during the time that Lowell Mason, who was to dominate the American church music of his day, was a bank clerk and choir director of the Independent Presbyterian Church there. Chance had brought together a well-schooled European musician and a talented American amateur. Mason became a pupil of Frederick L. Abel and when Mason finally succeeded in publishing the pioneer Boston *Handel and Haydn Society Collection of Church Music* (1822) *The Savannah Museum* carried the following endorsement (May 14, 1822) written by Abel before his premature death:

Having critically examined the manuscript copy of *The Handel and Haydn Society Collection of Church Music* I feel a pleasure in saying that the selection of tunes is not only judiciously made, but the parts are properly arranged, the Bass is correctly figured, and in no instance are the laws of counterpoint and thorough Bass violated as is the case in most American Musical Publications.

The emphasis on correctness is not only characteristic of the well-schooled German, but also conveys a note of justified pride in an apt scholar. The days of the homespun counterpoint of Billings were past, except in the Southern books. Here perhaps more than at any other single moment German theory and American psalmody were united in the person of Lowell Mason.

ALSEN was included in the *Handel and Haydn Society Collection* and its fresh simplicity makes us regret that Abel did not live to make a larger contribution to our music. We have selected a somewhat later text by the Presbyterian church musician Thomas Hastings. The poem has a folklike quality appropriate to Abel's tune.

Jesus, Saviour, Pilot Me   PILOT 7.7.7.D.
St. 1–3
Edward Hopper, 1871   John E. Gould, 1871

It was natural that a minister preaching to seafaring men should describe life as a voyage that could end only "in peaceful rest" with Christ as the pilot. When Edward Hopper wrote this poem he was pastor of the Church of Sea and Land, New York, which is now dwarfed by the Manhattan Bridge.

John Gould's tune, in a diminutive three-part song form, was composed for the poem. Written in the style of the gospel hymn, it has remained in use to the present day.

Jesus, Shepherd of Thy   BETHUNE 7.7.7.7.D.
  Sheep
George Washington Bethune,   Anon., 1863
  1863

In William Batchelder Bradbury's *The Key-Note* (1863), text and tune appear as above with the title "Teacher's Hymn." The tune may be by Bradbury. Although it is not specifically credited to him, the preface announced "a great variety of new church tunes." It is in a very concise three-part form in which each part consists of a four-bar phrase, with the opening phrase repeated.

This hymn is not among those mentioned in Julian's *Dictionary of Hymnology* in the article on George Washington Bethune. It is possible that it was written at Bradbury's request, who then named his tune after the author.

Jesus Spreads His Banner   ROCKWELL 8.7.8.7.D.
   O'er Us
St. 1, 2
Roswell Park, 1836   Anon., 1845

Of all of Roswell Parks' hymns, only this one for communion, which appeared in his *Poems* in 1836, has been widely used. Although not included in the hymnals of the Protestant Episcopal Church, his own denomination, it was reprinted in other hymnbooks in both this country and Great Britain.

Few tunes were provided for this meter in the 1830s. ROCKWELL was designed either for texts in 7.7.7.D. or in 8.7.8.7.D. It appeared in *The Psaltery,* edited by Lowell Mason and George J. Webb, a tune book described as a collection of new music in which undesignated tunes, with certain exceptions, were by the editors. However, ROCKWELL was not ascribed to Lowell Mason in Henry T. Mason's *Hymn-Tunes of Lowell Mason.*

Jesus, These Eyes Have   BOSTON C.M.
   Never Seen
St. 1–5
Ray Palmer, 1858   Uzziah C. Burnap, 1869

This hymn, like "Lord, My Weak Thought in Vain Would Climb" (q.v.), was contributed to *The Sabbath Hymn Book* (1858) of Edward A. Park and Austin Phelps. It is based on I Peter 1:8, "Whom having not seen, ye love; in whom, though ye see him not, yet believing, ye rejoice with joy unspeakable and full of glory." Julian notes that it "is accounted by many as next in merit and beauty to 'My Faith Looks Up to Thee.'"

The tune BOSTON was used for this text in the *Hymns and Songs of Praise* (1874), of Roswell D. Hitchcock, Zachary Eddy, and Philip Schaff. It first appeared in the 1869 Dutch Reformed *Hymns of the Church,* edited by Burnap.

Jesus, Thou Divine   LOVE DIVINE 8.7.8.7.D.
   Companion
St. 1–3
Henry Van Dyke, writ. 1909   George F. Le Jeune, 1887
   (altered), pub. 1910

This hymn, representing Christ as a presence among the workers, strikes a note characteristic of its period. It was published in 1910 in *Hymns of the Kingdom of God,* edited by Henry Sloane Coffin and Ambrose White Vernon. Although not included in the Presbyterian *Hymnal* of 1933, it has been used in a number of recent hymnals including H. Augustine Smith's *Hymns for the Living Age* (1923), where a special tune, COMPANION, was provided by J. Arthur Demuth. It has also appeared in *The Hymnal 1940* of the Protestant Episcopal Church, where it was associated with an earlier anonymous tune named PLEADING SAVIOUR that had appeared in the *Plymouth Collection* (1855).

We have preferred LOVE DIVINE, the most frequently sung tune by the English-American organist George F. Le Jeune, which has been used for the Van Dyke text by several American editors. Le Jeune's text was named for, and is generally sung to, Charles Wesley's "Love Divine, All Loves Excelling."

Jesu, to Thee My Heart I   LOB SEY DEM ALMÄCHTIGER
   Bow   GOTT L.M.
St. 1–6   Zahn 346
Nicolaus L. Zinzendorf, 1721   Johann D. Mueller, arr., 1754
John Wesley, trans. 1737

While John Wesley was on shipboard on his way to Georgia, he studied Count Zinzendorf's *Das Gesang-Buch der Germeine in Herrnhut* and made the earliest of the translations which are his chief contribution to hymnody. "Jesu, to Thee My Heart I Bow" was first printed in the *Collection of Psalms and Hymns* (Charleston, S.C., 1737). This collection showed the importance of hymn singing in the missionary work of the Wesleys and marked a beginning which was followed by the development of a native tradition of Methodist hymn singing.

A chorale seemed suitable to John Wesley's translation from the German. LOB SEY DEM ALMÄCHTIGER GOTT has been realized in four parts from the version for melody and figured bass in Johann D. Mueller's *Vollstandiges Hessen-Hanauisches Psalmen und Choralbuch.*

Joyfully, Joyfully Onward I   JOYFULLY, JOYFULLY
  Move   10.10.10.10.D.
St. 1–3
William Hunter, 1843   Abraham Down Merrill, 1845

This jubilant poem by William Hunter was included in his *Minstrel of Zion* (1854) to a different tune by Samuel Wakefield. Julian dates the poem 1843 and Brown and Butterworth (in *The Story of the Hymns and Tunes*), 1842. The melody is extraordinarily unstable, appearing in many variant forms. In *Hymns and Songs of Praise* (Roswell D. Hitchcock, Zachary Eddy, and Philip Schaff), the tune is dated 1845.

A Joyful Sound It Is   LOBT GOTT IHR CHRISTEN
                          ALLZUGLEICH 8.6.8.6.6.
St. 1, 4, 5, 7   Zahn 199
George Strebeck, 1795   Johann Martin Spiess, arr.
                                1745

Strebeck was an associate of John Kunze and a contributor to the first hymnbook in English for the Lutherans in and near New York, *A Hymn and Prayer-Book* (1795). Critics have dealt harshly with that pioneer effort. It must be admitted that the rhymes in the present poem are sometimes very inexact, *are* rhymed with *ear,* for example, and that such an expression as "consolates their minds" has an odd quaintness about it. Much of the text, however, has a simple directness that is far from unappealing.

LOBT GOTT IHR CHRISTEN ALLZUGLEICH has been taken from the second part of Spiess's *Davids Harpffen-Spiel,* which is called the *Geistliche Liebes-Posaune* ("Trombone of Spiritual Love") as an appropriate melody for Strebeck's poem. The last line of each stanza is to be repeated to fit the tune. The inner parts have been added in accordance with the figured bass given by Spiess.

It will be noted that Spiess figures the notes not present in bass or melody. Thus the first inversion of a triad is figured 6 or 3 to indicate the missing note. In bar 4, third quarter, Spiess figures $\frac{6}{3}$ according to the same principle where one would expect $\frac{6}{5}$.

Judah in Exile Wanders
Lam. 1:3, 4
George Sandys, 1638   William Lawes, 1648

George Sandys' version of the "Lamentations of Jeremiah" appeared in the 1638 edition of his *A Paraphrase upon the Divine Poems.*

This publication included laudatory verses by a number of his friends, among which were some lines "To my honoured Kinsman Mr. George Sandys on his admirable paraphrase" by Francis Wyatt. The poetry is in decasyllabic couplets, a form in which the poet delighted.

This setting, by William Lawes, was published after Sandys' death in *Choice Psalmes put into Musick for Three Voices.* The music is a good example of the chromatic style as practiced in England in the middle of the seventeenth century. Such words as *weep, mourne, lament* are "painted" in chromatic fashion.

The score is for two sopranos (G clef, second line; C clef, first line) and bass (F clef, fourth line) with a separate figured continuo part. The latter has been omitted here, but performers should note that the composer intended a keyboard accompaniment.

Judge Me, O God   HOPKINTON C.M.
Ps. 43: 1–4
Joel Barlow, 1785   Oliver Holden, 1796

In Oliver Holden's *Union Harmony* HOPKINTON was set to stanza 4 of Joel Barlow's version of Psalm 43, although Holden gives the first line of the stanza as "Now to thy altar, O my God" rather than "Then to thy altar." This psalm, omitted by Watts, was added by Barlow.

The tune is marked by an asterisk as "never before published" and it may be by Holden himself. Vigorous octaves and unisons alternate with passages in harmony in the second section. Counter in G clef notated an octave too high. Time signature ℭ. For other paraphrases by Barlow see "Along the Banks," and "O God of My Salvation, Hear."

Just As Thou Art   WOODWORTH L.M.
St. 1–3
Russell Sturgis Cook, 1850   William Batchelder Brad-
                                bury, 1849

This hymn was written to suggest Christ's answer to the petition expressed in Charlotte Elliot's "Just as I Am Without One Plea." It was published in the *American Messenger,* which Cook edited, and the author sent a copy to Miss Elliot. It was adopted by hymnals in Great Britain and the United States, often with alterations. A form sometimes found in American books begins with stanza 3, "Burdened with guilt, woulds't thou be blest?"

Bradbury's familiar tune WOODWORTH had appeared a year earlier as a setting for Elizabeth Scott's "The God of Love Will Sure Indulge" in the *Mendelssohn Collection* of Thomas Hastings and Bradbury. It has frequently been used for Miss Elliot's hymn and has been selected here for its American counterpart. See also "Dear Saviour, If These Lambs Should Stray."

Kindle the Taper	10.10.10.10.
St. 1–3	
Emma Lazarus, 1889	Jacob Singer, 1932

Emma Lazarus, who is best remembered for her sonnet to the Statue of Liberty, "Not like the giant of Greek fame," is represented by two hymns in the *Union Hymnal* of 1932, "Remember Him, the Only One," and "Kindle the Taper." The latter is a song for Chanukah, the Feast of Lights in the Jewish calendar. It was associated with a tune in the movement of a march by Jacob Singer.

Kind Words Can Never Die	6.4.6.4.6.6.6.4., with chorus
St. 1–4	
Abby Hutchinson, 1855	Abby Hutchinson, 1855
	B. W. Williams, arr. 1859

The period preceding the Civil War was the great period for singing family groups. Of two such groups whose songs are included in *American Hymns,* the Cheney family and the Hutchinson family, the former contributed more to the church music of its day and the latter more to the great causes of the period, antislavery and temperance. The theme song of the Hutchinsons, "The Old Granite State," was sung to the Millerite tune the OLD CHURCH YARD (q.v.) and many of their songs had moral or religious texts like "My Mother's Bible." "Kind Words Can Never Die" conveys an optimism as characteristic of the period as the host of songs and poems dwelling on the pangs of death.

Composition with the Hutchinsons was frequently a family matter, but "Kind Words" was the work of the one sister in a group of brothers, Abby Hutchinson.

Written as a solo song with piano accompaniment, it was adapted as a hymn for three voices in B. W. Williams' *Songs for the Sabbath School and Vestry* (Boston, Chicago, Cincinnati, 1859).

A King Shall Reign in	WYEFORD L.M.
Righteousness	
St. 1–4	
Sebastian Streeter, 1829	Henry Kemble Oliver, 1848

The text reproduced here, which has the subheading "Character of Christ," comes from *The New Hymn Book, Designed for Universalist Societies,* edited by Sebastian and Russell Streeter. WYEFORD was first published in *The National Lyre* (1848), edited by Oliver, Silas A. Bancroft, and Samuel P. Tuckerman. In his *Original Hymn Tunes* Oliver mistakenly gives 1851 as the date of composition.

Die Kleine Heerde Zeugen	O WELT, SIEH HIER DEIN
This Flock So Small	LEBEN 7.7.6.7.7.8.
St. 1–3	Zahn 2298
Anna Nitschmann, 1742	Christian Gregor, 1784
Sheema Z. Buehne, trans.	
1965	

Although Anna Nitschmann was in Pennsylvania only from 1740 to 1743 and was engaged in missionary work among the Indians, she still found time to write hymns among which is "Die Kleine Heerde Zeugen." The early Moravians were copious hymn writers and their hymnal was enlarged by successive supplements. This hymn was included in Appendix XI.

Our version of the designated chorale melody, O WELT, SIEH HIER DEIN LEBEN, has been taken from the Moravian *Choral-Buch,* edited by Christian Gregor, published in 1784. The original for soprano and figured bass has been realized in four parts.

Time signature ¢ ; note values reduced by half.

Laat ons den Herre Singen	SEI TANTO GRATIOSA
Oh, Sing to God	Irregular
St. 1–4	
Jacob Steendam, 1650	Giovanni Ferretti, c.1580
	Adrianus Valerius, arr. 1621

Like "Als ik des Herren Werk," this poem appeared in Steendam's *Den Distelfink.* The practice of writing religious verses to be sung to well-known tunes was common in the sixteenth and seventeenth centuries. Jacob Steendam's "Laat ons den Herre Singen" was written with the Italian song Sᴇɪ Tᴀɴᴛᴏ Gʀᴀᴛɪᴏsᴀ in mind. This five-part Neapolitan secular song, composed by Giovanni Ferretti about 1580, achieved great popularity. It was reprinted in Italy and appeared in Yonge's *Musica Transalpina* (London, 1588) to the English words "So gracious is thy sweet self." In Holland it is found in a number of collections including Valerius' *Nederlandsche Gedenckclanck* (1621).

Valerius has transformed the work into a solo song by arranging the lower voices for the lute. His accompaniment has been transcribed from lute tablature to modern staff notation.

Laborers of Christ! Arise   Kᴇɪᴛʜ S.M.
St. 1–4
Lydia Sigourney, 1836   Thomas Loud, 1838

Although Lydia Sigourney's poetic gifts were employed in writing hymns for Congregational, Baptist, and Universalist books, she felt it her duty to join the Episcopal Church when she married, because her husband was a member of that denomination. "Laborers of Christ! Arise," written for the Baptist publication *Select Hymns*, edited by James H. Linsley and Gustavus F. Davis, was placed there under the heading of "Tract Meetings," although it was a plea for home missionary work. It was, as Julian notes, "one of the most widely used of her hymns."

Daniel Read's Lɪsʙᴏɴ, Henry W. Greatorex's Lᴇɪɢʜᴛᴏɴ, and Lowell Mason's Bᴏʏʟsᴛᴏɴ are American tunes which have been sung to this text. We have preferred Kᴇɪᴛʜ, by Thomas Loud, from George Kingsley's *The Sacred Choir* (1838), where it was associated with Watts's "Welcome Sweet Day of Rest."

Laboring and Heavy Laden   Cᴏʟʟʏᴇʀ 8.7.8.7.
St. 1–4
Jeremiah E. Rankin, writ.   Leonard Marshall, 1852
   1855

Rankin's parting hymn "God Be with You Till We Meet Again" (q.v.) is still universally known where gospel hymns are sung. "Laboring and Heavy Laden" was found worthy of inclusion in such collections as Elias Nason's *Congregational Hymn Book* (1857) and the later *Songs for the Sanctuary* (1865) edited by Charles S. Robinson. Written in 1855 "for a sister who was an inquirer," it first appeared in print in the Boston *Recorder*.

Cᴏʟʟʏᴇʀ, by Leonard Marshall, was published in *The Harpsichord*

(1852), edited by Marshall in collaboration with Henry N. Stone. It is lyric in character, the stressed slurs and its inclination to the subdominant giving it a reflective and somewhat plaintive mood which accords well with the text.

Lamm Gottes Abgeschlachtet	NUN RUHEN ALLE WÄLDER
	7.7.6.7.7.8.
Slain Lamb of God	
St. 1, 4, 9, 11	Zahn 2293a
Nicolaus L. Zinzendorf, writ.	Johann Martin Spiess, arr.
1742	1745
Sheema Z. Buehne, trans.	
1965	

The Moravian *Geistliches Gesangbuch der Evangelischen Brudergemein von 1735 zum drittenmahl aufgelegt und durchaus revidirt* was enlarged by various appendices. The eleventh appendix, which contained hymns written in America by the religious leader Zinzendorf, was edited by him "from the camp before Wyoming in the great plain of Skehantowano." (The Wyoming in question was a valley in the northeastern part of Pennsylvania.) From this eleventh appendix "Lamm Gottes Abgeschlachtet" has been selected. It was written for the first Oecumenical Synod, Germantown, 1742, an event significant in relation to Zinzendorf's dream of uniting the German-speaking denominations in this country.

NUN RUHEN ALLE WÄLDER, one of the fine tunes associated with the Lutheran service, was arranged many times in the various chorale books. Modern musicians are likely to be most familiar with the masterly arrangements by Johann Sebastian Bach. Because it seems unlikely that earlier American congregations were familiar with the Bach arrangements, we have chosen an arrangement from the chorale book of Johann Spiess for melody and figured bass. The inner parts have been added in accordance with the figuring except in bar 6 and the parallel passage in bar 13. If we use a sixth as called for, the normal voice leading would produce fifths between tenor and soprano. We have therefore disregarded these figures.

Ein Lämmlein Geht	Hör Liebe Seele 8.7.8.7.
On Earth There Is a Lamb So Small	Zahn 252
St. 1, 2, 8, 13	
Nicolaus L. Zinzendorf, 1742	Balthasar Schmid, arr. 1748
Sheema Z. Buehne, trans. 1965	

This poem appeared with others written during Nicolaus L. Zinzendorf's American stay in Appendix xi of the Moravian hymnal. The first couplet was taken from a hymn by Paul Gerhardt, but with the third line Zinzendorf began to pursue his own course, like a musician who first plays a borrowed theme on which he then improvises in his own fashion. The four-line stanzas of Zinzendorf are simpler than Gerhardt's ten-line groupings which had been built on the plan 8.7.8.7.8.8.7.8.8.7.

It is interesting to note that the Moravian *Choral-Buch* of 1784 contained a melody for the Gerhardt text. The tune used here for Zinzendorf's tender poem appeared in 1748 in Balthasar Schmid's book of chorales for the text "Hör Liebe Seele." The two parts provided there (melody and figured continuo) have been realized here in four parts.

Lead On, O King Eternal	Rex Aeternus 7.6.7.6.D.
St. 1–3	
Ernest W. Shurtleff, writ. 1887, pub. 1888	Charles L. Ziegler, 1904

Frequently sung at baccalaureate services, this hymn was written in 1887 by Ernest Shurtleff for his own graduating class at Andover Theological Seminary. It appears in *The Pilgrim Hymnal* (1904) to a vigorous processional tune by Charles Ziegler, one of the editors, which was composed and named for it.

Lead Us, O Father, in the Paths of Peace	Willow 10.10.10.10.
St. 1–4	
William Henry Burleigh, 1868	John Zundel, 1855

Although he did not regard himself as a poet, Burleigh did write verse, including a number of hymns which were widely used here and in England. "Lead Us, O Father, in the Paths of Peace" is one of his best known hymns. It appeared in Charles Dexter Cleveland's *Lyra Sacra Americana* (1868), in the posthumous edition of the author's *Poems* (1871), and in the Unitarian *Hymns of the Spirit* (1937). The longing for peace expressed here is more poignant now because it is still unfulfilled.

WILLOW was published in Henry Ward Beecher's *Plymouth Collection* of 1855.

Let All Created Things	LENOX H.M.
St. 1–3	
Artis Seagrave, 1792	Lewis Edson, 1782

Artis Seagrave of New Jersey contributed twenty-one hymns, including "Let All Created Things," to the Universalist *Evangelical Psalms, Hymns, and Spiritual Songs* of 1792.

LENOX, a joyful fuguing tune in hallelujah meter, appeared a decade earlier in the *Chorister's Companion* of Simeon Jocelyn and Amos Doolittle. It became Edson's most popular tune.

Counter, C clef third line. Original key C major; time signature, ; tune in tenor.

Let Him with Kisses of His Mouth	OLD 119TH C.M.D.
Song of Sol. 1: 1–3	Frost 132
Anon., 1651	Richard Allison, arr. 1599

This passage from The Song of Songs appeared in "The Supplement, containing other Scripture Songs; placed in order as in the Bible," which was added to all editions of the *Bay Psalm Book* from 1651.

The OLD 119TH tune, which was first published in the Anglo-Genevan psalter of 1558, was taken into English usage in 1560. It became a favorite and is found in many collections since that time, including the 1698 edition of the *Bay Psalm Book,* the earliest edition extant with music, and Richard Allison's *The Psalmes of David.* Allison designed his psalter for a variety of vocal and instrumental combinations. "The plaine Song beeing the common tunne to be sung and plaide upon the Lute, Orpharyon, Citterne or Base Violl, seuerally or altogether, the singing part to be either Tenor or Treble to the Instrument, according to the nature of the voyce, or for fower voyces." The last possibility is chosen here.

Cantus, G clef, second line; altus, C clef, second line; tenor, C clef, third line; bassus F clef, third line. Time signature Ɔ ; note values reduced by half; transposed down a minor third. Altus, second line, third note, had D, making octaves with the bass. Line 3, note before last, sharp lacking in altus.

Let Me Go Where Saints Are Going	8.7.8.7.D., with chorus
St. 1–5	
Lewis Hartsough, writ. 1861, pub. 1867	Lewis Hartsough, writ. 1861, pub. 1867

Musical editor of Joshua Hillman's *The Revivalist,* Lewis Hartsough wrote both the words and music of "Let Me Go Where Saints Are Going" which appeared in William Batchelder Bradbury's *Clariona* of 1867. *The Revivalist* appeared in the following year and Hartsough included his own hymn in that volume. Hartsough's hymn is of the gospel type with chorus, though in this instance the chorus is sung to a repetition of the second strain. The folk elements of *The Revivalist* have been illustrated in such hymns as "Come, Precious Soul" (q.v.) and Hartsough's own "Come, Friends and Neighbors, Come." Hartsough's hymn, with others by John Stockton, Philip Phillips (q.v.), and William Batchelder Bradbury (q.v.), revealed the growing popularity of the gospel hymn which was largely to displace the folk hymn in the North.

Let the Deep Organ Swell	L.M.D.
St. 1, 2	
Constantine Pise, 1851	Nicola A. Montani, 1920

In a volume devoted to sacred music it seems appropriate to include a hymn addressed to Saint Cecilia, the patron saint of music and musicians. The text by Rev. Constantine Pise was associated with a tune composed for it in the *St. Gregory Hymnal,* edited by Nicola A. Montani. This hymnal contains not only many original hymns by the editor but also arrangements from Slovak and other traditional sources.

Let There Be Light   L.M.D.
St. 1–4
William M. Vories, 1909   Jacob Singer, 1932

This hymn for peace, which first appeared in the *Advocate of Peace* (1909), has enjoyed considerable use. It appears in H. Augustine Smith's *The New Church Hymnal* (1937), *Hymns for the Living Age* (1923), and the *Hymnal for American Youth* (1926), but not to a tune by an American composer. It is also included in the *Union Hymnal* of 1932 to an original tune by Jacob Singer, reproduced here.

Let Thy Kingdom   Nettleton 8.7.8.7.D.
St. 1–3, 6
Anon., version of 1831   Version of 1858

The early form of Nettleton appears in John Wyeth's *Repository of Sacred Music, Part Second* (1813), where it is called Hallelujah. It has been attributed to Wyeth, but he does not claim it and its character is that of a folk tune. No one seems to know why the name was changed to Nettleton. The tiny volume of tunes called *Zion's Harp,* which Asahel Nettleton published to provide tunes in the more unusual meters for the texts in his *Village Hymns* (1824), does not contain Nettleton. In the course of time the preferences of singers and editors were reflected in a shift from duple to triple meter and in modifications of the melodic line. Our setting comes from William Batchelder Bradbury's *Jubilee* of 1858.

Robert Robinson's "Come, Thou Fount of Every Blessing" became the almost invariable text. Earlier Nettleton had been associated with a camp-meeting text "Let Thy Kingdom," the association retained here. The text is reproduced as it appeared in Orange Scott's *New and Improved Camp Meeting Book* (1831).

Let Tyrants Shake Their Iron Chester L.M.
 Rod
St. 1, 3–5
William Billings. St. 1, 1770 William Billings, 1770
St. 2–4, 1778

In Chester Billings expressed the patriotism, the self-confidence, and the determination of Revolutionary New England. The people and the army received his music and sang it as their own. Frank Moore, the author of *Songs and Ballads of the American Revolution,* says that "The New England soldiers, who, during the war, were stationed in the Southern states, had many of his tunes by heart, and amused themselves by singing them in camp, to the delight of all who heard them."

Only the first stanza appeared with CHESTER in Billings' *New England Psalm Singer*. Elhanan Winchester reprinted this stanza and added eight more of his own in *Thirteen Hymns Suited to the Present Times* (2d ed., Baltimore, 1776). Billings republished CHESTER in 1778 in his *Singing Master's Assistant,* adding four stanzas which do not resemble any of the later stanzas in Winchester. There seems to be no reason to doubt that Billings wrote both the tune and the usual text. It is possible that Winchester saw the opening stanza in the *New England Psalm Singer* and thought that it should be amplified.

Counter, C clef, third line. Time signature $\mathcal{C}$; tune in tenor.

Let Us Break Bread Together   7.3.7.3. with chorus
St. 1–3
Traditional   Harmonized 1953

This spiritual is a communion hymn. "Let us break bread together" in the first stanza is followed by "Let us drink wine together" in the second. The melody came from Calhoun and the harmonization was made in 1953 for the Presbyterian *Hymnbook* of 1955. Like "Lord, I Want To Be a Christian" and "Were You There" it has taken its place in denominational hymnals.

Let Us Cheer the Weary
    Traveler
St. 1, 2
Traditional, arr. by Harry T.
    Burleigh, 1924

"Let Us Cheer the Weary Traveler" is a spiritual arranged by Harry T. Burleigh to celebrate his thirtieth year as baritone soloist at St. George's Church. It is a processional hymn for choir with organ accompaniment. The same melody was arranged by Samuel Coleridge-Taylor for piano solo in his *Twenty-Four Negro Melodies Transcribed for the Piano* (1904).

Life of Ages, Richly Poured SOLITUDE 7.7.7.7.
St. 1–5
Samuel Johnson, 1864 Lewis Thompson Downes,
1877

"Life of Ages, Richly Poured" appeared in the collection jointly edited by Samuel Johnson and Samuel Longfellow and published as *Hymns of the Spirit* in 1864. Henry Wilder Foote, in *Three Centuries of American Hymnody* (p. 240), has noted the similarity between Longfellow's "O Life That Maketh All Things New" and Johnson's "Life of Ages, Richly Poured." Both present a vision of the presence of the Holy Spirit, but the poems are quite distinct in form and expression.

SOLITUDE was given as the tune for Johnson's text in the Unitarian *Hymn and Tune Book* of 1877. It is characterized, as was George Hews's HOLLEY (q.v.), by an opening with chromatic neighboring tones.

Lift Your Glad Voices in TRUMPET
   Triumph on High   10.11.11.11.12.11.10.11.
St. 1, 2
Henry Ware Jr., 1817 Isaac B. Woodbury, 1854

The *Christian Disciple* in which this Easter hymn was first printed was a Unitarian periodical which Ware edited. From that source it was taken for Charles Dexter Cleveland's *Lyra Sacra Americana* (1868), Alfred P. Putnam's *Singers and Songs of the Liberal Faith* (1875), and various hymnals including the Unitarian *Hymn and Tune Book* (1877). In that volume it was set to a tune by Charles Avison commonly sung to "Sound the Loud Timbrel." Indeed the very unusual meter of Ware's poem leads one to suspect that it must have been written for this tune, which was long a favorite. In Edwin A. Bedell's *The Church Hymnary* (1894) the tune FILBY, named for its composer W. C. Filby, seems to have been composed for Ware's hymn. It is, however, too late for the text. An American tune written for "Lift Your Glad Voices," which enjoyed a considerable degree of popularity, was Isaac B. Woodbury's TRUMPET. It first appeared in the composer's *Cythara* (entered 1854). Lines 5 and 6 are treated as a duet for soprano and tenor. Not only is there no modulation in this setting, there is not even a single note foreign to the scale.

Like Noah's Weary Dove	S.M.
St. 1–5	
William Augustus Mühlen-berg, 1826	John Henry Hopkins Jr., 1882

This hymn was contributed to the Episcopal *Prayer Book Collection* of 1826. It depicts the church as the only refuge of the questing soul just as the ark was the only place where the dove sent forth by Noah could find rest. Shortened by some later editors to begin with stanza 2 or stanza 3, it is presented at full length here.

Hopkins not only wrote musical settings for his own poems but also a series of tunes for texts in the Episcopal hymnal. Among these are settings of Francis Scott Key's "Lord, with Glowing Heart I'd Praise Thee," and Mühlenberg's "Like Noah's Weary Dove," which were included in the third edition of his *Carols, Hymns, and Songs.* Here one distinguished Episcopal clergyman has composed music for a poem by another.

Like to the Grass That's Green Today	Essex's Last Good-Night L.M.
St. 1–3	
Peter Bulkeley, the Younger	Anon., 17th cent.

Peter Bulkeley, the Younger, wrote chiefly on religious themes. The present poem, in a familiar psalm meter, deals with the transitory character of man's life in lines that have the character of folk verse.

Essex's Last Good-Night was one of those adaptable tunes that served for mournful ballads like the one that provides its title as well as for a Christmas carol, "All You That in This House Be Here" (1661). Two harmonized versions have been preserved, one for lute (Univ. Lib. Camb. Lute MSS. Dd. vi, 48.) and the one used here from the *Elizabeth Rogers' Virginal Book.*

Transposed up a minor third.

A Little Kingdom I Possess	C.M.D.
St. 1–4	
Louisa May Alcott, writ. c. 1846	A. P. Howard, cop. 1873

A letter, written October 7, 1875, by Louisa May Alcott to Eva Munson Smith, tells of the origin of "My Kingdom." "I send you a little piece which I found in an old journal, kept when I was about thirteen years old . . . Coming from a child's heart, when conscious of its wants and weaknesses, it may go to the hearts of other children in like mood."

The tune, composed by A. P. Howard and originally published by Oliver Ditson & Company, was reprinted in *The Sunny Side* (1875), a book of Sunday-School songs which included poems by well-known American writers of the day. Miss Alcott's "O the Beautiful Old Story" has also been sung as a hymn.

The Lone Wild Fowl   Cwmafan L.M.
St. 1, 2
H. R. MacFayden, writ. 1923,   Philip James, 1927
   pub. 1927

This is H. R. MacFayden's only hymn. When he was a field worker for the Nashville Presbytery, he noticed a hymn-writing contest announced in *The Homiletic Review*. In a letter dated February 16, 1934, he recalled that "the hymn was written on a quiet Sunday afternoon in the fall or early winter of 1923 and sent to the *Review*. It was forgotten until I was surprised with an announcement that I had been awarded the third prize in the contest."

The imagery of the opening lines of the poem has a certain analogy with that of William Cullen Bryant's "To a Wild Fowl." The second couplet of both stanzas has the character of a refrain happily stressed in the music by the *pianissimo* and the sustained chords at this point.

Philip James's prize-winning tune was composed for this poem. First published in 1927, tune and text were included in *The American Student Hymnal* in 1928 and in the Presbyterian *Hymnal* of 1933. The composer retouched the tune after publication and these changes are incorporated in our version. A variant spelling is *Cymafan*.

Long as the Darkening Cloud   Fairlee L.M.
   Abode
St. 1–5
George Richards, 1792   Oliver Holden, 1793

The cloud and pillar of fire guided the Israelites on their journey to the Promised Land. George Richards has drawn a parallel between the Lord's guidance of ancient Israel and Christ opening "th' eternal gates of day" to all the nations. "Long as the Darkening

Cloud Abode" appeared in *Psalms, Hymns, and Spiritual Songs: Selected and Original* (1792). Although this hymn was reprinted in 1865 in *The Songs of the Sanctuary* and a hundred years after its publication in the *New Laudes Domini*, it was extensively altered in both instances. The reading here follows the original edition.

FAIRLEE is given as it appeared in Holden's *Union Harmony* of 1793. Time signature ℃ ; transposed down a minor third.

Lord, at This Closing Hour   KNOWLTON S.M.
St. 1–4
Eleazar Thompson Fitch,   Charles Zeuner, 1845
    1845

Fitch was one of the editors of *Psalms and Hymns for Christian Use and Worship* (1845) "prepared and set forth by the General Association of Connecticut." Three of the six poems which he contributed to that volume were more widely used than the others: "The God of Peace, Who from the Dead," "By Vows of Love Together Bound" (q.v.), and "Lord, at This Closing Hour." As the opening line makes clear, the last named is intended as a concluding hymn and it is one which might well be revived.

KNOWLTON, a quiet, lyric tune by the German-American organist Charles Zeuner, was one of the tunes contributed by him to *The Psaltery* (1845) of George Webb and Lowell Mason. The preface emphasizes that it was a volume of new music and singles out Zeuner as a notable contributor.

Lord, Deliver, Thou Canst   TAPPAN 7.7.7.7.
    Save
St. 1–5
Eliza Lee Follen, 1836   Charles Zeuner, 1845

This hymn against slavery is typical of the zeal for social reform which left its mark on the history and on many hymnbooks of the early nineteenth century. "Lord, Deliver, Thou Canst Save" appeared in *Songs of the Free* (1836) and passed into *Hymns for Christian Devotion* (1846) of John G. Adams and Edwin H. Chapin, *Hymns for the Church of Christ* (1853) of Frederic Henry Hedge and Frederic D. Huntington, and Henry Ward Beecher's *Plymouth Collection* (1855).

The pleading character of Zeuner's TAPPAN is well suited to a hymn of supplication. TAPPAN is found in *The Psaltery* (1845) of Lowell Mason and George J. Webb. It should be distinguished from

George Kingsley's tune with the same name (see "There Is an Hour of Peaceful Rest").

The Lord Descended from   MAJESTY C.M.D.
  Above
Ps. 18: 9, 10, 16, 17, 20, 21
Thomas Sternhold, 1561   William Billings, 1778

These verses from Psalm 18, Old Version, which depict the Lord as riding on the tempest, convey a sense of power and a touch of wild poetry which appealed to early New England congregations. The tune was one which deeply impressed Harriet Beecher Stowe. In *Pogunuc People* she wrote that "there was a grand wild freedom, an energy of motion, in the old 'fuguing' tunes of that day that well expressed the heart of a people courageous in combat and unshaken in endurance . . . Whatever the trained musician might say of such a tune as old 'Majesty,' no person of imagination and sensibility could ever hear it well rendered by a large choir without deep emotion. And when back and forth from every side of the church came the different parts shouting:

> On cherubim and seraphim
> Full royally he rode,
> And on the wings of mighty winds
> Came flying all abroad,—

there went a stir and a thrill through many a stern and hard nature." Mrs. Stowe was probably quoting from memory when she wrote "On cherubim and seraphim" instead of "On cherubs and on cherubims."

MAJESTY first appeared in Billings' *The Singing Master's Assistant.* Even when the works of the New England psalmodists had been reduced to a small group of favorites sung in "Old Folks' Concerts" MAJESTY was likely to be included. It may be found in such reminiscent collections as *The Billings and Holden Collection* (Boston, 1836), *Ancient Harmony Revived* (Hallowell, Maine, 1847), Leonard Marshall's *The Antiquarian* (Boston, 1849), D. H. Mansfield's *The American Vocalist* (Boston, 1849), and *Ye Centennial* (Boston, 1875).

Countertenor, C clef, third line. Time signature ₵; transposed down a minor third. On the last eighth of bar 14 the soprano has G$\sharp$ while the countertenor takes G$\natural$. Those who wish to avoid this effect may omit the G$\natural$ in the countertenor and sustain the E as a quarter note (though this produces octaves with the bass). Clashes of this kind appear in Elizabethan music and occasional instances may be found in the works of our early New England composers. It is worth noting that bar 14 was reproduced without change in *The*

Easy Instructor (1798) of William Little and William Smith. Robert Kemp (or his source) in *Old Folks' Concert Tunes* smooths the passage as suggested above. The doubling of the bass in a lower octave is characteristic of Billings. In such cases the lower note is intended for a supporting instrument such as the bass viol.

Lord God of Hosts	FAITHFUL LEGIONS
St. 1–4	11.10.11.10.
Shepherd Knapp, writ. 1907, pub. 1912	Edward Shippen Barnes, 1936

This hymn headed "We Work with Thee" was intended for the men's association of the Brick Presbyterian Church, New York, where Shepherd Knapp was assistant minister. It was included in *The Pilgrim Hymnal* (1912) where the second tune was J. Albert Jeffery's ANCIENT OF DAYS. FAITHFUL LEGIONS was named for this text. Composed in 1936, it was associated with Knapp's text in H. Augustine Smith's *The New Church Hymnal* of 1937.

The Lord Has a Child	
St. 1, 2	
Langston Hughes, writ. 1955	William Schuman, comp. 1956

This poem, imagining the singer as a child tenderly watched over by the Lord as Father, has been set as a unison song with piano or organ accompaniment by William Schuman. There is more than a touch of the popular song in Schuman's setting, which perhaps departs more widely from the conventions of hymn writing than any other in this section.

Lord, I Am Thine	BATH L.M.
St. 1, 4, 5, 7	
Samuel Davies, 1769	Version from James Lyon, 1761

This communion hymn, written as part of the sermon "Dedication to God argued from Redeeming Mercy," appeared in *Hymns Adopted to Divine Worship* by Thomas Gibbons and later in John Rippon's *Selection of Hymns from the Best Authors* (1787). It was in general use by the mid-nineteenth century and was one of the very few early American texts to gain and retain such popularity. Its simplicity of diction and its mood of almost childlike trust reveal Davies in a new light, though in the lines "Do Thou assist a feeble Worm/ the Great Engagement to perform" he uses the imagery of his period.

Lord, I Know Thy Grace Is Nigh Me	RATHBUN 8.7.8.7.
St. 1–5	
Hervey Doddridge Ganse, 1864	Ithamar Conkey, comp. 1847, pub. 1851

This poem of comfort was written while Ganse was resting on a winter evening in a farmhouse near Freehold, N.J., where he had paid a call of condolence. "I composed on my pillow in the darkness; completing the verses with no little feeling before I slept."

Published in the Reformed Dutch *Hymns of the Church* (1869), it was there associated with RATHBUN by Ithamar Conkey, but attributed to Henry Wellington Greatorex (q.v.). The tune did appear in the Greatorex *Collection of Psalm and Hymn Tunes* of 1851, even though it had been composed four years earlier.

Lord, in Thy Presence Here	LIBERTY HALL C.M.
St. 1, 5, 6, 9	
Jesse L. Holman, 1825	Anon., 1820

This hymn for the opening of worship first appeared in *Hymns, Psalms, and Spiritual Songs* (1st ed., 1825; 2d ed., 1829), edited by Rev. Absalom Graves. The original version contained nine stanzas, but it was shortened to six when reprinted in H. Miller's *Psalms, Hymns, and Spiritual Songs* (30th ed., 1842), Buck's *Baptist Hymn Book* (1842), and elsewhere.

A Southern tune seemed appropriate for an author who was born in Kentucky. LIBERTY HALL, folklike in character, appeared in *Beauties of Harmony* (2d ed.; 1816), by Freeman Lewis, and in a number of earlier Southern books, including Allen D. Carden's *Missouri Harmony* (1820) and John McCurry's *Social Harp* (1855). The tune, which lacks the sixth step, is plagal in range, extending from the fifth below to the fifth above the final. We reproduce the version from *Missouri Harmony*, which differs from that in *Beauties of Harmony*.

The Lord into His Garden Comes	Garden Hymn 8.8.6.6.D.
St. 1–6	
Anon., 1805	Anon., version of 1866

Julian traces the text of "The Lord into His Garden Comes" to Joshua Leavitt's *The Christian Lyre* of 1831, but it is earlier than that. In 1805 Jeremiah Ingalls printed three stanzas without music in his *Christian Harmony.* They follow a tune called Love Divine set to "To Him Who Did Salvation Bring." The melody of Garden Hymn has the movement of a penitent Celtic jig. Widely distributed, it appeared in Leavitt, in William Walker's *Southern Harmony* (1854), the *Jubilee Harp,* compiled by A. T. Gorham (1866), Joseph Hillman's *Revivalist* (1868), and elsewhere. The text and musical setting given here come from the *Jubilee Harp,* the music slightly modified.

Transposed down one step.

Lord, I Want To Be a Christian	
St. 1–5	
Traditional, transcribed by R. Nathaniel Dett	R. Nathaniel Dett, arr. 1957

"Lord, I Want To Be a Christian" seems to belong to the repertory of spirituals sung by the students of Hampton Institute. It appeared in R. Nathaniel Dett's *Religious Folk-Songs of the Negro* (1927) and, in a similar arrangement by Dett, in the *African Methodist Episcopal Zion Hymnal* (1957). It is the latter version, intended for congregational singing, that is presented here. In the chorus the soprano sets a pattern that is repeated by the lower voices in a way made familiar by many refrains in gospel hymns. This spiritual is one of those sung by white and mixed congregations since it was included in *The Hymnbook* of 1955, prepared for use in the several branches of the Presbyterian and Reformed churches.

Lord Jesus Christ, We Humbly Pray	Sursum Corda L.M.
St. 1–5	
Henry Eyster Jacobs, 1910, pub. 1917	Luther Reed, 1910, pub. 1917

Dr. Luther Reed's interest in plainsong, shown in 1901 by *The Choral Service Book,* is also revealed in Sursum Corda, in which the melody is derived from the "Plainsong Preface Melodies." This communion hymn with the text by Henry Eyster Jacobs appeared in the *United Lutheran Hymnal* of 1917. Note that this tune name was also used for an entirely different tune by Alfred Morton Smith ("Peace Is the Mind's Old Wilderness").

Lord! Lead the Way the   Bristol C.M.
   Saviour Went
St. 1–4
William Crosswell, writ. 1831,   Edward Hodges, 1848
   pub. 1860

Julian states that "Lord! Lead the Way the Saviour Went" was generally accepted as the best American hymn for benevolent occasions. Originally composed for the Howard Benevolent Society of Boston in 1831, it was included in Crosswell's posthumous *Poems* of 1860 and in *The Hymns of the Church* of 1892. The musical influence of the Church of England on the Episcopal service here was great and musicians trained in that tradition came to this country to serve as organists and to train choirs with boy sopranos. As they spent much of their professional life here and wrote compositions for American churches, it seems proper to include their work as a characteristic element in our tradition.

   Such a musician was Edward Hodges, whose Bristol was named for his English birthplace. It was included in two books published in 1848: *The National Lyre* (eds. Henry Kemble Oliver, S. Samuel Tuckerman, and Silas A. Bancroft) and Samuel Jackson's *Sacred Harmony*.

Lord, Many Times Thou   Te Deum C.M.D.
   Pleased Art
St. 1, 3, 5, 11   Frost 2
George Wither, 1641   Thomas Ravenscroft, arr.
                       1621

   George Wither's hymn "for them who intend to settle in Virginia, New England, or the like places" is the next to last piece in the third part of *Haleluiah; or, Britan's Second Remembrancer*. The author designed the volume "that all Persons, according to their Degrees and Conditions, may at all Times, and upon eminent Occasions, be remembered to praise God; and to be mindful of their Duties." In the preface Wither complains that lately "Poesie hath bin prophaned by unhallowed Suggestions" but adds that "to prevent these Errors and

Offences, Mr. Sandys, Mr. Herbert, Mr. Quarles, and some others have lately to their great commendations, seriously endeavoured, by tuning their Muses to divine Strains." Each of the poets mentioned had interesting relationships with the New World. Sandys settled in Virginia for a time. Herbert's works were in the library of Increase Mather. His hopes for the advancement of religion in the New World were stated in the famous lines: "Religion stands on tiptoe in our land/Ready to pass to the American strand." Quarles was consulted by the editors of the *Bay Psalm Book.*

Wither precedes his hymn with the note: "Many depart every yeare from this *Ile,* to settle in *Virginia, New England,* and other parts of America, whose happinesse I heartily desire; and whose contented well-being in those places, might perhaps be somewhat furthered by such *Meditations* as these: And therefore, to those who please to accept thereof, I have recommended my love in this *Hymn.* Sing this as, 'We praise Thee God.' " These are the opening lines of the hymn commonly attributed to St. Ambrose called the "Te Deum." It is associated here with a tune which first appeared in the English psalter of 1561. It is harmonized in the psalter printed by John Day in 1563. William Damon made three settings of this tune. The melody was also treated by John Farmer (1592), Richard Allison (1599), Thomas Ravenscroft (1621), and John Playford (1677).

Ravenscroft wrote the cantus in the C clef, first line; medius, C clef, third line; tenor or plainsong, C clef, fourth line; bassus, F clef, fourth line. Time signature C; note values halved.

Lord, My Weak Thought in Vain Would Climb　　　Louvan L.M.
St. 1–5
Ray Palmer, 1858　　　　　Virgil Corydon Taylor, 1846

Written for *The Sabbath Hymn Book* (1858), compiled by Edward A. Park and Austin Phelps, this is one of the most beautiful and enduring of Palmer's hymns. To this volume Palmer contributed four free translations and three original hymns. Two of the three remain in use and they sustain Palmer's position as one of the finest American hymn writers.

Louvan is the tune in Charles S. Robinson's *Laudes Domini* (1884) and this association is retained here. Louvan first appeared in 1846 in the composer's *Sacred Minstrel or American Church Music Book.*

Lord of All Being, Throned   Federal Street L.M.
   Afar
St. 1–5
Oliver Wendell Holmes, writ.   Henry Kemble Oliver, comp.
   1848, pub. 1859   1832, pub. 1835

This poem, entitled "A Sun-day Hymn," appeared in the *Atlantic Monthly* for December 1859, at the end of the last installment for the year of the "Professor at the Breakfast Table." The poet urged his readers to "join in singing (inwardly) this hymn to the source of light we all need to lead us and the warmth which can make us all brothers."

The Unitarian *Hymn and Tune Book* of 1877 employed Virgil C. Taylor's Louvan for this fine text. The *New Hymn and Tune Book* (1914) coupled Holmes's poem with Federal Street, the most famous tune by the Unitarian composer Henry Kemble Oliver, a choice which we have followed here. Oliver conceived it as a setting for the final stanza of Anne Steele's "So Fades the Lovely Blooming Flower." In 1834 when Lowell Mason (q.v.) was conducting a singing class in Salem, Oliver gave him his setting, which appeared in the *Boston Academy's Collection of Church Music* in 1835. The origin of the tune name has been variously explained. We follow Rev. Armin Haeussler (*The Story of Our Hymns*) in suggesting that it was named either for the street in Salem, Mass., where Oliver resided, or the street in Boston where he attended church as a child.

Lord of Each Soul   8.8.8.8.8.
St. 1–3
Paul Engle, writ. 1957   Harriett Johnson, comp. 1958

Poet Paul Engle wrote "Lord of Each Soul" to be set to music as one of our contemporary hymns. The somewhat unusual plan of the hymn involves a fifth line, "Lord of our Hand and Lord of Head," which in the opening stanza is a repetition of the previous line and is retained in the later stanzas as a refrain line. Harriett Johnson has given Paul Engle's poem a setting in chromatic style. Both here and in her setting to "Through Warmth and Light of Summer Skies" the "Amen" is conceived as an essential part of the music and should not be omitted.

Lord of Life, All Praise Excelling	GRAFTON STREET 8.7.8.7.
St. 1–4	
Clement Clarke Moore, 1808	P. K. Moran, 1828

"Lord of Life, All Praise Excelling" was the first hymn by an American to be accepted for use in the services of the Protestant Episcopal Church. It appeared in the *Prayer Book Collection* of 1808 as one of a number of additional hymns. The fundamental theme of the poem is the equality of people of high and low degree before the Lord, an idea not commonly treated by hymn writers of that period.

GRAFTON STREET appeared in Jonathan Mayhew Wainwright's *Music of the Church* (New York and Philadelphia, 1828). P. K. Moran was represented in that collection and in Wainwright's earlier *A Collection of Psalm, Hymn and Chant Tunes Adapted to the Service of the Protestant Episcopal Church* (New York, pref., 1823). Wainwright was himself an Episcopalian clergyman and his collection was designed especially for the Episcopal service. Although GRAFTON STREET is in minor it is gently reflective rather than melancholy. The melody is remarkably limited in range consisting as it does of only four notes.

Lord of My Heart's Elation	ADVENT 7.6.7.6.D.
St. 1–3	Seth Bingham, submitted
Bliss Carman, 1894	1957

This vigorous unison hymn is by Seth Bingham, whose original hymn tunes reflect his long interest in and practical experience with congregational singing.

As submitted ADVENT was associated with James Montgomery's "Hail to the Lord's Anointed." In *American Hymns* it is to be sung to Bliss Carman's "Lord of My Heart's Elation." It was H. Augustine Smith who recognized the suitability of this poem of courage and aspiration as a hymn by including it in his *American Student Hymnal* (1928).

Lord of the Worlds Below!	WORSHIP H.M.
St. 1–5	
James Freeman, 1799	Hans Gram, 1802

"Lord of the Worlds Below!" appeared in *A Collection of Psalms and Hymns* in 1799. It is set here to WORSHIP by Hans Gram.

The tune appeared in Samuel Holyoke's bulky *Columbian Reposi-*

tory (1802). Gram's harmony has been altered in line 3 to provide a clearer cadence in C major. The change, contrary to our usual editorial practice, affects one note of the tune. The last tenor note in line 3 was B♭, not C. Other lapses from academic propriety have been allowed to stand.

Countertenor in C clef, third line. Original key G major; tune in tenor. The first soprano notes in bars 3, 6, and the last bar of the first section were printed as appoggiaturas in Holyoke.

The Lord Our God Alone Is   CAMP L.M.
   Strong
St. 1–5
Caleb T. Winchester, writ.   Peter C. Lutkin, 1905
   1871

"The Lord Our God Alone Is Strong" was written for the dedication of the Orange Judd Hall of Science, Wesleyan University. Professor Winchester was a member of the Joint Commission responsible for *The Methodist Hymnal* of 1905 and Peter Lutkin, who composed CAMP for this text, was one of the music editors. One might speculate that Camp was named for John Spencer Camp, a Hartford organist, but *The Music and Hymnody of the Methodist Hymnal* says only that it was named for a friend.

The Lord's My Shepherd, I'll   PISGAH C.M.D.
   Not Want
Ps. 23: 1–6
Francis Rous, 1650   J. C. Lowry (?), 1820

This version of Psalm 23 has survived to the present in both the British Isles and the United States. PISGAH, a tune with folk characteristics, appeared in 1820 in Allen D. Carden's *Missouri Harmony*. It was attributed to J. C. Lowry, of whom nothing is known. It was sung not only in our own country, particularly in the South, but was also one of a number of American tunes sung in Scotland. Those who prefer to sing the text to a more nearly contemporary tune may turn to PSALM 18 ("I to the Hills Will Lift Mine Eyes") from the great Scottish psalter of 1635.

Lord, Thou Hast Promised   BELLEVILLE L.M.
St. 1–4
Samuel K. Cox, 1905   Peter C. Lutkin, 1905

The opening of this hymn is based on John 1:16 "And of his fullness have all we received, and grace for grace." It was published in the *Baltimore and Richmond Christian Advocate* and reprinted in *The Methodist Hymnal* of 1905.

BELLEVILLE was composed for *The Methodist Hymnal* by Lutkin, who, with Karl P. Harrington (q.v.), was one of the musical editors.

Lord, Who's the Happy Man   ST. DAVID C.M.
Ps. 15: 1, 2, 5, 7
Nahum Tate and Nicholas   Daniel Purcell, arr. c.1718
   Brady, 1696

With the appearance of the New Version by Tate and Brady, American churches close to the Anglican tradition were provided with a psalter more in accord with contemporary taste than the Old Version of Thomas Sternhold and John Hopkins. Psalm 15 was a favorite with Thomas Jefferson, who transcribed the first stanza into his own copy of Daniel Purcell's *The Psalms set full for the Organ or Harpsichord.* Daniel, brother of the celebrated Henry Purcell, had harmonized familiar psalm tunes in keyboard style and had provided them with instrumental interludes to be played between the lines. This and John Blow's harmonization of HACKNEY (q.v.) are important because they show how an organist of the period might actually accompany a psalm tune. This version may be compared with John Playford's simple harmonization of ST. DAVID, which has been included as the setting to Benjamin Keach's "How Glorious Are the Morning Stars" (q.v.).

Lo, What Enraptured Songs   PERSIA L.M.
   of Praise
St. 1–4
Sebastian Streeter, 1829   Thomas Whittemore, 1841

Streeter's text appeared in Whittemore's *The Gospel Harmonist* (1841) to the editor's tune. It had appeared earlier in the volume edited by Sebastian Streeter and his brother Russell, *The New Hymn Book, Designed for Universalist Societies* under the heading "Ascriptions to Christ."

PERSIA is a choir rather than a congregational tune, as is shown by the independent passages where the progress of the soprano is interrupted to permit other voices to be heard. Striking also is the unison for all voices beginning on the upbeat to bar 5, and the trumpetlike figure beginning in bar 7.

Make Ye a Joyful Sounding Noise	OLD 100TH L.M.
Ps. 100: 1–5	Frost, 114; Zahn 368
Anon., 1640	John Dowland, arr. 1621

This metrical version of Psalm 100 (A Psalm of Prayse) is accompanied by a tune first found in the 1551 edition of the French psalter for Psalm 134. Ten years later it was taken into the Anglo-Genevan psalter to William Kethe's familiar rendering of Psalm 100, "All people that on earth do dwell." The origin of the melody has been much discussed. Loys Bourgeois, the musical editor of the French psalter, may have been thinking of the *chanson* "Il n'y a icy celluy qui n'ait sa belle" or the Gregorian melody "Suaves Domine Christo jubente" when he "composed" the tune.

Shakespeare recognized the tune's popularity in a reference in *Merry Wives of Windsor* (II.1). Mistress Ford and Mistress Page are comparing Falstaff's love letters. Mistress Ford, wishing to emphasize the vast difference between Falstaff's words and his disposition, exclaims, "they do no more adhere and keep place together than the hundredth Psalm to the tune of Green Sleeves."

Lowell Mason reprinted the *Bay Psalm Book* version of Psalm 100 as late as 1845 in his *Psaltery*, perhaps to call to mind all that this psalm had meant to the early settlers. "Old Hundredth" is probably the only sixteenth-century psalm tune still universally known to Protestant churchgoers of the present day. Thomas Ravenscroft places it quite properly with the "French tunes" and prints a version by the great lutanist and composer John Dowland.

Cantus, C clef, first line; medius, C clef, third line; "tenor or playnsong," C clef, fourth line; bassus, F clef, fourth line. Time signature C ; note values halved; transposed up a major third.

Mary Lifted from the Dead St. 1–6	7.7.7.7.D.
William Alfred, writ. 1956	Theodore Chanler, comp. 1956

Theodore Chanler, a Catholic, when asked to write an original hymn tune for *American Hymns,* sought the collaboration of William

Alfred, a writer and educator who shared the same faith. "Mary Lifted from the Dead" was, therefore, written especially for music. The care with which the movement of the music is adjusted to varying verbal rhythms in different stanzas makes it difficult as a congregational hymn. A meticulous workman, Chanler's setting was modified twice after submission. As he wrote, "when errors are found there is nothing for it but to correct them."

Master, No Offering	LOVE'S OFFERING
St. 1–4	6.4.6.4.6.6.4.4.
Edwin Pond Parker, writ.	Edwin Pond Parker,
1888, pub. 1889	writ. 1888, pub. 1889

This poem, with its somewhat sentimental tune, has been widely used. Written in 1888 to be sung at the conclusion of a sermon, it was taken up by *The Christian Hymnal. The Pilgrim Hymnal* (1904) included it, and Rev. Charles L. Atkins has found that it appears in over sixty twentieth-century hymnals. Characteristic of its own period, it still appeals to a large group of American churchgoers.

The tune was composed by the author who, as pastor of the Second Congregational Church in Hartford, Conn., also wrote many tunes and arranged classical themes for his choir.

Med Gud och Hans Vanscap	ACK, SALIGA STUNDER
With God and His Mercy	11.11.11.6.6.11.
St. 1–5	
Carl Olof Rosenius	Oscar Ahnfelt, 185(?)

Oscar Ahnfelt was a spiritual troubadour who composed or arranged tunes to popular religious texts and wandered from place to place in Sweden singing them to his own guitar accompaniment. "Med Gud och Hans Vanscap" was especially popular with Swedish immigrants to the United States. The original was arranged for guitar or piano (though we reproduce only the piano accompaniment). It was included in the Augustana Lutheran hymnal of 1925, arranged in four-part harmony, with the English translation which we gave here.

Mighty One, Before Whose Face   LAYON 7.7.7.7.
St. 1–3
William Cullen Bryant, 1840   John Zundel, 1855

Although Julian dates this hymn 1840, he remarks that it "is probably earlier." Bryant's poem, with a number of others, is printed with John Zundel's STORRS in the *Plymouth Collection* (1855). Since this double tune requires two of the three stanzas, leaving us with only one for its repetition, it seemed better to choose a single tune by the same composer. Zundel was organist of the Plymouth Church, Brooklyn, and an editor of the *Plymouth Collection,* in which a number of his tunes appeared. LAYON has been transposed from A to G major.

Mine Eyes Have Seen the Glory   THE BATTLE HYMN OF THE REPUBLIC 15.15.15.16., with chorus
St. 1–4
Julia Ward Howe, 1862   William Steffe, 1852

Composed by William Steffe and first generally sung in the neighborhood of Charleston, S.C., to a text beginning "Say brothers, will you meet us," this tune was taken up by singers of all descriptions, among them soldiers of the Union army.

The version beginning "John Brown's body lies a-mouldering in the grave" developed among the singers of a battalion of Massachusetts soldiers nicknamed the "Tigers" who were at Fort Warren, Boston Harbor. The recent hanging of John Brown after the attack on Harper's Ferry was in everyone's mind. As it happened, a soldier in the "Tigers" was also called John Brown and some unknown soldier-humorist devised the line "John Brown's body lies a-mouldering in the grave" as a way of teasing a comrade. Soldiers on the march spread the tune wherever they went.

Julia Ward Howe was in Washington in December 1861, when she and her husband were spectators as Union troops went into action with this song on their lips. The Rev. James Freeman Clarke (q.v.), a Unitarian minister who was also present, suggested that Mrs. Howe write new words to the popular tune. That same night, with the events of the day still vivid in her mind, she wrote the lines familiar to every American,

> Mine eyes have seen the glory of the coming of the Lord.
> He is trampling out the vintage where the grapes of wrath
>   are stored

Her verses are remembered, but hers was by no means the only attempt to fit a new text to the familiar air. Edna Dean Proctor had already written an antislavery text for it. A later poem by Frederick L. Hosmer (q.v.) began,

> From age to age they gather, all the brave of heart and
>   strong;
> In the strife of truth with error, of the right against the
>   wrong.

The Morning Bright, with   MORNING C.M.
  Rosy Light
St. 1–3
Thomas O. Summers, writ. c.   Anon., 1861
  1846

Although the entire range of American hymns for children cannot be illustrated in this volume, certain outstanding examples are not to be ignored, especially when they attain the dignity of a reference in Julian's *Dictionary of Hymnology*. Thomas O. Summers, eminent in the Southern branch of the Methodist Episcopal Church of his day, rendered special services to hymnology as an editor of the *Songs of Zion* (1851) and the *Wesleyan Psalter* (1855). However, nothing he wrote was so widely circulated as two little hymns, one for morning, the other for the evening. Concerning the first he wrote:

My first child was born in January, 1845. When she was about a year old, as I was descending the Tombigbee River in a little steamer, I wrote a morning hymn for her on the back of a letter, transcribed it when I reached Mobile, and sent it to her at Tuscaloosa. That was the origin of "The Morning Bright."

This hymn, first published anonymously in the *Southern Christian Advocate*, was copied by other periodicals and hymnbooks. Summers' evening hymn, written for his second child, began "The daylight fades, the evening shades . . ."

The tune MORNING is usually listed as anonymous, although William R. Huntington, in his *The Church Porch* (New York, 1874), attributed it to "Hart." It was published in *Hymns & Music for the Young* (1861), by J. Freeman.

The Morning Light Is   WEBB 7.6.7.6.D.
  Breaking
St. 1–4
Samuel Francis Smith, 1832   George J. Webb, 1837

Samuel Francis Smith had hoped to become a missionary and two of his hymns were on missionary themes: "The Morning Light Is Breaking" and "Yes, My Native Land, I Love Thee." The former, inspired by an account written by the famous missionary to Burma, Adoniram Judson, was an early poem written while Smith was a theological student at Andover. Both Smith's hymn and George Duffield's "Stand Up, Stand Up for Jesus" (q.v.) are frequently sung to WEBB, also called MILLENNIAL DAWN. The association has been preserved here, although WEBB was originally composed for a secular text, " 'Tis Dawn, The Lark Is Singing." WEBB was first associated with Smith's poem in *The Wesleyan Psalmist* (1842), compiled by Moses Lewis Scudder.

Morning Star, O Cheering   MORNING STAR 7.7.6.7.
  Sight!
St. 1–4
Anon., c. 1870   Francis F. Hagen, comp. 1842

Francis F. Hagen is said to have composed this Christmas carol at Salem in 1842. It was originally set to a hymn by Johann Scheffler (1624–77). The present English text is said to have been adapted to Hagen's music shortly after 1870. It early became and has remained the favorite Christmas song of the Moravian Church in America. As early as 1856 it was described as "that grand old anthem, pride of Christmas even" in lines written by General William Emil Doster. In 1876 it was included in the Moravian hymnal with indications of the keyboard accompaniment. This example has been followed in *American Hymns*. Organists who wish to use the independent accompaniment may use the edition of Hans David published by G. Schirmer in 1939.

More Love
Anon., 1876   Anon., 1876

The title page of the Shaker *A Selection of Devotional Melodies* (Canterbury, N.H., 1876) bears the statement: "Simple in Arrangement,

Yet,—Inspirational" together with an appropriate quotation: "Whoso offereth praise glorifieth me" (Ps. 50:23). The text is in prose, as if improvised for the tune. "More Love" should be sung as a unison hymn, and the accompaniment provided here may be omitted.

More Love to Thee, O Christ   BETHANY 6.4.6.4.6.6.6.4.
St. 1–4
Elizabeth Payson Prentiss,   Lowell Mason, 1859
    writ. c.1856 pub. 1869

Sarah Flower Adams' famous hymn "Nearer My God to Thee" is inseparably associated in America with Lowell Mason's BETHANY. Brown and Butterworth, in their *Story of the Hymns and Tunes,* asked why Mason did not call his tune BETHEL instead of BETHANY, because the imagery of the poet in stanza 2 was based on Genesis 28:19, the passage in which Jacob called the place where the Lord appeared to him "Bethel." Actually, Mason had already used that name for a tune published in his *The Hallelujah* in 1854 and had set it to "Nearer My God to Thee." BETHANY was therefore a second tune for the same text, first published in the *Sabbath Hymn and Tune Book* of 1859.

Elizabeth Prentiss in a letter of 1870 wrote to explain that a hymn mentioned by her correspondent was not hers. She then went on to say, "I will enclose one that is, which my dear husband has kindly had printed; perhaps you will like to sing it to the tune of 'Nearer My God to Thee.' There is not much in it, but you can put everything into it as you make it your prayer." In view of the relationship of this American poem with Mason's famous tune, it seemed desirable to associate them here. A more recent tune for the same text was William Howard Doane's MORE LOVE TO THEE, published in 1868.

Mother Dear, O! Pray for Me   7.6.8.6.D., with chorus
St. 1–3
Anon.: st. 1, 1863; st. 2, 3,   Isaac B. Woodbury, 1850
    1867

This hymn to the Virgin Mary has enjoyed a persistent popularity with members of Catholic congregations but has been deplored by some of their leading scholars and musicians. It is a parody in the more specialized sense of that term: a secular song "spiritualized" by altering the text. It is included here as representative of its type. In spite of its popularity its origin was obscure until J. Vincent Higginson succeeded in tracing it.

The familiar melody by Isaac Woodbury was published in 1850. Its title was the same as that of the hymn, but was addressed to an earthly mother by her son. The opening stanza of the hymn had appeared earlier in *Peter's Catholic Harp* (1863), but with a different melody by A. Cull. This stanza was adapted to the Woodbury tune and the two remaining stanzas were added in an appendix to *The Sacred Wreath,* dated 1867.

The Music of His Steps
St. 1–4
William Hunter, 1854

THE ITINERANT'S DEATH L.M.

Samuel Wakefield, 1854

Perhaps no volume of hymns gives such a vivid picture of the life of the Methodist circuit rider or itinerant preacher as *The Minstrel of Zion* by William Hunter and Samuel Wakefield. Such titles as "The Prayer in the Wilderness" and "The Itinerant's Death" picture episodes of frontier life which have now passed into history. THE ITINERANT'S DEATH is marked "S.W.," the initials of Samuel Wakefield, joint editor of the collection.

The original setting was for soprano accompanied by a rather ill-contrived bass. The melody is here presented in the original key, but the bass has been rewritten and alto and tenor parts have been added for those who prefer a four-part setting.

My Country, to Thy Shore
St. 1–5
Theodore Chickering Williams, 1912

MACEDON 6.6.4.6.6.6.4.

Frederick Field Bullard, 1902

The metric pattern of this hymn is indelibly imprinted on the minds of all Americans, since it is that of "My Country, 'Tis of Thee." Williams' poem is also a national hymn, one envisaging "a new brotherhood of man" and the day when all mankind shall be one.

MACEDON, copyrighted in 1902, was published in the 1904 edition of *The Pilgrim Hymnal.* For further discussion of the tune, see "Christ for the World! We Sing."

My Days Are Gliding Swiftly By	SHINING SHORE 8.7.8.7., with chorus
St. 1–4	
David Nelson, writ. 1835	George F. Root, 1856

Ira D. Sankey, in *My Life and the Story of the Gospel Hymns* (1906), gives a romantic account of the origin of the text. David Nelson, who had been convinced of the evils of slavery, was driven from his plantation by slave-holding neighbors. While he was hidden on the bank of the Mississippi, which flowed between him and a safe haven on the Illinois shore, these lines came into his mind. He jotted them down on the back of a letter. He is said to have had the melody of LORD ULLIN'S DAUGHTER in mind, although his poem is now firmly associated with Root's tune.

SHINING SHORE is the best of Root's hymn tunes of the gospel type. Yet this is an opinion which he did not share. Root's mother had given him the poem from a newspaper clipping with the remark, "George, I think that would be good for music." Root read the poem and wrote down the melody which it suggested. Later he questioned whether so "simple and commonplace" a melody was worth harmonizing, but finally decided to do so. Julian dates the text 1835. It appeared in *The Sabbath Bell* (1856) with Root's tune. Apparently Root did not remember this publication, for in *The Diapason* (1860) he attributed his tune to the later *Sabbath Hymn and Tune Book* (1859). See also "Wayfarers in the Wilderness."

My Faith Looks Up to Thee	OLIVET 6.6.4.6.6.6.4.
St. 1–4	
Ray Palmer, writ. 1830, pub. 1832	Lowell Mason, 1832

Ray Palmer wrote his first hymn when, as a young graduate from Yale, he taught in a New York school for young ladies. Lowell Mason met the author in Boston a year or more after the poem was written and requested a hymn text. "The little book containing the hymn was shown him, and he asked for a copy. We stepped into a store together, and a copy was made and given to him, which, without much notice, he put into his pocket. On sitting down at home and looking it over, he became so much interested in it that he wrote for it the tune OLIVET, to which it has almost universally been sung." OLIVET made its appearance in *Spiritual Songs for Social Worship* (Boston, 1832), edited by Thomas Hastings (q.v.) and Lowell Mason. Originally published in three-part harmony as given here, it was subsequently altered and commonly printed in four parts. Original key G major.

Thomas Hastings' "Saviour, I Look to Thee," written in the same unusual meter as "My Faith Looks Up to Thee," appears to have been intended as a counterpart of that hymn.

My God, I Thank Thee St. 1–4 Andrews Norton, 1809	DUNBARTON L.M. William Selby, 1802

"My God, I Thank Thee," the first and most widely used of Norton's hymn texts, was first published in the *Monthly Anthology and Boston Review,* September 1809.

Few of William Selby's hymn tunes appear in American collections, but Samuel Holyoke's *Columbian Repository* includes two, PAUL'S STREET and DUNBARTON. Since Selby was the organist at King's Chapel in Boston which became a Unitarian church, DUNBARTON seemed a good choice as the setting for a Unitarian text. In the *Columbian Repository* it was associated with Isaac Watts's "Here at Thy Cross, My Dying God."

My Heart, How Very Hard It's Grown! (Singing at the Plough) St. 1–5 Cotton Mather, 1727	CAMBRIDGE C.M. John Playford, arr. 1677

Two poems from Cotton Mather's *Agricola* are included here: "My Heart, How Very Hard It's Grown!" and "When the Seed of Thy Word Is Cast." In the former, Mather compares the heart of the impenitent sinner to hardened ground which must be broken by the plough before it can receive the scriptural promises and truly repent. It has been set here to John Playford's arrangement of the CAMBRIDGE tune as found in his *The Whole Book of Psalms* (1677).

Time signature ¢ 3.

My Latest Sun Is Sinking Fast   THE LAND OF BEULAH C.M.,
St. 1–4   with chorus
Jefferson Haskell, 1860   William Batchelder Brad-
                                                    bury, 1862

This hymn has a brief verse (two couplets sung to a single repeated musical phrase) followed by a more extended rhythmic
chorus. This form reflects the practice of camp meetings and revivals where many of the songs followed the ancient pattern of solo
and response. The choral responses were easily learned, used the
same text for each stanza, and sometimes gained an independent life
since a favorite chorus might be attached to different hymns. "My
Latest Sun Is Sinking Fast" has an appealing simplicity. It appeared
in J. W. Dadmun's *Melodeon* (1860) to a tune by Dadmun, in Bradbury's *Golden Shower* to his THE LAND OF BEULAH, and Bradbury's
setting was included in Joseph Hillman's *The Revivalist* of 1868. The
latter collection, originally intended for the "praying band" of Troy,
N.Y., was extensively used and served to record and circulate religious folk songs.

My Shepherd Is the Living   CAMBRIDGE C.M.
   Lord
Ps. 23: 1–5   Frost 42
Thomas Sternhold, 1561   Edmund Hooper, arr. 1592

Thomas Sternhold's metrical version of Psalm 23 appeared in
1561 although the author died in 1549. The tune given here was
used for this psalm by William Daman in 1579, but was not called
CAMBRIDGE until 1621. In Thomas East's psalter it was harmonized
by Edmund Hooper and matched with Psalm 9. Richard Allison's
version of 1599 is associated with Psalm 12. In a modified form it
was sung in Scotland as LONDON TUNE. The tune was one of the first
common meter tunes to achieve popularity in the sixteenth century.
   Cantus, C clef, first line; altus, C clef, third line; tenor, C clef,
fourth line; bassus, F clef, fourth line. Time signature ¢ ; note values
halved.

My Soul Before Thee
  Prostrate Lies
St. 1, 3, 5, 6, 9, 11
C. F. Richter, 1704
John Wesley, trans. 1737

ZEUCH MEINEN GEIST L.M.

Johann Christoph Kühnau,
  arr. 1786

John Wesley had been deeply impressed by the singing of the Moravians who sailed with him to Georgia in 1735. As a result he made translations from the German such as "My Soul Before Thee Prostrate Lies" and "Jesu, to Thee My Heart I Bow." They were first published in the *Charleston Collection of Psalms and Hymns,* 1737. The German text, "Hier legt mein Sinn sich vor Dir Nieder" is by C. F. Richter and was first published in Johann Anastasius Freylinghausen's *Geist-reiches Gesang-Buch, den Kern alter und neuer Lieder . . .* (1704).

We do not know what tunes the Moravians sang but presumably they were chorale melodies like ZEUCH MEINEN GEIST, which we present in an arrangement by Johann Christoph Kühnau.

My Soul, Weigh Not Thy Life
St. 1–4
Leonard Swain, 1858

LABAN S.M.

Lowell Mason, 1854

This poem both in meter and thought closely parallels George Heath's well-known "My Soul Be on Thy Guard." With the heading "The Good Fight of Faith" it was published in *The Sabbath Hymn Book* (1848) without the name of the author, as was Swain's "My Soul, It Is Thy God."

Since Lowell Mason's LABAN is frequently sung to the Heath text, it seemed most appropriate to use it here with the very similar American text. Indeed, in Edwin A. Bedell's *The Church Hymnary* (1894) both texts are given with this tune. LABAN, first published in *Spiritual Songs for Social Worship* (1832), compiled by Mason and Thomas Hastings, was included in the *Boston Academy's Collection of Church Music* (1835). In Mason's *Hallelujah* (1854) the tune is provided with an instrumental interlude intended for the instrumental ensembles which accompanied the singers in many churches. It is this version which we reproduce.

My Soul Would Fain Indulge   ABERFORD C.M.
  a Hope
St. 1–6
Joseph Steward, 1799   G. K. Jackson, 1804

"My Soul Would Fain Indulge a Hope" by Joseph Steward, an editor of the *Hartford Selection,* is headed "Hoping Yet Trembling."

In Jackson's *David's Psalms,* ABERFORD is marked with an asterisk as an original tune. A peculiarity of the collection is the fact that tunes are printed twice: for melody and figured bass, and for four-part chorus "as used in Choirs for the further improvement of Psalmody in singing schools." It is this choral version of ABERFORD which is reproduced here.

Treble, G clef, second line; countertenor, C clef, third line; tenor, C clef, fourth line; bass, F clef, fourth line. Original key E♭ major.

Mysterious Presence! Source   CATON L.M.
  of All
St. 1–4
Seth Curtis Beach, writ. 1866   Henry Kemble Oliver, comp.
                                           1866, pub. 1875

This hymn, written for Visitation Day 1866, while Beach was a student at Harvard Divinity School, has been widely used as an opening hymn. In the *Unitarian Hymn and Tune Book* of 1877 the tune ILLA by Lowell Mason was assigned to it. In this volume it seemed more fitting to set the text to CATON, a tune composed the same year by Henry Kemble Oliver, who was himself a Unitarian. It was published in Oliver's *Original Hymn Tunes.*

När Vil Du, Jesu, Min   LOBE DEN HERREN
  Eländes Vandring Besluta?   14.14.4.7.8.
When Shall My Pilgrimage,
  Jesus My Saviour, Be
  Ended?
St. 1–3, 5
Andrew Rudman (?), c.1700   Anon., 1665
Ernest Edwin Ryden, trans.
  1970

Andrew Rudman published two little pamphlets containing hymns in Swedish: *Twenne Andelige Wisor* and *Naora Andelige Wisor.* If any of the hymns are original with Rudman they are the earliest written in Swedish in this country. That Rudman did write original hymns is shown by an entry in his diary for April 11, 1697: "I also wrote a hymn beginning 'O Gud, O Gud sa from.'" That at least some of the hymns in the second pamphlet were revisions or translations is indicated by remarks such as that for No. 5: "The fifth, better than before composed," or for No. 6: "The sixth improved from the German." Ryden suggested that Rudman might have reprinted hymns from the Swedenborg hymnal, a hundred copies of which had been sent here for the use of the Swedish settlers. Of the present hymn Ryden writes that "the poetry in the Swedish is very fine, and if Rudman really wrote it, he certainly was a gifted man."

The melody LOBE DEN HERREN, which may be the one to which this hymn was originally sung, comes from the *Stralsund Gesangbuch*. It is reprinted here as it appears in the Lutheran *Service Book and Hymnal* of 1958.

Nations That Long in Darkness Walked	MARBLEHEAD L.M.
Isa. 9: 2, 6, 7	
John Barnard, 1752	Version from Barnard, 1752

John Barnard's *New Version of the Psalms of David* also contains "several hymns out of the Old and New Testaments." The text here is a metrical version of Isaiah 9.

Barnard's version was sometimes bound with a supplement of tunes which included MARBLEHEAD. Presumably of English origin, the attractive tune is accompanied by voices which move in step with it in the manner of John Playford's *Whole Booke of Psalms*.

In the medius in line 2, bar 2, the second note was D, making fifths with the bass. In line 4, bar 1, the third note was E, in unison with the cantus.

Nobody Knows de Trouble I've Seen	
St. 1, 2	
Traditional, pub. 1927	R. Nathaniel Dett, arr. 1927

According to *Slave Songs* (1867), this song was a favorite in the black schools of Charleston, S.C., in 1865; it subsequently spread to the Sea Islands. Its presence in the Sea Islands at an early date is indicated by the tale that General Howard was moved to tears when he asked the people to sing this spiritual at a meeting called to quiet their impatience at the inaction of the government in disposing of confiscated lands. Yet the song was extremely fluid. The Charleston version lacked the syncopated rhythm at the opening of each section of the chorus, though a variant noted from Florida in *Slave Songs* possessed this peculiarity. Neither version began with the descending sixth which appeared in the Dett arrangement and which the modern hearer accepts as a characteristic feature. The melody is plagal in character, ranging from five to five of the scale with the tonic or tone of repose centrally located, or more precisely, a fourth above the lowest tone and a fifth below the highest.

No More Beneath the   Liberty C.M.
   Oppressive Hand
Anon., 1800   Stephen Jenks, 1800

This fuguing tune, which first appeared in New Haven in 1800 in Stephen Jenks's *The Musical Harmonist,* enjoyed lasting popularity. John Wyeth reprinted it in the second part of his *Repository of Sacred Music* (Harrisburg, Pa., 2d ed., 1820) and at the same time reduced it to three parts by simply omitting the countertenor. It is possible that the Southern books took it from Wyeth. At any rate, it appeared in *The Southern Harmony* (1835) in three parts, as in Wyeth. (Two notes only are different!) In the *Original Sacred Harp* (1936) this sturdy tune still survives, but S. M. Denson (one of the editors) added an alto part, evidently not realizing that Jenks himself had composed Liberty in four parts. Only one stanza appeared as text. The editors of the *Original Sacred Harp* ventured the remark that "He [Jenks] is supposed to have composed the words of this tune." This seems to be no more than an editorial speculation, yet a persistant search has revealed neither the name of the author nor the other stanzas.

   Countertenor, G clef, an octave too high. Time signature ℭ; tune in tenor.

Not Alone for Mighty Empire Geneva 8.7.8.7.D.
St. 1–4
William Pierson Merrill, writ. George Henry Day, 1940
   1909, pub. 1911

William Merrill has said that this prayer for patriotism based on justice and brotherhood "came out of a Thanksgiving service in Chicago, at which Jenkin Lloyd Jones offered a prayer which impressed me greatly by its emphasis on the spiritual national blessings and assets. I went home and wrote a rather diffusive hymn about it, and later made it over into the present one."

At the time when Day wrote GENEVA he was the organist of Trinity Church in that city. Tune and text were combined in *The Hymnal 1940* as they appear here.

Not Only Where God's Free 8.6.8.8.6.
    Winds Blow
St. 1–5
Shepherd Knapp, 1908   Edward Lawton, comp. 1957

In their willingness to work with the notes of a single scale the music of some of our contemporary composers is closer to the tunes of the sixteenth and seventeenth centuries than to those of the nineteenth century, which are modulatory in character. This sturdy unison hymn by Edward Lawton is severely diatonic. Aside from the longer cadence tones and one solitary pair of eighth notes, the melody strides along in uniform quarter notes. On the other hand, the free movement of the accompanying parts results in a prevailingly dissonant texture.

The text by Shepherd Knapp is the later of two hymns by him which have been included in twentieth-century hymnals. The other is "Lord God of Hosts." See the earlier setting of this poem by Kenneth E. Runkel.

Not Only Where God's Free   ETERNAL LIGHT 8.6.8.8.6.
    Winds Blow
St. 1–5
Shepherd Knapp, writ. 1908,   Kenneth E. Runkel, 1941
    pub. 1937

"Lord God of Hosts" (q.v.) and "Not Only Where God's Free Winds Blow" are two hymns by Knapp which have been widely sung. Some editors have altered the latter hymn to begin with stanza 2, "Dear God, the sun whose light is sweet," but the complete poem is presented here. It is perhaps natural that one who had served a church in metropolitan New York should write a hymn stressing God's presence in the city as well as in the countryside.

The tune ETERNAL LIGHT, selected for inclusion in *The Hymnal 1940,* was set to and named for Thomas Binney's "Eternal Light, Eternal Light." Written without a time signature, it is basically in $\frac{4}{4}$, yet the first complete bar contains three, and the second five, quarter notes, a freer pattern than is usual. This text has also been set to a tune commissioned from Edward Lawton for *American Hymns.*

Not to Us, Not unto Us, Lord   OLD 113TH 8.8.8.8.8.8.D.
Ps. 115: 1–18   Frost 125; Zahn 8308
Anon., 1640   Thomas Ravenscroft, arr.
                                            1621

This metrical version of Psalm 115, from the *Bay Psalm Book* of 1640, is to be sung to a famous melody, sometimes attributed to Thomas Greiter, which goes back to the early years of the sixteenth century. Zahn gives the date of the tune as 1526. It appeared in Calvin's first Strassburg psalter of 1539 to Psalm 36 and later to Psalm 68. From there it was taken into the Anglo-Genevan psalter of 1561 and so into English usage where it was associated with the text of Psalm 113. For this reason it was often called OLD 113TH. It is one of the tunes specifically mentioned in the "Admonition to the Reader" in the *Bay Psalm Book* of 1640. The metric pattern on the continent was 8.8.7.8.8.7.D., which became uniform octosyllabic lines in the English-speaking churches.

The militant words of Psalm 68, "Que Dieu se montre seulement," made it popular with Calvinist soldiers and it became a favorite war song in the period when Geneva was fighting for its independence. Bach used the melody with the German words "O Mensch bewein dein Sünde gross" in the *St. Matthew Passion.* In New England it lasted until the end of the eighteenth century. The Ravenscroft setting is given here, although there were earlier arrangements by Claude Goudimel and Richard Allison.

Cantus, C clef, first line; medius, C clef, second line; "tenor or playnsong," C clef, third line; bassus, F clef, third line. Original pitch; time signature C ;note values halved.

Now Behold the Saviour   PLEADING SAVIOUR 8.7.8.7.D.
   Pleading
St. 1–4
John Leland, 1791   William Hauser, arr. 1878

The text and music of this hymn are given as they appear in William Hauser's 1878 tune book, *The Olive Leaf.* The text, however, is earlier and was popular among the Baptists. Henry Burrage, who gives a variant first line, "Now the Saviour stands a-pleading," states that it was "found in most Baptist collections a half century ago" (i.e., c.1838). It was sung in the North as well as the South, for it is included in the *Plymouth Collection* (1855), compiled for Henry Ward Beecher's Brooklyn church.

Now Be the Gospel Banner   MISSIONARY HYMN 7.6.7.6.D.
St. 1, 2
Thomas Hastings, 1832   Lowell Mason, comp.
                              1823/24, pub. 1829

The MISSIONARY HYMN was written for and is usually sung to Reginald Heber's "From Greenland's Icy Mountains." Its creation dates back to the period when Mason was a bank clerk in Savannah, Ga. A copy of Heber's poem had been sent from England to a lady in that city who was anxious to obtain music to which it could be sung but knew of nothing suitable. Since Mason was locally known as an amateur composer she dispatched her son to him with the request that he set the poem to music. The boy returned after a short interval with the hymn we know. This is the story of the origin of a composition which has been sung countless times to the present day. There were four issues of the version for solo voice. It first appeared in a choral version in the seventh edition of the *Boston Handel and Haydn Society Collection of Church Music* in 1829 and it is this version for three voices which is reproduced here. In bar 11, soprano, the second C was originally an appoggiatura. In view of the enormous success of the tune it seems strange that Mason offered a choice of three different harmonizations as he did in his *The Hallelujah* (1854). In *The Psaltery* (1845) he suggested E or even D as more suitable keys for congregational singing. "It is often sung too fast: four moderate beats will give the right time."

Although Heber's text was so closely associated with the MISSIONARY HYMN, American poets have written lines to the familiar pattern. Deodatus Dutton's "On Thibet's Snow-Capt Mountain," published in 1831, was too obviously cast in the same mold as Heber's poem. We have preferred Thomas Hastings' "Now Be the Gospel Banner," which also expresses a hope for the universal victory of Christianity. It first appeared in *Spiritual Songs for Social Worship* (1832) to a different tune called GOSPEL BANNER.

Now Evening Puts Amen to
  Day
Paul Horgan, pub. 1942   Ernst Bacon, comp. 1942

Ernst Bacon's lively interest in the hymn as a characteristic American form is evident in his set of hymns for chorus with accompaniment for piano, four hands.

The evening hymn included here, however, was originally a part of the opera *A Tree on the Plains,* dating from 1942, commissioned by the League of Composers, with text by Paul Horgan. Of two versions of this hymn we prefer the simpler one in which the accompaniment simply doubles the voices except for the two opening chords.

Now from Labor and from   Toplady 7.7.7.D.
  Care
St. 1–3
Thomas Hastings, 1850   Thomas Hastings, comp.
                              1830, pub. 1832

Toplady, the most famous tune by Thomas Hastings, was named for Augustus N. Toplady and set to his famous hymn "Rock of Ages, Cleft for Me." The tune (called Rock of Ages) first appeared in *Spiritual Songs for Social Worship* (Utica, N.Y., 1832) in a simple three-part version for Air, 2d Treble, and Bass, although Hastings had composed it in 1830. It became one of the most widely sung and best-loved hymn tunes composed by an American and has been treated with great editorial freedom. Four-part arrangements have replaced the original version in three parts, and rhythmic variants abound. Compare the original version given here with the $\frac{6}{8}$ version in the *Plymouth Collection* (1855) or that in *The Methodist Hymnal* of 1905, where the notes on the word "ages" are equal instead of a dotted note followed by a shorter one. Although the tune is indelibly associated with Toplady's words, we have presented it in this volume with an American text, "Now from Labor and from Care," written by Hastings himself and included in his *Devotional Hymns and Religious Poems* (New York, 1850). Hastings must have found a stanza of six lines of seven syllables each congenial, for no less than eight of the poems included in his collection are written on that plan.

Now Help Us, Lord   8.6.8.6.6.
(The Collection)
"Stanzas from old hymns"   Charles E. Ives, comp. 1920

Charles E. Ives can hardly be said to have composed a congregational hymn, although his setting of Whittier's "O Sabbath Rest of Galilee" might be sung as a unison hymn, and his music for "Little Star of Bethlehem" is certainly a Christmas carol. However, his early experience as an organist made him familiar with the congregational singing of his day, and he had listened to camp-meeting singers with a sympathetic ear. Hymn tunes, like familiar patriotic songs, had significance for him as symbols, and they are quoted in his instrumental works. The finales of his violin sonatas are based on hymn tunes, notably the fourth, which uses Robert Lowry's familiar "Shall we gather at the river." The haunting melody in "On the Housatonic" has a resemblance to the opening theme of Beethoven's Fifth Symphony, but it is somewhat closer to Charles Zeuner's familiar MISSIONARY CHANT ("Thou Lord of Hosts Whose Guiding Hand") (q.v.). In "Now Help Us, Lord" the soprano enters after an organ prelude with George Kingsley's TAPPAN, and the "village choir" joins the soloist at the final cadence. It is a genre picture of a country church service which was included in the composer's privately printed *114 Songs by Charles E. Ives* in 1922. No doubt these stanzas with their message of mutual toleration had a special significance for Ives. We have been unable to identify them, perhaps because Ives did not quote the first stanzas of the hymns. See "There Is an Hour of Peaceful Rest" for Kingsley's own harmonization of TAPPAN.

Now Israel May Say, and   Psalm 124 10.10.10.10.10.
    That Truly
Ps. 124: 1, 2, 5–8   Frost 139
William Whittingham, 1556   William Daman, arr. 1579

Both text and tune have a long history. In 1551 Théodore de Bèze set his version of Psalm 124 to this tune. The fine metrical version in English by William Whittingham was first published in the English psalter of 1560. "Its rugged strength is perfectly matched by the noble Genevan melody, and in the revised form of 1650 it is sung with fervor in Scotland to this day" (Millar Patrick, *Four Centuries of Scottish Psalmody,* p. 33). It was harmonized in all the English psalters from John Day to John Playford. The version selected here is from Daman.

Time signature ¢ ; note values halved; tune in tenor; transposed down a whole step. In stanza 2, original reading "overwhelmed," not "o'erwhelmed"; stanza 3, "heaven" must have one syllable. Alto, line 1, notes 8 and 9 corrected to C instead of A. Note the diminished seventh, alto, line 4, notes 9 and 10. The rests between lines are retained as in Daman since they are a necessary part of the rhythmic scheme. See also the setting of this tune by Giles Farnaby ("Except the Lord That He For Us Had Been").

Now Let Our Hearts Their Glory Wake	VARIETY C.M.
(Settling in a New Habitation)	
St. 1–5	
Elizabeth Scott, 1806	Stephen Jenks, 1800

Elizabeth Scott of Norwich, England, had written hymns which remained in manuscript before she married Colonel Elisha Williams, formerly rector of Yale College, in January 1750/51 and sailed with him to America. If the hymns dealing with a change of residence had personal significance they must have been written shortly before that event. They are headed "Seeking Direction for a New Habitation," "Going to a New Habitation," and "Settling in a New Habitation." These poems were brought before the public by their inclusion in J. Dobell's *New Selections* of 1806. Dobell's collection was reprinted in Morristown, N.J., in 1815.

Since New Haven, Conn., was the "new habitation" where Elizabeth Scott settled, VARIETY by Stephen Jenks seemed a suitable choice.

Counter, G clef, second line, an octave too high. Time signature ℭ; transposed down one step. In bar 10 the bass is doubled in octaves and in bars 11 and 12 the upper note is sustained while the lower repeats in quarters. In similar passages in Billings, the basses sing the upper note leaving the lower one for the bass viol.

Nun Schlaff du Liebes Kindelein	LOBT GOTT IHR CHRISTEN ALLZUGLEICH 8.6.8.6.6.
Now Sleep My Little Child So Dear	
St. 1, 5–7	Zahn 199
Casper Kriebel, 1762	Balthasar Schmid, arr. 1748
Sheema Z. Buehne, trans. 1965	

This Christmas lullaby is from the first printed Schwenkfelder hymnbook of 1762. The dominant mood is a tender one. Other stanzas stress the belief that the mortal babe is born in sin and can be saved only by the intervention of the Christ Child. The complete text may be found in John Joseph Stoudt, *Early German-American Poetry: 1685–1830,* p. 159.

The chorale melody has been supplied and the middle parts added following the version for soprano and figured bass in the chorale book of Balthasar Schmid. Schmid assumes that the organist has both melody and bass before him. Thus a first inversion which would usually be marked $\frac{6}{3}$ is marked either 6 or 3, the figure supplying the note which the soprano does not have. The figure 3 in bar 3, second quarter, is missing in Schmid.

O Beautiful My Country
St. 1–3
Frederick Lucian Hosmer,
   1884

SALVE DOMINE 7.6.7.6.D.

Lawrence W. Watson, 1909

Similar in theme to Katherine Lee Bates's "O Beautiful for Spacious Skies" but expressing in poetic terms more of a reformer's zeal, this is among the best national hymns. It was first published in *Chicago Unity Festivals* in 1884.

In H. Augustine Smith's *Hymnal for American Youth* (1926) it was to be sung to SALVE DOMINE by Watson. This is a marching tune that follows the patterns made familiar by Anglican composers such as Smart, Barnby, and Dykes, but it is effectively realized within the limits of that style.

Ob Ich Deiner Schon Vergiss
Though My Thoughts
St. 1–3
Francis Daniel Pastorius
Sheema Z. Buehne, trans.
   1965

HIMMEL, ERDE, LUFT, UND
   MEER 7.7.7.7.

Johann Anastasius Freylinghausen, arr. 1704

Since Pastorius wrote verses in both his native German and in English, he is represented in this collection by both "Ob Ich Deiner Schon Vergiss" and "Great God, Preserver of All Things" (q.v.). The present German text has all the genial naïveté of a folk song. Each stanza concludes with the refrain line "Lieber Gott, vergiss mein nicht" varied in the last to "Und vergiss mein nimmer nicht."

The tune with its bass was taken from the *Geist-reiches Gesang-Buch, den Kern alter und neuer Lieder* . . . of Johann Anastasius Freylinghausen, published in Halle, 1704, where it was the melody for HIMMEL, ERDE, LUFT UND MEER. The inner parts as they appear here are editorial additions.

O Blest Estate, Blest from
  Above
Ps. 133: 1–3
George Sandys, 1636   Walter Porter, 1657

Walter Porter, English pupil of Monteverdi, speaks with enthusiasm of the "words of Excellent Sandys: Words so Pure and Proper, as that David Himself would have sung them with joy." Porter dedicated each of his settings of the psalm paraphrases of Sandys to a different person. This metrical version of Psalm 133 was dedicated to Sir John Thorowgood, whose brother Adam Thorowgood came to Virginia in 1621.

This is vocal chamber music in imitative style suitable for performance in the home. The vocal parts are soprano (C clef, first line) and bass. As the title indicated, the upper part might also be sung by a tenor. In addition to the part for the bass singer there is a part in score for the accompanist which is unusual for the period. The music has been compressed on two staves and an inner part added. The last measures marked "chorus" are for soprano and bass only.

O Child of Lowly Manger   EATON L.M.
  Birth
St. 1–5
Ferdinand Q. Blanchard,   George W. Chadwick, comp.
  writ. 1906, pub. 1909   1888, pub. 1895

Chadwick made his major contributions as composer, conductor, and educator. It cannot be said that his hymns represent him at his best. He treated the form in a frankly romantic style. He may have lacked the austerity which, perhaps, should never be entirely lacking in church music. Nevertheless he is too important a figure to be omitted in a collection of American hymns.

EATON was first published in 1895 in *Church Harmonies New and Old.* It is to be sung to Ferdinand Q. Blanchard's "O Child of Lowly Manger Birth," a hymn which traces the meaning of Christ's life as child, as teacher, and as leader.

O Christ of Bethlehem   S.M.
St. 1–3
H. Glenn Lanier, writ. 1954,   Richard Donovan, comp.
   pub. 1955   1956

Only a hymn which a congregation can understand and sing with understanding stands a chance of survival. In a sense the contemporary section of *American Hymns* is an attempt to widen that understanding. Yet some of the compositions here presented are suited only to chorus and others perhaps only to congregations with superior musical opportunities and with less resistance to novelty than usual. This unison hymn by Richard Donovan proceeds to the perhaps more difficult task of achieving musical distinction with complete practicability and with a simple diatonic structure. The shift in texture from four to three parts and back is of course due to the fact that this is an organ part. The one accidental, the E^b in bar 7, produces a colorful and unexpected major chord. The old contrapuntists used this procedure to avoid the forbidden diminished fifth on $E^{\sharp}$. Modern composers employ it for its archaic flavor.

O Could I Find from Day to   BETHEL C.M.
   Day
St. 1, 2, 3 (altered), 4
Benjamin Cleavland, 1792   Hibbard, 1800

A lay Baptist with a zeal for hymn writing, Benjamin Cleavland is remembered for this one hymn which has enjoyed a certain amount of popularity from 1792. First published in the author's *Hymns on Different Spiritual Subjects,* it was later included in the *Hartford Selection,* 1799. Asahel Nettleton, in his *Village Hymns* (1824), reduced the original six stanzas to four. Our reading for stanza 3 follows that in the *Hartford Selection.*

BETHEL, by Mr. Hibbard, may be found in Stephen Jenks's *The Musical Harmonist* (New Haven, Conn., 1800). The tune was there associated with Isaac Watts's version of Psalm 5, "Lord in the Morning."

Countertenor in G clef an octave too high. Time signature ↄ; tune in tenor; transposed down one step.

O Day of God, Draw Nigh   Day of God S.M.
St. 1-5
Robert B. Y. Scott, writ. 1937   Howard Boatwright, comp.
                                        1956

This hymn, composed for this volume, shows a contemporary composer writing in a manner which suggests the early New England psalm tune. The voluntary rudeness, the use of the cross relation (bar 6), and the modal character (mixolydian) are used in a way which is both archaic and contemporary in effect. Howard Boatwright had originally chosen an early New England text, Timothy Dwight's "I Love Thy Kingdom, Lord," and his music may be sung to that text. It is associated here with a more nearly contemporaneous hymn, Robert B. Y. Scott's "O Day of God, Draw Nigh."

O Day of Light and Gladness   Laufer 7.6.7.6.D.
St. 1-3
Frederick Lucian Hosmer,   Emily Swan Perkins, 1924
   writ. 1903, pub. 1904

This joyful Easter hymn by one of the most distinguished Unitarian writers of the late nineteenth century was written in 1903, just after the turn of the century. First published in *Hymns of the Ages,* edited by Louisa Loring (1904), it may also be found (with minor alterations) in *Unity Hymns and Chorals* (1911), in *The New Hymn and Tune Book* (1914), in *Hymns of the Spirit* (1937), and in *Hymns for the Celebration of Life* (1964).

   LAUFER, named for Calvin W. Laufer (q.v.), appeared in the later of the two collections of original hymn tunes which Miss Perkins published.

O'er Continent and Ocean   Patmos 7.6.8.6.D.
St. 1-3
John Haynes Holmes, 1917   Henry J. Storer, 1891

   The immediate occasion for writing this hymn was a "service of commemoration of a century of British American Peace" at the Church of the Messiah, Montreal, Canada, which was a part of the Unitarian General Conference of 1917. It was later selected for inclusion in *Hymns of the Spirit* (1937).

   "O'er Continent and Ocean" tells of the universal message of Christianity and of those who carry it "to all the sons of men." It is interesting to note the place names which appear in the first stanza and to remember that Holmes himself later visited Palestine in the interest of the Jews in 1929 and that he lectured in India in 1947–48.

The meter of the text is commonly associated with music in the movement of a processional hymn. Henry J. Storer's PATMOS, perhaps his most widely used tune, was written in the still dominant Victorian style of the period. See also "Outside the Holy City."

O'er Waiting Harp-Strings of   NORTON 8.4.8.4.
   the Mind
St. 1–7
Mary Baker Eddy, cop. 1887   Lyman Brackett, cop. 1887

The most notable hymns contained in the *Christian Science Hymnal* are those by Mary Baker Eddy. Her poems are distinguished in the hymnal by the number of tunes provided for them. In the 1932 edition there are five tunes for the poem beginning "O'er waiting harp strings of the mind." The tune NORTON was selected here because in style and date it is closest to that of the poem. Indeed both poem and musical setting appeared in the earliest *Christian Science Hymnal* (1892), although they had been copyrighted in 1887.

O for the Happy Hour   FIRTH 6.6.8.6.6.
St. 1–6
George Washington Bethune,   Sylvanus Billings Pond, 1841
   1843

"O for the Happy Hour" was first published in *Parish Hymns* (Philadelphia, 1843). Bethune included it in his *Lays of Love and Faith* (1847) and it appeared in many hymnals. In the Reformed Dutch *Hymns of the Church* (1869), edited by Uzziah C. Burnap, this text was to be sung to Lowell Mason's OLMUTZ.

Sylvanus Billings Pond's FIRTH, composed for Bethune's text, first appeared in his *United States Psalmody* (1841) and later in Isaac B. Woodbury's *Dulcimer* (1850).

O God, Above the Drifting   FOREFATHERS L.M.
  Years
St. 1–4
John Wright Buckham, 1916   Seth Bingham, submitted
                                              1957

Seth Bingham's settings of Psalm 84 and Psalm 148 won the J. B. Herbert Memorial Psalm Tune Competition in 1944 and 1951.

FOREFATHERS is appropriately named, associated as it is with a text dealing with the spiritual heritage which we have received from the pioneer forefathers. The harmonies have a gravity largely due to the free use of the Aeolian mode.

O God, Accept the Sacred   COMMUNION C.M.
  Hour
St. 1–3
Samuel Gilman, 1820   S. Hill, 1834

This closing hymn for a communion service was written by Samuel Gilman for Dr. Thaddeus M. Harris' *Hymns for the Lord's Supper* (1820) and was included in Henry D. Sewall's *A Collection of Psalms and Hymns,* published in the same year, and later in *Hymns for the Church of Christ* by Frederic Henry Hedge and Frederic D. Huntington (1853). In 1877 it appeared in the Unitarian *Hymn and Tune Book* where it was to be sung to COMMUNION by S. Hill. COMMUNION first appeared in Charles Zeuner's *Ancient Lyre* as a setting for Samuel Stennett's hymn, "Here at Thy Table, Lord, We Meet."

O God, Beneath Thy Guiding   BALTIMORE L.M.
  Hand
St. 1–4
Leonard Bacon, writ. 1833   Christopher Meinecke, 1831

Leonard Bacon's hymn was written for the New Haven bicentennial. The first line of the complete poem was "The Sabbath morn is as bright and calm." In an abbreviated form, and with the first line as given above, it was published in his *Psalms and Hymns* (1845) headed "For the twenty-second of December." It was to become Bacon's best-remembered and best-loved hymn.

It has usually been sung to DUKE STREET, and it is not easy to find an American tune of the period with the union of simplicity and strength which is required. Meinecke's BALTIMORE (also called

MARYLAND) seemed suitable in character. It was used in the North, as shown by its appearance in Alling Brown's *The Musical Cabinet* (New Haven, Conn., 1831).

O God, Great Father, Lord   BAPTISM L.M.
   and King
St. 1–5
E. Embree Hoss, 1903   Peter C. Lutkin, 1905

This hymn, written for a baptismal service conducted by Bishop Hoss at Walnut Ridge, Ark., November 1903, was first printed in the Nashville *Christian Advocate* shortly after that date. It was adopted by the Joint Commission responsible for *The Methodist Hymnal* (1905) to meet a need for a hymn suitable for the baptism of children.

Lutkin, one of the music editors for *The Methodist Hymnal,* composed BAPTISM for this text. It is a plain tune moving almost uniformly in half notes.

O God, I Cried, No Dark   RENASCENCE L.M.
   Disguise
St. 1–5
Edna St. Vincent Millay, 1917   Hugh Porter, 1927

H. Augustine Smith sought lyrics of high literary quality which might be used as hymns. This sensitive poem by Edna St. Vincent Millay is a record of a personal experience rather than the expression of a common aspiration. It first appeared in her *Renascence and Other Poems* in 1917.

Hugh Porter's setting was contributed to Smith's *American Student Hymnal* (1928), for which he was an associate editor. A different version appears in another hymnal compiled by Smith, the *New Hymnal for American Youth* (1930).

O God, in Whom the Flow of   L.M.
   Days
St. 1–4
Donald C. Babcock, writ.   Bernhard Heiden, comp.
   1956   1956

The Victorian hymn-tune writer was likely to accelerate or sustain the tones of his melody in order to make the sometimes unequal lines of his poems match the balanced flow of his musical phrases. Here, however, starting with a quatrain with eight syllables in each line the composer writes in three-bar phrases and the bars themselves are of unequal length. The interest is less in the harmony, which follows conventional patterns, than in a more fluent and varied rhythmic pattern and one which makes possible a more expressive musical reading of the poem. At first sight the stress on the word "of" in the second line of the first stanza seems amiss. However, a composer must consider what stress is best suited to the larger number of stanzas if there is a difference. In this instance the words "stands," "good," and "will" are all important and stressed in stanzas 2, 3, and 4. However, singers will be well advised to deal gently with the word "of" in stanza 1.

O God, in Whose Great Purpose	NEILSON 7.6.8.6.D.
St. 1, 2	
James G. Gilkey, writ. 1912	John H. Gower, 1894

The origin of this hymn may best be stated in Gilkey's own words:

My hymn "O God in Whose Great Purpose" was the baccalaureate hymn written for my class [1912 at Harvard College]. I had been elected class poet, and when an announcement was made that there would be a competition for the class's baccalaureate hymn, I submitted this hymn and it was presently chosen. It was first sung when our class held its baccalaureate service in June, 1912, in Appleton Chapel at Harvard. President Lowell of Harvard preached the sermon on that occasion. The hymn was written in spring of 1912.

The author wrote his poem to ALFORD, by the English church composer John B. Dykes. NEILSON, by John H. Gower, an English organist who settled in the United States, is given here. NEILSON was one of the new tunes in J. Ireland Tucker's musical edition of the Protestant Episcopal hymnal of 1892.

O God of My Salvation, Hear	OLD BRICK 8.8.8.D.
Ps. 88, st. 1–5	
Joel Barlow, 1785	Anon., 1806

Although the Connecticut Congregationalists used Barlow's version of the Psalms from 1785 to 1801 only, when it was superseded by that of Timothy Dwight, singers and composers evidently liked and continued to sing some of Barlow's verses.

OLD BRICK was published in the First Church collection (2d ed., 1806) with no composer indicated. The committee responsible for the collection spoke for the American composer in the preface: "In the knowledge and practice of sacred musick, as might be justly expected, the psalmodists of the elder continent are vastly superior to those of America. But is this fact a sufficient reason for the total disuse of American musick? . . . Instead of ridiculing the productions of our age and country, and indiscriminately condemning to oblivion the incipient efforts of the American composer, let us, while we reject his worst, commend his best."

The music of OLD BRICK has been rebarred in the first section to make the verbal and musical accents coincide. Countertenor, C clef, third line. Time signature 𝄵 throughout; tune in tenor; transposed down one tone. The sixth and seventh notes in the soprano were printed a step lower in the original.

O God of Stars and Distant Space	8.8.8.D.
St. 1–3	
John Franzen	Edwin Gerschefski, comp.
	1971

This hymn, which begins with an invocation to the "God of Stars and Distant Space," was written at the request of Albert Christ-Janer. It is presented here with the musical setting composed for it by Edwin Gerschefski. His music is notable because a distinctive harmonic coloration is obtained by very simple means. The music is entirely without dissonance and all the harmonies are in their simplest and strongest form (i.e., are fundamental triads).

O God of Youth	LYNNE 13.10.11.10.
St. 1–4	
Bates G. Burt, writ. 1935, pub. 1940	Bates G. Burt, 1940

This hymn of youth set to a tune by the author is reproduced here as it appeared in the Protestant Episcopal *Hymnal 1940*. The text was originally written for a high-school commencement in Pontiac, Mich. (1935). The tune used here, composed five years later, was named LYNNE for a granddaughter.

A nineteenth-century musician was likely to adjust the tones of his melody in order to form phrases of uniform length for poetic lines of varying length. Burt quite simply lets his notes follow the poetic line. Since his phrases consist of uniform quarter notes terminated by one or more longer notes, the longer lines contain more melodic tones. The barring is free and the usual metric signature is omitted since there are bars containing four, six, and eight quarter notes.

O God, Send Men   HUGHES HALL 11.10.11.10.
St. 1–4
Elizabeth Burrowes, 1966   Wilbur Held, 1970

The Hymn Society of America has sought, evaluated, and published a series of hymns on themes of special relevance. Its publication of *Contemporary Hymn Tunes* in 1970 was a parallel effort to expand our repertory of musical settings. We reproduce two compositions from this collection: Shirley L. Brown's HEARTHSIDE to Elinor Lennen's "Within the Shelter of our Walls" (q.v.) and the present example. "O God, Send Men" was published in 1966 as one of *Ten New Hymns on the Ministry.* It was associated with HUGHES HALL in *Contemporary Hymn Tunes.* Wilbur Held's rigorously diatonic tune has a certain bareness of sound, due in part to the movement in parallel fourths.

O God, though Countless   NORTHFIELD C.M.
   Worlds of Light
St. 1–4, 6
James D. Knowles, 1843   Jeremiah Ingalls, 1805

NORTHFIELD appeared in Jeremiah Ingalls' *Christian Harmony* and remained a favorite long after his time. We are told that Ingalls came home hungry and impatient and finally began to sing to the tune of NORTHFIELD:

> How long ye maidens, O how long
> Shall dinner still delay?
> Fly swift, ye maids, without delay
> And bring a dish of tea.

The text is by neither Ingalls nor John Leland, as has been claimed, but was an impromptu paraphrase of a passage from Isaac Watts. The opening line is based on "How long, dear Saviour, O how long," in stanza six of the twenty-first hymn by Watts. Although Ingalls was a Congregationalist, a number of the texts which he set came from Joshua Smith's *Divine Hymns or Spiritual Songs* (1797), a collection much used by the Baptists. In choosing a Baptist text we follow the example set by Ingalls himself. "O God, Though Countless Worlds of Light" by James D. Knowles, a Baptist, first appeared in *The Psalmist* (1843).

O God Whose Presence Glows in All	PILESGROVE L.M.
St. 1–4	
Nathaniel L. Frothingham, writ. 1828	Nahum Mitchell, 1816

Nathaniel Frothingham's hymn, written for the ordination of William P. Lunt, was popular over a considerable period. It was included in Lunt's *Christian Psalter* of 1841. It is the only hymn by Frothingham to remain in use in the twentieth century. Nahum Mitchell was a judge of the Court of Common Pleas when PILESGROVE was published in the *Bridgewater Collection,* edited by Benjamin Holt, Bartholomew Brown, and Mitchell. PILESGROVE is in the fourth edition of this collection and possibly in earlier editions.

O Gracious Jesus, Blessed Lord!	CHURCH STREET L.M.
St. 1–3	
Andrew Fowler, 1793	Jervis Henry Stevens, 1783/84

Like "Awake, My Soul! In Grateful Songs," this text comes from the slender volume of hymns published by Andrew Fowler in 1793.

Jervis Henry Stevens, like Peter Valton and Henry Purcell, was one of a group of composers active in Charleston, S.C., and associated with St. Michael's Church there. CHURCH STREET was preserved in the *Choirmaster's Book,* compiled by Jacob Eckhard (1809). Like other tunes from that source, it is for soprano and figured bass in accordance with which the inner parts have been added.

O Gracious Father of Mankind	CREEVELEA C.M.D.
St. 1–4	
Henry Hallam Tweedy, writ. 1925	Arthur Davis, 1927

Henry Wilder Foote, in his *Three Centuries of American Hymnody,* singled out three hymns by Tweedy for special comment: "Eternal

God Whose Power Upholds," "O Spirit of the Living God," and the present hymn. After expressing certain reservations he praises them as "the best contribution made by a Congregationalist to American hymnody in this century." The theme of "O Gracious Father of Mankind" is stated in the closing lines of the first stanza:

> Thou dost not wait till human speech
>   Thy gifts divine implore;
> Our dreams, our aims, our work, our lives
>   Are prayers thou lovest more.

CREEVELEA is the tune given for Tweedy's text in H. Augustine Smith's *The American Student Hymnal* (1928).

Oh, Day of Days   DAY OF DAYS 10.10.10.10.
St. 1–4
LeRoy V. Brant, 1930   Annabel Morris Buchanan,
                                       comp. 1955

Although Annabel Morris Buchanan is best known as a collector and a gifted arranger of folk hymns, she was also an Episcopalian organist and choir director for many years. Here and in "Green Plumes of Royal Palms" the texts are in the form of a sonnet, an unusual and difficult form to treat in hymn style. Mrs. Buchanan notes that her setting is for "Advent or Christmas Eve, especially for our midnight Christmas Eve communion service in the Episcopal Church."

O Hear My Prayer, Lord   PSALM 143 6.6.6.6.D.
Ps. 143: 1, 6, 8, 9   Frost 168; Zahn 8187a
John Craig, 1564/65   Anon., arr. 1635

John Craig contributed fifteen paraphrases to the Scottish psalter of 1564/65, including Psalm 143. The tune is very old. Franz M. Böhme cites a late fourteenth-century source (*Altdeutscher Liederbuch*, No. 539, Leipzig, 1877). Zahn's earliest version is 1527. Perhaps Craig or William Kethe became familiar with it during their Continental wanderings. It was taken over into the Scottish psalters from 1564 on. The version here is from the Scottish psalter of 1635.

Cantus, C clef, first line; countertenor, C clef, third line; tenor, C clef, third line; bassus, F clef, fourth line. Original pitch; time signature lacking; note values halved; tune in tenor. Those who wish to avoid the cross relation in line 2 may sing the suggested E^b in the countertenor part of the first chord. In line 8 the third chord contains a major seventh left by skip.

O Heaven Indulge	PSALM 34 8.8.8.6.D.
St. 1, 2, 5, 6, 9	Frost 383
Stephen Tilden, 1756	Henry Lawes, 1638

Tilden wrote his *Miscellaneous Poems* "to attempt to animate, and stir up the martial spirits of our Soldiery." The hymn chosen here had a special heading:

> The Christian Hero, or *New England's* Triumph;
> written soon after the success of our Arms at *Nova-Scotia*
> and the Signal Victory at *Lake George.*

The tune was composed by Henry Lawes for Psalm 34 in the metrical version by George Sandys. Since the original meter was 8.8.6.D., lines 2 and 5 have been repeated. Treble, C clef, third line; bass, F clef, third line. No key signature; time signature ¢ ; inner parts added.

Oh, Give Us Pleasure in the Flowers Today	
St. 1–4	
Robert Frost, 1913	Thomas Canning, comp. 1957

This hymn to the springtime beauties of nature by Robert Frost is presented here with a musical setting made for it by Thomas Canning. Frost wrote of New England in terms which have universal meaning. Canning's interest in New England and in its music is shown in his best-known work, the *Fantasy on a Hymn by Justin Morgan.* The poem does not have the regularity of line structure of the typical hymn, and the slurs in bars 7, 8, 9, and 10 are to be observed or disregarded depending on whether one or two syllables are available.

O Holy City Seen of John	RANGELEY 8.6.8.6.8.6.
St. 1–5	
Walter Russell Bowie, 1910	Henry M. Dunham, 1909

"O Holy City Seen of John" was first published in *Hymns of the Kingdom of God* (1910). Its origin is best stated in the words of the author: "It was written at the request of Dr. Henry S. Coffin, who wanted some new hymns that would express the conviction that our hope of the Kingdom of God is not alone some far off eschatological possibility but in its beginnings, at least, may be prepared for here on our actual earth."

RANGELEY was composed for the same collection where it appeared as a second tune for Dr. Bowie's text. When "O Holy City Seen of John" was reprinted in the Episcopal *Hymnal 1940* it was associated with MORNING SONG, an arrangement by Winfred Douglas of a folklike tune which first appeared in John Wyeth's *Repository of Sacred Music: Part II,* 1813.

O Holy, Holy, Holy Lord   BRIGHTON L.M.
St. 1–4
James Wallis Eastburn, writ.   Alling Brown, 1823
   1815, pub. 1826

This hymn to the Trinity, a *Ter Sanctus,* written in 1815, was first published in the important *Prayer Book Collection* of 1826 and then in other collections.

BRIGHTON appeared in Alling Brown's *The Musical Cabinet* (New Haven, Conn., 1823). Brown took some pains to make his book useful for the Episcopal service. "The particular metre tunes are marked to correspond with the classification of the Episcopal hymn book." Tunes were arranged by meter, which made it easy to make a selection by turning adjacent pages. Meters and stanza patterns were designated by a roman numeral to indicate the number of feet in the lines, followed by an arabic numeral that indicated the stanza pattern. Thus III was the symbol for stanzas with lines of seven or seven and eight feet; III.1 designated a quatrain with seven feet to the line; III.2, longer stanzas with sevens; III.3, stanzas with lines of seven and eight syllables. BRIGHTON is marked with a "B" as are the other original tunes by the editor. It is a somewhat florid tune which still reflects the influence of eighteenth-century psalmody.

Oh, When Shall I See Jesus?   MORNING TRUMPET 7.6.7.6.D.,
St. 1–5   with chorus
Anon., 1805   Benjamin Franklin White,
                                     arr. 1854

This camp-meeting text appeared in 1805 and later was included by a number of Southern editors. *The Original Sacred Harp* (1936) credited the text to John Leland, but this attribution is not supported by the earlier sources.

In such Southern books as William Walker's *Southern Harmony* (1854), W. H. and M. L. Swan's *Harp of Columbia* (1848), John G. McCurry's *Social Harp* (1855), and *The Original Sacred Harp,* the text is associated with MORNING TRUMPET, a tune of the folk type. We reproduce the three-voice arrangement from the 1854 edition of *Southern Harmony,* transposed down one step; tune in tenor.

O Jesus Christ, True Light of God   HERR JESU CHRIST DICH ZU UNS WEND L.M.

St. 1, 4–6
John F. Ernst, 1795   Version from John Christian Jacobi, 1732

This hymn, intended to be sung "at the beginning of the Service," comes from the appendix of John Christopher Kunze's *A Hymn and Prayer Book, For the Use of such Lutheran Churches as use the English Language* (New York, 1795). It may be compared with the chorale texts by Kunze and George Strebeck from the same volume which are also included in *American Hymns.*

The melody in this instance comes from a volume which Kunze mentions in his preface, the *Psalmodia Germanica,* first printed in London in complete form in 1732 and reprinted in New York in 1756. The original is for soprano and figured bass.

O Jesus, My Saviour, I Know Thou Art Mine   EXPRESSION 11.11.11.11.

St. 1–3
Caleb J. Taylor, 1814   Anon., 1844

This text was marked "T" in Thomas S. Hinde's *Pilgrim Songster* of 1814, the symbol used to designate poems by Caleb J. Taylor. William Hauser's *Olive Leaf* (1878) attributes the same hymn to John A. Granade. George Pullen Jackson traces the tune to the 1844 edition of *The Sacred Harp.* The single stanza given in the 1859 edition came from Peter D. Myers' *Zion Songster* (1836), and we have used the edition of 1876 in completing our text.

Tune in tenor; transposed down a perfect fourth. Jackson, in *Another Sheaf of White Spirituals* (No. 225), notates this tune as Dorian with raised sixth as he had heard it sung, although it is Aeolian in the *Original Sacred Harp* (1936). Those who wish to try this effect should sing F$^\sharp$ instead of F$^\natural$ in the melody. Annabel Morris Buchanan published an arrangement of a version of this tune in her *Folk Hymns of America* (1938).

O Kersnacht   9.9.8.D.
O Christmas Night
St. 1, 2, 4, 6
Henricus Selyns, writ. 1663   Traditional
Howard Murphy, trans. 1865

The wedding songs of the poets of New Amsterdam were usually in honor of a particular bride-to-be. This "Bruydtlofs-Liedt" ("Song in Praise of the Bride") was written by Henricus Selyns for Aegidius Luyck and Judith van Isendoorn. The records of the Reformed Dutch Church in New Amsterdam confirm the marriage and place it in 1663. The bridegroom was described as "Rector of the Latin School." Stanza 5, omitted in our hymn text, refers to the marriage:

> And as they bring this child before them,
> Luyck comes and marries Isendoorn,
> Standing before this Christ-like crib;
> And finds when her consent is shewn,
> Flesh of his flesh, bone of his bone,
> For Judith is his second rib.

In writing his poem Selyns had an earlier hymn in mind, "O Kersnacht, schooner den de daegen," by Vondel, which had appeared in 1637 in Klaerissen's *Bysbreyht van Aemstel*. Indeed, Selyns' opening line repeats that of the earlier poem with slight modifications.

That the tune for "O Kersnacht" was familiar at the time is shown by the fact that it was also indicated for the hymn "Het Heyl der Heyligen" in the third part of Jacob Steendam's *Den Distelfink* (1650). The version given here is a harmonization of the melody as given in Van Duyse in *Die melodie van het Nederlandische lied* (1902).

O King of Saints, We Give   WITNESSES 11.10.11.10.
   Thee Praise and Glory
St. 1–5
Mary A. Thomson, 1892   William H. Walter, comp.
                                  1889, pub. 1892

This hymn for All Saints' Day appeared with three other hymns by Mrs. Thomson in *The Church Hymnal* of 1892. A second hymn of this group, "O Sion Haste," has also been included in *American Hymns*. The provision of special hymns for the seasons and days of the church year is characteristic of the Episcopal church, thus the hymnals of this denomination are organized according to the calendar of the church year.

William H. Walter's WITNESSES, which was composed for this text, was contributed to the musical edition of *The Hymnal Revised and Enlarged* of 1892, edited by J. Ireland Tucker and William Rousseau.

O Life That Maketh All   ROSEHILL L.M.
   Things New
St. 1–4
Samuel Longfellow, writ.   Joseph Emerson Sweetser,
   1874, pub. 1876   1856

This hymn, stressing the essential unity of all seekers for truth, was originally intended for the second Social Festival of the Free Religious Association. The author published it in his *A Book of Hymns and Tunes for the Congregation and the Home* (1876). It was included in the Unitarian *Hymn and Tune Book for the Church and the Home* of 1877 and later in the *New Hymn and Tune Book* of 1914 and the *Hymns of the Spirit* of 1937.

ROSEHILL appeared in George F. Root's *Sabbath Bell* (1856) and was reprinted in Root's very successful *The Triumph* (1868) and elsewhere. It still appears in twentieth-century hymnals.

O Little Town of Bethlehem   ST. LOUIS 8.6.8.6.7.6.8.6.
St. 1–5
Phillips Brooks, writ. 1868   Lewis H. Redner, comp. 1868

This famous hymn on the birth of Christ was directly inspired by a visit Phillips Brooks made to the Holy Land in 1866. Later the author wrote:

I remember especially on Christmas Eve, when I was standing in the old church in Bethlehem, close to the spot where Jesus was born, when the whole church was ringing hour after hour with the splendid hymns of praise to God, how again and again it seemed as if I could hear voices that I knew well, telling each other of the 'Wonderful Night' of the Saviour's birth, as I had heard them a year before.

In 1868 he wrote the verses for his Sunday School at Holy Trinity Church, Philadelphia, and soon afterwards asked the organist and superintendent of the Sunday School, Lewis H. Redner, to set it to music. The latter put off the task until the night before Christmas. After falling asleep for a few hours he awoke with the melody in his head. Writing it down immediately he harmonized it the next day. According to Redner, the first performance was on December 27, 1868. The third stanza, included in a letter from Redner to Hubert P. Main (q.v.), was unpublished for years until restored by the Rev. Charles L. Atkins. This stanza was included in *The Hymnal 1940* of the Protestant Episcopal Church.

O Lord, Almighty God (The Song of Moses and the Lamb)
Rev. 15: 3
Anon., 1647

NUNC DIMITTIS C.M.D.

Frost 37
John Playford, arr. 1671

The 1647 edition of the *Bay Psalm Book* added spiritual songs, including "The Song of Moses and the Lamb." In *A Testimony to the Order of the Gospel, in the Churches of New England* (1701) by the Rev. John Higginson and the Rev. William Hubbard we read that "It is not yet forgot by some surviving witnesses of it, that when the Synod (in the year 1648) had finished the Platform of Church Discipline, they did, with an extraordinary elevation of soul and voice, then sing together the Song of Moses the Servant of God and the Song of the Lamb, in the fifteenth chapter of Revelation."

Our melody appeared as the tune for Psalm 19 in the Anglo-Genevan psalter of 1556. In 1560 it was associated with the "Nunc Dimittis," which was the text used by Thomas Ravenscroft (1621) and by Playford both in 1671 and 1677.

Altus, C clef, third line; countertenor, C clef, third line; tenor or common tune, C clef, fourth line; bassus, F clef, fourth line. Time signature ¢; note values halved. The lower G at the beginning of line 4 is intended for the instrumental bass.

O Lord, Bow Down Thine Ear
Ps. 86: 1, 4, 7, 9–11
Thomas Prince, 1758

SOUTHWELL S.M.

Frost 45
Version bound with Prince, 1755

This metrical version of Psalm 86 (like "Give Ear, O God, to My Loud Cry") appeared in *The Psalms, Hymns, and Spiritual Songs of the Old and New Testaments* . . . The edition is sometimes bound with a thin pamphlet containing standard tunes arranged in three parts. SOUTHWELL is included in this supplement. It first appeared as the tune for Psalm 25 in William Daman's *The former booke* (1591). Thomas Ravenscroft (1621) called it LONDON, while John Playford (1677) gave it the name which we use. It became a favorite tune in the New World and the versions in Thomas Walter's *Grounds and Rules of Music Explained* (Boston, 1721) and in John Tufts's *Introduction to the Art of Singing* (5th ed., Boston, 1726) were both ultimately derived from Playford's *Whole Book of Psalms* (1677).

We read B instead of C for line 2, note 2, in the middle part, and G instead of G♯ for line 3, note 1, in the upper part. We also prefer to make the second note long instead of the first in lines 1 and 2 (as in Tufts), since this fits the text better.

O Lord, How Lovely Is the Place	PSALM 84 L.M.D.
Ps. 84: 1–3	
Francis Hopkinson, adapted 1767	Version altered from Claude Goudimel, 1774

The text of "O Lord, How Lovely Is the Place" has been selected from *The Psalms of David, with the Ten Commandments, Creed, Lord's Prayer, &c In Metre Also, the Catechism, Confession, Liturgy &c Translated from the Dutch, For the Use of the Reformed Protestant Dutch Church of the City of New York* (New York, 1767). The services of a minister to preach in English in this church had been requested in a petition of May 3, 1762. The adaptation of English texts for the Psalms was entrusted to Francis Hopkinson. He performed his task by adapting the psalms of Tate and Brady to make them fit the meters of the Genevan tunes sung in the Dutch church.

The harmonies accompanying the melody of Psalm 84 are also taken from a volume associated with the Reformed Dutch Church of New York: *A Collection of the Psalm and Hymn Tunes: Used by the Reformed Protestant Dutch Church of the City of New York, agreeable to their Psalm Book, published in English, In Four Parts, Viz. Tenor, Bass, Treble, and Counter* (New York, 1774). This collection, intended for psalm singing in the home, was credited to "a number of the members of the said Church." It actually consisted of an adaptation of the Goudimel psalm tune arrangements of 1565. The result is much less satisfactory to us than the original settings, since the arrangements are marred by faulty voice leading and by an inept use of second inversions. The notation was simplified by writing all the parts in one clef, the C clef on the third line. However, this collection is of great historical importance, since it shows how the Goudimel psalms were actually sung in New York in the eighteenth century.

O Lord of Life   GREYLOCK C.M.D.
St. 1–3
Washington Gladden, 1897   Waldo S. Pratt, 1927

Although Waldo S. Pratt was best known as a scholar, hymnologist, and educator, he was also a well-schooled musician, as is evident from this tune, named for the mountain which towers above North Adams in Massachusetts. Written as a festival hymn, it was set to a text by Washington Gladden. It is a hymn of thanks for prophets and spiritual leaders, a plea for a continuing search for the meaning of nature, and a prayer:

> That word and life Thy truth may tell
> And praise Thee evermore!

O Lord Our God, Thy   AMERICA BEFRIEND C.M.D.
   Mighty Hand
St. 1–4
Henry Van Dyke, 1912   William Pierson Merrill, 1912

One of Van Dyke's best-known hymns is omitted in this volume. His "Joyful, Joyful, We Adore Thee" was intended to supply a text for the choral theme of Beethoven's Ninth Symphony and has been widely used in association with that theme. "O Lord Our God, Thy Mighty Hand" was published in 1912 in *The Continent* and was included in *Songs of the Christian Life* (1912) and in the Presbyterian *Hymnal* of 1933. It is reprinted here with the vigorous tune written for it by another Presbyterian clergyman, William Pierson Merrill.

O Lord, That Art My God   PSALM 145 L.M.D.
   and King
Ps. 145: 1–3, 8–10, 15, 19   Frost 170
John Craig, 1564/65   Anon., arr. bet. 1562–1566

A metrical version of Psalm 145 by John Craig, this text appears in the Scottish psalters from 1564 to 1635. As Dr. Millar Patrick pointed out, this text "remains second only to [William] Kethe's 100th in use and honour . . . a conclusive evidence of his [Craig's] powers." The harmony used is from the St. Andrews psalter of 1562–66 ("missing notes partly supplied from 1635 psalter") and is given through the courtesy of Miss Hilda Hutchinson. It may be the work of David Peebles. The popularity of these settings, "meet and apt for musicians to recreate their spirits," is illustrated by the fact that many of them reappear in the psalter of 1635. Undoubtedly they lasted for many decades after that.

In stanza 2, line 1, the singers must either sing the word "gracious" as three syllables with a note for each syllable, or reduce it to two, singing the first syllable to notes 6 and 7. Treble, C clef, second line; countertenor, C clef, third line; tenor or psalm tune, C clef, fourth line; bassus, F clef, fourth line. Key signature one flat; no time signature; note values halved.

O Lord, Thou Hast Been to the Land	PATER NOSTER or OLD 112TH 8.8.8.D.
Ps. 85: 1, 2, 7–13	Frost 180; Zahn 2561
Anon., 1640	George Kirbye, arr. 1621

Our text is Psalm 85 as it appears in the *Bay Psalm Book* of 1640. The noble melody of the PATER NOSTER first appeared in Schumann's *Geistliche Lieder* of 1539, set to "Vater unser im Himmelreich." It was taken into the Old Version of Thomas Sternhold and John Hopkins in 1560 to Coxe's version of the Lord's Prayer, "Our Father which in heaven art." The PATER NOSTER tune, also called the OLD 112TH, was listed in the "Admonition to the Reader" in the *Bay Psalm Book* of 1640. There are five different settings of the melody by Bach, two in the Johannes Passion, and three in separate cantatas. Our setting by George Kirbye comes from Thomas Ravenscroft's psalter where the melody is classified as a "High Dutch Tune."

Cantus, C clef, first line; medius, C clef, third line; "tenor or faburden," C clef, fourth line; bassus, F clef, fourth line. Original pitch; time signature C ; note values halved. In the original, tenor, line 3, the third note from the end is E instead of D. In the medius, line 5, the second note is F instead of E. Since the setting is predominantly Dorian rather than minor, it is presented with no signature as in the original.

O Lord, Turn Not Away Thy Face	THE LAMENTATION C.M.D.
St. 1, first half of 4, first half of 5	Frost 10
John Marckant (?), 1561	Robert William Parsons, arr. 1621

This well-known hymn, probably by John Marckant, is a devout prayer to God for mercy. It first appeared in 1561 in the *Psalms of*

David in English Metre of Thomas Sternhold and John Hopkins. The tune was harmonized in the 1563 publication of John Day, by William Daman, by John Farmer in Thomas East's psalter, by Robert William Parsons in Thomas Ravenscroft's psalter and twice by John Playford. Henry Ainsworth set his version of Psalm 32 to the same tune. As Waldo Selden Pratt observed: "With suitable harmony . . . this apparently monotonous lament takes on a singularly haunting beauty."

Cantus, C clef, first line; medius, C clef, third line; tenor, C clef, fourth line; bassus, F clef, fourth line. Original pitch; time signature C ; note values reduced by half. In the medius, lines 3 and 8, the two sixteenth-notes are given as C♯, B♮, rather than C♯, B♭, as in the original.

O Love Divine, That Stooped   CROWN POINT L.M.
    to Share
St. 1–4
Oliver Wendell Holmes, 1859   Henry Kemble Oliver, comp.
                                1873

This hymn and "Lord of All Being, Throned Afar" (q.v.) were included in the "Professor at the Breakfast Table," which appeared serially in the *Atlantic Monthly.* It was included in the Unitarian *New Hymn and Tune Book* (1914), *Hymns of the Spirit* (1937), and *Hymns for the Celebration of Life* (1964), as well as in the Congregational *Pilgrim Hymnal* of 1931.

CROWN POINT is one of the later tunes by Henry Kemble Oliver. Composed in 1873, it was published in the composer's *Original Hymn Tunes* of 1875.

O Love That Lights the   VITTEL WOODS C.M.
    Eastern Sky
St. 1–4
Louis F. Benson, writ. 1923,   Bradley Keeler, comp. 1924,
    pub. 1924   pub. 1925

"O Love That Lights the Eastern Sky" was written in February 1923, and appeared first in *Contemporary Verse,* December 1924.

VITTEL WOODS was composed expressly for the hymn in May 1924, by Benson's close friend Bradley Keeler. The poem with the music was published in Benson's *Hymns, Original and Translated* (Philadelphia, 1925).

O Mary, Don't You Weep,
  Don't You Mourn
St. 1–3
Traditional, pub. 1940   John W. Work, arr. 1940

"O Mary, Don't You Weep, Don't You Mourn" is presented here as it appeared in John W. Work's *American Negro Songs.* The chorus precedes, and its second phrase beginning "Pharaoh's army got drownded" is also used to conclude the verse section. This spiritual does not appear in *Slave Songs of the United States* (1867). The range of the tune is plagal (from 5 of the scale up to 4) and the seventh tone is missing. The text in which Mary of the New Testament is associated with the Old Testament Pharaoh of Exodus has the character of an improvisation as do the texts of many other spirituals.

O Master, Let Me Walk with   GLADDEN L.M.
  Thee
St. 1–4
Washington Gladden, 1879   Charles L. Ziegler, cop. 1902

The Pilgrim Hymnal was a notable contribution to liberal Christianity. More successful on the literary than on the musical side, it nevertheless brought forward a number of settings by American composers Frederick Field Bullard (q.v.), Henry J. Storer (q.v.), and Charles L. Ziegler were among the contributors. This hymn by Washington Gladden, an editor of *The Pilgrim Hymnal,* was first published in five stanzas in *The Sunday Afternoon,* a magazine which he edited. In 1880 it appeared in four stanzas in Charles H. Richard, *Songs of Christian Praise.*

Although Gladden himself wished his text sung to H. Percy Smith's MARYTON, we have preferred GLADDEN, composed by Charles L. Ziegler, a musical editor of *The Pilgrim Hymnal.*

O Master Workman of the   MOUNT SION C.M.D.
  Race
St. 1–3
Jay T. Stocking, 1912   Horatio Parker, comp. 1886,
                                pub. 1894

Watching carpenters at work on an Adirondack camp in 1912 gave Jay T. Stocking the idea of this hymn for young people: "The figure of the carpenter, as applied to Jesus, flashed on me as never before, and I sat down and wrote the hymn, almost, if not quite, in the exact form in which it now appears."

"O Master Workman of the Race" has been used in a number of twentieth-century hymnals, including the *Hymnal of the Evangelical and Reformed Church* (1941). MOUNT SION, a festive tune by Horatio Parker, is well suited to the double stanzas of the text.

On a Hill Far Away	THE OLD RUGGED CROSS
	12.8.12.8., with chorus
St. 1–4	
George Bennard, 1913	George Bennard, 1913

"On a Hill Far Away" was the most popular gospel hymn of its period. It was conceived in an unusual way—the subject first, next the music, and the words last of all. Written in 1913, it was first sung by the author in the home of Rev. and Mrs. L. O. Bostwick of Pokagon, Mich., and shortly thereafter was introduced to a convention at Chicago. The music conforms to the familiar pattern of verse and chorus. The melody of the verse begins with a sequence of notes a step above and a half step below F followed by a similar pattern around G. Such chromatic treatments are more characteristic of later gospel songs, and they detract from that folklike simplicity that the best early examples possess.

Once More, O Lord	CALVARY C.M.D.
St. 1–3	
George Washington Doane, writ. 1827	Christopher Meinecke, 1827

The complete form of this poem, beginning "He came not with His heavenly crown," was first published in *Hymns for Church and Home* (1860). It was later included in Doane's *Songs by the Way* (1875), where it was dated December 1827. It came into general usage among American Episcopalians through their *Additional Hymns* of 1865, but with the first three stanzas omitted. There the hymn began "Once more, O Lord, Thy sign shall be," the first line of the original fourth stanza.

The somber character of Meinecke's CALVARY seemed in harmony with Doane's text. It appeared in John Cole's *The Seraph* (1827), where the text was Samuel Wesley's "From whence these direful omens round." The leap of the octave between beats 3 and 4 in bar 2 will tend to place a stress on the upper note. This is admirable for stanza 2 where the exclamation "oh" falls on the high note. In the other stanzas singers are urged to attack the high note with discretion, keeping the meaning of the text in mind.

Once More, Our God, Vouchsafe to Shine!	Veni Creator L.M.
St. 1–3, 6	Frost 197; Zahn 367
Samuel Sewall, writ. 1700	John Playford, arr., 1671

These verses by Samuel Sewall were written to celebrate the new century. "Bell-Man said these verses a little before Break-a-day, which I printed and gave him." Trumpeters played jubilantly. Sewall noted the expense: "Trumpeters cost me five pieces 8." It was natural for Sewall, who led the psalm singing in church, to use one of the familiar psalm meters.

The tune chosen here for Sewall's encomium is Veni Creator. This ancient melody had been used in the French psalter of 1592 for Psalms 100, 131, and 142 and in Henry Ainsworth for Psalms 33, 81, and 104. Playford makes the tune minor rather than Aeolian and his melody for the last line is different.

His setting was intended for male voices: altus, C clef, third line; countertenor, C clef, third line; tenor, C clef, fourth line; bassus, normal F clef. The tune was in the tenor. However it is printed here as the soprano part. Our version may be sung by mixed voices. Those who wish to sing it with male voices must read the present soprano part an octave lower.

One More Day's Work for Jesus	7.6.10.6.10., with chorus
St. 1–3, 5	
Anna B. Warner, 1869	Robert Lowry, 1869

A letter from Rev. Benjamin M. Adams suggested the theme of this hymn which was entitled "The Song of a Tired Servant." The letter told of Mr. Adams' fatigue after a long day and of his joy in doing the work of the Lord. This poem appeared in Miss Warner's *Warfaring Hymns Original and Translated* (pref. 1869).

Robert Lowry wrote the tune which first appeared in *Bright Jewels* (1869). His setting reflects our natural speech rhythms in setting words like "nearer" and "dearer" to a short note on the accent followed by a longer one.

One Sweetly Solemn Thought   Nearer Home S.M., with
chorus
St. 1–3, 7 alt.
Phoebe Cary, writ. 1852   Philip Phillips, 1876

Written in the house of a friend "in the little back third-story bed-room, one Sunday [in 1852] after coming from church," this poem has been more widely sung than any other from the busy pens of the Cary sisters. One factor which makes a poem practical as a hymn is a uniform line structure from stanza to stanza. "One Sweetly Solemn Thought" is unusually irregular in this respect. We reprint the adapted form with added chorus as it appeared in *Gospel Hymns,* No. 2, in 1876, since this version was widely circulated.

The tune there by Philip Phillips was described by Brown and Butterworth, in *The Story of Hymns and Tunes,* as the most popular in their day. The date of publication of Nearer Home is not clear. Phillips himself dated it 1877 on the basis of its appearance in *Song Sermons.* However, it had already been published in *Gospel Hymns,* No. 2, in 1876 where it is marked "Philip Phillips, by per." Another tune composed for this text is Eben Tourjée's Cary. Richard S. Ambrose's Dulce Domum is more frequently used in recent hymnbooks.

Onward, Onward, Men of   Hall 8.7.8.7.D.
  Heaven!
St. 1–3
Lydia H. Sigourney, 1833   Abner Jones, 1836

Mrs. Sigourney's appeal for missionary effort is dated 1833 by Julian. He says it appeared in three books in that year, but he names only the *Supplement to the Christian Lyre.* It does not appear in the first edition (1831) of the *Supplement.*

In the preface to his *Evening Melodies,* Abner Jones paid tribute to "the lofty and measured expression of Old Hundredth, St. Anne, and other pieces of a similar character" but he points to a need for tunes that are "more easy of execution, and that possess more warmth, vigour, and animation of character than the pieces above alluded to." It is not easy to judge his compositions, since they are not identified, but Hall and Preparation (q.v.) appear to be his. Hall, granted the bare simplicity of its harmonies and the repetition of only two rhythmic patterns, has a vigor that must have appealed to singing schools. Thomas Hastings' Zion is somewhat similar in rhythmic design.

On Zion and on Lebanon   QUEBEC CHAPEL C.M.
St. 1–6
Henry Ustic Onderdonk,   John Paddon, 1828
  1826

In the *Prayer Book Collection* (1826) this poem and "When, Lord to This Our Western Land," which is also by Onderdonk, were included under the heading "For Missions to the New Settlements in the United States." In Isaiah 35:2, "The wilderness and the solitary place shall be glad for them," we find the idea which is developed in this hymn.

QUEBEC CHAPEL appeared in Jonathan Mayhew Wainwright's *Music of the Church* (New York and Philadelphia, 1828), a collection "adapted to the worship of the Protestant Episcopal Church in the United States." "Mr. John Paddon, Organist of St. Paul's in Boston," was mentioned in the preface as one who had made suggestions for the improvement of the collection. Those troubled by the proximity of the fifths and octaves in bar 3 may sing F in the alto and A in the tenor on the third beat.

O Ride On, Jesus
St. 1–4
Traditional, 1918   Version of Natalie Curtis
                               Burlin, 1918
                               Adapted by R. Nathaniel
                               Dett, 1927

This song from St. Helena's Island, S.C., is one of a series of Negro spirituals and secular songs notated from singers at Hampton Institute by Natalie Curtis Burlin. She also recorded the songs on an early Edison phonograph, although she preferred to use records to confirm or supplement notations obtained through repeated hearings of the singers. Her transcriptions are notable because all the parts were recorded and because she made a special effort to indicate dynamic patterns, verbal accents, and peculiarities of pronunciation. "O Ride On, Jesus" was later included in the *Religious Folk-Songs of the Negro* of R. Nathaniel Dett in a form better adapted for group singing. We have used the Dett version. The original transcription is in Book 1 of the *Hampton Series of Negro Folk-Songs* (New York: G. Schirmer, 1918).

O Risen Lord upon the   O Risen Lord L.M.
 Throne
St. 1–4
Louis F. Benson, 1895   Uzziah C. Burnap, comp.
          1898, pub. 1925

This hymn was originally written for the Presbyterian *Hymnal* of 1895 where the first line reads "O risen Christ, who from Thy throne." The revised version appeared in *The Hymnal* of 1911.

Uzziah C. Burnap was one of a number of musicians who wrote original tunes for Benson's hymns. His setting of this text, composed in 1898, was first printed in 1925 when Benson brought together his poems and the music his friends had composed for them in *Hymns Original and Translated.*

O Saviour of a World   Westfield 8.8.8.D.
 Undone
St. 1–3
Leonard Withington, 1857   Anon., 1845

This is a dramatic and forceful treatment of the theme of redemption through the blood of Christ, a treatment more characteristic of theological thinking a hundred years ago than of the present. Based on Philippians 2:5–8, the hymn was first published in Elias Nason's *Congregational Hymn Book* of 1857 and was republished in Charles S. Robinson's *Songs for the Sanctuary* (1865), where it was to be sung to Lowell Mason's Admah.

The tune selected for *American Hymns* is Westfield, which appeared in *The Psaltery* (1845), edited by Lowell Mason and George J. Webb. Marked "slowly and plaintively," it conveys a mood in harmony with the text. Though printed for L.M., the editor has noted its suitability for a six-line stanza by repeating the music for the first two lines. Of the music for the fifth line he says: "treble complains in one note, B."

O Seid im Arnscht   8.7.9.7., with chorus
O Earnest Be

         Recorded by Don Yoder,
          1951

That our German-speaking settlers brought with them a tradition of chorale singing has long been evident. It was Don Yoder who revealed, notably in his *Pennsylvania Spirituals* (1961), that there was also a more recent literature of camp-meeting songs in German. "O Seid im Arnscht" is one of these. It was recorded in 1951 by Don Yoder from the singing of Emma L. Yoder. Like many camp meeting songs and Negro spirituals it consists of a chorus ("O seid im Arnscht") which comes first and the verse section ("Es ist ein grosse Vilderniss") which follows. The latter is stanza 3 of "Kommt, Brüder, kommt, wir eilen fort" by Johannes Walter. Yoder states that this and "Wer will mit uns nach Zion gehn" are "the two most popular German hymns ever written in America." Yoder gives only the melody of this hymn. It may be sung in unison without accompaniment if desired.

O Sing to Me of Heaven

St. 1–4
Mary Stanley Bunce Dana, 1840

No Sorrow There S.M., with chorus

William Batchelder Bradbury, 1860

This hymn was published in the *Southern Harp* (1840), where Mrs. Dana set her poems to folk songs. We have preferred an American tune composed for this text by William Batchelder Bradbury, published in his *Cottage Melodies* (entered 1859, dated 1860) and repeated in *The Key-Note* (1863). The song consists of a short meter stanza followed by four lines in the same pattern which serve as chorus.

O Sion, Haste, Thy Mission High Fulfilling
St. 1–6
Mary A. Thomson, 1892

O Sion Haste 11.10.11.10., with chorus

Henry J. Storer, 1894

Among the relatively few new American texts which appeared in the Episcopal *Hymnal* of 1892 were four by Mary A. Thomson. Two have been chosen for inclusion in *American Hymns*, "O Sion Haste," a missionary hymn, and "O King of Saints" (q.v.) for All Saints' Day. Mrs. Thomson may reasonably be counted among American writers since she was only a girl when she came from England and her poems and hymns were written in this country.

The official hymnal of 1892 contained no music and a number of editions with tunes were published by individual initiative. The tune O Sion Haste by Henry J. Storer appeared in Charles L. Hutchins' *The Church Hymnal Revised and Enlarged* (1894).

O Son of Man, Thou Madest Known	SUTHERLAND L.M.
St. 1–4	
Milton S. Littlefield, writ. 1916, pub. 1920	Emma L. Ashford, 1905

There are relatively few hymns devoted to the spiritual values inherent in work well done. One such is Milton S. Littlefield's "O Son of Man, Thou Madest Known," written in 1916. It was published in *The School Hymnal* (1920), but was not included in such later hymnals of the author's own denomination as the Presbyterian *Hymnal* of 1933 and *The Hymnbook* of 1955.

SUTHERLAND, by Emma L. Ashford, appeared in *The Methodist Hymnal* of 1905 as the tune for Charles Wesley's "Holy, and True, and Righteous Lord."

O Thou Most High Who Rulest All	SONG 9 C.M.
St. 1, 4, 6, 9	Frost 344
Anne Bradstreet, writ. 1661/62	Anon., 1621

These verses were written by Anne Bradstreet "upon my dear and loving husband his goeing into England, Jan. 16, 1661." The Puritans composed religious verse so that the "memorial of God's mercies shall be the better preserved in our hearts," and Mistress Anne Bradstreet on one occasion wrote the verses "All Praise to him who hath now turn'd / My fears to Joyes, my sighes to song."

The tune set here to "O Thou Most High Who Rulest All" comes from George Wither's *The Songs of the Old Testament* (London, 1621) where it is used for Isaiah 26 (The Third Song of Esay). Wither does not name the composer, saying merely "I have endeavoured to procure from some of our best Musitians, such notes as (being easie, and proper to the matter) might the more accommodate them, for the singing now in use."

SONG 9 has been transposed down one tone. Alto and tenor parts have been added to the original soprano and unfigured bass.

O Thou, Who Didst Ordain   CHADWICK C.M.
   the Word
St. 1–3
Edwin Hubbell Chapin, 1846   Henry Kemble Oliver, 1835

This ordination hymn was one of a group of seven contributed by Edwin Hubbell Chapin to the Universalist *Hymns for Christian Devotion.* It has been associated here with the tune CHADWICK by the Unitarian composer Henry Kemble Oliver, which appeared in the *Boston Academy's Collection* (2d ed., 1835).

O Thou Whose Feet Have   LOG COLLEGE C.M.
   Climbed Life's Hill
St. 1–5
Louis F. Benson, writ. 1894,   George W. Warren, comp.
   pub. 1895   1894, pub. 1895

This well-known hymn for schools and colleges was written in Philadelphia, on February 2, 1894. Later that same year, December 5, 1894, George William Warren conceived the tune with which it is associated. Both appeared in the Presbyterian *Hymnal* of 1895.

O Thou Whose Gracious   PIXHAM L.M.
   Presence Shone
St. 1–4
Marion Franklin Ham, writ.   Horatio Parker, comp. 1901,
   1912, pub. 1914   pub. 1903

"O Thou Whose Gracious Presence Shone" was written in 1912 and passed into Unitarian usage through its inclusion in Unitarian hymnals from the *New Hymn and Tune Book* (1914) to *Hymns for the Celebration of Life* (1964). This meditative communion hymn is to be sung to Horatio Parker's lyric tune PIXHAM (see also "We Praise Thee, God, for Harvests Earned," which, too, may be sung to PIXHAM). Although Parker was associated with the Episcopal Church both by belief and professional affiliation, his tunes found their way into the hymnals of other Protestant denominations.

O Thou Whose Own Vast Temple Stands	ARMENIA C.M.
St. 1–4	
William Cullen Bryant, writ. 1835	Sylvanus Billings Pond, 1841

Bryant's best-known hymn, "O Thou Whose Own Vast Temple Stands," was composed in 1835, when a chapel on Prince Street, New York City, was to be dedicated. A variant reading of the opening line is "Thou, Whose unmeasured temple stands," which apparently first appeared in Alfred P. Putnam's *Singers and Songs of the Liberal Faith* (1875) and was subsequently adopted in a number of hymnbooks.

ARMENIA, which appeared in Pond's *United States Psalmody* (1841), is still in use in the twentieth century.

O Thou! Whose Presence Went Before	DEDICATION CHANT L.M.
St. 1–5	
John Greenleaf Whittier, writ. 1834, pub. 1844	Leonard Marshall, 1842

This occasional poem was written by Whittier "on the 4th of the 7th month, 1834," for the Anti-Slavery Meeting at Chatham Street Chapel, New York City. Ten years later it appeared in *Christian Hymns,* a Unitarian hymnbook.

Leonard Marshall's DEDICATION CHANT was included in the *Boston Musical Education Society's Collection,* edited by Benjamin V. Baker and Isaac B. Woodbury and published in Boston in 1842, the earliest date we have for this tune. It was reprinted in Marshall's own *Fountain of Sacred Song* (Boston, 1871), but there it was placed among the congregational tunes at the end, as if the composer considered it an established favorite.

O Turn Ye, O Turn Ye	EXPOSTULATION 11.11.11.11.
St. 1–5	
Josiah Hopkins, 1831	Anon., 1831

A Vermont pastor contributed this, his best-known hymn, to Joshua Leavitt's *The Christian Lyre.* Whether Hopkins was responsible for both tune and text is not there indicated; indeed his name is not given at all in connection with this hymn, although he is named as author of the other text which he contributed, "Why Sleep We, My Brethren?"

The tune was built on a major scale with no fourth step. Indeed the seventh step appears only as the penultimate note. Both of the melodies to the Hopkins' texts persistently use a dactylic rhythm (–∪∪) which gives them an air of similarity. "O Turn Ye" reappeared in Joseph Hillman's *The Revivalist* (1868) and was reprinted in a four-part version in the *Hymns and Songs of Praise* (1874) of Roswell D. Hitchcock, Zachary Eddy, and Philip Schaff. The setting given here is based on the melody and unfigured bass given in *The Christian Lyre*. The inner parts are editorial additions. Transposed from A to G major.

Our Bondage It Shall End   SAINTS BOUND FOR HEAVEN
                               Irregular

St. 1–3, 5, 6
Anon., 1835   J. King and William Walker,
                           arr. 1835

"Our bondage it shall end, by and by" is a rousing revival chorus in a variant of the distinctive Captain Kidd meter (the normal form alternates sixes and threes). See also "Remember, Sinful Youth" and "What Wondrous Love Is This." The editors of the *Original Sacred Harp* state that the tune appeared in "the first *Southern Harmony*" (1835). The arrangement for three voices attributed to J. King and to the editor, William Walker, reproduced here, was retained in the edition of 1854. It reappeared in William Hauser's *Hesperian Harp* (1848), with the addition of an alto part.

The melody is hexatonic, lacking the fourth step. The impression of major is strengthened by the one use of the seventh step in the sixth complete bar. Elsewhere this step is omitted by skipping from 6 to 8 of the complete scale or the reverse.

Time signature Ɔ ; tune in middle part; transposed down a minor third.

Our Father, by Whose Name   KING OF GLORY 6.6.6.6.8.8.8.
St. 1–3
F. Bland Tucker, writ. 1939,   Horatio Parker, 1894
    pub. 1940

The theme of this hymn is the family, and the author relates the members of the human family to the Persons in the Trinity. The opening stanza speaks of the Father, the second of Christ as the Son, and the third of the Spirit, the Holy Ghost, dwelling in the home.

Originally cast in 6.6.6.6.8.8., it was altered in *The Hymnal 1940* to fit the tune RHOSYMEDRE by the English composer John David Edwards. The tune KING OF GLORY appears in the 1894 edition of *The Church Hymnal* edited by Charles L. Hutchins, and later in *The Hymnal Revised and Enlarged* (1903), edited by Parker. Although Parker's tune is printed as 6.6.6.6.8.8., the fact that the last line is repeated makes it equivalent to the meter of Tucker's text.

Our Father, God	COTTAGE C.M.
St. 1–3	
Adoniram Judson, writ. 1825, pub. 1853	George F. Root, 1860

This fine metric version of the Lord's Prayer, remarkable for its brevity and its faithfulness to the original, is dated "Prison, Ava, March, 1825," and was written while the famous missionary was held a prisoner during the hostilities between Great Britain and Burma. Root's simple, chantlike setting is reproduced here as it appeared in the *Diapason*.

Our Father in Heaven	BAZETTA 6.5.6.5.D.
St. 1, 2	
Sarah Josepha Hale, 1831	Lowell Mason, 1845

Sarah Josepha Hale's "Our Father in Heaven," a paraphrase of the Lord's Prayer, was published in *Church Psalmody* (1831), edited by Lowell Mason and David Greene. See also Adoniram Judson's "Our Father, God." Although Mrs. Hale was a member of the Episcopal Church, her poem does not appear in hymnals of that denomination.

In Volume I of *The Sacred Harp* Mason set his own TAPPAN to this text. Later, in his *Psaltery* (ed. with George J. Webb, 1845), he used BAZETTA for the same poem.

Our Fathers' God	PURITAN L.M.
St. 1–5	
Benjamin Copeland, 1903	Henry M. Dunham, 1905

"Our Fathers' God" was first published in *Zion's Herald* (Boston, 1903) and became associated with the present tune in *The Methodist*

Hymnal of 1905, a hymnal markedly hospitable to the American composer. Peter C. Lutkin, Karl Harrington, David Stanley Smith, and others were represented in addition to Henry M. Dunham, the composer of PURITAN.

Like many American tunes of the late nineteenth and early twentieth centuries, PURITAN reflects the profound influence exerted by the Anglican collection *Hymns Ancient and Modern* (1861). The rather active lower parts, the chromatically altered chords, the transient modulations, all confirm this impression.

Our Father Which in Heaven   THE LORD'S PRAYER
  Art   8.6.8.6.8.6.D.
                                   Frost 11
Anon., 1561   John Farmer, arr. 1621

This simple version of the Lord's Prayer first appeared in the English psalter of 1561. The author is unknown. It was harmonized in John Day's psalter (1563), three times in William Daman, in Thomas East, in Richard Allison, and by John Farmer in Thomas Ravenscroft. Although most of the couplets follow the pattern 8.6., the second and third pairs are lengthened, making a more varied pattern than is usual.

Cantus, G clef, second line; medius, C clef, first line; tenor "or Playnsong," C clef, third line; bassus, F clef, fourth line. Time signature C ; note values halved; transposed down one step. We have read "e'en" for "even" in line 4 for a better adjustment of text to tune.

Our Father! While Our   CAPEN C.M.
  Hearts Unlearn
St. 1–6
Oliver Wendell Holmes, 1893   Leo R. Lewis, 1898

"Our Father! While Our Hearts Unlearn" illustrates Holmes's talent for occasional verse of fine quality. Originally written for the twenty-fifth anniversary of the Boston Young Men's Christian Union, it appeared in both *The New Hymn and Tune Book* (1914) and *Hymns of the Spirit* (1937). Henry Wilder Foote, in *Three Centuries of American Hymnody* (p. 247), suggested that this hymn, written almost at the end of Holmes's life, may reflect his own decision to become a Unitarian, thus rejecting the strict Calvinism of his early days.

CAPEN was composed by Leo R. Lewis, one of the editors of the Universalist *Church Harmonies New and Old* (Boston, 1898), in which it appeared.

Our Kind Creator   CHARITY L.M.
St. 1, 3, 5, 6
Solomon Howe, 1799   Solomon Howe, 1799

Solomon Howe wrote tunes and, in some instances, the texts to which they were to be sung. In his *The Worshipper's Assistant* (Northampton, Mass. 1799), a collection designed for beginners, he states that "if the Tunes here contained, can prove useful to Farmers and Mechanicks, the Author will have reason to be thankful." Howe preferred "tunes which go in score" (plain tunes) to the popular fuguing tunes. Our text in praise of singing is printed on the title page of *The Worshipper's Assistant.* It was natural that a man who was both singing master and clergyman should emphasize the values of hymn singing in the family circle, as Howe does in stanza 3. Howe himself set CHARITY to "Messiah's temper, calm and sweet."

Countertenor in C clef, third line. Time signature 𝄵 ; tune in tenor.

Our School Now Closes Out   THE TEACHER'S FAREWELL
                                  S.M., with chorus
St. 1–3
Edmund Dumas, 1858   Edmund Dumas, 1858

This hymn, taken literally, applies to a teacher bidding farewell to his students. Such songs, however, were sung at the end of a camp meeting before preacher and people dispersed, and we are probably intended to understand the present text in that sense. The Puritan congregations had both a preacher and a teacher, and the latter word may be used figuratively or with some tinge of its early meaning. Elder Edmund Dumas, a Primitive Baptist, wrote tune and text in 1858. His hymn, published in the 1869 edition of *The Sacred Harp,* was still included in the 1936 edition. It may also be found in *Good Old Songs,* compiled by C. H. Cayce (Martin, Tenn., 1913). However, in spite of the claims made for Dumas, the medody is essentially the same as that for the chorus "No sorrow there" attributed to E. W. Dunbar (1854).

The melody, in the middle part, is in the familiar folk idiom, plagal in range and pentatonic in scale (equivalent to a major scale with the fourth and seventh steps omitted). George Pullen Jackson compares it with a minor folk version of "Sing to Me of Heaven" (see *Down-East Spirituals and Others,* No. 205, p. 204).

Transposed down one step. In bar 2, last two eighths, the upper part moves in seconds with the middle part. The soprano may sing B C here. In bar 8, first two eighths, the upper and lower parts move in ninths. The bass may sing D C at this point. Consecutive octaves and fifths appear as in the original.

Our States, O Lord	Union C.M.
Ps. 21: st. 1, 3, 6	
John Mycall, 1776	Supply Belcher, 1794

John Mycall was one of the first American editors to attempt a revision of Watts's psalms that would be more American or at least not so outspokenly British. In Psalm 21, where Watts had the heading "Our King Is the Care of Heaven," Mycall substituted "America the Care of Heaven." Later editions of Mycall's version appeared until 1812.

Evidently Supply Belcher was familiar with his version, for in his *The Harmony of Maine* (1794) his tune Union is set to "Our States, O Lord." In stanza 1 the third line differs from that in Mycall, who has "And blest with thy salvation raise." Time signature ₵ .

Our Tense and Wintry Minds	S.M.
Hayden Carruth, writ. 1955	Roy Harris, comp. 1956

Hayden Carruth wrote this modern Christmas song, which contrasts our "tense and weary minds" with the "soft voices from afar" announcing the birth of Christ, at the request of Albert Christ-Janer. The poet wrote: "I think of the Christmas hymn as having a soothing and muted effect, but not too slow or dignified."

This is a unison hymn, "octave congregation or men unison, or women unison," to quote the composer's directions, with organ accompaniment. The melody, practical in range (an octave) and diatonic in character, is well suited for mass singing, while the harmonies of the organ part are much more freely treated. Rhythmically the richly scored chords follow the melody almost note for note. Weaker brothers and sisters in the congregation may be disconcerted to find that the upper notes in the organ part do not always coincide with the vocal melody.

Outside the Holy City	Patmos 7.6.8.6.D.
St. 1–4	
James G. Gilkey, writ. 1915	Henry J. Storer, 1891

The origin of this hymn is best stated in the author's own words:

My hymn "Outside the Holy City" was written in the spring of 1915, when I was a Middler at Union Seminary. My brother, Dr. Charles W. Gilkey, was at that time minister of the Hyde Park Baptist Church in Chicago. He asked me to write for him a Palm Sunday hymn which could be used by the children in his Sunday School at their exercises on Palm Sunday, 1915. In writing this hymn I used the same tune and the same metrical structure which I had used three years before in writing the baccalaureate hymn for my class at Harvard.

The baccalaureate hymn referred to was "O God, in Whose Great Purpose" (q.v.).

The tune which Gilkey had in mind for both texts was ALFORD by the English church composer John B. Dykes. In accordance with the editorial policy of *American Hymns* we have preferred PATMOS by the American composer Henry J. Storer, which appeared in his *Three Processional Hymns* (1891). Note that PATMOS has also been chosen for "O'er Continent and Ocean."

O Welch ein Licht	8.6.7.6.
What Splendid Rays	
St. 1–4	
Christian Gregor	John Antes, late 18th cent.
Anon., English trans. 1789	
St. 2, 3, and 4 revised by Kenneth G. Hamilton, 1957	

Christian Gregor, the dominant figure in Moravian church music of his period, wrote hymns and service music and edited the Moravian hymnals of 1778 and 1784.

John Antes composed twenty-five anthems and *Three Trios for Two Violins and Violoncello*. We reproduce the music and text of his fourth chorale from the collection published by the Moravian Music Foundation. The original figured bass has been worked out by Thor Johnson.

O Young and Fearless Prophet	COMRADES OF THE CROSS 7.6.7.6.D.
St. 1–6	
Samuel Ralph Harlow, writ. 1931, pub. 1935	Edward Shippen Barnes, 1927

The circumstances under which this hymn was written have been described by the author:

With my wife I was driving from Pittsfield to Northampton one spring morning. The words, "O young and fearless Prophet of ancient Galilee," kept singing through my mind. Gradually the entire hymn came to me, and as we had to stop by the road, I repeated them to my wife, who wrote them down. Shortly after writing them down, we started again on our trip and passed a man poorly dressed and looking very tired. My wife suggested that if we lived up to the words of the hymn we ought to pick him up, which we did. He was most grateful and told us that he had walked from Boston to Albany and out to Rochester, looking for work and finding none. He said: "Just as you passed I felt that I was at the end of my rope." He concluded, "Somehow when you think you are utterly forgotten, God shows you that you are not so forgotten as you think you are."

In recalling the incident the Harlows associated it with a passage in the hymn which was omitted in *The Methodist Hymnal* (1935), where it first appeared, but included here:

> Stir up in us a protest against unearned wealth,
> While men go starved and hungry who plead for work and
>   health;
> Whose wives and little children cry out for lack of bread,
> And spend their years o'erweighted beneath a gloomy
>   dread.

In 1927 Edward Shippen Barnes composed four tunes for H. Augustine Smith's *American Student Hymnal*. One, Comrades of the Cross, set there to Willard Wattles' "I Cannot Think or Reason," was chosen for Harlow's hymn.

A Parting Hymn We Sing   Brainard S.M.
St. 1–4
Aaron R. Wolfe, 1858   James Flint, 1849

This hymn, which is intended for the close of a communion service, was one of a group of seven texts contributed by Aaron R. Wolfe to *Church Melodies* by Thomas Hastings.

The course of the melody of Brainard runs so naturally and so smoothly that we may easily miss the fact that it is entirely formed of three-bar phrases except phrase three, corresponding with the long line, which is four bars long. Brainard appeared in 1849 in the *Collection of Church Music* edited by George F. Root and Joseph Emerson Sweetser.

The Past Is Dark with Sin and Shame	BADEN L.M.
St. 1–5	
Thomas Wentworth Higginson, 1846	Thomas Hastings, 1855

Higginson was a contributor to the *Book of Hymns*, edited by Samuel Johnson and Samuel Longfellow, at a time when all three were students at the Harvard Divinity School. Among the four hymns by Higginson were "To Thine Eternal Arms, O God" (q.v.) and "The Past Is Dark with Sin and Shame." The latter paints a gloomy picture of human history lightened only by the hopes expressed in the final stanzas.

It is associated here with BADEN by Thomas Hastings. Rev. Charles L. Atkins has traced this tune to the second edition of *Sacred Songs* (American Tract Society, 1855). The first edition, which appeared in 1842, does not include BADEN.

Peace Is the Mind's Old Wilderness	SURSUM CORDA 10.10.10.10.
St. 1–4	
John Holmes, writ. 1937, pub. 1943	Alfred Morton Smith, comp. 1941

This moving hymn, which equates the idea of peace with simple, everyday happenings, is a shortened and altered version of a poem that first appeared in 1943. In *Hymns for the Celebration of Life*, as here, it was to be sung to Smith's SURSUM CORDA. This tune, composed in 1941, was a later addition to the Episcopal *Hymnal 1940*.

Note that there is a different tune with the same name, composed by Luther Reed, and set to "Lord Jesus Christ, We Humbly Pray."

Permit Us, Lord, To Consecrate	SULLIVAN L.M.
St. 2, 4, 6, 9–11	
Joseph Green, 1766	William Billings, 1778

Our text consists of stanzas selected from the Ode which concludes Joseph Green's *An Eclogue Sacred to the Memory of the Rev. Dr. Jonathan Mayhew, who departed this life, July 8, anno salutis humanae 1766, aetatis 46.*

SULLIVAN appeared in Billings' *Singing Master's Assistant* (1778).

Countertenor, C clef, third line. Tune in tenor; transposed down one step.

Praise Him Who Makes Us Happy	NEVER ANOTHER 7.6.7.6.
St. 1–5	
Mark Van Doren, 1953	Virgil Thomson, comp. 1955

Mark Van Doren's "Praise Him Who Makes Us Happy" appeared in his *Spring Birth* (1953). This unconventional but moving song of praise finds its suitable counterpart in the simple chords of Virgil Thomson's setting. There are words in English ("happy, reason") in which the first syllable is both accented and short. This feature of our language is reproduced in the musical rhythm associated with these words in bars 2 and 6. The older authors called this rhythm effect the "Scotch snap."

Praise Now Your God	11.11.10.10., with chorus
St. 1–3	
H. P. Brucker, S.J., 1964	Jan Kern, 1964

"Praise Now Your God" was included in the *Hymnal for Christian Unity,* Catholic in origin but ecumenical in intent. Some of the hymns are of Protestant, some of Catholic origin, and several are by contemporary poets and composers. Among these is "Praise Now Your God" with its jubilant refrain. The sturdy tune that Jan Kern has written for it is predominantly diatonic with a modal character.

Praise Ye the Lord, O Celebrate His Fame	BABYLON 10.10.10.10.
Selected stanzas	
Peleg Folger, after 1755	Jacob French, 1802

This extensive poem is one of several included in the diary of Peleg Folger. Our selection of stanzas was made from the version printed in E. A. Duyckinck's *Cyclopaedia of American Literature,* which is itself abridged. The poem, a whaler's *De Profundis,* makes us realize the special significance that certain biblical passages had for thoughtful seafaring men. The story of Jonah must have seemed very real to a man who had been twice cast "into the dark abyss" from a wrecked whaling boat.

Although it seems improbable that a Quaker would have sung his own verses, we have ventured to suggest a tune to which they might be sung by others. BABYLON was published in Jacob French's *Harmony of Harmony* (1802) as a setting for Joel Barlow's popular version of Psalm 137: "Along the banks where Babel's current flows."

Treble, G clef, second line; countertenor, C clef, third line; tenor, G clef, second line; bass, F clef, fourth line. Time signature Ɔ.

Precious Child, So Sweetly Sleeping	PRECIOUS CHILD 8.7.8.7.7.7.
St. 1–4	
Anna Hoppe, writ. 1928, pub. 1932	Oscar R. Overby, arr. 1931, pub. 1933

It seems most appropriate that a Norwegian folk song associated with a religious text should be included in the *Concordia Hymnal* (1933), which was designed for the use of American Lutherans of Norwegian descent. "Precious Child, So Sweetly Sleeping" is a Christmas lullaby by Anna Hoppe.

The melody was arranged in a simple but effective fashion by Oscar Overby. The repeated G's in the bass at the opening and again in the fifth and sixth bars suggest the drones of pastoral instruments.

The Prince of Peace His Banner Spreads	ALL SAINTS NEW C.M.D.
St. 1–4	
Harry Emerson Fosdick, writ. 1931, pub. 1937	Henry S. Cutler, 1872

In the summer of 1931 Dr. Fosdick wrote three hymns: "God of Grace and God of Glory," "O God in Restless Living," and "The Prince of Peace His Banner Spreads." He wrote the latter "because I wanted to use the tune to which The Son of God Goes Forth to War is generally sung for a more laudable purpose than that military metaphor suggests."

The tune in question was Henry S. Cutler's ALL SAINTS NEW, which first appeared in the Episcopal *Hymnal with Tunes Old and New,* edited by J. Ireland Tucker. It was set there to the Reginald Heber text and this association has persisted to the present.

Proclaim the Lofty Praise
St. 1–4
Sarah Judson, 1829

ELDRIDGE S.M.D.

Thomas Hastings, 1847

It is curious that this poem by an American woman should have appeared in William Urwick's *Dublin Collection* of 1829, but no earlier American publication has been noted.

ELDRIDGE was included in the *New York Choralist* (1847), edited by Thomas Hastings and William Batchelder Bradbury. Hastings preceded the tune with a brief choral hallelujah which is omitted here, explaining in a footnote that "hallelujahs were sometimes used after this manner in the days of the Reformers."

purer than purest pure
e. e. cummings, 1950

STAR

Vincent Persichetti, 1956

The request to contribute a hymn to this collection so interested composer Vincent Persichetti that he produced a set of forty *Hymns and Responses for the Church Year,* which were published as Opus 68 by Elkan Vogel Company (1956). His choice of texts was both eclectic and highly personal. Among the poets whose poems he chose are John Quincy Adams, Emily Dickinson, Edna St. Vincent Millay, and e. e. cummings. The latter's "purer than purest pure" was first published in 1950 in the poet's *Xaire*. Marked "gently," the melody, largely Aeolian in character although freely harmonized and without its characteristic cadence, reproduces the mood of muted wonder set by the text.

Put Forth, O God, Thy
  Spirit's Might
St. 1–4
Howard Chandler Robbins,
  1937

CHELSEA SQUARE C.M.

Howard Chandler Robbins,
  comp. 1941
Ray Francis Brown, arr. 1941

"Put Forth, O God, Thy Spirit's Might" may be compared with hymns by William Pierson Merrill (q.v.) and Calvin W. Laufer (q.v.) in which the clergyman-poet was also the composer of the tune. In the present instance the poem appeared in H. Augustine Smith's *New Church Hymnal* (New York, 1937), of which Robbins was an associate editor. "The present tune, CHELSEA SQUARE, was hummed by the author/composer to Ray Francis Brown at the General Theologi-

cal Seminary, Chelsea Square, New York City," in 1941, according to
The Hymnal 1940 Companion, and it was Brown who harmonized it.

Qué Preciosas Mañanitas
Dawning Fair, Morning Won-
   derful
Traditional   Traditional

The missions in the Southwest trained musicians as well as ar-
tisans. Although the services were conducted in Latin, the value of
religious songs in the vernacular was well understood. What is left of
these devotional songs in Spanish has been preserved in manuscript
(like the "Alabados") or gleaned from oral tradition by folk song
collectors. "Qué Preciosas Mañanitas" was recorded by Anna
Blanche McGill and published in an article, "Old Mission Music," in
the *Musical Quarterly* (Vol. XXIV, p. 186).

The Ransomed Spirit to Her   WEBSTER L.M.D.
   Home
St. 1–3
William B. Tappan, 1824   George Kingsley, 1844

This text, which Julian pronounced "probably his [Tappan's] best
hymn," was first published in Asahel Nettleton's *Village Hymns* of
1824. The tunes indicated there were HAVERHILL and PHILADELPHIA.
HAVERHILL is by the English church musician Dr. Samuel Arnold.
Although two tunes called PHILADELPHIA are included in this collection, neither is suitable for the Tappan poem. However, George
Kingsley wrote his WEBSTER for this text. It appeared in 1844 in his
The Harp of David. It is a choir rather than a congregational tune
which requires both low and high notes from the soprano. Original
key, G major.

Read, Sweet, How Others   11.10.10.10.
   Strove
St. 1, 2
Emily Dickinson, writ. c.   Roy Harris, comp. 1956
   1861, pub. 1891

This setting of Emily Dickinson's tribute to faith and courage embraces the two stanzas of her brief poem. In this instance the com-

poser has written four vocal parts. These may be sung *a cappella* or with organ accompaniment. In the latter case an instrumental bass part is added, which may be played on the pedals. As in certain of the early psalm books the bar lines serve to show the division of the poem into lines rather than to indicate stressed syllables. Indeed most of the lines of the poem would normally be read with a stress on the second rather than on the first syllable.

Reine Liebe Sucht Nicht Sich
  Selber
Love That's Pure, Itself
  Disdaining
St. 3, 6, 8
Johann A. Gruber, 1748
Sheema Z. Buehne, trans.
  1965

Wo ist Wohl ein Süsser
  Leben 8.7.8.7.6.6.7.7.

Zahn 6519
Johann Balthasar König,
  1738

This hymn, which urges self-abnegation, "Lernet doch erst recht nichts seyn" ("Learn first rightly to be nothing"), suits Johann Gruber's pen name *Ein Geringer* ("a humble man").

The chorale melody Wo ist Wohl ein Süsser Leben, which matches the elaborate eight-line metrical plan of the poem, is given here in the version of König. The bass as well as the inner parts are editorial additions.

Rejoice, Let Alleluias Ring
St. 1–3, 6
Sister M. Cherubim Schaefer,
  O.S.F., 1951

C.M., with chorus

Sister M. Cherubim Schaefer,
  O.S.F., 1951

Although this hymn is for the choir rather than the congregation, we have included it to represent the important contribution of the author to Catholic hymnody. Sister M. Cherubim Schaefer was editor of the *Alverno Hymnal,* named for Alverno College in Milwaukee, which is our source. The interludes between the stanzas have been omitted here (except the first), but they may be found in volume II of the *Alverno Hymnal.*

Remember, Sinful Youth   SOLEMN THOUGHT
                                12.9.12.12.9.
St. 1–5
Anon., early 19th cent.   F. Price, arr. 1854

This warning against "carnal mirth" is one of a number of spiritu-alized secular songs in the so-called Captain Kidd meter, a meter used for the laments attributed to condemned malefactors, in this in-stance the famous pirate Captain Kidd, and named for him. These laments were printed as broadsides and sung and sold by wandering ballad singers. Probably the present example with its grim refrain is close to the original form. See also "What Wondrous Love Is This" for another hymn in the same meter. "Remember, Sinful Youth" ap-peared in 1805 in the *Christian Harmony* of Jeremiah Ingalls (q.v.) before the Southern singing masters took possession of it. Of special interest is William Walker's note: "I learned it from my dear mother (who now sings in heaven) when I was only three years old,—the first tune I ever learned."

It was thus known in the South as early as 1812. The version pre-sented in *American Hymns* comes from the 1854 edition of William Walker's *Southern Harmony,* where the arrangement is credited to F. Price.

Time signature ↄ; tune in middle part.

Remember Thy Creator Now   PRIMROSE C.M.
St. 1–4
Peter Long, 1878   Aaron Chapin, 1878

Text and music come from William Hauser's *Olive Leaf* (1878). A number of the most popular tunes in folk idiom are attributed to Chapin.

PRIMROSE appeared at least as early as Allen D. Carden's *Missouri Harmony* (1820), and in the Southern tune books it was usually sung to Watts's "Salvation, Oh the Joyful Sound." Hauser's *Olive Leaf* dif-fers from earlier Southern tune books (including the editor's own earlier *Hesperian Harp*), since the melody is sung by the soprano, not the tenor, and the harmony has lost much of the rude folk character and is in general conformity with the conventional idiom.

Original key, A major. In the last bar but one, the bass made oc-taves with the tenor on the two quarter notes. These have been cor-rected by analogy with bar 1.

Rise Up, O Men of God   Festal Song S.M.
St. 1–4
William Pierson Merrill, writ.   William H. Walter, 1894
  1911, pub. 1912

Of the two hymns by William Pierson Merrill, "Rise Up, O Men of God," and "Not Alone for Mighty Empire" (q.v.), both written after he became minister of the Brick Presbyterian Church, the first has been more widely used. It first appeared in the *Presbyterian Tribune* and was included in the Presbyterian *Hymnal* and in hymnals of other denominations.

Its challenging lines have been most frequently associated with Festal Song, perhaps the best-known tune of the distinguished American organist William H. Walter. Short meter may be the most difficult for the musician because its very brevity limits musical development. The fanfare with which this tune opens sets a mood that is maintained in the vigorous progressions which follow.

Roll, Jordan, Roll
St. 1–4
Traditional, pub. 1927   R. Nathaniel Dett, arr. 1927

"Roll, Jordan, roll" was a familiar refrain, popular with both white and black singers. George Pullen Jackson found it in John G. McCurry's *Social Harp* of 1855, and it is the first of the *Slave Songs* of 1867 where the editor claimed that it was widely distributed and frequently sung. The melody in *Slave Songs* is quite different from the version which R. Nathaniel Dett prints in his *Religious Folk-Songs of the Negro* (1927). The variable seventh of the scale is the striking feature of this melody, appearing in a most dramatic fashion as D♭ in bar 3, then as D♮, and then as D♭ again.

The Sabbath Day Was By   Dexter Street S.M.
St. 1, 2, 4, 6, 7
Howard Chandler Robbins,   Winfred Douglas, comp. 1940
  1929

The Episcopal *Hymnal 1940* was notable for the number of original tunes included in it. Dexter Street was composed by Winfred Douglas for "The Sabbath Day Was By" and was named by him for the street in Denver where he lived at the time. The text, "An Easter Carol for Children," was first published in a volume of poems, *Vita*

Nova (1929). When it was reprinted in the *Hymnal 1940* two stanzas were omitted and the first line altered from the original reading, "The Sabbath it was by."

Saints in Glory, We Together   Sing of Jesus 8.8.8.5.
St. 1–6
Nehemiah Adams, 1864   Luther O. Emerson, 1863

This jubilant song of praise made its earliest appearance in *Church Pastorals* (1864), edited by Adams. It has sometimes been attributed to S. E. Mahmied, a fanciful nom de plume.

Sing of Jesus, a contemporary tune by the Maine-born composer and singing master Luther O. Emerson, appeared in his *Harp of Judah* (1863). Although it does not bear his name, Emerson's practice in the volume was to indicate other sources and composers, leaving us to assume that the rest were by the editor.

Salve Jesu Pastor Bone   Salve Jesu S.M.D.
Wide Open Are Thy Hands
St. 1–3
Bernard of Clairvaux
Charles P. Krauth, trans.   Harold Lewars, comp. 1914,
   1870   pub. 1917

Charles P. Krauth was one of several Lutheran pastors who contributed translations to the *Hymnal and Service Book* of 1880. "Salve Jesu Pastor Bone" has been attributed to Bernard of Clairvaux, who died in 1153. It is associated here with a tune composed for it by the American organist Harold Lewars for the Lutheran hymnal of 1917. In the Lutheran *Service Book and Hymnal* of 1958 the translation by Krauth has been retained, but not the Lewars tune.

Saviour, Sprinkle Many   Faben 8.7.8.7.D.
   Nations
St. 1–3
Arthur Cleveland Coxe, 1851   John Henry Wilcox, 1849

This missionary hymn, based on Isaiah 52:15, was "begun on Good Friday, 1850, and completed 1851, in the grounds of Magdalen College, Oxford." Although Bishop Coxe served on the Episcopal Hymnal Committee (1869–71), none of his poems was included in the *Hymnal* of 1871 in accordance with his own wishes. The result was that this hymn, first published and in common use in England, was sung in America by members of other denominations only.

FABEN is the most widely known hymn tune by John Henry Wilcox, who was for a time organist of St. Paul's Episcopal Church in Boston. It is used to Coxe's text in the Methodist *Hymnal* of 1878.

Saviour, Thy Dying Love	6.4.6.4.6.6.6.4.
St. 1–4	
Sylvanus D. Phelps, 1871	Robert Lowry, 1871

This hymn, the work of two Baptist clergymen, first appeared in *Pure Gold* (1871), Robert Lowry's enormously successful Sunday-School songbook. It was later taken up in *Gospel Hymns, No. 1,* and has maintained its popularity to the present. It is included in the select list of the best-known hymns by Baptist writers in the *Encyclopedia of Southern Baptists* and in the Southern *Baptist Hymnal,* edited by Walter Hines Sims (Nashville, Tenn., 1956).

Although designed for Sunday-School use, this tune, without refrain, is quietly meditative in mood. The composer, by extending the musical setting for the short lines, has produced a tune which moves in uniform four-bar phrases.

Saviour, Who Thy Flock Art Feeding	PHILADELPHIA 8.7.8.7.7.
St. 1–4	
William Augustus Mühlenberg, 1826	Benjamin Carr, 1828

Of the four hymns that William Augustus Mühlenberg contributed to the *Prayer Book Collection* of 1826, "Saviour, Who Thy Flock Art Feeding" was to enjoy the widest use.

Carr's PHILADELPHIA was included in *Music of the Church* (1828), a collection edited by the English-American Episcopal minister Jonathan Mayhew Wainwright (q.v.). Transposed down one step. The soprano eighth notes in bars 2 and 4 were written as long appoggiaturas in the original. The trill in the bass, bar 16, is for the organist only.

See How the Rising Sun   Sutton S.M.
St. 1–3, 5–7
Elizabeth Scott, 1806   Version of 1812

Elizabeth Scott's "Morning Hymn," "See How the Rising Sun," was first published in J. Dobell's *New Selections* of 1806. Its first line, originally "See how the rising sun," has been altered to "See how the mounting sun" in Henry Ward Beecher's *Plymouth Collection* (1855) and to "See how the morning sun" in the *Hymnal of the Methodist Episcopal Church* (1878). We adhere to the original form. Dobell evidently printed this and other poems from manuscript copies made before Elizabeth Scott's departure from England.

Sutton is a graceful tune of English origin, popular in this country at least from 1771, when it was included in Daniel Bayley's imprint of Aaron Williams' *The American Harmony; or, Universal Psalmodist.* It is for four voices in that publication, but was sometimes reduced to three, as in the 1812 edition of William Little and William Smith's *The Easy Instructor.* (It should be noted that a different tune with the same name appears in the 1817 edition and probably in other editions. See Irving Lowens and Allen P. Britton, *"The Easy Instructor* (1798–1831): A History and Bibliography of the First Shape Note Tune Book," *Journal of Research in Music Education,* Spring 1953.)

Tune in middle part; transposed down one step. In the bass part, third bar before the end, the A♭ was printed in the form of a grace note. It is interpreted as an eighth preceded by a dotted quarter. Modern choir singers should omit the trill on the penultimate note.

Send Forth, O God, Thy   Holden C.M.D.
     Light and Truth
St. 1, 2
John Quincy Adams, 1841   Thomas Whittemore, 1841

John Quincy Adams, President of the United States (1824–29), was probably the only individual who held that high office who was also an accomplished hymn writer. His complete paraphrase of the psalms remains unpublished. However, the *Christian Psalter* (1841) edited by Dr. William P. Lunt, pastor of the Unitarian church which Adams attended, contained five of his hymns together with seventeen of his versions of the Psalms. "Send Forth, O God, Thy Light and Truth," which originally appeared in the *Christian Psalter,* was reprinted as recently as 1942 in C. B. Parker's *Worship in Song.*

Thomas Whittemore's Holden appeared in his *The Gospel Harmonist* (Boston, 1841). The continuous four-part texture of this

C.M.D. tune is relieved by a two-bar duet for soprano and alto marked *piano* at the beginning of the second half.

Shall Man, O God of Light   WASHINGTON L.M.
Ps. 88: second part, st. 1–4
Timothy Dwight, 1800   Timothy Olmstead, 1805

Timothy Olmstead's *The Musical Olio* is of special interest because he was familiar with Dwight's revision of the metric psalms of Isaac Watts. Perhaps he led the singing in a church in which it was used. However, although seven of the texts are credited to Dwight, only the present poem is original with him. (Even "Bless, O ye western world, your God," in spite of the opening line, is largely Watts.)

The preface of *The Musical Olio* states that some of the settings are in three parts and some in four. Some of his second parts are for countertenor (C clef) and some for second soprano; the tunes also vary in location since they may be in the tenor or the soprano. Evidently Olmstead tried to suit both the old and the newer practice.

WASHINGTON is for three voices with the tune in the first soprano. Olmstead strives for a fluent, graceful style without always achieving complete success. Editorial interference has been kept to a minimum, but the following adjustments have been made: first page of score, line 2, last note of bass was C$^\sharp$; second page: line 1, bar 3, soprano 1, the next to last note was C$^\natural$; line 2, bar 1, bass was a third higher in the original.

Shall We Gather at the River?   BEAUTIFUL RIVER 8.7.8.7.,
                                   with chorus
St. 1–4
Robert Lowry, writ. 1864,   Robert Lowry, writ. 1864,
  pub. 1865   pub. 1865

This hymn was written during the period when Robert Lowry was the pastor of a church in Brooklyn. He has told how it originated.

It was a time when an epidemic was sweeping through the city, and draping many persons and dwellings in mourning. All around friends and acquaintances were passing away to the spirit land in large numbers. The question began to arise in the heart with unusual emphasis, "Shall we meet again? We are parting at the river of death, shall we meet at the river of life?" Seating myself at the organ simply to give vent to the pent up emotions of the heart, the words and music of the hymn began to flow out, as if by inspiration.

First published in *Happy Voices* (1865), Philip Bliss and Ira D. Sankey included it in their *Gospel Hymns and Sacred Songs* that same year. It was widely circulated and sung.

In spite of the tragic circumstances attending the origin of this hymn, the melody has a jaunty air. Musically speaking, Lowry was attuned to the cheerful Sunday School hymn. For a very free treatment of the tune, see the finale of Charles E. Ives's Fourth Violin Sonata.

Shepherd, Show Me How To Go	GUIDANCE 7.5.7.5.D.
St. 1–3	
Mary Baker Eddy, cop. 1887	Lyman Brackett, cop. 1887

This poem by Mary Baker Eddy is perhaps more widely known than any other from the pen of the founder of Christian Science. It is coupled here with GUIDANCE, composed by Lyman Brackett, music editor of the earliest *Christian Science Hymnal* (1892).

Si Feliz Quieres Ser	10.9.10.9., with chorus
If You Happy Would Be	
St. 1–3	
Abraham Fernández, cop. 1955	Cosme C. Cota, 1955

Although the gospel hymn originated in the United States among English-speaking people, we have endeavored to indicate similar manifestations among Swedish settlers (see "Med Gud Och Hans Vanscap") and among German-speaking residents of Pennsylvania (see "O Sei im Arnscht"). The spread of Protestant doctrines among Spanish-speaking people has been fostered by the translation of favorite gospel hymns into Spanish and by the composition of popular hymns. "Si Feliz Quieres Ser," which is popular among Spanish-speaking Baptists in this country, is sung to a tune which has an affinity with Latin popular music and perhaps with Italian opera. It was published in *El Nuevo Himnario Popular* (1955).

Sing, My Soul
St. 1–4
Anon., 1805

SING, MY SOUL 7.7.7.7.

Ned Rorem, comp. 1955

This is the first of *Three Hymns* composed in France in 1955. Actually these hymns are for a trained choir and are not congregational hymns.

The text of "Sing, My Soul," chosen by the composer, may be of American origin. It has been traced to a *Collection* published in Baltimore in 1800, where it consists of three stanzas. In the *Episcopal Prayer Book Collection* of 1826, there are four stanzas and it is still included in the *Hymnal 1940*.

The pattern of the setting may be stated as a b a b. The first and second stanzas are set in lyric style in E major. For stanza 3 the opening melody is utilized, shifted up a third to G major. The final stanza returns to E major and to the melody of the second stanza, with more movement in the accompanying parts.

Sing to the Lord Most High
Ps. 100, st. 1–4
Timothy Dwight, 1800

NEW MILFORD 6.6.8.6.4.4.4.4.

Japhet Coombs Washburn,
c.1804

Watts presented two versions of Psalm 100, one headed "A Plain Translation," the other "A Paraphrase." Both reappear in Dwight's version of the Psalms, but the opening stanza of the paraphrase in which Watts referred to the "Northern Isles," Dwight recast in more general terms to avoid the reference to the British Isles. In addition, he gives a third version of his own "in the metre of the 148th psalm," i.e., in hallelujah meter. Dwight's paraphrase, presented here, has survived to the twentieth century, especially in Moravian usage.

NEW MILFORD may be found in Abraham Maxim's *Northern Harmony* (c.1804). It is a vigorous fuguing tune. Soprano, G clef, second line; countertenor, C clef, third line; tenor, G clef, second line; base, F clef, fourth line. Time signature ℭ; transposed down one step. In bar 4 we have read the third quarter note in the bass as F rather than E♭ to avoid the second between bass and tenor.

Sinner, Is Thy Heart at Rest?	FAIRFAX 7.7.7.7.

St. 1, 2, 4, 5
Jared B. Waterbury, 1831   Anon., 1831

With one exception all of Jared B. Waterbury's hymns which have enjoyed considerable use appeared in Joshua Leavitt's *The Christian Lyre* (1831). A number of hymns in this volume appeal to the uneasy conscience of the sinner, but the note of warning is also forcibly sounded, as in this poem. The warning note is even more noticeable in "See Sodom Wrapt in Fire":

> O sinner, mark thy fate!
> Soon will the Judge appear;
> And then thy cries will come too late;
> Too late for God to hear.

Such texts suggest the atmosphere of revivals of the period and form a type which cannot be ignored in a historical anthology.

FAIRFAX is retained here as the tune which Leavitt gives for this text, although in other volumes it is usually marked "German." In Charles Zeuner's *Ancient Lyre* (1834) there is a version in uniform half notes (except for the final whole notes in lines 1, 2, and 4) headed "The original Choral." Leavitt prints this tune in two parts, soprano and bass.

Sinners, Will You Scorn the Message?	BRANDYWINE 8.7.8.7.8.7.

St. 1–6
Jonathan Allen, 1801   Dr. Robert Rogerson, 1786

The *Memorial History of Bradford,* in reference to "Sinners, Will You Scorn the Message?" says that "The truer poesy of his [Allen's] nature appeared in later years, in the hymns which were inspired with the new life that came to him when the gospel of God became a new power . . . After one of [his] sermons, when the whole congregation was melted and in tears, they sang for the first time that sweet hymn which has been adopted by Christians all the world over as one of the precious songs of the church. It has given Mr. Allen fame in two continents. It was born in the revival of 1806." However, the text had already appeared in *Hymns Adapted to Public Worship, Collected from Various Authors* (Exeter, N.H., 1801), although without Allen's name.

The unusual meter of Allen's poem limits the choice of tune. Dr. Rogerson's BRANDYWINE, which appeared in the *Worcester Collection* (1786) seemed to be a suitable choice.

Sleep Sweetly   THE PILGRIM'S LOT 8.8.8.6.D.
St. 1–3, 5
Henry Timrod, 1866   Andrew Gramblin, 1835

Instead of the fiery and partisan battle hymns of this Southern poet we have selected this elegy, an "Ode Sung on the Occasion of Decorating the Graves of the Confederate Dead At Magnolia Cemetery, Charleston, S.C., 1867."

Since the original tune is unknown, we have set Timrod's text to a tune which, according to George Pullen Jackson, in *Another Sheaf of White Spirituals* (p. 160), appeared in William Walker's *Southern Harmony* in 1835. The tune has a folk character. The three-voice setting, as reproduced here, is transposed down a major third and rebarred. In *Southern Harmony* it is in $\frac{6}{8}$ throughout. The only change in note values, however, is in the final chord which was a dotted quarter tied to a dotted half in all voices in the original. Tune in middle part.

Slowly, by God's Hand   KNISELY 7.7.7.7.
    Unfurled
St. 1–4
William Henry Furness, writ.   George Frederick Bristow,
    1825, pub. 1840   1865

In his *Manual of Domestic Worship* (1840) Furness included his evening hymn "Slowly, by God's Hand Unfurled" and his morning hymn "In the Morning I Will Pray" (q.v.). The original reading of the first line was "Slowly, by Thy Hand unfurled," but both the 1853 *Hymns for the Church of Christ* of Frederic Henry Hedge and Frederic D. Huntington and the Unitarian *Hymn and Tune Book* of 1868 gave the reading which is retained here.

Three of Bristow's original hymn tunes, including KNISELY, were included in his collection *The Cantilena.* Two other tunes which appear in that volume are marked with an asterisk and may also have been Bristow's. The original text for KNISELY was "See My Shepherd Gently Guide."

Softly Fades the Twilight Ray   HOLLEY 7.7.7.7.
St. 1–5
Samuel Francis Smith, writ.   George Hews, 1835
    1832, pub. 1843

This hymn was first brought out in *The Psalmist: A New Collection of Hymns,* edited by Smith and Baron Stowe, a widely circulated Baptist collection which appeared in 1843.

George Hews's Holley was first issued in the *Boston Academy's Collection* (1835). It is a placid contemplative tune which has been widely used. In the original edition the first two lines were printed as a duet for soprano and alto. The tenor and bass, in small notes, were to be played on the organ.

Softly Now the Light of Day   Preparation 7.7.7.7.
St. 1–4
George Washington Doane,   Abner Jones, 1834
    writ. 1824

This tender evening hymn, written by George Washington Doane in 1824, has become one of the relatively few American hymns which have been generally sung for well over a century. George Hews's tune Holley ("Softly Fades the Twilight Ray") (q.v.) has been commonly associated with Doane's text.

We wish also to present Abner Jones's Preparation. In its complete simplicity, it seems a suitable expression of Doane's poem. Preparation was published in Jones's *Evening Melodies* of 1834.

Die Sonn Ist Wieder   9.9.8.8.
    Aufgegangen
The Sun Now Risen
St. 1, 8, 20
Johann Conrad Beissel, 1747   Johann Conrad Beissel, 1747

The hymns used at the Ephrata Community in Pennsylvania were published in 1747 as the *Turtel Taube*. The musical setting is taken from a manuscript volume of music for the hymns of the *Turtel Taube* in the possession of the New York Public Library. In spite of the profound impression which the singing at Ephrata made on contemporary visitors, the musical part writing is crude in the extreme. Yet Beissel's followers were singing not only in four, but also in six, seven, and eight parts at a time, when the only native publications were the two-voice psalm tunes in the *Bay Psalm Book* of 1698 and the little three-part settings in John Tufts and Thomas Walter.

The irregular barring in the original has been omitted except for the bars at the end of the lines. Soprano, C clef, first line; alto, C clef, third line; tenor, F clef, fourth line; bass, F clef, fourth line. A three-bar passage in the key of F immediately following the music given here has not been reproduced.

So Touch Our Hearts with   Worship C.M.
   Loveliness
St. 1–3
Gail Brook Burket, writ. 1955   Irving Fine, comp. 1955

"So Touch our Hearts with Loveliness" was sent to us in response to a request by Albert Christ-Janer.

The three stanzas on the themes of loveliness, holiness, and grace have been combined in a single extended setting by Irving Fine. He has given his setting the subtitle "Chorale," and a number of passages do indeed suggest the texture and movement of parts made familiar to us by the Bach chorale arrangements (bar 3 or bar 15, for example), although Fine uses a more dissonant harmony. The alternation of sevenths and ninths in tenor and bass (bars 18, 19, and 20) may prove disconcerting to less adventurous choir leaders, to say nothing of choir singers.

Sovereign and Transforming   Leverett 7.7.7.7.
   Grace
St. 1–4
Frederic Henry Hedge, writ.   Henry Kemble Oliver, comp.
   1829, pub. 1853   1842, pub. 1875

This poem appeared in *Hymns for the Church of Christ*, edited by Hedge and Frederic D. Huntington (1853), and was later included in the Unitarian *Hymn and Tune Book* of 1877 as well as the *New Hymn and Tune Book* of 1914. It was written for a special occasion, the ordination of H. D. Barlow, Lynn, Mass. (1829), but was later shortened, and in the briefer form became a suitable opening hymn. Henry Wilder Foote remarks that "few hymns in English make a grander invocation than the four stanzas now in common use."

Leverett was composed by Henry Kemble Oliver in 1842 and later included in his collected *Original Hymn Tunes* of 1875. It begins with chromatic neighboring notes like Holley (q.v.), or Mercy (q.v.), but is developed simply, without the cloying effects which often follow such an opening.

Spare Us, O Lord, Aloud We   Complaint L.M.
   Pray
Ps. 102: 2–4, 6
Isaac Watts, 1719   Parmenter, 1793

Harriet Beecher Stowe's tale "The Pearl of Orr's Island" deals with the Maine coast near Brunswick, where her husband was a professor at Bowdoin College. The seafaring folk there knew from their own experience the dangers of a great storm. This hymn, which was used as a prayer for the safety of those at sea, set the mood of one of her chapters.

They raised the old psalm-tune which our fathers called COMPLAINT, and the cracked, wavering voices of the women, with the deep, rough bass of the old sea captain, rose in the uproar of the storm with a ghostly, strange wildness, like the scream of the curlew or the wailing of the wind.

> "Spare us, O Lord, aloud we pray,
> Nor let our sun go down at noon;
> Thy years are an eternal day,
> And must thy children die so soon!"

The text sung by Mrs. Stowe's characters was a cento, derived from Watts's metric paraphrase of Psalm 102 (the version in long meter). The original first line read "It is the Lord our Saviour's hand."

The tune itself, by a composer spelled variously as Parmeter or Parmenter, was much sung in early New England. Proof of the lasting esteem in which it was held is its appearance in later anthologies such as the *American Vocalist* (Boston, 1849). Our own setting comes from the *Union Harmony* of Oliver Holden (2d ed., 1796).

The tune, perhaps originally Aeolian, has been provided with C#s, which not only bring it closer to D minor, but produce the forbidden melodic skip of an augmented second (second part, tenor, bar 2; treble, bars 6 and 8). All C#s are omitted here except in the countertenor, part one, bar 6 (note the cross relation with the soprano), and part two, bar 10.

Time signature Ɔ ; tune in tenor; transposed down one step.

The Spirit in Our Hearts St. 1–4 Henry Ustic Onderdonk, 1826	UTICA S.M. Charles Zeuner, 1834

This hymn of invitation and warning was included in the *Hymns of the Protestant Episcopal Church* in 1826. The author contributed eight other hymns as well as three psalm paraphrases to this collection, which marked the beginning of the use of native hymns by this denomination.

Charles Zeuner's UTICA appeared in his *The Ancient Lyre*.

Spirit of Life, in This New   De Pauw L.M.
  Dawn
St. 1–5
Earl B. Marlatt, writ. 1926,   Robert G. McCutchan, comp.
  pub. 1932   1928, pub. 1930

Few hymns have been created for the purpose of interpreting a doctrine to a perplexed college student. "Spirit of Life" was written to explain Marlatt's conception of the Trinity—"not three persons in One, but three cosmic, continuing manifestations of the one creative, redeeming, consoling Power of whom Jesus said, 'God is a Spirit, and they that worship Him must worship Him in spirit and in truth.' " A puzzled student had asked for a simpler explanation than the one Marlatt had given in class to which Marlatt in some exasperation had responded, "Did you want me to sing it?" "Well," responded the student, "it would help a lot if you could." Marlatt took the retort to heart and "Spirit of Life," earlier called "God Is a Spirit," was the result. The hymn was included in *The Methodist Hymnal* of 1932.

The tune there was Henry Percy Smith's Maryton. We have substituted De Pauw by a Methodist musician, Robert G. McCutchan. Composed in 1928 at Lake Winona, Ind., it was first published in *The Standard Hymnal* (1930).

Stand Up, Stand Up for Jesus   Webb 7.6.7.6.D.
St. 1–4
George Duffield Jr., 1858   George J. Webb, 1837

The dying words of Dudley A. Tyng were "Tell them to stand up for Jesus!" During the winter and spring of 1857–58 he had been a leading preacher at revival meetings in Philadelphia. While at his country home he went to see a corn-shelling machine operated by mule power. He came too near, the sleeve of his gown caught in the gears, and he was fatally injured. Duffield wrote his poem as a conclusion for a sermon preached on the following Sunday. The poem had been printed on a single sheet for the Sunday-School children and one of the copies was reprinted in a Baptist paper. Duffield approved a version reduced to four from the original six stanzas which was printed in Charles Dexter Cleveland's *Lyra Sacra Americana* in 1868.

Webb wrote his tune to " 'Tis Dawn, the Lark Is Singing" on a voyage from England to the United States in 1830. It was first published with this text in the *Odeon* (1837), edited by Webb and Lowell Mason. Its earliest use as a hymn tune was to S. F. Smith's "The

Morning Light Is Breaking" (q.v.) in *The Wesleyan Psalmist* (1842).
Not until 1861 was WEBB used for Duffield's poem in William Batchelder Bradbury's Sunday-School collection *The Golden Chain.*

The Stately Structure of This   PLAINFIELD C.M.D.
  Earth
Ps. 24, st. 1–3, 6, 7
Martha Brewster, 1757   Jacob Kimball, 1800

This pretty and picturesque, but very free, paraphrase of Psalm
24 is from Martha Brewster's book of poems published in New London, Conn.

Her verses are matched here with Jacob Kimball's PLAINFIELD, included in the *Essex Harmony* (Exeter, N.H., 1800) issued jointly by
Kimball and Samuel Holyoke. It is interesting to note that in this instance only Kimball gives both the time signature ¢, which indicates
four beats per bar, as well as the Italian term *allegro moderato.*

Countertenor, C clef, third line. Tune in tenor; transposed down
one step.

Such As in God the Lord Do   HIGH DUTCH TUNE
  Trust   8.8.8.8.6.6.
Ps. 125:1–4   Frost 144
William Kethe, 1561   Giles Farnaby, arr. 1621

This metrical setting of Psalm 125 by William Kethe is one of
twenty-five that the Scottish poet made for the Anglo-Genevan
psalter of 1561. The melody had already appeared in 1551 to a
translation of Psalm 21, by Théodore de Bèze, who was often called
Beza. Beza's meter, however, was 8.7.7.8.6.6. When Kethe lengthened the second and third lines the tune was modified by repeating
the penultimate notes of these lines.

Cantus, G clef, second line; medius, C clef, second line; tenor,
which has the psalm tune, C clef, fourth line; bassus, F clef, third
line. Original pitch; time signature C; note values halved.

The Summer Harvest   STRATFIELD L.M.
  Spreads the Fields
St. 1–5
Nathan Strong, 1799   Goff, version of 1793

Asahel Nettleton, in the preface to *Village Hymns,* speaks of his
search for revival hymns. "I had hoped to find in the style of genu-

ine poetry, a greater number of hymns adapted to the various ex-
igencies of a revival. Laborious research has, however, led me to
conclude that not many such compositions are in existence." This
statement should probably be read with emphasis on the phrase "in
the style of genuine poetry," since it seems clear that there had been
a considerable development of popular camp-meeting hymns by that
time. Strong's evangelistic "The Summer Harvest Spreads the
Fields" was one of the hymns which had been reprinted from *The
Hartford Selection of Hymns* (1799) in Asahel Nettleton's *Village Hymns*
(1824). It dwells on the great harvest of souls at Judgment Day and
emphasizes the fate of the rejected with characteristic grimness:

> Go, burn the chaff in endless fire,
> In flames unquenched, consume each tare.

The tunes indicated in *Village Hymns* are OLD HUNDREDTH, BATH,
and LEEDS. It has been set here to a fuguing tune by a little-known
American composer called Goff. STRATFIELD was published in two
collections in 1793, the *American Harmony* by Nehemiah Shumway,
which we follow, and the *Union Harmony* by Oliver Holden, which
contains variants.

Time signature ↄ. The tune was preceded by a measure of rests in
all parts, which is not included here. The dissonance caused by the
entry of the tenor on the last quarter of bar 17 is in the original.

The Sun and Moon So High and Bright	SONG 34 L.M.
Hab. 3: 11–13, 17, 18	Frost 362a
Anon., 1651	Orlando Gibbons, 1623

This text from the third chapter of Habakkuk was among the spiritual songs added to the *Bay Psalm Book* of 1651. The lines in which
Habakkuk declares that he would rejoice in God even though the fig
tree and olive should fail were not only selected for versification by
Massachusetts divines living in a land where neither would thrive,
but reappeared in later hymns, such as Henry Ustic Onderdonk's
paraphrase of the same passage:

> Although the Vine its fruit deny
> The budding fig-tree droop and die,
> No oil the olive yield.

SONG 34 is one of a group of tunes which Orlando Gibbons composed for the versified psalms of George Wither (q.v.). Since Gibbons wrote for soprano and unfigured bass, the alto and tenor parts

are editorial additions. The text may be sung by one voice, or in unison, to the organ or other keyboard instruments.

Sweet Rivers of Redeeming   Sweet Rivers C.M.D.
   Love
St. 1, 2, 4, 6, 7
John A. Granade, 1814   William Moore, 1859

This text, based on Revelations 22:1, antedates 1825. It has been traced to Silas M. Noel's *A Hymn Book, Containing a Copious Selection of Hymns and Spiritual Songs* (Frankfort, Ky., 1814) and to Thomas S. Hinde's *Pilgrim Songster* of the same year. The later version reproduced here comes from Jesse Mercer, *The Cluster of Spiritual Songs, Divine Hymns, and Sacred Poems* (5th ed., 1835, often called "Mercer's Cluster").

George Pullen Jackson stated that "William Moore, compiler of the *Columbian Harmony* (1825), claimed the song, and subsequent Southern rural compilers have allowed his claim to stand." The melody has folk affiliations. Although it contains all the tones of the major scale, the fourth step appears only once and there are a number of melodic figures in which it is avoided: 2-3-5, 5-2-3, and 6-5-3. It thus has some of the characteristics of a melody built on a gapped scale. Jackson related it to his Roll Jordan family and pointed to Pleasant Hill and Zion's Light as related tunes. Sweet Rivers was republished in *The Southern Harmony* (1854) and *The Sacred Harp* (1859).

Our score follows *The Sacred Harp;* tune in tenor; transposed down one tone.

Swell the Anthem, Raise the   Ascension 7.7.7.7.
   Song
St. 1–6
Nathan Strong, 1799   Jacob French, 1802

The editors of *The Hartford Selection* did not restrict themselves to hymns by Isaac Watts, but included originals by American hymnists. Of Nathan Strong's contributions his "Swell the Anthem, Raise the Song" was the most successful. Its popularity continued through the nineteenth century, and it is included in a number of hymnals published in the twentieth century.

The Hartford Selection named the tune Ascension for Strong's poem. Two American tunes had this title: one by Jacob French, which appeared in his *Harmony of Harmony* in 1802; the other in simple three-voice style appeared in Samuel Holyoke's *Christian Harmonist* of 1804. A Southern setting of Strong's text by W. H. Swan appeared in the composer's *New Harp of Columbia* (Nashville, Tenn., c.1867).

French writes the countertenor in the C clef, third line. Time signature ₵; transposed down one step.

Take Thou Our Minds, Dear Lord	Hall 10.10.10.10.
St. 1–4	
William H. Foulkes, writ. 1918	Calvin W. Laufer, comp. 1918

The origin of this hymn may best be given in the words of William H. Foulkes who wrote the poem. The place was the railroad station, Stony Brook, Long Island, New York, the year 1918.

Dr. Calvin W. Laufer approached me, and, humming a tune, said: "Dr. Foulkes, we need a devotional hymn for the young people that will challenge their hearts and minds. It has occurred to me that you might be in a mood to write a few verses for such a hymn." We then hummed the tune together so that I remembered it. As I went on in the train that morning the words of the first three stanzas came to me almost spontaneously.

The fourth stanza was added after the hymn had appeared in *Conference Songs* (1918). The complete text may be found in the Presbyterian *Hymnal* of 1933.

The tune, originally named Stony Brook, was rechristened Hall as a tribute to a mutual friend, the Rev. William Ralph Hall.

Tarry With Me, O My Saviour	Kidron 8.7.8.7.
St. 1–4	
Caroline Sprague Smith, writ. 1852	William Mason, comp. 1845, pub. 1848

This hymn, rejected by *The Messenger,* was published after a lapse of years in an Andover paper edited by Caroline Smith's sister, a Mrs. Terry. Originally in seven stanzas, *The Plymouth Collection* (1855) reduced the text to five, and the second stanza of this version dealing with the loss of friends in old age was omitted in *Hymns and Songs of Praise* (1874), edited by Roswell D. Hitchcock, Zachary Eddy, and Philip Schaff, and elsewhere.

KIDRON, one of a number of hymn tunes composed by William Mason, was included in *The National Psalmist* (1848), edited by his father, Lowell Mason, and George J. Webb.

Tell Me Not in Mournful Numbers	JACINTH 8.7.8.7.D.
(Psalm of Life)	
St. 1–6	
Henry Wadsworth Longfellow, 1839	Charles Beecher, 1855

This poem appeared as "A Psalm of Life" in the author's *Voices of the Night* (1839). Henry Ward Beecher's *Plymouth Collection* contained five hymns by Henry Wadsworth Longfellow, including translations from German and Spanish sources. Among them was "Tell Me Not in Mournful Numbers" set to JACINTH by Charles Beecher. The same poem appeared later in the Unitarian *Hymn and Tune Book* (1877) to Ithamar Conkey's RATHBUN (q.v.). In some instances stanza one is omitted; the poem then begins: "Life is real! Life is earnest." Beecher's tune has been retained here.

Tell Us, Ye Servants of the Lord	SYME C.M.
St. 1, 3–5	
William Staughton, 1836	Edward Hamilton, 1857

The motto line in this poem, "We would see Jesus," comes from John 12:21, the passage repeating the request of certain Greeks to the disciple Philip. The text first appeared in the 1836 *Select Hymns* of James H. Linsley and Gustavus Davis, where it is directed to be sung to DUNDEE. We have preferred an American tune.

SYME, by Edward Hamilton, was published in his *The Sanctus* (Boston, 1857) and repeated in the musical edition of *The Psalmist* which appeared in 1859. The tunes are classified in the preface, and SYME is called a "choral," which is described as a tune with a note to a syllable except for occasional passing notes.

There Is a High Place	10.10.10.10.
(One Music)	
St. 1, 2	
Edwin Markham, 1915	Alan Hovhaness, comp. 1957

A number of the larger compositions by Hovhaness are religious in spirit. This poem of Edwin Markham's, with its musical imagery and its vision of a remote and peaceful land, seems peculiarly suited to Hovhaness' character as a composer. The brief prelude (or interlude) for organ is followed by the voices of the choir which intone with complete rhythmic simplicity chords that are at the same time archaic and contemporary in atmosphere. The harmonies consist almost exclusively of the fundamental triad used in novel relationships.

There Is a Land Mine Eye	Altitude L.M.
Hath Seen	
St. 1–4	
Gurdon Robins, 1843	Leonard Marshall, 1852

This poem of a land where "those who meet shall part no more" appeared in *The Psalmist* (1843), edited by Samuel Francis Smith and Baron Stowe, without the author's name. It was included in *The Baptist Hymnal for Use in the Church and Home* (1883) where it was to be sung to Leonard Marshall's Altitude, and this association has been preserved here. There is an atmosphere of pastoral simplicity about Altitude, perhaps due to the use of triple meter, the thirds in the upper parts, and the legato slurs, which is in harmony with Gurdon Robins' poem. Altitude appeared in 1852 in *The Harpsichord*, edited by Marshall and Henry N. Stone.

There Is an Hour of Peaceful	Tappan 8.6.8.8.6.
Rest	
St. 1–4	
William B. Tappan, 1818	George Kingsley, 1838

The origin of this hymn was described by the author in his *Gems of Sacred Poetry*, 1860:

It was written by me in Philadelphia, in the summer of 1818, for the *Franklin Gazette*, edited by Richard Bache, Esq. and was introduced by him to the public in terms sufficiently flattering to a young man who then certainly lacked confidence in himself. The piece was republished in England and on the Continent, in various newspapers and magazines and was also extensively circulated in my own native land, where it has found a place in several hymn and music-books. It was published in my first volume of *Poems* in Philadelphia, in 1819, and soon after was set to music by A. P. Heinrich, Esq. in the same city.

Heinrich's setting for solo voice and piano was printed about 1820 as part of his *The Western Minstrel*. The Providence musician Oliver Shaw (q.v.), treated the same text as a vocal duet with piano accompaniment (entered 1833).

In 1838 George Kingsley published his *Sacred Choir* in which his tune TAPPAN appeared as a setting for the present hymn. Composers of that period tended to vary the texture of their tunes by treating passages as duets or trios, and Kingsley's setting of the words "A balm for every wounded breast" is a good example of the practice.

See also "Now Help Us, Lord," which is a free treatment of TAPPAN by Charles E. Ives. Charles Zeuner's TAPPAN is a different tune.

There Is No Name So Sweet on Earth   SWEETEST NAME 8.7.8.7., with chorus
St. 1–3
George Washington Bethune, 1858   William Batchelder Bradbury, 1861

This hymn, written in 1858, was included by William B. Bradbury in his Sunday-School collection *The Golden Chain* (1861). The text was inspired by the words: "God also hath highly exalted him, and given him a name above every name" (Phil. 2:9). Julian, on the authority of H. P. Main, ascribes the text to Bethune.

Bradbury's music, at once appealing and transparently simple, is in three-part form. After the opening part, the chorus adds a contrasting phrase, then concludes the stanza by returning to the beginning.

There's a Land That Is Fairer Than Day   SWEET BY-AND-BY 9.9.9.9., with chorus
St. 1–3
S. Fillmore Bennett, writ. 1867   J. P. Webster, comp. 1867

In 1867 S. Fillmore Bennett was a druggist with literary leanings and J. P. Webster a music teacher in Elkhorn, Wis. A sentence uttered by Webster in a despondent mood, "It will be all right by and by," provided Bennett with his theme. "The sweet by and by! Why would that not make a good hymn?" He immediately wrote down the verses as we know them and passed the manuscript to Webster who composed the tune. The hymn was published in circulars advertising *The Signet Ring* in 1868. A sheet music edition appeared in the same year. The setting is completely in the orbit of the gospel hymn. Particularly typical is the echoing of the upper voices by the lower in the chorus.

They Cast Their Nets in   GEORGETOWN C.M.
   Galilee
St. 1–4
William A. Percy, 1924 (al-   David McK. Williams, 1941
   tered)

First published in the author's *Enzio's Kingdom and Other Poems* in 1924, this poem was selected for *The Hymnal 1940*, where the original first stanza was omitted.

One of the trends evident in a number of the twentieth-century tunes published in *The Hymnal 1940* is an increased freedom from a rhythmic and metrical point of view. This freedom may in part result from studies of Gregorian song with its freer rhythms. In the present instance the poem is in C.M., the most usual of all meters. The composer broadens his opening and third line (those with eight syllables in the text) by a measure which contains six instead of four quarter notes. The second line moves in uniform fours. In the last line the composer, desiring to give special stress to the word "Lord," lengthens that note, which makes the penultimate measure five quarter notes in length.

They Pray the Best Who Pray   BISHOP L.M.
   and Watch
St. 1–4
Edward Hopper, writ. 1873,   Joseph P. Holbrook, 1874
   pub. 1874

Edward Hopper was pastor of the ancient Church of Sea and Land in downtown New York, a sailors' church, and it was natural that two of his three hymns should have nautical imagery, "Jesus, Saviour, Pilot Me" (q.v.) and "Wrecked and Struggling in Mid-Ocean." The present hymn is the exception. It appeared in *Hymns and Songs of Praise* (1874), edited by Roswell D. Hitchcock, Zachary Eddy, and Philip Schaff, where the hymn was dated 1873. The tune set there was Chapin's FOREST.

Holbrook describes himself as "Director of Music in the First Presbyterian Church, Brooklyn, New York" in his *Quartet and Chorus Choir* (1871). His BISHOP was in Duryea's *The Presbyterian Hymnal* of 1874.

Think Not When You Gather to Zion	9.8.9.8.D.
St. 1–4	
Eliza R. Snow, 1856	John Tullidge, 1857

Eliza R. Snow was perhaps the most prolific hymn writer among the Latter-Day Saints. Her "Think Not when You Gather to Zion" appeared in *Sacred Hymns and Spiritual Songs* (1856). John Tullidge, an English-born choral conductor, composed the setting which was first published in the *Psalmody* of 1857, which he edited.

This Is My Father's World	TERRA BEATA S.M.D.
St. 1–3	
Maltbie Davenport, 1901	Franklin L. Sheppard, 1915

Though Babcock's hymns were actually written in the nineteenth century, they were published in 1901 in a volume entitled *Thoughts for Everyday Living*. "This is my Father's world," a cento derived from one of his poems, has been widely used. It has been associated with a melody which Babcock's friend Franklin L. Sheppard arranged for it. Text and music first appeared together in *Alleluia,* a Sunday School hymnal, where the tune was marked "Traditional English Melody. Arranged by F.L.S. 1915." Sheppard himself said that the tune was one he had learned as a child from his mother. Some later editors have assumed that Sheppard was really the composer of the tune, but Mrs. Hugh Porter has settled the matter by locating the melody in an English hymnal under the name RUSPEL.

This New Day	NEW DAY 8.7.8.7.
St. 1–4	
Vail Read, writ. 1955	Gardner Read, comp. 1955

This is only one of the contemporary hymns in our anthology in which the text was written by a wife, the musical setting by the husband (see also "Hail, Oh Hail to the King," by Beatrice Quickenden and John St. Edmunds, and "All That I Am," by Verna Arvey and William Grant Still). In contrast to the more usual practice, Mrs. Read prefers to write her verses to preexistent music. "This new Day" is suitable for a baptismal hymn.

Here too the flowing and lyric melodic lines of the musical setting follow harmonic and formal patterns familiar and acceptable to the musical churchgoer. The composer wrote: "I have tried to create a singable work, but with harmony and voice leadings a bit more advanced than those found in the standard hymns."

Thou Art, O God, the God of Might	BURG 8.7.8.7.
St. 1–4	
Emily Swan Perkins, 1921 (altered)	Emily Swan Perkins, 1921

Emily Perkins dedicated herself to the cause of hymn singing in this country through her pioneer efforts as a founder of the Hymn Society of America, through her long service in that organization, and through the creation of the texts and the music of her own hymns. Two volumes of her hymns were privately published. "Thou Art, O God, the God of Might," first published in her *Stonehurst Hymn Tunes* (1921), was selected for inclusion in the Presbyterian *Hymnal* of 1933. It is set to her own tune, BURG, which has the character of a processional hymn.

Thou Art the Tree of Life	TREE OF LIFE 10.10.10.D.
St. 9, 10	
Edward Taylor, 1703	Henry Cowell, comp. 1955

Henry Cowell has written a large choral work on lines by the mystic minister-poet Edward Taylor in addition to the present hymn. His interest in early New England hymnody has been shown in his fuguing tunes, which suggest the New England psalm tune but which at the same time are developed in a personal and contemporary fashion. The setting of "Thou Art the Tree of Life," in its modal quality, the bareness of its fourths and fifths, reflects a similar practice. The melody is Dorian and is sung by both sopranos and tenors while altos and basses sing supporting parts.

Thou Art the Way   ATKINSON C.M.
St. 1–4
George Washington Doane,   John Cole, 1839
    1824

"This, in the judgment of many, is the first of American hymns, and one of the most admirable and useful in the English language." Such was the verdict of F. M. Bird, the distinguished hymnologist, in his article on Doane in Julian's *Dictionary of Hymnology*. At the present time Doane's "Softly Now the Light of Day" (q.v.) is his best-known and most-beloved hymn. "Thou Art the Way," first published in a volume of poetry *Songs of the Way* (1824), was made known by its inclusion in the Episcopal *Prayer Book Collection* (1826).

In *The Church Choir* of Joseph Muenscher, which was intended for the Episcopalians of the West, ATKINSON was set to Doane's text. George Kingsley's HEBER also appeared in the Muenscher collection to "Thou Art the Way," but Cole's tune has been preferred because of his long association with the Episcopal service.

Though Fatherland Be Vast   AMERICA THE BEAUTIFUL
                                       C.M.D.
St. 1–4
Allen Eastman Cross, 1918   William W. Sleeper, 1908

This poem was written in the war year of 1918 and was prefaced by a quotation from Edith Cavell, the English nurse shot by the Germans in 1915: "Standing as I do in view of God and eternity I realize that patriotism is not enough. I must have no hatred or bitterness for anyone." Beginning:

> Though Fatherland be vast and fair,
> Tho' Heav'n be e'er so near,
> Yet there's a land,
> That is to God more dear!

It develops the vision of the kingdom of God in language that has a certain general similarity to "O Mother dear, Jerusalem."

In H. Augustine Smith's *American Student Hymnal* (1928) it is associated with the tune CAVELL (PHOENIX) written for it by Leonard N. Fowles. We have preferred an American tune by William W. Sleeper dated 1908 and originally intended for Katherine Lee Bates's "America the Beautiful."

Though I Should Seek	HARMONIA L.M.
St. 1–5	
Henry Ustic Onderdonk,	Anthony Philip Heinrich,
1826	1832

Bishop Henry Ustic Onderdonk was an influential member of the committee that compiled the Protestant Episcopal prayer book collection of 1826 and his original hymns were written for it. These include "Though I Should Seek," which appears under the heading "Need of the Mediator."

Anthony Heinrich's contribution to American church music was slight. We turn rather to his ambitious compositions for orchestra which celebrate the American Indian or the glories of his adopted land. His setting of William B. Tappan's "There Is an Hour of Peaceful Rest" in his early *Western Minstrel* is a solo song rather than a hymn.

More to our purpose are the tunes HARMONIA and ANTONIA, which appeared in Nathaniel D. Gould's *National Church Harmony* (1832). ANTONIA, named for Heinrich's daughter, is somewhat Italianate in style like much of Heinrich's music. HARMONIA, with progressions which repeat like a chime of bells, is more original.

Thou Grace Divine,	HEBER C.M.
Encircling All	
St. 1–5	
Eliza Scudder, writ. 1852,	George Kingsley, 1838
pub. 1857	

Eliza Scudder was the niece of Edmund H. Sears (q.v.), distinguished Unitarian clergyman and hymn writer, and it was in her uncle's *Pictures of the Olden Time* (1857) that "Thou Grace Divine" first appeared. It subsequently appeared in *Hymns of the Spirit* (1864), edited by Samuel Johnson and Samuel Longfellow, in *The New Hymn and Tune Book* (1914), and in *Hymns of the Spirit* (1937).

George Kingsley's HEBER is similar in rhythm to such tunes as Thomas A. Arne's ARLINGTON (1744) and Deodatus Dutton's WOODSTOCK (1829), which (like the German "Tannenbaum") are characterized by a dotted eighth on the accent followed by a sixteenth. The high E in line 3 should not be unduly stressed where it falls on a word of little importance such as "in" in stanza 3.

Thou Long Disowned,   Geer C.M.
  Reviled, Oppressed
St. 1–5
Eliza Scudder, writ. 1860,   Henry Wellington Greatorex,
  pub. 1864   1849

This poem, first published in 1864 in *Hymns of the Spirit,* edited by Samuel Johnson (q.v.) and Samuel Longfellow (q.v.), was retained in the *New Hymn and Tune Book* of 1914. Few tunes characterized by musical learning have gained and retained a place in our hymnals. Tallis' Canon by the early English composer Thomas Tallis is a well-known exception. The tune Geneva, by the English-American John Cole, was perhaps the only American tune beginning with successive imitative entries to enjoy a long period of use.

Geer by Henry Wellington Greatorex consists musically of two seven-bar phrases in each of which the soprano is imitated by the tenor. Its first appearance, under the name Elim, was in 1849 in the *Collection of Church Music,* edited by George F. Root and Joseph Emerson Sweetser. When Greatorex transferred it to his *Collection of Psalm and Hymn Tunes* of 1851 he changed the name to Geer.

No time signature. Most modern editions reduce the note values by half.

Thou, Lord, Hast Been Our   French Tune or Dundee
  Sure Defense   C.M.
Ps. 90: 1, 2, 4–6   Frost 204
John Hopkins, 1562   Thomas Ravenscroft, arr.
                                         1621

This metrical version of Psalm 90 by John Hopkins appeared in 1562. All sixty psalm paraphrases which he contributed to the English psalter were in common meter, although he tended to rhyme alternate lines where Thomas Sternhold was satisfied to rhyme line 2 with line 4 and (in a double stanza) line 6 with line 8. This practice will be evident if Hopkins' version of Psalm 90 is compared with Psalm 18 or Psalm 23 by Sternhold. Psalm 90 will be familiar to readers in the form which Isaac Watts gave it: "O God, Our Help in Ages Past."

The familiar tune which we call Dundee was first printed in *The CL Psalms of David* (Edinburgh, 1615), edited by A. Hart, where it was called French Tune. Six years later Thomas Ravenscroft gave it the name by which it is generally known, although he spelled it Dundy.

Cantus, C clef, first line; medius, C clef, third line; tenor, C clef, fourth line; bassus, F clef, third line. Time signature C ; note values halved.

Thou Lord of Hosts, Whose Guiding Hand	MISSIONARY CHANT L.M.
St. 1–5	
Octavius Brooks Frothingham, 1846	Charles Zeuner, 1834

"Thou Lord of Hosts, Whose Guiding Hand" was included by Samuel Longfellow and Samuel Johnson in their *Book of Hymns,* which appeared in 1846, and in Alfred P. Putnam's *Singers and Songs of the Liberal Faith* (1875).

The term "chant tune" was a favorite designation with Zeuner. He not only uses it frequently for his own compositions, but also for compositions by others, for example, William Billings' LEBANON and Daniel Read's LISBON. It is not easy to define the type. MISSIONARY CHANT, the most famous example, is characterized by repeated notes and a limited range—both characteristics which facilitate a clear projection of the text. But repeated notes are not a feature of some of Zeuner's own chant tunes and many hymn tunes have a limited range. MISSIONARY CHANT, which is still sung, appeared in the composer's *Ancient Lyre* (1834).

Thou One in All, Thou All in One	CLONBERNE L.M.
St. 1–4	
Seth Curtis Beach, writ. 1884	Henry Kemble Oliver, 1875

Beach is remembered as a hymn writer for his "Mysterious Presence! Source of All" (q.v.), written while he was still a college student, and for his "Thou One in All, Thou All in One," written almost two decades later. The latter first appeared in the *Sunday School Service Book and Hymnal,* edited by Henry G. Spalding (1884). Five years later it was included in John Hunter's *Hymns of Faith and Life* (Glasgow, 1889). It is also to be found in the Unitarian *New Hymn and Tune Book* (1914) and in *Hymns of the Spirit* (1937). It is presented here with CLONBERNE, one of the later tunes of Henry Kemble Oliver, written in 1873, and included in his *Original Hymn Tunes* of 1875.

Thrice Blest the Man   100TH PSALM TUNE NEW L.M.
Ps. 1: 1–6
John Barnard, 1752   Version from John Tufts,
                              1726

This metrical version of the first Psalm by John Barnard is set to the 100TH PSALM TUNE NEW. The earliest appearance of the tune is in *An Introduction to the Singing of Psalm Tunes. In a plain & easy Method. With a Collection of Tunes in Three Parts. By the Rev. Mr. Tufts. The Fifth Edition. Printed from Copper-Plates, Neatly Engraven. Boston, in N. E. Printed for Samuel Gerrish. at the Lower End of Cornhill,* 1726. Irving Lowens believes that "for stylistic as well as historical reasons this piece is an American composition." If we accept this view, it is the earliest-known native composition from the New England area.

Thrice Welcome First and   ALL SAINTS L.M.
  Best of Days
St. 1–4, 6, 7
Isaac Chanler, 1745   William Knapp, version of
                              1767

"Thrice Welcome First and Best of Days" appeared in Chanler's diary entry for October 6:

I looked out at window and saw it Rain when it seemed likely to prove a wet day, at which I a little regretted. However upon a short recollection of thought I became quite resigned and thereupon laid myself down again and breathed forth my soul unto God and wrestled with him for his gracious presence and obtained my suit I went forth and expounded with a degree of comfort and freedom the 92 Psalm and sang a sabbath morning Hymn of my own composing.

The diary does not mention the tunes to which Isaac Chanler sang his own hymns and those by Isaac Watts which he mentions.

ALL SAINTS, which is still in common use, appeared in the composer's *A Sett of New Psalms and Anthems* (1738). Our score comes from the American edition of *Royal Melody Compleat, or the New Harmony of Sion,* published by Daniel Bayley.

Countertenor in C clef, third line. Tune in tenor; transposed down one step. The triplets in bar 10 were notated in eighth notes in the original.

Through the Dark the Dreamers Came	DREAMERS Irregular
St. 1–3	
Earl B. Marlatt, writ. 1927, pub. 1928	Mabel W. Daniels, comp. 1927, pub. 1928

Earl Marlatt, an associate editor of *The American Student Hymnal* in which these verses appeared, stressed the importance of including contemporary poems in such a collection in his preface. This gentle and poetic treatment of the quest of the three Wise Men suggests a comparison with the more familiar and earlier treatment of the same theme, "We Three Kings of Orient Are," by John Henry Hopkins Jr. (q.v.). Marlatt's poem is macaronic in the sense that the English lines are followed by a Latin refrain.

The setting, admirably suited to the quality of Marlatt's poem, begins in minor but gravitates to the relative major to correspond with the Latin refrain.

Through Warmth and Light of Summer Skies (Summertide)	C.M.
St. 1–4	
Austin Faricy, writ. 1957	Harriett Johnson, comp. 1958

Samuel Longfellow's " 'Tis Winter Now," set by Lockrem Johnson, is a seasonal hymn, as is this poem by Austin Faricy, written for inclusion in *American Hymns* and called "Summertide." It has been set to music by Harriett Johnson, who has added a soprano descant as a fifth voice to be sung at the end of the fourth stanza and in the concluding "Amen." The composition is perhaps better suited for performance by the choir than the congregation. When used as a congregational hymn a solo soprano from the choir might sing the descant.

Through Willing Heart and Helping Hand	THEODORE L.M.
St. 1–5	
Frederick Lucian Hosmer, 1909	Peter C. Lutkin, 1905

This warm and human poem of dedication appeared in the *New Hymn and Tune Book* (1914) and *Hymns of the Spirit* (1937). It began as a housewarming hymn:

> And gathered here, a household band,
> We light tonight the household fire,

and ended with a plea for kindling a spiritual fire in the hearts of those gathered together. The poem was inspired by the dedication of the Parish House of the First Unitarian Church in Berkeley, Calif., in 1909.

In *The Methodist Hymnal* (1905) THEODORE was associated with Benjamin Copeland's "Our Fathers' God, to Thee We Raise." An editor of the *Hymnal* characterized the tune as "strenuous," a term often applied to President Theodore Roosevelt. The tune name finally chosen was THEODORE.

Thus Spake the Saviour   ALHALLOWS TUNE L.M.
St. 1–3, 5, 7
Jeremy Belknap, 1795   William Selby, 1762

The tendencies which were to lead to Unitarianism were already manifest in the closing years of the eighteenth century. One of the volumes which marked this transition was Jeremy Belknap's *Sacred Poetry,* from which "Thus Spake the Saviour" has been selected.

ALHALLOWS TUNE was published in England before William Selby came to Boston. However since Selby was organist in King's Chapel, the first church in New England to adopt Unitarian doctrine, it seems appropriate to associate his tune with this Belknap hymn.

Thy Loving Kindness, Lord, I   WINTHROP L.M.
   Sing
St. 1–5
George Barrell Cheever, writ.   Anon., 1849
   1845, pub. 1851

Of the nineteen original hymns included in George Barrell Cheever's *Christian Melodies,* "Thy Loving Kindness, Lord, I Sing" was most widely used. It appeared in *Hymns and Songs of Praise* (1874), edited by Roswell D. Hitchcock, Zachary Eddy, and Philip Schaff, shortened to four stanzas. It is strange that Cheever's zeal for social reform left little or no impress either on his own hymns or on his selection of poems by others.

WINTHROP is a simple but effective tune from *A Collection of Church Music* (New York, 1849), edited by George F. Root and Joseph Emerson Sweetser.

Thy Mercies, Lord, to   PSALM 36 8.8.8.8.8.
    Heaven Reach
Ps. 36: 5–10   Frost 58
William Kethe, 1561   Anon., arr. 1635

The Scottish psalter was produced by a committee working under the authority of the General Assembly of 1561. William Kethe, "a Scotch divine, no unready rhymer," was one of this group and the first authorized Scottish psalter appeared as a result of their labors in 1564. Twenty-five of Kethe's versions, including the present example, had, however, appeared earlier in the *Foure Score and Seven Psalmes of David* (Geneva, 1561). The melody was borrowed from the French Genevan psalter, where it was used for Psalm 132 from 1551 on. It was regularly used in the Scottish psalters (1564–1635) for Psalm 36, though it was also quite generally associated with its original text, Psalm 132.

The fine Phrygian melody loses something of its special character as set in the Scottish psalter of 1635, since at the final cadence the last tone of the melody is treated as fifth step, not as final, thus avoiding the characteristic Phrygian cadence.

Treble, C clef, first line; countertenor, C clef, third line; tenor, C clef, fourth line; bassus, F clef, fifth line. Key signature B$\sharp$, i.e., B$\natural$, which merely shows that we are not in a flat key; no time signature; melody in tenor; transposed up a minor third.

Thy Praise, O God, in Zion   STONEHAM L.M.
    Waits
Ps. 65, st. 1, 3, 4, 6, 7
Jacob Kimball, 1793   Jacob Kimball, 1793

Jacob Kimball's paraphrase of Psalm 65 appeared in his tune book *Rural Harmony* to a tune of his own composition called STONEHAM and was later printed as a "new version" in Jeremy Belknap's *Sacred Poetry* of 1795.

Countertenor in C clef, third line. Time signature.

The Time Is Swiftly Rolling   HICKS' FAREWELL C.M.
    On
St. 1, 3, 5, 6, 9, 10
Berryman Hicks, 1835   William Walker, 1835

This very personal hymn, written by Baptist evangelist Berryman Hicks and "sent to his wife while he was confined in Tennessee by a fever of which he afterwards recovered," is characteristic of the songs of parting and death so popular a century and a half ago. In the *Harp of Columbia* (1848), by W. H. and M. L. Swan, four stanzas of the text appear to another tune credited to W. Atchly. Cecil Sharp recorded five versions of the song in the Appalachian Mountains in 1916 and 1918 (*English Folksongs from the Southern Appalachians*, II, 142–43). George Pullen Jackson published a version with a similar text in his *White Spirituals in the Southern Uplands* (p. 202). William Walker claimed the tune in the *Southern Harmony* of 1835 and it is still in the edition of 1854, which is our source.

The Time Will Surely Come Concord 6.6.8.8.6.
St. 1–4
Robert T. Daniel, 1833   Oliver Holden, 1793

Although the text by Robert T. Daniel is somewhat later in date than Oliver Holden's tune, its confident optimism seems well suited to the strong and jubilant strains of Concord. "The Time Will Surely Come" appeared in 1833 in the fourth edition of William Dossey's *The Choice: In Two Parts. Part I, containing Psalms and Hymns. Part II, containing Spiritual Songs,* a collection usually referred to as *Dossey's Choice.*

In Holden's *Union Harmony* (1793) the text associated with Concord is Isaac Watts's "The hill of Zion yields a thousand sacred sweets." Here, as in Holden's more famous Coronation, the second section begins with a passage for two voices which are later joined by the other two so that the section closes in full four-part harmony.

Countertenor in C clef, third line; in bar 9, last quarter, the counter has been altered to G although it is clearly an F in the original. Time signature ℭ; transposed down one whole tone.

'Tis Midnight and on Olive's Olive's Brow L.M.
 Brow
St. 1–4
William B. Tappan, 1822 William Batchelder Brad-
          bury, 1853

This hymn, captioned "Gethsemane" by its author, appeared in his *Poems* (Philadelphia, 1822). As is often the case, scripture texts form the basis of several verses; in this instance Luke 22:39, Mark 14:32, and Matt. 26:36.

Bradbury's tune, inspired by Tappan's text, was published in *The*

Shawm (1953), jointly edited by Bradbury and George F. Root (q.v.). The tune, within the compass of a sixth, is a tender chant. The first chord of the last line was figured $\frac{4}{3}$ instead of $\frac{4}{2}$ in the original.

'Tis the Gift To Be Simple

Traditional   Aaron Copland, arr. 1950

The melody and text of this Shaker song come from Edward D. Andrews' study of the Shakers entitled *The Gift To Be Simple.* Since dancing played a part in Shaker religious exercises it is not surprising to find references to bodily movement in the text. Aaron Copland used this melody as the subject of a set of five variations in Part VII of his ballet score *Appalachian Spring* (first performed in 1944). Later he chose it as the fourth of his *Old American Songs* (Set I, first performed in 1950), which is reproduced here.

'Tis Winter Now   L.M.
St. 1–4
Samuel Longfellow, 1864   Lockrem Johnson, comp.
                                                   1955

This setting of the winter verses of the nineteenth-century Unitarian poet is one of a set of four hymns by Lockrem Johnson. The melody, largely Dorian, suggests a folk song in which the sopranos carry the melody alone in the first stanza; sopranos and altos sing the second in two parts; the third is in major for four-part chorus; and the last in modal harmonies with both altos and tenors singing the melody. Thus the effect remains strophic, although each stanza receives a different treatment.

Today Beneath Benignant   CENTENNIAL HYMN 8.8.8.D.
   Skies
St. 1–4
Denis Wortman, 1881   John Knowles Paine, 1876

Two of Denis Wortman's poems were intended for special occasions: "Today Beneath Benignant Skies" for the laying of the cornerstone of a church, "God of the Prophets!" (q.v.) for the centenary of the New Brunswick Theological Seminary. Written in 1881, it was associated in Edwin A. Bedell's *The Church Hymnary* (1894) with the

CENTENNIAL HYMN of John K. Paine and the coupling has been retained here. Paine's tune, composed for the Philadelphia Centennial of 1876, was originally set to a text by Whittier.

To God Our Strength Shout Joyfully	FRENCH TUNE: PSALM 100 L.M.
Ps. 81, 1–6, first part of 7	Frost 322; Zahn 367
Henry Ainsworth, 1612	Claude Le Jeune, arr. 1601

Psalm 81 begins as an exhortation to praise God joyfully with psalms and musical instruments. In this it resembles Psalm 150. Later verses, omitted here, lament the disobedience of Israel to the commands of the Lord. The word "heast" means command; the King James version renders it as "statute."

The fine Phrygian tune for Psalm 100 was first introduced in the Genevan psalter of 1551, where it was also used for Psalm 131. Orentin Douen (in *Clément Marot et le psautier Huguenot*) considered it one of the best melodies in the Genevan repertoire. In 1598 it was adopted by the Lutherans. Omitted in the Old Version of Sternhold and Hopkins, it reappeared in John Playford's *Psalms & Hymns in Solemn Musick of four parts* (1671) as a melody for "Veni Creator." The Le Jeune setting of Psalm 100 has the melody in the tenor. We have preferred the version which he gives for Psalm 131, which places the same tune in the soprano.

Cantus, C clef, first line; altus, C clef, third line; tenor, C clef, fourth line; bassus, F clef, fourth line. Time signature ₵; note values halved. The original tune was diatonic throughout. In the Le Jeune setting the G is sharped in the cadence of the first line. The characteristic Phrygian cadence at the end should be noted.

To Show How Humble	MEAR C.M.
St. 1–4	
Anon., 1877	Anon., 1720

The rite of foot washing, recalling that Christ had washed the feet of the disciples (John 13:5), survived in the Eastern Church and in some Protestant denominations as an act symbolic of Christian humility. This hymn, one of three on this subject in the Mennonite hymnal of 1877, is also of interest because it was written in English, not German.

Tunes are indicated at the head of each hymn. The adoption of hymns in English brought a very general use of English and Ameri-

can tunes. Although MEAR was an English tune, it was familiar in
early New England and first appeared in Simon Browne's *Hymns and
Spiritual Songs* (London, 1720), where it is called MIDDLESEX. It later
appeared in Daniel Bayley's *Psalm Singer's Assistant* (1765) and in
Andrew Law's *A Select Number of Plain-Tunes* (1767 and after).

To Thee, Eternal Soul, Be Praise	GILDER L.M.
St. 1–5	
Richard W. Gilder, writ. 1903, pub. 1905	Arne Oldberg, 1905

"To Thee, Eternal Soul, Be Praise" was written for Wesleyan University's celebration of the two-hundredth anniversary of the birth of
John Wesley (q.v.). It appeared in *The Methodist Hymnal* of 1905 with
tunes by two Americans, Karl Harrington's WORSHIP and Arne Oldberg's GILDER, which is reproduced here. Oldberg's tune is written
in a style which has a certain affinity with that of the Lutheran
chorale.

To Thee, O God	BRIDGEWATER L.M.
St. 1–6	
Abiel Holmes, 1796	Lewis Edson, 1782

"To Thee, O God," with the title "My Times Are in Thy Hand," is
a free paraphrase of Psalm 31 which first appeared in 1796 in the
Family Tablet. The poem was signed "Myron," a pseudonym for the
Rev. Abiel Holmes, father of Oliver Wendell Holmes. Although the
hymns of Abiel Holmes have been forgotten, "My Times Are in Thy
Hand" reveals him as a fluent and literate writer of verse conceived
in a somewhat formal eighteenth-century style.

BRIDGEWATER was one of the most popular fuguing tunes of the
early nineteenth century. Published in 1782 in Edson's *The Choirmaster's Companion,* it was among the compositions included in Father
Robert Kemp's *Old Folks Concert Tunes* (before 1860). It was still familiar in the 1870s and was sung at retrospective concerts given by
Father Kemp and others.

The imitative passage in the second part of BRIDGEWATER is of the
most elementary description since the tones of the subject are merely
notes of the tonic chord.

Time signature ₵ . Bar 6 involves rude passing dissonances and
near-consecutive fifths. The passage has been allowed to stand,

partly because the reading was retained in later books such as *The Easy Instructor* by William Little and William Smith, but chiefly because the movement of the offending parts is good if we are willing to accept the dissonance incidental to their progress.

To Thee, O God, the Shepherd Kings	Woodstock C.M.

St. 1–6
John G. C. Brainard, 1845   Deodatus Dutton Jr., 1829

Headed "an agricultural hymn," this poem of the seasons appeared in *Psalms and Hymns for Christian Use and Worship* (1845). The picture of the farmer reading the Scriptures before his peaceful hearth has the flavor of a period when America was more rural than at present. Here, as so often, Watts has furnished a model. His lines

> His hoary frost, his fleecy snow
> Descend and clothe the ground;
> The liquid streams forbear to flow
> In icy fetters bound.

were particularly popular in the early nineteenth century when sung to the favorite tune called Winter.

Dutton is best remembered for Woodstock. Frank J. Metcalf (*American Writers and Compilers of Sacred Music*) suggests that it was named for the Connecticut town. First published in *American Psalmody*, edited by Elam Ives Jr., and Dutton, to an American text, "I Love to Steal Awhile Away" (q.v.) by Phoebe Hinsdale Brown, Woodstock was reprinted in *The Boston Academy's Collection* (1835), edited by Lowell Mason. It has been frequently republished and is still sung in the twentieth century.

To Thee, Then, Let All Beings Bend	Eroica L.M.

Ps. 145: selected lines
Nathaniel Evans, 1772   Benjamin Carr, 1820

"To Thee, Then, Let All Beings Bend" is a portion of a metrical paraphrase of Psalm 145 which appeared in the author's *Poems on Several Occasions* in 1772.

Benjamin Carr's Eroica, originally set to the last three verses of the Tate and Brady version of Psalm 103, is appropriately jubilant in style. It was first published in *The Chorister: A Collection of Chants &*

Melodies Adapted to the Psalms and Hymns of the Episcopal Church (Philadelphia, 1820). Carr provides a prelude and postlude in brilliant instrumental style. The indications *tromba* and *tutti* suggest the use of the trumpet stop and the full organ.

Transposed down a minor third.

To Thee the Tuneful Anthem Soars (New England Hymn) St. 1–3 Mather Byles, 1770	AMERICA 8.8.8.D. William Billings, 1770

AMERICA is the first tune in William Billings' first book, *The New England Psalm Singer*. The "New England Hymn" of Mather Byles was printed on the opposite page, "adapted to America Tune." It was thus distinguished both by its position and by the fact that the text was also given with the music. Indeed, at the bottom of page 1 Billings remarks, "No doubt the reader will excuse my not adapting words to all the tunes as it is attended with great inconvenience," a sentiment with which all editors of hymnbooks will agree.

The poem, in perhaps somewhat overenthusiastic eighteenth-century style, is well matched by the pompous and sonorous measures of Billings' tune. The note E, soprano, bar 3, last beat, is not sharped in the original.

To Thine Eternal Arms, O God St. 1–4 Thomas Wentworth Higginson, 1846	HAMBURG L.M. Lowell Mason, arr. 1825

"To Thine Eternal Arms, O God," like the author's "The Past Is Dark with Sin and Shame" (q.v.), was first published in *A Book of Hymns* (1846), edited by Samuel Longfellow and Samuel Johnson. Both hymns reappeared in the Unitarian *Hymn and Tune Book* of 1877 and in the *New Hymn and Tune Book* of 1914.

Lowell Mason was often at his best in his arrangements. HAMBURG was a free arrangement of a Gregorian melody taken from the Benedictus of Novello's Evening Service—not a very authentic source. Nevertheless, the result is a tune which is simple, dignified, and still widely sung. HAMBURG appeared in the fifth edition of the *Boston Handel and Haydn Society Collection* (1825).

Touch Thou Mine Eyes   LANHERNE 11.10.11.10.
St. 1–3
Marion Franklin Ham, writ.   Henry Hayman, 1904
   1911, pub. 1914

Written when the author believed that he might become blind, this expression of personal crisis transcends the immediate circumstances and broadens into an appeal for spiritual vision. Dated 1911, it was one of four hymns included in the Unitarian *New Hymn and Tune Book* of 1914.

   Henry Hayman contributed LANHERNE to the *Pilgrim Hymnal* of 1904, where it was set to another American text, Whittier's "O Brother Man, Fold to thy Heart thy Brother."

Trembling Before Thine   CONFIDENCE L.M.
  Awful Throne
St. 1–3, 7
Augustus L. Hillhouse, 1822   Samuel Holyoke, 1804

The terror of the sinner before the judgment of God was a characteristic theme of early American hymnody, though in this example the severity of the opening is tempered by the later passages telling of pardon granted and heavenly joys won. The extravagant rhetoric recalls the enthusiasms of the earlier Mather Byles. The couplet from stanza 5 describing the angels who "throned in floods of beamy day, symphonious in his presence play" is characteristic. The poem was written in Paris (after 1815), and was published in the *Christian Spectator* (New Haven, Conn., 1822). Its first appearance in a hymnbook may have been in Asahel Nettleton's *Village Hymns* in 1824.

   CONFIDENCE is a double tune which is further extended by repeating the second couplet of the second stanza. It appeared both in Holyoke's *Columbian Repository* (1802) and in his *Christian Harmonist* of 1804. The original time signature was ♩.

True Son of God, Eternal   L.M.
  Light
St. 1, 2, 4, 5
P. J. Cormican, 1920   Cyr de Brant, 1953

This tune by Cyr de Brant (J. Vincent Higginson) appeared in the *Pius X Hymnal* (1953) as a setting for the Latin hymn "Verbum supernum prodiens" by St. Thomas Aquinas. The composer suggested

"True Son of God, Eternal Light" by Father Cormican as a suitable American text. It first appeared in the *Catholic Hymnal* (1920), compiled by the Rev. John G. Hacker, S.J.

Trust in Me

Anon., 1876   Anon., 1876

Like "More Love" this Shaker hymn comes from Canterbury, N.H. It appeared in the *Selection of Devotional Melodies* published in "Shaker Village" in 1876. The text might be described as almost verse. It is unrhymed except for the opening couplet in the second part, and each part closes with a kind of refrain line "As you journey onward" and "While you journey heavenward." The melody is pentatonic, lacking the fourth and seventh steps.

Turn, Turn, Unhappy Souls,   CYRENE, C.M.
    Return
Henry Alline, 1791   Samuel Holyoke, 1791

Samuel Holyoke set these words by Henry Alline to CYRENE in *Harmonia Americana.* This setting is in four parts with the melody in the tenor. The note values in our version have been halved and the time signature correspondingly altered from $\frac{3}{2}$ to $\frac{3}{4}$. An interesting characteristic of this tune is the alternation of four-bar and three-bar phrases which correspond with the lines of eight syllables alternating with those of six.

The C clef, third line, is used for the countertenor part. In bar 3 the soprano and bass made parallel octaves. The bass has been altered from B♭ A to B♭ G A to avoid them.

The Twilight Shadows Round   CECILE C.M.D.
    Me Fall
St. 1–3
Ernest Edwin Ryden, 1925   Peter Johnson, 1925

This reflective hymn dealing with the problems and aspirations of old age was first published in the Augustana Lutheran hymnal of 1925, then in the *American Lutheran Hymnal* (1930), and in the *Service Book and Hymnal* (1958). It was the tune which inspired the text in this instance. After listening to Peter Johnson play the newly composed tune, Dr. Ryden remarked that it sounded like an evening hymn. "The Twilight Shadows Round Me Fall" was written as a suitable text. The tune was named for Dr. Ryden's first child, his daughter Cecile.

Unto Jehovah Sing Will I	FRENCH TUNE: PSALM 24
	8.8.8.D.
Exod. 15: 1–5, 10–13	Frost 326; Zahn 2665
Henry Ainsworth, 1617	Claude Le Jeune, arr. 1601

Henry Ainsworth's *Annotations upon the Second Book of Moses, Called Exodus* was issued at Amsterdam in 1617. The work is primarily a prose glossary, but Ainsworth included a metrical paraphrase of Exodus 15 and printed the Geneva tune to Psalm 24 to go with it. He had used the same tune for Psalm 61 in his *Booke of Psalms* (1612). It had first appeared in the "Pseudo-Roman" psalter of 1542. The definitive form of the melody appeared seven years later in *Pseaulmes cinquante de Dauid, mis en vers françois par Clément Marot.* Ainsworth omits a note of the Geneva tune in line 3 and again in line 6, as will be evident by comparing the tenor of the Le Jeune score with the Ainsworth melody, also shown.

Cantus, C clef, first line; altus, C clef, second line; tenor, C clef, third line; bassus, F clef, third line. Time signature ₵; note values reduced by half; transposed down a minor third. Altus, line 2, fourth note, was D, making octaves with bass. Sharp lacking in cantus, line 3, note before the last.

Unto Our God Most High We Sing	PLYMOUTH L.M.
St. 1–3	
John Vance Cheney, 1879	Simeon Pease Cheney, 1879

Simeon Pease Cheney published *The American Singing Book* (Boston, 1879) containing much music performed in Cheney family concerts as well as some of the famous older tunes of New England accompanied by biographical sketches of the composers.

PLYMOUTH, by Simeon Pease Cheney, set to a poem by his son John Vance Cheney, is printed here as it appeared in *The American Singing Book.*

The Voice of God Is Calling   MISSION 7.6.7.6.D.
St. 1–4
John Haynes Holmes, writ.   Horatio Parker, 1894
    1913, pub. 1914

Although the Unitarians were not alone in their zeal for social reform they were distinguished by it. Certain of the hymns of John Haynes Holmes develop this characteristic theme in terms of the twentieth century. "The Voice of God is Calling" is based on a verse from Isaiah 6:8, "Also I heard the voice of the Lord, saying, Whom shall I send, and who will go for us? Then I said, Here am I; send me." It interprets the biblical words as a call for leaders to work for the miners, the people of urban slums, "to loosen the bonds of shame and greed." This hymn has had extensive use. It appeared in *The New Hymn and Tune Book* (1914), *Hymns of the Spirit* (1937), and *Hymns for the Celebration of Life* (1964). Holmes wrote it for the Young People's Religious Union of Boston in 1913.

MISSION, a processional hymn, was contributed to J. Ireland Tucker's *Hymnal* of 1894.

Waked by the Gospel's   GANGES 8.8.6.8.8.6.
    Powerful Sound
St. 1, 3, 6–8
Samson Occom, 1801   S. Chandler, 1798

This hymn is usually attributed to Occom, a Mohegan Indian and a Presbyterian minister. The earlier form, given here, appeared in Josiah Goddard's *Collection* (Walpole, N.H., 1801). The altered form "Awaked by Sinai's Awful Sound" was more widely used. F. M. Bird, writing in Julian's *Dictionary of Hymnology,* does not think that Occom wrote the altered form; he traces it to the *Connecticut Evangelical Magazine* of July 1802. Occom's *Choice Collection of Hymns and Spiritual Songs* (1774) does not contain this hymn. It is commonly sung to the tune GANGES, which first appeared in *The American Musical Miscellany* as a setting for a poem, "The Indian Philosopher." The tune name came from the lines "On fancy's airy horse I rode . . . 'till on the banks of Ganges' flood . . . I stood." Asahel Nettleton chose GANGES as the tune for Occom's hymn in his *Village Hymns* (1824), and the music is included in his *Zion's Harp* (1824), which has tunes for the special meters in *Village Hymns.* The original song was for melody and bass, but it is arranged in four parts in *The Columbian Sacred Harmonist* (1808) by Oliver Shaw, Amos Albee, and Herman Mann, the version printed here. Countertenor, C clef, third line.

Time signature ₵; tune in tenor. In bar 4, and in the parallel passage in bar 12, the second note in the countertenor was E.

Wake, Isles of the South	ISLES OF THE SOUTH
	11.11.11.11.11.
St. 1–4	
William B. Tappan, 1822	William Hauser, 1848

William Tappan's hymn is an expression of the desire to convert remote peoples to the Christian faith that was so strong in the early nineteenth century. It was sung on a New Haven wharf as a group of missionaries were about to sail to the Sandwich Isles. The poem was published in the same year in Tappan's *Lyrics*. It was taken up by the Southern shape-note singers and was set there to a folk or folk-line tune claimed by the Georgian William Hauser in his *Hesperian Harp* (1848). It was included in the 1854 edition of William Walker's *Southern Harmony* and George Pullen Jackson noted that it was also in Walker's *Christian Harmony* of 1866. The character of the melody suggests that it may have been sung long before it was published.

Tune in tenor.

Wake the Song of Jubilee	AMBOY 7.7.7.7.D.
St. 1–3	
Leonard Bacon, 1823	Lowell Mason, 1845

Bacon published three of his own hymns, including "Wake the Song of Jubilee," in his *Hymns and Sacred Songs for the Monthly Concert*. He used the word *concert* not in its usual musical meaning but in the sense of a meeting in which those in attendance joined in prayers and hymns, in this instance for the success of missions. The hymn is thus a missionary hymn envisioning a day in which "the whole creation sings, 'Jesus is the King of Kings.'" From the Andover pamphlet this text passed in an altered form to an English publication, Josiah Pratt's *Three hundred and fifty portions of the Book of Psalms . . .* (London, 1829), and thence to the *Church Psalmody* of David Greene and Lowell Mason (1831). Bacon retouched the altered version of his early hymn and included it in the Appendix, which he prepared for Timothy Dwight's (q.v.) revised edition of Isaac Watts's *Psalms* (1833). Since that version embodied changes approved or made by the author it has been adopted here.

Lowell Mason repeatedly used his AMBOY for Bacon's text. It is reproduced here from *The Psaltery* (Boston, 1845), edited by Mason and George J. Webb. In the early New England tunes the tenor usually sang the melody. In Mason's time as now the soprano normally had the leading part. Nevertheless Mason's suggestion, "treble and tenor may be inverted," shows that he arranged the tune with both possibilities in mind. Original time signature 3. The return of the first section was indicated by D.C. in *The Psaltery*, but it is written out in full here.

Watchman, Tell Me	BUCHANAN 8.7.8.7.D.
St. 1–3, 6	
Anon., 1863	Version of 1866

This hymn is a dialogue between the Watchman and the Pilgrim, the Watchman asking a question in the first half of the double stanza, the Pilgrim answering in the second half. This dramatic form is more effective when men and women sit on opposite sides of the central aisle of a church and can sing antiphonally. The text, like those of many Adventist hymns, points to signs and portents that "the kingdom's very near."

The tune is a "Western Melody," a folk type sung at camp meetings and revivals in the South and West. Under the name OLNEY it appeared as early as 1820 in Allen D. Carden's *Missouri Harmony*. It is called BUCHANAN in the *Jubilee Harp* of 1866. Although all the notes of the scale are present in the melody, the fourth and seventh steps appear only as short unaccented tones. The text, with a different tune, appeared in 1863 in William Batchelder Bradbury's *Keynote*.

Wayfarers in the Wilderness	SHINING SHORE 8.7.8.7., with chorus
St. 1–4	
Alexander R. Thompson, 1869	George F. Root, 1856

It seems likely that this text was written to Root's folklike tune. Thompson's verses appear in the Reformed Dutch *Hymns of the Church with Tunes* as an alternate text together with "My Days Are Gliding Swiftly By" (q.v.), by David Nelson, the poem originally associated with Root's tune.

The structure of the melody provides for the four lines of the stanza in the first section. Two lines of the chorus are sung to new music while the remaining two are sung to the last four bars of the tune. Root credits this tune to the *Sabbath Hymn and Tune Book*.

We Are on Our Journey Home St. 1–5 Anon., version of Charles Beecher, 1855	MT. BLANC Irregular Anon., version of Charles Beecher, 1855

The congregational singing at Henry Ward Beecher's Plymouth Church in Brooklyn was famous in his day, and the *Plymouth Collection,* which he edited, is noteworthy as an early congregational hymnal which brought words and music together on the same page or on opposite pages in the way now usual. Henry Ward Beecher's brother Charles was, as the preface indicates, chiefly responsible for "the adaptation of words and the arrangements and harmonies of the music." He adapted the hymn "We Are on Our Journey Home" to a tune that was earlier associated with the text "There Are Angels Hovering Round." It will be found with the earlier text in the *American Vocalist* (1849), edited by the Reverend D. H. Mansfield.

We Are Watching, We Are Waiting St. 1–4 William O. Cushing, 1868	THE BEAUTEOUS DAY 8.7.8.7., with chorus George F. Root, 1868

This hymn is reproduced here as it appears in Root's *The Triumph* (1868). It had appeared earlier in *Chapel Gems.* The theme of the second coming of Christ was a favorite among folk hymnists around 1840. Such hymns as OLD CHURCHYARD ("You Will See Your Lord A-Coming") (q.v.) illustrate the earlier type. The present example takes the form of the hymn with chorus, a type made familiar by the *Gospel Hymns* of Dwight L. Moody and Ira D. Sankey. Root's music seems fresher and closer to the folk spirit than most of his compositions. Rhythmically it is distinguished by a free use of the "Scotch snap," in which a short accented note is followed by a longer and usually dotted longer note. Here the pattern is an eighth note followed by a dotted quarter.

We Bring No Glittering Treasures St. 1–3 Harriett C. Phillips, writ. c. 1848, pub. 1849	MIRIAM 7.6.7.6.D. Joseph P. Holbrook, 1865

This song of praise for children appeared in the Methodist hymnal of 1849 and was reprinted in its successor of 1878. In the latter it was set to MIRIAM, and this association has been retained here. The habit of returning to earlier phrases was characteristic of the simpler tunes of the period. Here the pattern of the music is A B C B. MIRIAM appeared in *Songs of the Sanctuary* (1865) and was later reprinted in two different meters ($\frac{6}{4}$ and $\frac{4}{4}$) in Holbrook's *Quartet and Chorus Choir* (1870).

Weeping Sinner, Dry Your	KESWICK 7.7.7.7.
Tears	
St. 1, 3, 7, 8	
Oliver Holden, 1806	Samuel Holyoke, 1804

The eight stanzas trace the life of Christ and show Him as the salvation of the "weeping sinner." It may have appeared in the *Young Converts Companion* (Boston, 1806).

The tune is from the *Christian Harmonist,* a book edited by Holyoke for Baptist congregations in 1804. Written for three voices in the simplest style, its mood of mild melancholy suits the text well. The seven-syllable lines fall naturally into the pattern of the normal four-bar musical phrase—two syllables each to three bars and one to the fourth and final bar.

Original time signature 𝄵 .

Welcome, Sweet Rest	PSALM 124 10.10.10.10.
St. 1–3	Frost 140
Michael Wigglesworth, 1662	Edward Millar, 1635

"Welcome, Sweet Rest," which is headed "Death Expected and Welcomed," appears at the end of Michael Wigglesworth's *Day of Doom.* The lyric character of the verse invites a musical setting.

Edward Millar's music appeared in the great Scottish polyphonic psalter of 1635. The countertenor has been notated an octave too high. With the countertenor in its real register the scoring suggests three male voices with the boy sopranos high above them. However, the parts have the usual names: Treble, G clef, second line; countertenor, C clef, fourth line; tenor, C clef, fourth line; bassus, F clef, fifth line. The rude dissonances in the cadence of line 2 and the parallel fifths (tenor and bass) at the close of line 3 are in the original.

Welcome, Ye Hopeful Heirs   ELM STREET 8.8.8.8.8.
   of Heaven
St. 1–4
Phoebe Hinsdale Brown,   A. Eastman, 1835
   1824

This hymn, headed "Welcome to Young Converts," was first published in Asahel Nettleton's *Village Hymns,* where it was to be sung to
BLENDON, BATH ("Lord, I Am Thine") (q.v.), or PORTUGAL.
   ELM STREET, which was included in Henry E. Moore's *New Hampshire Collection* (2d ed., 1835), has been set to "Welcome, Ye Hopeful
Heirs of Heaven," in this volume as a tune of New England origin of
nearly the same period. The form of the tune, which contains five
phrases, requires the repetition of the last line of each stanza.

We Love the Venerable   HERMON C.M.
   House
St. 1–6
Ralph Waldo Emerson, 1833   Lowell Mason, 1839

"We Love the Venerable House" has a special interest since it
marks a moment of decision in Emerson's life. In 1832 he relinquished his position as minister of the Second Unitarian Church of
Boston, thus turning decisively toward his future career as writer
and lecturer. Written in 1833, it was intended for the ordination of
his successor, Rev. Chandler Robbins, who published it in his *Hymns
for Christian Worship* (1854). Samuel Johnson and Samuel Longfellow
later included it in *Hymns of the Spirit* (1864).
   From the point of view of the singer Emerson has created a difficulty in placing the third syllable of the word "venerable" in a position which is normally stressed. By choosing a tune in $\frac{3}{2}$, HERMON by
Lowell Mason, we have tried to lessen this difficulty, since the offending syllable now appears on an unaccented beat. HERMON first
appeared in Lowell Mason's periodical publication, *The Seraph*
(June 1839).

We Praise Thee, God, for   PIXHAM L.M.
   Harvests Earned
St. 1–5
John Coleman Adams, writ.   Horatio Parker, comp. 1901,
   1911, pub. 1914   pub. 1903

This hymn, giving thanks for future fields of action rather than
for present blessings, was written by a Universalist clergyman, John

Coleman Adams, in 1911. It was given a place in the Unitarian *New Hymn and Tune Book* of 1914, but the tune provided there was the well-known processional hymn CAMDEN, by the English composer John Baptiste Calkin.

We have set Adams' text to a dignified tune by Horatio Parker which, though conventional in conception, displays the sure musical instinct and mastery of his medium which characterized that composer. It appeared in *The Hymnal* (1903), which Parker edited. Although Parker was associated with the Episcopal Church, his tunes found their way into the hymnals of other Protestant denominations. Note that PIXHAM has also been used for "O Thou Whose Gracious Presence Shone."

We Praise Thee, If One Rescued Soul St. 1–4 Lydia H. Sigourney, 1846	MEINECKE L.M. Anon., 1848

Headed "For a Temperance Anniversary," this hymn was included under "Philanthropic Subjects" in the Universalist *Hymns for Christian Devotion* (1846) of John G. Adams and Edwin H. Chapin. It is coupled here with a tune called MEINECKE, perhaps named for or composed by Christopher Meinecke, a musician of German birth who settled in Baltimore, where he was organist of St. Paul's Protestant Episcopal Church. The Rev. Charles L. Atkins has traced this tune to S. Jackson's *Sacred Harmony* of 1848 and *A Tune-Book Proposed for the Use of Congregations of the Protestant Episcopal Church* (New York, 1858).

We Read of a People St. 1–3, 5, 6 Anon., 1852	GOSPEL LIBERTY 11.8.11.8.D. Anon., 1852

This versified plea for tolerance is selected from *A Sacred Repository of Anthems and Hymns* . . . (Canterbury, N.H., 1852). It was written in a simplified notation in which the tones of the scale were represented by letters. In spite of the fact that this is a song of persecution, the melody is sprightly, suggesting a derivation from the country dance. This characteristic is less astonishing with the Shakers than with other sects, since a special form of dancing was a part of their religious exercises. Though it was published as an unaccompanied melody, it is provided here with accompanying parts that may be played or sung.

Were You There
St. 1–3
Traditional   Winfred Douglas, arr. 1940

The Hymnal 1940 appears to be the earliest hymnal of a major denomination to include spirituals for congregational singing, although there is a group of spirituals in H. Augustine Smith's *The American Student Hymnal* of 1928. "Were You There When They Crucified My Lord" was arranged by Winfred Douglas from the version in William E. Barton's *Old Plantation Hymns* (1899). This simple account of Christ's crucifixion and resurrection has since been published in other hymnals including the Presbyterian *Hymnbook* (1955), the *Service Book and Hymnal* of the Lutheran Church (1958), and the Congregational *Pilgrim Hymnal* (1958).

We Shall Overcome   10.7.9.7.
Selected lines
Anon., sung before 1947

Under leaders like Martin Luther King "We Shall Overcome" has become the symbol of the movement of black people against lack of equal opportunity, against segregation, and against discrimination. The movement owed something to Mohandas Gandhi in its emphasis on nonviolence, and it operated through sit-ins, boycotts, and freedom marches. It developed its own literature of songs, some of them spirituals sung with a new emphasis some, like "We Shall Overcome," with folk roots reshaped to meet the needs of the movement.

We Thank Thee, Lord   FIELD 10.10.10.10.
St. 1–4
Calvin W. Laufer, writ. 1919,   Calvin W. Laufer, writ. 1919,
  pub. 1921   pub. 1921

This hymn of gratitude for the opportunities of Christian service grew out of one of many luncheon discussions between Laufer, then a field secretary of the Board of Publication and Sunday School Work of the Presbyterian Church, and Herbert H. Field, at that time minister of the Flatbush Presbyterian Church of Brooklyn.

The tune composed by Laufer to fit his own words was named FIELD, in honor of his friend and luncheon companion. It is a tune possessed of the virtues of simplicity and melodious appeal, though the harmonic treatment suggests the amateur. It is reproduced here in the form given it by the composer.

We Three Kings of Orient
  Are
St. 1–5
John Henry Hopkins Jr.,
  writ. 1857, pub. 1863

KINGS OF ORIENT 8.8.8.6.,
  with chorus

John Henry Hopkins Jr.,
  writ. 1857, pub. 1863

This folklike Christmas carol was published in the author's *Carols, Hymns and Songs.* Julian dates the first edition as 1862, but a note in the copy at the Union Theological Seminary states that the volume "as such appeared in December 1863, though all, or nearly all, of the pieces in it appeared separately before, during the six or seven years previous." It has taken its place with such favorite American carols as "O Little Town of Bethlehem" and "It Came Upon the Midnight Clear."

We Will Not Fear
David Diamond, 1955

David Diamond, 1955

The text of this short choral composition is in prose, although the refrainlike repetitious "We will not fear" and (at the end) "Fearful though they be" help in emphasizing the close of the two sections into which this brief work is divided. These few bars succeed in conveying a sense of grandeur. The bold unisons alternate with dissonant responses patterned as superposed fourths in bar 16 and superposed fifths in the last four bars.

We Would See Jesus
St. 1–4
Anna B. Warner, 1852

KERMODE 11.10.11.10.

Luther O. Emerson, 1872

Anna B. Warner liked to include hymns in her novels. Thus the child's hymn "Jesus Loves Me, This I Know" (q.v.) appeared in her *Say and Seal* in 1859. Her best-known hymn, "We Would See Jesus," was written in a mood of pathetic longing which had a particular appeal for readers of her day. It must have been written before February 1, 1851, since an entry in the diary of her sister, Susan Warner, mentions it. It was published in Anna Warner's novel *Dollars and Cents* in 1852. In 1858 she included "We Would See Jesus" in her *Hymns of the Church Militant.*

KERMODE appeared in 1872 in the *Standard,* edited jointly by Emerson and H. R. Palmer. Marked "E" to indicate that it was by Emerson, it was set to an American text, "Come unto Me, When Shadows Darkly Gather," by Catherine H. Watterman (q.v.).

What Glorious Vision	Song 12 10.10.10.10.
St. 1, 2, 7, 10, 11	Frost 347
Thomas Cradock (?), writ. c.	Anon., 1621
1759	

"The Prospect" is the sixth poem from a manuscript entitled "Crurulia, Part the 2d," formerly in the possession of the Cradock family, but now in the collection of the Maryland Historical Society. These poems may have been written by Thomas Cradock, though positive proof is lacking. The account in Sprague, *Annals of the American Pulpit,* speaks of "hymns on various subjects and for different occasions" which "show not only his evangelical views but the cheerful and lively tone of his poetry." This description fits the enthusiastic character of "The Prospect." The poems are undated and the manuscript has numerous corrections in a second hand. In the first poem, "The Check," stanza 7 dwells on the lot of the colonies which "Cou'd late a Wolfe, can yet an Amherst boast." Wolfe died in 1759, Amherst was appointed Governor of Virginia in 1763. If Cradock wrote these lines they may be dated between 1759 and 1770, when Cradock himself died.

The anonymous tune was originally printed in George Wither's *Songs of the Old Testament.*

Tune in C clef, third line; transposed down a perfect fifth; inner parts have been added.

What Happiness Can Equal	L.M.D.
Mine	
St. 1–4	
John David, 1840	John David, 1840

This Catholic hymn for solo soprano with organ accompaniment is entitled "Aspirations after Communion." It first appeared in Richard Garbett's *The Morning and Evening Services of the Catholic Church . . . for the use of the Diocese of Boston.* The composer's name does not appear above his hymn, but in the index it is given as "Bishop David."

What If the Saint Must Die	Sudbury S.M.D.
(A Poem on the Resurrection)	
St. 1, 2, 8, 9, 14, 15	
John Peck, 1773	William Billings, 1770

This hymn, like "Here Is a Song," comes from Peck's long poem, "A Description of the Last Judgment." The setting by Billings appeared in the *New England Psalm Singer*. Though the text deals with death and resurrection, the mood of the music is confident and joyful and the melody has more than a suggestion of a country dance. Countertenor, C clef, third line.

What Ship Is This?	OLD SHIP OF ZION Irregular, with chorus
St. 1–4	
Samuel Hauser (?), c.1800	Thomas W. Carter, arr. 1844

The ship which will "safely land us on Canaan's bright shore" takes its place with the "sweet chariot" and the "gospel train" in folk hymnody. The text has been so widely sung that it exists with at least two different tunes and with numerous textual variants, both white and Negro. The form chosen here is what William Hauser (q.v.) called the "Georgia Version" (*Olive Leaf*, 1878). He adds that the text was "written perhaps sixty or seventy years ago by the Rev. Samuel Hauser, this editor's paternal uncle," which would place the origin of the text in the first years of the nineteenth century.

The tune is in a major scale which lacks the seventh step. It appeared in the *Sacred Harp* (1844 ed.) in an arrangement for three voices, attributed to Thomas W. Carter. Tune in tenor; transposed down a whole step.

What Wondrous Love Is This	WONDROUS LOVE 12.9.12.12.9.
St. 1–3, 5, 7	
Anon., early 19th cent.	Anon., 1854

This beautiful melody has been preserved in many Southern tune books and has been recorded from folk singers in the Southern Appalachians. Tune and text conform to the distinctive Captain Kidd meter, which had previously served to preserve in verse the dying words of that worthy. See also "Our Bondage It Shall End" and "Remember, Sinful Youth." The poem appears in Jesse Mercer, *The Cluster of Spiritual Songs, Divine Hymns and Sacred Poems* (5th ed., after 1835), but manuscript notes by F. M. Bird trace it back to an earlier collection (Silas M. Noel, 1814). William Hauser, who was careful to record what information he had, attributed the text to "Rev. Alex Means, A.M., M.D., D.D., L.L.D." in his *Olive Leaf* (1878).

The melody is based on six tones rather than on the complete scale, since the third step is omitted. Annabel Morris Buchanan, who has made an effective arrangement of a version learned from her father and grandfather in her *Folk Hymns of America,* points out that traditional forms are generally Dorian, printed versions usually Aeolian. George Pullen Jackson confirms this tendency by noting that he has "heard the country folk sing this tune with the Dorian raised sixth." The setting included here is from William Walker's *Southern Harmony* (1854), where it is attributed to "Christopher." Singers who wish to test the effect of the Dorian scale may sharp the C's in the melody.

Original time signature ℭ ; tune in tenor. In bar 18 the second bass note is G. We have preferred F♯ as in the parallel passage in bar 6. This reading also appears in the setting in William Hauser's *Hesperian Harp* (Philadelphia, 1848), p. 234.

What Wondrous Love Is This　　12.9.12.12.9.
St. 1–4
Traditional　　　　　　　　Annabel Morris Buchanan,
　　　　　　　　　　　　　　arr., cop. 1934

This well-known folk hymn, like "Where Are Now the Hebrew Children?" is presented here in two versions—the earlier from William Walker's *Southern Harmony,* the later from *Twelve Folk Hymns,* edited by John Powell—to facilitate a comparison between the two harmonizations, each typical of its own period.

When God Descends with　　CORINTH 8.8.8.8.8.
　 Men to Dwell
St. 1–5
Hosea Ballou I, 1808　　　　Amos Blanchard, 1803

The Universalist *Hymns Composed by Different Authors* (1808) contained 199 of Ballou's poems, including "When God Descends with Men to Dwell." It was repeated in other collections, including the Universalist *Church Harmonies New and Old* of 1895.

CORINTH belongs to the same period as Ballou's text. First published in *Village Harmony,* it persisted in such retrospective collections as *Continental Harmony* (1857), *Ancient Harmony Revived* (1840), and the *Stoughton Collection* (1828). A different tune with the same name is set to "Hail, Tranquil Hour of Closing Day" (q.v.).

Transposed down a whole step. The suggested B♮s in bars 7 and 16 are not in the *Village Harmony.* However, such later collections as *Ancient Harmony Revived* add them. In bars 15 and 16 the alto and tenor, although individually satisfactory, are dissonant with each other.

When Israel Was in
  Egypt's Land
St. 1–3, 17, 18
Traditional, version from
  Jubilee Songs, 1872

This wonderful song of deliverance from oppression appeared in the repertory of the Jubilee Singers of Fisk University in substantially the form familiar to most Americans today. The parallel between the Israelites enslaved in Egypt and the Negro in bondage in our own land was stressed in lines like:

> We need not always weep and moan
>   Let my people go;
> And wear these slavery chains forlorn,
>   Let my people go.

We have noted that the chorus precedes the verse in early versions of many spirituals (for example, "Didn't My Lord Deliver Daniel" in this collection). In "Go Down, Moses" not only does the chorus follow but the opening section is divided into two short unison or solo sections, each followed by the harmonized command, "Let My People Go."

When Our Earthly
  Sun Is Setting   8.7.8.7., with chorus
St. 1–4
Edwin H. Nevin, 1863   Stephen Collins Foster, 1863

This hymn is perhaps Stephen Collins Foster's most successful venture in the style of the gospel hymn with chorus. It appeared in *The Athenaeum* (1863) and was probably contributed to the collection at the suggestion of Horace Waters, who was the editor. The text, by Edwin H. Nevin, dwells on sentiments suitable to death-bed scenes before passing with some abruptness to the rousing chorus with its hope of reunion in heaven.

When Shall We All Meet   PARTING FRIENDS 7.7.7.7.7.7.
  Again?
St. 1–3
Anon., 1831   Anon., 1831

This hymn is supposed to have been written by three Indians who had been fellow students at Dartmouth College. It was commonly sung as a farewell at the close of religious exercises. According to Brown and Butterworth, in *The Story of the Hymns and Tunes,* the three friends did finally meet there again after almost fifty years. They improved the occasion by writing another hymn, to be sung to the same tune, which began:

> Parted many a toil-spent year,
> Pledged in youth to memory dear,
> Still to friendship's magnet true,
> We our social joys renew . . .

"When Shall We All Meet Again?" appeared in Joshua Leavitt's *The Christian Lyre* (1831) in a version for melody and unfigured bass. It was included in William Walker's *Southern Harmony* (1835) in a three-part arrangement with the melody somewhat altered and in the tenor. Joseph Hillman's *The Revivalist* (1868) gave the melody in another and less attractive form. Our version follows that of Leavitt, with the addition of alto and tenor parts that may be played or sung.

When Sun Doth Rise	Landaffe C.M.
St. 1–3	Frost 241
Roger Williams, 1643	Thomas Ravenscroft, arr.
	1621

This, like "If Birds That Neither Sow Nor Reap" (q.v.), is from *A Key into the Language of America.* The second stanza, dealing with the star lore of the Indians, is one of many passages which shows Williams' interest in the Indians and his knowledge of their ways. It will be noted that the comparison drawn between Indians and English is to the disadvantage of the latter.

In stanza 3, line 3, the dotted slurs and ties in the music must be used since this line has only six syllables. Ravenscroft calls Landaffe a Welsh tune.

Cantus, C clef, first line; medius, C clef, second line; tenor or "playnsong," C clef, third line; bassus, F clef, third line. Time signature C; note values halved; transposed down a minor third. We have retained the original signature of three sharps, since there are more D♮s in the score than D♯s.

When the Seed of Thy Word Is Cast	PSALM 41 C.M.D.
(The Sower a Singer)	
St. 1–4	
Cotton Mather, 1727	John Playford, 1677

This poem, like "My Heart, How Very Hard It's Grown!" appeared in Cotton Mather's *Agricola.* There is no indication that these verses were to be sung, but they are well suited to music. "When the Seed of Thy Word Is Cast" is based on the parable of the sower (Matt. 13:3).

The poem is here set to John Playford's arrangement of the tune to PSALM 41 as published in his *While Book of Psalms* (1677).

Transposed one step down; melody in top part.

When Thickly Beat the Storms of Life	ZEPHYR L.M.
St. 1–4	
Gurdon Robins, 1843	William Batchelder Bradbury, 1844

Although *The Psalmist* (1843), edited by Samuel Francis Smith and Baron Stowe, lists "When Thickly Beat the Storms of Life" as anonymous, it was one of two hymns by Gurdon Robins included in that volume. The other was "There Is a Land Mine Eye Hath Seen" (q.v.). The present poem, headed "God A Rock," has been associated here with the tune ZEPHYR by the contemporary educator and composer William Batchelder Bradbury, who was also a Baptist. In *The Keynote* Bradbury dates this tune 1847. He knew that it had appeared in the *New York Choralist* (1847) which he had edited with Thomas Hastings, but he evidently forgot that it had appeared three years earlier in *The Psalmodist,* another tune book which he had produced with Thomas Hastings.

When Thy Heart with Joy O'erflowing	WOODLAWN 8.5.8.3.
St. 1–5	
Theodore Chickering Williams, 1891	Robert L. Sanders, 1934

This hymn of brotherhood, dated 1891, was included in the Unitarian *New Hymn and Tune Book* (1914), *Hymns of the Spirit* (1937), and

Hymns for the Celebration of Life (1964). WOODLAWN was composed by Robert L. Sanders for *Hymns of the Spirit,* of which he was a music editor.

When Wild Confusion	HACKNEY C.M.
Wrecks the Air	
(The God of Tempest)	
St. 7, 8, 11, 14	
Mather Byles, 1795	John Blow, c.1718?

This judgment hymn is the latter part of a longer poem beginning "Thy dreadful Pow'r, Almighty God," included in an appendix to the psalter of Nahum Tate and Nicholas Brady (1760), edited in part by Byles. Evidently Jeremy Belknap was the first to print the shortened form beginning with stanza 7 in his *Sacred Poetry* (1795), and this form (with alterations) was still included in Henry Ward Beecher's *Plymouth Collection* (1855) and the *Baptist Praise Book* (1871).

The exuberant rhetoric of Byles's poem makes a more elaborate musical treatment not inappropriate and it is presented here with a version of HACKNEY "set full" by the English organist and composer John Blow. This version in free keyboard style and with interludes between the lines may be compared with the simple three-voice arrangement of the same tune which is set here to Thomas Prince's "Give Ear, O God, to My Loud Cry." HACKNEY appeared in John Playford's *Whole Book of Psalms* (1677), but it was naturalized here at an early date. It was included among the tunes published in the 1698 edition of the *Bay Psalm Book* and also in the collection of tunes bound with Thomas Prince's revision of that work in 1758.

When Winds Are Raging	REST 11.10.11.10.
Still, Still with Thee	
St. 1–5, St. 1–6	
Harriet Beecher Stowe, 1855	Charles Beecher, 1855

Three hymns by Mrs. Stowe appeared in the famous *Plymouth Collection* (1855) edited by her brother Henry Ward Beecher, with the assistance of another brother, Charles, as music editor. They were all in the same meter and were all to be sung to the tune REST by Charles Beecher.

Of the three, "That Mystic Word of Thine" is given in a shorter version beginning "Abide in me, O Lord, and I in Thee." One may surmise that Beecher's tune was written for "When Winds Are Raging." At any rate, that was the text associated with the tune in the Plymouth hymnal. Its parallel between spiritual peace and the unbroken repose of the ocean depths has led some editors to call it the "Sabbath of the Sea." It is perhaps not too fanciful to associate the wide leaps of the second phrase of the melody with the "billows wild."

Although "Still, Still with Thee" has been criticized for its romantic imagery, it is not only typical of its period but has retained popularity with many singing congregations down to the present. Based on Psalm 139:18, it was written two years before its publication while the author was paying a summer visit to a friend who noted that "she often arose in the morning at half-past four and went out to enjoy the birds and the dawn."

Where Are the Hebrew Children?	THE HEBREW CHILDREN
	7.7.7.6.8.8.8.6.
St. 1–3	
Anon., often attributed to Peter Cartwright, 1835	David Walker, arr. 1841

According to the *Original Sacred Harp* "Peter Cartwright used this tune in his camp meetings long before it was ever placed in notation. It is one of the old melodies of America and has for a long time been quite a favorite of many of the older people." Cartwright did not claim this hymn as his own although it has often been attributed to him. Based on Daniel 3:21, "These men were cast into the midst of the burning fiery furnace," the singers ask in turn of the whereabouts of the twelve apostles and the holy Christians and answer that all are "Safe in the promised land."

David Walker's arrangement of THE HEBREW CHILDREN appeared in the 1854 *Southern Harmony*. *The Sacred Harp* (1859) prints the same arrangement, ascribed to B. F. White. A Negro version entitled "Wonder Where Is Good Ole Daniel" may be found in *Religious Folk-Songs of the Negro* by R. Nathaniel Dett. Readers should compare this version with the arrangement of the same hymn by Annabel Morris Buchanan, also included.

Where Cross the Crowded   KIEL L.M.
   Ways of Life
St. 1–6
Frank Mason North, writ.   Peter C. Lutkin, 1905
   1903

   This hymn by a Methodist pastor and editor was written as a plea for a Christian solution of the conflicts and tragedies of modern urban living. Although Caleb T. Winchester, a member of the Joint Commission for the 1905 *Methodist Hymnal,* suggested the writing of this hymn, it appeared first in the *Christian City.*

   Because Peter Lutkin's forebears and those of his wife had come from Denmark three of his tunes were named for places in that country. KIEL was the birthplace of his wife's great grandfather.

Wherein Consists the High   DUKES TUNE C.M.
   Estate
Question 28, st. 1–5   Frost 203
Ebenezer Dayton, 1769   Thomas Ravenscroft, arr.
                                  1621

   When Ebenezer Dayton used rhyme to help his students in learning the shorter catechism, he was employing an age-old device. From early times lessons had been chanted, presumably because it was agreeable to the students and easy for the teacher to be sure that all his students were studying their lessons. The stanzas of Dayton selected here deal with the resurrection of Christ.

   In accordance with Dayton's suggestion that his lines should be sung to the most usual psalm tunes we have chosen DUKES TUNE, one of the common meter tunes from Ravenscroft's psalter of 1621.

   Cantus, C clef, first line; medius, C clef, third line; tenor, C clef, fourth line; bassus, F clef, fourth line. Note values halved.

Where Is Our Holy Church?   OXNAM S.M.
St. 1–5
Edwin H. Wilson, writ. 1928,   Robert G. McCutchan, 1930
   pub. 1937

   " 'Where Is Our Holy Church?' was written in France in the summer of 1928, following my first season as minister of a Unitarian church." Such was Edwin H. Wilson's account of the origin of a hymn which "has been used in many ordinations or installation services in the liberal churches."

Robert G. McCutchan's vigorous short-meter tune OXNAM, which has also been used for William Pierson Merrill's "Rise Up, O Men of God," has been selected as an appropriate setting for Wilson's hymn of aspiration.

Where Nothing Dwelt But Beasts of Prey	WHITESTOWN L.M.
Ps. 107, last part: 3–5, 7	
Isaac Watts, 1718	How'd, 1800

The last part of Psalm 107 in the version of Isaac Watts was headed "Colonies planted, or nations blest & punished. A psalm for New England." Our text begins with stanza 3, the part most directly concerned with the lot of the early settlers.

In Allen D. Carden's *Missouri Harmony* (1820), WHITESTOWN is the tune and no composer is given. In *Southern Harmony* (1854) the same tune is attributed to Ward. Although this tune persisted longest in the South, it was of Northern origin and is found in *The Musical Harmonist* (New Haven, Conn., 1800) of Stephen Jenks; there the composer named is How'd. The part writing reveals a concern for a good melodic movement in individual parts and a considerable indifference to forbidden parallel movements and incidental dissonance.

Time signature ⊃ ; countertenor notated an octave too high; melody in tenor.

Where Now Are the Hebrew Children?	8.8.8.6.D.
St. 1–4	
Traditional	Annabel Morris Buchanan, arr., cop. 1934

Southern folk hymns are unusual in the fact that they first appear harmonized, distinguishing them from folk songs, which were for the most part collected as unharmonized melodies that were later harmonized for performance. However, many folk hymn melodies have been reharmonized in the twentieth century to satisfy performers and listeners who might find the original folk harmony rude and bare. To make a comparison possible we print two settings of "What Wondrous Love Is This" and "Where Now Are the Hebrew

Children?" The latter appears as printed in *The Sacred Harp* (1859 ed.) and as harmonized by Mrs. Buchanan in *Twelve Folk Hymns*, edited by John Powell (J. Fischer, 1934). Note that Mrs. Buchanan's text adds the word "now" to the opening line. This collection also contains arrangements by Hilton Rufty and by the editor.

While I Am Young	HAPPY CHOICE 8.8.6.6.D.
St. 1–4	
Silas Ballou, 1785	Jeremiah Ingalls, 1805

This simple and touching hymn for young people was published in Silas Ballou's *New Hymns on Various Subjects*.

A tune published by a musician who directed the choir in Newbury, Vt., seemed a suitable match. The melody of HAPPY CHOICE has folk characteristics. Jeremiah Ingalls' setting appeared in 1805 in his *Christian Harmony*.

While O'er Our Guilty Land, O Lord	DELHI L.M.D.
St. 1, 2, 4–6, 8	
Samuel Davies, 1756	Samuel Holyoke, 1791

Davies liked to drive home the point of a sermon with a hymn. The present example, as well as "While Various Rumors Spread Abroad," was printed with the sermon of which it formed a part under the title *Virginia's Danger and Remedy, and Occasioned by a severe Drought in sundry parts of that Country, and the defeat of General Braddock.* In the opening stanza and later in stanza five (six of the original) Davies juxtaposed lines dealing with his two themes: "Revive our withering fields with rain, / Let peace compose our land again." Thomas Gibbons, in his *Hymns adapted to Divine Worship* (London, 1769), prints the hymn as Davies wrote it. In John Rippon's *Selection of Hymns from the Best Authors* (1787, first American edition, New York, 1792), the lines relating to the drought are omitted. (The first stanza in Rippon is made from the two first lines of the first stanza plus the last two lines of the original second stanza.) The result was a hymn suited to times of national danger that could be used as a fast-day hymn. Both forms were used. We give the poem in its original form.

In Samuel Holyoke's *Harmonica Americana* (Boston, 1791) DELHI is given as the tune for the Davies poem. Holyoke was opposed to the fuguing tune and considered that "sentiment and expression ought to be the principal guide in vocal music."

Original time signature 𝄵.

While o'er the Deep Thy Servants Sail	HARTFORD L.M.
St. 1–4	
George Burgess, 1845	Jonathan Mayhew Wainwright, 1830

"While o'er the Deep Thy Servants Sail" is the altered form in which Burgess' earlier psalm version "Lord in Thy Name We Spread the Sail" passed into usage. The date of the original version is unknown, but it was published in the author's *Poems* of 1868. The modified form was published in the Connecticut *Psalms and Hymns for Christian Use and Worship* (1845) and was probably altered for that volume. Julian remarked that this hymn was to be found "in almost every recent American collection but that of the Protestant Episcopal Church," the denomination of the author. It has been set here to HARTFORD by Jonathan Mayhew Wainwright, whose *Psalmodia Evangelica* appeared in 1830 in New York.

Bar 10, tenor originally B♭, C making fifths with the alto; bar 12, first note in tenor originally D. The anticipatory $^6_4$ chord (bar 10, last quarter) is strange. In bars 14–15, the near octaves between tenor and bass appear thus in the original.

While We Lowly Bow Before Thee	ALVAN 8.7.8.7.4.7.
St. 1–3	
Daniel C. Colesworthy, 1857	Lowell Mason, 1854

This, perhaps the best-known hymn by Daniel Colesworthy, appeared in Elias Nason's *Congregational Hymn Book* of 1857 and then was selected for inclusion in hymnals with a wide circulation: Charles S. Robinson's *Songs for the Sanctuary* (1865) and his *Laudes Domini* (1884). In the latter volume it was given with Lowell Mason's ALVAN as the tune, an association preserved here.

ALVAN has much of the naïveté of the German folk song. It is marked with an asterisk in Mason's *The Hallelujah* to show that it was published there for the first time. Many of the tunes, including ALVAN, were provided with interludes. "They have been prepared, not for the organist who is able to play his own impromptu interludes, but rather for the purpose of furnishing other instruments with something better than the constant repetition of the last line."

Whilst In This World I Stay	IN CRETE 10.10.10.D.
Meditations 17–20	
Philip Pain, 1668	Anon., after 1571

The constant theme of Pain's *Daily Meditations* is the transitory character of human life and the immediate prospect of death. This preoccupation seems doubly pathetic in view of the author's early death in a shipwreck. The text selected here is for "July 23. The second day," and it consists of Meditations 17–20.

"In Crete, when Daedalus first began" is the opening line of an Elizabethan ballad associated with a tune preserved in three lute tablatures. The melodic line is clearest in William Ballet's Lute Book. The last two bars, missing in the Ballet manuscript, have been taken from the Folger tablature. The ornaments in the upper part are to be played by the accompanying instrument while the voice sings the notes of the tune. In stanza 3 we suggest slurring the first two notes in bar 2 and omitting the word "all."

Who Has Our Redeemer	7.6.7.6., with chorus
Heard	
St. 1–4	
Stephen Collins Foster, 1863	Stephen Collins Foster, 1863

This hymn, with words and music by Stephen Collins Foster, first appeared in *The Athenaeum* (1863). In spite of technical awkwardness—Foster was less at home in four-part writing than in the song with piano accompaniment—this song sustains a gentle, pleading mood without the mawkishness that mars others of his hymns. The echo in the second bar of the chorus is likely to remind the singer of the use of this device in the chorus of "Old Black Joe."

Who Here Can Cast His Eyes	INVITATION L.M.
Abroad	
St. 1–5	
Abiel Holmes, 1796	Jacob Kimball, 1793

Abiel Holmes, better known as a biographer and historian than as a poet, was the "Myron" who contributed sixteen poems including this "Hymn—Written at Sea" to a thin volume, *A Family Tablet Containing a Selection of Original Poetry,* in 1796. The publication seems truly to have been a family affair since Holmes's first wife, a daughter of Ezra Stiles, president of Yale, appeared as "Myra" with eight poems, while Ruth Stiles ("Louise") and Dr. Ezra Stiles Jr. ("Eugenis") wrote three each.

In the preface to his *The Rural Harmony,* Jacob Kimball stated that he "aimed at originality in his compositions, and endeavored to deviate (as far as he deemed it justifiable) from the common style; where he has given in to it, he has attempted to improve it by a particular attention to the harmony." What is apparent over one hundred and fifty years later is the freshness and rhythmic drive of his fuguing tunes, the best of which were in major. INVITATION first appeared in Kimball's *The Rural Harmony* to the text, "Come my beloved, haste away." An indication of its popularity is the fact that it was included in the *Old Folks Concert Tunes* of Father Robert Kemp (repeatedly issued from c.1860 to 1889), which contained and recalled a type of music that had largely passed out of use.

Countertenor in alto clef. Time signature 𝄵 ; tune in tenor; transposed down one step. Tenor, bar 9, first quarter, has D, here corrected to C.

Whoso Would See This Song of Heavenly Choice	How Can the Tree
Lines 43–66	10.10.10.D.
John Wilson, 1626	Anon., 1576

These lines are from the introduction of John Wilson's *Song of Deliverance,* which is decasyllabic in contrast to the prevailing ballad meter. The poem, first published in London in 1626 before Wilson came to this country, was reprinted in Boston after his death. It is a narrative of the "wonderful defeat of the Spanish Armada," of the plagues of 1603 and 1625, of the Gunpowder Plot of 1605, and of the "downfall of Blackfryers" during a sermon by a Jesuit priest in 1623. "Confess We All, Before the Lord" (q.v.) is another excerpt from the poem.

The anonymous music chosen for Wilson's text was a setting for "How Can the Tree" by Thomas, Lord Vaux. It is scored for solo voice accompanied by four viols. The accompanying parts have been compressed on two staves and may be played on a keyboard instrument. Note values reduced by half. In bar 8 the viols rested on the third quarter instead of sustaining as here. A version of this music to "How Can the Tree" appeared in William Barley's *New Book of Tablature* (1596).

Why Do We Mourn   China C.M.
  Departing Friends?
St. 1, 3, 5, 6
Isaac Watts, 1707   Timothy Swan, 1801

This rude tune, indelibly associated with Watts's funeral hymn "Why Do We Mourn Departing Friends?" was sung by New Englanders in the presence of their dead for a century. Watts's text appeared in Book II of his *Hymns and Spiritual Songs* with the heading "The Death and Burial of a Saint."

Harriet Beecher Stowe, in *The Pearl of Orr's Island,* speaks of China as "that strange, wild warble, whose quaintly blended harmonies might have been learned of moaning seas or wailing winds." It has been reprinted from Timothy Swan's only collection, *New England Harmony* (Northampton, Mass., 1801).

Countertenor, G clef, second line, written an octave too high. Tune in tenor; transposed down a major third.

Why Linger Yet upon the   Wider Ways C.M.
  Strand?
St. 1–4
Louis F. Benson, writ. 1897,   Uzziah C. Burnap, comp.
  pub. 1925   1898, pub. 1925

The poem beginning "Why linger yet upon the strand?" with its musical setting has been taken from Benson's anthology *Hymns, Original and Translated.* This call for spiritual courage equal to that of seafaring men was appropriate to the Maine coast where it was written (Bar Harbor, August 8, 1897). First published in the author's *Hymns and Verses* (1897), the text was revised before its inclusion in his collected hymns.

Burnap composed Wider Ways in 1898, but it remained in manuscript until it was published with Benson's text in 1925.

Why, Lord?   Why, Lord 10.10.10.
St. 1–3
Mark Van Doren, 1935   Anthony Donato, comp. 1957

"Why, Lord?" was included in Van Doren's *A Winter Diary and Other Poems.*

This somber but moving hymn is treated with the utmost simplicity from a rhythmic point of view; indeed all the voices move together throughout the piece. The treatment, too, is strophic. The harmonies, however, individually consonant, begin and close in the old Dorian scale, but are placed in colorful and striking relationships in the intermediate bars (6, 7, and the opening of bar 8). The choir director will need to urge his singers to carry the text of stanza 2 through bar 7, not phrasing after the first chord as they did in the first stanza.

Why Should Vain Mortals Tremble	BUNKER HILL 11.11.11.5.
St. 1–3, 8, 10, 13, 15	
Nathaniel Niles, 1775	Andrew Law, 1781

The somewhat bombastic ode of Nathaniel Niles has a historical importance that its literary merits alone would hardly justify.

The tune, attributed to Andrew Law, is given here as it appears in his *Select Number of Plain Tunes Adapted to Congregational Worship.* The musical problem presented by the poem is the unsymmetrical balance of three long lines followed by a short one. Law treats each of the long lines as a four-bar phrase, but adds a two-bar interlude for soprano and bass after line 2, which balances the two-bar setting of the short line at the end.

An expression of the upsurge of patriotic fervor which followed the Battle of Bunker Hill, this ode was issued as a broadside in Norwich, Conn. in 1795. In 1781 Andrew Law published it with his tune in his *Select Number of Plain Tunes.*

Countertenor, C clef, third line. Time signature ₵. The tune begins with half rests in all parts. These have been omitted here.

Wilt Thou Not Visit Me?	VINGROVE 6.10.6.10.
St. 1–5	
Jones Very, 1839	Henry Kemble Oliver, 1860

"Wilt Thou Not Visit Me?" was one of the poems included in Jones Very's *Essays and Poems* (1839). It later appeared in the *Book of Hymns* (1846), edited by Samuel Longfellow and Samuel Johnson. The great discrepancy in the length of the lines in this hymn presented a special problem to the musician. Charles Beecher is credited with WATERBROOK, the tune given for this text in the *Plymouth Collection* (1855), although this may be an arrangement. In John S. Adams' *Vestry Harmonies* (1857) OMNISCIENCE was apparently composed for Very's poem by J. D. W. (J. D. Willard). A later setting by

Arthur Foote called SALEM appeared in the Unitarian *Hymns for the Church Universal* (1890).

Oliver has treated the lines of six syllables as two-bar sections. The first line of ten syllables became a three-bar phrase, while the final line is broadened by the use of half notes to five bars. Tune and text were included in Oliver's *Collection of Church Music* (1860).

With All My Heart, Jehovah, I'll Confess	FRENCH TUNE: PSALM 8 10.10.10.10.
Ps. 9: 1, 2, 10, 11, 13, 20	Frost 321; Zahn 923
Henry Ainsworth, 1612	Claude Goudimel, arr. 1565

It seems probable that when the Pilgrims sang such lines as "Jehovah, strike in them a dread dismay; Let heathens know weak men they be," they thought of their own situation and of the ever-present danger of an Indian attack. The melody which Ainsworth used had appeared as the tune for Psalm 8 in the French psalter of 1542, called "Pseudo-Roman" because the title page stated that it was "printed at Rome by order of the Pope," even though it was actually published in Strassburg under Protestant auspices. It is similar to a popular song, "Si ton amour," which was published in Tilman Susato's *Chansons à quatre parties* (Anvers, 1544/45).

Claude Goudimel set the melody twice: in 1564 with the melody in the superius and in 1565 with the melody in the tenor. It is the later and simpler version which we have selected. The melody passed into Lutheran usage in 1592. The meter of the French text was 11.11.10.10., which Ainsworth altered to 10.10.10.10.

Superius, C clef, first line; countertenor, C clef, third line; tenor, C clef, fourth line; bassus, F clef, third line. Original pitch; time signature lacking; note values halved. The conventional rests after each line are omitted here.

With Christ and All His Shining Train	HYMN ON THE DIVINE USE OF MUSIC L.M.
St. 1–3	Frost 201
Thomas Prince, 1758	John Playford, arr. 1677

Thomas Prince added fifty hymns to his revision of the *Bay Psalm Book* entitled *Psalms, Hymns, and Spiritual Songs of the Old and New Testaments*. While most are by Isaac Watts, this hymn is by the reviser. The addition of man-made devotional verse to metrical paraphrases of passages from the Bible was an important step in the transition from psalmody to congregational hymn singing.

The HYMN ON THE DIVINE USE OF MUSIC was published by Playford in 1677. It is among the hymn tunes in the *Supplement to the New Version of Psalms by Dr. Brady and Mr. Tate* (5th ed., 1704) and was included in the musical supplement bound with Prince's revision.

Time signature 3; note values reduced by half.

Within These Doors	CORONATION C.M.D.
Assembled Now	
St. 1–4	
Oliver Holden, before 1808	Oliver Holden, 1793

Oliver Holden's CORONATION is the one American tune written during the eighteenth century that has enjoyed general and uninterrupted popularity to the present day. This statement cannot be made of William Billings, whose tunes have been sung continuously only by the shape-note singers in the South. The present vogue for Billings in other circles has the character of a revival. CORONATION belongs to the vigorous, marching type of tune with many repeated notes in which our forefathers delighted. Only after the double bar does the texture thin to soprano and bass for two bars. Otherwise the tune is for four voices throughout with five-voice chords at the final cadence for extra fullness. In the *Select Hymns* of James H. Linsley and Gustavus F. Davis (1836) the Holden text, designed for the "opening of a conference meeting," is directed to be sung to CORONATION. This text is used here in preference to "All Hail the Power of Jesus' Name" by the English hymn writer Edward Perronet, which has always been associated with CORONATION. The tune name comes from the phrase "and crown him Lord of all" in the Perronet text.

Countertenor, C clef, third line. Time signature ℭ; tune in tenor; transposed down one step. In *Union Harmony*, Vol. 2, the first chord in bar 8 has A in the countertenor. We read G following Holden's own revision in his *Worcester Collection of Sacred Harmony* (7th ed., 1800). Similarly, in bar 9, last quarter, and bar 10, first three quarters, we read G in the countertenor instead of F$^\sharp$.

Within the Shelter of Our	HEARTHSIDE 8.6.8.8.6.
Walls	
St. 1–3	
Elinor Lennen, cop. 1961	Shirley L. Brown, 1970

"Within the Shelter of Our Walls" was published by the Hymn Society of America in 1961 as one of *Thirteen New Marriage and Fam-*

ily Life Hymns. It was included in the Society's *Contemporary Hymn Tunes* of 1970 with this setting by Shirley L. Brown. The use of triplets lends a certain flexibility to the march of uniform quarter notes. The tune is completely diatonic with an aeolian coloration.

Word of God, Across the Ages
St. 1–3
Ferdinand Q. Blanchard, 1952

WORD OF GOD 8.7.8.7.D.

Richard Donovan, comp. 1956

This vigorous contemporary example of a processional hymn composed for *American Hymns* is set to a text chosen and first published by the Hymn Society of America as one of *Ten New Hymns of the Bible* (1952).

The World, the Devil, and Tom Paine
St. 1–3
Anon., 1807

COME AND GO ALONG WITH ME L.M.

Anon., 1868

This camp-meeting hymn in praise of the Methodists was selected from a little collection *Hymns and Spiritual Songs* (Richmond, Va., 1807), edited by Stith Mead. Resolutely partisan in point of view, it singles out Tom Paine as one of the three great spiritual enemies. It expresses the rollicking vigor, the downrightness, and the denominational rivalries of the frontier.

COME AND GO ALONG WITH ME appeared in Joseph Hillman's *Revivalist* in 1868. Its dancelike character suggests a folk origin. The optional lower parts are editorial additions.

Ye Realms below the Skies
St. 1–4
Hosea Ballou II, 1829

SPRING STREET 6.6.6.6.8.8.8.

Thomas Whittemore, 1841

This hymn, headed "Glory of God's Works," was published in *The New Hymn Book, Designed for Universalist Societies,* by Sebastian and Russell Streeter. It was one of the two hymns by the author still included in *Church Harmonies New and Old* in 1895. In Thomas Whittemore's *The Gospel Harmonist* (1841) it was set to SPRING STREET, a tune by the editor. Whittemore states in his preface that "there are no hymn books so fruitful in odd, or particular metres, as the collections of the Messrs. Streeters and of H. Ballou, 2d. We have no hesitation in saying there is no collection of music extant, which furnishes tunes for *every* variety of metre in those books except this work." This tune book was thus planned with special reference to Universalist usage.

Ye Scattered Nations   SYMPHONY 10.10.10.10.D.
Ps. 66: selected lines
Thomas Cradock, trans. 1754   Justin Morgan, 1790

In addition to writing hymns which remained in manuscript, Thomas Cradock published *A Poetical Translation of the Psalms of David from Buchanan's Latin into English Verse* (London, 1754), dedicated as an old scholar to "Mr. John Hargreaves, some time MASTER of Trentham SCHOOL in the County of Stafford . . . In Acknowledgment of the pious Care that he took in my Education." Cradock's paraphrase of Psalm 66 is included here.

Few American tunes were composed for this meter. SYMPHONY, by Justin Morgan, made its first appearance in the *Federal Harmony* of Asahel Benham.

Soprano, countertenor, and tenor, G clef, second line; bass, F clef, fourth line. Original key E♭ major; time signature ꜱ.

Yoke Soft and Dear   ACH GOTT UND HERR 8.7.8.7.
St. 1, 3, 10
John Christopher Kunze,   Adapted from the version of
   1795   J. G. Schmauk, 1847

In his preface John Kunze, the editor of *A Hymn and Prayer-Book, For the Use of such Lutheran Churches as use the English Language* (New York, 1795), described the difficulties experienced by German Lutherans who lived in large cities and who settled among English-speaking people, whose children gradually lost their knowledge of the German tongue. Even at that time services in English were already established in certain New Jersey and New York congregations and this volume was intended for their use.

Kunze's original hymns, which were printed in the appendix and signed with a "K," have been harshly treated by the critics. Louis F. Benson dismissed them as "didactic prose." It is quite true that Kunze's verses are frequently awkward and his imagery quaint and surprising. In stanzas not included in the hymn as printed here the figure of the pews "yielding milk and honey" (stanza 7) is an instance of this kind as is the description of the worshiper shutting his ears "to worldly cares and to the roaring lion" (stanza 9). Nevertheless, they represent a critical turning point in the development of the Lutheran Church in this country that cannot be ignored in a historical collection.

ACH GOTT UND HERR is adapted from the version published in the *Deutsche Harmonie oder Mehrstimmige Gesange für deutsche Singschulen und Kirchen,* compiled by J. G. Schmauk. It must be confessed that his arrangements leave something to be desired and the harmony as presented here has been somewhat altered. Schmauk, in his preface, remarked "that in every human work there are shortcomings to be found and to be improved."

Young and Radiant, He Is   8.7.8.7.D.
  Standing
St. 1–4
Allen Eastman Cross, 1921   Louis Adolphe Coerne, 1921

Allen Eastman Cross, whose poetic gift found expression in two volumes of poetry, wrote two hymns depicting Christ as a youth: "The Hidden Years at Nazareth" and "Young and Radiant, He Is Standing." Written in a marching meter, this hymn has been matched with a jubilant processional tune composed and named for it. First published in 1921, text and tune appeared again in H. Augustine Smith's *Hymns for the Living Age.*

You That Have Been Often   OSCEOLA 11.11.11.11.
  Invited
Anon., 1845   Thomas Commuck, melody
                                 1845, Thomas Hastings,
                                 arr. 1845

This hymn is from a curious collection, *Indian Melodies,* by Thomas Commuck. In the preface he asserted pathetically that such a production was not expected from the despised Indian, claimed that he published the collection to aid in the support of a numerous family, and appealed to fellow Methodists to sustain his efforts. The melodies were by Commuck. In only one instance did he state that a tune, OLD INDIAN HYMN, was traditional among the Indians.

OSCEOLA is an attractive minor tune in four regular four-bar phrases dominated by a persistent rhythm like a drum beat expressed by a quarter followed by two eighth notes. Neither the scale nor the form of the melody reveal Indian characteristics, although it is possible that Hastings rather than Commuck added the sharps which make it a minor, rather than an Aeolian tune. The text by an unknown author has the character of a hortatory camp-meeting text.

You Will See Your Lord A-Coming St. 1–3, 5, 7, 9 Anon., 1843	OLD CHURCHYARD Irregular Anon., 1849

This song, "You Will See Your Lord A-Coming," was the best-known of those sung by the Millerites, members of a sect who not only believed in the Second Coming of Christ but were willing to set the year 1843 as the year of His return. "You Will See Your Lord A-Coming" was sung at baptisms in eastern New York and at cemeteries where the Millerites gathered to be near their friends who were buried there, hoping to join them at the moment of the resurrection. Undaunted when the expected event failed to materialize, the more enthusiastic of them were still chanting an appropriately altered version a decade later:

> O praise the Lord, we do not fear
> To tell the world he'll come next year,
> In eighteen hundred fifty-four
> The saints will shout their sufferings o'er.

The text of this revival song appeared at the beginning of Jerome Himes's *Millennial Harp* (1843) and our version has been taken from that volume.

The arrangement of the music comes from *The American Vocalist* (Boston, 1849), edited by D. H. Mansfield. Original key, F major. The fifth tenor note in the next to last measure is A in Mansfield. The old hymn was further transformed by the famous Hutchinson family, who used the tune as the basis for their own song "The Old Granite State."

BIOGRAPHIES OF AUTHORS
AND COMPOSERS

Alonzo J. Abbey, American composer; b. 1825; d. 1887.

The scant details we have on the life of Alonzo J. Abbey are gleaned from *Hymns and Hymn Writers of the Church* (New York, 1911), by Charles S. Nutter and Wilbur F. Tillet. Yet Abbey's tune COOLING (q.v.), which first appeared in 1858 in *The American Choir*, was popular not only in the nineteenth century but is also included in at least ten twentieth-century hymnals, and this in a period when many American tunes of the past century have been discarded. Abbey apparently knew Artemas N. Johnson, editor of *The American Choir*, for thirty-seven of his tunes were included in Johnson's later *Empire Collection* (1862) and nine in his *Alleghany Collection* (1867). Abbey was also active as an editor of Sunday School hymnals, for which he wrote many tunes. Among the hymnals were *Songs of the Bible* (1873, with N. A. Ogden) and *The Banner of Victory* (1881, with M. J. Munger). The preface of the latter book states that the same editors had published an earlier and very successful book called *White Robes*.

Frederick L. Abel, musician; b. Ludwigslust, Mecklenberg-Schwerin, 1794; d. Savannah, Ga., Sept. 23, 1820.

Frederick L. Abel was a grandnephew of Karl Friedrich Abel, a noted gambist and contemporary of J. S. Bach. His father, a violinist, taught his two sons both violin and piano, when they were still very young. The children gave a trial performance when the younger, J. L. Abel, was nine years old. It so impressed those present that several volunteered to provide free instruction for the brothers. Two years later their father took them on a concert tour of northern Germany. The venture was not a financial success, and Frederick turned to a business career until 1817, when he left Germany and came to the United States.

He taught music in Savannah, Ga. Respected for his character, his temperate way of life, and his zeal for his profession he enjoyed the friendship of his pupils and their families and was always welcome in their homes. In 1815 Lowell Mason (q.v.), then twenty-three, came to Savannah as a bank clerk. He studied harmony and musical composition with Abel, who was his first well-trained teacher. Abel did much to prepare Mason for the musical career which really began

on his return to Boston in 1827. *The Savannah Museum* noted the arrival of Mason's first collection, *The Handel and Haydn Society Collection of Church Music* (1822), which was warmly recommended by F. L.
Abel, who signed himself "Professor of Music."

In 1819 Abel's brother, J. L. Abel, came to Savannah from Germany, intending to settle there and teach piano, cello, and guitar.
The two brothers, reunited after so long a time, had only a year
together before Frederick's death of yellow fever on September 23
was reported in *The Georgian* of October 10, 1820. His estate, valued
at $2400, was put into the hands of administrators, and the contents
of his home were sold at auction. The inventory, testifying to a wide
range of interests, included watches, guns, tools, a microscope, musical instruments, a quantity of music of all sorts, paintings, and books.
See ALSEN ("Jesus, Merciful and Mild").

Joseph Achron, composer and violinist; b. Lozdzeye, Lith-uania, May 1, 1886; d. Hollywood, Calif., April 29, 1943.

Joseph Achron began the study of violin and music theory at the
age of five and gave his first public concert in Warsaw at age eight.
He studied at the St. Petersburg Conservatory under Leopold Auer
and Anatol K. Liadow and, later, with Maximilian Steinberg. In 1913
he directed the violin and chamber music department of the Khar-
kov Conservatory. After service in the army from 1916 to 1918 he
conducted master classes in violin and chamber music in the Lenin-
grad Artist's Union.

In 1925 Achron came to the United States. After nine years in
New York he moved to Hollywood, where he translated Rimsky-
Korsakov's *Practical Manual of Harmony* into English. His *Golem Suite*
(1932) was performed at the Venice International Society of Contemporary Music Festival. The Third Violin Concerto, Opus 72
(1933), was commissioned by Jascha Heifetz. His film ballet *Spring
Night (A Night with Pan)* dates from 1935. He was one of the composers represented in the *Union Hymnal* by original tunes, including
the one to Penina Moise's "God Supreme! to Thee We Pray" (q.v.).

John Coleman Adams, Universalist minister; b. Malden, Mass., Oct. 25, 1849; d. Hartford, Conn., June 22, 1922.

John Coleman Adams was the son of John G. Adams (q.v.). He
was educated at Tufts College (A.B., 1870; B.D., 1872). After his ordination to the Universalist ministry in 1872 he served churches in

Newton (1872–80) and Lynn, Mass. (1880–84); Chicago (1884–90); Brooklyn (1890–91); and Hartford (1901–22). See "We Praise Thee, God, for Harvests Earned."

John G. Adams, Universalist minister; b. Portsmouth, N.H., July 30, 1810; d. Melrose Highlands, Mass., May 4, 1887.

Ordained in 1833, Adams was active in Claremont, N.H.; Malden and Worcester, Mass.; Providence, R.I.; Lowell, Mass.; and Cincinnati, Ohio. He joined Edwin Hubbell Chapin in assembling and editing a Universalist hymnbook, *Hymns for Christian Devotion* (1845), and was editor and compiler of *The Gospel Psalmist* (1861) and *Vestry Harmonies* (1868). Altogether he wrote some twenty books and pamphlets, most of which were distinctly Universalist in character. See "Heaven Is Here" and the hymn tune THORNTON ("In God's Eternity").

John Quincy Adams, 6th President of the United States, author of a metrical version of the psalms; b. Braintree (now Quincy), Mass., July 11, 1767; d. Washington, D.C., Feb. 2, 1848.

John Quincy Adams early gained a knowledge of foreign countries and served as additional secretary in the negotiations which concluded the Revolutionary War. After graduating from Harvard in 1787 he studied law but did not practice it. He was occupied instead with a variety of diplomatic missions. When Thomas Jefferson became President, Adams returned to the United States and was elected a state senator (1802) and in the following year a member of the United States Senate. He became Secretary of State in 1817 and played an important part in the acquisition of Florida and in the formulation of the Monroe Doctrine. In 1824 he was elected President, but the opposition of the Jacksonians prevented his reelection. At the age of sixty-four he again served as senator and worked for the repeal of the "gag rule," which the pro-slavery legislators had introduced.

Adams wrote, but did not publish, a complete metrical version of the psalms, some of which were included in William P. Lunt's *Christian Psalter* (1841). His diary records his feelings when his version of Psalm 65 was sung in church. "Were it possible to compress into one pulsation of the heart the pleasure which, in the whole period of my life, I have enjoyed in praise from the lips of mortal man, it would not weigh a straw to balance the ecstasy of delight which streamed from my eyes as the organ pealed and the choir of voices sung the praise of Almighty God from the soul of David, adapted to my native tongue by me." "Sure to the Mansions of the Blest" was a burial hymn and "Alas! How Swift the Moments Fly" was written for the two-hundredth anniversary of the Congregational Church of Quincy, Mass. (1859). Adams himself was a Unitarian. See "Send Forth, O God, Thy Light and Truth."

Nehemiah Adams, Congregational minister; b. Salem, Mass., Feb. 19, 1806; d. Boston, Mass., Oct. 6, 1878.

Nehemiah Adams received his early education at the Salem Latin School. In 1826 he graduated from Harvard and in 1829 from Andover Theological Seminary. At thirty-four he became pastor of the Union Congregational Church of Boston. On the twenty-fifth anniversary of his service there a celebration was arranged at which Rufus Choate was the principal speaker. On the same occasion Henry Kemble Oliver (q.v.), who had taught Adams at the Latin School, recalled him as "a quiet, sedate, unassuming, faithful, confiding boy."

During Adams' pastorate he made a vigorous defense of orthodox Trinitarian Congregationalism as opposed to Unitarianism. His views were published under the title *Why Am I a Trinitarian Congregationalist?* He believed that the problem of slavery should be solved by the South, and his arguments on that question, entitled *A South-Side View of Slavery,* were printed in 1854. His hymns appeared in *Church Pastorals* (1864), which he edited. See "Saints in Glory, We Together."

Felix Adler, educator and reformer; b. Alzey, Germany, Aug. 12, 1851; d. New York City, April 24, 1933.

Felix Adler was six years old when his family emigrated to the United States. His father was a rabbi, well known and highly regarded. Felix graduated from Columbia College in 1870. Four years later he joined the faculty of Cornell University as Professor of Hebrew and Oriental Literature. A second period of teaching began in 1902 when he became professor of political and social ethics at his alma mater, now called Columbia University. During the years between the two professorships he organized, in New York, the Society for Ethical Culture and made it a force for the improvement of education. He also helped to establish a district nursing service, championed child labor laws, and urged investors to erect model tenements. In addition he wrote a number of books, original in thought and forceful in expression: *Creed and Deed,* published in 1877; *The Moral Instruction of Children* (1903); *Marriage and Divorce* and *The Religion of Duty* (both 1905)—all titles which reveal his preoccupation with moral problems in the lives of average people. See "Hail the Glorious Golden City."

Oscar Ahnfelt, wandering Swedish singer of popular religious songs; b. Gullarp, May 21, 1813; d. Karlshamn, Sweden, April 22, 1882.

Accompanying himself on the guitar Oscar Ahnfelt sang melodies which he composed or adapted to poems by Lina Sandell and Carl Olof Rosenius. Indeed, the popularity of the hymns by Lina Sandell was largely due to his performances. Jennie Lind, who was herself a Pietist, heard Ahnfelt and gave him the money to publish the two volumes of songs dedicated to her. They are so arranged that they can be performed with either guitar or piano accompaniment. When Swedish immigrants came to the United States they remembered these songs, and the one most frequently sung at their services was the one included here. It was published in the Augustana Lutheran hymnal of 1925. See his tune Ack, Saliga Stunder to the text "Med Gud och Hans Vanscap" by Carl Olof Rosenius.

Henry Ainsworth, author of a psalter; b. Swanton Morley, Norfolk, England, 1571; d. Amsterdam, Netherlands, late 1622 or early 1623.

Admitted to Caius College, Cambridge, on December 15, 1587, Henry Ainsworth resided there as a scholar for four years. Learned, sincere, earnest, and uncompromising, Ainsworth attached himself to the Separatist religious movement and became a leader in one of the "Brownist" groups. Fleeing English persecution, Ainsworth arrived in Amsterdam in 1593 where he supported himself as a porter to a bookseller. Later he became a teacher and minister of one of the churches in that city. During the time of his ministry he wrote many religious tracts and exegetical commentaries which served to establish for the English nonconformists a tradition of learning and culture. Even those who despised his sect admired his attainments in rabbinical and Oriental literature.

His translations from the Hebrew Psalms were first printed in Amsterdam in 1612. Having studied the Hebrew text, which few of the earlier translators could do, Ainsworth was able to correct some of the errors of the Sternhold-Hopkins psalter. "I follow the Original text," he wrote in the preface, "where more are to be seen than our English can well admit of; serving both to shew the sense, and to read with consideration." The psalter was entitled *The Booke of Psalms: Englished Both in Prose and Metre.* Copies were brought to the Plymouth Bay Colony and used there. See "Except the Lord, That He for Us Had Been," "Fire in My Meditation Burned," "How Long, Jehovah?" "I Minded God," "In the Distress upon Me," "I Spread Out unto Thee My Hands," "To God Our Strength Shout Joyfully," "Unto Jehovah Sing Will I," "With All My Heart, Jehovah, I Confess" (from Ainsworth's *Annotations upon the Second Book of Moses Called Exodus*), and "Give Ear, O Heavens, to That Which I Declare" (from *Annotations upon the Fifth Book of Moses Called Deuteronomie*).

Louisa May Alcott, author; b. Germantown, Pa., Nov. 29, 1832; d. Boston, Mass., March 6, 1888.

For two years Louisa May Alcott lived in Germantown, Pa., where she was born. Then the family moved to Boston and six years later to Concord, Mass. Her peripatetic father, Bronson Alcott, visionary schoolteacher, peddler, and writer, moved from job to job and town to town. When she was eleven he gave his family an experience in cooperative living by joining two English friends in an experimental community called Fruitlands, which they set up near Harvard. Louisa's earliest instruction was given her by her idealistic father; later she had Thoreau for a teacher. Throughout her life Ralph Waldo Emerson remained her idol and a lifelong family friend.

Poverty early drove her to work. She started her breadwinning career as a doll's dressmaker; then worked at teaching, sewing, and even domestic service for a short period. For fifteen years she wrote potboilers which yielded five or ten dollars apiece. During ten of those years she taught school. In 1860 fifty dollars received for an *Atlantic* story seemed unbelievably munificent. Her first book, *Flower Fables* (1854), was a group of tales originally written for Emerson's daughter Ellen. When the Civil War came she volunteered for service in a military hospital. For months she worked, writing her experiences to her family in a series of letters which she made into *Hospital Sketches,* published in 1863. Its success encouraged her, but intensive literary work had to be postponed because she left her nursing service in a state of physical collapse. In 1863 she took a trip to Europe to regain her health. She stayed a year and returned home to go to work again.

A novel, *Moods,* was published in 1865. It showed promise, but she did not really develop as a novelist until she discovered her real talent, writing for young people, particularly girls. *Little Women* was published in 1868. It was an immediate success, was translated and sold abroad, and continued to sell well for a long time. The family life of her girlhood, which provided material and atmosphere for the story combined with the author's love of people and happy point of view, lent it an appeal that was timeless. It became the most popular girls' book ever written in America. *Little Men* (1871) inspired by the doings of her nephews, followed. She bought a home in Concord, "Orchard House," and established her parents and immediate family in it, thus becoming the chief support of the household for the rest of her life.

Other titles of hers include: *An Old Fashioned Girl* (1870), *Shawl Straps* (1871), *Work* (1873), *Lulu's Library* (3 vols., 1885–89), and *Jo's Boys* (1886). Buoyant as her nature was, her dual role of writer and head of a family was finally too heavy. Her ardor in the causes of abolition and woman suffrage also took a heavy toll of her time and energy. The overwork which caused her death prevented her from fully developing her talent. What she did write, however, gave pleasure to a vast and well-defined circle of readers.

Although she herself stated that she had written only one hymn, four of her poems were so used, including "A Little Kingdom I Possess" (q.v.) and "O the Beautiful Old Story," which was included in *The New Hymn and Tune Book* (1914).

William Alfred, poet and educator; b. New York City, Aug. 16, 1922.

William Alfred early showed an interest in poetry and was assistant editor of *The American Poet* from 1941 to 1944. After spending the years 1943 to 1946 in the U.S. Army, he studied at Brooklyn College (B.A., 1948) and at Harvard (M.A., 1949, and Ph.D., 1954). He joined the Harvard faculty in 1954, has been professor of English since 1963, and in 1975 was named Andrew R. Kenan Jr. Professor of English. In 1953 he received the Literary Association award of Brooklyn College, in 1960 he was a Creative Arts grantee from Brandeis, and in 1956 an Amy Lowell Traveling Poetry scholar. His publications include *The Annunciation Rosary* (1948), *Agamemnon* (1954), and *Hogan's Goat* (1956). See "Mary Lifted from the Dead," set to music for *American Hymns* by Theodore Chanler.

Jonathan Allen, Congregational minister; b. Braintree, Mass., 1749; d. Bradford, Mass., March 6, 1827.

Jonathan Allen graduated from Harvard in 1774, then studied theology with Rev. Ephraim Judson at Taunton, Mass. In 1781 he was ordained at Bradford, Mass., and, after some differences of opinion on his qualifications had been resolved, he was chosen by the congregation of the First Church of Bradford to be its fifth pastor. His view of a minister's duties was solemn, but he did not hesitate to enter into the festivities of Bradford. A contemporary remembered him as wearing short breeches with silver knee buckles, a cocked hat topping a powdered wig, and often taking his deacon along to a merrymaking.

At the turn of the century a religious revival sobered Bradford and seemed to intensify Parson Allen's spiritual power. He is said to have moved his congregation to tears by one of his sermons, at the conclusion of which they sang his own revival hymn, "Sinners, Will You Scorn the Message?" (q.v.). "Go, Ye Heralds of Salvation" was written in 1812 for a farewell service for two women members who were leaving for missionary work.

When Bradford Academy was incorporated in 1804, Allen was chosen its first president. In 1813 he helped form the Philendian Society, dedicated to helping women who volunteered to give moral and educational training to neglected children. He was active, too, in a society to discourage intemperate drinking, although he did not advocate total abstinence.

When age diminished the pastor's activity, his congregation provided a "colleague pastor," whose installation provided a memorable occasion. After the religious service, Parson Allen led a procession from the church to the town common, where "refreshing liquids" were offered to everyone at the church's expense. When a full-time successor had to be appointed, the old minister presided over the induction services. He died three years later. His hymn, "Great Is the Lord, the Heavenly King," was sung at the two hundredth anniversary of the founding of the First Church of Bradford.

Richard Allen, founder and first bishop of the African Methodist Episcopal Church; b. Philadelphia, Pa., Feb. 14, 1760; d. March 26, 1831.

Born a slave, Richard Allen was bought by a farmer in the vicinity of Dover, Del. Religiously inclined, he began to hold services in his master's home. The latter made it possible for him and his family to become free. At first Allen studied and supported his family by chopping and carting wood. After serving as an itinerant, preaching in New Jersey, Pennsylvania, and Maryland, he was received as a minister at the first conference of the Methodist Church in Baltimore in 1784. For a time Allen accompanied Richard Watcoat and Bishop Asbury on their travels. When he settled in Philadelphia in 1786, he preached to Negroes and from time to time at St. George's Methodist Church. His idea of providing a special church for his people was opposed by both whites and his own people until black worshipers were forcibly ejected from the body of the church and ordered to the gallery. The Free African Society was formed in 1787 and Allen persuaded most of the black worshipers to join him in establishing what was called the African Methodist Episcopal Church dedicated by Bishop Asbury in 1794. He was first deacon (1799), then elder (1816). Other congregations were organized, until in 1816 there were sixteen with Allen as bishop. He compiled two hymnbooks and left an autobiography (1793). Nine of the hymns in his *A Collection of Hymns & Spiritual Songs from Various Authors* (1801) cannot be identified and may be by Allen. His rare *Pocket Hymn Book* appeared in 1818. "The God of Bethel Heard Her Cries" (q.v.) appeared in his autobiography.

S. Allen, fl. mid-nineteenth century.

S. Allen contributed the tune ABBY ("Immortal Soul, Forever Full") to *The Psaltery* (Boston, 1845) of Lowell Mason and George J. Webb.

Henry Alline, Freewill Baptist preacher and hymn writer; b. Newport, R.I., June 14, 1748; d. North Hampton, N.H., Feb. 2, 1784.

Although Henry Alline had had no formal schooling when he moved to Nova Scotia as a boy of twelve, he developed a talent for writing hymns, some containing passages describing the beauties of that region. From 1776 to 1783 he served as minister to the people of the pro-Loyalist settlements of Nova Scotia, traveling to them on snowshoes or on horseback. His *Hymns and Spiritual Songs* was published posthumously in Boston in 1785. Later editions (Dover, N.H., 1795 and 1797, and Stonington-port, Conn., 1802) testify to its popularity. Thirty-seven of the hymns were printed in an important Baptist collection, *Hymns Original and Selected for the Use of Christians* (1805), by Elias Smith and Abner Jones, and "Amazing Sight! The Saviour Stands" (q.v.) appeared in Asahel Nettleton's *Village Hymns*

(1824). See also "Hard Heart of Mine" and "Turn, Turn, Unhappy Souls, Return."

Richard Allison, "gentleman practitioner" of music and composer; fl. late 16th, early 17th cents.

The first work of Richard Allison (Alison), *The Psalmes of David in Meter* (1599), was dedicated to the Countess of Warwick and contained a complimentary sonnet by John Dowland. The collection, designed for domestic use, was composed for solo voice with instrumental accompaniment (lute, orpharion, cittern, and bass viol) or for four voices. See BENEDICTUS ("Fire in My Meditation Burned") and OLD 119TH ("Let Him with Kisses of His Mouth"). Allison had earlier contributed psalm settings to Thomas East's *Whole Booke of Psalmes* (1592). *An Houre's Recreation in Musicke, apt for Instruments and Voyces* appeared in London in 1606. The statement that this collection was "for the most part with two trebles, necessary for such as teach in private families" suggests that Allison was so employed. The dedication to his patron, Sir John Scudamore, Knight, whom he thanks for "those quiet dayes which by your goodnes, I have enjoyed," may indicate that Allison had been a member of his household.

Lewis R. Amis, Methodist minister; b. Maury Co., Tenn., Dec. 7, 1856; d. Pulaski, Tenn., 1904.

Lewis R. Amis graduated from Vanderbilt University in 1878. In the same year he joined the Tennessee Conference of the Methodist Episcopal Church, South, as an itinerant preacher. Later he became pastor of a church at Pulaski, Tenn., not far from his birthplace, and there he remained until his death. See "Jehovah, God, Who Dwelt of Old."

John Antes, Moravian pastor, missionary, and composer; b. Frederick, Pa., March 24, 1740; d. Bristol, England, Dec. 17, 1811.

John Antes was a student in the Moravian school, Bethlehem, Pa., from 1752. Gifted in music, he was also a skilled workman with an inventive mind. A violin which he made in 1759 still exists. He later made a viola and a cello. Twenty-five of his anthems and twelve chorales survive. He left America in 1764 and spent the years from 1765 to 1769 learning the trade of watchmaker. In 1769 he entered the Moravian ministry and became the first American missionary to Egypt. He was imprisoned and beaten at the order of a bey who hoped to extort money from him. While recovering from this ordeal, he composed his three string trios. Settling in Fulneck, England, he was in charge of the finances of the Moravian congregation there. A notation by Joseph Haydn shows that he knew Antes as a composer. Antes sent a number of his inventions to the Leipzig *Allgemeine Musikalische Zeitung* in 1806, including a method for tuning the violin and suggestions for an improved violin bow and piano hammers. When he retired from his post in Fulneck in 1808, he and his wife moved to Bristol. See his chorale tune set to Christian Gregor's "O welch ein Licht" ("What Splendid Rays").

Verna Arvey, pianist and journalist; b. Los Angeles, Calif., Feb. 16, 1910.

Verna Arvey was educated in the public schools of Los Angeles and studied piano privately with Marguerite d'Aleria, Rose Cooper Vinetz, Alexander Kosloff, and Ann Eachus. She concertized in the United States and Latin America and appeared as soloist with Raymond Paige's orchestra over the CBS network and, in 1939, with the Los Angeles Philharmonic Orchestra under Otto Klemperer, playing William Grant Still's *Kaintuck,* which the composer dedicated to her.

Verna Arvey has contributed articles to *Etude,* the *New York Times, Musical Courier, Musical America, Chesterian* (London), *American Dancer, Opera and Concert, Ritmo* (Madrid), *Musical Digest,* and *American Mercury.* She has been on the staff of *Opera and Concert* since 1947. In 1939 she was the author of a monograph on William Grant Still and in 1941 Dutton published her book *Choreographic Music.*

Since her marriage to William Grant Still in 1939 she has supplied texts for many of Still's compositions. Among these are *Lenox Avenue* (commissioned by CBS); *Rhapsody for Soprano;* the ballet, *Miss Sally's Party;* and many songs. See her "All That I Am."

Emma L. Ashford, organist and composer; b. Newark, Del., March 27, 1850; d. Nashville, Tenn., Sept. 22, 1930.

Emma Ashford's musical talent was evident at an early age. At twelve she was an organist in Kewanee, Ill. After her marriage to

John Ashford, she moved with him to Nashville, where he was superintendent of buildings and grounds at Vanderbilt University. Emma Ashford composed church music and hymn tunes. Among the latter were EVELYN and SUTHERLAND ("O Son of Man, Thou Madest Known") (q.v.), published in *The Methodist Hymnal* of 1905.

Richard K. Avery, innovative Presbyterian minister and composer; b. Visalia, Calif., Aug. 26, 1934.

Richard K. Avery graduated from the University of Redlands and attended Union Theological Seminary in New York City. In 1959 he became pastor of the First Presbyterian Church of Port Jervis, N.Y. He stresses the use of contemporary music and dramatic presentations as an aid to worship. With his choirmaster, Donald Marsh, he wrote *Hymns Hot and Carols Cool; More, More, More;* and *Alive and Singing.* See "And the Cock Begins to Crow."

Donald C. Babcock, Methodist minister and college professor; b. Minneapolis, Minn., 1885.

Donald C. Babcock was educated at the University of Minnesota (A.B., 1907; A.M., 1908) and at Boston University (S.T.B., 1912). Ordained a Methodist minister, he held pastorates in the state of Washington and in New England between the years 1908 and 1918. From 1918 to 1944 he was professor of history at the University of New Hampshire. Appointed professor of philosophy in the same institution in 1944 he served in that position until his retirement in 1956.

His publications include *Man and Social Achievement, An Introduction to Social Achievement* (1929), and two volumes of poems: *For Those I Taught* (1951) and *New England Harvest* (1953). See "O God, in Whom the Flow of Days."

Maltbie Davenport Babcock, Presbyterian minister and hymn writer; b. Syracuse, N.Y., Aug. 3, 1858; d. in Italy, May 18, 1901.

Educated at Syracuse University and Auburn Theological Seminary, Maltbie Davenport Babcock became a top-rank student in both schools, excelling in scholarship, athletics, dramatics, and music. He was a natural leader with a magnetic personality which attracted people to him throughout his life. After his ordination to the Presbyterian ministry he became pastor of a church in Lockport, N.Y. When Brown Memorial Church in Baltimore called him to its pulpit, he accepted the post and stayed fourteen years. In 1899 he was asked to succeed Dr. Henry Van Dyke at the Brick Presbyterian Church in New York City. Eighteen months after his installation in that pulpit, he died while on a Mediterranean tour.

Shortly after his death his hymns were published for the first time in a book of verse, *Thoughts for Everyday Living*. See "Be Strong! We Are Not Here to Play" and "This Is My Father's World."

Samuel Babcock, compiler and composer; fl. late 18th cent.

Frank J. Metcalf's *American Psalmody* lists a singing book, *Middlesex Harmony*, by Samuel Babcock, which appeared in both Watertown, Mass., and Boston in 1795, with a second edition in Boston in 1803. That Babcock was also a composer, as was usual with compilers of this period, is indicated by two tunes: SPRINGFIELD, in Andrew Law's *Select Harmony* (1779), and NEWTON ("Dear Brethren, Are Your Harps in Tune?") (q.v.), in Jacob French's *Harmony of Harmony* (1802). Genealogical accounts of the Babcock family furnish no clue which would enable us to identify our compiler.

Ernst Bacon, composer, pianist, and educator; b. Chicago, Ill., May 26, 1898.

Ernst Bacon studied at Northwestern University, the University of Chicago, and the University of California (M.A., 1935). He studied music privately in Chicago, and later specialized in composition with Karl Weigl in Vienna and Ernest Bloch in San Francisco. After appearing as concert pianist in Europe and the United States, Bacon became instructor in piano at the Eastman School of Music and assistant conductor of the Rochester Opera Company (1925–28). He became director of the School of Music at Syracuse in 1945 and composer-in-residence in 1947. Bacon is a prolific composer whose accomplishments have been recognized by a Pulitzer Traveling Scholarship in 1932 and Guggenheim fellowships in 1939 and 1942. His compositions include *Ford's Theatre* (1943) and the *Enchanted Island* (1954), both for orchestra, and a *Sonata for Cello* (1948). He has been deeply influenced by our native hymn music, as may be seen in his *Five Hymns* for mixed chorus with piano or organ (1952) and "Now Evening Puts Amen to Day" (q.v.), from his opera *A Tree on the Plains*.

Leonard Bacon, Congregational minister and educator; b. Detroit, Mich., Feb. 19, 1802; d. New Haven, Conn., Dec. 23, 1881.

Leonard Bacon's father, a Congregational missionary, had settled in Detroit, where he hoped to convert the Indians. After attending Yale, Leonard went to Andover Theological Seminary. His *Hymns and Sacred Songs for the Monthly Concert* (Andover, Mass., 1823), the first American collection of missionary hymns, appeared while he was a student there. "Wake the Song of Jubilee" (q.v.) was one of the three original hymns included. In 1825 he was called to the Centre Church in New Haven and his hymn "Here, Lord of Life and Light, to Thee" was written for his installation. Bacon was a member of the editorial committee for *Psalms and Hymns for Christian Use and Worship* issued in 1845 for the General Convention of Connecticut. It included five of his own hymns. In 1866 Bacon was appointed professor at the Yale School of Divinity. An excellent debater, he was prominent as a writer and lecturer on slavery. He helped found *The New Englander* and was active in founding *The Independent,* one of the most influential religious publications of the late nineteenth century. See "O God, Beneath Thy Guiding Hand," written in 1833 for the bicentennial of the founding of New Haven, and "Hail, Tranquil Hour of Closing Day."

Benjamin F. Baker, singer, choir director, and educator; b. Wenham, Mass., July 10, 1811; d. Boston, Mass., March 11, 1889.

From 1841 to 1847 Benjamin F. Baker taught music in the schools of Boston as Lowell Mason's (q.v.) successor. In addition he served as vice-president of the Handel and Haydn Society (1844–49) and was active as a vocal soloist. He was principal and head of the department of voice of the Boston Music School, which he founded in 1851. The closing of the school in 1868 marked the end of his own career.

Baker was co-editor of a series of choir and chorus books: *The Boston Musical Education Society's Collection,* with Isaac B. Woodbury (q.v.) (Boston, 1842), *Choral,* with Woodbury (Boston, 1845), *The Haydn Collection of Church Music,* with L. H. Southard (1850), *Melodia Sacra,* with Artemas N. Johnson and Josiah Osgood (q.v.) (1852). *The Haydn Collection* was typical of its period in including melodies from Haydn, Handel, Mozart, Beethoven, and others arranged as psalm tunes. In addition to hymn and psalm tunes, glees, and anthems, Baker composed three rather grandiloquent cantatas: *The Storm*

King, The Burning Ship, and *Camillus the Conqueror.* He published *Thorough Bass and Harmony* in 1870 and was for a time an editor of *The Boston Musical Journal.*

A lasting reminder of the work of Benjamin Baker is the annual Worcester music festival. Baker helped a local musician, Edward Hamilton (q.v.), organize the first festival. See his WALLINGFORD ("In Pleasant Lands Have Fallen the Lines").

Thomas Baldwin, Baptist evangelist and minister; b. Bozrah, Conn., Dec. 23, 1753; d. Waterville, Maine, Aug. 29, 1825.

Thomas Baldwin lost his father at an early age. When his mother remarried he went with her to Canaan, N.H. He married there at age twenty-two. After several successful terms as his town's representative in the legislature, he began the study of law, but the death of his first child turned him to religion. In 1780, when two visiting Baptist ministers held services in Canaan, he became a convert and was baptized a year later. After his ordination in 1783 he spent seven years as an evangelist. He then accepted an offer from the Second Baptist Church of Boston and, in 1790, became its pastor. He served until his death. A number of his hymns were included in Baptist collections. "From Whence Doth This Union Arise?" (q.v.) still survives in the South.

Hosea Ballou 1, Universalist clergyman and hymn writer; b. Richmond, N.H., April 30, 1771; d. Boston, Mass., June 7, 1852.

Hosea Ballou grew up in frontier poverty; largely self-taught, he learned to write on birch bark. His books were the Bible and an almanac. At the age of eighteen Ballou joined the Baptist church. Through his older brother David and others he was influenced by Universalist teachings and was excommunicated in 1791. He came in contact with John Murray at the New England General Convention of Universalists and began to preach. He supported himself by teaching school in Rhode Island and Massachusetts while he preached as an itinerant. His success led Elhanan Winchester (q.v.) to summon him in 1794 for an unsolicited ordination. After his marriage in 1796 Ballou continued his circuit preaching, first from Dana, Mass., and later from Barnard, Vt. His period of eminence was spent in Boston (1817–52) where he was pastor of the Second Church. He, with Abner Kneeland and Edward Turner, edited the

Universalist *Hymns Composed by Different Authors* (Walpole, Mass., 1808) which includes 109 of his hymns. In 1821 he edited a hymnal with Edward Turner called *The Universalist Hymn Book: A New Collection.* See "Dear Lord, Behold Thy Servants," "In God's Eternity," and "When God Descends with Men to Dwell."

Hosea Ballou II, Universalist clergyman and college president; b. Guilford, Vt., Oct. 18, 1796; d. Medford, Mass., May 27, 1861.

Hosea Ballou II was a son of Asahel Ballou and grandnephew of Hosea Ballou I (q.v.), both early converts to Universalism. His early education was in the public school in Halifax, Vt., where his father had settled as a farmer and maker of spinning wheels and chairs. Although he showed exceptional ability in his studies with his Latin tutor, a local clergyman, he was not permitted to go to college because his parents feared proselyting influences. At seventeen he went to assist his granduncle with a school in Portsmouth, N.H. There he obtained enough theological training to become a pastor in Stafford, Conn., in 1817. After much itinerant preaching, he married and accepted a larger pastorate in the New Universalist Church of Roxbury, Mass., in 1821, where he also conducted a private school for boys. In 1838 he moved to a pastorate in Medford, Mass., where he fostered public schools and supervised the study of ministerial candidates. During those years Ballou helped edit the *Universalist Magazine* (1822), the *Universalist Expositor* (1830–40), and the *Universalist Quarterly and General Review* (1844–56).

After he taught himself German, French, and Greek, in addition to the Latin and Hebrew he already knew, he published the *Ancient History of Universalism* (1829), which ran to four editions. In recognition of his scholarship the Board of Overseers of Harvard College elected him to membership (1843–58) and made him an honorary Doctor of Divinity in 1845. In 1854 he was made a member of the Massachusetts Board of Education.

Spurred on by his zeal, his denomination incorporated Tufts College in 1852 and appointed him first president, a post he held from 1854 to 1861 while teaching both history and philosophy in that institution. His writings have been preserved in *Hosea Ballou, 2d, D.D.: His Origin, Life, and Letters* (1896), written by Hosea Starr Ballou. See "Ye Realms below the Skies."

Silas Ballou, Universalist layman and hymn writer; b. Cumberland, R.I., Feb. 24, 1753; d. Richmond, N.H., Feb. 10, 1837.

Silas Ballou's *New Hymns on Various Subjects* was published in Worcester, Mass., in 1785 (2d ed., Newbury, Vt., 1797). Twenty-five of his hymns were included in *Evangelical Psalms, Hymns, and Spiritual Songs. Selected from Various Authors* (Philadelphia, 1792). See "Almighty God in Being Was" and "While I Am Young."

James Henry Bancroft, b. Boston, Mass., 1819; d. there Aug. 25, 1844.

Though James Henry Bancroft intended to become a Congregational minister he was unable to realize his goal because of poor health. His "Brother, Though from Yonder Sky," which was reproduced in a number of books as a funeral hymn, was written for a fellow student at Andover (Dudley Leavitt), who died after a brief illness in 1842. It was first published in the following year in *The Psalmist: A New Collection for the Use of Baptist Churches.*

Joel Barlow, poet and diplomat; b. Redding, Conn., March 24, 1754; d. Cracow, Poland, Dec. 24, 1812.

Joel Barlow was educated at Dartmouth and Yale, from which he graduated at the head of his class, receiving a degree in 1778. He studied law, then theology, and was licensed to preach in the Congregational Church. He served as a chaplain in the Revolutionary War (1780–83). During that time he was associated with his college friends Timothy Dwight and David Humphreys. After the war he settled in Hartford, Conn., resumed the study of law, and started a weekly gazette called *The American Mercury.* He gained a reputation as a poet who composed popular patriotic songs and as the author of a long poem *Columbia.* The General Association of Connecticut selected him to revise Watts's version of the psalms. Published in 1785, it was entitled *Doctor Watts' Imitation of the Psalms of David, Corrected and Enlarged by Joel Barlow.* Barlow's critics felt that the text of Watts had been revised too freely. In particular, President Ezra Stiles of Yale noted, "Mr. Barlow is an excellent poet; yet he cannot retouch Watts to advantage." In spite of opposition Barlow's version attained four editions, but was finally rejected by the Connecticut Congregationalists who had authorized it, partly because Barlow during his stay in France was suspected of being "an infidel."

Barlow's later career was chiefly concerned with affairs abroad. He lived in Paris for seventeen years. As consul of the United States in Algiers he concluded treaties (1795) with the Barbary States that secured the release of more than one hundred captives. In 1805 he returned to the United States and purchased a home in Georgetown, Washington, D.C. Appointed by President Madison in 1810 as Minister Plenipotentiary to France he again moved to Paris and entered into negotiations with Napoleon. While the latter was conducting his Russian campaign he sent for Barlow to meet him in conference in Poland. Barlow's hardships on the journey led to his death in Cracow. Distinguished honors were paid to his memory in both France and the United States. See "Along the Banks," "Judge Me, O God," and "O God of My Salvation, Hear."

John Barnard, Congregational minister and psalmist; b. Boston, Mass., Nov. 6, 1681; d. Marblehead, Mass, Jan. 24, 1770.

After John Barnard received an M.A. from Harvard, Governor Dudley appointed him a chaplain of the army which was to go to Acadia and Port Royal in 1707. On his return Barnard became an itinerant preacher. In 1709 he sailed to Barbados and then to London, where he stayed for almost a year. Barnard continued to preach but was also active as a wine- and ale-taster. He took this opportunity to meet clergymen, many of whom hoped to find posts in New England churches through his good offices.

Although he returned to the United States in 1710, he did not obtain a permanent pastorate until 1716. He and Edward Holyoke had been nominated two years earlier for the church in Marblehead, Mass. Since the congregation could not agree on a single choice, it split, and a new meeting house was erected. Barnard went to the old church where he stayed for the remainder of his life.

His *New Version of the Psalms* (1752) was designed to replace the obsolescent expressions of the *Bay Psalm Book* with the language of Barnard's own time. It also turned from the close renderings of the older version to a freer and more consciously literary style. See "Nations That Long in Darkness Walked" and "Thrice Blest the Man."

Edward Shippen Barnes, organist and composer; b. Seabright, N.J., Sept. 14, 1887; d. Idylwild, Calif., 1958.

Edward Shippen Barnes studied organ with Professor Van Dyke at the Lawrenceville School. At Yale University he studied with

Harry B. Jepson and Horatio Parker (q.v.) in 1910 and 1911, then went to Paris where his teachers were Louis Vierne, and, at the Schola Cantorum, Vincent D'Indy and Abel Decaux.

On his return to New York he was organist at the Church of the Incarnation (1911–12) and at the Rutgers Presbyterian Church (1913–24); in Philadelphia at Saint Stephen's Church (1924–38), and in Santa Monica, Calif., at the First Presbyterian Church (from 1938). He composed two symphonies, three suites, and shorter pieces for organ, several Episcopal services, cantatas (*The Comforter, Remember Now Thy Creator,* and *Christmas*) as well as instructive material for organ students and collections for junior choirs.

See HOLMES ("God of the Nations, Near and Far"), FAITHFUL LEGIONS ("Lord God of Hosts"), and COMRADES OF THE CROSS ("O Young and Fearless Prophet").

Maro L. Bartlett, vocalist, conductor, and educator; b. Brownhelm, Ohio, Oct. 25, 1847; d. Des Moines, Iowa, 1919.

Maro L. Bartlett received his first musical instruction in a country singing school. Later, as a student at Oberlin Conservatory, he prepared for a career in music. After his graduation he became conductor of the Philharmonic Society in Meadville, Pa. From Meadville he went to Orange, N.J., to join the public-school system as music supervisor. He then moved to New York, appearing as a bass soloist in oratorio concerts in various cities while teaching in the New York public schools. In 1880 he moved to Chicago, where he conducted the Mozart Club, directed the music in the First Congregational Church, and headed the vocal department of Chicago Musical College. Leaving Chicago he went to Des Moines to become director of the Des Moines College of Music. Drake University of that city gave him a Doctor of Music degree in 1889. See TEMPLE ("Jehovah, God, Who Dwelt of Old").

Seth Curtis Beach, Unitarian minister; b. near Marion, Wayne Co., N.Y., Aug. 8, 1837; d. Watertown, Mass., Jan. 30, 1932.

Seth Curtis Beach received his higher education at Antioch and Union colleges. He graduated from Harvard Divinity School in 1866 and his subsequent ministerial work included pastorates in Augusta, Maine; Dedham, Mass.; Bangor, Maine; and Wayland, Mass. He retired to Watertown, Mass., in 1911. One sermon, "Our Martyred President," was a tribute to the memory of President Garfield. Two other published sermons, dated September 1 and 25, 1881, were delivered in the First Church in Dedham. In 1886, at the celebration of the 250th anniversary of the incorporation of the town, his hymn "To Him Who Formed the Rolling Spheres" was sung. On November 18 and 19, 1888 the First Church observed its 250th "Gathering." As chairman of the general committee in charge of arrangements Seth Beach preached the commemorative sermon. See "Mysterious Presence! Source of All" and "Thou One in All, Thou All in One."

John C. Bechler, composer, teacher, Moravian pastor, later bishop; b. Oesel, an island in the Baltic Sea, Jan. 7, 1784; d. Herrnhut, Germany, April 15, 1857.

John C. Bechler was in the United States from 1806 to 1836. During that time he taught theology in the Seminary at Nazareth, Pa., and served Moravian churches in Philadelphia; Staten Island; and Lititz, Pa. He found time to compose rather extensively, writing hymns, anthems, and ariettas. Of special interest for our anthology is a collection entitled *VIII Hymns Selected from the Common Prayer Book of the Episcopal Church* (New York, c.1813). See Hymn 6 ("Awake, My Soul, In Grateful Songs").

Charles Beecher, minister and educator; b. Litchfield, Conn., Oct. 1, 1815; d. Georgetown, Mass., April 21, 1900.

Charles Beecher, a son of Lyman Beecher and the youngest brother of Henry Ward Beecher and Harriet Beecher Stowe, prepared for college at the Boston Latin School and at Lawrence Academy in Groton where his brother George was headmaster. He graduated from Bowdoin College in 1835, then studied theology at Lane Seminary in Ohio. He was for a time a student and teacher of music in Cincinnati. Licensed to preach by the Presbytery of Indianapolis, he was ordained pastor of the Second Presbyterian Church at Fort Wayne, Ind., in 1844. In 1851 he became pastor of the First Congregational Church in Newark, N.J., where his pronounced antislavery views were an obstacle to fellowship with the other Protestant churches in the city. He was installed as minister of the First Congregational Church at Georgetown, Mass., in 1857. From 1870 to 1877 he resided in Florida, where he was for two years state superintendent of public instruction. After serving as acting pastor of the church in Wysox, Pa. (1885–93), he moved again to Georgetown, where he spent the remaining years of his life. He was one of the musical editors of Henry Ward Beecher's *Plymouth Collection* (1855) and author of several hymns. Julian mentions two: "There's Rest in the Grave" and "We Are on Our Journey Home" (q.v.). The latter, however, was adapted from an old revival hymn. See also JACINTH ("Tell Me Not in Mournful Numbers") and REST ("When Winds Are Raging").

Johann Conrad Beissel, religious leader and hymn writer; b. Eberlach, the Palatinate, April 1690; d. Ephrata, Pa., July 6, 1768.

The posthumous child of a drunken baker, Johann Conrad Beissel lost his mother when he was eight years old. He was apprenticed to a baker who taught him to play the violin. Converted in his twenty-seventh year, he almost immediately revealed a pietistic bent and accepted celibacy as a primary requirement for deep devotion to God. Because of his views Beissel was banished from the Palatinate. Two of his friends, Stiefel and Stuntz, persuaded him to go to America with them, and they set sail in 1720, arriving in Boston in the autumn of that year.

In 1728 Beissel founded the "Economy," a Community of Seventh Day Baptists, at Ephrata, Pa. In 1732 he was joined by some of the Solitary Brethren, Sisters, and married couples who pledged themselves to continence. At first the Solitary Brethren and Spiritual Virgins were quartered in the same building, a fact which gave rise to suspicion and bitter persecution. The community grew until it contained several hundred members. Later the men and women lived in separate dwellings; the Sisters were veiled, and both sexes were garbed in hoods and cowls. The colony excelled in the printing of books and the illumination of manuscripts.

Beissel's *Mystische und Sehr Geheyme Spruche,* printed by Benjamin Franklin in 1730, was one of the earliest American publications containing German poetry. More important was the 1747 hymnal *Das Gesang der Einsamen und Verlassenen Turtel-Taube,* which was printed on the Ephrata press. The music that Beissel composed for these hymns has been preserved in manuscript. Beissel also left a treatise on harmony. Both the treatise and his actual compositions reveal his limitations as a composer. Nevertheless the singing of the choir which he developed in the Ephrata community impressed visitors as strange and other-worldly. When we consider that Beissel produced the earliest substantial body of identifiable compositions in the American Colonies, their importance becomes evident. See "Die Sonn ist wieder aufgegangen."

Supply Belcher, pioneer choir leader and composer; b.
Stoughton, Mass., April 10, 1752; d. June 9, 1836.

Supply Belcher studied music with William Billings, who was in
Stoughton in 1774. Shortly after the outbreak of the Revolutionary
War Belcher moved to a farm near Canton, Mass., and opened a tav-
ern. Musical people of the town formed the habit of meeting there.
Belcher served under Washington in the army. Poor after he was
mustered out, he decided to try his luck in a new place and moved to
Hallowell, Maine, in 1785 and six years later to Sandy River Town-
ship, later Farmington, Maine.

Belcher served Farmington as its principal magistrate, as select-
man, and several times as its representative in the Massachusetts
legislature. Each Sunday he led the singers in the Old Center Meeting House while John Titcomb accompanied on his flute. The
Squire's own singing, however, was rated second to his violin playing. He went with a member of the Stoughton Musical Society
to the Harvard Commencement of 1792 just to hear the music.
When Hallowell Academy celebrated the close of its first year in
1796, Belcher conducted the music. His collection, *The Harmony of
Maine,* was published in 1794. Many of Belcher's tunes were named
for towns in Maine, such as BATH, FARMINGTON, and YORK. See
UNION ("Our States, O Lord").

Daniel Belknap, singing master, compiler, and composer; b.
Feb. 9, 1771, Framingham, Mass.; d. Pawtucket, R.I., Oct. 31,
1815.

Daniel Belknap's education was limited to the elementary school in
Framingham. Later he was active there as farmer and mechanic. He
possessed musical gifts which he cultivated to such purpose that he
was able to teach others by the time he was eighteen. In 1812 he
moved to Pawtucket where he later died of a fever.

Belknap's first publication was *The Harmonist's Companion* (Boston,
1797), followed by the *Evangelical Harmony* (Boston, 1800), *The Middlesex Collection of Sacred Harmony* (Boston, 1802), and *The Village Compilation of Sacred Music* (Boston, 1806). His last collection, *The Middlesex Songster, containing a collection of the most approved songs now in
use* (Dedham, Mass., 1809), included BELKNAP'S MARCH. See his
BLUE HILL ("Dear Lord, Behold Thy Servants").

Jeremy Belknap, Congregational clergyman and author; b. Boston, Mass., June 4, 1744; d. there June 20, 1798.

Jeremy Belknap's mother was a niece of Mather Byles (q.v.); his father a leather dresser and a furrier. Belknap entered Harvard before he was fifteen and taught school at Milford, Mass., for a year or two after his graduation. While teaching he was also studying for the ministry, and in 1766 he was installed as pastor of the Congregational Church in Dover, N.H. Although he was appointed chaplain to the New Hampshire troops at Cambridge during the Revolution, he could not accept because of ill health. In 1786 Belknap resigned at Dover and in 1787 was called to the Federal Street Church in Boston, where he continued as minister during the rest of his life.

Belknap's reputation rests chiefly on his *History of New Hampshire* (1784–92), a three-volume work which is remarkable for its style, research, and impartiality. About 1787 he amused himself by writing *The Foresters,* a humorous allegory on the rise of the British colonies in America. He wrote a plea for the abolition of slave traffic in 1788. His two-volume *American Biography* (1794–98) dealt with the lives of the early explorers and colonial leaders. In addition to his historical work he wrote a biography of Isaac Watts and in 1795 published *Sacred Poetry: consisting of Psalms and Hymns adapted to Christian Devotion in public and private.* This volume satisfied only those Congregational churches which were evolving toward Unitarian doctrine and was long used by them.

In the summer of 1790 Belknap formulated plans for an antiquarian society and the following January attended the meeting which established the Massachusetts Historical Society (incorporated 1794). Belknap was its first corresponding secretary. See "Far from Our Friends," "How Often Have Our Restless Foes," and "Thus Spake the Saviour."

Nathan S. S. Beman, Congregational and Presbyterian pastor; b. Canaan (now New Lebanon), N.Y., Nov. 27, 1785; d. Carbondale, Ill., Aug. 8, 1871.

Nathan Beman was trained in an academy at Poultney, Vt., and the grammar school at Williamstown, Mass. He entered Williams College in 1803, transferred to Middlebury in 1804, and graduated in 1807. While principal at Lincoln Academy, Newcastle, Maine, he studied theology, was licensed to preach in 1809, and was ordained as pastor of the Third Congregational Church of Portland, Maine, in 1810. Illness compelled him to seek a milder climate and he moved to Hancock, Ga., where he established a school and a Presbyterian church. In 1822 he accepted a call from the First Presbyterian Church in Troy, N.Y. After occupying the pulpit there for forty years, he retired in 1863 and spent the last years of his life in Carbondale, Ill., with his daughter.

Williams and Middlebury colleges granted him honorary degrees. He was Moderator of the Presbyterian General Assembly of 1831 and, as an abolitionist, took an active part in the debates (1837–38) that led to the dismemberment of the church. His *Sacred Lyrics,* published at Troy in 1832, was enlarged and reissued in 1841. The later edition with the title altered to *Church Psalmist* was used by the New School Presbyterians. Beman is remembered for three hymns: "Jesus, We Bow Before Thy Throne," "Hark, the Judgment Trumpet Sounding," and "Jesus, I Come to Thee" (q.v.).

George Bennard, Methodist evangelist; b. Youngstown, Ohio, 1873; d. Reed City, Mich., Oct. 11, 1958.

George Bennard first worked with the Salvation Army and was later ordained in the Methodist Episcopal Church. He made his home in Reed City, Mich., where he engaged in evangelistic work. He is best remembered for the well-known THE OLD RUGGED CROSS ("On a Hill Far Away") (q.v.).

Anna Elizabeth Bennett, librarian and writer; b. Brooklyn, N.Y., July 1914.

Anna Elizabeth Bennett's father was a physician and her mother a pianist. Graduated from Adelphi College in 1935 and from the Pratt Library School in 1937, she thereafter worked in libraries in several cities, including New York, Lansing, Mich., Morristown, N.J., and Brooklyn.

In 1953 Lippincott published her children's book, *Little Witch;* and in 1954 the Fine Editions Press published a book of her poems, *Cantabile.* She now lives in Southampton, N.Y., and devotes her full time to writing. See "Hush Thee, Princeling," with music composed by Norman Dello Joio for *American Hymns.*

S. Fillmore Bennett, druggist; b. Eden, N.Y. June 21, 1836; d. Illinois, 1898.

S. Fillmore Bennett was a schoolteacher in Illinois and later an editor and druggist in Wisconsin. During the Civil War he served in the army. See "There's a Land That Is Fairer Than Day."

Louis F. Benson, Presbyterian minister and hymnologist; b. Philadelphia, Pa., July 22, 1855; d. there Oct. 10, 1930.

Benson intended to be a lawyer, and it was only after seven years in that profession that he prepared for the ministry at the Princeton Theological Seminary. His first charge was the Church of the Redeemer, Germantown, Pa. where he remained until 1892. He then pursued a career as hymn book compiler and authority on liturgics and hymnology, teaching the former at the Auburn Theological Seminary and the latter at the Princeton Seminary.

Among the books which he edited are: *The Hymnal* (Presbyterian) (1895), *The Hymnal for Congregational Churches* (1896), *The Chapel Hymnal* (1898), and *The School Hymnal* (1900). In collaboration with Henry Van Dyke (q.v.) he edited *The Book of Common Worship of the Presbyterian Church in the U.S.A.* (1905). His *Christian Song* (1926) best represents his personal preferences. He also wrote several books in the field of hymnody. *The English Hymn, Its Development and Use in Worship,* first published in 1915, remains a standard work in its field. His *Hymns Original and Translated* included both Benson's own hymns and the music which had been composed for them by contemporary musicians. See "O Love That Lights the Eastern Sky," "O Risen Lord upon the Throne," "O Thou Whose Feet Have Climbed Life's Hill," and "Why Linger Yet upon the Strand?"

George Washington Bethune, pastor of the Reformed Dutch Church; b. New York City, March 18, 1805; d. Florence, Italy, April 27, 1862.

George Washington Bethune entered Columbia College in his fifteenth year. There he studied three years before entering Dickinson College at Carlisle, Pa., where his father's friend, John M. Mason, was the president. After graduating from Dickinson (1823) he studied for two years in the Theological Seminary at Princeton. Licensed to preach by the Second Presbytery of New York in 1826 he went to Savannah, Ga., as a missionary to sailors and blacks.

Ordained in 1827 Bethune became pastor of the Reformed Dutch Church of Rhinebeck, N.Y. (1827–30), of the Reformed Dutch Church of Utica, N.Y. (1830–34), of the First Reformed Dutch Church of Philadelphia (1834–37), of the Third Church of the same city (1837–50), and of the Reformed Dutch Church in Brooklyn Heights (1850–59). Ill health caused him to resign from this pastorate and, after a trip to Europe, he returned to New York where he became an associate pastor of St. Paul's Reformed Dutch Church.

Bethune was repeatedly honored with invitations to other pastorates, to professorships, and to presidencies of colleges. Both New

York University and the University of Pennsylvania offered him their highest administrative posts. In 1838 he received an honorary D.D. from the University of Pennsylvania.

His publications were numerous: several volumes of a theological or homiletic nature as well as *Lays of Love and Faith and Other Poems* (1848); his edition of Izaak Walton's *Compleat Angler* (1847); *British Female Poets* (1848), with biographical and critical notices; and a post-humous work, *Lectures on the Heidelberg Catachism* (1864). See "Jesus, Shepherd of Thy Sheep," "O for the Happy Hour," and "There Is No Name So Sweet on Earth."

Emma Frances Bevan, translator; b. Oxford, England, Sept. 25, 1827; d. 1909.

The daughter of Rev. (later Bishop) Philip Nicholas Shuttleworth, Emma married R. C. L. Bevan, a banker, in 1856. Her contributions to hymnology are to be found in a volume of translations from the German entitled *Songs of Eternal Life,* which she published in 1858, and in the later *Songs of Praise for Christian Pilgrims,* which appeared in 1859. A number of her translations have come into use. Her "Rise, Ye Children" is the best translation of Justus Falckner's "Auf ihr Christen" (q.v.), although the meter differs from that of the original.

William Billings, singing master and composer; b. Boston, Mass., Oct. 7, 1746; d. there Sept. 26, 1800.

On his father's death William Billings was apprenticed to a tanner, and it is said that he chalked his early tunes on the walls of a bark mill. He was largely self-taught, gathering what he could from elementary treatises by William Tans'ur (q.v.) and others. In spite of physical disabilities—one sightless eye, a withered arm, legs of different length, and a rasping voice—he was an enthusiastic and successful singing master and a popular composer. One of his schools, held in Stoughton, Mass. (1774), led to the formation of the Stoughton Musical Society (founded 1786), the oldest society of its kind still in existence.

Billings compiled and published six collections of church music which include his original compositions: *The New England Psalm Singer* (Boston, 1770), the first edition of which was engraved by Paul Revere; *The Singing Master's Assistant* (1778, "Billings' Best"); *Music in Miniature* (Boston, 1779); *The Psalm Singer's Amusement* (1781); *The Suffolk Harmony* (1786); and *The Continental Harmony*

(1794). His CHESTER ("Let Tyrants Shake Their Iron Rod") (q.v.) became the hymn of the Revolution. He composed and advocated "fuguing tunes" but also composed plain tunes and anthems. He introduced the bass viol and pitch pipe into church choirs. See also PARIS ("Behold with Joy"), SAVANNAH ("From Whence Does This Union Arise?"), THOMAS-TOWN ("Great God, How Frail a Thing Is Man"), AMHERST ("Hail to the Joyous Day"), JORDAN ("Hark! Tis the Saviour of Mankind"), WEST SUDBURY ("Here Is a Song"), MAJESTY ("The Lord Descended from Above"), SULLIVAN ("Permit Us, Lord, to Consecrate"), AMERICA ("To Thee the Tuneful Anthem Soars"), and SUDBURY ("What If the Saint Must Die").

Abraham W. Binder, music director and composer; b. New York City, Jan. 13, 1895; d. there Oct. 10, 1966.

Educated at Columbia University (1916–20), where he was a Rosenthal Fellow, Abraham Binder later received the honorary Bachelor of Music degree from the New York College of Music in 1922. In 1918 he became director of the School of Music for the Young Men's Hebrew Association of New York. He conducted the Jewish Choral Society until 1965. Binder joined the staff of Hebrew Union College of the Jewish Institute of Religion in 1922 and was appointed professor of liturgical music in 1937; he was also director of music at the Stephen Wise Free Synagogue. Binder was guest conductor of the Manhattan Symphony Orchestra and of the Palestine Symphonic Ensemble. In 1941 he organized the conference on "The Status of Synagogue Music in America." He was also chairman of the committee on "Music of All Faiths" for the National Federation of Music Clubs in 1949. His compositions include *Ha-Chalutzim Overture; Holy Land Impressions; Concertante for String Orchestra; Rhapsody for Piano and Orchestra; Lament—in the Memory of the Defenders of the Warsaw Ghetto; Hibbath Shabbath; Evening Service for the New Year; Kabbalath Shabbath; Amos on Times Square,* a choral poem; *Israel Reborn,* a choral poem; and *Requiem Yiskor,* an oratorio. Binder was the musical editor of *New Palestinian Folk Songs: Book I,* 1925, *Book II,* 1932, *Palestine in Song, Pioneer Songs of Palestine, The Jewish World in Song,* and the *Union Hymnal* (3d ed., 1932), and of a book on biblical chant. See Binder's tunes to "Come, O Sabbath Day," and "In Mercy, Lord, Incline Thine Ear."

Seth Bingham, organist, college teacher, and composer; b. Bloomfield, N.J., April 16, 1882; d. New York City, Jan. 21, 1972.

Seth Bingham studied organ at the age of fourteen and directed his first choir when he was seventeen. While at Yale he studied organ with Harry B. Jepson and composition with Horatio Parker. He received his bachelor's degree in 1904 and won first prize in organ playing. In 1906–07 he studied composition with Vincent D'Indy and organ with Charles-Marie Widor and Alexandre-Félix Guilmant in Paris. He received the degree Bachelor of Music from Yale in 1908 and the Steinert prize in composition. In the following year he became a fellow of the American Guild of Organists. After teaching at Yale from 1908 to 1920, Bingham became a member of the Music Department of Columbia University, where he remained from 1920 to his retirement in 1954. For thirty-five years he was organist and choir director at the Madison Avenue Presbyterian Church (1913–1948).

His *Wall Street Fantasy* (1912) was played by the New York Philharmonic and his *Passacaglia* (1918) by the Boston Symphony Orchestra. *Wilderness Stone,* for narrator, soloists, chorus and orchestra, is a setting of an episode from Vincent Benét's *John Brown's Body.* Bingham wrote much for organ including a *Concerto for Brass, Snare Drum, and Organ* (1954). See his ADVENT ("Lord of My Heart's Elation") and FOREFATHERS ("O God, Above the Drifting Years").

Amos Blanchard, singing master, compiler, and composer; fl. early 19th cent.

In the list of subscribers printed at the end of Samuel Holyoke's *Columbian Repository* in 1802, Amos Blanchard's residence is given as Exeter, N.H. In 1823, on Monday and Friday evenings, Blanchard taught at a school for instruction in sacred music at the Methodist Chapel on Sewall Street in Salem, Mass. His terms were two dollars and a quarter, one-half payable in advance. His *Newburyport Collection of Sacred European Music* (Exeter, N.H., 1807) was followed by *The American Musical Primer* (Exeter, 1808). CORINTH ("When God Descends with Men to Dwell") (q.v.) appeared in *Village Harmony* in 1803, perhaps earlier.

Ferdinand Q. Blanchard, Congregational minister; b. Jersey City, N.J., July 23, 1876; d. 1968.

Ferdinand Q. Blanchard spent his early years in Newton, Mass. He served churches in Southington, Conn., and East Orange, N.J., before going to Cleveland, Ohio, where he was pastor of the Euclid Avenue Congregational Church for thirty-six years, resigning to become pastor emeritus. During his years in Cleveland he was an active participant in numerous religious, civic, and philanthropic organizations. From 1942 to 1944 he served as Moderator of the Congregational Christian Churches, the highest office in his denomination. See "O Child of Lowly Manger Birth" and "Word of God, Across the Ages."

William G. Blanchard, music educator; b. Greencastle, Ind., Sept. 5, 1905.

William G. Blanchard was the son of Dean William M. Blanchard of De Pauw University, a prominent layman of the Methodist Church who served as a delegate to the General Conferences in 1920, 1924, and 1932. The younger Blanchard studied music at De Pauw and at the School of Music of the University of Michigan. In 1936 he joined the faculty of Pomona College in California as an instructor of music. He became assistant professor in 1939 and associate professor in 1946. See GODWIN ("God of the Strong, God of the Weak").

Philip Bliss, singing evangelist and composer of gospel hymns; b. Clearfield Co., near Rome, Pa., July 9, 1838; d. Ashtabula, Ohio, Dec. 29, 1876.

A log cabin was the first home of Philip Bliss. After he had been baptized by a minister of the Christian denomination he joined a neighboring Baptist church. Although he was musical as a child, it was not until he was nineteen that he was able to take music lessons. Later that year he attended a convention in Rome led by William Batchelder Bradbury. In 1860 he attended a Normal Academy of Music in Geneseo, N.Y., after which he set up as a music teacher himself, going about with an old horse, Fanny, and a twenty-dollar melodeon. In 1863 he sent a song to Root and Cady, a Chicago music publishing firm, requesting a flute as payment. Root sent him the flute, and this contact led Bliss to move to Chicago, where he promoted the interests of the firm by organizing conventions and giving concerts. He met Dwight Moody in 1869 and later traveled as a singing evangelist with Major D. W. Whittle. Bliss and his wife died in the burning wreckage of a train. He shared in and contributed much to the enormous vogue of the gospel hymn, particularly through his *Gospel Songs* (1874), *Gospel Hymns and Sacred Songs* (1875), and *Gospel Hymns No. 2* (1876), the last two with Ira D. Sankey. See "Almost Persuaded."

John Blow, English organist and composer; b. Newark-on-Trent (Nottinghamshire), Feb. 1648/9; d. Westminster (London), Oct. 1, 1708.

As a boy John Blow sang in the Chapel Royal (1660–61), studied organ with Christopher Gibbons, and became organist of Westminster Abbey in 1668. This post passed to Blow's gifted pupil Henry Purcell in 1679, but Blow was reappointed after Purcell's untimely death in 1695. Blow also served as Master of the Children (1674), Master of the Choristers at St. Paul's (1687), and organist (1677) and composer (1699) to the Chapel Royal. His masque *Venus and Adonis* is really a miniature opera. In addition to songs and church music he published a collection of familiar psalm tunes "set full" for the organ. The copy at the Research Library, Lincoln Center, is bound with Daniel Purcell's *The Psalm Tunes set full for the Organ or Harpsichord*, a similar collection. Both are of interest because they show how an organist accompanied congregational singing. See Blow's setting of HACKNEY ("When Wild Confusion Wrecks the Air"). For a similar setting by Daniel Purcell see ST. DAVID ("Lord, Who's the Happy Man").

Howard Boatright, violinist, composer, and teacher; b. Newport News, Va., March 16, 1918.

Howard Boatright gave his first violin recital at the age of fourteen, and appeared in Town Hall, New York City in 1942. In 1943 he became associate professor of violin at the University of Texas. A growing interest in composition led him to resign that position to go to Yale for study with Paul Hindemith in 1945. In 1948 he joined the Yale faculty as assistant professor of the theory of music and upon the retirement of Hugo Kortschak in 1952, he became conductor of the University Orchestra. In addition to his responsibilities at Yale, Boatright served as concertmaster of the New Haven Symphony and director of music at St. Thomas' Episcopal Church.

He was a Fulbright lecturer in India in 1959–60 and spent 1960 in studying violin playing in South India assisted by a grant from the Rockefeller Foundation. From 1964 to 1971 he was dean of the School of Music at Syracuse University.

Among his compositions are a *Quartet for Clarinet and Strings* (1958), a setting of the *Passion According to St. Matthew* (1962), the *Canticle of the Sun* (1963) for chorus, soloist, and orchestra, and *The Slings of Death* (1966), as well as service music for the Episcopal Church and a complete service for Reformed Jewish worship. See his setting of "O Day of God, Draw Nigh," composed for *American Hymns.*

Arnold G. H. Bode, organist and clergyman; b. Dungog, New South Wales, Australia, July 22, 1866; d. Sierra Madre, Calif., Aug. 10, 1952.

Arnold Bode's early activities included work as organist at Cuddeston College, as a curate of a church in one of London's slums, and as chaplain in the home of the High Sheriff of Nottingham. Following his residence in England he migrated, at the age of thirty-three, to the United States where he became canon of the Cathedral of St. John in the Wilderness at Denver, Colo. From that post he went to Laramie, Wyo., where he was dean of St. Matthew's Cathedral and director of the School of Music at the University of Wyoming. In 1913 he began several years of service in country parishes around Los Angeles. He was active in the labor movement. A member of the Musicians' Union, he was elected to the Central Labor Council. See LARAMIE ("I Know Not Where the Road Will Lead").

George H. Boker, poet, dramatist, and diplomat; b. Philadelphia, Pa., Oct. 6, 1823; d. there Jan. 2, 1890.

George H. Boker graduated in 1842 from the College of New Jersey (now Princeton), where he was a contributor to the *Nassau Monthly.* He was married in 1844, spent a year in Europe, and returned to Philadelphia to study law, but soon turned to writing. Boker's first play, *Calaynos* (1849), was performed in Philadelphia. His most successful drama, *Francesca da Rimini,* appeared in New York in 1855 and was revived as late as 1902.

Although a Democrat, he was strongly pro-Union during the Civil War. In 1862 he helped found the Union League in Philadelphia (the first to be formed in this country) and served as its secretary and later its president. *Poems of the War* (1864) gave evidence of his sympathies.

In 1871 Boker was appointed minister to Turkey where he developed into an extremely able diplomat, although he had to contend with indifferent cooperation at home. In 1875 he was transferred to Russia as minister plenipotentiary. He established a cordial relationship with the czar. Recalled in 1878 he returned to Philadelphia where he was a great influence in the city's social and literary life. See "God, To Thee We Humbly Bow."

Matthew Bolles, Baptist minister; b. Ashford, Conn., April 21, 1769; d. Hartford, Conn., Sept. 26, 1838.

Matthew Bolles was the son of a Baptist minister. Early in life he pursued a business career, and it was not until the year 1812 when he was forty-three that he preached his first sermon at Pleasant Valley, Lyme, Conn., and there he was settled as minister after his ordination in 1813.

From 1817 to 1838 he preached successively at Fairfield, Conn., Milford, N.H., and Marblehead and Bridgewater, Mass. He was described as "able, eloquent, and full of the Holy Ghost."

"Here, Lord, Retired, I Bow in Prayer" (q.v.) appeared in *Select Hymns,* compiled by James H. Linsley and Gustavus F. Davis (Hartford, Conn., 1836).

Walter Russell Bowie, Episcopal rector and educator; b. Richmond, Va., Oct. 8, 1882; d. Washington, D.C., April 23, 1969.

Bowie prepared for college at the Hill School. After graduating from Harvard (B.A. 1904) he went to the Virginia Theological Seminary to prepare for the ministry (B.D. 1908, D.D. 1919). Upon his ordination as deacon he was first rector in Greenwood, Va. at Emmanuel Church (1908–11) and subsequently was rector of St. Paul's Church, Richmond, Va. (1911–23) and finally of Grace Church, New York City (1923–39). In 1939 Bowie accepted a professorship in practical theology at Union Theological Seminary, which he held until 1950. He also served as dean of students from 1945 to 1950. In 1950 he became professor of homiletics at the Theological Seminary in Virginia. During his teaching career he held lectureships at Philadelphia Divinity School, Yale Divinity School (1935), and Seabury-Western Theological Seminary (1939).

While in Virginia he had edited the *Southern Churchman*. He served on his denomination's Commission of Faith and Order and on the committee which in 1946 produced the *Revised Standard Edition* of the Bible. Author of numerous books (*The Story of the Bible, The Bible Story for Boys and Girls, Finding God Through St. Paul, The Master, The Living Story of the New Testament*), his hymns are included in English as well as American hymn books.

Lyman Brackett, composer and music editor; fl. late 19th cent.

Lyman Brackett was music editor of the first *Christian Science Hymnal* (1892) to which he contributed ninety-nine tunes. The current hymnal includes five of them, among them the familiar composition GUIDANCE, the best-known musical setting for "Shepherd, Show Me How to Go" (q.v.), by Mary Baker Eddy (q.v.). Copyrighted in 1887, GUIDANCE was one of the earliest tunes written especially for a poem by Mrs. Eddy. Today it is the theme music for most Christian Science radio and television broadcasts. See also NORTON ("O'er Waiting Harp-Strings of the Mind").

William Batchelder Bradbury, composer, compiler, and pioneer in Sunday School music; b. York, Maine, Oct. 6, 1816; d. Montclair, N.J., Jan. 7, 1868.

At the age of fourteen William Batchelder Bradbury went to Boston where he lived with Sumner Hill, who taught him harmony. He enrolled in Lowell Mason's choir at the Bowdoin Street Church and in the Boston Academy. At Mason's request he went to Machias, Maine, and later to St. John's, New Brunswick, where he conducted music classes. In 1841 Bradbury became organist at the Baptist Tabernacle in New York City where he stayed until 1847. There he organized free singing classes and juvenile music festivals which facilitated the introduction of music into the New York public schools. He spent the years from 1847 to 1849 in England and Germany where he studied music and teaching methods. On his return to the United States he devoted his time to composing, compiling collections, conducting music festivals, and participating in normal institutes.

Perhaps *The Jubilee* (1858) was his most successful singing book. Such Sunday-School books as *Fresh Laurels* and the "Golden" series were widely used. His tuneful hymns, harmonized with the utmost simplicity, exactly suited the popular taste of his day. HE LEADETH

ME ("He Leadeth Me, O Blessed Thought") and THE LAND OF BEU-LAH ("My Latest Sun Is Sinking Fast") were early gospel hymns and JESUS LOVES ME (q.v.) was long a favorite Sunday-School hymn. See also ROLLAND ("Almighty God, Thy Constant Care"), PASSAIC ("As Flows the Rapid River"), FULTON ("Brother, Though from Yonder Sky"), WOODWORTH ("Dear Saviour, If These Lambs Should Stray" and "Just As Thou Are"), NO SORROW THERE ("O Sing to Me of Heaven"), SWEETEST NAME ("There Is No Name So Sweet on Earth"), OLIVE'S BROW (" 'Tis Midnight and on Olive's Brow"), and ZEPHYR ("When Thickly Beat the Storms of Life").

William Bradford, governor of Plymouth Colony; b. Austerfield, Yorkshire, 1589/90; d. Plymouth, May 9, 1657.

William Bradford came to Plymouth on the *Mayflower* in 1620 and succeeded Governor Carver the following year. He was elected to this office no less than thirty times; his tenure, though not continuous, spanned the period from 1621 to 1656. He conciliated the Indians by affirming the treaty with Massasoit. Exercising his unusually extensive powers with discretion, he did much to establish the infant colony. Although perhaps intended as a personal narrative, his *History of Plymouth Plantation* is the most revealing document about the early years of this settlement. In an intolerant age, he was relatively tolerant in matters of religion and, although he was primarily a successful administrator, he found time to be a not unsuccessful poet. See "And Truly It Is a Most Glorious Thing."

Anne Bradstreet, one of the first poets in colonial America; b. Northampton, England, c.1612; d. Andover, Mass., Sept. 16, 1672.

Anne Dudley Bradstreet was probably born at Northampton, England, where her father, Thomas Dudley, was a steward on the estate of the Puritan Earl of Lincoln. At sixteen she married Simon Bradstreet, son of a nonconformist minister who had been forced to emigrate to Holland. In 1630, when Anne Bradstreet was eighteen, she came with her husband, mother, and father to the Bay Colony. First settling at Newtown (Cambridge), then at Ipswich, she moved to North Andover about 1644. While she was writing poetry she moved in the leading political and social circles, for her father became governor in 1634. She had eight children; among her descendants were Richard Henry Dana, Wendell Phillips, and Oliver Wendell Holmes.

The Tenth Muse Lately Sprung Up in America was published in London in 1650 (2d ed., Boston, 1678). In her later years she composed a group of *Meditations*. See her "As Spring the Winter Doth Succeed" and "O Thou Most High Who Rulest All."

Nicholas Brady, author; b. Bandon, County Cork, Ireland, Oct. 28, 1659, d. Richmond, Surrey, England, May 20, 1726.

After attending Westminster, Nicholas Brady studied at Christ Church, Oxford, and Trinity College, Dublin, receiving the D.D. from the latter institution. He was appointed Prebendary of Cork. During the Irish war he sided with William of Orange and was able to save his native town from burning on three occasions. He went to London bearing a petition from Bandon, became minister of St. Catherine and Cree's, Lecturer of St. Michael's, Wood Street. He was Chaplain to the King and (1702–05) incumbent at Stratford-on-Avon. He may have held more than one of these posts at the same time. With Nahum Tate, he was co-author of the 1696 "New Version" of the Psalms. The New Version was brought to this country by John and Charles Wesley in 1735 for use in their services in the New World. It was gradually taken up here by such Episcopal churches as were willing to abandon the Old Version of Sternhold and Hopkins. Brady also published sermons, a translation of the *Aeneid,* and a play, *The Rape, or the Innocent Imposters.* See "Lord, Who's the Happy Man."

John G. C. Brainard, lawyer, editor, and poet; b. New London, Conn., Oct. 21, 1796; d. there Sept. 26, 1828.

John Brainard graduated from Yale in 1815, prepared himself as a lawyer, and practiced for a time in Middletown, Conn. In 1822 he went to Hartford where he edited the *Connecticut Mirror,* a "weekly political and literary gazette" to which he contributed poems. He published a volume of poetry in 1825. He returned to his native town in 1827 where he died of tuberculosis in the following year. "His person was small and well-formed, his countenance mild and indicative of the kindness and gentleness of his nature." He was a friend of Whittier, who wrote his biography. See his "To Thee, O God, the Shepherd Kings."

Cyr de Brant (J. Vincent Higginson), organist, hymnologist, and composer; b. 1896.

J. Vincent Higginson, whose pen name is Cyr de Brant, attended New York University (B.M., 1929; M.A., 1938), the Institute of Musical Art, and the Pius X School of Sacred Music, and also studied music with A. Madely Richardson. He served as organist of St. Sylvester's Church, Brooklyn, N.Y., and composed and edited music for Catholic hymnals. He taught at New York University and the Pius X School and lectured on hymnody at the summer school of Notre Dame University. Long associated with the *Catholic Choirmaster* which he edited for some years, he was also active in the American Hymn Society, as president and associate editor of its publication *The Hymn*. He was made a fellow of the American Hymn Society in 1953 and a Knight Commander of St. Gregory by Pope John XXIII in 1961. See the tune set here to "True Son of God, Eternal Light," published under Higginson's pen name, Cyr de Brant.

LeRoy V. Brant, organist; b. Lexington, Neb., Dec. 3, 1890.

A lineal descendant of Chief Joseph Brant (Thayendenagea) of the Six Nations, LeRoy Brant was educated in the public schools of Julesburg, Colo., Petaluma, Calif., and the Conservatory of the College of the Pacific of San Jose, Calif. His degrees include B.Mus., College of the Pacific (1913), and M.Mus., Chicago Musical College (1924). He was also an associate (1919) and choirmaster (1942) of the American Guild of Organists and an associate of Trinity College, London (1937).

Brant taught music in San Jose for more than thirty-five years and was director of the Institute of Music, which he founded there in 1919. He served as organist and choirmaster of the Trinity Episcopal Church (1926–44), organist of the San Jose Scottish Rite Bodies, and conducted the Municipal Chorus and the Choral Guild of San Jose.

A writer for musical periodicals, Brant published two volumes of verse: *Beauty* (1930) and *Immortal Singers* (1936). See "Green Plumes of Royal Palms" and "Oh, Days of Days," both set to music by Annabel Morris Buchanan for *American Hymns*.

Jean de Brebeuf, Jesuit missionary; b. Condé-sur-Vire, Normandy, March 25, 1593; d. Quebec, March 16, 1649.

Jean de Brebeuf became a member of the Society of Jesus in 1617. In 1625 he began work in Quebec where he founded a mission at a place called Ihonatiria on Lake Huron. The mission could not be sustained because of the intense opposition of the local Indians. In spite of this reverse he continued to preach and to make converts. To celebrate Christmas, the Indians "built a small chapel of cedar and fir branches. . . . Even those who were at a distance of more than two days' journey met at a given place to sing hymns in honor of the new-born child." The carol "Jesous Ahatonhia" ("Let Christian Hearts Rejoice Today") (q.v.) may have been composed in 1641 when Brebeuf could not travel because of a fractured shoulder. He was taken captive and killed by hostile Indians in 1649.

Martha Brewster, poet; b. Lebanon, Conn., April 1, 1710; d. date unknown.

Described as an "authoress" in the Brewster genealogy, Martha Wadsworth was married to Oliver Brewster on March 22, 1732. They had two children, Oliver, and presumably Martha Brewster, went to live in Bernardston, Mass., in 1765. Oliver held various minor town offices there until 1776, after which his name disappears. There is no record of Martha's death.

A book of poems by Martha Brewster was printed and sold by John Green, New London, Conn., in 1757. Several are "acrosticks," most are serious and contemplative. Among the titles are: "On the Day of Judgment," "The 24th Psalm Paraphrased," "A Prayer," "To the Subjects of the Special Grace of God and Its Opposers." A few of the poems are about people: "A poem to the memory of Dr. Watts," "To the memory of that worthy man, Nathaniel Burt of Springfield." There is one on "Braddock's Defeat." More personal are "A letter to some Christian friends" and "A word of advice reserved for my two grandsons, being yet babes." See "The Stately Structure of This Earth."

George Frederick Bristow, composer, organist, and educator; b. Brooklyn, N.Y., Dec. 19, 1825; d. New York City, Dec. 13, 1898.

George Frederick Bristow was the son of an English musician who came to New York in 1825 to serve as organist at St. Patrick's Cathedral. He began his musical training at an early age, and at eleven he was playing the violin at the Olympia Theater. He became one of the directors of the Philharmonic Society when it was founded in 1842 and played first violin in the orchestra. After eleven years with the

Society he resigned both posts because he believed that American composers of the day were inadequately represented on the programs. He later resumed his association with the Society. From 1851 to 1862 he conducted the Harmonic Society, where he continued his efforts to get the works of American composers performed.

Bristow was organist in several churches. From 1854 until he died he was a visiting teacher in the New York public schools. The music critic W. J. Henderson considered him "a most earnest man, filled with real love for his art, and self-sacrificing in labor for the benefit of those . . . who . . . strove to push American music into artistic prominence."

His opera *Rip Van Winkle,* produced in New York on September 27, 1855, ran four weeks at Niblo's and was third in popularity in the list of offerings at the city's theaters. It was revived in 1870.

Among Bristow's other works were two oratorios, *Praise God* (1860) and *Daniel* (1867); two cantatas, *The Great Republic* and *Niagara;* anthems, songs, pieces for the organ, piano, and violin; and six symphonies. His second symphony was first played in 1856, the third in 1859, and the *Arcadian Symphony* in 1874. A number of original hymn tunes were included in *The Cantilena* (1861). At the time of his death he was working on an opera, *Columbus.* See KNISELY ("Slowly, By God's Hand Unfurled").

Andrew Broaddus, Baptist clergyman and preacher; b. Caroline Co., Va., Nov. 4, 1770; d. Dec. 1, 1848.

Although his father was a zealous Episcopalian, Andrew Broaddus was converted to Baptist views and joined the church of Upper King and Queen in 1789. He decided to become a minister and preached to local meetings, displaying superior talents as a speaker. He was ordained in 1791. He served a number of local congregations and, as his reputation grew, he received calls from metropolitan congregations. What Henry Burrage calls a "constitutional timidity" made him decline all of these except that from the First Baptist Church of Richmond, Va., where he remained only six months. For the remainder of his life he continued to preach to the rural congregations he had earlier served. He was editor of the *Dover Selection of Spiritual Songs* which contained his "Help Thy Servant" (q.v.).

Phillips Brooks, preacher; b. Boston, Mass., Dec. 13, 1835; d. there Jan. 23, 1893.

After attending the Boston Latin School, Brooks entered Harvard (A.B. 1855), where he came under the influence of Emerson and

Theodore Parker. After a short period of rather unsuccessful Latin teaching at the Boston Latin School, he decided to become a minister and, after completing his studies at the Virginia Theological Seminary, was ordained as a deacon (1859). His first charge was the Church of the Advent in Philadelphia. In 1862 he became rector of Holy Trinity Church in Philadelphia and in 1868 rector of Trinity Church in Boston. After twenty-two years there, he was appointed Bishop of Massachusetts in 1891, two years before he died.

Brooks was generally considered one of the most eminent American preachers of his day. His "O Little Town of Bethlehem" (q.v.) is among the most familiar of American Christmas carols.

Alling Brown, music teacher, editor, and composer; fl. mid-19th cent.

Alling Brown is listed as "professor of music" in New Haven, Conn., directories from the late 1830s to 1859/60. *The Gamut* (New Haven, 1822) was followed by *The Musical Cabinet: A Collection of Sacred Music* (New Haven, 1823 and 1831). Brown also contributed a song to *The True Masonic Chart* (New Haven, 1824). See BRIGHTON ("O Holy, Holy, Holy Lord").

Phoebe Hinsdale Brown, author; b. Canaan, N.Y., May 1, 1783; d. Marshall, Ill., Oct. 10, 1861.

An orphan at an early age, Phoebe Hinsdale lived with relatives and friends and was often badly treated. She did not learn to read or write until she was eighteen and then had only three months' schooling. After her marriage to Timothy H. Brown, a house painter, she resided in several towns in Connecticut and Massachusetts, but it was in Monson, Mass., that she wrote most of her hymns. Two of her daughters married ministers, and a son, the Rev. S. R. Brown, went to Japan as the first American missionary.

When Asahel Nettleton was compiling his *Village Hymns* (1824), he visited Mrs. Brown, and she gave him four of her hymns, among them the well-known "I Love to Steal Awhile Away" (q.v.) and "Welcome, Ye Hopeful Heirs of Heaven" (q.v.).

Unschooled though she was, Mrs. Brown became a frequent contributor to periodicals. Several of her essays appeared in the *Religious Intelligencer,* published by Deacon Nathan Whiting at New Haven. Her "Tales of Real Life" and several poems came out in *The Pearl* at Hartford. Later she published two Sunday-school books, *The*

Village School and *The Tree and Its Fruits.* At her death she left behind an unpublished autobiographical manuscript of over four hundred pages.

Ray Francis Brown, organist; b. Roxbury, Vt., June 23, 1897; d. New York City, March 23, 1964.

After receiving both the B.A. and B. Mus. from Oberlin, Brown remained there to teach organ (1925–27) serving also as organist of St. Andrew's Church, Elyria, Ohio. He next went to Fisk University in 1927 to head the music school there. In 1933 he was in London studying with Sydney H. Nicholson and Ernest Bullock. On his return he began his long association with the General Theological Seminary, teaching church music and serving as organist. In 1957 he became director of music. Concurrently he played the organ and directed the choir at St. Clement's Church, New York City (1936–38), Christ Church, Bronxville (1938–43), the Church of the Resurrection (1943–54), and Calvary Church (from 1957), both in New York City.

Lecturer in the School of Sacred Music at Union Theological Seminary from 1948 to 1957 Brown also edited two books: *The Oxford American Psalter* (1949) and (with Morton Stone) *Anthems of the Day* (1952), both published by Oxford University Press. In 1956 he was given an honorary Mus.D. by the University of the South. Active on the Tunes Committee while the *Hymnal 1940* was being compiled, Brown also served on the Joint Commission on the Revision of the Hymnal. He was a member of the Council of the American Guild of Organists. See his arrangement of CHELSEA SQUARE ("Put Forth, O Lord, Thy Spirit's Might"), a tune by Howard Chandler Robbins.

Samuel R. Brown, clergyman and missionary to Japan; fl. mid-19th cent.

Samuel Brown possessed what appears to have been a family gift for music (his grandfather, George Hinsdale Brown, composed the tune HINSDALE). Samuel's tune MONSON (q.v.) was often sung to "I Love to Steal Awhile Away" by his mother, Phoebe Hinsdale Brown.

Shirley L. Brown, music teacher and tune writer; b. St. Louis, Mo., Feb. 27, 1925.

After graduating from MacMurray College with a B.M., Shirley Brown went to the Eastman School of Music in Rochester (M.M., 1947). She returned to MacMurray College to teach theory and piano from 1947 to 1949, then went to the University of Texas where she taught theory. After her marriage to Gene M. Brown in 1954, they moved to the Boston area. Mrs. Brown has conducted choirs and a handbell ensemble and now teaches music at St. Anne's School in Arlington and leads a chorus at Bethany, a facility for retarded women in Lincoln, Mass. She composed two spiritual songs for *Sound of Living Waters: Songs of the Spirit.* See HEARTHSIDE ("Within the Shelter of Our Walls").

William Cullen Bryant, poet and editor; b. Cummington, Mass., Nov. 3, 1794; d. New York City, June 12, 1878.

William Cullen Bryant was educated at home, in the public schools, and at Williams College. After writing indignant satires against Jefferson's administration in a book entitled *The Embargo* (1808), he wrote "Thanatopsis" and "To a Waterfowl," but left them unpublished. He pursued a career in law which lasted until 1825. In 1817 "Thanatopsis" was accidentally published in the *North American Review,* and his fame as a poet dates from that time.

In 1821 he was invited to read "The Ages," a Phi Beta Kappa poem, at Harvard Commencement, and later that year he published his first mature book of *Poems.* He also contributed poems to the *United States Literary Gazette* in 1824–25. In 1825 he became co-editor of the *New York Review* and *Athenaeum Magazine* and, a little later, of the *New York Evening Post.* Assuming the full editorship of the *Post* in 1829, he held that position for almost fifty years. By 1840 he had become a leading Democratic editor, but his stand on the slavery issue led him to join the new Republican party. He allied his newspaper with the Republican organization and when Lincoln made his famous Cooper Union speech in 1860, it was Bryant who introduced him.

A writer of poetry (*The Fountain,* 1842; *The White-Footed Deer,* 1844; *A Forest Hymn,* 1860; *Thirty Poems,* 1864; *Hymns,* 1869; *The Little People of the Snow,* 1873; *Among the Trees,* 1874; and *The Flood of Years,* 1876), he also published some prose (*Letters of a Traveller* and collected *Orations and Addresses*). See "As Shadows Cast by Cloud and Sun," "Mighty One, Before Whose Face," and "O Thou Whose Own Vast Temple Stands."

Annabel Morris Buchanan, folklorist; b. Groesbeck, Limestone Co., Texas, Oct. 23, 1888.

Annabel Morris Buchanan graduated from the Landon Conservatory, Dallas, in 1907 and from the Guilmant Organ School in New

York in 1923. She also studied with John Powell. She taught music in Oklahoma and Texas for eight years and for three years at Stonewall Jackson College in Abington, Va. In September 1939 she delivered a paper entitled *Modal and Melodic Structure in Anglo-American Folk Music* at the first International Music Congress held in America. Co-founder of the Virginia State Choral Festival, Mrs. Buchanan was also co-founder of the White Top Music Festivals (1931–41) and director of the White Top Folklore Conference, both held at Marion, Va. She is the author of *Folk Hymns of America* (1938), *American Folk Music* (1939), and editor of two series: *White Top Folk Song Series* and *Early American Psalmody.* Her PALM SUNDAY ("Green Plums of Royal Palms") and DAY OF DAYS ("Oh, Day of Days") were composed for *American Hymns.* See also her arrangements of "What Wondrous Love Is This" and "Where Now Are the Hebrew Children?"

Dudley Buck, organist and composer; b. Hartford, Conn., March 10, 1839; d. Orange, N.J., Oct. 6, 1909.

When Dudley Buck was sixteen he was given his first music lessons; his talent was then so apparent that his father gave him a thorough musical education in this country, followed by studies in Leipzig, Dresden, and Paris. Upon his return to Hartford in 1862 he was appointed organist at the Park Church. His second church position was at St. James' Church in Chicago, where the manuscripts of all his early compositions were lost in the great fire. In 1871 he went to St. Paul's in Boston. He served as organist of the May Festival in Cincinnati in 1875 and later that year went to New York to assist Theodore Thomas in conducting concerts in Central Park. He then moved to Brooklyn, where he served as organist in three churches during the next twenty-seven years: St. Anne's (1875–77), Holy Trinity (1877–1902), and Plymouth Church (1902). The Plymouth post was a brief one, and the last he held before his retirement.

During his long career Dudley Buck was one of the leading teachers of music in the East. Among his pupils were W. H. Neidlinger and Harry Rowe Shelley. His *Studies for Pedal-Phrasing* was widely used by students and organists. He composed eighteen cantatas, both sacred and secular, and his organ compositions include a *Grand Sonata, Sonata No. 2, Triumphal March, Impromptu and Pastorale.* The variety of his secular music is shown by a partial list: a comic opera, *Deseret;* four *Tone Pictures;* a symphonic overture, *Marmion.* He wrote much service music for the Episcopal Church including the *Festival Te Deum in E♭.* His *Motet Collection* (1864) was so well received that he published a second collection.

See his tune to "God of our Fathers, Bless This Our Land," by John Henry Hopkins Jr.

John Wright Buckham, Congregational minister and theologian; b. Burlington, Vt., Nov. 5, 1864; d. March 30, 1945.

John Wright Buckham was educated at the University of Vermont, where he gained his A.B. degree in 1885 and an honorary D.D. in 1904. He was ordained in 1888 after graduation from Andover Theological Seminary. His first charge was the Second Church in Conway, N.H. In 1890 he accepted a call from the Crombie Street Church in Salem, Mass., where he remained for thirteen years. In 1903 he joined the faculty of the Pacific School of Religion, retiring with the rank of professor emeritus in 1937. He was chosen to deliver the Nathaniel W. Taylor Lectures at Yale University in 1914.

Devoted to the study of the philosophy of religion, Buckham wrote numerous books and articles in periodicals. Some of his best-known titles are: *Whence Cometh Help* (1902), *Christ and the Eternal Order* (1906), *Personality and the Christian Ideal* (1908), *Mysticism and Modern Life* (1915), *Progressive Religious Thought in America* (1919), *Religion as Experience* (1922), and *Personality and Psychology* (1936). See "Hills of God, Break Forth in Singing" and "O God, Above the Drifting Years."

Sheema Z. Buehne, educator and translator; b. Philadelphia, Pa., Sept. 21, 1910.

After receiving an A.B. from Bryn Mawr College in 1931, Sheema Buehne became a Fellow of the Institute of International Education at the University of Berlin in 1931–32. Pennsylvania State University awarded her the A.M. in 1950 and the Ph.D. in 1960. An instructor at Pennsylvania State University (1947–55), the Friends' Central School, Philadelphia, and the Baldwin School, Bryn Mawr, she became Professor of German at Rutgers University, retiring in 1974. Professor Buehne has been active as a translator and an officer in both the American Translators' Association and the Delaware Valley Translators' Association. She made a group of translations from the German for *American Hymns*. See "Be Glorified Eternally," "I Am the Lord," "Jehovah, Lord and Majesty," "Jesus, Come on Board," "Lord, Dear God! To Thy Attending," "Love That's Pure, Itself Disdaining," "Now Sleep My Little Child So Dear," "On Earth There Is a Lamb So Small," "Slain Lamb of God," "This Flock So Small," and "Though My Thoughts."

Stephen G. Bulfinch, Unitarian minister and author; b. Boston, Mass., June 18, 1809; d. East Cambridge (now Boston), Oct. 12, 1870.

Son of the famous architect, Charles Bulfinch, Stephen was nine when the family moved to Washington, D.C., where his father planned the rebuilding of the Capitol, which had been burned by the British in 1814. Stephen graduated in 1827 from Columbian College in that city and for the next three years studied theology at the Harvard Divinity School. He was ordained a Unitarian minister in January 1831, by Dr. Samuel Gilman. He next occupied the pulpit in Unitarian churches in Pittsburgh, Pa., and Washington, D.C. In 1845 the Unitarian Church of Nashua, N.H., called him to its pulpit. He remained there until 1852, when he went to Dorchester, Mass. An honorary D.D. degree was bestowed on him by his alma mater in 1864. In the following year he moved to East Cambridge, now Boston.

Bulfinch's original hymns were published in *Contemplations of the Saviour* (1832), *Poems* (1834), *Lays of the Gospel* (1845), and *Harp and the Cross* (1857), a collection of hymns, which he edited. He also contributed six hymns to Leonard J. Livermore's Unitarian *Hymn and Tune Book for the Church and the Home* (Boston, 1868).

Other publications include: *The Holy Land and Its Inhabitants* (1834), *Communion Thoughts* (1850), *Palestine and the Hebrew People* (1853), *Honor, or the Slaveholder's Daughter* (1864), *Manual of the Evidences of Christianity* (1866), and *Studies in the Evidences of Christianity* (1866). See "Hail to the Sabbath Day."

Peter Bulkeley, the Younger, merchant and physician; b. Concord, Mass., Aug. 12, 1643; d. Fairfield, Conn., 1691.

Peter Bulkeley was a member of the class of 1662 at Harvard, although the record does not show that he received a degree. The following year he moved with his widowed mother to Fairfield, Conn., and there combined the activities of merchant and physician. Married and the father of five children, he somehow found time to write poetry as had his father, a pastor and founder of the town of Concord. The quality of the son's verse was better than that of Peter Bulkeley, the Elder, and it was above the average of that written by the author's contemporaries. All but one of his poems were religious. His longest, "A Loving Conference had with Christ and the deceast Soul," a dialogue, was interesting as an expression of a fairly liberal Puritan's concept of salvation. See "Like to the Grass that's Green Today."

Amos Bull, singing master and composer; b. c.1744; d. date unknown.

In an advertisement in a New Haven newspaper in 1766 Amos Bull asked for subscribers for a forthcoming book. He gave his age as twenty-two. We do not know whether the book was ever printed. In 1775, in an advertisement asking for subscribers to a volume, *Universal Harmony,* Oliver King mentioned a Mr. Bull as a New York singing master. In 1805 Amos Bull advertised for pupils in Hartford, Conn. He planned to open a school to teach the three R's "with other learning useful and necessary in common life" as soon as six scholars had registered for the first quarter term, at a tuition fee of two dollars. The advertisement also mentioned that he received "constant supplies of goods" including "clock and watch files."

In her manuscript reminiscences his granddaughter, Eliza Hopkins, describes him as "a man of much taste," "a fine musician." His oldest daughter, Lucy Ball, "became a proficient upon the harp-composed musick for it." Amos Bull himself "played the violin and bass viol and published a musick book for a choir of singers which he volunteered to teach and lead in the South Presbyterian Church (so called) in Hartford—a famous choir for many years." This book *The Responsary,* which was published in 1795, was described on the title page as "a collection of church musick, set with second trebles instead of counters, and peculiarly adapted to the use of the New England Churches." See NEWMARK ("Amazing Sight! the Saviour Stands") and PSALM 46 ("By Babel's Streams").

Frederick Field Bullard, composer; b. Boston, Mass., Sept. 21, 1864; d. there June 24, 1904.

Frederick Field Bullard attended the Massachusetts Institute of Technology, but in his twenty-fourth year turned from science to music and went to Munich, where he studied composition and organ with Josef Rheinberger for four years. On his return to Boston he became known as a composer of songs and choral music. Bullard edited a number of collections of songs and wrote a series of Christmas and Easter cantatas and several part-songs. The glee clubs of his time and their audiences enjoyed his "Stein Song" and "Barney McGee." Also popular was "A June Lullaby," "From Dreams of Thee," "Song of Pan," and "The Sisters." He was musical adviser for the first edition of *The Pilgrim Hymnal* (Boston, 1904), to which he contributed eight original tunes and an arrangement. See HOSMER ("From Age to Age They Gather") and MACEDON ("My Country, to Thy Shore").

George Burgess, Episcopal rector and bishop; b. Providence, R.I., Oct. 31, 1809; d. at sea near Haiti, April 3, 1860.

Although two hymns by George Burgess, "The Harvest Dawn is Near" (q.v.) and "While O'er the Deep Thy Servants Sail" (q.v.), were very widely used, they do not appear in hymnals of his own denomination. Educated at Brown University (B.A. 1826) he became a tutor there before going to Germany for two years as a student. On his return he served Christ Church, Hartford, Conn. as rector (from 1834) but in 1847 became bishop of Maine and rector of Christ Church in Gardiner. The principal sources for his hymns are *The Book of Psalms Translated into English Verse* (1839) and his *Poems* (1868). He also published *The American Metrical Psalter* in 1864. His biography, written by his brother, was published in 1869.

Gail Brook Burket, writer; b. Stronghurst, Ill., Nov. 1, 1905.

Gail Brook Burket received her Bachelor of Arts degree from the University of Illinois in 1926 and her Master's degree from Northwestern in 1929. The author of six books, hundreds of published poems, and numerous articles, she is a free-lance writer who appears frequently on poetry programs. Mrs. Burket is active in literary, journalistic, and historical organizations. Married to Dr. Walter Cleveland Burket, a well-known surgeon, she has three daughters and has lived in Evanston, Ill. since 1929. See "So Touch Our Hearts with Loveliness," with music composed by Irving Fine for *American Hymns,* and "From Countless Hearts," set by Paul Nordoff.

Harry T. Burleigh, singer, composer, and arranger of spirituals; b. Erie, Pa., Dec. 2, 1866; d. Stamford, Conn., Sept. 12, 1949.

Harry T. Burleigh's gifts as a vocalist were evident when he was still a schoolboy, and he began to sing in synagogue and church choirs when he was sixteen. He applied for a scholarship to the National Conservatory of New York and was finally successful when Mrs. Edward MacDowell intervened to obtain a second hearing for him. As a student he met Antonin Dvořák, who was then director of the Conservatory, and Dvořák's interest in Negro spirituals was stimulated by hearing Burleigh sing them. In 1894 Burleigh became soloist in the choir of St. George's Protestant Episcopal Church, a post he held for fifty-two years. In 1900 he accepted a similar post at

Temple Emmanuel, where he remained for twenty-five years. His major contribution as a composer was a large group of spirituals arranged for solo voice and piano, which opened the song recital to spirituals and created a new audience for them. It seems strange that, in spite of his long experience as a church singer, he did not treat more spirituals in the form of the hymn. In addition to the arrangements which he made for Dorothy Bolton's *Old Songs Hymnal,* only two arrangements of spirituals as hymns have been found. McKEE, which is an arrangement of "I Know the Angels Done Changed My Name" from *Slave Songs,* was published in *The Hymnal 1940.* See his arrangement of "Let Us Cheer the Weary Traveler."

William Henry Burleigh, Unitarian author and editor; b. Woodstock, Conn., Feb. 12, 1812; d. Brooklyn, N.Y., March 18, 1871.

William Burleigh was apprenticed to a printer and then became a writer and publisher. He published *The Christian Witness* and *The Temperance Banner* in Pittsburgh. Later he edited *The Christian Freeman.* His hymns, some of which had appeared earlier in periodical literature, were gathered in *Poems* (1841; enl. ed., 1871, with a biography by his wife). He was a zealous advocate of social reform, working for the New York State Temperance Society, 1849–55. In the latter year he was appointed Harbor Master for New York, a post he held till 1870. See "Abide Not in the Realm of Dreams" and "Lead Us, O Father, in the Paths of Peace."

Natalie Curtis Burlin, collector of folk songs and folk tales; b. New York City, April 26, 1875; d. Paris, Oct. 23, 1921.

After musical studies here and abroad Natalie Curtis Burlin became an authority on Indian songs and legends, publishing *Songs of Ancient America* in 1905 and *The Indian's Book* in 1907. Of her four collections of *Negro Folksongs,* two contain spirituals as sung by members of the Hampton Choir. Not only the melodies but also the accompanying parts were carefully notated showing us how they were sung in 1918. See "O Ride On, Jesus."

Uzziah C. Burnap, businessman and musician; b. Brooklyn, N.Y., 1834; d. there 1900.

Uzziah Burnap was for many years a well-known dry-goods merchant in Brooklyn and New York. He studied music in Paris, graduating from the University of Paris with a degree in music. A prolific composer, he wrote many songs and hymn tunes and served for thirty-seven years as organist of the Reformed Church in Brooklyn Heights. He was a gifted improviser, ranking with Dudley Buck. He was the music editor of two books for his denomination: *Hymns of the Church* (1869) and an abridgement called *Hymns of Prayer and Praise* (1871). With John K. Paine (q.v.) and James Flint (q.v.), he edited the music of *Hymns and Songs of Praise* (1874). See SCHELL ("Floods Swell Round Me, Angry, Appalling"), BOSTON ("Jesus, These Eyes Have Never Seen"), O RISEN LORD ("O Risen Lord Upon the Throne"), and WIDER WAYS ("Why Linger Yet Upon the Strand?").

Elizabeth Burrowes, author and poet; b. 1885.

Elizabeth Burrowes, now of Berkeley, Calif., had earlier been a resident of Englewood, N.J. An ordained elder of the Presbyterian Church, she later joined an interracial church, the South Berkeley Community Church. For it she wrote an anniversary hymn entitled "Almighty God, We Pray Thee Still to Guide Us." Her "God of the Ages by Whose Hand," first published by the Hymn Society in 1958, has been chosen for inclusion in the new Methodist hymnal. "O God, Send Men," one of *Ten New Hymns on the Ministry* published by the Hymn Society in 1966, was later included in their *Contemporary Hymn Tunes* (1970) as the text for Wilbur Held's HUGHES HALL.

Bates G. Burt, Episcopal priest; b. Wheeling, W.Va., Dec. 21, 1878; d. Edgewood, Md., April 15, 1948.

For a quarter of a century Bates G. Burt was in Pontiac, Mich. where he served as rector of All Saints' Church. To *The Hymnal 1940* he contributed his hymn "O God of Youth" and from 1946 he served on his denomination's Joint Commission on the Revision of the Hymnal.

A graduate of Kenyon College (M.A., 1901), he later pursued theological studies at the Seabury Divinity School (1902). His ordination as deacon was in 1903, as priest 1904. In World War I he went to France as chaplain (1918–19).

Mather Byles, Congregational minister and poet; b. Boston, Mass., March 15, 1706; d. there July 5, 1788.

Mather Byles, a descendant of John Cotton and Richard Mather, graduated from Harvard at nineteen. He entered the ministry, was ordained in 1733, and accepted the call to be the first pastor of a newly organized church on Hollis Street in Boston. Noted for his scholarly sermons and quick wit, he held that post until 1776. He and his friend Joseph Green (q.v.) were prominent literary figures of the period. The Revolutionary War brought him trouble, which he took with aplomb. Because he made no secret of his strong Toryism, he was removed from his pulpit and placed under arrest. Tried by his church and, in 1777, by the civil authorities, he was sentenced to deportation. That sentence was later remanded to imprisonment in his home. Inevitably being a wit and punster, he called the guard who marched in front of his house an "Observe-a-Tory," and he once persuaded the man to go on an errand for him, while he himself, during the interim, marched back and forth in the guard's place. When finally free he did not seek another pulpit, but lived in retirement until his death.

Byles was a tall, well-built man with a strong, musical voice and fine skill as a speaker. From boyhood he wrote poetry, devotional or contemplative. *A Collection of Poems by Several Hands* (Boston, 1744) contained several written by him. He contributed essays and verses to the *New England Weekly*. Watts (q.v.), Swift, and Pope were among his correspondents. Pope sent him a copy of his translation of *The Odyssey*. At home Byles was widely known and his witticisms smilingly awaited. He was married twice, first to a niece of Governor Belcher and then to a daughter of Lieutenant Governor Tailer.

In addition to numerous sermons he published various short pieces, such as "The Conflagration" (1729) and a collection of verse, *Poems on Several Occasions* (Boston, 1744). Three of his hymns were included in an *Appendix* to Tate and Brady (q.v.) (1760), which he edited in part. See "Great God, How Frail a Thing Is Man," "Great God, Thy Works," "To Thee the Tuneful Anthem Soars," and "When Wild Confusion Wrecks the Air."

Edward N. Calisch, Reform rabbi; b. Toledo, Ohio, June 23, 1865; d. Richmond, Va., Jan 7, 1946.

After graduating from Hebrew Union College in 1887, Edward Calisch served as rabbi in Peoria, Ill., and, from 1891, in Richmond, Va. He was President of the Central Conference of American Rabbis from 1921 to 1923. In the *Union Hymnal* of 1932 stanzas three and

four of the hymn "God Supreme! To Thee We Pray" (q.v.) are by
Calisch.

Thomas Canning, composer and educator; b. Brookville, Pa., 1911.

Thomas Canning pursued undergraduate studies at Oberlin
(B.M., 1936), where he was a composition student under Norman
Lockwood. He then went to the Eastman School of Music (M.A.,
1940), where his teachers included Bernard Rogers and Howard
Hanson. Canning taught music theory and composition at Morning-
side College, Sioux City, Iowa, Indiana State College, Indiana, Pa.,
and the Royal Conservatory of Music, University of Toronto. In
1946 he returned to the Eastman School as a teacher, a period broken in 1961–62 when he served as exchange professor at the University of Hull. Appointed associate professor at the new Creative Arts
Center, West Virginia University, in 1963, he was promoted to full
professor in 1967. Canning's *Fantasy on a Hymn by Justin Morgan* for
two string quartets and string orchestra has enjoyed a substantial
success and was recorded by Howard Hanson and by Leopold Stokowski. His COVENANT HYMN appeared in the Methodist hymnal of
1966. See his setting of Robert Frost's "Oh, Give Us Pleasure in the
Flowers Today," composed for *American Hymns.*

George Careless, Mormon musician of English birth; fl. 19th cent.

George Careless composed the music for "The Morning Breaks"
at the request of the captain on whose ship he came to the United
States in 1864. A number of his tunes were highly esteemed, notably
a setting of Eliza Snow's "Though Deep My Trials," and he was an
important contributor to the Mormon *Psalmody* of 1889. Careless
and John Tullidge conducted classes in sightsinging using the English tonic sol-fa method. Their success in developing capable
singers is illustrated by a performance of the *Messiah,* which Careless
conducted at the Salt Lake Theater in June 1875, claimed to be the
first performance of the work between New York and San Francisco.
See the tune for "Arise, O Glorious Zion," by William G. Mills.

Bliss Carman, poet; b. Fredericton, N.B., Canada, April 15, 1861; d. New Canaan, Conn., June 8, 1929.

Bliss Carman was educated at the University of New Brunswick (A.B., 1881; A.M., 1884), the University of Edinburgh (1882–83), and Harvard (1886–88). The University of New Brunswick conferred on him the honorary LL.D. in 1906. After 1888 he made his home in New York and New Canaan, Conn. From 1890 to 1892 he edited *The Independent* (New York) and in 1894 *The Chap-Book* (Boston). In 1893 he published his own first notable poetry in *Low Tide on Grand Pré: A Book of Lyrics.* His poems filled with youthful buoyancy and love of nature combined with a carefree gypsy spirit brought him wide popularity. They also initiated a revolt against the scholarly and rather anemic poetry of his time.

Carman wrote *Songs from Vagabondia* (1894), *More Songs from Vagabondia* (1896), and *Last Songs from Vagabondia* (1901) all in collaboration with Richard Hovey. More than twenty volumes followed which included *Behind the Arras: A Book of the Unseen* (1895), *Ballads of Lost Haven: A Book of the Sea* (1897), *Sappho* (1904), *Pipes of Pan* (1906), *Echoes from Vagabondia* (1912), *The Rough Riders and Other Poems* (1909), *April Airs: A Book of New England Lyrics* (1916), and *Wild Garden* (1929). He also wrote essays: *The Friendship of Art* (1904), *The Making of Personality* (1908), and *The Kinship of Nature* (1913). See "Lord of My Heart's Elation."

Benjamin Carr, music publisher and composer; b. London, Sept. 12, 1768; d. Philadelphia, Pa., May 24, 1831.

Benjamin Carr received his musical education from Dr. Samuel Arnold and Charles Wesley II (1757–1834). When he was twenty-five, the Carr family migrated to America and in 1794 set up as music dealers in three American cities. Benjamin established two separate businesses: at 136 High Street in Philadelphia and 131 William Street, New York City. His success is indicated by the large number of imprints under his name. "Yankee Doodle" and "Hail Columbia" were first printed in the United States by Carr in his *Federal Overture* of 1794. (There had been an earlier Scottish imprint of "Yankee Doodle.")

Carr's participation in concerts began in the spring of 1794, and from that time he often appeared in concerts and opera as harpsichordist and singer. His opera *The Archers of Switzerland* was produced on the night of April 18, 1796, by the American Company in New York and later in Boston. It is the first American opera from which excerpts still survive. He was long the organist of St. Peter's

Church in Philadelphia and was music director of St. Joseph's Catholic Church there from 1801. His *Masses, Vespers, Litanies, Hymns, Psalms, Anthems & Motets* (1805) was for Catholic use and his *Collection of Chants and Tunes for the Use of the Episcopal Church in the City of Philadelphia* was intended for Episcopal churches. According to instructions in his will, he was buried in the churchyard of St. Peter's. See PHILADELPHIA ("Saviour, Who Thy Flock Are Feeding"), EROICA ("To Thee, Then, Let All Beings Bend"), and Carr's setting of the DIES IRAE (same).

Hayden Carruth, poet and critic; b. Waterbury, Conn., Aug. 3, 1921.

Hayden Carruth received his early education at Mitchell Grammar School in Woodbury, Conn., and at the High School in Pleasantville, N.Y. After finishing his studies at the University of North Carolina (A.B., 1942), he did graduate work at the University of Chicago (M.A., 1948). During World War II he served two years in Italy and in the A.A.F.

In 1954 Carruth received the Bess Hokin Prize and in 1956 the Vachel Lindsay Prize, both awarded by *Poetry* magazine. His poetry and criticisms have been published widely in journals and periodicals.

Editor of *Poetry* (1949–50), Carruth has been an associate editor at the University of Chicago Press (1950–52) and editor of *Perspectives USA* (1953). Since 1954 he has devoted full time to his own writing. See "Our Tense and Wintry Minds," which was set to music by Roy Harris for *American Hymns*.

Thomas W. Carter, composer or arranger; fl. mid-19th cent.

Thomas Carter was represented by seven hymns in the *Sacred Harp* (1844). The notes in that volume confess that "but little is known of Professor Thomas W. Carter outside the music credited to him in the *Sacred Harp*. . . . He was a member of the Southern Musical Convention from the time of its organization until after the war, and also a member of the Chattahoochie Musical Convention from the time it was formed until after the war." See his version of the OLD SHIP OF ZION ("What Ship Is This?").

Peter Cartwright, itinerant preacher; b. Amherst Co., Va.,
Sept. 1, 1785; d. near Pleasant Plains, Sagamon Co., Ill., Sept.
25, 1872.

Peter Cartwright was the son of a veteran of the War of Independence who took his family to Kentucky in 1790. There Peter grew up in frontier surroundings, received little education, and spent his time gambling and horse racing until 1801 when he heard John Page preach. In June of that year he was received into the Methodist Church; in the autumn of 1802 he became a licensed minister and was given the Livingston circuit around the mouth of the Cumberland River. Ordained a deacon, then presiding elder, he was transferred to Kentucky, and in 1823 was sent to the Illinois conference where he was presiding elder in two or three different districts until 1869. See "Our Bondage It Shall End" and "Where Are the Hebrew Children?", both sometimes attributed to him.

Phoebe Cary, poet; b. Hamilton Co., Ohio, c.10 miles north
of Cincinnati, Sept. 4, 1824; d. Newport, R.I., July 31, 1871.

Alice Cary, Phoebe's older sister, taught her the art of making verses. Their schooling was meager and few books were available to them, but they persisted in sending their poems to various papers and magazines. John Greenleaf Whittier wrote them an early letter of encouragement. In 1849 a publisher agreed to issue a small volume of their verse for which he proposed to pay them a hundred dollars. On the strength of that promise the sisters decided to take a trip to New York. They called on Whittier, who recorded the event in the following lines:

> Years since (but names to me before),
> Two sisters sought at eve my door;
> Two song birds wandering from their nest,
> A gray old farmhouse in the West . . .

In 1850 Alice moved to New York and Phoebe joined her the following year. While their verse was widely read in its own day, Phoebe Cary's chief contribution to hymnology lies in the hymn "One Sweetly Solemn Thought" (q.v.).

George W. Chadwick, composer, teacher, and administrator; b. Lowell, Mass., Nov. 13, 1854; d. Boston, Mass., April 4, 1931.

The Chadwick family was a musical one. George's older brother Fitz Henry taught him piano and they played the Beethoven symphonies as piano duets. George learned to play the organ, began to try his hand at composition, and commuted to Boston for music lessons. In 1876 he taught music at Olivet College; in 1877 he went to Germany where he studied in Leipzig with Jadassohn. His *Rip Van Winkle Overture,* written at that time, was performed in Dresden and Boston. Chadwick continued his studies in organ playing and composition with Josef Rheinberger in Munich. He returned to the United States in 1880. Among his pupils were Horatio Parker (q.v.), Sidney Homer, and Arthur Whiting. Chadwick joined the faculty of the New England Conservatory of Music in 1882 and became director in 1897, a post he held until his death in 1931.

Although Chadwick composed in most forms his symphonies (three in number), his dramatic overtures, and his four *Symphonic Sketches: Jubilee, Noel, Hobgoblin,* and *A Vagrom Ballad* (1907) constitute the best of his production. Rhythmic vigor and a jaunty and carefree spirit distinguish his works. The use of folk material is exceptional with him, although in *Jubilee* he does utilize the melody of a spiritual. Although Chadwick played the organ as a young man, his heart was really in his compositions for orchestra. His hymns ARMSTRONG and PEACE were written in a sentimental, romantic style which does not represent the composer's best qualities. He contributed four hymn tunes, EATON ("O Christ of Lowly Manger Birth") (q.v.), MURRAY, PENITENCE, and TUTTLE, to the *Universalist Church Harmonies New and Old* of 1895.

S. Chandler, fl. late 18th cent.

Frank J. Metcalf states in his *American Writers and Compilers of Sacred Music* that S. Chandler was active at Troy, N.Y., around 1800, though he gives no source. Chandler's tune ENFIELD was printed at least twice during the eighteenth century: in Andrew Law's *Art of Singing* (1794) and in Oliver Holden's *Union Harmony* (1796 ed.). It was taken up in Ananias Davisson's *Kentucky Harmony* (Harrisonburg, Va., c.1815). Perhaps Freedman Lewis' *Beauties of Harmony* (c.1813) was the intermediary. Chandler was even better known by "The Indian Philosopher" published in *The American Musical Miscellany* (Northampton, Mass., 1798). This tune under the name GANGES was used for Samson Occam's "Waked by the Gospel's Powerful Sound"(q.v.).

Isaac Chanler, Baptist preacher and diarist; b. Bristol, England, May 10, 1700; d. Nov. 30, 1749.

Isaac Chanler came to the United States c. 1733. At first he served the people along the Ashley River, near Charleston, S.C. His work was so effective that in 1736 the Ashley River Church was organized with twenty-eight charter members. Later another church was established by a group at Euhaw, where Chanler preached on alternate Sundays. For some time he had been the only regular Baptist minister in the region, and his death at forty-nine left his congregations without a spiritual leader. His diary, which gives a vivid portrayal of the life of a pioneer preacher, is also our source for his hymns. See "Awake My Soul, Betime• Awake," and "Thrice Welcome First and Best of Days."

Theodore Chanler, composer; b. Newport, R.I., April 29, 1902; d. Boston, Mass., July 27, 1961.

Theodore Chanler was educated at Middlesex School (1916–18), Browning School (1919–21), Brasenose College, Oxford (1923–24), and the Institute of Musical Art (1919–21). He also studied privately with Ernest Bloch in Cleveland (1921–23) and Nadia Boulanger in Paris (1924–26). From 1945 to 1947 he taught theory and composition at the Peabody Conservatory; from 1947 to 1959 he was a teacher at the Longy School in Boston.

In 1940 Chanler received the League of Composers Award (for *Five Rhymes for Peacock Pie,* a soprano song cycle written to poems by Walter de la Mare for Dorothy Maynor); in 1944 he was a Guggenheim Fellow. He was a member of the executive board of the League of Composers and a regular contributor to *Modern Music* until it suspended publication. In 1934 he was a music critic for the *Boston Herald.*

His principal compositions include: *Sonata for Violin and Piano* (1927), *Eight Epitaphs* (1936); *The Second Joyful Mystery,* for two pianos and women's chorus (1943); *The Children,* a cycle of nine songs set to poems by Leonard Feeney (1945). His opera *Pot of Fat* received a New York performance in 1956. See his setting of "Mary Lifted from the Dead," composed for *American Hymns.*

Chapin, surname of members of a musical family, fl. 18th cent.

A prominent member of the family was Amzi Chapin, cabinet maker and singing master, who was born in North Carolina in 1768 and died in Northfield, near Cleveland, Ohio. He was active in North Carolina, Kentucky, Pennsylvania, and Ohio. There is a brief biographical sketch in *Early Western Pennsylvania Hymns & Hymn-Tunes 1816–1846,* edited by Jacob A. Evanson and George Swetnam. More recently attention has been directed to Lucius Chapin, Amzi's brother. See Charles Hamm, "The Chapins and Sacred Music in the South and West" (*Journal of Research in Music Education,* VIII, 2, 91–98), who points out seven musical Chapins. Since attributions are often vague and sometimes contradictory it seems more prudent to use the family name only. We include PRIMROSE ("Remember Thy Creator Now") taken from William Hauser's *Olive Leaf* and there attributed to Aaron Chapin who is not otherwise known. Allen D. Carden's *Missouri Harmony* (1820) prints this same tune without attribution and William Walker's *Southern Harmony* (1854) and Benjamin Franklin White's *Sacred Harp* (1859) have only Chapin.

Edwin Hubbell Chapin, Universalist minister; b. Union Village, N.Y., Dec. 29, 1814; d. New York City, Dec. 26, 1880

After attending school in Bennington, Vt., Edwin Chapin became a popular lecturer and preacher. With John G. Adams (q.v.) he edited an important collection of hymns for the Universalist Church entitled *Hymns for Christian Devotion* (Boston, 1846). His pastorates were Richmond, Va. (1838–40), Charlestown (1840–46), and Boston, Mass. (1846–48), and New York City (1848–80). See "Hark! Hark! With Harps of Gold" and "O Thou Who Didst Ordain the World."

George Barrell Cheever, crusading preacher; b. Hallowell, Maine, April 17, 1807; d. Englewood, N.J., Oct. 1, 1890.

George Barrell Cheever entered Bowdoin College at fourteen and taught school during the summer. He enrolled in Andover Theological Seminary but left without graduating, since he felt that he could not promise to preach. After an interval he returned, confident that he did indeed wish to preach and was licensed in 1835. His pastorate at the Howard Street Church of Salem, Mass., was followed by a trip abroad to restore his health. On his return he went to the Allen Street Presbyterian Church, but again his health failed and he went to Switzerland. In 1846 he became the pastor of a new Congregational church in New York City, the Church of the Pilgrims. He retired in 1867 and moved to Englewood, N.J.

Cheever was in the forefront of the controversies of his day, defending Congregational doctrine against the Unitarians, the Cherokee Indians against the state of Georgia, active in promoting the cause of temperance, and an ardent abolitionist. Among his many publications was *Christian Melodies* (1851), which contained "Blest Be the Wondrous Grace" (q.v.) and "Thy Loving Kindness, Lord, I Sing" (q.v.).

John Vance Cheney, poet and editor; b. Groveland, N.Y., Dec. 29, 1848; d. May 1, 1922.

John Vance Cheney was a son of Simeon Pease Cheney of the Cheney singers. In his later years he became a resident of California. One of his poems, "The Man with the Hoe, A Reply," is included in the *Home Book of Verse*. A representative list of his works includes: *Caxton Club Scrap-Book,* a compilation of early English verses; *The Old Doctor,* a romance; a collection and arrangement of Simeon Pease Cheney's *Native Wood Notes Wild* (a pioneer study of bird songs); an edition of inaugural addresses of the presidents from Washington to Lincoln; *The Golden Guess,* essays on poetry; *Lyrics; Poems* (in several editions); and a compilation, *Memorable American Speeches.* See his "Unto Our God Most High We Sing," with music by his father, Simeon Pease Cheney.

Simeon Pease Cheney, singing master and student of bird songs; b. Meredith, N.H., April 18, 1818; d. Franklin, Mass., May 10, 1890.

The Cheneys were a gifted singing family from Vermont who may be compared to the better-known Hutchinson family of New Hampshire. The group consisted of one sister, Elizabeth, and four brothers, Moses Ela, Nathaniel, Simeon Pease, and Joseph. Simeon Pease Cheney was a gifted singer and teacher. He married Christiana Vance (?) in June 1847, at Groveland, N.Y. They had two sons, John Vance Cheney, a poet, and Albert Baker Cheney. Simeon was a keen observer of bird life, particularly bird songs. He used to search out the haunt of a bird, then visit the spot with pitch pipe and paper, generally early in the morning. His observations and his notations appeared first in the form of a series of articles in the *Century Magazine,* later, after his death, in the volume *Native Wood Notes Wild* (Boston, 1892).

The American Singing Book, which he edited, appeared in 1879 and was advertised as containing "the original music of the Cheney family." A special feature was the biographical section (advertised on the title page as worth the price of the volume). Each singing master is represented by an original composition followed by a brief account of his life. A number of the biographies were based on personal knowledge of the subject and thus are of special interest.

Evidently Simeon had his share of self-esteem, if we may credit a letter by his brother Moses, who remarked that "he is such a great Being that all you and I can expect of him is the pleasure of his permission to worship him." See his PLYMOUTH, set to a text ("Unto Our God Most High We Sing") by his son John Vance Cheney.

F. Melius Christiansen, teacher and choral director; b. Eidsvold, Norway, April 1, 1871; d. Northfield, Minn., June 1, 1955.

F. Melius Christiansen and his brother Karl came to the United States in 1888. After settling in Ashland, Wis., Christiansen led the band in Marinette and played the organ in the Lutheran Church. In 1892 he attended Augsberg College and, after a year there, transferred to the Northwestern Conservatory of Music in Minneapolis (1892–94).

In 1897 Christiansen married and took his bride to Europe, where the couple stayed two years while he studied at the Royal Conservatory of Music at Leipzig. After a son was born in 1898, the three returned to Minneapolis. In 1902 Christiansen was asked to become director of music at St. Olaf College in Northfield, Minn. Leaving his family in Minneapolis, he tried the job for a year, decided he liked it, and stayed for forty-one years. He is best remembered for developing the St. Olaf Lutheran Choir, which made its first tour in 1911. The choir, which made annual tours in this country and two in Europe, was widely acclaimed for its superior *a cappella* singing. Melius Christiansen retired in 1944 and was succeeded by his son Olaf. Melius was associate editor of the *Lutheran Hymnary* (1913). See FLOWERS OF LOVE ("I Know a Flower So Fair and Fine").

James Freeman Clarke, Unitarian and unaffiliated pastor; b. Hanover, N.H., April 4, 1810; d. Boston, Mass., June 8, 1888.

James Freeman Clarke was named for his step-grandfather, Dr. James Freeman, in whose home his boyhood was spent. He took his A.B. at Harvard College in 1829 and completed his course in the Harvard Divinity School in 1833.

Clarke began his preaching career in Louisville, Ky. (1833–40), finding the slave-holders quite different from his friends in the anti-slavery circles of Boston. During this period of service he established, with two friends, *The Western Messenger,* a periodical which, as the organ of political liberalism, lasted six years and contained truly distinguished writing. Its scholarly editor made translations of Goethe and Schiller for it; Emerson sent him many poems besides "The Humble Bee" and "The Rhodora"; and John Keats sent, via his brother who had settled in Louisville, his "Hymn to Apollo," and others.

Urged by William Ellery Channing to come back to Boston because firmer preaching was needed there, Clarke went, not only to preach, but to propose the organization of a new church: "not a congregation of Unitarians, but a Church of Christ." The name chosen for the church was "The Church of the Disciples." Its atmosphere simple, homelike, and fraternal in the best sense, it allowed no pew-holding. One lifelong member was Julia Ward Howe (q.v.). Its appeal to young, independent thinkers drew in so many from remote districts that it became known as "The Church of the Carry-alls." Serving as pastor there from 1841 to 1888 Clarke edited a *Service Book* (1844) which contained a number of hymns. It was the first American collection to include Sarah Flower Adams' "Nearer, My God, to Thee." See "Brother, Hast Thou Wandered Far?" and "Dear Friend, Whose Presence in the House."

Benjamin Cleavland, Baptist hymn writer; b. Windham, Conn., Aug. 30, 1733; d. Horton (later Wolfville), N.S., March 9, 1811.

Benjamin Cleavland's first marriage, to Mary Elderkin, when he was twenty-one, gave him twelve children. One son, Nathan, became a Baptist minister. A second marriage, in 1784 to Sarah Hibbert, was childless. Cleavland was one of the New Englanders who, when the Acadians were driven from Nova Scotia, settled upon land thus left vacant.

A small book of hymns by Benjamin Cleavland was issued in Norwich, Conn., in 1790, with the title *Hymns on Different Spiritual Subjects.* By 1792 it had gone into a fourth edition. See "O Could I Find from Day to Day."

Louis Adolphe Coerne, composer and educator; b. Newark, N.J., Feb. 27, 1870; d. Boston, Mass., Sept. 11, 1922.

After graduating from Harvard Louis Adolphe Coerne studied with Josef Rheinberger in Munich (1890–93). *Hiawatha,* a symphonic poem composed at this time, was played in Germany and later by the Boston Symphony Orchestra (1894). After a period during which he taught in the United States, Coerne returned to Germany (1899–1902). Once more in the United States he taught at Smith College (1903–04). In 1905 Harvard gave him the first Ph.D. degree awarded by an American university in the field of music. His thesis, *The Evolution of Modern Orchestration,* was published in 1908. He was the first American to obtain an operatic performance in Germany with his *Zenobia,* presented at Bremen in 1905 during a third period of residence there. During a final period in the United States he was again active as a teacher. His opera *A Woman of Marblehead,* Opus 40, was not performed. See his SON OF MAN, set to Allen Eastman Cross's "Young and Radiant, He Is Standing."

John Cole, composer and organist; b. Tewksbury, England, 1774; d. Baltimore, Md., Aug. 17, 1855.

John Cole came to the United States in 1785. He led a band which was especially well liked during the War of 1812. Cole's first musical studies in this country were under such teachers as Andrew Law (q.v.), Thomas Atwell, and Ishmael Spicer (q.v.). In 1797 he began publishing music and continued in that business almost as long as he lived. In his later years he had the assistance of his son as partner.

Cole won a fine reputation as organist and director of church music during a long period of activity at St. Paul's Episcopal Church in Baltimore. He was in charge of most of the special programs of sacred music which were given in that city, and he conducted several oratorios. A persistent and vigorous opponent of the music of the New England psalmodists, he was locally successful in replacing their compositions by smoother and more conventional music in the prevailing English style.

GENEVA was his most popular tune. (It should be distinguished from the much later tune by George Henry Day which has the same name.) His published collections included: *Episcopalian Harmony* (1800 and 1811), *A Collection of Psalm Tunes and Anthems* (Boston, 1803), *Beauties of Psalmody* (3d ed., 1827), *Divine Harmonist* (1808), *Ecclesiastical Harmony* (1810), *Minstrel Songs* (1812), *Devotional Harmony* (1814), *Songs of Zion* (1818), *The Seraph* (1821, 1822, 1827), *Sacred Melodies, Union Harmony* (1829—printed with character notes), *Laudate Dominum* (1842 and 1847), and *Music for the Church* (1844). All of these collections save the second were published in Baltimore. See ATKINSON ("Thou Art the Way").

Daniel C. Colesworthy, printer and editor; b. Portland, Maine, July 14, 1810; d. 1893.

Daniel C. Colesworthy, author of "A Little Word in Kindness Spoken," was a descendant of an old Boston family. One forebear took part in the Boston Tea Party. Colesworthy attended a school, noteworthy in its day, of which his father was also a graduate, and the son wrote an account of it in *John Tileson's School.* When Daniel Colesworthy was a young man he worked in a printing shop and from 1840 to 1844 he edited the *Portland Tribune.* He was later a bookseller in Boston.

His published writings are varied: *Sabbath School Hymns* (1833), *The Gem,* also entitled *The Wreath* (Boston, 1843), *A Group of Children and Other Poems* (1868), *The Old Bureau and Other Tales* (1861), *The Year* (1873), and *John Tileson's School* (1887). See "While We Lowly Bow Before Thee."

Benjamin Colman, Congregational clergyman; b. Boston, Mass., Oct. 19, 1673; d. there Aug. 29, 1747.

Benjamin Colman received his preparatory schooling at the hands of the famous schoolmaster Ezekial Cheever and was graduated from Harvard in 1692. The following year he began to preach at Medford, Mass. Two years later he set out on a trip to England, which was then at war with France. On the way, Colman's ship was attacked by a French privateer; in the ensuing naval engagement his ship was captured and he spent some time as a prisoner in France. Finally an exchange included him and he was sent to England. There he preached very successfully and made friends with prominent dissenting clergymen.

In 1699 Boston called him back to be the first pastor of the Brattle Street Church, where he occupied the pulpit until the last Sunday of his life. His oratory was splendid and many of his sermons were published. In 1724 he was elected president of Harvard, but declined to serve. He was, however, active in raising funds for both Harvard and Yale. He was awarded the honorary D.D. by the University of Glasgow.

A large family survived Colman, who was married three times. His son-in-law, Rev. Ebenezer Turell, published an interesting biography of him. Among his works were a number of poems, including one written in 1707 on the death of Rev. Samuel Willard entitled "Elijah's Translation," and a tract advocating inoculatjon against smallpox, a moot question of the day. See "God of My Life!"

Thomas Comer, singer, conductor, teacher, and organist; b.
1790; d. 1862.

The diversity of Thomas Comer's musical interests was characteristic of his period. In 1837 we find him with Louis Ostinelli in charge
of the music of the Tremont Theater in Boston. In the same year
they were jointly responsible for organizing the Boston Musical Institute, one of the short-lived groups that split off from the older
Handel and Haydn Society. The title page of *The Boston Musical Institute's Collection of Church Music* (1840) describes Comer as organist of
historic King's Chapel. In 1847 he was the organizer of the Boston
Musical Fund Society which gave orchestral concerts for the benefit
of needy musicians. See EAST HAYES ("Abide Not in the Realm of
Dreams").

Thomas Commuck, fl. mid-19th cent.

A small volume of *Indian Melodies* by Thomas Commuck, a Nar-
raganset Indian, was published in 1845 with tunes which had been
harmonized by Thomas Hastings (q.v.). The preface to the book was
signed by Commuck and dated at Manchester, Wisconsin Territory,
in 1845. In it he explained that he gave his tunes the names of Indian chiefs, women, and places, because he wanted to pay a tribute
of respect to the memory of tribes nearly or perhaps totally extinct,
and to show courtesy to tribes he knew personally. PEQUET, CUM-
MANCHE, QUAPAW were among the titles. Also included was OLD IN-
DIAN HYMN, a tune which the Narragansets believed had been
heard in the air by tribes living along the Atlantic coast many years
before the white men arrived. Later, when their descendants visited
a church of the white settlers in Plymouth Colony, they heard the
same tune sung and were able to join in.

Commuck claimed that he was the first "son of the forest" to un-
dertake such a task. In 1836 he began to study singing by established
rules. Although he had no teacher, he had access to a few books on
the subject. He was a poor man, with a family of seven children, and
was apparently a convert to the Methodist faith. He hoped his book
would make money, not only to help his family but also to enable
him to help some of the needy of his people. See OSCEOLA ("You
That Have Been Often Invited").

Ithamar Conkey, church singer and organist; b. Shutesbury, Mass., 1815; d. Elizabeth, N.J., April 30, 1867.

Ithamar Conkey is listed among the members of the choir of Trinity Church in New York City for 1848. In 1850 he was bass soloist in Calvary Episcopal Church. From 1852 to 1854 he took part in services at Trinity Church. In 1861 he was bass and leader of the quartet choir in the Madison Avenue Baptist Church. He was sought as a soloist in oratorio performances. His tune RATHBUN ("Lord, I Know Thy Grace Is Nigh Me") was widely used, but the facts concerning its origin have been variously stated. It is often dated 1847, but Philo Adams Otis, in *The Hymns You Ought to Know,* states that it was composed in 1849 when Conkey was organist of the Central Baptist Church of Norwich, Conn., and that it was named for Mrs. Beriah S. Rathbun, the leading soprano of the choir.

Mrs. M. A. W. Cook, editor; b. July 23, 1806; d. Sept. 15, 1874.

Mrs. M. A. W. Cook, wife of the Rev. Parsons Cook, was the editor of *The Puritan Recorder.* Mrs. Cook's hymn "In Some Way or Other, the Lord Will Provide" (q.v.) was included in Ira D. Sankey's English collection *Sacred Songs and Solos* (1873) and in *Gospel Hymns and Sacred Songs* (1875), published in this country by Sankey and Philip Bliss. It is credited there to *Hallowed Songs.*

Russell Sturgis Cook, Congregational minister; b. New Marlboro, Mass., March 6, 1811; d. Pleasant Valley, N.Y., Sept. 4, 1864.

Russell Sturgis Cook began the study of law at Syracuse, N.Y., but abandoned it for the ministry. In 1832 he entered the Theological Seminary at Auburn, N.Y. He received his degree in 1834 and became a pastor of the Congregational Church at Lanesborough, Mass. At the end of a year, when he had lost his voice as a result of a bronchial infection, he resigned his charge and became an agent for, and later the secretary of, the American Tract Society in New York City. During his years with the Society he edited a monthly paper, the *American Messenger.* In 1857 he resigned to accept the secretaryship of the New York Sabbath Committee. He retired in May 1864. He is known for one hymn, "Just As Thou Art" (q.v.).

Benjamin Copeland, Methodist minister and poet; b. Clarendon, N.Y., June 14, 1855; d. Buffalo, N.Y., Dec. 1, 1940.

Benjamin Copeland was one of four brothers who were ordained as Methodist ministers. Educated at Genesee Wesleyan Seminary, he was admitted on trial to the Genesee Conference in 1877. Two years later he was granted full membership and for forty-two years served in twenty-two churches in western New York State. Copeland founded five churches, four in Buffalo, where he continued to live after his retirement in 1919. In 1892 he became secretary of the Methodist Union. In 1918 the honorary degree of S.T.D. was conferred on him by Syracuse University. The author of four volumes of poetry, he also wrote hymns including "Christ's Life Our Code" and "Our Fathers' God."

Laura S. Copenhaver, teacher and Lutheran leader; b. Marion, Va., Aug. 29, 1868; d. there Dec. 18, 1940.

Laura Copenhaver's father, John Jacob Scherer, was the founder of Marion College and served as its president for about thirty years. Her sister Mary was dean of women; another sister, Mrs. E. C. Cronk, was a writer and missionary leader; a brother, John, was pastor of a Lutheran church in Richmond for fifty years. Laura spent her whole life in Marion. She early revealed a literary talent and, in addition to becoming a teacher at her alma mater, she was made chairman of the education committee of the Woman's Missionary Society of the United Lutheran Church. In later life she was in great demand as a speaker at various religious conferences.

Through Mrs. Copenhaver's initiative the Missionary Society started work among the mountaineers of the South. She encouraged native craftsmanship among the mountain people of her section of the state. See "Heralds of Christ."

Aaron Copland, American composer; b. Brooklyn, N.Y., Nov. 14, 1900.

Aaron Copland studied with Nadia Boulanger in Paris and composed an organ concerto which she played in this country with the New York Philharmonic under Walter Damrosch (1924) and with Koussevitsky and the Boston Symphony. His early *Music for the Theatre* (1925) and his Piano Concerto (1926) were influenced by jazz. As he matured he tended to write both accessible works—often with a folk atmosphere—and works in a more dissonant, abstract style. Among the former are his ballets *Appalachian Spring* (1944), *Billy the Kid* (1938), and *Rodeo* (1942), and his film scores for *Of Mice and Men* (1939), *The Red Pony* (1948), and *The Heiress* (1948). Among the latter are the *Piano Variations* (1930), the *Piano Sonata* (1939–41) and the *Third Symphony* (1945). He included a setting of the Shaker melody " 'Tis the Gift To Be Simple" (q.v.) in his *Old American Songs*, Set i, and one of a Southern folk hymn, "Zion's Walls," in Set ii.

P. J. Cormican, S.J., educator and parish priest; b. Lurgan Co., Galway, Ireland, 1858; d. Buffalo, N.Y., 1945.

P. J. Cormican became a Jesuit in 1880, studied for the priesthood at Woodstock College in Maryland, and was ordained in 1894. After teaching in Jesuit colleges from 1895 to 1927 he went to St. Michael's Church in Buffalo, N.Y. In 1929 he became a parish priest at St. Anne's Church in that city and remained there the rest of his life. See his "True Son of God, Eternal Light."

Henry Cowell, composer, pianist, and ethno-musicologist; b. Menlo Park, Calif., March 11, 1897; d. Shady, N.Y., Dec. 10, 1965.

Henry Cowell began to study the violin at the age of five. Largely self-educated at first, he later studied with Charles Seeger at the Berkeley campus of the University of California, with Percy Goetschius at the Institute of Musical Art (1919), and with Arnold Schoenberg in Berlin. From his boyhood he had an interest in Eastern music first aroused by performances of Chinese opera in San Francisco. Cowell was a pupil of Erich von Hornbostel (1931–32). He studied South Indian music in Madras, Japanese court music, and Iranian music.

Cowell was active as a concert pianist seeking special effects in his piano compositions by the use of "tone clusters" played with fist or forearm, harmonics, glissandos on the undamped strings, and plucked tones. His formal debut at Leipzig (1923) was followed by five tours in Europe, one in the Soviet Union (1928), and fifteen transcontinental tours in this country.

His compositions were numerous and varied. He wrote eight compositions called *Hymn and Fuguing Tune*, which were inspired by the early New England singing masters. Other works, like his *Homage to Iran* (1959), reflected his interest in Eastern music. His *Mosaic*

Quartet (No. 3, 1935) is an example of "open-ended form" where the performers select the sections they wish to play and play them in any order they choose. Perhaps the symphonies form the most continuous series of compositions. Symphonies 5 (1949), 7 (1952), 11 (1954), 15 (1961) and 16 (1962) have been recorded. Cowell composed his TREE OF LIFE ("Thou Art the Tree of Life") especially for *American Hymns.*

Samuel K. Cox, minister and educator; b. Boston, Mass., July 16, 1823; d. Nov. 27, 1909.

Son of a Methodist minister and cousin of Bishop John C. Keener, Samuel Cox received an excellent education in the Boston schools. In 1844 he joined the Maryland Conference of the Methodist Protestant Church, of which his father had been one of the organizers in 1828. After filling various pastoral charges in Washington, D.C., and elsewhere, he became professor of Mental and Moral Philosophy at Madison College, Uniontown, Pa., in 1853. He spent a few years in that position before he moved to Virginia, then to Alabama, in both of which states he engaged in educational work.

In 1866 he joined the Methodist Episcopal Church, South, in which he served as educator and pastor in several cities, among them Washington and Baltimore. Editor of the *Episcopal Methodist,* the *Baltimore Christian Advocate,* and the *Baltimore and Richmond Christian Advocate,* he was a member of the committee which compiled (1886–88) the hymnbook of the Methodist Episcopal Church, South. It was the official hymnal for that denomination until it was replaced by the 1905 edition of *The Methodist Hymnal,* which represented both branches of American Methodism. See "Lord, Thou Hast Promised."

Arthur Cleveland Coxe, Protestant Episcopal bishop, author, and hymn writer; b. May 10, 1818, Mendham, N.J.; d. Buffalo, N.Y., July 20, 1896.

At ten years of age Arthur Cleveland Coxe was sent to preparatory school at Pittsfield, Mass. In his sixteenth year he entered New York University. Excelling in literature and writing, he graduated in 1838. He attended the General Theological Seminary of New York from which he graduated in 1841. Ordained that same year, he became rector of St. Anne's Church, Morrisania, N.Y. In 1842 he accepted a similar post at St. John's in Hartford, Conn., and in 1854 moved to Grace Church in Baltimore.

At the outbreak of hostilities which led to the Civil War he upheld the Union cause against great opposition. When the rectorship of Calvary Church was made vacant by the resignation and removal of the Rev. Dr. Hawks to Baltimore, Coxe was called to New York City to take his place. Chosen in 1864 to be bishop co-adjutor of Western New York, he became diocesan bishop the following year. He remained in Buffalo for the rest of his life.

Coxe favored neither the liberal trends of his time nor those within his church, and was in opposition when Phillips Brooks was elevated as bishop. Since he believed that the authorized version of the Bible was a precious common heritage, he opposed attempts to modernize its text. A contributor of poetry to journals and periodicals from his college days, Coxe published *Christian Ballads* in 1840, followed by another volume of verse in 1842. See his "Father, Who Mak'st Thy Suffering Sons," "In the Silent Midnight Watches," and "Saviour, Sprinkle Many Nations."

Thomas Cradock, clergyman and teacher; b. Bedfordshire, England, 1718; d. Baltimore Co., Md., May 7, 1770.

Thomas Cradock was a university graduate and the brother of a Protestant Archbishop of Dublin who served from 1772 to 1778. Coming to Maryland in 1744, Cradock became rector of St. Thomas' Parish in Baltimore Co., Md., a post he retained as long as he lived, even through a period of invalidism. In 1747 he advertised to receive young men as boarders in his home in the town of Owings Mills and to teach them Latin and Greek at a fee of $53 a year. The school became famous and his own reputation for excellence as a teacher and adviser was solidly established. Many of his students came from the southern counties of the state.

He reared his family, three sons and a daughter, on a large plantation which had been a gift to his wife from her father. Cradock's will, made in 1770, disposed of the acres which he had acquired as well as the home plantation which his wife had inherited. Besides the land, slaves were left to members of the family, as were the furnishings of the house, globes, telescopes, and books, including a twelve-volume *History of the World*.

A Poetical Translation of the Psalms of David from Buchanan's Latin into English Verse by Cradock was printed in London, 1754, for Mrs. Ann Cradock at Wells, Somersetshire. It is thought that she was the author's mother. A later edition (1756) had the title *A New Version of the Psalms of David* and a dedication to "His Excellency, Horatio Sharpe, Esq., Governor of the Province of Maryland, and the Hon. James Hamilton, Esq., late Governor of the Province of Pennsylvania." Some unsigned poems were found among Cradock's papers. See "What Glorious Vision" and "Ye Scattered Nations."

John Craig, Reformed clergyman and contributor to the Scottish psalter; b. 1512; d. Dec. 12, 1600.

John Craig became a Dominican monk after study at St. Andrews, but left Scotland under suspicion of heresy. With the help of Cardinal Pole at Rome he became master of novices in the Dominican monastery at Bologna. There he found a copy of Calvin's *Institutes* which influenced him so profoundly that he adopted the Reformed faith. On leaving the monastery he was taken by the Inquisition and imprisoned at Rome in a pit into which the Tiber flowed as the tide rose. He was sentenced to be burned to death on August 19, 1559, but disorders broke out after the death of Pope Paul IV, the prison was opened, and Craig fled. He was able to elude pursuit and to return to Edinburgh in 1560. He preached there in Latin for a time, since he had been away so long that he had lost his command of his own Scottish tongue. He was minister with John Knox at St. Giles' (1563), chaplain to King James, and minister at Holyrood (1579). Craig made fifteen contributions to the Scottish psalter of 1564/65, among which his second version of Psalm 145 was notable. Since most of his versions were in unusual meters, only three were retained in the Scottish psalter of 1650 (second versions of Psalms 136, 143, and 145). See "O Hear My Prayer, Lord" and "O Lord, That Art My God and King."

Fanny J. Crosby, blind hymnist; b. Southeast, N.Y., March 24, 1820; d. Bridgeport, Conn., Feb. 12, 1915.

At the age of twelve Fanny Crosby entered the New York City School for the Blind (where Grover Cleveland was secretary) and remained there as a teacher for twenty-three years. In 1858 she married Alexander Van Alstyne, a blind musician, also a teacher at the school. Through her long residence in New York she kept her church membership at the old John Street Methodist Episcopal Church. Her later years were spent at Bridgeport, Conn., where she died at the age of ninety-five. Fanny Crosby was the most prolific of the many writers who published texts for Gospel and Sunday-School hymns. She was eight when she wrote her first hymn and she continued for eighty years, using not only her own name but also two to three hundred pen names. For many years she was under contract to furnish three hymns a week to Bigelow and Main, publishers of books of the gospel song type. She said that she often composed as many as six or seven hymns a day. Many have been long forgotten, but a number have shown persistent vitality. It must be granted that in her special genre she succeeded admirably in what she set out to do. Among the composers who wrote tunes for her texts were William Howard Doane, George F. Root, William Batchelder Bradbury, and Robert Lowry. See "Blessed Assurance, Jesus Is Mine" and "Jesus, Keep Me Near the Cross."

Allen Eastman Cross, Congregational minister and hymnist; b. Manchester, N.H., Dec. 30, 1864; d. there April 23, 1942.

Allen Eastman Cross attended preparatory school at Phillips Andover Academy. His college was Amherst and he prepared for the Congregational ministry at Andover Seminary from which he later received the degree of Doctor of Divinity. His first pastorate was at Cliftondale, Mass. He went on to Springfield Park Church at Springfield, Mass., and to the Old South Church in Boston, where he served as associate pastor with Dr. George A. Gordon from 1901 to 1911. In 1911–12 he traveled around the world visiting missions of all denominations.

Cross's last pastorate began in 1914 in the First Congregational Church of Milford, Mass.; he retired in 1925 and returned to New Hampshire. He was the author of a volume of poems, *Pass on the Torch* (1929), and of *Thunder Over Jerusalem* (1936). During his retirement he contributed to various newspapers and periodicals. Since his death his hymns have continued to be reprinted in many newly published hymnals. See "The Gray Hills Taught Me Patience," "Though Fatherland Be Vast," and "Young and Radiant, He Is Standing."

William Crosswell, Episcopal pastor and hymnist; b. Hudson, N.Y., Nov. 7, 1804; d. Boston, Mass., Nov. 9, 1851.

William Crosswell took a law course at Yale, graduating in 1822. After graduation he turned to the Episcopal ministry and studied theology at Hartford College. He was rector of Christ Church, Boston; St. Peter's, Auburn, N.Y.; and, in Boston again, at the Church of the Advent which he founded. His sudden death occurred there at the conclusion of a service. See "Lord! Lead the Way the Saviour Went."

e e cummings, poet and painter; b. Cambridge, Mass., Oct. 14, 1894; d. New York City, 1962.

e e cummings (Edward Estlin Cummings) took his B.A. at Harvard in 1915 and his M.A. the next year. Before the United States entered World War I he joined the Norton Harjes Ambulance Unit in France. During his service in it he was mistaken for a spy, seized, and held prisoner for six months, an experience out of which he wrote *The Enormous Room* (1922). On his return home he served as a private in his country's army at Camp Devens, Mass. After the war he spent two years in New York, followed by several in Paris, where he studied art. Cummings had a one-man show of his paintings at the American British Art Center in 1944 and at the Rochester Memorial Gallery in 1945.

His first volume of poetry, *Tulips and Chimneys,* was published in 1923. Several more volumes have come out since then: *XLI Poems* (1925), *&* (1925), *is 5* (1926), *Christmas Tree* (1928), by e e cummings (no title, 1930), *C I O P W* (1931), *ViVa* (1931), *No Thanks* (1935), *Tom* (1935), *1/20* (1936), *Collected Poems* (1938), *50 Poems* (1940), *One Times One* (1944), *Santa Claus* (1946), *Xaipe* (1950), *Poems 1923–1954* (1954). A travel diary of his visit to Russia, published in 1933, was entitled *Eimi.* His only play, *him,* was produced by the Provincetown Players in 1928. In 1953 Cummings delivered the Charles Eliot Norton Lectures at Harvard. He received several awards: the Fellowship of the Academy of American Poets in 1950, the National Book Award in 1955, the Boston Arts Festival Poetry Award, and the Bollingen Prize in Poetry at Yale in 1957. He was a member of the National Academy of Arts and Letters.

An article by John Finch in the *New England Quarterly* describes Cummings as "New England Prodigal" and expresses the opinion that this challenging and uniquely gifted poet had "become a left-wing spokesman for the same state of mind which, on the right, animates the acid resignation of Robert Frost." See "purer than purest pure."

Evelyn Atwater Cummins, editor and civic worker; b. Poughkeepsie, N.Y., May 17, 1891.

After attending the National Cathedral School, Washington, D.C., and the Masters School, Dobbs Ferry, N.Y., Evelyn Atwater became the wife of the Rev. Alexander G. Cummins, rector of Christ Church, Poughkeepsie, N.Y. She was active as a writer and citizen. Publications with which she was connected are: *The Chronicle* (associate editor, 1926–46; publisher, 1946–47), *The Living Church* (1926–29); and *Poughkeepsie Evening Star* (1940–43).

Mrs. Cummins' civic activities include work as a member of the Poughkeepsie War Council (1940–46), of the Diocesan Board of Religious Education (1938–40), and the Federal Council of the Churches of Christ of America (1941–42); as director of the Visiting Nurses Association (1939–42), and the YWCA (1938–43); as a trustee of the Poughkeepsie City Library (1942–48), and of Vassar Brothers Hospital (1940–47). The first female police commissioner in New York state, she served Poughkeepsie in that capacity in the period 1948–50. She was commissioner of both the police and fire departments and a member of the police advisory board of the New York State Safety Division. See "I Know Not Where the Road Will Lead."

William O. Cushing, minister and writer of hymns; b. Hingham, Mass., Dec. 31, 1823; d. Lisbon Center, N.Y., Oct. 19, 1902.

Convinced at the age of eighteen that he wanted to be a minister, William O. Cushing's first charge was at Searsburg, N.Y. There he married Rena Proper on February 4, 1854. After serving as pastor in several communities he returned to Searsburg because of his wife's ill health. She died on July 13, 1870. When what was called "creeping paralysis" deprived him of his voice and his employment as a minister, he found a home at Lisbon Center, N.Y., with Rev. and Mrs. E. E. Curtis. He turned with success to writing texts for Sunday School songs and hymns of the gospel type. See "We Are Watching, We Are Waiting."

Henry S. Cutler, organist and choir director; b. Boston, Mass., Oct. 13, 1824; d. there Dec. 5, 1902.

Henry Cutler studied organ in Boston, then went abroad, first to Frankfurt in 1844, then to England, where his admiration for the choral service as performed in English cathedrals was decisive in determining his own later career. His first post on his return to the United States was as organist of Grace Church, Boston, but it was at the Church of the Advent (from 1852) that he developed a choir with boy singers which won wide acclaim for the manner in which it performed the choral services. In 1858 he went to Trinity Church, New York City, at first on a temporary basis that later became permanent. When he arrived there were two women in the choir in addition to boys. Here he formed another all male choir, which made

its first appearance in surplices when the Prince of Wales visited on
October 7, 1860. Cutler later served as organist in Brooklyn, Providence, Philadelphia, and Troy, N.Y. After his retirement in 1885 he
returned to Boston. Among his publications were the *Trinity Psalter*
(1864) and *Trinity Anthems* (1865). See ALL SAINTS NEW ("The Prince
of Peace His Banner Spreads").

Sewall Sylvester Cutting, Baptist preacher and editor; b.
Windsor, Vt., Jan. 19, 1813; d. Brooklyn, N.Y., Feb. 7, 1882.

When Sewall Cutting was still a small boy his family moved from
Windsor, Vt., his birthplace, to Westport, N.Y. At the age of four-
teen he was baptized and became a member of the Baptist church.
Four years later he matriculated at Waterville College, and after two
years' attendance decided to transfer to the University of Vermont.
There he took his degree in 1835, leading his class in scholarship.

In 1836 he was ordained in West Boylston, Mass., and took the
pulpit of its Baptist church. In 1837 he went to the Baptist Church
of Southbridge, Mass., where he occupied the pulpit until 1845. For
the next ten years he held positions in organized religious work:
editor of the *Baptist Advocate* (later the *New York Recorder*), corresponding secretary of the American and Foreign Bible Society, and
editor of the *Christian Review,* among them.

In 1855 he acepted an invitation from the University of Rochester
to fill the post of professor of rhetoric and history. After thirteen
years he resigned to become secretary of the American Baptist Educational Commission. Then for three years he served as corresponding secretary of the American Baptist Home Mission Society.

Cutting was known as a clear-minded, useful man, and he left a
long record of speaking and publishing in the Baptist field. In 1841
he issued *Hymns for the Vestry and Fireside.* Of its 390 hymns three
were his own compositions: "Spirit! On Restless Wing," "Green the
Hillside, Ever Fair," and "Father! We Bless the Gentle Care." His
best-known hymn was "God of the World, Thy Glories Shine" (q.v.),
first published in James H. Linsley and Gustavus F. Davis, *Select
Hymns* (Hartford, Conn., 1836). See also "Gracious Saviour, We
Adore Thee."

William Daman, arranger; b. Liège, c.1550; d. England, by
1593.

William Daman (or Damon), "one of her maiesties musitions," was
brought to England between 1561 and 1564 by Thomas Sackville,

Lord Brockhurst. Little is known of his life, but he was obviously well-trained in polyphony. His *Psalmes of David in English Meter with notes of foure partes set unto them* was issued in 1579 by John Day at the instigation of the goldsmith John Bull "to the use of the godly Christians for recreatyng themselves in stede of fond and unseemely Ballades." Daman was considerably annoyed that they had been published without his knowledge since he had written them for the "pleasuryng of his private frend." This collection kept the church tune in the tenor and is an unpretentious example of plain counterpoint. Of particular interest is the appearance in this volume of four common meter tunes which later were to become extremely popular under the names OXFORD, CAMBRIDGE, CANTERBURY, and SOUTHWELL. Indeed, all except the first appear in this collection in arrangements by other composers.

His *The Former Booke of the Musicke of M. William Damon* is in more elaborate counterpoint or motet style; in the first book "the tenor singeth the church tune," while in the second "the highest part singeth the church tune." The work was published after the composer's death by his friend William Swayne "for the recreation of such as delight in Musicke." See PSALM 25 ("I Lift My Heart to Thee") and PSALM 24 ("Now Israel May Say, and That Truly").

Mary Stanley Bunce Dana, poet; b. Beaufort, S.C., Feb. 15, 1810; d. Texas, Feb. 8, 1883.

Mary Stanley Bunce married Charles E. Dana in 1835 and in 1838 she went with him to Bloomington, Iowa. After his death in 1839 she returned to South Carolina. She published the *Southern Harp* in 1840 and the *Northern Harp* in the following year. In these volumes her verses were set to melodies some of which were of folk, or at least of popular, origin. Her "I'm a Pilgrim and I'm a Stranger," for example, is to be sung to an "Italian Air, Buona Notte." We have placed "O Sing to Me of Heaven" (q.v.) with the Presbyterian hymns, although Mrs. Dana was later a Unitarian and finally an Episcopalian. In 1851 she married Rev. Robert D. Shindler and moved to Texas with him.

Robert T. Daniel, Baptist missionary; b. Middlesex Co., Va., June 10, 1773; d. Paris, Tenn., Sept. 14, 1840.

Baptized in 1802, Robert T. Daniel became a member of the Holly Springs Baptist Church, Wake Co., N.C., and was ordained the fol-

lowing year. One of the first missionaries to work for the North
Carolina Baptist Benevolent Society, he served regions which had no
established churches and was the founder of the First Baptist
Church of Raleigh in 1812. Widely known as a persuasive and eloquent preacher he widened the field of his activities to include Virginia, Mississippi, and Tennessee. He summarized his labors when in
1833 he stated that "during the years of my ministry I have traveled
about sixty thousand miles, preached about five thousand sermons,
and baptized more than fifteen hundred people. Of that number
many now are ministers, twelve of whom are men of distinguished
talents and usefulness." See "The Time Will Surely Come."

Mabel W. Daniels, composer; b. Swampscott, Mass., Nov. 27, 1879; d. Boston, Mass., March 10, 1971.

Mabel W. Daniels was the daughter of a one-time president of the
Handel and Haydn Society. A graduate of the Girls' Latin School,
Boston, she finished magna cum laude at Radcliffe College in 1900.
She studied composition with George W. Chadwick and with Ludwig
Thuille in Munich. In 1911 she received two prizes offered by the
National Federation of Music Clubs: one for a song, *Villa of Dreams,*
and the other for two three-part songs, *Voice of My Beloved* and *East-
ern Song.*

Miss Daniels composed two operettas for students of Radcliffe.
She also wrote *Desolate City* (a poem for baritone and orchestra, first
performed at the MacDowell Festival, 1913); *Peace with a Sword* (for
mixed voices and orchestra, first performed by the Handel and
Haydn Society, 1917); *Songs of Elfland* (for women's voices, flute,
harp, strings, and percussion); *Exultate Deo* (for mixed voices and
orchestra, composed for the fiftieth anniversary of Radcliffe); *Deep
Forest* (introduced by the Boston Symphony); *Pirate's Island; In the
Greenwood;* and *Fairy Scherzo* (played by several orchestras).

A trustee of Radcliffe College, Miss Daniels received an honorary
A.M. from Tufts College (1933), and a Mus.D. from Boston Univer-
sity in 1939. The author of *An American Girl in Munich* (1905), she
was a member of the American Composers Alliance and the Mac-
Dowell Colony. See DREAMERS ("Through the Dark the Dreamers
Came").

John David, B.M., Catholic missionary and musician; b. Coueron, France, June 4, 1761; d. Nazareth, Ky., July 12, 1841.

John David prepared for the priesthood in Nantes and was ordained in 1785. He became a teacher in the seminary at Angers

where he also served as bursar until it was attacked during the French Revolution. In 1791 he came to the United States where he served as a missionary in Maryland, as a teacher of philosophy at Georgetown College, Washington, D.C., and as provisional head of St. Mary's Seminary in Baltimore. In 1811 he traveled to Kentucky where he was for many years the Superior of St. Thomas' Seminary at Bardstown. In 1832 he was consecrated as the second bishop of Bardstown, a post which he relinquished the following year. He not only played the organ but also composed church music including the setting for "What Happiness Can Equal Mine."

Samuel Davies, Presbyterian pastor and educator; b. New Castle, Del., Nov. 3, 1723; d. Princeton, N.J., Feb. 4, 1761.

Samuel Davies was licensed to preach in 1746 and ordained an evangelist in 1747. He began his mission in Hanover County, Virginia. In that state, where dissenters were frowned upon, Davies made the cause of nonconformists his own and in a few years had built up a strong Presbyterian membership. In 1752 he issued *Miscellaneous poems, chiefly on divine subjects. In two books. Published for the religious entertainment of Christians in General.* Over twenty years later Philip Vickers Fithian examined a copy and observed: "I saw a small Book of Hymns moral and religious by President Davies, here, that charmed me exceedingly—Great American Genius! I highly venerate thy strong abilities; all thy Labours are both useful and entertaining."

In 1753 Davies was commissioned by the Synod of New York to visit the British Isles with Gilbert Tennant to raise funds for the College of New Jersey (now Princeton University). His fame as an orator caused him to be invited by George II to occupy the pulpit of the Chapel Royal. On his return to Virginia in 1755, he was largely instrumental in founding the first presbytery in that state. Two years later, after the death of Jonathan Edwards, the trustees named Davies president of the College of New Jersey. He died in office in 1761.

Among the students at the college during Davies' administration was James Lyon (q.v.) of the class of 1759, and Davies subscribed for four copies of *Urania,* a tune book edited by Lyon which appeared in 1761. Among Davies' manuscripts were sixteen hymns which were published by Dr. Thomas Gibbons, an English Independent minister, in his *Hymns Adapted to Divine Worship* (London, 1769). Seven of these were later republished in John Rippon's *A Selection of Hymns from the Best Authors* (New York, 1787). Davies thus became the earliest native-born American hymn writer whose hymns had general acceptance. See "Eternal Spirit, Source of Light," "Lord, I Am Thine," and "While o'er Our Guilty Land, O Lord."

Abijah Davis, Presbyterian pastor; b. Deerfield Township, Cumberland Co., N.J., 1763; d. Millville, N.J., Aug. 1817.

Abijah Davis was the youngest of five boys. At twenty-one he married. His father gave him a small farm, but he soon sold it and went to the College of Philadelphia to study for the ministry. That course finished, he studied further with Rev. Robert Smith in Pequa, Pa. He was finally licensed to preach by the Philadelphia presbytery and around the year 1790 he settled in Cape May. Ten years later he moved to Millville, N.J., where he died.

His parishioners considered him a strong-minded and orthodox thinker, a man of melancholy disposition. When he was in his teens he resolved to begin an original version of the Psalms by the time he reached the age of forty. He kept the resolution. For ten years he worked on the project, called *An American Version of the Psalms of David: suited to the state of the Church in the present age of the world, by Abijah Davis, Minister of the Gospel at Millville, New Jersey* (Millville, N.J., 1813). See "Blest Is the Man Whose Tender Breast."

Arthur Davis, composer.

Arthur Davis wrote the tune CREEVELEA (q.v.), which was published in H. Augustine Smith's *American Student Hymnal* in 1928. It had first appeared in the *Homiletic Review* in 1927.

Ozora S. Davis, Congregational minister and educator; b. Wheelock, Vt., July 30, 1866; d. Chicago, Ill., March 15, 1931.

Before Ozora Davis enrolled at Dartmouth College, he had decided that he wanted to enter the Congregational ministry. After earning his A.B. degree (1889), he studied at the Hartford Theological Seminary and the University of Leipzig (M.A.; Ph.D., 1896). He became an ordained minister in 1896. His first pastorate at First Church in Springfield, Vt. (1896–99), was followed by others at Central Church, Newtonville, Mass. (1899–1904); and South Church, New Britain, Conn. (1904–08). In 1908 he accepted the presidency of Chicago Theological Seminary, where he remained until 1920.

Davis was the author of several books, among them: *John Robinson—The Pilgrim Pastor* (1903), *The Pilgrim Faith* (1913), *Using the Bible in Public Address* (1916), *Meeting the Master* (1917), *International Aspects of Christianity* (1919), *The Gospel in the Light of the Great War* (1919), *Evangelistic Preaching* (1921), and *Preaching and the Social Gospel* (1922).

Dartmouth College conferred an honorary D.D. (1909) on Davis and Colorado College an honorary LL.D. (1920). In 1927 he became moderator of the National Council of the Congregational Church. See "At Length There Dawns the Glorious Day."

George Henry Day, organist and choirmaster; b. New York City, Sept. 13, 1883; d. Geneva, N.Y., Nov. 23, 1966.

George Henry Day was a choirboy at Trinity Chapel in New York City. In 1903 he studied organ with Dr. G. Edward Stubbs and served as his assistant organist at St. Agnes' Chapel in New York. In 1909 Day became a fellow of the American Guild of Organists and later served as a member of its council (1915–16). From 1911 to 1916 he was organist and choirmaster at St. Peter's Episcopal Church in New York, at the same time serving as visiting choirmaster at St. Paul's in Westfield, N.J.

Until 1913 Day held, in addition to his musical positions, a purely commercial one. After studying accounting and commercial law at New York University he became assistant auditor of the Gorham Manufacturing Company. In 1913 he resigned from the Gorham firm to make music his sole occupation. He took special courses at Columbia University and in 1915 graduated from the New York College of Music.

Day served as organist and choirmaster in churches in Youngstown, Ohio; Wilmington, Del.; Rochester, N.Y.; and finally in 1935, at Trinity Church, Geneva, N.Y. While at Wilmington he studied composition with Edward Shippen Barnes (q.v.) and Orlando Mansfield. In 1923 he received the Mus.D. from Lincoln-Jefferson University.

Among Day's compositions the Christmas cantata, *Great David's Greater Son* (1928) has probably been most often performed. His tune GENEVA ("Not Alone for Mighty Empire") (q.v.) was named for Geneva, N.Y., and EDSALL for Samuel Edsall, the rector of Trinity Church in neighboring Auburn. The tunes MY MASTER, ROCHESTER, MARTINEAU, and DECISION were published in H. Augustine Smith's *The New Hymnal for American Youth* (1930).

Ebenezer Dayton, teacher; fl. mid-18th cent.

In 1769 Ebenezer Dayton was "of Brook-haven, and late School-Master in *Newport, Rhode Island.*" In that year he published *A Consise, poetical Body of Divinity, Published in Three separate Parts Each a Pam-*

phlet, in which he turned each question of the shorter catechism "into a Divine Hymn, in the form of a Question and Answer; and fitted to the several Metres, and suitable to be sung in Families and private Meetings of Societies; for the Instruction of Persons of all Ages and Capacities, to whom they are dedicated." It was probably used to educate the young, since a knowledge of the catechism determined by a series of questions was a prerequisite to church membership. See "Wherein Consists the High Estate."

Charles F. Deems, clergyman and hymnist, b. Baltimore, Md., Dec. 4, 1820; d. New York City, Nov. 18, 1893.

Charles F. Deems founded and was pastor of the (unaffiliated) Church of the Strangers during the years that Alice and Phoebe Cary (q.v.) were members of his parish in New York. With Phoebe he compiled a hymnal, *Hymns for All Christians,* which was published in 1869. See "I Shall Not Want: In Deserts Wild."

Norman Dello Joio, composer, pianist, and organist; b. New York City, Jan. 24, 1913.

Norman Dello Joio is the son of an accomplished organist and composer who was in turn the descendant of a long line of Italian musicians. After graduating from All Hallows School in 1930, he was enrolled at the College of the City of New York from 1932 to 1934. In 1936 he studied at the Juilliard Institute of Musical Art; from 1939 to 1941 at the Juilliard Graduate School; and, during the period 1941–42, at the Yale School of Music. Between 1945 and 1950 he taught in the music department of Sarah Lawrence College. He later taught composition at the Mannes College of Music in the city of New York.

A recipient of the Elizabeth Sprague Coolidge award in 1937, Dello Joio won the Town Hall Composition award in 1941. He received Guggenheim Fellowships in 1943 and 1944, a Pulitzer prize in 1947, and a grant of the Music Critics Circle in 1949. A director of the American League of Composers, he is also a member of the board of the American Music Center. In 1957 Lawrence College at Appleton, Wis., presented Dello Joio with an honorary degree.

The composer's works include a ballet, *On Stage* (1945); *Ricercari* (1946) for piano and orchestra; *Variations-Chaconne-Finale* (1947); *Concertante for Clarinet and Orchestra* (1949); *New York Profiles* (1949) for orchestra; *The Triumph of St. Joan* (1950), an opera commissioned by the Whitney Foundation; *Psalm of David* (1950) for chorus and orchestra; *Song of Affirmation* (1951) for soprano, chorus, narrator, and orchestra; *The Tall Kentuckian* (1952), a score for a musical play; *Song of the Open Road* (1952) for chorus; *The Listeners* (1956), songs. In April 1956, NBC's Opera Theater presented a television production of his opera *The Trial at Rouen*. See his LULLABY composed for *American Hymns* to a text ("Hush Thee, Princeling") by Anne Elizabeth Bennett.

R. Nathaniel Dett, composer, arranger, and educator; b. Drummondsville (now Niagara) Ont., Oct. 11, 1882; d. Battle Creek, Mich., Oct. 2, 1943.

R. Nathaniel Dett's musical gifts were evident at an early age. He studied at Oberlin Conservatory (B.M., 1908), Columbia University, the Eastman School of Music (M.A.), Harvard University, the American Conservatory in Chicago, and the University of Pennsylvania. He studied composition with George W. Andrews, Rosseter G. Cole, Arthur Foote, and Nadia Boulanger (summer, 1929).

In 1920 Dett won Harvard's Francis Booth prize in composition and the Bowdoin prize for his essay "The Emancipation of Negro Music." In 1927 he received the first award of the Harmon Foundation for Creative Music. Oberlin College and Howard University both conferred the honorary Doctor of Music on him. He was president of the National Association of Negro Musicians, 1924–25.

From 1908 to 1911 Dett taught at Lane College, Jackson, Miss. He was also on the staff at the Lincoln Institute, Jefferson City, Miss. (1911–13), Hampton Institute (1913–20, 1921–31), Sam Houston College (1935), and Bennett College (1937–41). In 1930 he organized the Hampton Choral Union and toured with it in both the United States and Europe. Among his compositions, his *In the Bottoms* for piano (containing his popular "Juba Dance"); choruses, many of which are based on spirituals; and his oratorio *The Ordering of Moses* are notable. See "Nobody Knows de Trouble I've Seen" and "Roll, Jordan Roll" from his *Religious Folk-Songs of the Negro* (1927), as well as "Lord, I Want To Be a Christian" and "O Ride On, Jesus."

David Diamond, composer; b. Rochester, N.Y., July 9, 1915.

David Diamond studied at the Cleveland Institute of Music in 1928. From 1930 to 1934 he attended the Eastman School of Music, studying with Bernard Rogers. He later worked with Roger Sessions at the New Music School and with Paul Boepple at the Dalcroze Institute (1934–36). The summers of 1937 and 1938 were spent at Fountainebleau where he studied with Nadia Boulanger. He received Guggenheim Fellowships (1938 and 1941), the Prix de Rome cash award in 1942, and the Paderewski Prize in 1943. His *First Symphony* (1940) was performed by Dimitri Mitropoulos; a *Second Symphony* written in 1941 was introduced by the Boston Symphony Orchestra. In 1945 Diamond composed both his *Third* and *Fourth Symphonies*. The latter was performed in 1948 by the Boston Symphony under Leonard Bernstein and was later recorded. Diamond's music for *The Tempest* dates from 1944, the same year in which his *Rounds* for string orchestra was composed. It was followed by music for *Romeo and Juliet* (1947) and by *Timon of Athens, Portrait after Shakespeare* (1949). *The World of Paul Klee* (1957) is a set of connected impressions for orchestra based on paintings by the Swiss artist. Diamond provided both the words and the music to "We Will Not Fear" for *American Hymns*.

Emily Dickinson, poet; b. Amherst, Mass., Dec. 10, 1830; d. there May 15, 1886.

Daughter of Edward Dickinson, a prominent lawyer of Amherst, Mass., Emily Dickinson was educated at Amherst Academy for one year and at Mount Holyoke Female Seminary under Mary Lyon. Her life was outwardly eventless for she lived quietly at home. During her last twenty-five years she became a recluse, secluding herself from all but the most intimate friends. Although she never married, she had intellectual friendships with several men who influenced her life. One, a law student in her father's office, introduced her to stimulating books and urged her to take seriously her vocation as a poet. Religious questionings prompted by his early death led her to appeal for guidance to Rev. Charles Wadsworth of Philadelphia, whom she met in 1854. In her later life she initiated a literary correspondence with Thomas Wentworth Higginson (q.v.), whom she knew only through his articles in *The Atlantic Monthly*. She occasionally showed a few of her poems to Samuel Bowles, Dr. J. G. Holland, and Helen Hunt Jackson, all close friends.

For the most part, however, she wrote in secret, and before her death composed well over 1,000 brief lyrics, based on small observations, tiny ecstasies, candid insights, and speculations on the timeless mysteries of love and death. She could express feelings of deepest poignancy in terms of wit, and the greatest essentials in precise, brief, often colorful metaphors. From the chaotic mass of manuscripts found after her death six volumes have since been published.

See "If I Can Stop One Heart from Breaking," and "Read, Sweet, How Others Strove," the latter set to music for *American Hymns* by Roy Harris.

George Washington Doane, Episcopal bishop and educator; b. Trenton, N.J., May 27, 1799; d. Burlington, N.J., April 27, 1859.

The family of George Washington Doane moved to New York from Trenton and, as a child, he attended the school of a notable linguist, Rev. Dr. Edmund Barry. When Doane was ten the family moved again, to Geneva, N.Y., where he went to a preparatory school. After studying law for a short time in New York, he gave it up to enter a class in theology taught by Professor (later Bishop) Brownell, while teaching part time to support his mother and sisters. In 1821 he was ordained a deacon in Christ Church, New York City, and became assistant rector at Trinity. There he was ordained a priest in 1823.

In 1824 Doane joined the faculty of a newly established college in Hartford, Conn., now Trinity College. He was also a most successful field fund-raiser for the college. During his years at Trinity he was an associate editor of the *Episcopal Watchman*.

When he was twenty-five his first book was issued: *Songs by the Way, Chiefly Devotional*. It contained his "Softly Now the Light of Day" (q.v.) and "Thou Art the Way" (q.v.). In 1828 he became assistant rector at Trinity Church in Boston and, two years later, on the death of the rector, Doane succeeded him. In 1829 he married Eliza Perkins of Baltimore. In 1832 he was elected second bishop of New Jersey. Settling then in Burlington, N.J., he assumed the duties of the rectorship of St. Mary's in that city the following year. After founding a school for girls, St. Mary's Hall in 1837, he established Burlington College, a training school for holy orders, in 1846. See also "Fling Out the Banner" and "Once More, O Lord."

William Croswell Doane, Episcopal bishop and educator; b. Boston, Mass., March 2, 1832; d. Albany, N.Y., May 17, 1913.

Son of the eminent Protestant Episcopal bishop, George Washington Doane (q.v.), William Croswell Doane followed closely in his father's footsteps. Educated at Burlington College, N.J. (A.B., 1850; M.A., 1852), which his father had founded, and at Trinity College (M.A., 1863), where his father had taught, he was ordained a deacon by his father in 1853, a priest in 1856. After serving as rector of St. Mary's Church in Burlington (1853–60); of St. John's, Hartford, Conn. (1860–64); and of St. Peter's, Albany, N.Y. (1867–69); he became the Bishop of Albany in 1869.

During his years in Burlington he also taught English literature at Burlington College; while he was at Hartford he lectured on the same subject at Trinity (1863–67). From 1892 he was a regent, from 1902 to 1909 a chancellor, of the University of the State of New York. Like his father, he had an interest in education, and was responsible for the founding of St. Agnes School for Girls in Albany.

Doane received a number of honorary degrees: the D.D. from Columbia (1867), Trinity (1886), Oxford (1888), and Dublin (1901); the LL.D. from Union (1880), Cambridge (1886), Hobart (1890), and the University of Pennsylvania (1902). Hobart also gave him the D.S.T. in 1890, and Union conferred on him the Doctor of Canon Law degree.

Doane's chief literary work was a life of his father entitled *Life and Writings of the Second Bishop of New Jersey* (4 vols., 1860). He later published a book of verse, *Rhymes from Time to Time* (1892), and wrote *Mosaics, or the Harmony of a Collect Epistle,* and *Gospel for the Sundays of the Christian Year.* He served as chairman of the commission which compiled the Protestant Episcopal *Hymnal Revised and Enlarged* (1892). See "Ancient of Days, Who Sittest Throned in Glory."

William Howard Doane, business executive and amateur musician and composer; b. Preston, Conn., Feb. 3, 1832; d. South Orange, N.J., Dec. 24, 1915.

William Howard Doane was the choir leader while a student at Woodstock Academy. He composed his first piece at the age of sixteen. At first associated with his father's cotton manufactury in 1850, he joined the J. A. Fay Company of Norwich, Conn., a maker of woodworking machinery. As managing partner he moved to Cincinnati in 1860 and later became president of the firm. He joined the Baptist Church at an early age and was long the Sunday School superintendent of the Mount Auburn Baptist Church in Cincinnati. He was also a strong supporter of the YMCA.

Doane was a prolific composer of Sunday School and gospel hymns. His first collection was *Sabbath School Gems* (1862), followed by *Silver Spray* (1867) and *Songs of Devotion* (1868). Later he was associated with Robert Lowry in producing collections published by Bigelow and Main, New York. See his NEAR THE CROSS ("Jesus, Keep Me Near the Cross"). Other familiar tunes by Doane are SAFE IN THE ARMS OF JESUS, THE OLD, OLD STORY, PASS ME NOT, MORE LOVE TO

THEE, O CHRIST, EVERY DAY AND EEVERY HOUR, RESCUE THE PERISH-
ING, and DRAW ME NEARER.

Christopher Dock, early Mennonite schoolmaster and music
teacher; b. Germany, date unknown; d. near Morristown,
N.J., 1771.

Christopher Dock is said to have been drafted into the army and
then discharged because he refused to bear arms. He came to Pennsylvania in about 1714 and opened a Mennonite school on the Skippack, beyond Morristown, where many German Protestants had settled. Ten years later he gave it up because of poor attendance and
bought a farm from the Penns near Germantown where he taught
during the summer. In 1738 he returned to the Morristown area
and opened two schools, one in Skippack and one in Salford, teaching three days alternately in each.

Dock's *Schul-Ordnung*, completed August 8, 1750, but not published until 1770, was probably the first treatise on schoolteaching
published in America, and it gives a complete picture of a Pennsylvania country school. Dock devised a "note-board," a narrow black-
board used in teaching the children music with three musical staves
on each side. In his old age Dock published "Rules of Conduct" in
Sauer's *Geistliches Magazien*, including several hymns and spiritual
songs. Death came to him in the autumn of 1771 while he was on his
knees in prayer beside the desk in his schoolroom. See "Ach Kinder,
wollt ihr lieben?"

Anthony Donato, educator, composer, and conductor; b.
Prague, Neb., March 8, 1909.

Anthony Donato was educated at the University of Nebraska
(1926–27) and the Eastman School of Music (Mus.B., 1931; Mus.
M., 1937; Ph.D., 1947), where he was a member of the Rochester
Philharmonic Orchestra. He studied violin with Gustave Tinlot,
composition with Howard Hanson, Edward Royce, and Bernard
Rogers, and conducting with Eugene Goosens. He has been head of
the violin departments of Drake University (1931–37), Iowa State
Teachers College (1937–39), and the University of Texas (1939–46),
where he also taught composition and orchestration. In the summer
of 1947 he taught composition at the Eastman Summer School.
Since 1947 he has been professor of theory and composition and
conductor of the chamber orchestra at Northwestern University.

From 1951 to 1952 he was on leave from that post while he lectured on contemporary American music in England and Scotland on a Fulbright grant.

Donato's chamber music compositions include three string quartets (the first received an award from the Society for the Publication of American Music in 1946), *Drag and Run* (Composers Press publication award, 1946), two violin sonatas, *Sonatina for Three Trumpets* (1947), and *Sonata for Horn and Piano* (1950, commissioned by the National Association of Schools of Music). Among Donato's orchestral compositions are two symphonies, a *Sinfonietta* (1936), *Elegy for Strings* (1938), *Prairie Schooner Overture* (1947), *Andante for Strings* (1948, from the first string quartet), *Suite for Strings* (1948), and *The Plains* (Composers Press Publication, 1953). *The March of the Hungry Mountains* (1949) is for chorus and orchestra and *Solitude in the City* (1954, commissioned by Thor Johnson), for orchestra with narrator. See Donato's setting of Mark Van Doren's "Why Lord?" which was composed for *American Hymns*.

Richard Donovan, composer, organist, and educator; b. New Haven, Conn., Nov. 29, 1891; d. Middletown, Conn., Aug. 22, 1970.

Richard Donovan was educated at the Yale School of Music (Steinert Prize and Mus.B., 1922; honorary M.A., 1947) and at the Institute of Musical Art (1914–18). He studied organ with several teachers including Charles-Marie Widor in Paris.

A member of the faculty of the Taft School (1920–23), Smith College (1923–28), the Institute of Musical Art (1925–28), Finch Junior College (1926–40), Donovan joined the Yale School of Music in 1928, becoming associate professor in 1940, professor in 1947, and Battell Professor of the Theory of Music in 1954. In the summers of 1946 and 1947 he was on the staff of the Middlebury College Composers Conference and in 1948 a visiting member of the music faculty at the University of Southern California.

Organist of Christ Church and conductor of the Bach Cantata Club in New Haven for several years from 1932, he was also conductor of the New Haven Symphony and of the Yaddo Chamber Orchestra in 1937 and 1940. Donovan was one of the group interested in the development of music at Yaddo following the Festival of American Music there in 1932 and his own music has often figured on its programs.

Donovan's compositions comprise works for orchestra: *Woodnotes* (symphony for chamber orchestra), 1926; *Smoke and Steel* (symphonic poem), 1932; *Overture for Orchestra,* 1946; compositions for chorus and chamber music. His *Design for Radio* won a Publication Award in a 1945 contest sponsored by Broadcast Music, Inc. Several of his compositions were recorded by the Office of War Information for broadcast to foreign countries during World War II. Donovan composed *Two Chorale Preludes on American Folk Hymns* (1947) for organ. See his settings for "O Christ of Bethlehem" and "Word of God, Across the Ages," which were composed for *American Hymns.*

Eliakim Doolittle, schoolteacher, singing master, and composer; b. Cheshire, Conn., Aug. 28, 1780; d. Argyll, N.Y., April 1850.

Eliakim Doolittle entered Yale at an early age and later taught school and conducted singing classes in Connecticut. In 1802 he went to live in Hampton, N.Y., where he continued his teaching. He was popular and highly regarded, even considered a genius by some. A gifted musician, he was religious by nature, a zealous reader of the Bible, and a member of the Congregational Church.

In 1806 Doolittle published *The Psalm Singer's Companion,* containing forty-one hymn tunes and an anthem of his composition. EXHORTATION was the best-liked and longest remembered. His song "The Hornet Stung the Peacock" celebrated an engagement in the War of 1812 in which the English man-of-war *Peacock* was sunk by the American ship *Hornet.* It was embellished with an engraving by the composer's brother Amos Doolittle.

Always a wanderer, tempermental and unstable, Doolittle began to show signs of insanity. For some years after his first breakdown he managed to continue his work. During his last years, spent mainly in Pawlet, Vt., he became a solitary wanderer, often ragged and wild-looking. See SOLEMNITY ("Almighty God in Being Was").

Winfred Douglas, canon of the Episcopal church and authority on plain song; b. Oswego, N.Y., Feb. 15, 1867; d. Peekskill, N.Y., Jan. 18, 1944.

Winfred Douglas, educated at Syracuse University (B.Mus., 1891), was an instructor in vocal music there. He prepared for the ministry at St. Andrew's Divinity School, Syracuse, N.Y. After his investiture as deacon (1893) he became a curate at the Church of the Redeemer, New York City, a post which he had to relinquish to seek a more favorable climate when he contracted a lung disease. He was first in Denver as a minor canon at St. John in the Wilderness (from 1894). After further study at St. Matthew's Hall, he was ordained a priest and instituted services at Evergreen, Colo. He served the mission there from 1897 to 1907. In the latter year he became canon of St. Paul's Cathedral, Fond du Lac, Wis., but continued associations as honorary canon there from 1911 and at St. John's from 1934.

Douglas' studies of church music in England, France, and Germany, particularly those with the Benedictines of Solesmes, then (1904) on the Isle of Wight, made him an acknowledged authority on Gregorian music. At the Community of St. Mary, Peekskill, N.Y., where he became director of music from 1906 he was able to apply his knowledge of Gregorian song to the performance practise there and to edit Gregorian music with English texts. He also published collections of plainsong in a form suited to American usage. His book *Church Music in History and Practice* (1937) is the most extended statement of his views. He was the musical editor of both the 1916 and 1940 editions of the Protestant Episcopal hymnal. See "Were You There" and DEXTER STREET ("The Sabbath Day Was By").

John Dowland, English lutanist and composer; b. Ireland, December 1562; d. London, Jan 21, 1626.

John Dowland was a celebrated lute virtuoso of his time with Bachelor of Music degrees from both Oxford and Cambridge. Before the age of twenty he was in the service of Sir Henry Cobham, who in 1579 became English ambassador in Paris. When Cobham was recalled in 1583, Dowland stayed on with his successor. He probably returned to England in 1584–85. Invited to Germany by the Duke of Brunswick he traveled extensively in that country and later served the musical Maurice Landgrave of Hesse-Cassel. From Germany he went to Italy for a stay of several years. On November 11, 1598, Dowland was appointed lutanist to Christian IV of Denmark, who had married Anne, sister of James of Scotland. He received the very large salary of 500 dalers per annum, a sum that rivaled the salaries of high officers of state. During this period some of Dowland's pieces were written at Elsinore, in the castle made famous by his contemporary Shakespeare in *Hamlet*.

Leaving Christian's service on February 24, 1606, Dowland returned to England where recognition came to him in his later years. As a performer on the lute he was without rival in Europe, but his lasting fame rests on his ability as a composer. Of his four volumes the first three were described as books of *Songs or Ayres*, and that of 1612 is entitled *A Pilgrimes Solace*. Dowland was particularly successful at writing sad, mournful songs. He made six settings of psalm tunes, five in Thomas East's collection of 1592, and another in Thomas Ravenscroft's of 1621. See his arrangement of OLD 100TH ("Make Ye a Joyful Sounding Noise").

Lewis Thompson Downes, composer; b. 1827; d. 1907.

Lewis Thompson Downes is remembered for the tune SOLITUDE ("Life of Ages, Richly Poured") (q.v.), composed in 1850 and widely used. Robert G. McCutchan suggests that he was an organist active in Providence, R.I.

Jacob Duché, Anglican preacher; b. Philadelphia, Pa.,
Jan. 31, 1738; d. Jan. 3, 1798.

Jacob Duché graduated from the Academy of Philadelphia in 1757. One of his classmates was Francis Hopkinson, his future brother-in-law. After graduation he made a trip to England and studied two years at Cambridge, but did not take a degree. On his return he obtained a license and became assistant preacher at Christ Church and its offshoot, St. Peter's. In 1760 he married Elizabeth Hopkinson and in the same year traveled to Easton, Pa., as clerk to the governor of Pennsylvania on a treaty-making visit to the Indians. He then resumed his church duties and succeeded Dr. Peters as rector.

After he had been twice chosen to give the opening prayer before the Continental Congress, Duché was appointed chaplain, but resigned after three months. When British troops approached Philadelphia, Duché prayed for the king, was arrested at the church door, and imprisoned. Shortly thereafter he wrote to General Washington, urging him to resume his allegiance to the crown, secure the repeal of the Declaration of Independence, and seek peace. As a result Duché was obliged to leave the country in 1777 and take refuge in England. He was appointed secretary and chaplain of an English orphan asylum, where his hymns were written. He was able to return to the United States in 1792. See "Chilled by the Blasts of Adverse Fate" and "Great Lord of All, Whose Work of Love."

Thomas Spence Duché, artist; b. U.S., fl. 18th cent.

Thomas Spence Duché, the son of Jacob Duché, went to England with his father. He was evidently musical since an article in the *New Church Magazine* states that he composed the tune for Psalm 68 in *The Hymns and Psalms Used at the Asylum or House of Refuge for Female Orphans* (c.1785). In the "new and enlarged edition" of 1801 the melody of Hymn 14, "On the Excellency of the Bible," is also his. That he was a natural rather than a trained musician seems probable since the bass (at least for the first melody) was supplied by his friend François Hippolyte Barthélémon, a famous violinist and composer for the theater of the period. See HYMN ON THE EXCELLENCY OF THE BIBLE ("Chilled by the Blasts of Adverse Fate") and HYMN FOR WHITSUNDAY ("Great Lord of All, Whose Work of Love").

William E. Dudley, Congregational minister; b. Leintwardine, Shropshire, England, Oct. 4, 1887.

William Dudley studied for the ministry at Hartley College, Manchester, before going to Canada as Home Missionary pastor. He continued his studies at the University of North Dakota and at Wesley College. After serving as minister in Winona and Minneapolis, Minn.; Brooklyn, N.Y. (1929); Toledo, Ohio (1942); St. James United Church, Montreal (1948); Trinity United Church, Charlottetown, Prince Edward Island (1948–49); he went to Holyoke, Mass., as pastor of the Second Congregational Church (1949). He received the degree of Doctor of Law from Defiance College in 1943. See "The City, Lord, Where Thy Dear Life."

George Duffield Jr., Presbyterian minister; b. Carlisle, Pa., Sept. 12, 1818; d. Bloomfield, N.J., July 6, 1888.

George Duffield's great-grandfather, the Rev. George Duffield (1732–90), was a chaplain in the Revolutionary Army and the Continental Congress. His father, the Rev. George Duffield (1796–1868), who had held pastorates in Carlisle and Philadelphia, in New York and Detroit, was also regent of the University of Michigan from 1840 to 1848.

George Duffield Jr. studied at Yale University and Union Theological Seminary, and held pastorates in Brooklyn; Philadelphia; Bloomfield, N.J.; Galesburg, Ill.; and Adrian, Saginaw, Ann Arbor, and Lansing, Mich. He died at the home of his son, the Rev. Samuel Willoughby Duffield, an excellent hymnologist who wrote *English Hymns, Their Authors and History* (1886). See "Stand Up, Stand Up for Jesus."

William Duke, preacher, writer, and teacher; b. Patapsco Neck, Baltimore Co., Md., Sept. 15, 1757; d. Elkton, Md., 1840.

William Duke began to preach when he was sixteen. Licensed as an "exhorter" he served small churches for seven years. Then, in broken health, he devoted himself to the study of Latin and Greek. By 1785 he was able to take holy orders in the Protestant Episcopal Church. He was rector of various parishes in Maryland for a time, but the small and uncertain salaries paid in accordance with a "voluntary" system had to be supplemented. Equipped to teach, Duke took a position in an academy at Elkton, Md., and then went successively to St. John's College, Annapolis, to Charlotte Hall School in St. Mary's County, and finally back to the Elkton Academy, where he died.

Duke published anonymously a small collection, *Hymns and Poems on Various Occasions* (1790), wrote an article scoring the prevalence of infidelity in France, and contributed to the *Theological Repertory.* He left a valuable library which his daughter gave to St. James College, Washington County, Maryland. See "Hail Our Incarnate God!"

Edmund Dumas, singing master and preacher; d. 1884.

Active in Georgia, Edmund Dumas was a member of the Southern and Chattahoochee Conventions which brought singers together for annual gatherings. He was one of those responsible for the revision of the *Sacred Harp* of 1869. In the Denson edition of 1936 he was still represented by eight compositions or arrangements: THE DYING MINISTER (1854), WHITE (1856—named for Benjamin Franklin White, the compiler of the *Sacred Harp*), VAIN WORLD, ADIEU (1856), THE TEACHER'S FAREWELL (1858—both words and music by Dumas), REES (1859—"for J. P. Rees, one of his musical brethren"), EDMONDS (1869), THE GOSPEL POOL (1869), and MULLINS (1869—named for Elder John Mullins, a friend and a Primitive Baptist preacher). For THE TEACHER'S FAREWELL see "Our School Now Closes Out."

Henry M. Dunham, organist and choirmaster; b. Brockton, Mass., July 29, 1853; d. Brookline, Mass., May 4, 1929.

Henry Dunham was educated at Boston University, where he studied the organ under George E. Whiting. The music department later separated from the university to become the nucleus of the New England Conservatory. A trip to Europe after he had finished college was cut short by a call to come home and take the position left vacant by his teacher. For fifty years Dunham was identified with the New England Conservatory. Organist and choirmaster of the Porter Church in Brockton, the Ruggles Street Church and the Shawmut Church in Boston, and the Harvard Church in Brookline,

Dunham was also a conductor of the Gounod Club of Brockton and the Orphean Club at Lasell Seminary. The music department of Lasell was almost entirely his creation.

His works for the organ include *The Organ School, Passacaglia in G Minor, In Memoriam, Fantasia and Fugue in D Minor,* and four sonatas. Other compositions are *Duo Concertante* for violoncello and piano, *Evening in Venice* (strings, tympani, organ), *While All Things Were in Quiet Silence* (anthem), *Salve Regina* (women's chorus), *Aurora* (tone poem for organ and orchestra) and *Easter Morning* (symphonic poem). See RANGELEY ("O Holy City Seen of John") and PURITAN ("Our Fathers' God").

Deodatus Dutton Jr., Presbyterian preacher and musician; b. Monson, Mass., Dec. 22, 1808; d. New York City, Dec. 16, 1832.

Educated at Washington (now Trinity) College from which he was graduated as class poet in 1828, Deodatus Dutton Jr. was a precocious musician. By the time he was fourteen years of age he had become organist at Center Church in Hartford. Licensed to preach by the Third Presbytery of New York, but never ordained, he died at the age of twenty-four while pursuing his theological studies. In 1830 Dutton, with Elam Ives Jr., published *The American Psalmody.* A writer of hymn texts as well as tunes, he wrote words for hymns in *The Juvenile Lyre,* by Lowell Mason and Elam Ives Jr. (Boston, 1831). See LAWRENCE ("Here, Lord, Retired, I Bow in Prayer") and his best-known tune WOODSTOCK ("To Thee, O God, the Shepherd Kings").

Timothy Dwight, minister, poet, and president of Yale; b. Northampton, Mass., May 14, 1752; d. New Haven, Conn., Jan. 11, 1817.

A grandson of Jonathan Edwards, Timothy Dwight was precocious and is said to have learned the alphabet in one lesson and to have read the Bible at the age of four. At thirteen he entered Yale where, although he neglected his studies for two years, he was rivaled only by Nathan Strong when he graduated in 1769. He taught at the Hopkins Grammar School for two years before becoming a tutor at Yale. For six years he taught mathematics, rhetoric, and oratory at Yale, then returned to Northampton, his health somewhat broken by teaching and study. His epic poem *The Conquest of Canaan* was finished in 1774, although it was not published until 1785. Licensed to preach in 1777, he became a chaplain in the army and served at West Point. There he wrote *Columbia,* an ode. After a year in the army, his father's death forced his return. A preacher and farmer, he managed to support his family and to serve in the legislature. He was minister in the Congregational Church at Greenfield (1783–95) and principal of an academy there. Dwight succeeded Ezra Stiles as president of Yale (1795–1817). In 1800 he published a new version of the psalms of Watts which included "I Love Thy Kingdom, Lord," "Shall Man, O God of Light," and "Sing to the Lord Most High." See also "As Down a Lone Valley," the last stanza of Dwight's *Columbia.* His *Travels in New England and New York* (1822) is a valuable and detailed account of his observations.

James Wallis Eastburn, Episcopal rector and poet; b. London, Sept. 26, 1797; d. at sea, Dec. 2, 1819.

In 1803 the family of James Wallis Eastburn emigrated to New York where the father established a bookstore. Eastburn graduated from Columbia College in 1816. After trying journalism for about a year he went to Bristol, R.I., to study theology under Bishop Griswold. Ordained a deacon in 1818 he became rector in Accomac County, Va. Eastburn collaborated with Robert C. Sands in writing a narrative poem *Yamoyden* based on the life of King Philip, the famous Indian leader. By the summer of 1818 it was almost completed. Early in the winter of 1819 ill health prompted Eastburn to take a trip to the Canary Islands carrying the manuscript with him. He died on his fourth day at sea. Sands corrected obvious errors and published the poem in 1820. Eastburn's hymn "O Holy, Holy, Holy Lord" (q.v.), written in 1815, was published in the *Prayer Book Collection* of 1826 and in other hymnals. His "Mountains of Israel" was included in Rufus W. Griswold's *Sacred Poets of England and America* (New York, 1848), "Strangers No More We Wildly Rove" in Charles Dexter Cleveland's *Lyra Sacra Americana* (1868).

A. Eastman, tune composer; fl. early 19th cent.

Nothing is known of the life of A. Eastman, whose tune Elm Street ("Welcome, Ye Hopeful Heirs of Heaven") (q.v.) appeared in Henry E. Moore's *New Hampshire Collection* (1835). Many American singing books contain a number of compositions by obscure composers who may have been pupils, associates, or correspondents of the editor. Some of these compositions are tuneful and attractive.

Mary Baker Eddy, founder of Christian Science and hymn writer; b. Bow, N.H., July 16, 1821; d. Chestnut Hill, Mass., Dec. 3, 1910.

Mary Baker was educated by tutors at home and at the Academy in Tilton, N.H. She early wrote poetry and prose which appeared in New England publications. In 1843 she married Major George W. Glover of Concord, who resided in Charleston, S.C. He died six months after their marriage, and Mrs. Glover returned to New Hampshire, where her only child was born. She taught in a private school and in the New Hampshire Conference Seminary for the next ten years. Her marriage to Dr. Daniel Patterson, a dentist of Franklin, N.H., ended in divorce in 1873. Her third husband, Asa Gilbert Eddy, was one of the first of her followers to practice Christian Science publicly. After his death in 1882, Mrs. Eddy lived at Chestnut Hill near Boston until her own death in 1910.

Through years of widowhood, ill health, and other adversities, Mrs. Eddy had searched for religious meaning in the events of her life. In 1866 she felt that her understanding was deepened by the remarkable healing of an ailment. She believed that she had found the divine laws underlying Christ's works and called her discovery Christian Science. Her principal work was *Science and Health* (1875). See her hymns "O'er Waiting Harp-Strings of the Mind" and "Shepherd, Show Me How to Go."

Zachary Eddy, pastor and hymnbook editor; b. Stockbridge, Vt., Dec. 19, 1815; d. 1891.

After his ordination to the Presbyterian ministry Zachary Eddy became a missionary for the church in western New York and, for a time, in Wisconsin. From 1850 to 1855 he was pastor of a Congregational church in Warsaw, N.Y., then, following a second pastorate in Northampton, Mass., he was installed at a Dutch Reformed church in Brooklyn in 1867. From 1871 to 1873 he served a Congregational church in Chelsea, Mass., after which he moved to a church of the same denomination in Detroit, where he remained until 1884.

He was the principal editor of the Dutch Reformed *Hymns of the Church with Tunes* (1869) and collaborated with Roswell D. Hitchcock and Philip Schaff on *Hymns and Songs of Praise* (1874). See "Floods Swell Around Me, Angry, Appalling," and "Jesus, Enthroned and Glorified."

Lewis Edson, singing master and composer; b. Bridgewater, Mass., Jan. 22, 1748; d. Woodstock, Conn., spring 1820.

The family of Lewis Edson was descended from an early settler of Salem, Mass., who had moved from there to Bridgewater. As he grew up, Edson was taught the blacksmith's trade. When trouble began to brew between England and the colonies the Edson family, who were Tory sympathizers, found themselves part of an uneasy minority in the community, so they migrated to the western part of the state. Lewis Edson was married in 1770 at the age of twenty-two and six years later moved to New York. He taught singing there as well as in western Massachusetts and Connecticut. He was often called "the great singer."

DEERFIELD, LENOX, and BRIDGEWATER, all named for towns in Massachusetts, were first printed in *The Chorister's Companion,* a collection of church music published in New Haven in 1782. The book was printed for and sold by Simeon Jocelyn and Amos Doolittle. Edson was also represented in Olin Brownson's *Select Harmony* (1783), in Asahel Benham's *Federal Harmony* (1790), in Chauncey Langdon's *The Beauties of Psalmody,* and in *The Meridian Harmony,* compiled in 1808 by Zedekiah Sanger. With Lewis and Thaddeus Seymour, Edson was compiler of *New York Selection of Sacred Music,* first issued in 1809 and reissued several times, until 1816.

In 1817 Edson moved back to New England and spent his three remaining years in Woodstock, Conn. His LENOX (q.v.) "Let All Created Things" was popular over a longer period than any other tune of its day, with the single exception of Oliver Holden's CORONATION (q.v.) ("Within These Doors Assembled Now"). See also BRIDGEWATER ("To Thee, O God").

David H. Ela, presiding elder of the Methodist Episcopal Church; b. Canaan, Maine, 1831; d. Oct. 7, 1907.

David H. Ela was religiously inclined from childhood and became a church member at the age of nine. Although he was trained to be a printer and machinist, he decided to enter Wesleyan University. He graduated with honors in 1857 and, in 1876, he received the degree of D.D. from Cornell University. For two years he was principal of the East Greenwich Seminary. His hymn "The Chosen Three, On Mountain Height" (q.v.) was written in 1877 and published in *The Methodist Hymnal* of 1878.

Luther O. Emerson, composer and compiler; b. Parsonfield, Maine, Aug. 3, 1820; d. Hyde Park, Mass., Sept. 29, 1915.

Luther Emerson's father gave him a cello which he mastered sufficiently to play with the local choir. After studying in local schools he attended Dracut Academy in Massachusetts. When he decided on music as a career, he chose to study with Isaac B. Woodbury (q.v.), then prominent as a teacher. Emerson directed a choir in Salem, Mass., from about 1840. In 1847 he married the musical daughter of a Boston merchant. After six years' residence in Salem, Emerson went to Boston as organist of the Bulfinch Street Church where he stayed for four years. He then moved to Greenfield, Mass., to take charge of the music in the Second Congregational Church there. He also became head of the music department of Power's Institute at nearby Bernardston. Later he devoted his time to conventions and to his numerous collections for singing schools, Sunday Schools, and churches.

Emerson was extremely prolific as a composer and industrious as editor and compiler, publishing a long series of tune books. Among his most popular collections for church were: *The Romberg Collection of Sacred Music* (1852), *Harp of Judah* (1863), *The Jubilate* (1866), and *Choral Worship* (1884). See ASPIRATION ("Father! I Own Thy Voice"), SING OF JESUS ("Saints in Glory, We Together"), and KERMODE ("We Would See Jesus").

Ralph Waldo Emerson, lecturer, essayist, and poet; b. Boston, Mass., May 25, 1803; d. Concord, Mass., April 27, 1882.

Ralph Waldo Emerson is regarded as a founder of the transcendental movement. He graduated from Harvard in 1821. He then served for three years as assistant in his brother William's school for young ladies in Boston. In 1825 he entered the Harvard Divinity School. In 1829 he became associate minister of the Second Church in Boston. In 1829 he married Ellen Louisa Tucker, who died early in 1832. In that same year he resigned his pastorate because of doubts about the communion ritual.

In 1833 Emerson made a tour of England and the continent, where he met Carlyle, Coleridge, Wordsworth, and Landor. Upon his return he went to live with his mother in the old manse in Concord. In 1835 he married Lydia Jackson of Plymouth. They settled in a spacious old house in Concord, where Emerson spent the rest of his life. He took no active part in the reform movements of his day, although he firmly stated his position on such subjects as slavery and emancipation.

Julian lists only two hymns by Emerson: "Out of the Heart of Nature Rolled," a cento from a longer poem, and "We Love the Venerable House" (q.v.).

Paul Engle, poet and educator; b. Cedar Rapids, Iowa, Oct. 12, 1908.

Paul Engle was educated at Coe College, Cedar Rapids (A.B., 1931), the State University of Iowa (A.M., 1932), and Columbia University (1932–33). He went to England as a Rhodes scholar, receiving the A.B. from Merton College, Oxford, in 1936 and the A.M. in 1939. At the State University of Iowa he was professor of English in charge of the creative writing program from 1937. In 1953–54 he was a Guggenheim Fellow. He has published *American Child* (1945) and *The World of Love* (1951). See "Lord of Each Soul."

Laurentius Erhardi, cantor and teacher; b. Hagenau, Elsass, 1598; d. 1667.

Laurentius Erhardi was a teacher in Saarbruch, Strassburg, and Hagenau. From 1640 he was cantor and a member of the staff of the Frankfurt *Gymnasium.* Erhardi is remembered for his *Harmonisches Chor und Figural Gesang-Buch* published in Frankfurt in 1659. The music was for four to six voices, mostly with figured bass. In addition to his songbook he published a *Compendium musices Latino-germanicum* (1660, or 1640, according to Ernst Ludwig Gerber, in *Historisch-biographisches Lexikon der Tonkunstler,* 1790–92). See DIE HELLE SONNE IST DAHIN ("Great God, Preserver of All Things").

John F. Ernst, Lutheran pastor and teacher; fl. late 18th cent.

John F. Ernst contributed religious verse to the first American Lutheran hymnal in the English language, the *Hymn and Prayer Book,* edited by John Christopher Kunze (q.v.) in 1795. Ernst's contributions were designated by the letter "E." His career in the ministry began in Greenwich, N. J., in the 1780s. He later moved to New York where he preached in Clavarack and Athens. In 1798 he was appointed to the faculty of Hartwick Academy, a Lutheran school in Otsego County. From 1797 to 1802 he was "Pastor of Hartwick Patent." He delivered a sermon at Fort Plan, on January 28, 1800, to "the civil and military officers, the members of Franklin and St. Paul's lodges, and the citizens of Montgomery County." After 1802 he returned to Pennsylvania, where he had first settled. See "O Jesus Christ, True Light of God."

Nathaniel Evans, Anglican clergyman and author; b. Philadelphia, Pa., June 8, 1742; d. Haddonfield, N.J., Oct. 29, 1767.

Nathaniel Evans was educated at the Philadelphia Academy, which had recently been established by Benjamin Franklin and which later became the University of Pennsylvania. Placed in a counting house for training in business, he was so manifestly unhappy that his father permitted him to return to the Academy when he had finished his apprenticeship. Although he did not graduate, the Academy conferred an honorary M.A. degree upon him in 1765. Highly commended by the citizens of Philadelphia, he went to England where, through the sponsorship of the Society for the Propagation of the Gospel in Foreign Parts, he was ordained a clergyman. He returned to this country as a missionary to Gloucester County, N.J. Within two years he died from tuberculosis and was buried in Christ Church, Philadelphia.

Evans was one of the group who gathered around Francis Hopkinson (q.v.) in Philadelphia. His principal works include: *An Ode on the Late Glorious Successes of His Majesty's Arms* (1762), *The Love of the World Incompatible with the Love of God* (1766), and *Poems on Several Occasions: With Some Other Compositions* (1772). See "To Thee, Then, Let All Beings Bend."

Benjamin H. Everett, composer; fl. 19th cent.

Benjamin H. Everett was a brother of L. C. Everett (1818–67) and Asa Brooks Everett (1828–75). They were Virginia born and studied music in Boston. L. C. Everett went abroad for advanced study in Leipzig. The Everetts' outlook and training were quite different from that of the locally educated Southern singing masters in the folk tradition. They used conventional staff notation instead of shape notes and devoted much effort to teacher training. By about 1850 they had developed a group of fifty music teachers who followed their methods and used their books. Their work in the South has been compared with that of Lowell Mason in the North. Perhaps their parents were musical, and "Holden," Benjamin Everett's middle name, may have been given in memory of Oliver Holden (q.v.).

Benjamin assisted his brother Asa in compiling *The Sceptre* (1871), from which we have taken his BETTEVER'S CHANT.

Justus Falckner, first pastor ordained in Pennsylvania; b. Langen-Reinsdorf near Crimmitschau, Zwickau district, Saxony, Nov. 22, 1672; d. Newburgh, N.Y., 1723.

Justus Falckner was the younger brother of Daniel, who eventually became a leader in the Theosophical Brotherhood in Europe as well as on the Wissahickon creek. Both Falckner brothers were educated as theologians, and Justus was first a student of philosopher Thomasius at Leipzig. Later he studied at Halle where he cultivated the art of hymnody and was intimately associated with the German Pietist August Herman Francke, who taught him Oriental languages. In August 1700 he accompanied his brother Daniel, who had just completed a successful mission in Europe, to Pennsylvania. Several others came with them to the community on the Wissahickon creek. Elected a burgess of the German borough shortly after his arrival, Justus Falckner continued his theosophical studies in solitude under the guidance of Magisters Johannes Kelpius (q.v.) and Seelig.

On November 24, 1703, at Wicaco, Pa., he was ordained by pastors of the Swedish church including Andrew Rudman (q.v.) and according to Swedish ritual to the ministry of the Lutheran Church to labor among the scattered followers in the adjoining provinces of New Jersey and New York. Falckner immediately left Philadelphia for his missionary field and, from that time until his death in 1723, worked among the Low Dutch and High German Lutheran congregations, with New York and Albany the centers of his activity. His preaching stations were situated along the Hudson, in East New Jersey, and on Staten Island. See "Auf, Ihr Christen."

Norma Farber, soprano and poet; b. Boston, Mass., Aug. 6, 1909.

Norma Farber was educated at Wellesley (A.B.) and Radcliffe (M.A.) colleges. She further enriched her general and musical education with long periods of study abroad. A singer as well as a poet, she received a *premier prix* in singing in Belgium, with the award qualified "avec la plus grand distinction, félicitations du jury."

A woman of wide-ranging interests and many talents, she has been active in Boston's musical community as a soprano who gave accomplished recitals of lieder and art songs. More recently she has gained a reputation as a poet of virtuosic ability, one who may be considered in the conservative avant garde. Scribner's has brought out a collection of her verse, and her poems appear regularly in periodicals. See her "Bow Down, Mountain."

Austin Faricy, critic and poet; b. St. Paul, Minn., 1911.

Austin Faricy earned an A.B. summa cum laude in 1931 at the University of Minnesota. As a Rhodes scholar at Oxford he earned a B.A. in 1935 and a Master's degree in 1936. He has taught at the University of Minnesota (1934–35), Stephens College (1936–40), and the University of Texas (1940–41). He was lecturer in Humanities in the Extension Service of the University of California (1946–51), lecturer in Humanities and Semantics at the University of Hawaii (1955–59), and lecturer in English at the University of Osaka in Japan (1960–61).

At Stephens College Faricy published *The Humanities* with Louise Dudley in 1940. As a student he had poems published at the University of Minnesota and Oxford. He wrote extensively on music, theater, and art in the Hawaii *Star-Bulletin* from 1954 to 1960. See "Through Warmth and Light of Summer Skies," set to music for *American Hymns* by Harriett Johnson.

John Farmer, composer of madrigals and religious music; fl. late 16th cent.

Little is known of John Farmer's life, except that he apparently served as organist for Christ Church Cathedral in Dublin in 1596 and 1597 and that he was living in London at the time of the publication of his madrigals in 1599. Entitled "The first set of English Madrigals to Foure Voices," the collection contained seventeen pieces.

Although Farmer's madrigals are of an unpretentious character, his "Fair Phyllis I saw sitting all alone" has long been a favorite. He was one of the most important contributors to Thomas East's *Whole Booke of Psalmes* (1592). He set not only all the canticles and hymns (twelve in number) which were prefixed to the psalms proper, but also five of the psalm tunes themselves. See THE COMPLAINT OF A SINNER ("How Long, Jehovah?") from East and the setting of THE LORD'S PRAYER ("Our Father Which in Heaven Art") from Thomas Ravenscroft (1621).

Giles Farnaby, composer; b. Truro, Cornwall, England, c.1565; d. London, Nov. 1640.

Records show that Giles Farnaby was married at Bishopsgate and that he graduated Mus.B. at Oxford on July 7, 1592. One of his sons was baptized at St. Mary-le-Bow in 1598. His set of *Canzonets to Fowre Voyces* (1598) contained twenty-four compositions for four voices as well as a rare example of an eight-part English madrigal. His compositions are distinguished by chromatic harmonies, striking rhythms, texture, and great individuality of style. His set was prefaced by commendatory verses by Anthony Holborne, John Dowland (q.v.), and Richard Allison (q.v.).

As a writer for the virginals Farnaby ranks high, second only to William Byrd in that period. Over fifty of his virginal pieces were included in the *Fitzwilliam Virginal Book.* A contributor to Thomas East's *Whole Booke of Psalmes* (1592), he was also represented in Thomas Ravenscroft's *Whole Booke of Psalmes* (1621). See his setting of the FRENCH TUNE: PSALM 124 ("Except the Lord, That He for Us Had Been") from East and of the HIGH DUTCH TUNE ("Such As in God the Lord Do Trust") from Ravenscroft.

Harry Webb Farrington, Methodist minister and author; b. Nassau, the Bahamas, July 14, 1880; d. Asbury Park, N.J. Oct. 27, 1930.

Harry Webb Farrington's mother died when he was still a baby, and he was sent to Baltimore. He learned his surname only when he met relatives while attending a school at Williamsport, Pa. After joining the Methodist Church at Darlington, Md., he prepared for the ministry at Dickinson Seminary and Syracuse University. He received the degree of S.T.B. from Boston University in 1910, then went to Harvard where he studied with Professor Josiah Royce and won his M.A.

After serving several congregations in New England he went to Gary, Ind., and subsequently New York City where he instituted courses in religion for public school children. During World War I he served as athletic director to the French troops. He was subsequently assistant pastor of Grace Church, New York. He returned to the field of religious education in 1920–23 as director of education for the Methodist Child Welfare League and for the period 1924–28 as lecturer in that field and in social ethics. He died after an accident had left him completely paralyzed. In 1932 his wife issued a collected edition of his poems.

Farrington, who was deeply interested in hymns, left notes on them in *Valley and Visions.* A Christmas song, "I Know Not How That Bethlehem's Babe" (q.v.), written in 1910 while the author was a graduate student at Harvard won a prize as the best Christmas hymn written by a student. In 1927 he received an award from the *Homiletic Review* for his hymn "Dear Lord, Who Sought at Dawn of Day."

Giovanni Ferretti, Italian composer of *canzoni;* b. Venice (?) c.1540; d. date unknown.

Giovanni Ferretti may have been a pupil of Andrea Gabrieli. By 1569 he was in Ancona, where he was *maestro di cappella* at the cathedral. Carlo Schmidl (in *Dizionario universale dei musicisti,* Milan, c.1890) asserts that he was choirmaster at the Santa Casa in Loreto (1580–82 and 1596–1603).

During his lifetime Ferretti composed two books of six-voiced *canzoni alla napoletana* (1573 and 1575) and five similar books for five voices (1567–85). His *canzoni* were popular throughout Europe and were adapted to other texts. The example contained in this volume, for instance, was published in a version for solo voice and lute in Adrianus Valerius' *Nederlandtsche Gedenkclanck* of 1621 and 1626. See SEI TANTO GRATIOSA ("Laat Ons Den Herre Singen").

Irving Fine, composer and educator; b. Boston, Mass., Dec. 3, 1914; d. Aug. 23, 1962.

After receiving his A.B. (1937) and M.A. (1938) degrees from Harvard, Irving Fine spent one year in France studying with Nadia Boulanger. On his return he became a member of the Music Department at Harvard: teaching fellow (1939–42), instructor (1942–45), assistant professor (1946–50). In 1950 he was composer-in-residence at Brandeis University and from 1952 until his death he was professor and chairman of the School of Creative Arts. His *String Quartet* (1952) has been recorded; *The Serious Song: Lament for String Orchestra* (1955) and *Diversions* for orchestra (1960) were Louisville commissions; and a *Symphony* (1962) has been performed by the Boston Symphony. Fine's WORSHIP ("So Touch Our Hearts with Loveliness") was composed for *American Hymns.*

Eleazar Thompson Fitch, liberal theologian and educator; b. New Haven, Conn., Jan. 1, 1791; d. there Jan. 31, 1871.

After graduating from Yale in 1810, Eleazar Thompson Fitch attended Andover Theological Seminary. He succeeded Timothy

Dwight as Professor of Sacred Theology at Yale in 1817 and his lectures were so successful that a department of theology was formed which developed into the Yale Divinity School. Fitch retired as professor emeritus in 1861. See "By Vows of Love Together Bound" and his best-known hymn, "Lord, at this Closing Hour."

James Flint, Unitarian minister and hymn writer; b. Reading, Mass., Dec. 10, 1779; d. Salem, Mass., March 4, 1855.

James Flint studied the classics with Rev. Eliab Stone, his local pastor, then attended Harvard, from which he graduated in 1802. He taught at Andover Academy and then in Dedham where he prepared himself for the ministry with Rev. Dr. Bates. He became the pastor at East Bridgewater in 1806 and at the same time taught privately students who wished to enter Harvard. He was called to the East Church in Salem in 1821 where he remained for thirty years. He received the D.D. from Harvard in 1825. The collection of hymns in use in Salem had been compiled by Rev. William Bentley, a distinguished predecessor and diarist. That collection was replaced by *A Collection of Hymns for the Christian Church and Home* compiled by Flint and published in 1845. It contained a number of his own hymns including "In Pleasant Lands Have Fallen the Lines" (q.v.).

James Flint, organist, music editor, and composer; b. 1822; d. date unknown.

James Flint worked with Uzziah C. Burnap and John K. Paine in editing the music of *Hymns and Songs of Praise* (1874) of Roswell D. Hitchcock, Zachary Eddy, and Philip Schaff and is described there as "Organist in Orange, New Jersey." Two of his original hymn tunes, SCHEFFER and HARVILLE, appeared in that volume. Flint was again associated with Burnap in editing *Anthems of the Church: A Collection of Sacred Music for Quartette and Chorus Choirs* (Cleveland: S. Brainard's Sons, 1875). See BRAINARD ("A Parting Hymn We Sing").

Peleg Folger, mariner; b. Nantucket, Mass., Oct. 13, 1734; d. there May 26, 1789.

Great-grandson of Peter Folger (who was Benjamin Franklin's grandfather), Peleg Folger spent his life on a farm until he reached the age of twenty-one, when he went to sea. For several years he was engaged in the cod and whaling industries. He is known for the journal he kept of his voyages, written in a more scholarly manner than his limited education would suggest. Some of the verses in his journal were quoted in Obed Macy's *History of Nantucket* (1880). When he retired from the sea he became a local sage whose counsel was highly regarded by his neighbors. He was a member of the Society of Friends. See "Praise Ye the Lord, O Celebrate His Fame."

Eliza Lee Follen, Unitarian author; b. Boston, Mass., Aug. 15, 1787; d. Brookline, Mass., Jan. 26, 1860.

When Eliza Lee and the German-born Karl Follen were married in 1828, he was an instructor at Harvard. Although he later entered the Unitarian ministry and began to preach in and near Boston, he continued to teach. Mrs. Follen and he made their home a center of university social life.

At the end of a five-year term as professor, Follen left the university and the couple took a western trip with a party of which their friend Harriet Martineau was also a member. After their return Follen accepted the pastorate of the First Unitarian Church of New York. When his stand against slavery caused him to resign his pastorate, the family returned to Boston. After two lean years he took the pulpit of the Unitarian Society of East Lexington, Mass.

In December 1839, Mrs. Follen accompanied him, as usual, on one of his trips to New York and was taken ill there. Dr. Follen was engaged to dedicate a new church in East Lexington before his wife was able to travel. Reluctantly he left her with friends and took the boat for Boston. It was an old vessel, the *Lexington*. On Long Island Sound fire broke out aboard and in the disaster that followed Karl Follen perished.

Mrs. Follen wrote a biography of him, a small volume in which is reflected her full and interesting life as the wife of a friendly, unassuming man of brilliant mind and Christian character.

See "Lord Deliver, Thou Canst Save."

Harry Emerson Fosdick, preacher and author; b. Buffalo, N.Y., May 24, 1878; d. New York City, Jan. 13, 1964.

Harry Emerson Fosdick attended Colgate University (A.B., 1900), Union Theological Seminary (B.D., 1904), and Columbia University (A.M., 1908). He later received many honorary degrees. Fosdick's first charge after ordination was the First (Baptist) Church of

Montclair, N.J. (1904–05). At Union Theological Seminary he taught homiletics (1908–15) and later practical theology (1915–46). From 1919 to 1926 he was preacher and associate minister at the First Presbyterian Church of New York; in 1919 he accepted the pastorate of the Park Avenue Baptist Church, which became Riverside Church on its move to its present location overlooking the Hudson River. He was a pioneer in preaching over the radio under the auspices of the Federal Council of Churches of Christ. A prolific writer on religious themes, he also wrote three hymns which have had considerable usage. See "The Prince of Peace His Banner Spreads."

Stephen C. Foster, song composer; b. Lawrenceburg, now part of Pittsburgh, Pa., July 4, 1826; d. New York City, Jan. 13, 1864.

Educated in the Allegheny and Athens academies, Stephen C. Foster entered Jefferson College at Canonsburg in July 1841. His early predilection for music, which had led him to compose "The Tioga Waltz" for four flutes while he was at Athens Academy, contributed to his dislike of formal education and he left school in August 1841. Although he published "Open Thy Lattice, Love" in that year, his parents did not consider a musical career suitable for him and he was sent to Cincinnati to keep books for his brother who was in business there. While he was in that city a number of his minstrel ballads achieved great popularity ("O Susanna," "Louisiana Belle," "Away Down South"). In 1848 they were published in *Songs of the Sable Harmonists* and he returned to his parents' home in Allegheny City to devote himself exclusively to music.

Music hall entertainers of the time were largely minstrels, the most famous being Christy's troupe. In 1851 Foster sold E. P. Christy the privilege of singing his songs from manuscript before their publication, an arrangement that proved profitable for both of them. That year "The Old Folks at Home" was published, and in 1852 "Massa's in the Cold, Cold Ground" appeared. The year following saw the publication of "My Old Kentucky Home" and "Old Dog Tray," which sold 125,000 copies within eighteen months of its appearance.

In 1860 Foster took up permanent residence in New York. Although he continued to compose he was unable to repeat his earlier successes. His last years were spent in obscurity, made miserable and squalid by his intemperance. After a short illness he died in the charity ward of Bellevue Hospital. "Old Black Joe" (1860) was the only memorable composition of his last years. Most of his hymns were contributed to the *Athenaeum* (1863) edited by Horace Waters. See his tune for "Oh! 'Tis Glorious," and his text and tune for "Who Has Our Redeemer Heard."

William H. Foulkes, minister; b. Quincy, Mich., June 26, 1877; d. Smithtown, N.Y., Dec. 9, 1961.

After graduating from the College of Emporia in Kansas in 1897, William H. Foulkes studied at the McCormick Theological Seminary in Chicago. Awarded the Bernadine Orme Smith Fellowship he spent a year at New College, Edinburgh, Scotland. He served Presbyterian churches in Elmira, Ill., Portland, Ore., New York, City, Cleveland, Ohio, and Newark, N.J. He was appointed General Secretary of the Board of Ministerial Relief and Sustentation (1913–18) and Chairman of the New Era Movement. In addition Foulkes served as a member of the General Council of the Presbyterian Church and in 1937 was elected moderator of the General Assembly. He was also a contributor to the *Handbook to the Hymnal* (1935). See "Take Thou Our Minds, Dear Lord."

Andrew Fowler, Episcopal minister and writer; b. Guilford, Conn., June 10, 1760; d. Dec. 29, 1850.

A native of Guilford, Conn., Andrew Fowler entered Yale at nineteen, a convinced Presbyterian. When he had been in college but a few months he joined the church and became a lay reader. Denied access to Yale's library of Anglican writings, young Fowler found them elsewhere and, as a result, became an Episcopalian. After graduating from Yale he took holy orders and moved to New Rochelle where he kept a school. Ordained a deacon by Bishop Provoost on Staten Island in 1789, he advanced to the priesthood one year later. His first parish was Christ Church, Oyster Bay, N.Y. (1790), followed by a joint rectorship of the Manors of Cortland and Garrison (1792–94). Subsequent rectorships were in Bedford, N.Y.; Shrewsbury, Middletown, Spottswood, and Coles Town, N.J.; in Philadelphia; and in Bloomingdale, N.Y. In 1806 Fowler went to Charleston, S.C. He served as missionary at Edisto Island, Columbia, and Wilmington, S.C. When Spain ceded Florida to the United States in July 1821, the American residents of St. Augustine organized church services, which Fowler conducted for two years. His small book, *Hymns,* was written before hymn singing was authorized by his denomination. See "Awake, My Soul! In Grateful Songs," and "O Gracious Jesus, Blessed Lord!"

John Franzen, Methodist minister and poet; b. Oct. 29, 1904.

John Franzen graduated from Ohio Wesleyan University in 1932, then went to Yale Divinity School (S.T.B., cum laude, 1935). He served as parish minister for thirty-five years, then became consultant and counselor to patients at the Meriden, Conn., Regional Center. He has written three volumes of poetry: *Comments* (1966), *And for Another Matter* (1968), and *Potential Unlimited* (1971). See "O God of Stars and Distant Space," written for *American Hymns.*

Enoch W. Freeman, Baptist clergyman; b. Minot, Maine, Dec. 16, 1798; d. Lowell, Mass., Sept. 22, 1835.

Born into a farm family, Enoch W. Freeman, at age eighteen, went to Hebron Academy near his home. At the end of a year he started teaching in the town of Wiscasset. Under the influence of a sermon he had heard, he turned to religion a year later and not only joined the Baptist Church, but felt called to the ministry. He entered Waterville College, and while still a student began to preach. Ordained in 1827, he settled in Lowell, Mass. in the following year as minister of the First Baptist Church, and there he remained.

A Selection of Hymns, Including a few Originals (Exeter, N.H., 1829), a volume "designed to aid the Friends of Zion in their private and social worship," contains seven of his own hymns. His best known is the first in the collection, "Rouse Ye at the Saviour's Call." See "Hither We Come, Our Dearest Lord."

James Freeman, Unitarian; b. Charlestown, Mass., April 22, 1759; d. Boston, Mass., Nov. 14, 1835.

James Freeman graduated from Harvard in 1777 and in 1782 became a reader in King's Chapel, Boston. Ordained in 1787, he remained as minister of that church until 1826. The "first avowed preacher of Unitarianism in the United States," he led the congregation in the transition from Episcopalian to Unitarian doctrine. In 1799, with Joseph May, a layman of the parish, he published *A Collection of Psalms and Hymns* to replace the "New Version" which had been in use there for eighty-six years. His "Lord of the Worlds Below!" (q.v.) is derived from James Thomson's *The Seasons.*

Robert Freeman, Baptist, then Presbyterian minister; b. Edinburgh, Scotland, Aug. 4, 1878; d. Pasadena, Calif., June 29, 1940.

Robert Freeman came to the United States in 1896. He graduated from Allegheny College at Meadville, Pa., and from Princeton Seminary. An honorary Doctor of Letters was conferred on him by the College of Wooster. In his early ministry he served Baptist churches in McKeesport, Pa., and Binghamton, N.Y. Later he became pastor of Presbyterian churches in Buffalo, N.Y., and Pasadena, Calif. A moderator of the Synod of California, he was also president of the board of trustees of Occidental College in Los Angeles and a director of the San Francisco Theological Seminary. He wrote many poems and published several books including: *The Hour of Prayer, The Land I Live In and Other Verses, New Every Morning,* and *What About the Twelve?* See "Braving the Wilds All Unexplored."

Jacob French, psalmodist and compiler; b. Stoughton, Mass., July 15, 1754; d. date unknown.

The *New American Melody* of Jacob French was published in Boston in 1789, his *Psalmodist's Companion* in Worcester, Mass., in 1793, and *Harmony of Harmony* in Northampton, Mass., in 1802. See his BABYLON ("Praise Ye the Lord, O Celebrate His Fame") and ASCENSION ("Swell the Anthem, Raise the Song").

Philip Freneau, mariner, journalist, and poet; b. New York City, Jan. 2, 1752; d. near Freehold, N.J., Dec. 19, 1832.

Educated by tutors, Philip Freneau entered the sophomore class at the College of New Jersey (now Princeton) at the age of fifteen. When the Revolution broke out he became an enthusiastic writer, turning out pamphlet satires aimed at the British: *General Gage's Soliloquy* (1775) and *General Gage's Confession* (1775). As a secretary to a prominent planter he spent three years at Santa Cruz. His impressions were recorded in such poems as "The Jamaica Funeral" and "The House of Night." Captured by the British and released, Freneau returned to America to find the Revolution at its height. He shipped as supercargo of a brig plying between the Azores and New York and was captured by a British man-of-war. Remanded to the prison ship *Scorpion* in New York harbor, he received brutal treatment and nearly starved. He later described his experiences in *The*

British Prison Ship: A Poem in Four Cantos (1781). He sailed as master of a brig bound for Jamaica in 1784 and for several years lived in the Caribbean engaged in the Atlantic coast trade. He was shipwrecked once, narrowly escaping death, and later outrode a hurricane that destroyed most of the West Indies shipping.

When the national government moved from New York to Philadelphia Freneau was offered a job as translating clerk in the Department of State under Jefferson. He moved to Philadelphia in 1791 and was soon issuing the *National Gazette* as an antidote to John Fenno's aristocratic *Gazette of the United States.* Fenno was a beneficiary of Hamilton, but Freneau spoke for the views of Jefferson and Madison. A passionate democrat and able supporter of the French Revolution, Freneau, more than any other journalist of his time, expressed the democratic spirit of the new republic. When the *National Gazette* was suspended on October 26, 1793, Freneau returned to his country home in New Jersey. In December 1832, while returning home from the country store, he lost his way in a blizzard and perished. See "By Babel's Streams."

Johann Anastasius Freylinghausen, Lutheran pastor; b. Gandersheim, Duchy of Brunswick, Germany, Dec. 2, 1670; d. Feb. 12, 1739.

Johann Freylinghausen entered the University of Jena in 1689. He journeyed to Erfurt to hear the preaching of the Pietists August Hermann Francke and J. J. Breithaupt and remained there (1691–92) with the latter. Three years later he became assistant to Francke in Glaucha. In 1715 Francke became the pastor of St. Ulrich's in Halle and Freylinghausen became his associate and son-in-law. In 1727, on Francke's death, he replaced him as pastor.

Freylinghausen was important among the German Pietists not only as a hymn writer but as a composer. His *Geist-reiches Gesang Buch den Kern alter und neuer Lieder . . .* with its second part, *Neues Geist-reiches Gesang Buch wie auch die Noten der unbekannten Melodeyen und dazu gehörige nützliche Register in sich haltend,* appeared in 1704, and a complete and enlarged edition in 1714. Although the composers of most of the new tunes contained in the volumes remain unknown, twenty-two are thought to be by Freylinghausen himself. In general, the music lacks the severe simplicity of the finest of the old chorale tunes; it is more subjective in character and turns somewhat away from the true church style and towards the devotional *Lied.* The chorales CHRISTI WAHRES SEELENLICHT ("Ein von Got Geborner Christ") and GOTT SEY DANCK IN ALLER WELT ("Ob Ich Deiner Schon Vergiss") have been selected from Freylinghausen's collection.

Robert Frost, American poet; b. San Francisco, Calif., March 26, 1874; d. Boston, Mass., Jan. 29, 1963.

It was not until Robert Frost went to England in 1912 that his work was understood and appreciated. His earliest volumes of verse, *A Boy's Will* (1913) and *North of Boston* (1914), were published there. When he returned to the United States in 1915, the tide had turned and in later life the quality of his work was recognized to an unusual degree. He settled in New Hampshire near Franconia and later in Vermont. The *Complete Poems* appeared in 1949. Although his poems have been widely read and highly esteemed, only one appears to have attracted the attention of hymnbook editors. It is "O, Give Us Pleasure in the Flowers Today," included in the Unitarian *Hymns for the Celebration of Life* (1964). Thomas Canning composed a new setting of the poem for *American Hymns*.

Nathaniel L. Frothingham, educator and Unitarian pastor; b. Boston, Mass., July 23, 1793; d. there April 4, 1870.

Nathaniel L. Frothingham graduated from Harvard in 1811. While he was yet a student he delivered a poem at the installation of President John Thornton Kirkland in 1811. After teaching in the Boston Latin School he was, for a short time, a private tutor and then in 1812, at the age of nineteen, an instructor in rhetoric and oratory at Harvard. Meanwhile he studied theology and in 1815 was ordained pastor of the First Church in Boston. Because of ill health he resigned that charge in 1850.

The author of more than fifty published sermons Frothingham contributed numerous religious and literary articles to *The Christian Examiner, The North American Review,* and other periodicals. In 1852 he published *Sermons in the Order of a Twelve-month. Metrical Pieces* appeared in 1855, followed by a second part in 1870. A member of the Massachusetts Historical Society and the Academy of Arts and Sciences, Frothingham received an honorary D.D. from Harvard in 1836. See "O God Whose Presence Glows in All."

Octavius Brooks Frothingham, Unitarian minister and author; b. Boston, Mass., Nov. 26, 1822; d. there Nov. 27, 1895.

The father of Octavius Brooks Frothingham, Nathaniel L. Frothingham, wrote occasional hymns, one of which has survived, "O God, Whose Presence Glows in All" (q.v.). The son, after receiving the A.B. from Harvard in 1843, attended the Harvard Divinity School, graduating in 1846. His first charge was in Salem where he was minister of the North Church (1847–55). Later pastorates were in Jersey City (Independent Liberal Church, 1855–59) and New York (Third Congregational Unitarian Society, 1859–79). Although he served Unitarian churches he held independent views and was president of the Free Religious Association. His graduation hymn, "Thou Lord of Hosts, Whose Guiding Hand" (q.v.), was written for the class of 1846 at the Harvard Divinity School.

Margaret Fuller, teacher and author; b. Cambridge, Mass., May 23, 1810; d. in shipwreck, July 19, 1850.

Margaret Fuller's natural precociousness was exploited by her father, who put her through a rigorous training which turned her into a "youthful prodigy." Reading early became her habit and her passion. Her remarkable endowments were so well cultivated that she became one of the unquestionably brilliant women of her era.

Following her father's death in 1835 she taught languages in Bronson Alcott's school and, in 1837, became principal teacher in the Green Street School, Providence, R.I., a post she held for two years. From 1839 to 1844 she lived near Boston, during which time she published a translation of Eckermann's *Conversations with Goethe* and one of the corespondence between Karoline van Günderode and Bettina von Arnim. During that time she also conducted classes in conversation for ladies. These classes, which met with great success, were designed to systematize thought on the part of her students and were organized around philosophical and social subjects.

In 1840 Margaret Fuller started a magazine, *The Dial,* a poetical and philosophical magazine representing the views of Transcendentalism. Ralph Waldo Emerson (q.v.) and George Ripley were her colleagues. Her *Summer on the Lakes in 1843,* published in 1844, was one of the most graphic delineations of its period. In 1845 she published *Woman in the Nineteenth Century,* an elaboration of an essay from *The Dial,* an important milepost in the modern movement for women's rights.

A two-year residence in New York (1844–46), where she had been invited by Horace Greeley to write literary criticism for *The Tribune,* produced another book, a selection from some of her articles, *Papers on Literature and Art.* In 1846 she took a trip to Europe, visiting England, France, and Italy. After taking up residence in Italy she married the Marchese Giovanni Angelo Ossoli, a disciple of Mazzini. During the siege of Rome in 1848–50 she took charge of one of two hospitals there while her husband fought on the walls.

In May 1850 the couple, with their child, sailed for the United States. Their ship was wrecked off Fire Island, N.Y., and they drowned. Her manuscript on the struggle for freedom in Italy was lost with them. See "Jesus a Child His Course Begun."

William Henry Furness, Unitarian minister; b. Boston, Mass., April 20, 1802; d. Philadelphia, Pa., Jan. 30, 1896.

William Henry Furness reached the venerable age of ninety-four years, seventy of which he spent as pastor of the First Unitarian Church of Philadelphia, serving as pastor for fifty years and pastor emeritus for the remaining twenty-one. A graduate of Harvard and holder of the longevity record for his class, he found a congenial classmate in Ralph Waldo Emerson (q.v.) and was, like Emerson, opposed to slavery. At twenty-three he married Annis Pulling Jenks of Salem, Mass. Their son became a successful portrait painter. See his hymns "In the Morning I Will Pray" and "Slowly, by God's Hand Unfurled," both of which appeared in his *Manual of Domestic Worship* (1840).

Thomas H. Gallaudet, pioneer teacher of the deaf; b. Philadelphia, Pa., Dec. 10, 1787; d. Hartford, Conn., Sept. 10, 1851.

In 1800 Thomas Gallaudet and his family moved to Hartford. He attended Yale, graduating in 1805, and Andover Theological Seminary, from which he graduated in 1814. Ill health prevented his becoming a minister. Gallaudet met Alice Cogswell, a deaf child, in Hartford. Her father, with the help of friends, sent Gallaudet abroad to study techniques for the education of the deaf. Gallaudet returned with Laurent Clerc, a brilliant teacher from Paris, and with him raised money for the first American school for the deaf. It opened in Hartford in 1817 with Gallaudet as its first principal. He served until 1930. Despite ill health Gallaudet trained a number of men who became heads of similar schools. After retirement he remained in Hartford where he devoted himself to educational and philanthropic causes. See "Jesus, in Sickness and in Pain."

John Gambold, Moravian bishop; b. Puncheston, Pembrokeshire, England, April 10, 1711; d. Haverfordwest, Pembroke, Wales, Sept. 13, 1771.

John Gambold graduated from Christ Church, Oxford, as B.A. in 1730 and received the M.A. in 1734. After becoming Vicar of Stanton Harcourt, Oxfordshire, his religious convictions changed, and in October 1742, he gave up his charge and became a member of the United Brethren and in 1754 a bishop. He was active as both a writer of original hymns and a translator of hymns from the German into English. The translation of Nicolaus L. Zinzendorf's "American hymn" "For Us No Night Can Be Happier" (q.v.), which appeared in *A Collection of Hymns of the Children of God in All Ages, From the Beginning to Now* (London, 1754), has been attributed to Gambold.

William Channing Gannett, Unitarian minister and hymn writer; b. Boston, Mass., March 13, 1840; d. Rochester, N.Y., Dec. 15, 1923.

William Channing Gannett was enrolled at Harvard at the age of sixteen and graduated with the class of 1860. After teaching school for a year in Newport, R.I., he entered Harvard Divinity School. He withdrew to go South to work among freedmen. Serving first at Port Royal, S.C., he later worked in Savannah after Sherman's army had captured that city. Some of his observations of the time were published in "The Freedmen at Port Royal," which appeared in the *North American Review* in 1865. In June of that year Gannett went abroad to study in Germany. On his return he resumed his work at Harvard Divinity School from which he graduated in 1868.

As a young Unitarian minister Gannett served pastorates in Milwaukee (1868–70) and in East Lexington, Mass. (1871–72), before spending three years writing *Ezra Stiles Gannett,* a biography of his father that incidentally included an interesting history of New England Unitarianism. From 1877 to 1883 he was pastor of a church in St. Paul, Minn., and from 1887 to 1889 in Hinsdale, Ill. In 1889 he was called to the pulpit of the Unitarian Church in Rochester, N.Y., where he remained for the rest of his life.

Although Gannett did not achieve prominence as a minister, his writings were widely read and among Unitarians he was regarded as a strong defender of liberalism and individualism. In collaboration with Jenkin Lloyd Jones he wrote *The Faith That Makes Faithful* (1887). Other writings included: *A Year of Miracle* (1882), *The Childhood of Jesus* (1884), *Studies in Longfellow, Whittier, Holmes, and Lowell* (1898), *Of Making One's Self Beautiful* (1899), *A Wicket Gate to the Bible* (1907), *The Little Child at the Breakfast Table . . . Little Prayers for Morning, Bed-Time, and Household Thanksgivings* (1915). With Frederick Lucian Hosmer (q.v.) Gannett published *The Thought of God in Hymns and Poems* (1885, 1894, 1918) and with Hosmer and J. V. Blake, *Unity Hymns and Chorals* (1880, revised 1911). See "From Heart to Heart" and "He Hides within the Lily."

Hervey Doddridge Ganse, Dutch Reformed, later Presbyterian clergyman; b. near Fishkill, N.Y., Feb. 27, 1822; d. Chicago, Ill., Sept. 8, 1891.

In 1825 the family of Hervey Doddridge Ganse settled in New York City where Ganse attended Columbia College, graduating in 1839. He prepared for the ministry in New Brunswick, N.J., and, after his ordination in 1843, held pastorates at Freehold, N.J., and at the Madison Avenue Collegiate Church in New York City. He later became a Presbyterian and was pastor at St. Louis, Mo., and secretary of the Presbyterian Board of Aid for Colleges and Academies. See his "Lord, I Know Thy Grace Is Nigh Me."

Edwin Gerschefski, pianist, composer, and educator; b. Meriden, Conn., June 10, 1909.

After graduating from Yale (Ph.B. and Mus.B.) Edwin Gerschefski studied piano for two years at the Matthay School in London. He was also a pupil of Artur Schnabel and Joseph Schillinger. A number of his tours as concert pianist and composer were under the auspices of the Association of American Colleges. After serving as head of the music department at Converse College and at the University of New Mexico, he accepted a similar post at the University of Georgia in 1965. See his setting of John Franzen's "O God of Stars and Distant Space," which was commissioned for *American Hymns*.

Orlando Gibbons, English composer; b. Oxford, Dec. 25, 1583; d. Canterbury, June 5, 1625.

Orlando Gibbons came from a well-known family of English musicians. His father William and his brother Edward were both church musicians of the time. In 1596 he entered the choir of King's College, Cambridge, and from 1604 was organist of the Chapel Royal. After taking a Mus.B. degree at Cambridge in 1606 he probably took another at Oxford in 1607. In 1619 he became chamber musician to the king and in 1623 was appointed organist at Westminster Abbey, where he served for two years. On April 2, 1625, he conducted the music for the state funeral of King James I. Following James's death Gibbons, as a member of the Chapel Royal, attended the new king, Charles I. In less than two months after the death of James, Gibbons himself died of apoplexy and was buried in Canterbury Cathedral, where a monumental tablet was placed in his honor.

His secular music included madrigals, music for viols, solo songs with accompanying parts for viols, and virginal music. He was a renowned performer both on the virginals and the organ. His church music included about forty anthems, most of them verse anthems in which the fuller sound of the choir alternated with passages for solo voice. The others were full anthems in polyphonic style. Gibbons wrote no church music to Latin texts and thus differs from most of the Tudor composers. None of his religious music was published during his lifetime except two short compositions in William Leighton's *Teares or Lamentacions of a Sorrowful Soule* (1614) and sixteen tunes to George Wither's *Hymns and Songs of the Church* (London, 1623). See SONG 24 ("And Truly It Is a Most Glorious Thing"), SONG 4 ("The Angels Sung a Carol"), SONG 1 ("Hail, Holy Land"), SONG OF THE THREE CHILDREN ("In Heaven Soaring Up"), and SONG 34 ("The Sun and Moon So High and Bright").

Richard W. Gilder, editor and poet; b. Bordentown, N.J., Feb. 8, 1844; d. Nov. 18, 1909.

Richard W. Gilder was the son of the Rev. William Henry Gilder, a Methodist minister who conduced a seminary for girls. Richard served in the Civil War as an army chaplain and as a private in the First Philadelphia Artillery, after which he entered railroad work as a paymaster. Soon he drifted into newspaper work. After several years with the *Newark Daily Advertiser,* he founded, with R. Newton Crane, the *Newark Morning Register.* In 1870 he accepted the assistant editorship of *Scribner's Monthly* (later *The Century*), of which he became editor in 1881. He has been credited with a revolution in magazine management. A popular speaker at universities and on commemorative occasions, he received honorary degrees from Harvard, Yale, and Princeton. Active in many civic and social projects, he was chairman of the New York Tenement House Commission, worked for effectiveness in international copyrights, and was president of the New York Free Kindergarten Association. He published ten volumes of poems during his writing career. See "God of the Strong, God of the Weak" and "To Thee, Eternal Soul, Be Praise."

James G. Gilkey, minister, author, and educator; b. Watertown, Mass., Sept. 28, 1889; d. Westerly, R.I., July 15, 1964.

James G. Gilkey was educated at the Boston Latin School, Harvard (A.B., 1912; A.M., 1913), Union Theological Seminary (B.D., 1916),

and the Universities of Berlin and Marburg, Germany. He received
honorary D.D. degrees from Colgate University (1925), Colby College (1934), the University of Vermont (1935), the honorary Litt.D.
from Marietta College (1937) and the American International College, Springfield, Mass. Ordained to the Presbyterian ministry in
1916, he served as assistant in the Presbyterian Church at Bryn
Mawr, Pa., 1916–17, and was the minister of the South Church
(Congregational) in Springfield from 1917. He was professor of Biblical Literature at Amherst (1923–30) and a trustee of Springfield
College.

Gilkey wrote a number of books: *A Faith for the New Generation*
(1926), *Secrets of Effective Living* (1927), *The Certainty of God* (1928),
Solving Life's Everyday Problems (1930), *Meeting the Challenge of Modern
Doubt* (1931), *Managing One's Self* (1932), *What Can We Believe?*
(1933), *You Can Master Life* (1934), *Getting Help from Religion* (1936),
The Problem of Following Jesus (1938), *A Faith To Affirm* (1940), *How To
Be Your Best, God Will Help You* (1943), *When Life Gets Hard* (1945),
and *Gaining the Faith You Need* (1948). See "O God, in Whose Great
Purpose" and "Outside the Holy City."

Samuel Gilman, Unitarian minister and author; b. Gloucester,
Mass., Feb. 16, 1791; d. Kingston, Mass., Feb. 9, 1858.

Samuel Gilman graduated from Harvard in 1811 and was a University tutor from 1817 to 1819, when he received a call from the
Unitarian church in Charleston, S.C. After he had preached a trial
sermon there, Gilman hurried back to Gloucester to marry Caroline
Howard, whose father had been one of the "Indians" involved in the
Boston Tea Party. He remained with the Charleston church until he
retired. His *Memoirs of a New England Choir* was an entertaining account of his own early experiences. He contributed to the *Christian
Examiner*, the *North American Review*, and the *Southern Quarterly*. See
his "O God, Accept the Sacred Hour."

Joseph Henry Gilmore, Baptist minister and educator; b. Boston, Mass., April 29, 1834; d. Rochester, N.Y., July 23, 1918.

In 1858 Joseph Henry Gilmore completed his studies at Brown
University with highest honors and entered Newton Theological Institution from which he graduated in 1861. In 1862 he was ordained
and became the pastor of the Baptist Church in Fisherville, N.H. In
1863 and 1864 he acted as private secretary to his father, then the

governor of New Hampshire. At the same time he was an editor of the *Concord Daily Monitor.*

He returned to the ministry as pastor of the Second Baptist Church in Rochester, N.Y. (1865–67), where he also served as acting professor of Hebrew in Rochester Theological Seminary (1867–68). In 1868 he became professor of logic, rhetoric, and English literature at the University of Rochester, from which he retired as professor emeritus in 1908.

Besides magazine articles Gilmore published several textbooks, including *The Art of Expression* (1876) and *Outlines of English and American Literature* (1905). He was the author of several hymns, of which "He Leadeth Me, O Blessed Thought" (q.v.) was most widely sung.

Washington Gladden, Congregational preacher and hymn writer; b. Pottsgrove, Pa., Feb. 11, 1836; d. Columbus, Ohio, July 2, 1918.

Washington Gladden's father died before he was six and he was cared for by his grandfather and uncle. The latter encouraged him to leave the farm. Gladden worked for a time on the *Owego Gazette* and, in 1855, entered Owego Academy. In 1856 he was accepted as a sophomore by Williams College. There he attended the Saturday morning sessions conducted by the President, Mark Hopkins. After receiving his license to preach, he became pastor of the Congregational Church of LeRaysville, Pa., and in 1860 of the First Congregational Church, Brooklyn. A physical collapse caused by overwork forced Gladden to move to a smaller church in Morrisania, N.Y. He served on the Christian Commission during the Civil War. He met General Grant and President Lincoln in the field and was in New York at the time of the draft riots.

His concern with industrial relations was made evident in a course of lectures delivered to workingmen and their employers while he was pastor of the Congregational Church of Springfield, Mass. (from 1875). He was again confronted with an industrial crisis at his next pastorate in Columbus, Ohio (1883), where the Rocky Valley strike was in progress. Gladden's social concern is best shown in "O Master, Let Me Walk with Thee" (q.v.). See also "O Lord of Life." He was associate editor of *The Pilgrim Hymnal* (1904), to which he contributed "Behold a Sower from Afar."

Goff, fl. late 18th cent.

Goff appears to be known only by the tunes he composed. STRAT-FIELD appeared in *The American Harmony* (1793) by Nehemiah Shumway. In Oliver Holden's *Union Harmony* of the same year it was included in a variant form as was SUTTON (NEW). Daniel Read (q.v.), in the *Columbia Harmonist* (No. 4, 1810), included SUTTON (NEW) and referred to the composer as E. Goff. STRATFIELD (q.v.) ("The Summer Harvest Spreads the Fields") found its way South where it appeared in Allen D. Carden's *Missouri Harmony* (1820) and was still included in the *Original Sacred Harp* of 1936. The editors of the latter publication referred to it as "one among the old time minor melodies." They were uncertain of its origin. "It is believed to be an English tune or composed in the early settlement of this country."

Adoniram J. Gordon, minister, editor, and author; b. New Hampton, N.H., April 19, 1836; d. Feb. 2, 1895.

A descendant of John Robinson of Leyden, Adoniram Gordon graduated from Brown University at age twenty-four and entered the Baptist ministry. By 1869 he was pastor of the Clarendon Street Baptist Church in Boston and in 1871 was an editor of *The Service of Song for Baptist Churches*. In 1872 he published his own collection entitled *The Vestry Hymn and Tune Book*. One of his hymns, "O Spirit's Anointing, For Service Appointing," was written in the summer of 1886 while he was at the Moody School for Bible Study in Northfield, Mass. He composed it at the suggestion of a group of students who visited colleges throughout the country to stimulate interest in foreign mission work and to recruit students for the school's next summer session.

Gordon served on the Board of Trustees of Newton Theological Institution and on the Board of Fellows of Brown University, which gave him the honorary degree of doctor of divinity in 1878. He was, for a time, editor of a monthly periodical, *The Watchword,* and author of *In Christ, or the Believer's Union with His Lord* (1872), *Congregational Worship* (1872), *Grace and Glory* (1880), *Ministry of Healing* (1882), and *The Two-Fold Life* (1883). Gordon was also a successful hymn tune composer. Four of his tunes were in use in the twentieth century: GORDON (q.v.) ("Hear, Hear, O Ye Nations"), CARITAS, LOVE, and MY JESUS I LOVE THEE.

Gustav Gottheil, rabbi, religious leader, and hymnbook compiler; b. Pinne, Prussia, May 28, 1827; d. New York City,
1903.

Educated at the University of Berlin and the Berlin rabbinical
college, Gustav Gottheil became assistant minister of the Berliner
Reformgemeinde during his student days. From 1860 to 1873 he
was rabbi at Manchester, England; in two of the most noteworthy
sermons which he preached there he attacked those who declared
the institution of slavery to be sanctioned by Mosaic Law.

In 1873 he came to New York as assistant rabbi to Dr. Samuel
Adler at Temple Emanu-El and in the following year succeeded
him, serving as rabbi until 1899, when he became emeritus. He
founded the Emanu-El Sisterhood of Personal Service, the Emanu-
El Preparatory School, the Association of Eastern Rabbis, and took
an active part in the deliberations of the Central Conference of
American Rabbis when it merged with the Eastern Association.
Gottheil was vice-president of the Federation of American Jewish
Zionists, chairman of the revision committee of the *Union Prayer
Book,* and one of the governors of Hebrew Union College.

In 1887 Gottheil published *Music to Hymns and Anthems for Jewish
Worship,* one of the first Jewish hymnbooks printed in the United
States, on which was largely based the first edition of the *Union Hym-
nal,* generally used by Reform Jewish congregations throughout the
country. Among his written works are *Sarah* and *Sun and Shield* (New
York, 1896), a survey of Judaism.

One of the founders of the New York State Conference of Religions, he was a representative of Judaism at the Parliament of
Religions held at the Chicago World's Fair in 1892. A Gustav Gottheil lectureship in Semitic languages was founded at Columbia University on the occasion of his seventy-fifth birthday. See "Come, O
Sabbath Day."

Louis Moreau Gottschalk, concert pianist and composer; b.
New Orleans, La., May 8, 1829; d. Rio de Janeiro, Dec. 18,
1869.

Louis Moreau Gottschalk received his first newspaper publicity
when he appeared at the organ of the Cathedral of Saint-Louis in
New Orleans at the age of seven as a substitute for his teacher who
was indisposed. His own career was to take a different direction, and
he became a brilliant concert pianist and a composer of salon pieces
and larger works, some of them based on Creole, Negro, and Latin-
American popular and folk music. His only real link with hymnology

comes from the vogue for arranging a variety of music, often from instrumental sources, as hymn tunes. "The Last Hope" by Gottschalk, an enormously popular piano piece, was so arranged, and under the names GOTTSCHALK or MERCY ("Holy Spirit, Truth Divine") was extensively used. It is included here as the only example of its type.

Claude Goudimel, composer; b. Besançon, France, 1505; d. Lyons, France, Aug. 27, 1572.

Claude Goudimel was famous for the polyphonic treatment of French psalm tunes. Two of his *chansons* were included in the first volume of de Chemin's anthology of 1549 and his works were found in most later *chanson* collections. The first of his eight collections of *Pseaumes en forme de motets* was issued in 1551. In 1557 Goudimel was living at Metz, but it is not known on what date he joined the Protestants. In 1565 he was godfather to a child in the Huguenot community. Goudimel left Metz between 1565 and 1568 to seek a safer region. He returned to his native Besançon and later went to Lyons where he perished in the St. Bartholomew's Day massacre, August 27, 1572. His body was thrown into the Saône River the next day.

Palestrina knew Goudimel's Mass *Audi filia*, since themes from it appear in the Roman master's *Missa Brevis*. Goudimel's settings of the *Amours de Ronsard* are very fine. After his death Jean Bavent of Lyons published *La Fleur des chansons des deux plus excellents musiciens de ce temps à sçavoir de Lassus et de Claude Goudimel* (1574).

Goudimel's importance to Protestant church music lies in two settings of the French tunes for the complete psalter: *Les CL pseaumes de David, mis en musique à quatre parties* (Paris 1564, Geneva 1565) was in simple note against note counterpoint, while in *Les CL pseaumes de David nouvellement mis en musique à quatre parties* (1551) he treated the traditional melodies in a more elaborate fashion. See his settings of the FRENCH TUNES for PSALM 120 ("Give Ear, O Heaven, to That Which I Confess"), PSALM 23 ("In the Distress Upon Me"), and PSALM 8 ("With All My Heart, Jehovah, I'll Confess"), and for PSALM 84 ("O Lord, How Lovely Is the Place").

Hannah Flagg Gould, poet; b. Lancaster, Mass., Sept. 3, 1789; d. Newburyport, Mass., Sept. 5, 1865.

Hannah Flagg Gould's family moved to Newburyport, Mass., when she was still a child. Her *Poems* were published in 1832, 1835, and 1841. Several hymns have been made from them. See "Day of God! Thou Blessed Day."

John E. Gould, composer and compiler; b. Bangor, Maine, 1822; d. Algeria, March 4, 1875.

John E. Gould, the son of a sea captain, was deeply interested in music and began composing early in life. By the age of thirty, when he opened a music store on Broadway in New York City, he had already written a large amount of music and, with Edward L. White, had published four books: *The Modern Harp* (1846), *The Wreath of School Songs* (1847), *The Tyrolean Lyre* (1847), and *The Sunday School Book* (1848). Later he issued *Harmonia Sacra* (1851) and *Songs of Gladness for the Sunday School* (1869).

After living in Bergen Heights, N.J., where he married Josephine Barrows, Gould moved to Philadelphia. There he formed a partnership with William Gustavus Fischer. They conducted a music establishment under the name of Gould and Fischer. See GOULD ("Calm on the Listening Ear of Night") and his last tune, PILOT ("Jesus, Saviour, Pilot Me").

Nathaniel D. Gould, singing teacher and compiler; b. 1781; d. 1864.

Nathaniel Gould's surname was Duren, but in order to qualify for an inheritance from an uncle he added *Gould*. "Deacon Gould," as he was known, lived in Boston and from 1820 taught singing and penmanship throughout New England. In his *History of Church Music in America* (Boston, 1853) he stated that he was the first instructor to teach children singing by a systematic method. His earliest schools for juveniles were held in Boston, Cambridge, and Charleston, Mass.

WOODLAND (q.v.), ("Dear Lord and Father of Mankind") was the best known of Gould's original hymn tunes. Like Lowell Mason (q.v.), Gould introduced melodies from the great classic masters and arranged them as psalm tunes in his publications, including *National Church Harmony* (1832). Although this practice would be questioned today, it was defended in Gould's own time as an advance in taste.

John H. Gower, organist and choirmaster; b. Rugby, England, 1855; d. 1922.

John H. Gower was educated at Oxford and was organist and master of music at Trent College, Nottingham, from 1876 to 1887.

In the latter year he came to the United States and settled in Denver, Colo., where he had mining interests. After serving as organist and choirmaster at St. John's Cathedral, he worked in the same capacity at the Central Presbyterian Church in Denver. In 1893 he accepted a similar post at the Church of the Epiphany in Chicago. His compositions included a collection of *Original Tunes* published in 1919 as well as songs, part-songs, and a cantata, *The Good Shepherd*. See NEILSON ("O God in Whose Great Purpose").

Hans Gram, organist and composer; b. Denmark, 18th cent.

Hans Gram studied music in Sweden and emigrated to Boston before 1790. In 1795 he played the organ at the Brattle Street Church. He was associated with Oliver Holden and Samuel Holyoke in editing *The Massachusetts Compiler* (Boston, 1795). "The Death Song of an Indian Chief" has attracted attention because it deals with an indigenous subject and is the first composition published in orchestral score in this country. Gram is represented by one tune, WORSHIP (q.v.) ("Lord of the Worlds Below!"), in Samuel Holyoke's monumental *Columbian Repository* (1802).

Andrew Gramblin, composer; fl. early 19th cent.

Andrew Gramblin is known to us by the five tunes bearing his name which appear in William Walker's *Southern Harmony* (1st ed., 1835): MILLEDGEVILLE, THE PILGRIM'S LOT (q.v.) ("Sleep Sweetly"), MISSION, PROSPECT OF HEAVEN, and the NARROW WAY. The name is also spelled Grambling and the title "Rev." indicates that he was a minister. In the Southern tune books such credits often indicate the arranger rather than the composer of the tune, and the heading for MILLEDGEVILLE says "Original parts from Rev. A. Grambling."

John A. Granade, Methodist itinerant and hymnist; b. May 9, 1770 (?); d. Tenn., Dec. 6, 1807.

John A. Granade was one of the most influential evangelists of his time and was distinguished among his brethren as the "Western Poet" and composer of the Pilgrim Songs. He was a schoolteacher who sought to become a Methodist preacher after his third conversion. The Western Conference admitted him on trial in 1801. His piety and zeal were recognized, but a "certain hardness and stubbornness of temper" were also noted. In 1804 the Conference granted his request for a location. He went to Tennessee, married in 1805, and died two years later.

Many camp-meeting hymns are of uncertain origin; many are variously attributed. James B. Finley, in *Sketches of Western Methodism* (Cincinnati, 1854), was referring to the hymns of Granade when he wrote: "I have not seen any of them in their natural dress for many years, and fear they are out of print. Some vestiges of them, occasionally found in compilations, are so mangled and distorted that the author, if living, would hardly recognize them." Perhaps the best source is Thomas S. Hinde's *Pilgrim Songster* (Cincinnati, 1st ed., 1810), where the hymns by Granade are indicated by the letter "G." See "Come All Ye Mourning Pilgrims" and "Sweet Rivers of Redeeming Love."

John Grave, Anglican poet; fl. mid-17th cent.

John Grave is known to us as the author of a long poem dated "Virginia, The beginning of the 3d month," published in 1662. He states that his "outward habitation" was then in Virginia and the poem was written for "some of his Friends in England." The cento presented here begins "If Thou Wilt Hear."

Henry Wellington Greatorex, organist, choirmaster, and composer; b. Burton-on-Trent, Derbyshire, England, Dec. 24, 1813; d. Charleston, S.C., Sept. 10, 1858.

Descended from a line of church musicians Henry Wellington Greatorex was trained in church music. He came to the United States in 1836 to become the organist of the Central Church, Hartford, Conn., a post he held for two years. He then left the city for a time, and when he returned he was associated with St. John's Church. His next posts were in New York City where he played the organ at St. Paul's Church from 1846, and from 1851 directed the choir and was organist at the Calvary Church.

After a residence of seven years in New York, Greatorex moved to Charleston, S.C., where he died of yellow fever. His second wife, Eliza Pratt, was a well-known artist who excelled in pen-and-ink sketches.

His *Collection of Psalm and Hymn Tunes* (1851) was highly esteemed and long used. It contained thirty-seven original tunes and a number of the compiler's own arrangements. See LEIGHTON ("The Harvest Dawn Is Near") and GEER ("Thou Long Disowned, Reviled, Oppressed").

Joseph Green, merchant and author; b. Boston, Mass., 1706; d. London, Dec. 11, 1780.

Graduated from Harvard in 1726, Joseph Green went into business and was for a time a distiller. He had a pew in the First Church and at one time served on its standing committee.

As the Revolution approached he became a Royalist. He refused to sign the non-importation agreement of 1769 and, in 1774, joined in a protest to Governor Hutchinson against the cause of the patriots. The governor appointed him a counsellor to the province, thus testifying to his confidence in Green's loyalty. After his house was defaced by patriots, Green refused the appointment and took refuge in London (1775). Named in the act of banishment passed in Massachusetts in 1778, he died in London.

Known in his own time as a wit and a poet, his reputation was rivaled by that of his friend Mather Byles (q.v.). Like Byles he contributed to the *Collection of Poems by Several Hands.* Green's occasional verse included *A Parody on a Hymn by Mather Byles.* (See Byles's "Great God, Thy Works" and note.) Green wrote one fine serious poem, *An Eclogue Sacred to the Memory of the Rev. Dr. Jonathan Mayhew.* See his "Permit Us, Lord, To Consecrate."

Christian Gregor, Moravian bishop and composer; b. Dirsdorf, Silesia, Jan. 1, 1723; d. Herrnhut, Holland, Nov. 6, 1801.

Christian Gregor was minister of music in Herrnhaag in 1748. He became successively deacon, presbyter and, in 1789, bishop. He was a fine organist and the writer of many hymn texts. Gregor was chiefly responsible for the editing of the *Gesangbuch der evangelischen Brueder-Gemeinen* of 1778 and a volume of chorales, *Choral-Buch enthaltend alle zudem Gesangbuche der Evangelischen Brueder-Gemeinen vom Jahre 1778 gehörige Melodien* (1784), which included original tunes. Among his own compositions a "Hosanna" was reprinted in a number of collections published in this country. See MEINE HOFFNUNG STEHET FESTE ("Auf Ihr Christen"), NUN BITTEN WIR ("Gluckselger Ist Uns Doch Keine Nacht"), VON DEM TROST AUS JESU LEIDEN ("Guter Gott! Dir Ich Befehle"), and O WELT, SIEH HIER DEIN LEBEN ("Die Kleine Heerde Zeugen"). "What Splendid· Rays" (q.v.) is a translation of a German text by Gregor.

Edmund Grindal, Archbishop of Canterbury; b. 1519 ?, d. London, July 6, 1583.

A graduate of Cambridge, Edmund Grindal's gifts were recognized by ecclesiastical preferment, but his appointment as bishop was prevented by the accession of Queen Mary to the throne. Grindal found it prudent to go abroad where he became one of the Strassburg exiles. He returned to England on Mary's death in 1559 and was immediately recognized as a leader among the Protestant clergy. He became Archbishop of Canterbury in 1575, but was suspended from his functions for six months for failure to comply with Queen Elizabeth's orders regarding the Puritans. His friends persuaded him to submit to Elizabeth to some degree, and she restored him to most of his functions by the end of 1582. See "Give Peace in These Our Days, O Lord."

Alexander V. Griswold, Episcopal bishop; b. Simsbury, Conn., April 22, 1766; d. Boston, Mass., Feb. 15, 1843.

Alexander V. Griswold stayed on his parents' farm until he was ten years old. He then went to live with an uncle who was rector of the Simsbury parish. During the Revolution his father attempted to remain neutral and one of his Loyalist uncles moved to Nova Scotia. His own early marriage and his family's impoverishment kept young Griswold from entering Yale as he had planned. Until he was twenty-eight he cultivated a small farm and read law. In 1794, after being persuaded by a group of his friends, he offered himself as a candidate for holy orders in the Protestant Episcopal Church. In 1795 he was made deacon, then ordained priest by Bishop Seabury at Plymouth, Conn. For ten years he served churches in Plymouth, Harwinton, and Northfield. He had to continue farming in order to eke out his small salary. After becoming rector of St. Michael's Church, Bristol, R.I., in 1804, he was elected bishop of the Eastern Diocese in 1810. Consecrated at Trinity Church in New York City (1811), he continued as rector in Bristol until 1830 when he took charge of St. Peter's in Salem, Mass. Five years later he resigned to devote himself completely to his Episcopal duties.

An unassuming and friendly man, Griswold had force and firmness as well as administrative skill. He extended his diocese from twenty-two churches and sixteen clergy to one hundred churches and five organized dioceses.

Evangelical and Low Church in his sympathies, he published (1827–28) in the *Episcopal Register* of Vermont a series of articles on prayer meetings, which later appeared in book form, *Remarks on*

Social Prayer Meetings (1858). His reply to the progress of the Oxford Movement was contained in *The Reformation, A Brief Exposition of Some of the Errors and Corruptions of the Church of Rome* (1843). Two other titles of his are *Prayers Adapted to Various Occasions of Social Worship* (1835) and *Discourses on the Most Important Doctrines and Duties of the Christian Religion* (1830). See his "Holy Father, Great Creator."

Johann A. Gruber, religious leader; b. Schaffhausen, Germany, 1694; d. Germantown, Pa., 1763.

The son of Eberhard Ludwig Gruber, who was a leader of the Congregation of the True Inspiration, Johann Gruber came to Pennsylvania in 1726. Using the pen name *Ein Geringer* ("a humble man"), he became the "liaison man between Pennsylvania sectarianism and the radical Pietists in Europe." Gruber was the most important unattached religious leader in colonial Pennsylvania. See "Reine Liebe sucht nicht sich selber."

Nicolai F. S. Grundtvig, poet and theologian; b. Zealand, Sept. 8, 1783; d. Denmark, Sept. 2, 1872.

Nicolai Grundtvig was educated at the University of Copenhagen. He made a special study of Icelandic and wrote a "Northern Mythology" and a long epic poem, "The Decline of Heroic Life in the North." In 1810 he preached his first sermon. The theological views expressed in it offended the churchmen and their outrage led him to retreat to his father's parish to work there as pastor's assistant. From 1816 to 1819 he edited a polemical paper, wrote, and preached. His rationalist views won him an active following, but when Grundtvig opposed, in print, an important professor of theology, he was prosecuted, fined, and could not preach for seven years. He spent that period traveling and issuing theological works of his own. Returning to the pulpit in 1832, he continued to preach until his death. His mark upon his country's literature was strong—he was called the Danish Carlyle.

In 1861 his king appointed him a titular bishop, without a see. He published a hymnbook that made a decided change in Danish church services, for it used hymns by the nation's poets. Patriotism was a part of Grundtvig's religion. He established schools in which his country's poetry and history were part of the curriculum. He believed that the Apostles' Creed should be the overall authority in the church, with all other parts of the Bible secondary. He wrote about 1,500 hymns.

Grundtvig was three times married, last at the age of seventy-six. See "I Know a Flower So Fair and Fine."

Francis F. Hagen, Moravian teacher and pastor, b. Salem, N.C., Oct. 30, 1815; d. Lititz, Pa., July 7, 1907.

Francis F. Hagen is best remembered as the composer of the carol MORNING STAR ("Morning Star, O Cheering Sight!) (q.v.), which has remained in use for over a century within his denomination. The same gift for simple but characteristic melody was revealed in a few anthems, a cantata, and an overture. Hagen edited several volumes of a series called the *Church and Home Organist's Companion.*

Sarah Josepha Hale, author and editor; b. Newport, N.H., Oct. 24, 1788; d. Philadelphia, Pa., April 30, 1879.

Sarah Josepha Hale was educated by her mother and an older brother, a student at Dartmouth. In October 1813, she married David Hale, a Newport lawyer. With his encouragement she wrote occasional articles for local newspapers. After her husband died in 1822 she turned to writing to support her five sons. Her first novel, *Northwood; A Tale of New England* (Boston, 1827), attracted some attention. She was named editor of a new monthly, the *Ladies' Magazine,* and moved to Boston in 1828. As her influence grew, she became identified with various charities and patriotic undertakings, most notably with the completion of the Bunker Hill Monument. In 1837 the *Ladies' Magazine* passed into the hands of Louis Godey of Philadelphia, became *Godey's Lady's Book,* and with Mrs. Hale as editor became the best-known periodical of its period and type. After her sons were educated, Mrs. Hale moved to Philadelphia and was completely identified with *Godey's Lady's Book* for the rest of her life. Her *Woman's Record* (1853, 1869, 1876) had over 1,500 biographies designed to show the influence of women on society and literature. See her "Our Father in Heaven."

Amanda Benjamin Hall, author; b. Hallville, Conn., July 12, 1890.

Amanda Benjamin Hall was educated in private schools in Norwich, Conn. She studied art in Rome, short story writing at New

York University, and English versification at Columbia University. In 1923 she married John Angell Brownell (officer, U.S. Navy) and had one son, born in 1925.

A contributor for several years to such magazines as *Harper's, Century, North American Review, Poetry, Saturday Review of Literature, Yale Review,* and *The Lyric,* she wrote three novels: *The Little Red House in the Hollow* (1918), *Blind Wisdom* (1920), and *The Heart's Justice* (1922). Among her books of poetry are *The Dancer in the Shrine* (1923), *Afternoons in Eden* (1932), *Cinnamon Saint* (1937), *Honey Out of Heaven* (1938), *Unweave a Rainbow* (1942) and, recently, *Frosty Harp.*

In 1924 Amanda Benjamin Hall was awarded a prize for her "Ballad of Three Sons." She also won a prize given by the Poetry Society of America for her "The Dancer in the Shrine" and "I'll Build My House." See "It Seems That God Bestowed Somehow," set to music by Virgil Thomson for *American Hymns.*

Marion Franklin Ham, Unitarian minister, author, and hymn writer; b. Harveysburg, Ohio, Feb. 18, 1867; d. Arlington, Mass., July 23, 1956.

Educated in the schools of Harveysburg, Ham worked as a newspaper reporter and bank clerk in Chattanooga, Tenn. Ordained to the Unitarian ministry in 1898 he held his first pastorate in Chattanooga (1898–1904); in 1904 he was called to the First Church of Dallas, Texas. In 1909 he moved to Massachusetts where he served at Reading (1909–34) and at Waverley (1934–42). Though he retired in 1942, he preached in Gardner, Mass., from 1943 to 1945. He received a D.D. degree from Meadville Theological School, Chicago, 1942.

Ham's publications include a number of collections of poems and hymns: *The Golden Shuttle* (1896), *Songs of the Spirit* (1932), *Songs of Faith and Hope* (1940), *The King of Love* (song for church choir, 1941), *Christmas Bells* (song for church choir, 1941), *O Mother-Heart* (1941), *Keeper of the Flame* (1945), *Freedom* (1950), *Songs at Sunset* (1951), *Songs of a Lifetime* (1953), *In a Rose Garden* (1954). In 1914 he also published a book of stories in Negro dialect, *The Kinchin Stories.* Many of the hymns in his books were first published in the *Christian Register* and *Boston Transcript.*

Henry Wilder Foote, in *Three Centuries of American Hymnody* (p. 341), stated that his hymns "constitute the choicest contribution to the 'songs of the spirit' made by an American in this century." See "As Tranquil Streams," "O Thou Whose Gracious Presence Shone," and "Touch Thou Mine Eyes."

Edward Hamilton, bass soloist, composer, and compiler; b. Worcester, Mass., Jan. 6, 1812; d. unknown.

Edward Hamilton came of a family in which his father, grandfather, and great grandfather were all performers of unusual ability. Though he was intended for the legal profession, he forsook the law for music in 1837. He conducted the Mozart Society in Worcester and that city was the center of his activities, although he taught music in larger centers in his home state and to a limited extent in New Hampshire. In 1851 he became choir director at the Essex Street Church in Boston. Endowed with a remarkable bass voice he appeared as soloist in oratorio performances, notably in Handel's *Judas Maccabeus.*

With William Batchelder Bradbury, Edward Hamilton published *Songs of Sacred Praise or American Collection* (Boston, 1845). In 1858 he and Benjamin F. Baker (q.v.) originated the Worcester Musical Convention which later developed into the Worcester Festival. See SYME ("Tell Us, Ye Servants of the Lord").

Phoebe Ann (Coffin) Hanaford, pioneer woman preacher and author; b. Nantucket, Mass., May 6, 1829; d. Rochester, N.Y., June 2, 1921.

Born of Quaker parents, Phoebe Ann Coffin displayed an early aptitude for preaching. She began to teach at the age of sixteen; at twenty she married Dr. Joseph Hanaford of Cape Cod, a teacher, writer, and physician. They went to live in Newton, Mass., where she taught for a year. Although born a Quaker, she was in turn Episcopalian, Baptist and, finally, Universalist. In 1865, at her father's suggestion, she preached a sermon to neighbors at Siasconset. The following year she was invited to Canton, N.Y., to substitute for Rev. Olympia Brown and did so with success. Dr. Brown urged Mrs. Hanaford to enter the ministry. After finishing her preparatory studies, she was called in 1868 to the First Universalist Church, Hingham, Mass. She thus became the first woman ordained as a minister in New England. Mrs. Hanaford subsequently served churches in Waltham, Mass.; New Haven, Conn.; and Jersey City, N.J. In 1884 she was called to the Church of the Holy Spirit in New Haven where she remained until her retirement six years later. She published both verse and prose, including a *Life of George Peabody* and *Women of the Century.* See "Cast Thy Bread upon the Waters."

Chadwick Hansen, educator and poet; b. Benton Harbor, Mich., Feb. 15, 1926.

Chadwick Hansen grew up in Scarsdale, N.Y., where his father was pastor of the Baptist Community Church, and was educated in the public schools of Scarsdale and Bronxville. His college work was done at two institutions: Yale (B.A., 1948) and the University of Minnesota (M.A., 1951; Ph.D., 1956). At Yale he was given a Bursary Scholarship and in 1948 he won the Henry P. Wright Memorial Prize for creative writing. At the University of Minnesota he was a member of the honorary fraternity for creative writing and the Arts Council of the Walker Art Center.

His nonacademic experience has been extremely varied, for he has worked as a merchant seaman, a photographer, and a printer's devil. During his years as a graduate student he owned a phonograph store which specialized in jazz, one of his permanent passions. His three years in the U.S. Navy (1943–46) interrupted his college studies and provided him with unforgettable memories of World War II.

In 1954–55 he held a Ford Teaching Internship in American Studies at the University of Minnesota. Since 1955 he has been on the English and Humanities staff at Pennsylvania State University, where he is an assistant professor of English literature. He spent the year 1960–61 on leave as a Fulbright lecturer in American literature at the University of Graz in Austria.

Hansen has had poetry published in the *AAUP Bulletin, Antioch Review, Beloit Poetry Journal, CEA Critic, Folio, Harper's,* and *Pivot*. Several of his articles on jazz have appeared in *The Record Changer* and the *American Quarterly*. His book, *Modern Fiction: Form and Idea in the Contemporary Novel and Short Story* (with Deborah S. Austin and Ralph W. Condee), was published in 1959 by Pennsylvania State University Press.

In 1947 he married Betty Jane Richards. They are the parents of four daughters. See "Creator of Infinities" which is associated with a tune composed by Howard Hanson for *American Hymns*.

Howard Hanson, composer, conductor, and administrator; b. Wahoo, Neb., Oct. 28, 1896.

Howard Hanson was educated at Luther College in Wahoo, at the school of music of the University of Nebraska, at the Institute of Musical Art in New York, and at Northwestern University from which he received the Mus.B. degree in 1916. He was a member of the music department staff at the College of the Pacific in 1916. From 1919 to 1921 he served as dean of the Conservatory of Fine

Arts. In the latter year he became a Fellow of the Academy of Rome. His long association with the Eastman School of Music began in 1924 when he was appointed director. Hanson was a vigorous and effective champion of the American composer, and the first of a long series of orchestral concerts featuring native works was presented in 1925. Probably no one of his period was more active in recording American works, thus bringing them to a wider audience.

Hanson was a voluminous composer, conservative and even romantic in outlook, as is clear from his *Symphony No. 2* (1930) subtitled *Romantic Symphony*. There were five symphonies in all, the last the *Sinfonia Sacra* (1955). Among the choral works we may enumerate the *Lament of Beowulf* (1925) and *The Cherubic Hymn* (1949). His *Merry Mount* (1933), which includes a scene in which the Puritans sing in church, was commissioned by the Metropolitan Opera. The hymn tune which he composed for *American Hymns* is associated with the text "Creator of Infinities" by Chadwick Hansen.

Henry Harbaugh, pastor and theologian; b. Waynesboro, Pa., Oct. 28, 1817; d. Dec. 28, 1867.

Henry Harbaugh grew up on his father's farm. In the hope of getting a better education he went to Ohio in 1836. He worked as a carpenter, studied, and became a schoolteacher and writer. In 1840 he went to Mercersburg, Pa., and was enrolled as a preparatory student at Marshall College. He spent almost three years at Marshall and at Mercersburg Theological Seminary. Licensed to preach by the synod at Winchester, Va., he became the pastor of the German Reformed Church at Lewisburg in 1844 and was ordained the following January. After serving seven years at Lewisburg, he moved to the First Reformed Church in Lancaster, Pa. He remained there until 1860 when he resigned his post. His aversion to intemperance, his advocacy of a liturgical service, and his stern, moralizing attitude in his writings had made him unpopular. After three years as pastor at Lebanon, Pa., he became professor of didactic and practical theology at Mercersburg Seminary. His works include *Hymns and Chants for Sunday Schools* (1861) and his Pennsylvania-German verse which was collected under the title *Harbaugh's Harfe* (1870). See his "Jesus, I Live to Thee."

Samuel Ralph Harlow, Congregational minister and educator; b. Boston, Mass., July 20, 1885; d. Oak Bluffs, Mass., Aug. 21, 1972.

Samuel Ralph Harlow was educated at Harvard (A.B.), Columbia (M.A.), and Hartford Theological Seminary (Ph.D.). In 1912 he received his theology diploma from Union Theological Seminary. Ordained as a Congregational minister on February 5, 1912, he began pastoral work at the Spring Street Presbyterian Church while he was still a student at Union Theological Seminary. From 1912 to 1922 he was chaplain and head of the sociology department at International College, Smyrna, Turkey, and in 1923 he joined the Smith College department of religion.

During World War I he served as religious director of the YMCA in the Brest area of France. He was also general secretary of the Student Volunteer Movement for the Near East from 1919 to 1922. From 1922 to 1923 he acted as New England field secretary of the American Board of Commissioners for Foreign Missions. Since he was fluent in the languages of the Near East and knew conditions there, he was frequently consulted by the United States government.

The author of several books, Samuel Ralph Harlow is best known as the author of the hymn "O Young and Fearless Prophet" (q.v.), which first appeared in *The Methodist Hymnal* of 1935.

Karl P. Harrington, college teacher and composer; b. Somersworth, N.H., June 13, 1861; d. Middletown, Conn., Nov. 14, 1953.

Educated at Wesleyan University in Middletown, Conn., Karl P. Harrington was, from the time of his graduation in 1882 until his retirement as professor in 1929, actively engaged in teaching Latin. He held college positions in North Carolina and Maine as well as in Connecticut. He and Peter C. Lutkin (q.v.) were musical editors of *The Methodist Hymnal* of 1905. He was known to thousands of college men for his song "Mrs. Winslow's Soothing Syrup," which has been performed by glee clubs for many years. See COPELAND ("Christ's Life Our Code").

Roy Harris, composer; b. Lincoln Co., Okla., Feb. 12, 1898.

Roy Harris was born in a log cabin on land staked out by his father during the Cimarron Rush. The Harris family moved to the San Gabriel Valley, Calif., when he was six years old. At the age of eighteen he operated his own farm and, during the early twenties, drove a butter and egg truck. Educated in the San Gabriel Valley public schools, he attended the University of California in Los Angeles for one year (1919–20). His mother was his first music teacher. He later studied with Arthur Farwell and Modeste Altschuler. Awarded a Guggenheim Fellowship for 1928 (renewed 1929), he spent the period in Paris studying with Nadia Boulanger. From 1930 to 1933 he held a Creative Fellowship from the Pasadena Music and Art Association and from 1933 to 1938 he taught theory and composition at the Westminster Choir School. A position as composer-in-residence at Cornell University (1941–43) was followed by a number of similar appointments at other institutions.

Howard Hanson conducted his first orchestral composition, *Andante,* in 1926. His Third and Fifth Symphonies were commissioned by Serge Koussevitsky for the Boston Symphony Orchestra and the Seventh by the Koussevitsky Foundation. The Third has become one of the classics of American music. The *Quintet for Piano and Strings* (1937) is important among his chamber works. His interest in American folk song is revealed in short settings for piano and, on a larger scale, in the *Folk-Song Symphony* (1940). Harris composed settings of Emily Dickinson's "Read, Sweet, How Others Strove" and Hayden Carruth's "Our Tense and Wintry Minds" for *American Hymns.*

Lewis Hartsough, Methodist editor and hymnist; b. Ithaca, N.Y., Aug. 31, 1828; d. Mount Vernon, Iowa, Jan. 1, 1919.

Lewis Hartsough joined the Oneida Conference of the Methodist Episcopal Church in 1851. Editor of *Spiritual Songs* (1858) and *Sacred Melodies* (1864), he was also co-editor of *The Sacred Harmonist* in the latter year. Hartsough was musical editor of Joshua Hillman's *The Revivalist* (Troy, N.Y., 1868) and joint editor of *Beulah Songs* (Philadelphia, 1879). During a stay in the Rocky Mountains to restore his health he became the first superintendent of the Utah Mission. He spent his later years in Mount Vernon, Iowa. Hartsough's hymns were of the gospel type and "I Hear Thy Welcome Voice" was much sung. Four of his tunes, WELCOME VOICE, CONSECRATION, ROYAL WAY, and LET ME STAY are in use in the twentieth century. See "Let Me Go Where Saints Are Going" and THE PASTOR'S APPEAL ("Come, Friends and Neighbors, Come").

Jefferson Haskell, author; b. Thompson, Conn., Nov. 6, 1807; d. date unknown.

Jefferson Haskell's hymn on old age, "My Latest Sun Is Sinking Fast" (q.v.), was published in J. W. Dadmun's *Melodeon* (1860) and later in William Batchelder Bradbury's *Golden Shower* (1862).

Thomas Hastings, hymn writer and composer; b. Washington, Conn., Oct. 15, 1784; d. New York City, May 15, 1872.

Thomas Hastings was twelve when his family moved by sleigh and ox sledge to Clinton, N.Y. At eighteen he was leading the village choir; at twenty-two he was a singing master. He had a curious knack for reading a score from any angle and eventually became extremely nearsighted.

His first real success was *Musica Sacra; or Springfield and Utica Collections United* (1816, reprinted every year until 1836). As the title indicates, the book combined his own *Utica Collection* with Solomon Warriner's *Springfield Collection. Spiritual Songs for Social Worship* (Boston, 1832), which he edited with Lowell Mason, was designed for revival meetings.

In 1832 twelve churches in New York City urged him to come to that city. He complied and spent the rest of his life there. In spite of the seriousness with which Hastings pursued his ideals, his tunes have less character and are harmonized with less skill than those of such contemporaries as Lowell Mason. He was a voluminous composer of both hymns and hymn tunes: tune and hymn—TOPLADY ("Now from Labor, Now from Care"); hymns—"Hail to the Brightness of Zion's Glad Morning," "Jesus, Merciful and Mild," and "Now Be the Gospel Banner"; tunes—LUTHER ("Jesus, I Come to Thee), BADEN ("The Past Is Dark with Sin and Shame"), and ELDRIDGE ("Proclaim the Lofty Praise"); and, as arranger—OSCEOLA ("You That Have Been Often Invited").

Edwin Francis Hatfield, Presbyterian minister and hymnologist; b. Elizabethtown, N.J., Jan. 9, 1807; d. Summit, N.J., Sept. 23, 1883.

Edwin Francis Hatfield graduated from Middlebury College in 1829 and from Andover Seminary in 1831. His first Presbyterian ministry was in St. Louis, Mo. (1832–35). In 1835 he accepted a call to the Seventh Presbyterian Church in New York City where he remained for twenty-one years. From 1856 to 1863 he served as pastor of the North Presbyterian Church in New York. He did not preach after this, although he remained active in supervising church work. In 1883 the General Assembly of his church elected him Moderator; he discharged his duties with precision and diligence until his death.

After his death his *Poets of the Church* was published by his son. Dr. Hatfield's *Freedom's Lyre,* which appeared in 1840, contained twenty-four of his poems; ten written by him were included in his *Church Hymn Book* of 1872. See his "Hallelujah! Praise the Lord."

William Hauser, Methodist minister, doctor, and hymn compiler; b. near Bethania, N.C., Dec. 23, 1812; d. Wadley, Ga.,
Sept. 15, 1880.

William Hauser (or Houser) was just two years old when he lost
his father, and he received only a rudimentary education. He had a
keen desire to learn, however, and was able to overcome this early
handicap. He became a member of the Methodist Church in 1827,
received a license to preach in 1834, and spent two years as a circuit
rider. He married in 1837 and two years later went to Virginia, evidently because he wanted to gain a knowledge of Latin and Greek at
Emory and Henry College. He moved to Georgia in 1841, where he
became a schoolmaster while studying medicine with Dr. Samuel B.
Clark. In 1843 he set up for himself and gained the reputation of
being one of the most eminent practitioners in Georgia. In addition
he was for a time assistant editor of the *Blister and Critic* and the
Oglethorpe Medical Journal and taught physiology and pathology at
Oglethorpe Medical College (1859–60). Hauser's interest in music
and hymn singing led him to compile two tune books: *The Hesperian
Harp,* a large collection in four-shape notation, published in
Philadelphia in 1848; and *The Olive Leaf* (1878), in which he adopted
Jesse Aikin's seven-shaped notes. Hauser noted certain hymns as he
heard them sung and claimed others as his own. In his earlier book
the melody is in the tenor and the harmony in folk style. In *The Olive
Leaf* the melody has been transferred to the soprano, the harmony is
more conventional, and the influence of the gospel hymn is appar-
ent. See Pilgrim ("Come, All Ye Mourning Pilgrims"), Pleading
Saviour ("Now Behold the Saviour Pleading"), and Isles of the
South ("Wake, Isles of the South").

John Hay, statesman, diplomat, and author; b. Salem, Ind.,
Oct. 8, 1838; d. Newburg, N.H., July 1, 1905.

After graduating from Brown University in 1858, John Hay studied law in the office of Abraham Lincoln and was admitted to the
bar in Springfield, Ill., in 1861. He served as Lincoln's secretary until
the President's death in 1865. Hay was secretary of the U.S. legation
at Paris (1865–67), at Vienna (1867–69), and at Madrid (1869–70).
When he returned to this country he became an editorial writer for
the *New York Herald Tribune.* From 1879 to 1881 he was first assistant
secretary of state, and at the inauguration of President McKinley he
was appointed ambassador to Great Britain, from which post he was
transferred in 1898 to that of secretary of state. He remained in that
office until his death.

His publications included *Pike County Ballads* (1871), *Castilian Days* (1871), *Poems* (1890), and, with John G. Nicolay, *Abraham Lincoln: A History* (1890).

A few of his poems were used as hymns. "Lord, from Far-Severed Climes We Come" was written for the fifteenth international convention of Christian Endeavor. Hay was affiliated with the Presbyterian Church of the Covenant in Washington for many years. See his "Defend Us, Lord, From Every Ill."

Henry Hayman, composer; b. 1820; d. 1894.

Henry Hayman composed the tune LANHERNE ("Touch Thou Mine Eyes") (q.v.), which was included in *The Pilgrim Hymnal* of 1904 and reprinted in H. Augustine Smith's *Hymnal for American Youth* of 1919.

Frederic Henry Hedge, Unitarian minister, scholar, and author; b. Cambridge, Mass., Dec. 12, 1805; d. there Aug. 21, 1890.

Frederic Henry Hedge early learned to read the Latin classics and a family friend, George Bancroft, later a famous historian, prepared him for college. He was ready for Harvard at the age of twelve, but his father sent Frederic and George Bancroft on a trip to Europe. The pair spent four years abroad, studying the German classics. When Hedge came home, he entered Harvard and graduated, class poet, in 1825. He transferred to Harvard Divinity School where his intimacy with Emerson began. Ordained in 1829, Hedge was pastor in West Cambridge, Mass., for six years. He later preached in Bangor, Maine; Providence, R.I.; and Brookline, Mass.

During his years in Bangor he was associated with the transcendental movement, and the Transcendentalist Club there was known as "Hedge's Club." Those years also saw the completion of his major work, *Prose Writers of Germany*. An influential leader in the Unitarian movement, Hedge was president of the Society from 1859 to 1862. A member of the Harvard faculty from 1857 to 1882, he taught ecclesiastical history and German. With Frederic D. Huntington he edited *Hymns for the Church of Christ* (1853). His translation of "A Mighty Fortress Is Our God" has been much sung in this country. See his "Sovereign and Transforming Grace."

Bernhard Heiden, German-American composer; b. Frankfurt-am-Main, Germany, August 24, 1910.

Bernhard Heiden had early private instruction in piano, harmony, and theory. From 1929 to 1933 he studied at the State Academy for Music in Berlin, majoring in composition with Paul Hindemith and conducting with Julius Pruewer. During his last year there he won the Mendelssohn Prize in composition. From 1935 to 1943 he lived in Detroit, Mich., during which time he became a faculty member of the Art Center Music School, a staff arranger for Radio Station WWJ, and founder and conductor of the Detroit Chamber Orchestra, which gave gallery concerts at the Detroit Institute of Arts. He also served as organist at Holy Trinity Lutheran Church and made appearances as lecturer and harpsichordist.

Between 1943 and 1945 he was assistant bandmaster of the 445th Army Service Forces Band. At the end of this period he entered Cornell University where he studied musicology under Donald Grout, receiving his M.A. in 1946. Appointed assistant professor of music at Indiana University in 1946, he became professor in charge of composition there. He received the Fine Arts Quartet Composition Award from the ABC network in 1951 for his *String Quartet No. 2* and two commissions from the Fromm Music Foundation (1955) for his *Memorial for Orchestra* and for his *Serenade for Bassoon and Strings.* His major works include two symphonies, three string quartets, two sonatas for piano, and an opera, *The Darkened City* (performed 1963). Among his titles are: *Euphorion: Scene for Orchestra; Quintet for Horn and Strings; Trio for Piano, Violin and 'Cello; Sonata for Violin and Piano; Sonata for Horn and Piano; Sonata for Piano, Four Hands.* See his setting of Donald C. Babcock's "O God in Whom the Flow of Days," composed for *American Hymns.*

Anthony Philip Heinrich, Bohemian-American composer; b. Schönbüchel, Bohemia, May 11, 1781; d. New York City, May 3, 1861.

Anthony Philip Heinrich's compositions for large orchestra, some of which celebrated such themes as the American Indian (*Indian Carnival, Manitou Mysteries*) and the history of his adopted land (*The Columbiad*—"commemorative of events from the landing of the Pilgrim fathers to the consummation of American liberty"), constitute his chief interest to the student.

Heinrich inherited important wholesale and banking interests from a foster uncle. Musically inclined, he purchased in Malta a Cremona violin which he learned to play. While in the United States on a business trip he lost a considerable fortune when the Austrian government went bankrupt. It was then, at the age of thirty, that he turned to music for his livelihood. He married a Boston girl, took her to Bohemia where their daughter was born, and returned to the United States leaving the little Antonia with relatives. Shortly after their return his wife died. On two European trips Heinrich sought his daughter in vain. While her father was trying to find her in Europe, Antonia had come to the United States. They were eventually reunited.

In 1823 Heinrich was organist of the Old South Church in Boston for a brief period. In addition to HARMONIA ("Though I Should Seek") (q.v.) and ANTONIA (named for his daughter), Nathaniel D. Gould's *National Church Harmony* (1832) also contained Heinrich's short anthems "On Judah's Plain" and "The Death of a Christian."

Heinrich's efforts at composition had begun in 1818. His early works were collected in *The Dawning of Music in Kentucky* (1820). His contact with Indians at Bardstown may have caused him to celebrate their life and legends in music. His trips to Europe (1827, 1834) brought him neither musical fame nor financial security, but a festival performance in New York in 1842 gave a measure of recognition to one who had proudly described himself as an American composer.

Wilbur Held, organist and choir director.

After graduating from the American Conservatory and the Union Theological Seminary, Wilbur Held studied in France with Marcel Dupré and André Marchal. Since 1946 he has been on the faculty of the Ohio State University College of the Arts, where he is professor of organ and church music. Professor Held has also served as organist and choirmaster of the Trinity Episcopal Church (from 1949). He has composed extensively for his instrument and for choir. A number of his compositions for organ are based on hymn or psalm tunes like his *Suite of Passion Hymn Settings* (1966). In addition to HUGHES HALL ("O God, Send Men") (q.v.) he has composed the following hymn tunes: PRAYER FOR PEACE (1965), which received a prize from the Trinity Presbyterian Church, Atlanta, Ga.; "Father, Lead Us to Thy Table" (1974); COLUMBUS, to the text "Like a Miracle of Heaven" (1974); and "Come This Advent" (1974).

Everett Helm, composer; b. Minneapolis, Minn., July 17, 1913.

When Everett Helm graduated from Harvard in 1935 he was awarded the John Knowles Paine traveling fellowship. He studied with Francesco Malipiero in Italy and with Vaughan Williams in England. On his return to the United States he became chairman of the music department of Western College in Ohio (1943–44). He spent the years 1944 to 1946 concertizing in South America. From 1948 to 1950 he served under the Military Government of Germany as theater and music officer. A number of his works, including *Adam and Eve,* an arrangement of a medieval mystery play (Wiesbaden, 1951), and the *Concerto for Five Instruments* (Donaueschingen Festival, 1953), received first performances in Germany. His opera *The Siege of Tottenburg* was presented by the South German Radio Station in 1956 and his ballet *Le Roy fait battre tambour* by the Frankfurt Opera (1956). *Brasiliana,* a suite for piano (1955–56), grew out of Helm's South American experiences. *Three Gospel Hymns for Orchestra* (1955), on the other hand, utilizes themes characteristic of the United States. *Zweites Konzert für Klavier und Orchester* (1956) was a Louisville commission. Later compositions include a *String Quartet, No. II,* and a *Sinfonie da camera* (both 1962). See the setting for Robert Nathan's "Christian, Be Up," composed for *American Hymns.*

James Hewitt, violinist, organist, and composer; b. Dartmoor, England, June 4, 1770; d. Boston, Mass., Aug. 1, 1827.

James Hewitt may have studied violin with Giovanni Battista Viotti and been the principal violin of the Court Orchestra in London in 1792. Accounts published in New York City state that he took part in the Hanover Square and Professional Concerts. His activities in New York, in Boston, and in Augusta, Maine, were varied. He organized and performed in concerts; he led theatrical orchestras (Old America Company and, later, the Park Theatre Orchestra in New York City). He had a New York publishing business from 1798, the successor to Carr's Musical Repository. Among his ballad operas *Tammany* (a lost work) is frequently cited because of its native theme. He wrote and published an original setting of the "Star Spangled Banner." His *The Battle of Trenton* has been revived and recorded. In addition to these secular activities, he was organist of Trinity Church in New York and Trinity Church in Boston. His original hymn tunes are in Samuel Holyoke's *Columbian Repository* (1802) and in his own *Harmonia Sacra* (Boston, 1812). See his Lang ("All-Knowing God, 'Tis Thine to Know").

George Hews, piano manufacturer, organist, and composer; b. Jan. 6, 1806, Weston, Mass.; d. July 6, 1873, Boston, Mass.

George Hews was active as a music teacher in Boston from 1830. He sang countertenor in the Handel and Haydn Society and served as its vice-president from 1854 to 1858. One of the earliest manufacturers of pianos in this country, he established his business in 1840; several patents were granted to him for improvements in piano design, one of them styled the "Hews Patent American Action."

Hews served for some years as organist in the Brattle Street Church. Meetings of the Harvard Medical Association, of which he was made an honorary member, were held in his rooms in Boston from 1848 to 1851. Among his compositions were not only hymn tunes (published in the *Boston Academy's Collection of Church Music,* 1835; *The Sacred Lyrist* by J. and H. Bird, 1847; and in *The Service of Song for Baptist Churches,* 1871), but also secular music, instrumental and vocal. Hews's hymn tune HOLLEY ("Softly Fades the Twilight Ray") (q.v.) has retained its popularity to the present.

Hibbard, an obscure tune writer; fl. late 18th cent.

The composer of BETHEL ("O Could I Find from Day to Day") (q.v.), Hibbard is probably identical with the S. Hibbard who composed the widely used tune EXHORTATION.

Berryman Hicks, Baptist revivalist; b. Spartanburg Co. (now Cherokee Co.), S.C., July 1, 1778; d. Little Buck Creek, Spartanburg, S.C., June 11, 1839.

Berryman Hicks joined the State Line Church in 1800 and was soon licensed to preach. With a co-worker, Elder Drury Dobbins, he ranged the countryside holding revivals. So great was their popularity that the names Hicks and Dobbins became household words. Hicks, who possessed poetic talent, composed numerous hymns and spiritual songs which became popular. He was also an excellent performer on the violin.

Because of his talents, his fine physique, and attractive appearance he was dubbed "the Apollo of the Broad River Association" in his earlier days. Later, when he had financially embarrassed a bondsman, Deacon E. Jones, who suffered severely for Hicks's shortcomings, he was dropped by his Baptist brethren. His death was not recorded in the minutes of the Baptist Association. See "The Time Is Swiftly Rolling On."

J. Vincent Higginson, *see* Cyr de Brant.

Thomas Wentworth Higginson, author; b. Cambridge, Mass., Dec. 22, 1823; d. there May 11, 1911.

Thomas Wentworth Higginson graduated from Harvard in 1841. Although he was inclined towards the ministry, he was not impressed by the theological students at Harvard. He later overcame his doubts and entered Harvard Divinity School, from which he graduated in 1847. After ordination, he became pastor of the First Congregational Society in Newburyport (1847–50) and of the Free Church at Worcester, Mass. (1852–58). This was his last parish, and he subsequently devoted himself to literature and to such liberal causes as abolition and women's suffrage.

An ardent and active friend of the black people, Higginson advocated the rights of the slaves with action as well as words. He was wounded in the attempt to rescue Anthony Burns, a fugitive slave, from kidnappers in Boston. A personal friend of John Brown, he aided in the organization of bands of emigrants from the North to colonize Kansas in 1856. He fought in the Civil War as colonel of a regiment of black soldiers, the first enlisted in South Carolina. In 1864 he was discharged from the army after being wounded. Prominent as a contributor to the *Atlantic Monthly,* he was also the author of *Outdoor Papers* and *Malbone.* Higginson's hymns, written while he was a divinity student, were contributed to *Hymns of the Spirit* (1864), edited by Samuel Johnson and Samuel Longfellow. See "The Past Is Dark with Sin and Shame" and "To Thine Eternal Arms, O God."

S. Hill, organist, teacher, and compiler; fl. mid-19th cent.

S. Hill is evidently identical with Sumner Hill. An EVENING HYMN by S. Hill was published in *The Musical Reporter* of March 1841. The first edition (1849) of *The Bay State Collection* by A. N. Johnson mentioned "other compilers." In the edition of 1850 Sumner Hill's name was added as was that of Josiah Osgood. A recommendation of *Cantica Laudis* published in *The Choral Advocate* of January 1851, identified Hill as an organist and professor of music in Boston. See COMMUNION ("O God Accept the Sacred Hour").

Augustus L. Hillhouse, expatriate author; b. Dec. 9, 1792; d. near Paris, March 14, 1859.

Augustus L. Hillhouse attended Yale, but in 1816 his father sent him abroad in the hope that he would recover from the periods of depression and withdrawal to which he was subject. Hillhouse traveled in the south of France, visited Geneva, and then settled in Paris. From 1817 to 1819 he tried to revive interest in religion in his circle. These gatherings led to regular services following the Congregational and Presbyterian forms of worship. During this period he sent home a copy of his one hymn, "Trembling Before Thine Awful Throne" (q.v.). Hillhouse devoted his later years to a projected work to be called *The Political Experience of the United States Applied to Europe*. After its completion he had planned to return to the United States. Instead, he died in a village near Paris, where he had gone in an attempt to recuperate from an illness. The villagers, who knew him only as "Monsieur Auguste," walked in a procession to the little cemetery where he was buried.

Arthur J. Hodge, fl. late 19th cent.

Arthur J. Hodge was the author of "Five Were Foolish" (q.v.), which appeared in *Good as Gold* (1880), a collection compiled by Robert Lowry and William Howard Doane.

Edward Hodges, English cathedral organist and composer; b. Bristol, England, July 20, 1796; d. there Sept. 1, 1867.

Edward Hodges had earned a doctor's degree at Cambridge and had been organist of three Bristol churches before he came to this country in 1838 with the intention of playing at the cathedral in Toronto. He found his situation there so unsatisfactory that he went to New York, playing at Trinity Church, St. John's Chapel, and Trinity Chapel, as well as teaching in the boys' choir school. When Hodges was attacked by a disabling illness in 1858, he was given a leave of absence, later extended to a year, and he went back to England. Although he returned in 1860, he was still unable to play and in 1863 he resigned and went back to Bristol.

Hodges was important among the English cathedral organists brought here to train boy singers and to establish choral services in Episcopal churches. In addition to service music, much of it unpublished, he wrote a number of hymn tunes published in *The Trinity Collection of Church Music* (1864). See his BRISTOL ("Lord! Lead the Way the Saviour Went").

Balthasar Hoffman, Schwenkfelder hymn writer; b. Harpersdorf, Germany, 1686; d. July 11, 1775.

Balthasar Hoffman came to Pennsylvania in 1734 with a group of about forty Schwenkfelder families who had settled in Saxony after an earlier flight from persecution in Silesia. The Schwenkfelders, German Protestant followers of Casper Schwenkfeld, possessed a voluminous literature of hymns, which remained in manuscript because they were forbidden the use of the printing press. After their arrival in Pennsylvania they undertook the compilation of a hymnbook. Hoarded collections of hymns were brought together, money raised, and an editor, Rev. Christopher Schultz, selected. Schultz had already rearranged and copied the hymns being used by the sect in the mother country. This manuscript contained 106 "Epistellieder" by Balthasar Hoffman. Balthasar was the father of Christopher Hoffman, who was six years old when the family arrived in Pennsylvania. Christopher became a Schwenkfelder minister and was the transcriber of a Schwenkfelder manuscript hymnbook of 1758–60. Both father and son were naturally involved in the preparation of the first printed Schwenkfelder hymnbook in America, published by Christopher Saur in 1762. It contained thirty-nine hymns by the father. See "Gebenedyt sey allzeit."

Joseph P. Holbrook, music editor and hymn tune composer; b. near Boston, Mass., 1822; d. 1888.

Joseph P. Holbrook was music editor of Charles S. Robinson's *Songs of the Church* (1862), of his later *Songs for the Sanctuary* (1865), of the *Baptist Praise Book* (1872) and, with Eben Tourjée, of the *Hymnal of the Methodist Church with Tunes* (1878). Robinson, in the preface of *Songs of the Church*, paid tribute to Holbrook, commending his faithfulness, skill, and taste, and characterizing his original tunes as "among the best" in the collection. See Bishop ("They Pray the Best Who Pray and Watch") and Miriam ("We Bring No Glittering Treasures").

Oliver Holden, preacher, compiler, and composer; b. Shirley, Mass., Sept. 17, 1765; d. Charlestown, Mass., Sept. 4, 1844.

In 1786 the Holden household left Shirley and settled in Charlestown, Mass. The Battle of Bunker Hill had been fought and, since Charlestown had been burned by the British, there was work for a carpenter. Holden prospered there, not only as a carpenter but also in the real estate business. When a newly organized Baptist church needed land on which to build, he gave it to them. After a time he became the leader and preacher of a church called the Puritan Church during the fifteen years of its existence.

Eventually he gave up carpentry to run a successful music store and to teach music. He published: *American Harmony* (Boston, 1792), *Union Harmony* (Boston, 1793), *The Modern Collection of Sacred Music, Sacred Dirges, Hymns and Anthems, Commemorative of the Death of George Washington* and *Plain Psalmody* (all in 1800), and the *Charlestown Collection of Sacred Songs* (Boston, 1803). He also edited later editions of the Worcester Collection (from 1797) and with Hans Gram and Samuel Holyoke, *The Massachusetts Compiler* (Boston, 1795). There are tunes by Holden in *New England Sacred Harmony* (1803), edited by Benjamin Holt Jr., and others in the *Suffolk Collection of Church Music,* of which Holden is said to have been a compiler.

Holden, however, wrote hymn texts as well as tunes. Nineteen poems marked "H" were included in a little volume which Holden edited entitled *The Young Convert's Companion: A Collection of Hymns for the Use of Conference Meetings* (Boston, 1806). "All those who seek a throne of grace," which first appeared in this volume was long used though in an altered form and with the first line changed to "They who seek the throne of grace." For tune and hymn, see CORONATION ("Within These Doors Assembled Now"), his most celebrated tune, and still in use; hymns—"How Sweet Is the Language of Love" and "Weeping Sinner, Dry Your Tears"; tunes—ABERDEEN ("Th'Almighty Spake and Gabriel Sped"), HOPKINTON ("Judge Me, O God"), FAIRLEE ("Long As the Darkening Cloud Abode"), and CONCORD ("The Time Will Surely Come").

Jesse L. Holman, judge; b. Mercer Co., Ky., Oct. 22, 1783; d. March 28, 1842.

Jesse L. Holman joined the Baptist Church of Clear Creek when he was sixteen. A lawyer who opposed slavery, he found it advisable to move across the Ohio River to Indiana. He ran successfully for the Indiana Legislature in 1814, but resigned his seat within the year to accept an appointment as presiding district judge. Two years later he was elevated to the post of judge of the state supreme court. He was narrowly defeated when he was a candidate for the United States Senate in 1831, but in 1835 became a United States district judge.

In 1834 he was ordained, and while covering his circuit on judicial duty he often made speeches on various topics concerned with religion: missions, Bible study, temperance. Two of his hymns, "Lord, in Thy Presence Here" (q.v.) and "Ho! All Ye Sons of Sin and Woe" were published in *Hymns, Psalms, and Spiritual Songs* (1828) edited by Absalom Graves.

Abiel Holmes, Congregational clergyman and historian; b. Woodstock, Conn., Dec. 24, 1763; d. Cambridge, Mass., June 4,1837.

Abiel Holmes, the father of Oliver Wendell Holmes, graduated from Yale in 1783 and was ordained in New Haven on September 15, 1785. His first post was in Midway, Ga., where he remained from 1785 to 1791, although for part of this period (1786–87) he taught at Yale. The First Church in Cambridge, Mass., was his next pastorate, and he remained there thirty-seven years.

Holmes's *Life of Ezra Stiles D.D., LL.D.* (1798) was based on manuscripts left him by the president of Yale. *American Annals* (1805), a comprehensive history of the United States, was republished with a different title in 1829. He was a member and, from 1798 to 1833, corresponding secretary of the Massachusetts Historical Society. See "To Thee, O God," and "Who Here Can Cast His Eyes Abroad."

John Holmes, author and educator; b. Somerville, Mass., Jan. 6, 1904.

John Holmes, the son of John Haynes Holmes (q.v.), attended Tufts College, graduating with a B.S. in 1929. After a year at Harvard he returned to Tufts where he taught English. He wrote a hymn, "O Lord of Stars and Sunlight," for the 125th anniversary of the American Unitarian Association, in addition to four hymns published in the Unitarian *Hymns for the Celebration of Life* (1964). See "Peace Is the Mind's Old Wilderness."

John Haynes Holmes, liberal minister and champion of civil liberty; b. Philadelphia, Pa., Nov. 29, 1879; d. New York City, April 4, 1964.

John Haynes Holmes graduated from Harvard summa cum laude in 1902 and received the S.T.B. in 1904. He was later awarded a D.D. degree by the Jewish Institute of Religion in 1930, by St.

Lawrence University in 1931, and by Meadville Theological School in 1945. His honorary degrees included a Litt.D. from Benares Hindu University in 1947 and an H.H.D. from Rollins College in 1952. He was ordained and installed as minister of the Third Religious Society (Unitarian) at Dorchester, Mass., in 1904. Later he served as pastor of the Church of the Messiah (later called the Community Church) in New York from 1907 to 1949, the year of his retirement.

Active in the affairs of the Unitarian Church from 1908 to 1918, Holmes left the denomination and became an Independent in 1919. He became vice-president of the NAACP in 1909, a director of the American Civil Liberties Union in 1917 (chairman of its board in 1939), president of the All World Gandhi Fellowship in 1929, as well as a participant in numerous local and national civic activities.

In 1929 Holmes was sent on a special mission to Palestine and in 1933 he won the annual Gottheil medal for service to the Jews. He held the Watumull Foundation Lectureship to India in 1947 and 1948.

Author of many books in the field of religion and sociology since 1912 (*The Second Christmas,* 1943; *The Affirmation of Immortality, Ingersoll Lecture,* Harvard, 1947; *My Gandhi,* 1953), his sermons were published annually in the Community Pulpit series. From 1921 to 1946 he was editor of *Unity,* published in Chicago. See his "God of the Nations, Near and Far," "O'er Continent and Ocean," and "The Voice of God Is Calling."

Oliver Wendell Holmes, doctor, poet, and essayist; b. Cambridge, Mass., Aug. 29, 1809; d. Boston, Mass., Oct. 7, 1894.

Oliver Wendell Holmes attended Phillips Academy and graduated from Harvard in 1829. After studying medicine in Boston and Paris, he received the M.D. from Harvard in 1836. Holmes was professor of anatomy at Dartmouth (1838–40) when he went to Harvard to become Parkman Professor of Anatomy and Physiology (1847–82).

Reared in a Calvinist household, he became an influential Unitarian. The hymn "Our Father! While Our Hearts Unlearn" (q.v.) records his change in belief. He was a founder and an important contributor to the *Atlantic Monthly.* He is remembered for essays like those in *The Autocrat of the Breakfast Table* (1858) and its successors. His early "Old Ironsides" was followed by poems such as "The Last Leaf," and "The Boys" (written for the thirtieth reunion of his class). See also "Angel of Peace, Thou Hast Wandered Too Long," "Lord of All Being, Throned Afar," and "O Love Divine, That Stooped to Share."

Benjamin Holt, composer, teacher, and compiler; b. 1774; d. March 9, 1861.

Benjamin Holt married a daughter of the Rev. Thomas Baldwin, pastor of the Second Baptist Church in Boston. Holt was elected in 1817 as the second president of the Handel and Haydn Society, after serving as one of the original trustees. Following his service as president he was made a trustee (1819–23).

In 1803 Holt published *The New England Sacred Harmony,* a fifty-six page collection containing twenty-two of his own tunes. The remainder of the volume consisted chiefly of selections from English composers. In collaboration with Bartholomew Brown and Nahum Mitchell, Holt edited the important *Bridgewater Collection* (Boston, 1802 to 1839—later editions were entitled *Templi Carmina*). See WOODSTOWN ("Great God, the Followers of Thy Son").

Samuel Holyoke, composer, compiler, and singing master; b. Boxford, Mass., Oct. 15, 1762; d. Concord, N.H., Feb. 7, 1820.

Samuel Holyoke was born into a family which had produced ministers and educators. His mother's father, Oliver Peabody, had been minister to the Natick Indians. His father's uncle, Edward Holyoke, had been president of Harvard; and his father, settled for life as was then the custom, served the Congregational Church at Boxford for nearly half a century. A graduate of Harvard himself, Samuel Holyoke was to choose the life of a wandering music teacher.

Samuel Holyoke taught singing classes from Massachusetts to New Hampshire, in later years aiding himself with a clarinet. He was active in the yearly concerts given by the Essex Musical Association, some of which took place in his father's church in Boxford.

Harmonia Americana, the first collection of Holyoke's own music, was published in Boston in 1791. See ARNHEIM ("Great God, Thy Works"), SUNBURY ("Hard Heart of Mine"), CYRENE ("Turn, Turn, Unhappy Souls, Return"), and DELHI ("While O'er Our Guilty Land, O Lord"). In the preface he defended the simplicity of his tunes. Because it was essential for vocal music, he adapted his compositions to the rules of pronunciation. He put in no fuguing pieces, he said, "because the parts, falling in one after another, each conveying a different idea, confuse the sense and render the performance a mere jargon of words." His second appearance in print was in *The Massachusetts Compiler* (Boston, 1795), the editing of which he shared with Hans Gram (q.v.) and Oliver Holden (q.v.). Each editor put in one of his own tunes; the rest were from European sources.

In September 1790, the *Massachusetts Magazine* printed Holyoke's song "Washington" and from time to time published other pieces by him: "The Pensive Shepherd," "Sally, a Pastoral," and "Terraminta." For Washington's funeral he set to his own music two of Isaac Watts's hymns: "Hark from the Tombs" and "Beneath the Honors." There is a record of their being performed at Newburyport in January 1800. He also wrote two odes to Washington "to be performed at the Brattle Street Church [Boston] on Wednesday, February 19, 1800."

The largest collection of music made in this country up to that time was his *The Columbian Repository of Sacred Harmony* (1802). Dedicated to the Essex Musical Association, it offered 734 tunes and was published in Exeter, N.H. Distributed by subscription at three dollars, *The Columbian Repository* did not sell well, although it was Holyoke's most ambitious work. In 1804 his *Christian Harmonist,* a book of 195 pages, was printed at Salem, Mass. It contained "a set of tunes adapted to all metres," two anthems, and a funeral dirge, and was designed for use in Baptist churches. See SUNCOOK ("How Sweet Is the Language of Love"), CONFIDENCE ("Trembling Before Thy Awful Throne"), and KESWICK ("Weeping Sinner, Dry Your Tears"). Two books which Holyoke had printed in 1807 were unimportant as music: *Vocal Companion* and *Instrumental Assistant.* The latter gave instruction for violin, German flute, clarinet, bass viol, and hautboy. The best known of Holyoke's hymn tunes was ARNHEIM, which was long and widely used.

C. Hommann, violinist, organist, and pianist; fl. mid-19th cent.

C. Hommann was active in Philadelphia until 1857 when he left and was not heard from again. He was organist at Christ's Church and the Dutch Reformed Church. He is said to have composed a great quantity of music most of which was never performed. An organ voluntary, parts for an orchestral overture, and three string quartets have been preserved at the Free Library of Philadelphia. In *Cantus Ecclesiae* (1844), edited by W. H. W. Darley and J. C. R. Standbridge, there are ten hymn tunes by Hommann including ABERCROMBIE ("Holy Father, Great Creator") (q.v.). There is also a short anthem of his composition (Psalm 47) and a tune by Standbridge called HOMMANN.

Edmund Hooper, organist and composer; b. in Halberton, Devon, c.1553; d. July 14, 1621.

Edmund Hooper may have been a chorister in Exeter Cathedral. He was with the choir of Westminster Abbey about 1581 and on December 3, 1588, he was appointed organist. Hooper was one of the ten composers who made settings for *The Whole Book of Psalmes* published by Thomas East in 1592. On March 1, 1603/04 he was sworn a gentleman of the Chapel Royal and on May 9, 1606, he was appointed organist of Westminster Abbey. He held both posts until he died. Two of his compositions were in Leighton's *Teares or Lamentaciouns of a Sorrowful Soule* (1614). Hooper also contributed to Thomas Ravenscroft's psalter of 1621. See his settings of LONDON ("The Heavens Do Declare") and CAMBRIDGE ("My Shepherd Is the Living Lord").

John Hopkins, teacher, rector, and contributor to the "Old Version"; b. probably in Gloucestershire, England, c.1520; d. Great Waldringfield, Suffolk, Oct. 23, 1570.

John Hopkins was admitted B.A. at Oxford in 1544. He took holy orders and became a schoolmaster, apparently in Suffolk. It is known that he was rector of Great Waldingfield, Suffolk, on August 12, 1561.

The first edition containing Thomas Sternhold's (q.v.) metrical versions of the Psalms was undated. The second, which appeared in 1549, was posthumous. It was only in the third edition, of 1551, that a group of seven psalms by Hopkins was added. In the preface Hopkins said that his psalms should not be "fathered on a dead man," adding that they were "not in any part to be compared with his [Sternhold's] most exquisite doings." Both men wrote in the popular ballad meter, but Sternhold was satisfied to rhyme only even-numbered lines (abcb) while Hopkins also rhymed the other pairs (abab). Compare Sternhold's version of Psalm 23 ("My Shepherd Is the Living Lord") with Hopkins' version of Psalm 90 ("Thou, Lord, Hast Been Our Sure Defense"). In the psalter of 1561 fourteen more versions by Hopkins were added, and in the definitive edition of 1562, there were thirty-nine more—making a total of sixty, the largest contribution by any author.

John Henry Hopkins Jr., designer, musician, and poet; b. Pittsburgh, Pa., Oct. 28, 1820; d. Hudson, N.Y., Aug. 14, 1891.

John Henry Hopkins Jr. attended the University of Vermont (A.B. 1839), then moved to New York City where he was a reporter but at the same time prepared himself for a career as a lawyer. He received his M.A. at the University of Vermont (1845) and then studied for the ministry at the General Theological Seminary, graduating in 1850. Though Hopkins was successively deacon (1850) and priest (1872), and served as the rector of churches in Plattsburg (Trinity Church) and Williamsport, Pa. (Christ Church), his distinctive contribution to his church was in the arts.

He remained in the Seminary after graduation as the first teacher of music there (1855–57), serving also as the editor of the *Church Journal* (1853–68). His talents for design were expressed in stained glass, episcopal seals, and other church forms. His hymn texts and tunes show him as poet and musician. His *Carols, Hymns, and Songs* (1863) reached a fourth edition in 1882. His *Canticles Noted with Accompanying Harmonies* (1866) enjoyed a considerable success. "We Three Kings of Orient Are" (q.v.) has outlasted his other works and is still among the best loved and most frequently sung of American carols. See also the Easter carol "Alleluia! Christ Is Risen Today," "God of our Fathers, Bless This Our Land," and the unnamed tune to "Like Noah's Weary Dove."

Josiah Hopkins, Congregational missionary and minister; b. Pittsford, Vt., April 25, 1786; d. Geneva, N.Y., June 27, 1862.

Josiah Hopkins was more or less self-educated, but he did study theology with his pastor, the Rev. Holland Weeks, and with Rev. Lemuel Haynes, a famous mulatto pastor, in the adjacent town of Rutland, Vt. Licensed to preach by the Pawlet Association in 1809, he served first as a missionary in the Lake Champlain area, then was called to the Congregational Church of New Haven, Vt., in 1809, where he was ordained. He had an influence on the students of the neighboring college at Middlebury and was given an honorary D.D. degree by that institution in 1843. In 1830 he accepted a post at the First Presbyterian Church in Auburn, N.Y., where he served until 1846.

The editor of *Conference Hymns* (Auburn, N.Y., 1846), Hopkins also contributed to Joshua Leavitt's *The Christian Lyre* (New York, 1831). Two of his best-known hymns were "O Turn Ye, O Turn Ye" (q.v.) and "Why Sleep We, My Brethren?"

Francis Hopkinson, musician, author, and inventor; b. Philadelphia, Pa., Sept. 21, 1737; d. there May 9, 1791.

Francis Hopkinson was probably taught music by James Bremner, organist of Christ Church, whom Hopkinson later succeeded. Vestry minutes of this church and of St. Peter's record Hopkinson's services as instructor "in the art of psalmody." His first appearance in a public concert may have been in 1757 as harpsichord accompanist at the first performance of the *Masque of Alfred the Great,* given at Philadelphia College (now the University of Pennsylvania). Hopkinson was an undergraduate at the time. He later received a master's degree, studied law, and was admitted to the bar.

The harpsichord was his favorite instrument; one of his inventions was a method of quilling it to improve the tone. He urged Thomas Jefferson to interest manufacturers in his invention when Jefferson went abroad in 1784. In 1766 Hopkinson journeyed to England. He had earned part of the money for his trip by adapting the Psalms in English for the Reformed Dutch Church in New York (see "O Lord, How Lovely Is the Place"). One letter mentions the "pleasure of hearing the *Messiah* and other solemn Pieces of Musick performed by the best hands." His allegorical-political oratorial entertainment, *The Temple of Minerva,* presented in Philadelphia in 1781, praised the American alliance with France. Only the text survives.

From the time of his marriage at the age of thirty-one to Ann Borden of Bordentown, N.J., he held various public offices. He was a delegate to the Continental Congress, a signer of the Declaration of Independence, and the first Secretary of the Navy. He was later made Judge of the Admiralty from Pennsylvania.

Seven Songs for the Harpsichord (really eight, since one song was added too late to change the title page) was published in 1788 and dedicated to George Washington. It is important as the first collection of secular songs published in this country. One of these songs, "My Days Have Been so Wondrous Free," was apparently composed as early as 1759. Hopkinson also published *A Collection of Psalm Tunes with a Few Anthems, Some of Them Entirely New for the Use of the United Churches of Christ and St. Peter's Church in Philadelphia* (1763).

In a letter to his wife, John Adams described this man of various interests and skills as "pretty, little, curious, ingenious; his head not bigger than an apple; genteel and well bred," and "very social." His three-volume *Miscellaneous Essays and Occasional Writings* (Philadelphia, 1792) established Hopkinson as an author. It contains "Arise and See the Glorious Sun" (q.v.) and "At Length the Busy Day Is Done" (q.v.). See also his PHILADELPHIA, the tune for his "Arise and See the Glorious Sun."

Anna Hoppe, Lutheran hymn writer; b. 1889; d. 1941.

Anna Hoppe's parents were German immigrants who settled in Milwaukee, Wis. Her gift for writing religious poetry revealed itself when she was only eleven. Her education was limited since she had to leave school after the eighth grade to go to work. During her lunch hour she often typed the hymns she had written while traveling to work. The Augustana Lutheran hymnal of 1925 contained twenty-three of her hymns and the *American Lutheran Hymnal* (1930), eight. Besides her own compositions she translated many hymns from German into English and at least one from the Norwegian. In 1927 her poems were collected in a volume called *Hymns of the Church Year*. Her ambition to write a thousand hymns remained unrealized, although she did write approximately five hundred. See "Precious Child, So Sweetly Sleeping."

Edward Hopper, Presbyterian pastor and hymnist; b. New York City, Feb. 17, 1818; d. April 23, 1888.

Edward Hopper earned degrees from New York University (1839) and Union Theological Seminary (1842). Lafayette College gave him the honorary D.D. in 1871. He held Presbyterian pastorates at Greenville, N.Y.; Sag Harbor, a whaling port on Long Island; and the Church of the Sea and Land in New York City. Although Hopper wrote several hymns, all of which were at first published anonymously, he is best known for "Jesus, Saviour, Pilot Me" (q.v.). First published in the *Sailor's Magazine* in 1871 and a few months later in *The Baptist Praise Book,* the identity of the author was learned nine years later when he was invited to write a new hymn for the anniversary service of the Seaman's Friend Society. He brought instead a copy of "Jesus, Saviour, Pilot Me" and read it, thus revealing for the first time that he was the author. See also "They Pray the Best Who Pray and Watch."

Paul Horgan, American author; b. Buffalo, N.Y., Aug. 1, 1903.

Paul Horgan was educated at the New Mexico Military Institute (1920–23) in Roswell, N.M. After working with the production staff of the Eastman Theatre in Rochester, N.Y. (1923–26), he became librarian at the New Mexico Military Institute (1926–42), and assistant to the president (1947–56). On active duty with the U.S. Army from

1942 to 1946, he was later assigned to temporary active duty in 1950. Horgan was awarded the Legion of Merit as Chief, Army Information Branch of the Information Division, War Department. A lecturer at the Graduate School of Letters, University of Iowa, from February to June 1946, he became a Guggenheim Fellow in 1947–48. From 1948 to 1955 he was president of the board of directors of the Roswell Museum.

His works include: *Men of Arms* (1931); *The Fault of Angels* (1933), which won the Harper Prize novel competition that year; *No Quarter Given* (1935); *Main Line West* (1936); *From the Royal City* (1936); *The Return of the Weed* (1936); *A Lamp on the Plains* (1937); *Far from Cibola* (1938); *Figures in a Landscape* (1930); *The Habit of Empire* (1941); *A Tree on the Plains* (1942), an opera with music by Ernst Bacon; *Yours, A. Lincoln* (1942), a drama; *The Common Heart* (1942); *The Devil in the Desert* (1952), the biographical introduction to the *Diary and Letters of Josiah Gregg* (Vol. I, 1941; Vol. II, 1942); *Great River: The Rio Grande in North American History* (1954); and *Humble Powers* (1954). *Great River* won a Pulitzer prize in its publication year. His "Now Evening Puts Amen to Day" comes from *A Tree on the Plains,* an opera libretto set by Ernst Bacon (q.v.).

Frederick Lucian Hosmer, hymn writer and Unitarian minister; b. Framingham, Mass., Oct. 16, 1840; d. Berkeley, Calif., June 7, 1929.

After completing his undergraduate studies at Harvard (B.A., 1862), Frederick Lucian Hosmer continued at the Harvard Divinity School (B.D. 1869) and began his career as a Unitarian minister in the same year. His ministerial charges were: First Congregational Church, Northboro, Mass. (1869–72); Second Congregational Church, Quincy, Ill. (1872–77); First Unitarian Church, Cleveland, Ohio (1878–92); Church of the Unity, St. Louis, Mo. (1892–99); and First Unitarian Church, Berkeley, Calif. (1900–15).

During his lifetime he published *The Way of Life* (1877), *Unity Hymns and Chorals* (with William Channing Gannett and J. V. Blake, 1880; enl. ed., 1911), and *The Thought of God in Hymns and Poems* (with Gannett, 1885), in which fifty-six of his own hymns appeared.

Hosmer was a student of hymnology as well as a hymn writer. He lectured on this subject at Harvard Divinity School (1908) and at the Pacific Unitarian School for the Ministry (1912). He was considered one of the most original and powerful Unitarian hymn writers of his period. See "From Age to Age They Gather," "Hear, Hear, O Ye Nations," "O Beautiful My Country," "O Day of Light and Gladness," and "Through Willing Heart and Helping Hand."

E. Embree Hoss, educator, pastor, and bishop; b. Washington Co., Tenn., April 14, 1849; d. April 23, 1919.

E. Embree Hoss was a graduate of Ohio Wesleyan and of Emory and Henry College in Virginia. In 1870 he was ordained a minister in the Methodist Episcopal Church, South. Appointed pastor in Knoxville, Tenn., that same year he remained there until 1872. Then, after spending two years in San Francisco, he accepted a post in Asheville, N.C. During the years between 1876 and 1881 he was a professor at Martha Washington College in Abingdon, Va. From that professorship he was called to the vice-presidency and later the presidency of Emory and Henry College. Professor of Church History at Vanderbilt University (1885–90), he later edited the Nashville *Christian Advocate* (1890–92). In May 1902, he was elected bishop at Dallas, Texas. He was a member of The Joint Commission which produced *The Methodist Hymnal* of 1905. See "O God, Great Father, Lord and King."

Alan Hovhaness, composer; b. Somerville, Mass., March 8, 1911.

Alan Hovhaness was precocious both as performer and composer and was studying harmony and counterpoint in college while he was still a high-school student. At the New England Conservatory of Music (1932) he studied composition with Frederick Converse and piano with Heinrich Gebhard. Later Hovhaness worked with Bohuslav Martinu at Tanglewood. He conducted concerts of his own works in Boston (1947) and New York (1947 and 1949). After teaching at the Boston Conservatory of Music from 1948, Hovhaness moved to New York in 1951, where he has devoted all his time to composition. His work has been assisted by a number of grants including those from the National Institute of Arts and Letters, the Guggenheim Foundation (1953 and 1955), the Columbia Broadcasting System (1953, *Easter Cantata*), the Fromm Foundation (1954, *Stars*), and the Louisville Orchestra (1953, *Concerto No. 7 for Orchestra;* 1959, *Magnificat,* Opus 157). He has been influenced by Armenian and Eastern music, and his compositions were warmly received during a tour of Japan (1960). Other compositions are *Mysterious Mountain,* Opus 132, and *Symphony No. 4,* Opus 165. His hymn tune to Edwin Markham's "There Is a High Place" was especially composed for *American Hymns.*

A. P. Howard, writer of carols for Christmas and Easter; b. 1838; d. 1902.

A. P. Howard may have lived in Longwood (now a part of Brookline, Mass.); certainly all of his music was published in Boston. Armin Haeussler gives a list of his publications in *The Story of Our Hymns* to which his *Selected Christmas Carols* (1892) should be added. See his unnamed setting for Louisa May Alcott's "A Little Kingdom I Possess."

How'd, composer; fl. late 18th cent.

How'd was the composer of a fine tune called WHITESTOWN ("Where Nothing Dwelt But Beasts of Prey") (q.v.), which first appeared in Samuel Jenks's *The Musical Harmonist* (New Haven, Conn., 1800). Nothing is known of the composer. All we have is the history of the tune, which was a deserved favorite. In John Wyeth's *Repertory of Sacred Music* (1810) the composer's name was spelled Howel. Evidently WHITESTOWN passed from Wyeth to the Southern collections. It appeared in *Southern Harmony* (1835), attributed to Ward, and was included in the *Original Sacred Harp* (1936), although the composer's name was given there as Howell.

Julia Ward Howe, poet, essayist, and reformer; b. New York City, May 27, 1819; d. South Portsmouth, R.I., Oct. 17, 1910.

Julia Ward Howe was privately educated and grew up as a member of enlightened and distinguished circles in New York City. She married Samuel Gridley Howe in 1843, and they spent the following year abroad, during which time she formed friendships with leaders and writers in several countries. On the Howes' return they settled in Boston. They were sympathetic toward the Abolitionist movement and became enthusiastic crusaders. Mrs. Howe helped her husband edit *The Commonwealth,* an antislavery paper.

Her "Battle Hymn of the Republic," written during the Civil War, is still sung as an expression of the ideals of that period. Julia Ward Howe published a number of collections of poetry from 1854. Her later works include a study of Margaret Fuller (1883) and her *Reminiscences* (1899). Always in the forefront of liberal causes, she worked for the Unitarian movement, women's suffrage, prison reform, and international peace. See "Mine Eyes Have Seen the Glory."

Solomon Howe, composer and hymnist; b. North Brookfield, Mass., Sept. 14, 1750; d. New Salem, Mass., Nov. 18, 1835.

A Dartmouth graduate (1777), Solomon Howe was, at various times, a preacher, teacher, farmer, and printer. He may also have been a singing master in Greenwich, Mass., since all three of his collections were issued while he lived there. They were *The Worshipper's Assistant* (Northampton, 1799), which contained the rudiments of music as well as psalm tunes "adapted to the weakest capacities"; *The Farmers Evening Entertainment* (Northampton, 1804); and *Divine Hymns on the Sufferings of Christ* (1805). The first two have tunes and texts; the third texts only. See CHARITY with Howe's text "Our Kind Creator."

Langston Hughes, author and poet; b. Joplin, Mo., Feb. 1, 1902; d. New York City, May 24, 1967.

Langston Hughes studied at Columbia University (1921–22) and Lincoln University, Pa. (B.A., 1929). The latter institution honored him with the Litt.D. in 1943. He worked as a seaman on voyages to Europe and Africa and lived in Mexico, Paris, and Italy. In 1925 he won first prize in a contest for Negro writers offered by *Opportunity* magazine. In 1926 he won the Witter Bynner undergraduate poetry prize contest; later he received the Harmon gold award for literature (1930), a Guggenheim Fellowship (1935), a Rosenwald Fellowship (1941), a $1,000 grant from the National Institute of Arts and Letters (1946) and the Ainsfield-Wolfe award for the best book on race relations (1954).

Hughes's career was exceptionally varied. He spent a year in the Soviet Union (1932–33), served as a Madrid correspondent for the *Baltimore Afro-American* (1937), was a columnist on the *Chicago Defender,* a poet in residence at the University of Chicago Laboratory School (1949), a lyricist and radio writer, dramatist (*Mulatto,* produced at the Vanderbilt Theatre in New York, 1935), and librettist (for William Grant Still's opera *Troubled Island* and for some of the lyrics in the Elmer Rice–Kurt Weill musical *Street Scene*). Many of his poems have been set to music and he toured the country giving readings of them.

He is the author of *Weary Blues* (1926), *Fine Clothes to the Jew* (1927), *Not Without Laughter* (1930), *Popo and Fifina* (with Arna Bontemps, 1932), *The Dream Keeper* (1932), *The Ways of White Folks* (1934), *The Big Sea* (an autobiography, 1940), *Shakespeare in Harlem* (1942), *Fields of Wonder* (1947), *One-Way Ticket* (1949), *Simple Speaks His Mind* (1950), *Montage of a Dream Deferred* (1951), *Laughing to Keep from Crying* (1952), *The First Book of Negroes* (1954), *First Book of Rhythm* (1954), *First Book of Jazz* (1954), *First Book of the Caribbean* (1955), and *Simple Stakes a Claim* (1957). See "Heaven, Heaven, Heaven Is the Place" and "The Lord Has a Child."

William Hunter, editor, educator, and hymn writer; b. May 26, 1811, near Ballymoney, County Antrim, Ireland; d. Alliance, Ohio, Oct. 18, 1877.

William Hunter was brought to this country as a child and taken to York, Pa., where his family settled. He attended Madison College at Uniontown, Pa., from which he graduated in 1833. After a short period of teaching he was licensed to preach. In 1836 he began his work as an editor and for three different periods (1836–40, 1844–52, and 1872–76) edited *The Pittsburgh Conference Journal,* afterwards called *The Pittsburgh Christian Advocate.* He became a member of the faculty of Alleghany College in 1855 and remained there for fifteen years, teaching Hebrew and biblical literature.

An author of a large number of hymns he was also the editor of *Minstrel of Zion* (1854), *Select Melodies* (1851), and *Songs of Devotion* (1859). In these collections he included 125 of his own hymns. In 1876 he was appointed one of a committee of twelve by the General Conference of the Methodist Church to revise the hymnal, which was published in 1878 as the *Hymnal of the Methodist Episcopal Church.*

During intervals between his literary endeavors he was presiding elder and pastor in the West Virginia Conference. He later became minister of the Methodist Episcopal Church in Alliance, Ohio. See " 'Go, Bring Me,' Said the Dying Fair," "Joyfully, Joyfully Onward I Move," and "The Music of His Steps."

Abby Hutchinson, vocalist; b. Milford, N.H., 1829; d. New York City, Nov. 24, 1892.

A quartet composed of Abby Hutchinson and her three brothers, Judson, John, and Asa, made the singing Hutchinsons famous. After her marriage to Ludlow Patton in 1849, both joined the brothers on tour until Abby was stricken with a serious illness. She then decided to lead a more leisurely and comfortable life. Her disconsolate brothers could do no more than induce her to join them in occasional concerts in or near New York.

Abby is best remembered by a simple song which she used to sing, "Kind Words Can Never Die" (q.v.). It was appropriate that a member of a group that evidently advocated the emancipation of the slave should publish spirituals. She arranged and published five of the melodies which she heard at a freedman's meeting. She also published a setting of Tennyson's "Ring Out Wild Bells," which was used in concerts by her family. Her last public appearance as a singer, with her brother John and the Negro leader Frederick Douglass, was at a meeting for the unveiling of a statue of Senator John P. Hale on August 9, 1892.

Abby Bradley Hyde, hymn writer; b. Stockbridge, Mass., Sept. 28, 1799; d. Andover, Conn., April 7, 1872.

During her school years in Litchfield, Conn., Abby Bradley was under the pastoral care of Dr. Lyman Beecher. In 1818 she married the Rev. Lavius Hyde (1789–1865) and went with him when he took up his first pastoral charge at Salisbury, Conn.

During the years that he served as pastor in several Connecticut and Massachusetts towns she wrote a number of poems and hymns on religious themes. Leonard Bacon (q.v.) reprinted two of her hymns earlier published in the *Religious Intelligencer* for his *Collection of Monthly Concert Hymns* at the Andover Theological Academy.

When the Rev. Hyde took new duties at Bolton, Conn., in 1822, Mrs. Hyde found there the Rev. Asahel Nettleton, the revivalist, recovering from an attack of typhus fever. During his convalescence he compiled his *Village Hymns,* in which he included nine hymns by Mrs. Hyde. Thirty-four appeared in the revised and enlarged edition of 1851. See "And Canst Thou, Sinner, Slight," and "Dear Saviour, If These Lambs Should Stray."

William deWitt Hyde, administrator, author, and minister; b. Winchendon, Mass., Sept. 23, 1858; d. Brunswick, Maine, June 29, 1917.

After losing both his parents early in life, William deWitt Hyde was brought up by relatives in Keene, N.H. Graduated from Phillips Academy in Exeter (1875), he entered Harvard and received his degree in 1879. After a year spent at Union Theological Seminary he completed his course at Andover in 1882. A postgraduate year was notable chiefly for Hyde's renewed contacts with George Herbert Palmer of Harvard, his spiritual father, whose Hegel seminar he attended.

Ordained to the Congregational ministry in 1883, he became pastor of a church in Paterson, N.J. During his two years in Paterson he published two technical articles on theology which attracted considerable attention. In June 1885, when he was twenty-eight years old, he was appointed seventh president of Bowdoin College, where for thirty-two years, he administered the affairs of an expanding college with distinction and excellence. In constant demand as a lecturer Hyde was chosen to give the chief address at the Louisiana Purchase Exposition in St. Louis in 1904. He was appointed a trustee of Phillips Exeter in 1898 and became an overseer of Harvard in 1915. He took the lead in founding the Maine Interdenominational Commission in 1890, of which he was president as long as he lived. Through its success, by his advocacy of church unity in a series of articles in *Forum* and by active cooperation, he contributed importantly to the evolution of the Federal Council of Churches of Christ in America.

Although he wrote several other volumes, Hyde's most popular books were *Practical Ethics* (1892); *From Epicurus to Christ* (1904), republished as *The Five Great Philosophies of Life* (1911); and *Self-Measurement* (1908).

As religious leader, author, teacher, and college president he wielded much influence on the intellectual life of his time. See his "Creation's Lord, We Give Thee Thanks."

Jeremiah Ingalls, singing master, composer, and choir leader; b. Andover, Mass., March 1, 1764; d. Hancock, Vt., April 6, 1828.

Jeremiah Ingalls gave up the trade of cooper to become a musician. In 1787 he moved to Newbury, Vt., and four years later married Mary Bigelow. In the same year he was chosen to lead the singers in the First Church and in 1803 was made a deacon. The Newbury choir became locally famous and travelers would plan to stay over Sunday to hear the singing. Ingalls built a large house on his farm and ran a tavern for several years. In 1810 he was removed as deacon and excommunicated. Because the tavern proved unprofitable, he sold it and went to Rochester, Vt., where he stayed for a short time before he moved to Hancock, Vt., where he died.

Ingalls' one collection, *Christian Harmony* (Exeter, N.H., 1805), has become famous as an early source for folklike melodies. It contains his best-known tunes, such as UNION HYMN, NEW JERUSALEM, NORTHFIELD ("O God, Though Endless Worlds of Light") (q.v.), and HAPPY CHOICE ("While I Am Young") (q.v.), occasional pieces like his ELECTION ODE and ELECTION HYMN, and a funeral piece for Judith Brock of Newbury. See also RICH PROVISION ("Dear Happy Souls").

Charles E. Ives, insurance executive and innovative composer; b. Danbury, Conn., Oct. 20, 1874; d. New York City, May 19, 1954.

Charles was the son of a music teacher and bandmaster who had an inquiring turn of mind, who was interested in acoustics, and who encouraged his son's musical studies. Elam Ives Jr. (1802–1864), tune composer and compiler, was one of his distant ancestors. Charles Ives graduated from Yale in 1898. While there he studied with Horatio Parker. During his undergraduate days he was active as an organist in both Danbury and New Haven. From 1900 to 1902 he was organist and choirmaster at the Central Presbyterian Church in New York City. He developed a very successful insurance business which he carried on until his retirement in 1930.

Ives's major compositions were written between the years 1906 and 1916. During World War I he wrote nothing. In 1919 his piano sonata *Concord, Massachusetts, 1840–1860* was published, as was the accompanying volume *Essays before a Sonata.* In 1922 he issued a privately printed collection of 114 songs composed over a thirty-year period.

With the recording of the *Concord Sonata,* the second, third, and fourth symphonies, the four violin sonatas, and a sampling of the songs, Ives's position as a gifted and prophetic American composer became clearer. He wrote anthems, psalm settings, carols, religious solo songs, but perhaps no congregational hymn tunes. Yet the tunes of the popular hymns of his day were an important part of the melodic store which gave his music that homely and local flavor which is as native to it as his daring experimentation. The finales of the four violin sonatas and the group of solo songs based on hymn tunes will illustrate that phase of his creative activity. See "Now Help Us, Lord."

G. K. Jackson, organist and composer; b. Oxford, England, 1745; d. Boston, Mass., Nov. 18, 1822.

As a boy G. K. Jackson was a chorister in the Chapel Royal where James Nares was organist. In 1784 he sang tenor at the Handel Commemoration and in 1791 received the degree of Mus.D. from St. Andrew's College. He came to this country in 1796, landing in Norfolk, Va., later moving to Alexandria, Baltimore, Philadelphia, Elizabeth, N.J., and New York City where he was choir director at St. George's Chapel (1801). In 1800 he announced a music school at Newark. He was in Boston from 1813, although this period was broken by a stay in Northampton, Mass. (March 1813–April 1815). In Boston he was the organist of leading churches and of the

Handel and Haydn Society. With Gottlieb Graupner and his wife and Francis Mallet he gave oratorio performances. He was also active as a publisher. (See Richard J. Wolfe, *Secular Music in America, 1801–1825,* for a list of imprints.) His *David's Psalms* (New York, 1804), *A Choice Collection of Chants for Four Voices with a Gloria Patri and Sanctus* (Boston, 1816), and *The Choral Companion and Elucidation of Dr. G. K. Jackson's Chants* (Boston, 1817) are relevant to our subject. It was Dr. Jackson who persuaded the Handel and Haydn Society to publish Lowell Mason's important *Handel and Haydn Society Collection of Church Music* (Boston, 1822) with the addition of original tunes. He was remembered as a very portly man, somewhat impassive, but of good understanding. He died in reduced circumstances. See his ABERFORD ("My Soul Would Fain Indulge a Hope").

John Christian Jacobi, organist and compiler; b. Germany, 1670; d. London, Dec. 14, 1750.

John Christian Jacobi settled in London where he became Keeper of the Royal German Chapel, St. James' Palace, in about 1708. He retained the position until his death. He is important because of his collection, which presented German chorales with texts translated into English. *A Collection of Divine Hymns Translated from the High Dutch: Together with their Proper Tunes and Thorough Bass* appeared in London in 1720. It was reissued in 1722 in an enlarged and altered form as *Psalmodia Germanica* and with an addition of a second part in 1732. (The edition noted by Robert Eitner was that of 1732. See his *Biographisch-bibliographisches Quellenlexicon,* Leipzig, 1899–1904.) See HERR JESU CHRIST DICH ZU UNS WEND ("O Jesus Christ, True Light of God").

Henry Eyster Jacobs, educator, author, and administrator; b. Gettysburg, Pa., Nov. 10, 1844; d. July 8, 1932.

The son of a minister, Henry Eyster Jacobs attended Gettysburg Academy (1853–57) and Pennsylvania College (now Gettysburg College) A.B., 1862; A.M., 1865). He received his D.D. in 1877 and L.L.D. in 1891 from Thiel College. Muhlenberg College conferred the S.T.D. on him in 1907.

After spending a year in the study of history and law, Jacobs became a tutor at Pennsylvania College (1864–67), principal at Thiel Hall (1868–70), professor of ancient languages (1880–81), and professor of Greek (1881–83). In 1883 he became professor of systematic theology in the Lutheran Theological Seminary, Mt. Airy, Pa., where he served as secretary of the faculty (1885–94), dean (1894–1920), and president (1920–27). At the end of his term as president he was succeeded by his son Charles Michael. In 1895 he lectured on Lutheran liturgics at Union Theological Seminary in New York.

Apart from numerous articles published in theological journals, he was co-editor (with J. A. W. Haas) of the *Lutheran Cyclopedia,* an editor of the *Documentary History of the Pennsylvania Ministerium,* an author of *Lutheran Movement in England* (1891), *History of the Lutheran Church in America* (American Church History Series, Vol. iv, 1893), *Elements of Religion* (1894), *Commentary on Romans* (1896), *Commentary on I Corinthians* (1897), *Life of Martin Luther* (1898), *German Emigration to Pennsylvania* (1899), *Summary of Christian Doctrine* (1905), and *Lincoln's Gettysburg World Message* (1920). He was also a translator of note and a contributor to periodicals. See "Lord Jesus Christ, We Humbly Pray."

Henry S. Jacobs, rabbi and educator; b. Kingston, Jamaica, 1827; d. New York City, Sept. 12, 1893.

Henry S. Jacobs studied with the Rev. N. Nathan in Kingston while he served as headmaster of the Jewish Free School there. As a young man he later became rabbi of the English and German Synagogue in the same city.

In 1853 he emigrated to the United States where he was elected rabbi of a Portuguese Congregation, Beth Shalome, in Richmond, Va. From 1858 to 1862 he lived in Charleston, S.C., where he served the Jewish congregation in the same capacity. He later held similar posts in other cities: Columbia, S.C.; Augusta, Ga.; and New Orleans (1866–73). In the latter city he made many friends and was elected one of the commanding officers of the Masonic Fraternity in the state of Louisiana. His eloquent speech and distinguished appearance gave him a distinction which commanded attention. While he worked in the South he was particularly successful in the administration of religious schools.

On March 4, 1876, Jacobs was installed as rabbi of Congregational B'nai Jeshurun in New York City for a term of office that commenced officially on January 1, 1877, and ended in 1893. For the use of that congregation he published, in 1889, a large musical work entitled *The Synagogue Service.* See "How Goodly Is Thy House."

Philip James, conductor, composer, and educator; b. Jersey City, N.J., May 17, 1890; d. Southampton, N.Y., Nov. 1, 1975.

Philip James attended public schools in New York City and the College of the City of New York. During World War I he served in the infantry and, after the armistice, conducted General Pershing's Headquarters Band. James was an instructor in the music department of Columbia University and head of the New York University music department from 1933 to 1955. He directed the Bamberger Symphony Orchestra for Station WOR from 1929 to 1936.

In 1927 James received the first prize offered by *The Homiletic Review* for a hymn tune and in 1932 his satirical suite *Station WGZBX* won a $500 National Broadcasting Company award. In a contest organized by the New York Philharmonic Symphony Society his *Bret Harte* overture (1937) received an honorable mention and was conducted by John Barbirolli. The Juilliard Foundation Publication Award went to his *Suite for Strings* and a prize offered by the New York Women's Symphony Orchestra to *Song of the Night*. See Paumanok ("All the Past We Leave Behind"), Tregaron ("And Have All the Bright Immensities"), and Cwmafan ("The Lone Wild Fowl").

J. Albert Jeffery, organist and choirmaster; b. Plymouth, England, Oct. 26, 1855; d. Brookline, Mass., June 4, 1929.

J. Albert Jeffery succeeded to his father's position as organist at St. Anne's Cathedral, Plymouth, when he was a boy of fourteen. He went abroad to perfect his playing under such masters as Karl Reinecke (Leipaig Conservatory), Franz Liszt (Weimar), and Ferdinand C. W. Praeger (Paris). At Leipzig he received an honorary doctorate after his graduation from the Conservatory of Music, a most unusual distinction. He arrived in the United States in 1876 and became a leading musician in Albany, N.Y., developing a chorus, taking charge of the music in St. Agnes School, and playing organ in the recently completed All Saints Cathedral. He left Albany in 1893 and settled in Yonkers, N.Y., where he played at the First Presbyterian Church, but later joined the staff of the New England Conservatory as a piano teacher. See Ancient of Days (same).

Stephen Jenks, singing master, composer, and compiler; b. New Canaan, Conn., 1772, d. Thompson, Ohio, June 5, 1856.

While Stephen Jenks was living at Ridgefield, Conn., his first book, *The New England Harmonist,* was published (Danbury, Conn. 1800). A thin volume of sixteen pages, it was expanded and republished within the year under the title *The Musical Harmonist.* Amos Doolittle engraved this enlarged edition but when it was republished in 1803 it was set in type. *The Delights of Harmony* was published in New Haven in 1804. It too was engraved by Doolittle of New Haven and contained tunes by the engraver, by Daniel Read, by Oliver Holden, and by Jenks himself. *The Delights of Harmony or The Norfolk Compiler,* printed by the Manns in Dedham, Mass., appeared in 1805. In *The Hartford Collection of Sacred Harmony* (1807) Jenks was assisted by Elijah Griswold and John C. Frisbee. *The Harmony of Zion, or the Union Compiler* was predominantly a collection of tunes by European composers though there were compositions by Jenks himself and by other Americans.

Such tune names as Norwalk, North Stamford, and Pound Ridge may recall singing classes held in Connecticut and nearby New York.

Little is known about Jenk's personal life. His first wife died in Ridgefield in 1800, leaving two sons. He had six children by his second wife, whom he married in Providence. He went to Thompsonville, Ohio, in 1829 where, as Metcalf tells us, he made drums and tambourines until his death. See Desolation ("Along the Banks"), Evening Shade ("The Day Is Past and Gone"), Liberty ("No More Beneath the Oppressive Hand"), and Variety ("Now Let Our Hearts Their Glory Wake").

Harriett Johnson, music critic; b. Minneapolis, Minn., Aug. 31.

Harriett Johnson studied music at the Juilliard School of Music. Among her teachers were Olga Samaroff Stokowski, Rubin Goldmark, and Bernard Wagenaar. She has been active as a lecturer and as music critic of the *New York Post* (from 1943). She has composed music for children (*Chuggy and the Blue Caboose, Pet of the Met*), *Five Instrumental Preludes for Five Plays by William Inge,* and *Three Questions* for Piano (1972). Her settings of Paul Engle's "Lord of Each Soul" and Austin Faricy's "Through Warmth and Light of Summer Skies" were commissioned by *American Hymns.*

Lockrem Johnson, pianist and composer; b. Davenport, Iowa, March 15, 1924.

Lockrem Johnson grew up in Spokane and Seattle, Wash., and was educated at the Cornish School of Music and the University of Washington, both in Seattle. He studied composition with George Frederick McKay and John Verrall.

Johnson has been active as teacher, conductor, and pianist. He has been an associate in music on the University of Washington faculty (1947–49), a pianist for the Seattle Symphony Orchestra (1948–51), musical director in the Eleanor King Dance Company, and a private teacher of piano and theory. From 1946 to 1951 he spent a great deal of time in concert work in the Pacific Northwest and Alaska. After holding a Guggenheim Fellowship in 1952–53, he became educational director for the Mercury Music Corporation (1953–54) in New York and later head of the Orchestra Department. He has also been head of the Catalogue and Production Department for the C. F. Peters Corporation.

Johnson has had a variety of experience, including extensive copying and editing work on a free-lance basis, conducting musical comedy in New England summer stock, and playing a calliope in a parade at Coney Island. Founder of Dow Music Publishers in 1954 he has since that time been its director.

His compositions include six piano sonatas, three violin sonatas, two violoncello sonatas, a chamber opera (*A Letter to Emily*), a dance-drama (*She*), piano works (*Chaconne, Ricercare, Vacation Waltzes*), and choral pieces (*A Suite of Noëls*).

In addition to his Guggenheim Fellowship, Johnson has received two first prizes and an honorable mention in National Federation of Music Clubs contests. His works have been played at Composers' Forums in New York and Philadelphia, in Europe, over the NBC, CBS, and ABC networks, and at several festivals including Ojai and Tanglewood. See his setting of Samuel Longfellow's " 'Tis Winter Now," composed for *American Hymns*.

Peter Johnson, organist, choir director, and educator; b. Trolla, Ljungby, Sweden, July 28, 1870; d. 1966.

Peter Johnson came to the United States at the age of 10. Red Wing, Minn., became his home. He studied music at the Northwestern School of Music in Minneapolis, graduating in 1900 with the highest honors in his class. After serving as organist in various churches in Minnesota, he became director of the school of music at Augustana College, Rock Island, Ill. Later he served for many years as organist and choir director of Gustavus Adolphus Church in St. Paul, Minn. He also assisted in editing the music of the Augustana Lutheran Hymnal of 1925, to which he contributed nine hymn tunes. See his CECILE ("The Twilight Shadows Round Me Fall").

Samuel Johnson, hymn writer and pastor; b. Salem, Mass., Oct. 10, 1822; d. North Andover, Mass., Feb. 19, 1882.

Samuel Johnson was educated at Harvard College (A.B., 1842) and the Harvard Divinity School (graduated, 1846), where he was a classmate of O. B. Frothingham, T. W. Higginson, and Samuel Longfellow, who became his intimate friend and collaborator. Both Longfellow and Johnson developed an interest in the custom inaugurated at Harvard in 1842–43 of composing original hymns for possible selection and inclusion in the historical *Record* of the Divinity School. Both had hymns in the *Record* of 1846. During their student days they compiled their first hymnal, *A Book of Hymns for Public and Private Devotion* (1846), to which a Supplement was added in 1848. In 1864 they published a revised edition, *Hymns of the Spirit.* Because it represented a liberal outlook and was characterized by a fresh viewpoint it marked an epoch in the development of American hymnody. To all these publications Johnson contributed original hymns of lasting merit.

Johnson, who looked with distaste upon all parties, sects, lodges, and other organized forms of social groups, organized a Free Church in Lynn, Mass., and never allowed it to affiliate with the Unitarian denomination. He served as its pastor from 1853 to 1870 when he retired and returned to his native Salem. He devoted most of his time there to lecturing and to literary pursuits. After his father's death in 1876 he moved, with a sister, to a farm at North Andover, where he died.

He was the author of *The Worship of Jesus in its Past and Present Aspects* (1868) and *Oriental Religions and Their Relation to Universal Religion* (1872). See "Father, in Thy Mysterious Presence Kneeling," "I Bless Thee, Lord, for Sorrows Sent," and "Life of Ages, Richly Poured."

Abner Jones, tenor, music teacher, and compiler; fl. early 19th cent.

Abner Jones must have lived for a time in Carroll, N.Y., since his son Darius was born there in 1815. Director of the New York Institute of Sacred Music in 1835, Jones evidently devoted special attention to the musical education of the young, for in May 1835, he presented the children of the Seventh Presbyterian Church in a concert designed to demonstrate their proficiency and to provide funds for continuing that work. Frank J. Metcalf speculates that he may have moved to Newark in June of the same year since an Abner D. Jones was second vice-president of the Handel and Haydn Society there in 1835. The fact that his son, Darius Eliot Jones (q.v.), was active in Newark lends some support to that view. However, in 1854 the father was described as a "professor of Music in New York."

Jones's publications include: *Psalmodia Evangelica* (New York, 1830); *Medodies of the Church* (1832), containing five original hymn tunes; and *Evening Melodies* (1834). *Church Melodies* (1832) was a collection of hymn texts. He also published a metric version of *The Psalms of David* (1854). In the preface he explains that he had been unable to publish the book earlier, partly because of lack of funds and partly because he had been overwhelmed by the death of two daughters. In 1860 he published *The Psalter Defined and Explained*. See HALL ("Onward, Onward, Men of Heaven") and PREPARATION ("Softly Now the Light of Day").

Darius Eliot Jones, musician, editor, and minister; b. Carroll, N.Y., Oct. 18, 1815; d. Aug. 10, 1881.

Darius Eliot Jones, the son of Abner Jones (q.v.), worked in New York City and Newark, N.J. When Mason Brothers of New York, for whom he had worked, decided to publish a periodical called *The Choral Advocate* in 1854, they chose Jones and George J. Webb as assistant editors under Lowell Mason. Jones was then music director of the Plymouth Church in Brooklyn where John Zundel (q.v.) was organist. When Henry Ward Beecher, the pastor, decided that a new hymnal was needed in his church, he turned to Jones. The resulting volume was published in 1851 as *Temple Melodies*. In it Abner Jones was represented by six tunes and Darius Eliot Jones by two, one of which was STOCKWELL ("Father, Hear the Prayer We Offer," q.v.), his most famous tune, although it had previously appeared in 1850 in Lowell Mason's *New Carmina Sacra*. *Temple Melodies* was the first hymnal used by Congregational churches which provided the texts with tunes.

Darius Eliot Jones later moved to Chicago where he edited the *Congregational Herald*. He decided to prepare himself for the ministry, attended Iowa College, and after graduation became the pastor of churches at Columbus City and Newton Center, Iowa. He resigned in 1863 to become treasurer of the Iowa General Association. He worked for the American Bible Association and still later served his alma mater, Iowa (later Grinnell) College as agent. Although he did not accept another pastorate, he was to serve a number of churches within the state as interim minister. In 1869 he published *Songs for the New Life* which contained eighteen of his tunes.

Adoniram Judson, pioneer missionary; b. Malden, Mass., Aug. 9, 1788; d. at sea, April 12, 1850.

Adoniram Judson studied for the ministry at Andover Theological Seminary. After reading Claudius Buchanan's *Star of the East,* based on a sermon delivered in Bristol, England, in 1809, he decided to devote himself to foreign missionary work. On the voyage to Calcutta his religious beliefs were altered and he became a Baptist on his arrival in 1812. Because of the East India Company's opposition to his work in Calcutta, Judson went to Rangoon, Burma. The Judsons and his medical colleague, Dr. Price, were in Ava when the news of the capture of Rangoon by English troops reached that place. Judson and Dr. Price were imprisoned and survived only because Mrs. Judson went to the prison every day with food. Worn out by her exertions, Mrs. Judson died in 1826. After his release in 1827, Judson continued his work at Maulmein. He married Sarah Hall Boardman in 1834. By 1845 her health had deteriorated and they sailed for the United States, but she died off the island of St. Helena. In 1846 Judson married Emily Chubbuck as his third wife and returned with her to Rangoon.

His main literary work was the translation of the Bible into Burmese. He wrote a number of hymns which found their way into Baptist usage. See "Come Holy Spirit, Dove Divine," and "Our Father, God."

Sarah Hall Judson, Baptist missionary and poet; b. Alstead, N.H., Nov. 4, 1803; d. near St. Helena, Sept. 1, 1845.

Sarah Hall's family moved to Salem, Mass., where she joined the First Baptist Church. Her acquaintance with George Dana Boardman began after he read one of her poems, and in 1825 they were married. They went as missionaries to India where he died in 1831. Three years later she married Adoniram Judson (q.v.) and continued missionary work with him. After eleven years of this service, Mrs. Judson's health steadily declined, and the family set sail for home on April 26, 1845. On the voyage she seemed to be somewhat better, but a final relapse ended in her death off the island of St. Helena, where she was buried.

Mrs. Judson had written verse from her thirteenth year, at which age she rendered David's lament over Saul into verse. Later she rewrote that poem and included it in her volume *Life.* Mrs. Judson's biography was written after her death by Emily Chubbuck Judson ("Fanny Forester"), who became Dr. Judson's third wife. See "Proclaim the Lofty Praise."

Frank Kasschau, organist, choral director, and teacher; b. New York City, 1884; d. Ridgewood, N.J., April 6, 1944.

Frank Kasschau was associated with the Bridgeport, Conn., Oratorio Society and the Orpheus Club of Newark, N.J. He also served as organist in churches in Brooklyn and Ridgewood. See his BROOKLYN ("The City, Lord, Where Thy Dear Life").

Benjamin Keach, evangelist, pastor, and hymn writer; b. Stoke-Hammond, Buckinghamshire, England; d. Horsleydown, Southwark, England, 1704.

Religiously inclined from early years, Benjamin Keach joined a Baptist church while he was still very young and at eighteen began to preach. For ten years he was an evangelist in towns throughout Buckinghamshire. He experienced considerable hardship and was often persecuted for being a Baptist and a Nonconformist. When in 1664 he published *The Child's Instructor: or a New and Easy Primer,* he was brought before a Lord Chief Justice, sentenced to a fine, imprisonment, and the pillory. In 1668 he went to London to become pastor of a Particular Baptist Church, which first met in private houses and finally moved to Horsleydown, Southwark.

Keach introduced "conjoint singing" in his London congregation. Although he did not visit America himself, Elias Keach, the only son of his first marriage, came to Pennsylvania where he established two churches and may have introduced the singing of hymns among Baptists in this country. It is certain that a group of Welsh Baptists in Delaware added an article on the duty of singing psalms to the Confession of Faith which they adopted in 1716.

Keach wrote a great many hymns. A collection of nearly three hundred, entitled *Spiritual Melody,* was published in 1691. At his death he left a total of forty-two published works, in addition to prefaces and introductions written for books by others. See "How Glorious Are the Morning Stars."

Bradley Keeler, expatriate American pianist and composer; d. Nov. 11, 1933.

Bradley Keeler lived in Lausanne, Switzerland, but spent time in Paris and made short trips to the United States. He was an intimate friend of Louis Benson, the distinguished hymnologist, some of whose texts he set to music. See VITTEL WOODS ("O Love That

Lights the Eastern Sky"). He established a trust fund at Yale University for the education of young composers.

Matthias Keller, German-American musician; b. Ulm, Germany, March 20, 1813; d. Boston, Oct. 13, 1875.

Matthias Keller is best remembered for his prize-winning AMERICAN HYMN ("Angel of Peace, Thou Hast Wandered Too Long") (q.v.), originally composed for his own text but later sung after the Civil War in Patrick S. Gilmore's Peace Jubilee of 1869 to the "Ode to Peace" which Oliver Wendell Holmes wrote for the occasion. Keller was trained as a musician in Stuttgart and Vienna. After playing first violin in the Royal Chapel in the latter city, he became an army bandmaster for a period of seven years. When he first arrived in the United States in 1846 he became a violinist in the Philadelphia theaters. In 1807 he entered the field of violin-making with his "Patent Steam Violin Manufactory." He conducted English opera in New York for a time, then settled in Boston where he died. Most of his numerous compositions were songs and pieces in dance form like the *Ravel Polka* (1846). The text of the AMERICAN HYMN was his own. He also wrote *A Collection of Poems,* published in 1874.

Johannes Kelpius, hymnologist, musician, and mystic; b. Transylvania, Germany, 1673 (?); d. in Pennsylvania, 1708.

Johannes Kelpius was educated at the University of Altdorf near Nuremberg, graduating with honors in 1689. During the course of his studies Kelpius became a follower of Philip Jacob Spener, founder of the Pietists. Later, in London, he met Jane Leads, the head of the Philadelphists, another mystical sect. Members of such groups were opposed for their unorthodox views, and Kelpius decided to go to Pennsylvania where greater religious liberty might be enjoyed. With some forty followers he sailed on the *Sara Maria,* landing at Philadelphia on June 23, 1694. The next day he and his followers went to Germantown, where German emigrants were already settled under the leadership of Francis Daniel Pastorius. Kelpius and his Theosophists acquired a tract of 175 acres on the highest point of which was a log house known as the Tabernacle. Here the Hermits of the Wissahickon lived for ten years, preaching, teaching, and cultivating a large garden, probably the first attempt to grow medicinal herbs in America. Kelpius tried to unite the German sects in Pennsylvania. He and his followers seem to have been the first to own an organ and other instruments for use in musical services. Among his manuscript hymns is "Ich liebe Jesus noch allein" (q.v.).

William Kethe, writer of metrical versions of the Psalms; fl. 16th cent.

Little is known about the life of William Kethe, who may have been Scots by birth. He was among those who fled from England when Queen Mary ascended the throne, for the *Brieff discours off the troubles begonne at Frankford* (1575) places him there in 1555 and at Geneva in 1557. In 1558 he went to Basel, Strassburg, and elsewhere to confer with English refugees, returning the following year to report their views. In addition the *Discours* states that he was at Havre with the forces commanded by the Earl of Warwick in 1563 and "in the north" in 1569. Kethe was settled as rector of Childe Okeford, near Blandford, in 1561, retaining this post until c.1593, although it is not clear whether or when he was actually in residence there.

The twenty-five psalm versions by Kethe included in the Anglo-Genevan psalter of 1561 were retained in the Scottish psalter of 1564–65, but only nine were chosen for the English psalter of 1562. Kethe's rendering of Psalm 100 was added in 1565. This psalm was the only one transferred to the Scottish psalter in 1650. A version of Psalm 104 is sometimes found in greatly altered form in modern hymnals. One of Kethe's sermons preached before the Sessions at Blandford, January 17, 1571, was printed by John Day in the same year and dedicated to Ambrose, Earl of Warwick.

Kethe's translations of the Psalms in the psalter of 1561 had been made at Geneva, with foreign models before him. All but five had a tune, and all except one of them had been borrowed from the Geneva psalter. This edition brought into English use four celebrated psalm tunes: OLD HUNDREDTH, OLD 104TH, OLD 113TH, and OLD 134TH, better known as ST. MICHAEL. See "Such as in God the Lord Do Trust" and "Thy Mercies, Lord, to Heaven Reach."

Clive Harold Kilgore, accountant and musician; b. 1889.

Clive Harold Kilgore studied piano, organ, theory, and composition in Pittsburgh. He was organist and choirmaster for the Zion Church in Corapolis, Pa., and worked with the Mendelssohn Choir in Pittsburgh. A composer of anthems and choral works, he also composed two Lenten cantatas. See PAX ("God of Peace, In Peace Preserve Us").

Jacob Kimball, singing master; b. Topsfield, Mass., Feb. 22, 1761; d. there Feb. 6, 1826.

The son of a musical blacksmith who was chosen to "set ye psalms and sit in ye elder's seat," Jacob Kimball marched in 1775 as a drummer boy in a Massachusetts militia regiment (May 2 to October 2). After graduating from Harvard (1780) he read law. The Salem pastor and diarist William Bentley noted (December 7, 1795) that Kimball "intended to set up as a lawyer in Maine." However, music teaching and composing were to be his real work. Although his talents were recognized, he was unable to maintain himself in his later years and he died in the poor-house in his native town.

Kimball published *The Rural Harmony* (Exeter, N.H., 1793) and *The Essex Harmony* (Exeter, N.H., 1800). His version of Psalm 65, beginning "Thy praise, O God, in Zion waits," was included in Jeremy Belknap's *Sacred Poetry* (Boston, 1795) and is reprinted here to the author's STONEHAM. See also his STOCKHOLM ("Ah! Lovely Appearance of Death!"), PLAINFIELD ("The Stately Structures of This Earth"), and INVITATION ("Who Here Can Cast His Eyes Abroad").

J. King, editor; fl. early 19th cent.

J. King was a coeditor of *The Sacred Harp* with Benjamin Franklin White. A number of tunes are still credited to him in the *Original Sacred Harp* of 1936. He is said to have died shortly after the first edition appeared in 1844. However, Absalom Ogletree, a former pupil of White, called King a fine singer and stated that he had met him in Hamilton, Ga., in 1850. See SAINTS BOUND FOR HEAVEN ("Our Bondage It Shall End"), credited jointly to King and William Walker.

George Kingsley, hymn tune composer and compiler; b. Northampton, Mass., July 7, 1811; d. there March 14, 1884.

Through his own efforts George Kingsley acquired a knowledge of the technique of music and learned to play both the organ and the piano. By the time he was eighteen he was established as an organist in the Old South Church and the Hollis Street Church in Boston. For ten years he taught music at Girard College in Philadelphia, where he also directed the teaching of public school music.

Kingsley, who began to write hymn tunes as early as 1838, published a number of music books, some with Lowell Mason (q.v.).

Beginning with the *Sunday School Singing Book* (1832) he compiled ten music books by 1865, among them: *The Harmonist* (1833), *The Social Choir* (1836), *The Sacred Choir* (1st ed., 1838), *The Harp of David* (1844), *The Young Ladies' Harp* (1847), *Templi Carmina* (1853), and *The Juvenile Choir* (1865). His three-volume series, *The Social Choir*, has been called one of the best collections of its kind ever made.

Kingsley spent his later years in Northampton, where his music library was given to the Forbes Library. See WARE ("Complete in Thee, No Work of Mine"), FERGUSON ("Down to the Sacred Wave"), FREDERICK ("I Would Not Live Alway"), WEBSTER ("The Ransomed Spirit to Her Home"), TAPPAN ("There Is an Hour of Peaceful Rest"), and HEBER ("Thou Grace Divine, Encircling All").

George Kirbye, English composer of madrigals; d. Bury St. Edmunds, Oct. 1634.

George Kirbye (Kirby) was probably a native of Suffolk, where he apparently spent a great deal of his life. He contributed more settings of tunes to Thomas East's *Whole Booke of Psalmes* (1592) than any of the other composers represented except John Farmer. In 1597 he himself published what he referred to as the "first fruites of my poore knowledge in Musicke," a set of madrigals (24) for four, five, and six voices. The volume was dedicated to two of the daughters of Sir Robert Jermyn of Rushbrooke where Kirby lived as music master or musician. In 1601 he wrote a six-part madrigal for the *Triumphs of Oriana,* a collection of madrigals dedicated to Queen Elizabeth. See his arrangements of OLD 148TH ("Blessed Is Everyone") and PATER NOSTER or OLD 112TH ("O Lord, Thou Hast Been to the Land").

Mrs. Joseph F. Knapp, composer of Sunday School and gospel hymns; b. March 8, 1839; d. July 10, 1909.

At the age of sixteen Phoebe Palmer married Joseph Fairchild Knapp, a prominent Sunday School worker who became a successful businessman and the founder of the Metropolitan Life Insurance Company. She published more than five-hundred gospel songs. In addition to *Notes of Joy* she joined Bishop Simpson in compiling *Bible School Songs* (1873). One of her best-known compositions is a setting of "Blessed Assurance, Jesus Is Mine" (q.v.) by her friend Fanny J. Crosby.

Shepherd Knapp, Presbyterian minister and author; b. New York City, Sept. 8, 1873; d. Jan. 11, 1946.

Shepherd Knapp graduated from Columbia College in 1894 and earned his B.D. at Yale in 1897. During his life he held three pastorates: First Congregational Church in Southington, Conn. (1897–1900), Brick Presbyterian Church, New York City (assistant pastor, 1901–03), and Central Congregational Church, Worcester, Mass. (1908–36).

Shepherd Knapp was the author of a *History of the Brick Presbyterian Church* (1908), *On the Edge of the Storm* (1921), *Old Joe and Other Vesper Stories* (1922), and *The Liberated Bible: The Old Testament* (1941). See "Lord God of Hosts" and "Not Only Where God's Free Winds Blow," whose text appears both with the tune ETERNAL LIGHT by Kenneth E. Runkel and also with music composed by Edward Lawton for *American Hymns*.

William Knapp, parish clerk and composer; b. Wareham, England, 1698; d. Dorsetshire, 1768.

William Knapp may have been of German descent. Active in rural centers (he was called "a country psalm singer"), he may have been the organist in Wareham, where he was born, and in Poole, the scene of his later activities. Knapp was certainly the parish clerk of the Church of St. James, Poole, for thirty-nine years. His *A Sett of New Psalms and Anthems in four parts . . . and an Introduction to Psalmody after a plain and familiar manner* dates from 1738. His *New Church Melody and a sett of Anthems, Psalms and Hymns in four parts* followed in 1753. His tune ALL SAINTS ("Thrice Welcome, First and Best of Days") or WAREHAM has been sung to the present.

James D. Knowles, editor, minister, and educator; b. Providence, R.I., July 6, 1798; d. Newton, Mass., May 9, 1838.

James D. Knowles learned the printing trade as a boy, displayed talent as a writer, and was joint editor of *The Rhode Island American* when only twenty-one. After his baptism in 1820 he decided to prepare himself for the ministry, entering the Theological Seminary in Philadelphia, continuing his studies at Columbian College, Washington, D.C., and graduating with highest honors in 1824. In 1825 he accepted a call to the Second Baptist Church in Boston. There he remained until 1832 when the precarious state of his health caused him to relinquish the post to become professor in the Newton Theological Institution. He was only forty when he was struck down by smallpox. His hymn "O God, though Countless Worlds of Light" (q.v.) appeared in 1843 in *The Psalmist.*

Johann Balthasar König, choral conductor and compiler; b. Waltershausen, near Gotha, Germany, Jan. 1691; d. March 1758.

Johann König joined the town musicians of Frankfort-on-the-Main in 1703, presumably as a singing boy, then became a member of the group under the direction of Telemann from 1711 to 1721. In addition he was choir director in the Church of St. Catherine in 1718 or 1719. After serving under Telemann's successor Bodinius (1721–27), he became the music director, continuing at St. Catherine's and also taking charge of the music at the Barefoot Friars' Church (*Barfüsser-kirche*) and teaching vocal music at the Gymnasium. His choirs were an important factor in the cultural life of the town since he gave many performances of such important choral works as cantatas and oratorios. His *Harmonischer Lieder-Schatz, oder Allgemeines evangelischen Choral-Buch* (1738) is said to have been the most comprehensive collection of its century. See the melody Wo IST WOHL EIN SÜSSER LEBEN ("Reine Liebe Sucht Nicht Sich Selber").

Charles P. Krauth, Lutheran pastor and leader; b. Martinsburg, W.Va., March 17, 1823; d. Philadelphia, Pa., Jan. 2, 1883.

The son of a Lutheran clergyman, Charles P. Krauth graduated from Gettysburg College and Seminary, was ordained as a pastor, and soon came to be recognized as one of the foremost leaders of conservative Lutheranism in the United States as well as a scholar and theologian of outstanding ability. In 1864, when the Lutheran Seminary in Philadelphia was founded, Krauth was appointed professor of dogmatics. He also taught philosophy at the University of Pennsylvania. Later he became a leader in the organization of the General Council, a federation of Lutheran synods, and served as its first president from 1870 to 1880. For a long period he was editor of *The Lutheran* and *The Lutheran Church Review.* Among his publications was *The Conservative Reformation and its Theology* (1872). His translations "The Happy Christmas Comes Once More" (after Nicolai F. S. Grundtvig) and "Wide Open Are Thy Hands" (q.v.) (after

Bernard of Clairvaux) are retained in the Lutheran *Service Book and Hymnal* of 1958.

August Kreissman, singer, teacher, and conductor; b. Saxony, 1823; d. 1879.

August Kreissman was born in Saxony and returned to spend his last years there. His long period of activity in Boston, from 1849 to 1876, contributed to the advancement of music in this country. His compositions in A. N. Johnson's *The Handel Collection of Church Music* (Boston, 1854) included hymn tunes and an anthem, "Sing, O Heavens." He was the conductor of the Orpheus Club of Boston. See ROCKPORT ("I Bless Thee, Lord, for Sorrows Sent").

Caspar Kriebel, Schwenkfelder hymn writer; fl. mid-18th cent.

Nothing is known of the life of Caspar Kriebel except that he apparently came to Pennsylvania with the forty emigrating families of Schwenkfelders who arrived in Philadelphia on September 24, 1734. To their first hymnbook, printed in Pennsylvania by Christopher Saur (1762), he contributed seven hymns. See "Nun schlaff du liebes Kindelein."

Johann Christoph Kühnau, cantor, composer, and compiler; b. Volkstadt near Eisleben, Feb. 10, 1735; d. Berlin, Oct. 13, 1805.

A town musician in Aschersleben taught Johann Christoph Kühnau music. Kühnau prepared for a teaching career by attending an institute in Klosterbergen and was appointed to the polytechnic high school (*Realschule*) in Berlin. He used this opportunity to complete his musical education by studying composition with Johann Philipp Kirnberger. After teaching in Trinity School he was appointed cantor of Trinity Church in 1788. Performances of major choral works by his choir were an important feature of the cultural life of Berlin. See his ZEUCH MEINEN GEIST ("My Soul Before Thee Prostrate Lies").

John C. Kunze, pastor, translator, and editor; b. Artern, near Mansfeld, Germany; d. New York City, July 24, 1807.

John C. Kunze was chiefly responsible for the publication of *A Hymn and Prayer-Book, For the Use of Such Lutheran Churches as Use the English Language* (New York, 1795), the first American Lutheran hymnbook in English. It contained the earliest surviving translation of Luther's catechism made in this country. Moreover, the appendix contained original hymns, perhaps more remarkable for their quaintness than for their poetic qualities, by Kunze as well as by his associates John F. Ernst (q.v.) and George Strebeck (q.v.).

Kunze attended the University of Leipzig, from which he graduated in three years. He then taught classics for three more years while he studied theology. He was persuaded to accept a post in Pennsylvania, and after his ordination in 1770 he set sail for Philadelphia in company with two sons of Henry Melchoir Mühlenberg, the founder of the Lutheran Church in America. He became assistant pastor of the Church of St. Michael and Zion in Philadelphia, succeeding Mühlenberg as first pastor when the latter resigned in 1776. He was active in establishing a school for the education of candidates for the Lutheran ministry and he also served as professor of German at the University of Pennsylvania and as official translator to Congress from 1775. He and his family lived in Philadelphia during the difficult period when it was occupied by British troops during the Revolution.

In 1784 Kunze was called to New York City, where he served for twenty-three years as pastor of Christ Church, which then stood at Frankfort and Allen Streets. He became a trustee of Columbia University and professor of German and Oriental Languages. New York's Christopher Street still bears his name, for the country home of the Kunze family was located there. Kunze pioneered in conducting the Lutheran church service in English because he realized that the church's growth depended on it, and he trained the first Lutheran pastors in this country. Although he was buried in a Lutheran cemetery on Carmine Street in New York, his final resting place is in a vault of the Lorillard family at St. Mark's. He left a library in many languages and a valuable collection of coins now owned by the New York Historical Society. See "Yoke Soft and Dear."

H. Glenn Lanier, Methodist minister; b. Welcome, N.C.

H. Glenn Lanier received his A.B. degree from High Point College in 1945 and his B.D. degree from Duke University Divinity

School in 1949. He began to write poetry at the age of thirteen and is the author of some 400 poems and hymn texts, two of which, including "O Christ of Bethlehem" (q.v.) have been honored by the Hymn Society of America.

Sidney Lanier, poet, flutist, and composer; b. Macon, Ga., Feb. 3, 1842; d. Lynn, N.C., Sept. 7, 1881.

Sidney Lanier was of Huguenot descent on his father's side, Scottish and American on his mother's. As a child he was passionately fond of music. At the age of fourteen he entered Oglethorpe College, where, after graduation, he held a tutorship. From 1861 to 1865 he served in the Civil War, returning home with broken health. In 1867 he took a first novel to New York. He went to Texas for his health in 1872. In 1873 he secured an engagement as first flutist in the Peabody concerts in Baltimore.

Gradually he did more writing and studying. In 1879 he was made a lecturer on English literature at Johns Hopkins University. In 1880 he published *The Science of English Verse,* which had been preceded by a small volume of verse in 1877. *The English Novel* was published posthumously in 1883, as were the final edition of his *Poems* (1884), *Letters: 1866–1881* (1899), and *Shakspere and His Forerunners* (1902). A poem, "Into the Woods My Master Went" (q.v.), has been used occasionally as a hymn.

Orlando di Lasso, composer; b. Mons, Hainaut, 1532; d. Munich, June 14, 1594.

When Orlando di Lasso (or Orlandus Lassus) was a choir boy at St. Nicholas Church, the beauty of his voice attracted so much attention that he was thrice kidnapped. When he was twelve years old, Ferdinand Gonzaga, Viceroy of Sicily, obtained permission from his parents to take him into his service at Palermo and later at Milan. After 1548 he served in the courts of other Italian noblemen and in 1552 was named Maestro di Cappella of San Giovanni Laterano, a great honor for such a young man. He later traveled in France and in 1554 visited England, shortly after Philip of Spain had married Mary Tudor. Settling in Antwerp later in that year he published a book of madrigals and motets. In 1556 he was invited with other Belgians to the court of Duke Albert V of Bavaria. At first director of Albert's chamber music, he later succeeded Ludwig Daser as chapel master in 1562, remaining at that post until his death.

The rest of his life was spent in Munich, save for trips to Rome to obtain singers (1562, 1571, 1574, 1578, and 1585) and to Paris in 1571. Lasso was so much appreciated by the Catholic world that he was ennobled by the Emperor Maximilian II (December 7, 1570) and made a Chevalier of the Golden Spur by Pope Gregory XIII (April 6, 1571).

Orlando di Lasso represents the culmination of the era of polyphony in the Netherlands; his mastery of both sacred and secular musical forms made him one of the most versatile and international musicians of his time. The total number of his compositions amounted to over 2,000. His musical curiosity was great; although a Catholic he set three of Clément Marot's metrical versions of the psalms which had been adopted by the Huguenots. The setting of the De Profundis melody ("I Spread Out Unto Thee My Hands") (q.v.) (Psalm 130: Du fond de ma pensée) is first found in *Le Premier Livre de chansons à quatre parties . . . Composées par M. Orlando di Lassus, Maistre de la Chapelle de l'excelentissime & illustrissime Duc de Bauière.* Anvers, 1564.

Mary Artemisia Lathbury, writer and editor; b. Manchester, N.Y., Aug. 10, 1841; d. Oct. 20, 1913.

Mary Artemisia Lathbury was the daughter of a Methodist minister and the sister of two brothers ordained to the ministry. At an early age she developed a talent for composing verses and illustrating them. Later she became widely known as a contributor to children's periodicals. In 1874 Dr. John H. Vincent, who at that time was Secretary of the Methodist Sunday School Union, engaged her as his assistant in the editorial department. Through her work with him she became an important partner in promoting the Chautauqua Movement. The Chautauqua Assembly at Lake Chautauqua, N.Y., was located on the site of an old Methodist camp-meeting ground. The programs there, instituted under Bishop Vincent's direction, gave rise to "Chautauqua," the series of summer lectures and concerts given in many major communities in the late nineteenth and early twentieth centuries.

At Bishop Vincent's request she wrote two hymns in 1877 for use at Chautauqua, "Break Thou the Bread of Life" (q.v.) and "Day Is Dying in the West" (q.v.).

Calvin W. Laufer, church musician and pastor; b. Brodheads-
ville, Pa., April 6, 1874; d. Philadelphia, Pa., Sept. 21, 1938.

Calvin W. Laufer was educated at Franklin and Marshall College
(B.A., 1897; M.A., 1900) and trained at Union Theological Seminary
(1900). He was ordained to the Presbyterian ministry and held pastorates at the Steinway Reformed Church, Long Island City, N.Y.
(1900–05); and the First Presbyterian Church, West Hoboken, N.J.
(1905–14).

Appointed a field representative of the Presbyterian Board of
Publication and Sunday School Work (1914–24) he later became
field representative of the Presbyterian Board of Christian Education (1925–38) and assistant editor of that denomination's musical
publications (1925–38). He was associate editor of the new Presbyterian *Hymnal* (1933) and the *Handbook to the Hymnal* (1935). Laufer
was long associated with Dr. Louis F. Benson (q.v.) in his work on
hymnology. Since he was musical he wrote tunes as well as texts for
hymns.

Keynotes of Optimism (1911), *The Incomparable Christ* (1914), *The
Bible—Story and Content* (1924), *Junior Church School Hymnal* (1927),
Songs for Men (1928), *The Church School Hymnal for Youth* (1928),
Primary Worship and Music (1930), *Hymn Lore* (1932), and *When the
Little Child Wants to Sing* (1935) are books that Laufer wrote or edited
during his lifetime. See HALL ("Take Thou Our Minds, Dear Lord")
and FIELD ("We Thank Thee, Lord").

Andrew Law, singing master and pioneer in the use of shape
notes; b. Milford, Conn., March 21, 1749; d. Cheshire, Conn.,
July 13, 1821.

In his "Old Time Music and Musicians" (*Connecticut Quarterly*,
1895, 1, 371) N. H. Allen states that by 1770, Andrew Law was teaching flute and violin. He attended Rhode Island College (now Brown
University), studied theology, and was licensed to preach in 1776.
He did preach in Chesterfield, Mass., in 1777. He had already
taught singing as an undergraduate, and this rather than the ministry was to be his occupation. He taught singing classes in New England, Pennsylvania, New Jersey, and Maryland.

Law had conservative but high aims for American church music.
He opposed the use of instruments in church and disapproved of
the fuguing tune. Although his collections include American tunes,
he favored the works of minor English church composers. He was
an industrious compiler, and the complex history of his publications
may be studied in Richard A. Crawford's *Andrew Law: American*

Psalmodist. The earliest, *Select Harmony,* appeared in Cheshire, Conn., in 1778. *A Select Number of Plain Tunes Adapted to Congregational Worship* (1781) was a thin pamphlet which might be bound in at the end of a psalm book. Law's most ambitious collection was *The Art of Singing* (1794), which consisted of three parts: *Musical Primer, Christian Harmony,* and *Musical Magazine.* They were sold separately, combined in various ways, and frequently reprinted.

Law claimed that by 1786 he had worked out a system of notation, in which a note head of a given shape was associated with the syllables mi, fa, sol, la, and with the sounds they represented. However, his application for the copyright for the 1803 edition of his *Musical Primer* was filed after the publication of *The Easy Instructor* by William Little and William Smith. (Law calls the 1803 edition the fourth, but it is really the third.) The two books use the same shapes for the note heads (square, oval, diamond, and triangle), but there were differences in associating the shapes with the syllables. In Smith and Little the notes are appropriately placed on a five-line staff, while in Law the notes follow on the same level, thus losing the advantage of associating a higher or lower pitch with a higher or lower position on the staff. Law defended his four-character system against those who wished to use seven characters, one for each note of the scale. However, when he published his *Art of Playing the Organ and Pianoforte* (1809) he conceded that a system with seven characters, which he describes, is better suited to keyboard instruments.

Law did not associate his name with any of the tunes he published, but ARCHDALE and BUNKER HILL ("Why should Vain Mortals Tremble") (q.v.) are generally considered to be his.

Henry Lawes, singer and composer; b. Dinton, Wiltshire, England, Jan. 5, 1595; d. London, Oct. 21, 1662.

Henry Lawes received his musical education from John Cooper (Coperario). On January 1, 1626, he was sworn as an epistler of the Chapel Royal and, in the following November, he became one of the gentlemen of the Chapel. He later assumed the position of clerk of the cheque. In 1633 he composed the music for Thomas Carew's masque *Coelum Britanicum,* performed at court, and in 1634 the music for Milton's masque *Comus,* which was performed at Ludlow Castle on Michaelmas night with Lawes acting the part of the Attendant Spirit.

A Paraphrase Upon the Psalms of David by George Sandys, with music by Lawes dates from 1637, and in 1648, on the occasion of the death of William Lawes, his elder brother, he published *Choice Psalmes put into Musick for Three Voices . . . Composed by Henry and*

William Lawes, Brothers and Servants to His Majestie. The first thirty compositions in the volume were by Henry, followed by "A Pastoral Elegie to the memorie of my deare brother William Lawes" and other memorial pieces.

Comedies and Tragi-Comedies, with other poems by Mr. William Cartwright, the Ayres and Songs set by Mr. Henry Lawes, which was published in London (1651), contained no music, but some of his songs appeared in John Playford's *Select Musical Ayres* of 1652, 1653, and 1659, and in another collection, *The Treasury of Music* (1669).

During the Civil War and the Interregnum Lawes apparently suffered financial losses, but at the Restoration in 1660 he was reinstated to his court appointments. For the coronation of Charles II he composed the anthem *Zadok the Priest*. Fragments of eight or ten other anthems by Lawes have been found in an old choir book of the Chapel Royal and the words of several of his anthems exist in Clifford's *Divine Services and Anthems* (1664).

Henry Lawes was highly esteemed by his contemporaries both as composer and performer. Milton praised him in both capacities, and Herrick regarded him as one of the renowned singers of the time. See PSALM 9 ("As Spring the Winter Doth Succeed"), PSALM 10 ("The Boundary of Jehovah"), and PSALM 34 ("O Heaven Indulge"), all composed for the George Sandys *Paraphrase* of 1637.

William Lawes, composer; b. Salisbury, England,
May 1, 1602; d. Chester, England, Sept. 1645.

William Lawes, like his brother, Henry, received his musical education from John Cooper (Coperario). A member of the choir of Chichester Cathedral until 1602, he was sworn a gentleman of the Chapel Royal on January 1, 1602/03. He resigned his place in May 1611, but was readmitted in October of the same year. Lawes joined Simon Ives in composing music for James Shirley's masque *The Triumph of Peace,* presented at Whitehall on Candlemas Night, 1633/34, and afterwards given in the Merchant Taylors' Hall. He also wrote the music for Davenant's masque *The Triumph of the Prince D'Amour,* performed in 1635 in the Middle Temple.

At the outbreak of the Civil War Lawes took up arms for the King and was shot at the siege of Chester. In spite of his distinguished position, none of his works were published during his lifetime. They include songs, catches, suites, and fancies for viols, as well as settings of psalms which appeared posthumously in *Choice Psalms* (1648) compiled by his brother Henry. See his setting of "Judah in Exile Wanders."

Edward Lawton, organist, conductor, and educator; b. Newport, R.I., Aug. 30, 1911; d. Berkeley, Calif., Feb. 21, 1967.

A graduate of the Roxbury Latin School, Edward Lawton attended Harvard, graduating with a B.A. in 1934. During his undergraduate days he was also active as organist and choir director. As a John Knowles Paine Fellow he studied composition with Francesco Malipiero in Venice and was awarded a certificate in musical composition by the Liceo Benedetto Marcello. Appointed as assistant in the New York Public Library in 1936, he went to the Berkeley campus of the University of California in the same year as instructor. He became conductor of the University Chorus in 1939, performing a wide range of choral works, notably those of the twentieth century. The appearances of the University Chorus with the San Francisco Orchestra were memorable. Lawton was promoted to assistant professor in 1940, to associate professor in 1946, and in 1952 to professor. He played an important part in the development of choral music in California through his own activity as a conductor, by developing student conductors, and by serving as a judge in choral competitions. See the setting for Shepherd Knapp's "Not Only Where God's Free Winds Blow," which was composed for *American Hymns.*

Emma Lazarus, poet and translator; b. New York City, July 22, 1849; d. there Nov. 19, 1887.

Born of wealthy Jewish parents, Emma Lazarus was educated by private tutors. Very precocious, she published in 1866 a volume, *Poems and Translations,* that was reissued with additions in 1867. Though it was privately printed, it attracted the attention of Ralph Waldo Emerson (q.v.), who invited her to spend a week at his home in Concord. They kept up a lifelong correspondence and she dedicated her second book, *Admetus and Other Poems* (1871), to him. In 1874 she published her first prose work, *Alide: An Episode of Goethe's Life,* and in 1876, a poetic drama, *The Spagnoletto.* She became an active contributor to periodicals, especially *Scribner's Monthly* and *Lippincott's Magazine.* In 1881 her *Poems and Ballads of Heinrich Heine* appeared.

Although she had been trained in Jewish history, she considered herself an internationally minded writer until the persecution of Russian Jews from 1879 to 1883. When the refugees began arriving at Ward's Island, she led in organizing efforts for their relief. In 1882 she published *Songs of a Semite* and in 1883 she wrote a noteworthy article, "The Jewish Problem," for *Century Magazine.* Other articles followed. Her sonnet to the Statue of Liberty was chosen to be placed on its pedestal in 1886.

At the height of her powers she was stricken with cancer. She died at the age of thirty-eight. See "Kindle the Taper."

Olav Lee, pastor and educator; b. Trysil, Norway, May 21, 1859; d. May 22, 1943.

After studying for a year at the Hamar Normal School, Olav Lee came to the United States in 1877. In 1878 he entered Lutheran College, where he spent five years, receiving the A.B. and A.M. degrees. Lee then attended Lutheran Seminary for two years, Capital University for a year, and the University of Wisconsin for a year. In 1886 he began pastoral work in Northwood, N.D., and remained there until 1890. He later served in several towns in Minnesota and Wisconsin. From 1890 to 1894 he taught at Augustana College and then at St. Olaf College. From 1889 to 1908 he worked for the deaf and for general charities. He was the translator for the St. Olaf Choir Series. To the *Concordia Hymnal* of 1933 Lee contributed an original hymn, "How Blessed Is the Host in White," and seven translations, including "I Know a Flower So Fair and Fine" (q.v.).

Claude Le Jeune, Huguenot composer; b. Valenciennes, Flanders, 1528; d. Paris, March 29/31, 1600/1601.

Claude (Claudin) Le Jeune received his early training in Flanders, then moved to Paris where his first publication was issued in 1554. Six years later he entered the service of the Duc D'Anjou, brother of Henry III, and in 1578 accompanied the duke to Holland, where he spent several years at the court of William of Orange.

Le Jeune played an important role in the revival of ancient meters, setting to music secular poems and psalms in patterns imitating Greek and Latin poetry, the so-called *"musique mesurée."* He was the principal composer of the Académie de Baïf, a society dedicated to music and poetry and a return to classic models. In 1595 Le Jeune was appointed Chamber Composer to Henry IV and in the following year was given the right to publish, sell, and distribute his works for ten years. Probably he had then completed the *Dodéchachorde contenant douze Psaumes de David.* However, it was not until he secured a similar privilege from the States General of the Netherlands that he published this work in 1598. Two other complete settings of the Genevan psalter were published after Le Jeune's death. One, *Les 150*

Pseaumes de David (1601), became exceedingly popular and was issued in Dutch and German editions. The other, *Pseaumes de David mis en musique à III parties,* appeared in three books: 1602, 1608, and 1610. See his settings of the FRENCH TUNES for PSALM 100 ("To God Our Strength Shout Joyfully") and PSALM 24 ("Unto Jehovah Sing Will I").

George F. Le Jeune, organist and choirmaster; b. London, June 18, 1841; d. Staten Island, N.Y., April 11, 1904.

A pupil of Joseph Barnby and George A. Macfarren in London, George F. Le Jeune went to Montreal in 1863 where he studied organ with George Carter at the Cathedral. When he came to the United States he played in churches in Hartford, Conn., Philadelphia, And New York. In 1876 he accepted the post of organist at St. John's Chapel of Trinity Parish, N.Y.C. Le Jeune was a fine choirmaster with a special gift for training boys' voices. His boy choir at St. John's was one of the best in this country. Le Jeune also gave many organ recitals in New York City and elsewhere. One of his pupils, G. Edward Stubbs, played at St. Agnes, another of the Trinity chapels. The influence of the English cathedral school is apparent in his compositions. See LOVE DIVINE ("Jesus, Thou Divine Companion"), the best known of Le Jeune's tunes.

John Leland, preacher and evangelist; b. Grafton, Mass., May 14, 1754; d. Jan. 14, 1841.

Although his formal education was limited to what he could learn in the schools of Grafton, John Leland felt a call to the ministry and in 1775 was licensed as a Baptist preacher. In 1776 he went to Orange, Va., preaching wherever he could find hearers. He strongly supported legislation that severed the ties between the Episcopal Church and the state and worked zealously to secure the adoption of the state constitution.

In Massachusetts again from 1792 Leland settled in Cheshire which served as a pivot for his activities as Orange had in Virginia. He claimed he had baptized 1,524 people, preached 8,000 sermons, and published 30 pamphlets.

In 1801 Leland took a tour which made him a nationally known figure. When the farmers of Cheshire conceived the idea of sending the biggest cheese in America (1,450 pounds) to President Jefferson, Leland went to Washington by ox-team with it and preached along the way.

His *Sermons, Addresses, Essays, and Autobiography* was published by his niece, Miss L. F. Greene, at Lanesboro, Mass., in 1845. See "The Day Is Past and Gone," and "Now Behold the Saviour Pleading."

Elinor Lennen, author and educator; b. Kansas.

Elinor Lennen is a member of the Disciples of Christ and is active in the field of religious education in the McCarty Memorial Christian Church in Los Angeles. A member of the California Writers Guild and the Poetry Society of Southern California, she has dealt chiefly with religious themes. Her "Within the Shelter of Our Walls" (q.v.) appeared as one of the *Marriage and Family Life Hymns* issued by the Hymn Society of America in 1961.

J. W. Lerman, composer; b. 1865; d. 1935.

J. W. Lerman is credited with two tunes included in *The Methodist Hymnal* of 1935, both apparently written in the early twentieth century. See CORWIN ("At Length There Dawns the Glorious Day").

Harold Lewars, American composer; b. 1882; d. 1915.

The Hymnal of the United Lutheran Church in America (1917) contains six compositions by Harold Lewars, including his SALVE JESU ("Salve Jesu Pastor Bone") (q.v.).

Ralph P. Lewars, organist and music educator; b. Mahanoy City, Pa., March 20, 1883.

Ralph Lewars was educated at Gettysburg where he attended high school and college. He received both the B.A. (1903) and the M.A. (1908) degrees from Gettysburg College. He graduated from the Sternberg Conservatory of Music in Philadelphia in 1905, and from 1923 to 1933 he was a pupil of pianist Albert Jonas of New York. In 1935 he received an honorary Mus.D. from Susquehanna University, Selinsgrove, Pa.

Lewars' professional posts included service as organist at the First Presbyterian Church of Philadelphia (1908–20) and the Lutheran

Church of Holy Communion (1920–60). He also served as director of music in two institutions: the Philadelphia School of Musical Art (1915–25) and the Philadelphia Institution for the Blind at Overbrook, Pa. (1929–41).

A teacher of piano, organ, and composition, Lewars composed anthems, hymn tunes, settings for the Introits and Graduals, and antiphons for the Psalter. See his FESTAL DAY ("Come, All Ye People").

Leo R. Lewis, music educator; b. South Woodstock, Vt., Feb. 11, 1865; d. Cambridge, Mass., Sept. 8, 1945.

Leo R. Lewis was associated with Tufts College, where he was department head from 1895 to his death. His chief contribution to hymnology was made through the Universalist *Church Harmonies New and Old* (Boston, 1898), which he edited jointly with Charles R. Tenney and to which he contributed fourteen tunes. He received his A.B. from Tufts in 1887 and his M.A. from Harvard two years later. He then went to Munich where he studied with Josef Rheinberger. His publications were largely instructive in character. They included *The Ambitious Listener* (1928), *The Gist of Sight Singing* (1929), and *Experiencing Music* (1929). He also edited the *Tufts Song Book* (1906, 1915) and the *Book of Tufts Music* (1922). His *Symphonic Prelude to a Blot on the 'Scutcheon* was performed in Boston in 1925. See CAPEN ("Our Father! While Our Hearts Unlearn").

G. B. Lissart, organist and composer; fl. late 19th cent.

G. B. Lissart was the organist of Grace Church at Medford, Mass., where Rev. Charles L. Hutchins was rector. His tunes appeared in *The Church Hymnal Revised and Enlarged* (1894) and *Carols Old and Carols New,* both edited by Hutchins. Of particular interest is BANNER, composed for George Washington Doane's familiar and militant hymn "Fling Out the Banner!" (q.v.).

Milton S. Littlefield, Presbyterian minister; b. New York City, Aug. 21, 1864; d. June 12, 1934.

Milton Littlefield was educated at Johns Hopkins University and the Union Theological Seminary. He became a Presbyterian minister and helped edit two hymnbooks, one of which was *Hymns of Worship and Service for the Sunday School.* Two of his own hymns, "O Son of Man, Thou Madest Known" (q.v.) and "Come, O Lord," became well known, although neither of them was incorporated in the *Presbyterian Hymnal* of 1933.

Peter Long, fl. 19th cent.

Peter Long, author of "Remember Thy Creator Now," which appeared in William Hauser's *Olive Leaf* (1878), was described there as a Primitive Baptist of Greenville, Ill.

Henry Wadsworth Longfellow, poet and educator; b. Portland, Maine, Feb. 27, 1807; d. Cambridge, Mass., March 24, 1882.

Henry Wadsworth Longfellow prepared for college at private schools and entered Bowdoin as a sophomore. A number of the poems he wrote before graduation were published, and after graduation the college offered him a professorship of modern languages if he would prepare for it by studying abroad. He lived in Europe from 1826 to 1829. On his return he became professor of modern languages and college librarian. In 1831 he married a former classmate. He went back to Europe for a year to prepare for a post at Harvard. While in Rotterdam his young wife died suddenly. Longfellow managed to continue his work and returned in 1835 to become professor of modern languages at Harvard. In 1843 Longfellow remarried. In 1854 he resigned his professorship to devote his time to writing. When his second wife was burned to death in 1861, his creative work ended for a time. In 1868 he returned to Europe once again, this time as a celebrity.

Longfellow's fame as a literary figure exceeded that won by any earlier American writer. Lines from such poems as *Evangeline, Hiawatha,* and "The Village Blacksmith" became household words. He was not attracted to the hymn, as was his brother Samuel, but a number of his poems were adapted for this purpose. See his carol "I Heard the Bells on Christmas Day" and "Tell Me Not in Mournful Numbers."

Samuel Longfellow, Unitarian minister and hymnist; b. Portland, Maine, June 18, 1819; d. there Oct. 3, 1892.

Samuel Longfellow, the youngest brother of the poet Henry Wadsworth Longfellow, prepared for college at the Portland Academy. One of his closest friends during his youthful days was Edward Everett Hale with whom he carried on a lifelong correspondence. At the age of sixteen he entered Harvard College from which he graduated in 1839. After teaching three years he enrolled in the Harvard Divinity School, where Samuel Johnson (q.v.) was his classmate. During their days together as students they collaborated on the compilation of a hymnbook for Unitarian congregations. Called *A Book of Hymns for Public and Private Devotion,* it appeared in print the year of their graduation, 1846.

Ordained a Unitarian minister Samuel Longfellow first settled in Fall River, Mass. For the ordination ceremony in 1848 his brother Henry wrote a hymn. After serving at Fall River for three years he resigned to spend the next two years in Europe. In 1853 he accepted a pastorate in Brooklyn and in 1860 in Germantown, Pa. He resigned in 1882 to write a biography of his brother, Henry Wadsworth Longfellow. He went to Craigie House in Cambridge, Mass., where he worked diligently on the book which was published in 1886.

In 1859 Longfellow produced a small book called *Vespers* for his own Unitarian Society in Brooklyn and in 1860 *A Book of Hymns and Tunes* (revised 1876). *Hymns of the Spirit,* a second book by Johnson and Longfellow, was published in 1864. Johnson's hymns are among the best of their period. See "Again as Evening's Shadow Falls," "Holy Spirit, Truth Divine," "O Life That Maketh All Things New," and " 'Tis Winter Now" (with a tune composed by Lockrem Johnson for *American Hymns*).

Thomas Loud Jr., musician and piano maker; fl. early 19th cent.

Thomas Loud's father came to New York from England in about 1816, manufactured pianos there, and died in 1834. The son, who was established in Philadelphia as early as 1812, pursued his father's craft and was also active as pianist, organist, and director of the Musical Fund Society. He and three brothers, in a firm known as the Loud Brothers, made pianos. The firm was dissolved in 1824, the same year in which Loud's *Psalmist* was published in Philadelphia. The title page describes him as "organist of St. Andrews Church."

KEITH ("Laborers of Christ! Arise") (q.v.) is included in George Kingsley's *The Sacred Choir* (1838), where it is attributed to T. Loud. KEITH is not in Loud's own collection, but the tune (in D rather than E♭ major) appears in the *Cantus Ecclesiae* (1844) of W. H. W. Darley and J. C. R. Standbridge, where it is among the tunes for which the editors claim copyright. Although both the Darley-Standbridge and Kingsley publications omit the "Jr.," it seems reasonable to assign the composition to the son.

J. C. Lowry, tune composer or arranger.

In the 1854 edition of *Southern Harmony* William Walker ascribed three settings to Lowry: PISGAH ("The Lord's My Shepherd") (q.v.), MORNING STAR, and THE TRAVELLER (where the initials J. C. were added). PISGAH also appeared, without attribution, in Allen D. Carden's *Missouri Harmony* of 1820. In "The Folk Element in Early Revival Hymns and Tunes" (*Journal of the Folk-Song Society*, VIII, 1927–31), Anne G. Gilchrist considers it an American variant of an English folk tune. On the other hand, the English editor of *The Methodist Hymn Book* (1933) calls it "an American melody." In both England and Scotland it was sung under the misleading name COVENANTERS. What seems clear is that it was first printed here as a hymn and later reprinted in England and Scotland.

Robert Lowry, Baptist minister, editor, and composer; b. Philadelphia, Pa., March 12, 1826; d. Plainfield, N.J., Nov. 25, 1899.

Robert Lowry joined the Baptist Church at an early age and soon became an active Sunday-School worker and chorister. At the age of twenty-one he decided to enter the ministry and enrolled at Bucknell University where he graduated as valedictorian (B.A., 1854; M.A., 1857). He served as pastor at West Chester, Pa. (1854–58), New York City (1859–61), Brooklyn (1861–69), and Lewisburg, Pa. (1869–75). During his Lewisburg pastorate he was also professor of belles-lettres at Bucknell and received an honorary D.D. from that institution in 1875. His last ministry, begun in 1875, was in the Park Avenue Church of Plainfield, N.J. During the years 1880–85 he traveled in Europe, the Southwest, and Mexico, then returned to Plainfield.

The firm of Bigelow and Main, successor to the Bradbury Company, selected Lowry as editor of their Sunday-School book *Bright*

Jewels. Later William Howard Doane (q.v.) was associated with him in the issue of other songbooks: *Pure Gold* (1871), *Royal Diadem, Welcome Tidings, Brightest and Best, Glad Refrain, Good as Gold, Joyful Lays, Fountain of Song, Bright Array,* and *Temple Anthems.*

See "Shall We Gather at the River?" for which he wrote both text and tune, and the tunes for "One More Day's Work for Jesus," "Saviour, Thy Dying Love," and "Five Were Foolish" (THE DOOR WAS SHUT).

Peter C. Lutkin, organist, educator, and administrator; b. Thompsonville, Wis., March 27, 1858; d. Evanston, Ill., Dec. 27, 1931.

Peter C. Lutkin was the youngest of six children and, when both his parents died suddenly, was early thrown on his own resources. His education was obtained in the Chicago public schools and in the choir school of St. James's Church, the Protestant Episcopal Cathedral. He distinguished himself there as solo singer and when only fourteen served as organist. With the endorsement of such Chicago musicians as Regina Watson, Clarence Eddy, and Frederick Grant Gleason, Lutkin was able to go abroad. In Berlin he studied with A. Haupt, O. Raif, and W. Bargiel; in Paris with Moritz Moszkowski; and in Vienna with Stepanoff and Theodor Leschetizky. After his European studies, he was active in Chicago as organist and choirmaster, first at St. Clement's Church (1884–91), later at St. James's Church (1891–96), and from 1888 was in charge of theoretical studies at the American Conservatory.

Lutkin's most important contribution to music education was as the organizer and first dean of the school of music at Northwestern University (from 1896). The acapella choir which he organized was the first group of the kind in the Middle West. He was the initiator and from 1908 to 1930 the conductor of the North Shore Festival.

His lectures on sacred music at Western Theological Seminary in Chicago were published in 1910 in *Music in the Church.* President of the Music Teachers' National Association in 1911 and again in 1920, he served on the editorial boards of *The Methodist Hymnal* of 1905 and the Episcopal *Hymnal* of 1918. See PATTEN ("Almighty God, with One Accord"), JOSHUA ("Defend Us, Lord, from Every Ill"), CHARITY ("If I Can Stop One Heart from Breaking"), LANIER ("Into the Woods, My Master Went"), BELLEVILLE ("Lord, Thou Hast Promised"), CAMP ("The Lord Our God Alone Is Strong"), BAPTISM ("O God, Great Father, Lord, and King"), THEODORE ("Through Willing Hearts and Helping Hands"), and KIEL ("Where Cross the Crowded Ways of Life").

James Lyon, composer, compiler, and Presbyterian minister;
b. Newark, N.J., July 1, 1735; d. Machias, Maine, Dec. 25,
1794.

James Lyon attended the College of New Jersey (Princeton) and
composed the music for commencement (1759). His *Urania or a
Choice Collection of Psalm-Tunes, Anthems and Hymns* appeared in 1761
(2d ed., 1787; 3d ed., 1773). Princeton conferred the M.A. on him in
1762. *The Lawfulness, Excellency and Advantages of Instrumental Musick
in the Public Worship of God* (1763), which advocated the use of the
bassoon, cello, double bass, and organ during church services, was
probably his. After being licensed to preach, Lyon was ordained by
the Synod of New Brunswick in 1764. The next year he settled in
Halifax, Nova Scotia. After a short stay in Onslow, Nova Scotia,
where he had difficulty in supporting himself, he accepted a call to
Machias, Maine and settled there in 1772. He died there in 1794.
Lyon must be regarded as an American primitive among our composers. His *Urania* was the earliest native collection of its kind and
established a pattern which was taken up by later compilers. BATH
("Lord, I Am Thine") is given as it appears in *Urania*. See also PSALM
104 ("Eternal Spirit, Source of Light").

Robert G. McCutchan, musician, educator, and hymnologist;
b. Mount Ayr, Iowa, Sept. 13, 1877; d. Claremont, Calif.,
May 15, 1958.

Robert G. McCutchan graduated from Park College, Mo., in 1898
and spent the next two years teaching and arranging concerts. In
1904 he took his Mus.B. degree at Simpson College, Iowa, and then
accepted a professorship at Baker University, Baldwin City, Kans.,
where he remained for six years. During that period he organized
the musical conservatory there. He decided to study in France and
Germany and while in Berlin directed the choir of the American
church. On his return to the United States he was made dean of the
School of Music at De Pauw University. Five years later he was
elected president of the Indiana Music Teachers Association and, in
1920, became secretary of the Music Teachers National Association.
   In 1917, under the auspices of the Indiana State Council for Defense, McCutchan promoted community singing and completed a
book on music as a social force. An editor of *The Methodist Hymnal*
(1935), he published *Our Hymnody* in 1937, a manual for use with the
hymnal, and, in 1957, *Hymn Tune Names*. He was also music editor of
Standard Hymns and of *The Junior Church School Hymnal*. See DE PAUW
("Spirit of Life, in This New Dawn") and OXNAM ("Where Is Our
Holy Church?").

H. R. MacFayden, Presbyterian pastor; b. Bladen Co., N.C.,
Feb. 1, 1877.

The son of a Presbyterian minister, H. R. MacFayden served the
Presbyterian Church at Pinetops, N.C. See "The Lone Wild Fowl."

Alexander Mack I, founder of the Church of the Brethren; b.
Schriesheim, near Schwarzenau, Germany, Aug. 3, 1679; d.
Germantown, Pa., Jan. 31, 1735.

A Presbyterian educated in the Calvinist faith, Alexander Mack I
attended one of the German universities. He was known as a studi-
ous and thoughtful young man who learned the trade of a miller
and assisted in caring for the many vineyards owned by his family.

Married at the age of twenty-one to a girl from the same community he became the father of five children; two daughters died in
Germany, three sons (Valentine, John, and Alexander Jr.) later accompanied their father to America.

In 1708 Mack and his wife and six friends with Pietist leanings
were baptized in the River Eder, thus forming a pioneer church of
eight members. They were known in Germany as the Taufers or
Tunkers. Since they were often persecuted and imprisoned, Mack
gradually lost his patrimony, his vineyards, and his profitable mill,
paying the fines continually levied against him and his associates. In
1713 he published his book *Plain View of the Rites and Ordinances of
the House of God and the Groundsearching Questions.* In 1720 some of
the Brethren sailed for America under Peter Becker's leadership,
while the others fled to Holland. Among the Holland group were
Alexander Mack and his three surviving sons. After living nine years
there in Westervain, West Friesland, they decided to join the American emigrants. Departing as a congregation from Rotterdam they arrived in Philadelphia on September 15, 1729.

Their friends had prepared a log cabin for the use of the founder
of their church. Six years later Mack died and was buried in the
upper burying ground, sometimes known as Axes' burying ground,
in Germantown. His body rested there until November 13, 1894,
when it was removed to the cemetery at the Church of the Brethren
in Germantown. See "Ich bin ein Herr."

Thomas Mackellar, author; b. New York City, Aug. 12, 1812;
d. Dec. 29, 1899.

Thomas Mackellar went to work for the publishers Harper &
Brothers when he was fourteen. Seven years later he moved to Phila-

delphia and was employed by the type-foundry firm of Johnson and Smith. He advanced from proofreader to foreman and eventually became a partner. The firm's incorporation, from 1860 on, was under the name of Mackellar, Smith, & Jordan.

"Bear the Burden of the Present" appeared in his volume of poems *Lines for the Gentle and Loving,* which came out in 1853. The year 1866 saw the publication of *The American Printer* by Mackellar as well as a number of poems and hymns. Of the latter, "At the Door of Mercy Sighing" (q.v.) was first published in his *Rhymes Atween Times* (1872). "Book of Grace and Book of Glory" was printed first in *Hymns and a Few Metrical Psalms* (Philadelphia, 1883), which contained seventy-one of his hymns and three songs. He also wrote "Draw Nigh to the Holy," and "There is a Land Immortal."

Hubert P. Main, composer and editor; b. Ridgefield, Conn., Aug. 17, 1839; d. Oct. 7, 1925.

Hubert Main was educated in district school and at singing-schools taught by his father, Sylvester Main, and others. In 1854 he went to New York, where he started work as an errand boy. After a variety of jobs he had his first experience in compiling music books in 1855 when he helped his father edit *The Sunday School Lute* by Isaac B. Woodbury. In 1859 William Batchelder Bradbury asked Sylvester Main to assist him in compiling *Cottage Melodies,* and from that time on they worked together sporadically until Bradbury's death in 1868. During those years young Main assisted his father in editing books published by Woodbury and Bradbury.

In November 1864, Hubert Main went to Cincinnati to work for the Philip Phillips Company, where he served as bookkeeper and arranger. In 1866 he assisted Philip Phillips (q.v.) in the compilation of a new Methodist Episcopal hymn and tune book, for which Main prepared most of the copy and read all the proofs. In 1867 he officially joined the Bradbury firm and at its dissolution became a part of the Bigelow and Main Company, where he remained until his death.

Main, who had composed hymn tunes from the age of fifteen, wrote over a thousand settings for hymns and anthems as well as much secular music during his lifetime. He was an inveterate collector of old music books. In 1891 he sold to the Newberry Library in Chicago over 3,500 volumes, now known as the Main Collection. It includes more than two hundred American music books published between 1721 and 1810. See his tune for "In the Silent Midnight Watches."

John Marckant, English ecclesiastic and psalmist; fl. 16th cent.

Incumbent of Clacton Magna (1559) and of Shopland (1563–68), John Marckant is known as the writer of a few hymns and poems. It is thought that the initial "M" attached to four psalms in the English psalter (1562) indicated his authorship. In the 1565 edition of that volume one of the psalms usually bearing this initial bore the name "Marckant" in full, and an edition of 1606 had his name modified as "Market." See "O Lord, Turn Not Away Thy Face."

Edwin Markham, poet; b. Oregon City, Ore., April 23, 1852; d. Staten Island, N.Y., March 7, 1940.

Edwin Markham's father ran a store in Oregon City. When Edwin was about five, his mother left his father in Oregon, took her children to a valley near Sacramento, Calif., and bought a ranch where she raised wheat and sheep and cattle.

By the age of fifteen Markham had had only one year's schooling, but his literary bent interested a young teacher in the district, who introduced him to poetry. The boy ploughed rough farmland for a dollar an acre to buy a dictionary and copies of the English poets. In 1872 he graduated from San Jose Normal School. His first teaching position was in a remote California mountain settlement where he had to help build the schoolhouse. He became head of the Teachers Training School in Oakland in 1899.

Markham's first published poem was *The Gulf of Night* (1880), but it was *The Man with the Hoe,* after Millet's painting, that brought him wide recognition. From 1900 to 1905 he lived comfortably on earnings from his writing, but some unfortunate investments left little for his later years. See "There Is a High Place" with the setting by Alan Hovhaness for *American Hymns.*

Earl B. Marlatt, Methodist educator and administrator; b. Columbus, Ind., May 24, 1892; d. Winchester, Ind., June 13, 1976.

Earl B. Marlatt was educated at De Pauw University (A.B., 1912), Boston University (S.T.B., 1922; Ph.D., 1929), the University of Berlin and Oxford University (1922–23), and was a national fellow in religion (1924–25). He was an associate editor of the *Kenosha* (Wis.) *News* (1917–18) before he entered the U.S. Army where he served during World War I as a lieutenant in the field artillery.

In 1923 Marlatt became associate professor of philosophy at Boston University; in 1925 he attained a full professorship, and from 1938 to 1945 served as dean of the School of Theology there. In 1946 he became professor of religion, Perkins School of Theology at Southern Methodist University, Dallas.

Marlatt was invited to give lectures at Wellesley College (from 1928), at the Old South Church in Boston (1932–35), and De Pauw University (1941). De Pauw gave him the honorary degree of Litt.D. in 1931.

Member of a number of learned societies and a poet of distinction (*Chapel Windows*, 1924; *Cathedral*, 1937) he has written many hymns and served as associate editor of *The American Student Hymnal* (1928). See "Spirit of Life, in This New Dawn" and "Through the Dark the Dreamers Came."

Donald S. Marsh, composer and singer; b. Akron, Ohio, Sept. 5, 1923.

Donald S. Marsh graduated from the University of Houston (B.S. and M.S.), where he specialized in art, music, and the theater. After a period of activity in theatrical, night club, and television productions in New York City, he settled in Port Jervis, N.Y., where he became choirmaster of the First Presbyterian Church and director of a dramatic group called the Presby Players. With Richard K. Avery (q.v.) he wrote *Hymns Hot and Carols Cool; More, More, More;* and *Alive and Singing.* See "And the Cock Begins to Crow."

Simeon B. Marsh, singing master and editor; b. Sherburne, N.Y., June 1, 1798; d. Albany, N.Y., July 14, 1875.

Simeon Marsh's parents had moved from Wethersfield, Conn., to a farm at Sherburne, N.Y., where he was born. When he was seven he was singing in a children's choir, but he did not have instruction in music until he was sixteen. At the age of nineteen he began to teach in singing schools in towns nearby.

His first contact with a musician of more than local reputation was with Thomas Hastings, who was teaching in Geneva, N.Y. in 1817. In 1837 he published a newspaper in Amsterdam, N.Y. called *The Intelligencer* (later *The Recorder*) and later, when he returned to Sherburne, he started the *Sherburne News.* In Schenectady, where he taught music to children without charge, Marsh published three books for young people, hand-setting the type and doing all the work necessary to produce them. For thirty years he taught choirs and singing schools at various places within the limits of the Albany Presbytery. He returned to his native town in 1859 where he led the choir, was superintendent of the Sunday school, and gave class instruction in voice, violin, and piano.

At the age of twenty-two he married Eliza Carter of Hamilton, N.Y. His son, John Butler Marsh, also became a musician, teaching organ and voice in Elmira Female College, Elmira, N.Y. After Eliza Marsh's death, her husband went to live with one of their sons in Albany.

Among Marsh's compositions were *The Saviour,* a cantata for mixed voices, and *The King of the Forest.* His well-known MARTYN (see "Brother, Hast Thou Wandered Far"), a tune so simple that a beginner might sing it, is usually sung to "Jesus, Lover of My Soul."

Leonard Marshall, tenor, educator, and composer; b. Hudson, N.Y., May 3, 1809; d. date unknown.

Leonard Marshall went to Boston, where he studied music with John Paddon and organist Charles Zeuner (q.v.). He sang with and led the vocal quartet at the Twelfth Congregational Church from 1821 to 1857, later was director of the choir at the Tremont Temple for ten years, and was in charge of the music of other Boston churches for shorter periods, notably the Bowdoin Square Baptist Church, the Charles Street Baptist Church, and the Harvard Square Baptist Church.

He appeared as principal tenor soloist with the Boston Handel and Haydn Society and in concerts in the New England area. As time passed he devoted more time to music education and to organizations such as the National Summer School of Music and the Eastern section of the American Institute of Normal Methods. He composed songs such as "Don't Give Up the Ship" and "The Mountaineer," and edited collections of music including the *Antiquarian* (1849), *Harpsichord or Union Collection* (with Henry N. Stone, 1852), and *The New Sacred Star* (1865). He also edited a number of church music books. See COLLYER ("Laboring and Heavy Laden"), DEDICATION CHANT ("O Thou! Whose Presence Went Before"), and ALTITUDE ("There Is a Land Mine Eye Hath Seen").

Daniel Gregory Mason, composer, author, and educator; b. Brookline, Mass., Nov. 20, 1873; d. Greenwich, Conn., Dec. 4, 1953.

Daniel Gregory Mason's grandfather was Lowell Mason (q.v.); his father was a founder of the Mason and Hamlin piano company; and

William Mason (q.v.), a Liszt pupil and a distinguished pianist, was his uncle. Daniel Gregory Mason attended Harvard where he studied with John Knowles Paine. After graduation he continued his musical studies with George W. Chadwick in Boston, with Percy Goetschius in New York, and later with Vincent D'Indy in Paris. He taught music at Columbia University from 1910, became department chairman and, in 1929, MacDowell Professor. He retired in 1940.

Mason was a literate and informed writer on music; his books, too numerous to list here, did much to inform public taste in this country. His compositions moved largely within the orbit of Brahms, but some impressionist influence is apparent in certain later works. Although he was not among the composers who sought an American naturalism through the use of Negro and Indian melodies, he nevertheless wrote an attractive *Quartet on Negro Themes* (Opus 19); as well as *Fanny Blair, Folk Song Fantasy for String Quartet* (Opus 28); and a *Suite After English Folk Songs* (Opus 32). His most frequently played orchestral work was Opus 27, *Chanticleer, Festival Overture;* the work he regarded as his finest was *Symphony No. 3, A Lincoln Symphony* (Opus 35). See DEED ("All Praise to Thee.").

Lowell Mason, influential church musician; b. Medfield, Mass., Jan. 8, 1792; d. Orange, N.J., Aug. 11, 1872.

Lowell Mason's father and grandfather were musical and his four sons were active in the field of music. Although neither Mason nor his family contemplated music as a profession, he learned to play every instrument available to him. In 1812 he went to Savannah, Ga., where he found employment as a bank clerk. He was a member of the Independent Presbyterian Church there and in addition played the organ, led the choir, helped to organize the Sunday School, the only one in Savannah at the time, and was its superintendant. In Savannah Mason studied with his first well-trained teacher, Frederick L. Abel, a native of Germany who had recently settled there.

Mason's compilation of psalm and hymn tunes patterned on William Gardiner's *Sacred Melodies* remained unpublished until he met Dr. G. K. Jackson, who persuaded the Boston Handel and Haydn Society to publish it. The *Boston Handel and Haydn Society Collection of Church Music,* published in 1822, was immediately successful. As a result Mason moved to Boston, where he became a leader in the field of church and choral music. He led the choir in the Bowdoin St. Church where Lyman Beecher was the minister and presided over the most prestigious choral group of the period, the Handel and Haydn Society. *Juvenile Psalms,* Mason's first children's music book, appeared in 1829. By 1838 he had succeeded in introducing music into the curriculum of the Boston public schools. The date is significant, because it marked the first appearance of music in the public-school system. On Mason's first trip to Europe in 1837 he was able to observe the teaching of music according to the principles developed by Pestalozzi. After his return from Europe he made New York City his business headquarters and Orange, N.J., his home. He was an industrious and conspicuously successful composer and compiler of books for singing classes, church services, and juvenile instruction. He extended his influence by lectures, normal classes, and conventions. See MERIBAH ("Arise, Ye Saints of Latter Days" and "Jesus, Enthroned and Glorified"), HENLEY ("Come Unto Me, When Shadows Darkly Gather"), DOWNS ("Dear Friend, Whose Presence in the House"), SUCCOTH ("God of the World, Thy Glories Shine"), CORINTH ("Hail, Tranquil Hour of Closing Day"), WESLEY ("Hail to the Brightness of Zion's Glad Morning"), BENSON ("In the Morning I Will Pray"), ERNAN ("Jesus a Child His Course Begun"), BETHANY ("More Love to Thee, O Christ"), OLIVET ("My Faith Looks Up to Thee"), LABAN ("My Soul, Weigh Not My Life"), MISSIONARY HYMN ("Now Be the Gospel Banner"), BAZETTA ("Our Father in Heaven"), HAMBURG ("To Thine Eternal Arms, O God"), AMBOY ("Wake the Song of Jubilee"), HERMON ("We Love the Venerable House"), and ALVAN ("While We Lowly Bow Before Thee").

William Mason, pianist and teacher; b. Boston, Mass., Jan. 24, 1829; d. New York City, July 14, 1908.

William Mason, the third son of Lowell Mason (q.v.), studied piano in Boston and made his debut at the age of seventeen. He went abroad and became a member of Liszt's circle at Weimar. When he returned to the United States in 1854 he toured as a concert pianist and was probably the first in this country to give recitals without an assisting artist. He made New York City his permanent residence and after 1868 devoted himself to piano teaching. His pieces for the piano, which numbered forty, were in graceful, idiomatic, and often brilliant salon style. *Silver Spring* was a particular favorite. His hymn tunes appear to have been youthful productions written at the request of his father. For example, the ten tunes in *The National Psalmist* (1848), edited by Lowell Mason and George J. Webb (q.v.), were probably composed while William Mason was in Germany. One, KIDRON ("Tarry with Me, O My Saviour") (q.v.), was dated 1845.

Cotton Mather, author and minister; b. Boston, Mass.,
Feb. 12, 1662/63; d. there, Feb. 13, 1727/28.

Cotton Mather, the son of Increase Mather, was minister of the
Second Church of Boston from 1685 to 1727/28. In 1688 and 1689,
when the colonists opposed the royal governor, Mather was one of
their leaders. He was less successful when William Phips succeeded
to the governorship. He was made a fellow of Harvard in 1690, but
gave up the office after his father was ousted from Harvard's presidency in 1701.

Probably Mather's most fearless public service was his advocacy of
inoculation for smallpox in 1721. In his own time his fame was international. He corresponded with distinguished European scholars,
was elected to the Royal Society in 1713, and received an honorary
degree from the University of Aberdeen in 1710. Justly famous for
his scholarship, his list of publications reached 450. Mather believed
in witchcraft, and his publications and his statements influenced those
responsible for the trials at Salem in 1692.

His *Psalterium Americanum* (Boston, 1718) was written in blank
verse. The psalms could be sung in either long or common meter by
including or omitting material in parentheses. See "Eternal God,
How They're Increased" and "I Lift My Eyes up to the Hills." In his
Agricola (Boston, 1727) he drew spiritual lessons from the activities
of the farmer. The poems included, although not designed for singing, are in meters familiar to every psalm singer. See "My Heart,
How Very Hard It's Grown!" and "When the Seed of Thy Word Is
Cast."

Abraham Maxim, singing master and composer; b. Carver,
Mass., Jan. 3, 1773; d. Palmyra, Maine, 1829.

Abraham Maxim, a farmer's son, was of little use on the farm
because he was so preoccupied with the tunes that went through his
head. He is said to have been a pupil of William Billings (q.v.) of
Boston. When he came of age he went to Turner, Maine, married
there, taught singing school, and became the father of a large family
of singers. In 1827 the family moved to a farm in Palmyra, where he
also taught music. He suffered a stroke and died while returning
home after a session of his singing class.

Maxim's first book, *The Oriental Harmony* (Exeter, N.H., 1802) contained only his own compositions. *Northern Harmony,* (c.1804), his
most popular book, reached a fifth edition in 1819. His favorite
tunes BUCKFIELD and TURNER were named for towns in Maine. See
his COLUMBIA ("Columbia, Trust the Lord").

Claude Means, organist and choirmaster; b. Cincinnati, Ohio, May 12, 1912.

Claude Means became an organist and choir director in Episcopal churches and a composer of service music. In his early years he sang in the choir of the Denver Cathedral of St. John in the Wilderness, where he afterward was assistant organist. In 1933 he was at All Saints' Church in the same city, where he played the organ and directed the choir. After a period of advanced study in New York City with David McK. Williams (q.v.) and Normal Coke-Jephcott he resumed his career at Christ Church, Greenwich, Conn. (from April 1934). In 1941 he was accepted as a Fellow of the American Guild of Organists. He spent the period from October 1942 to March 1946 in military service.

Among his published compositions are a Jubilate, a Benedictus, and the anthems, "Lord of All Power and Might," "The King Rides Forth," and "O Come and Mourn." See SEABURY ("Creation's Lord, We Give Thee Thanks").

Christopher Meinecke, pianist, organist, and composer; b. Germany, 1782; d. Baltimore, Md., Nov. 6, 1850.

Christopher Meinecke received his musical education from his father, who was organist to the Duke of Oldenburgh. He left Germany when he was only eighteen, disembarked at Baltimore, and there he remained. In 1817 he returned to Europe where he stayed for two years. During that period he visited Beethoven, who praised a piano concerto which Meinecke had composed. Among his other compositions were sacred music, secular songs, and variations for piano. A Te Deum of his composition, performed in Baltimore by the choir of St. Paul's Church, where he was organist, was favorably reviewed in the *Euterpiad.* His Opus 25 was a Mass given in Leipzig. Sixty-two psalm and hymn tunes, which he composed for the choir of St. Paul's, as well as his favorite Gloria Patri, were included in John Cole's *Music for the Church* (1844). He never married. His death revealed an estate of $190,000 amassed by clever investing in real estate. See his BALTIMORE ("O God, Beneath Thy Guiding Hand") and CALVARY ("Once More, O Lord"). The tune MEINECKE ("We Praise Thee If One Rescued Soul") was probably named for him.

Abraham Down Merrill, Methodist minister and revivalist; b. Salem, N.H., March 7, 1796; d. April 29, 1878.

With no more education than the district school provided, Abraham Down Merrill had settled down to farm work until at the age of twenty-four he attended a local revival meeting and was not only converted but also convinced that he should himself become a minister. He began to preach and was accepted as a minister by the Methodist Episcopal Church in 1822. He was considered a persuasive preacher, eager to promote revivals, and his hymns have the character of revival songs. See GEORGE ("The Gloomy Night of Sadness") and JOYFULLY, JOYFULLY (same).

William Pierson Merrill, clergyman; b. Orange, N.J., Jan. 10, 1867; d. New York City, June 19, 1954.

William Pierson Merrill earned an A.B. degree from Rutgers in 1887, an M.A. in 1890, and a B.D. from Union Theological Seminary the same year. Ordained to the Presbyterian ministry in 1890, he served in pastorates at Trinity Church, Chestnut Hill, Pa. (1890–95), Sixth Church, Chicago (1895–1911), and the Brick Presbyterian Church, New York (1911–38). In 1917 Merrill declined the presidency of Union Theological Seminary. Active in the Hymn Society of New York and president of the board of trustees of the Church Peace Union, he was the author of several books whose major theme was world brotherhood.

Merrill's honorary degrees included a D.D. from Rutgers (1905) and from New York University (1923), the S.T.D. from Columbia (1927), and the L.H.D. from Rollins (1933). He was the author of *Faith Building* (1885), *Faith and Sight* (1900), *Footings and Faith* (1915), *Christian Internationalism* (1919), *The Common Creed of Christians* (1920), *Liberal Christianity* (1925), and *Prophets of the Dawn* (1927). Merrill, like Calvin Laufer and Howard Chandler Robbins, was a distinguished clergyman who possessed musical as well as literary gifts. He composed the tunes AMERICA BEFRIEND for Henry Van Dyke's "O Lord Our God, Thy Mighty Hand" (q.v.) and MARCUS WHITMAN for Robert Freeman's "Braving the Wilds All Unexplored" (q.v.). See also his "Not Alone for Mighty Empire" and "Rise Up, O Men of God."

Edward Millar, editor of the Scottish psalter of 1635.

Edward Millar graduated from Edinburgh University in 1624 and became a teacher of children in Blackfriars Wynd. Distressed by the discords produced by singing various settings of a given psalm tune at the same time, he compiled a psalter utilizing earlier harmonizations and correcting them where necessary. A manuscript version of Psalm 150 bound with Andro Hart's psalter of 1615, inscribed "E. Millar 2 Aprile 1626," seems to be evidence that he also composed settings. That he found favor with Charles I is shown by his appointment in 1634 to the "Kirk and parochine of Sanct Marie Kirk of the Lowis, lyand in Atrick Forrest." In the following year Millar became Master of the Music in the Chapel Royal and the harmonized psalter which he prepared was published. It seems likely that some of these psalm settings were sung as anthems before the king under Millar's direction. His fate during the Civil War is unknown, as is the date of his death. See the setting of PSALM 124 ("Welcome, Sweet Rest"), ascribed to Millar.

Edna St. Vincent Millay, poet; b. Rockland, Maine, Feb. 22, 1892; d. near Austerlitz, N.Y., Oct. 19, 1950.

Edna St. Vincent Millay was educated at Barnard and Vassar colleges (B.A., 1917). She later received honorary degrees from Tufts, the University of Wisconsin, and Russell Sage. Encouraged by her mother she began writing verse in her childhood, and she was still a student when her first major poem "Renascence" (which appeared in *The Lyric Year,* 1912) aroused general interest by its note of fresh beauty. The year she graduated from Vassar she published her first volume of poetry, *Renascence and Other Poems* (1917).

After college Edna St. Vincent Millay moved to New York's Greenwich Village where she continued to write, joined the Provincetown Players, and published three plays in verse, *Aria da Capo* (1921), *The Lamp and the Bell* (1921), and *Two Slatterns and a King* (1921). In 1921 she also issued *A Few Figs from Thistles* and *Second April,* and in 1923 she was awarded a Pulitzer prize for *The Harp-Weaver and Other Poems.*

That same year she married Eugene Boissevain and moved to a farm near Austerlitz, N.Y. Other books produced in her rural surroundings were: *The King's Henchman,* libretto for an opera by Deems Taylor (1927), *The Buck in the Snow* (1928), *Fatal Interview* (1931), *Wine from These Grapes* (1934), *Conversation at Midnight* (1937), *Huntsman, What Quarry?* (1939), *Make Bright the Arrows* (1940), *There Are No Islands Any More* (1940), *Collected Sonnets* (1941), *Murder of Lidice* (1942), and *Collected Lyrics* (1943). She became almost a recluse after the death of her husband in 1949. She died alone in her farmhouse a year later. See "O God, I Cried, No Dark Disguise."

Anne Langdon Miller, violist; b. New York City, Jan. 6, 1908.

Anne Langdon Miller studied at the Institute of Musical Art and the David Mannes School of Music. She later served as the principal viola player in the Vermont State Symphony Orchestra. In 1948 she entered the Community of Poor Clares. See VERMONT ("Give Peace, O God, the Nations Cry").

William G. Mills, hymnist.

William G. Mills may have been of English origin, but one can only speculate until something more about his life comes to light. His "Arise, O Glorious Zion" (q.v.), with music by George Careless, appeared in the Mormon hymnal *The Latter-day Saints' Psalmody* of 1889. Nothing of Mills is known beyond this fact. Indeed, Michael F. Moody, executive secretary of the Church of Jesus Christ of Latter-day Saints, was unable to state that Mills was a member of the Mormon Church.

Nahum Mitchell, lawyer and public official; b. East Bridge-water, Mass., Feb. 12, 1769; d. there, Aug. 1, 1853.

Nahum Mitchell combined a career as jurist and public official with an active interest in church music and composed one tune of lasting merit. He attended Harvard where he earned both the B.A. and M.A. degrees after which he went to Plymouth to prepare himself as a lawyer. He was state representative (1803–05 and 1839–40), judge of the Court of Common Pleas (1811–21), state senator (1813–14), member of the governor's council (1814–20), and state treasurer (1822–27). He was also elected to the House of Representatives in Washington for a term.

The *Bridgewater Collection of Sacred Music* (1802 and later), one of the most successful of its period, was the work of three men: Benjamin Holt, Bartholomew Brown, and Mitchell, although their names do not appear on the title page. John W. Moore asserts in his *Complete Encyclopedia of Music* that Mitchell was a compiler of *LXXX Psalm and Hymn Tunes for Public Worship* (1810), sometimes called *The Brattle Street Collection,* but Mitchell's name does not appear in it. See PILESGROVE ("O God Whose Presence Glows in All").

Penina Moise, author; b. Charleston, S.C., April 23, 1797; d. there Sept. 13, 1880.

Penina Moise had a limited education. When she was twelve, her father died and she had to leave school to help with the family. She showed great literary aptitude, and she wrote articles for newspapers and for *Godey's Lady's Book.* A collection of poetry, *Fancy's Sketch Book,* appeared in 1833.

She was superintendent of the Sabbath School of the Charleston synagogue and her *Hymns Written for Hebrew Congregations* appeared in 1847. This hymnal was used by the synagogue in Charleston and by other congregations in the South. During an outbreak of yellow fever in 1854 she devotedly cared for the sick. Penina Moise left Charleston during the Civil War but returned to open a school with her sister Rachel. Her eyesight gradually failed and she became blind. Her hymnal was a notable pioneer effort. The current *Union Hymnal* includes an altered version of her "God Supreme! To Thee We Pray" (q.v.).

Nicola A. Montani, composer and authority on Gregorian chant; b. Utica, N.Y., Nov. 8, 1880; d. Philadelphia, Pa., Jan. 11, 1948.

After studying music in the United States Nicola A. Montani went to Rome where he was a student of Lorenzo Perosi and Filippo Capocci. In 1905–06 he studied Gregorian chant with Dom Mocquereau and Dom Endine. On his return to this country he was organist and choirmaster in Philadelphia at St. John the Evangelist (1923–24) and in New York at St. Paul's Church (from 1925). He was also active as a teacher. To promote and improve the performance of Gregorian chant and the masterpieces of the early polyphonic composers he organized the Society of St. Gregory (1914) and the Catholic Choral Club, later called the Palestrina Choir. He was a Knight Commander of the Order of St. Sylvester and a member of the Pontifical Institute of Sacred Music. He composed much church music and was the editor of the *St. Gregory Hymnal* (Philadelphia, 1920). See his setting of "Let the Deep Organ Swell" by the Rev. Constantine Pise.

William Vaughn Moody, poet and playwright; b. Spencer, Ind., July 8, 1869; d. Colorado Springs, Colo., Oct. 17, 1910.

The son of a steamboat captain, William Vaughn Moody grew up in New Albany, Ind. After teaching school to earn money for college, he arrived at Harvard in September 1889, with twenty-five dollars in his pocket. While supporting himself and a sister, he attended college and was one of the editors of the *Harvard Monthly.* After earning his A.B. degree in 1893, he received an A.M. in 1894. He taught English at Harvard (1894–95), and at the University of Chicago (1895–99, 1901–07). He spent 1899–1900 in Boston and East Gloucester working on his *Poems,* published in 1901. This volume was preceded by *The Masque of Judgment* (1900). His prose drama *A Sabine Woman* (first performance, Chicago, 1906) was given again in New York with the title *The Great Divide. The Faith Healer* (1909) was less successful. At his death he left an unfinished play, *The Death of Eve.* See his "I Stood Within the Heart of God," with the setting which Quincy Porter composed for *American Hymns.*

Clement Clarke Moore, scholar and author; b. New York City, July 15, 1779; d. Newport, R.I., July 10, 1863.

After studying with tutors Clement Clarke Moore attended Columbia College, graduating in 1798 at the head of his class. Moore had inherited a large estate in what is now Greenwich Village, and in February 1819, he offered to the City of New York sixty lots (including the present Chelsea Square) for the building of a theological school. Prior to this the General Convention of the Protestant Episcopal Church had authorized a diocesan seminary (1817) and Moore became professor of biblical learning. In 1825 the diocesan seminary merged with the General Theological Seminary, a merger made possible by Moore's gift. Moore became professor of Oriental and Greek literature and continued in that post until 1850. In 1851 he helped to establish St. Peter's Church, near the seminary, and became its first organist. He is best remembered for his ballad " 'Twas the Night Before Christmas." His "Lord of Life, All Praise Excelling" (q.v.) has been widely used.

Douglas Moore, composer and educator; b. Cutchogue, N.Y., August 10, 1893; d. Greenport, N.Y., July 25, 1969.

Douglas Moore grew up in Cutchogue and Brooklyn and was educated at the Hotchkiss School and Yale (B.A., 1915). He entered the Yale School of Music, where his teachers were David Stanley Smith and Horatio Parker (B.M., 1917). In World War I Moore spent two years in the United States Navy. From 1919 to 1921 he was in Paris, where he studied with Vincent D'Indy at the Schola

Cantorum. On his return he was curator and director of music at the Cleveland Museum of Art while he studied with Ernest Bloch (1921–22). As the recipient of a Pulitzer scholarship in 1925, he returned to Paris where he worked with Charles Tournemire and Nadia Boulanger. In 1926 he was appointed associate in the Department of Music, Columbia University. He became a Guggenheim fellow in 1934. Moore attained the full professorship in 1940, when he also became executive officer. In 1943 he was named MacDowell Professor of Music. He retired in 1962.

Author of two books, *Listening to Music* (1932) and *From Madrigal to Modern Music* (1942), he is best known for compositions which reveal his interest in Americana, as in his orchestral suite *The Pageant of P. T. Barnum* and his operas: *The Devil and Daniel Webster, The Ballad of Baby Doe,* and *Carry Nation.* His tune for Henry Hallam Tweedy's "Eternal God, Whose Power Upholds" was composed for *American Hymns.*

William Moore, fl. early 19th cent.

William Moore's *Columbian Harmony* was registered on April 2, 1825, in the District of West Tennessee. An introduction, a section on the rudiments of music, and remarks on the art of singing are followed by 180 pages of music. Moore justifies his omission of certain musical signs by Davisson's example and the wording of his introduction echoes that of Davisson's *Kentucky Harmony* (1815). Eighteen of the songs in the *Columbian Harmony* bear Moore's name. Of these HOLY MANNA enjoyed considerable popularity in the South. WILSON and LEBANON were presumably named for his home county and its county seat. SWEET RIVERS (same) (q.v.) is an especially fine melody in folk style. Moore locates and dates it: West Tennessee, Wilson Co., March 1825.

P. K. Moran, organist, cellist, composer, and music publisher; d. New York City, Feb. 10, 1831.

P. K. Moran's career in the United States dates from 1817 when he came to New York from Dublin with his wife, who was a singer. He lived in New York from 1818 to 1830 according to city directories and taught piano according to an advertisement in the *New York Evening Post* (June 8, 1820). In 1822–23 he had a music store and piano salesroom; in 1825 he was a cellist in the orchestra for the Garcia Opera Company. He was also active as a publisher (see Richard J. Wolfe, *Secular Music in America, 1801–1825* [1964], for a list of his publications), and was organist at Grace Church. For Jonathan Mayhew Wainwright's *Collection of Psalm, Hymn & Chant Tunes* (New York, 1823) he made the reductions in close score for organ which were a special feature of this publication, and to it he contributed St. John and a chant. In Wainwright's *Music of the Church* there are four tunes by Moran: Mühlenberg, Moran, Grafton Street ("Lord of Life, All Praise Excelling") (q.v.), and Litany. That he was organist of St. John's Chapel in 1830 is shown by a reference in Wainwright's *Psalmodia Evangelica.*

Morelli, fl. before 1820.

A Giuseppe Morelli (born in 1736), Italian by birth, became a singer at the court of Cassel. Was he the composer of the tune called Morelli's Lesson which appeared in two New England collections of music for the fife: Hazeltine's *Instructor in Martial Music* (Exeter, N.H., 1820) and Alvan Robinson's *Massachusetts Collection of Martial Musick* (Exeter, N.H., 1820)? The tune has not been traced to earlier sources. Robinson also included tunes by such European composers as Stamitz, Haydn, and Kotzwara (two marches from his famous *Battle of Prague*). Morelli's Lesson was not only taken up by our native fifers and fiddlers, but was also adapted as a hymn tune. See "As Down a Lone Valley."

Justin Morgan, singing master and horse breeder; b. West Springfield, Mass., 1747; d. Randolph, Vt., March 2, 1798.

Although his father was a farmer, Justin Morgan was too frail for such work. He taught district school and special classes in penmanship and music. His earnings were increased by a small tavern on the Connecticut River and by stallions that he kept for breeding. He was considered honest and polite and a good teacher. He married in 1777 and a year later moved to Randolph, Vt., where he served as lister and town clerk and continued to teach. Mahlon Cottrell, the stage driver on the route from Royalton to Montpelier, often saw Morgan riding his horse to his singing schools.

Morgan's wife died in 1791. By spring 1793 he could no longer support his children and they were brought up by neighbors. He left an estate valued at $160.13; his creditors received thirteen cents on the dollar. His famous horse, the progenitor of the Morgan breed, is not listed among his assets.

Morgan published no singing book of his own, but such tunes as AMANDA and MONTGOMERY were highly esteemed, as was his JUDGMENT ANTHEM. See AMANDA ("How Often Have Our Restless Foes"), which appears with five other Morgan tunes in Andrew Adgate's *Philadelphia Harmony, Part II* (1803), and SYMPHONY ("Ye Scattered Nations").

Johann D. Mueller, German conductor and compiler; fl. mid-18th cent.

Johann Mueller's significance in our field comes from his influential *Vollstimmiges Hessen-Hanauisches Psalm und Choralbuch* (1754). He cultivated a simpler treatment of the chorale melody without excessive chromaticism following the example of Johann Christian Graupner. See his arrangement of LOB SEY DEN ALMACHTIGER GOTT ("Jesu, to Thee My Heart I Bow") and SEELENBRAUTIGAM, JESU GOTTES LAMM ("Jesu, Komm Herein").

William Augustus Mühlenberg, clergyman and educator; b. Philadelphia, Pa., Sept. 16, 1796; d. New York City, April 8, 1877.

William Augustus Mühlenberg was a grandson of Henry Melchior Mühlenberg, who established the Lutheran Church in America. Baptized a Lutheran, he attended St. James Episcopal Church, Philadelphia, with his mother, and grew up an Episcopalian. Educated at the University of Pennsylvania (1815), he prepared for the ministry under Bishop White and Jackson Kemper, was installed as deacon (1817) and priest (1820). Serving first as rector of St. James's Church in Lancaster, Pa. (1820–26), he became rector of George's, Flushing, N.Y. (1826–28). He was active as an educator, establishing a boys' school, Flushing Institute, in 1828, and St. Paul's College on Long Island in 1838. He was in England in 1843 and on his return went to the Church of the Holy Communion in New York City as rector. While there he established a boys' choir and was responsible for the building of St. Luke's Hospital.

Muhlenberg's *A Plea for Christian Hymns* (1821) influenced the General Convention which established a committee to compile a hymnal. Muhlenberg, who published *Church Poetry* (1823), a volume of hymns intended for his own congregation, served on this committee which compiled what was generally called the *Prayer Book Collection*. Four of his own hymns appeared in this volume. See his "I

Would Not Live Alway," "Like Noah's Weary Dove," and "Saviour, Who Thy Flock Art Feeding."

James R. Murray, composer and music editor; b. Ballard-Vale, Mass., March 17, 1841; d. Cincinnati, Ohio, March 10, 1905.

James R. Murray studied at the North Reading Musical Institute (1856–59), where his teachers were Lowell Mason, William Batchelder Bradbury, George J. Webb, and George F. Root. He was a musician in the Union Army from 1862 and he wrote his first song, *Daisy Deane,* in Virginia in 1863. He worked for the music publishing firm of Root and Cady until the Chicago fire. He then went to Andover and taught in the public schools until 1881, when he went to work for the John Church Company in Cincinnati. His last project was an edition of the Wagner operas for which he made an English translation. His MUELLER is still widely known as the tune for "Away in a Manger" (q.v.).

John Murray, founder of American Universalism; b. Alton, Hampshire, England, Dec. 10, 1741; d. Boston, Mass., Sept. 3, 1815.

John Murray's father became a friend and follower of John Wesley and the son responded to this influence and, when he went to London, to that of George Whitefield. In 1759, however, Murray was exposed to the preaching of James Relly and, after reading his *Redemption,* subscribed to the doctrine of universal redemption and was excommunicated from Whitefield's Tabernacle. In July 1770, he sailed from Gravesend for America on the brig *Hand-in-Hand.*

Murray's arrival in America was afterwards viewed by him as a call to found a church. When the brig grounded on a shoal in Cranberry Inlet, N.J., much of the cargo was put on a sloop with Murray in charge. On going ashore he found a farmer, Thomas Potter, who had prayed for the appearance of a preacher in whose belief all men were universally dear to God. Murray became an itinerant preacher with headquarters at "Good Luck," Potter's farm. In 1772 invitations to preach took him to New England. In 1773 and 1774 he continued to preach, to attract audiences, and to inspire antagonism from other religious groups. Befriended in Gloucester by Winthrop Sargent, he preached in Sargent's mansion and eventually married his daughter (1788). His appointment (May 1775) as chaplain to the Rhode Island regiments encamped near Boston was opposed by other chaplains but upheld by General George Washington.

In January 1779, sixty-one residents of Gloucester formed the Independent Church of Christ with Murray as their pastor. When the members refused to pay taxes for the support of the First Church, their goods were sold at auction. They in turn brought suit under the new constitution of Massachusetts. After extended litigation they obtained a favorable verdict (June 1786). In 1793 Murray was installed as pastor of the Universalist Society in Boston and, since by that time he was responsible for a family, he accepted a modest salary. His pastoral activities were ended by a paralytic stroke. See "Hark! 'Tis the Saviour of Mankind."

John Mycall, schoolteacher and printer; b. Worcester, England; d. Newburyport, Mass., 1833.

John Mycall taught school at Amesbury, Mass. Although he had served no apprenticeship in the art of printing he was ingenious and able to learn all he needed to know. He bought a share in the printing firm of Lunt & Tinges and half a year later became sole owner. After conducting the business successfully for twenty years he moved to a farm in Harvard, Mass., and later to Newburyport. During his residence at Harvard he delivered "A funeral address on the death of the late General George Washington," which was printed in 1800.

His importance for hymnology lies in the fact that he printed in Newburyport, in 1781, the first edition of Watts's psalms in which the patriotic references to Great Britain and to her monarch were replaced by expressions more appropriate to the American colonies. Ezra Stiles, president of Yale, approved of this edition and tells us that the alterations were made "with the Advice & Assist of neighbors ministers & others." It was thus a committee product, but Stiles does not name the other members. See "Our States, O Lord."

R. N., fl. 1849.

In *The Devotional Harmonist* (New York, 1849) there are ten tunes attributed to R. N. *The Devotional Harmonist* was a collection chosen by a committee appointed by "the choristers of the Methodist Episcopal Churches of this city [New York], Brooklyn, Williamsburg, and Jersey City," which was edited by Charles Dingley. The preface noted both that the tunes had been "drawn largely" from *The Methodist Harmonist* and that "a number of original tunes, contributed by various friends residing in this city and elsewhere," were also included. A check of *The Methodist Harmonist* of 1831 shows that none of the tunes by R. N. appeared therein. Apparently R. N. was one of the aforementioned "friends." See WHITEFIELD ("Come, Let Us Tune Our Loftiest Song").

Robert Nathan, author; b. New York City, Jan. 2, 1894.

· After attending private schools here and in Switzerland, Robert Nathan went to Harvard University. In 1924–25 he was a lecturer in the School of Journalism at New York University. He became known as poet and dramatist with numerous publications, but was also interested in music and composed a violin sonata as well as songs. In 1935 he was elected a member of the National Institute of Arts and Letters. He was also a charter member of PEN and a member of ASCAP. See his "Christian, Be Up."

David Nelson, surgeon, minister, and educator; b. Jonesborough, Tenn., Sept. 24, 1793; d. Oakland, Miss., Oct. 17, 1844.

David Nelson was educated at Washington College (graduated 1810) and took his M.D. degree in 1812 at Philadelphia. He became a surgeon in a Kentucky regiment during the War of 1812 and narrowly missed death on an expedition into Canada. After surviving campaigns in Alabama and Florida he returned to Jonesborough at the end of the war and, after marriage, started a medical practice. Although he had belonged to the Presbyterian Church, he had more or less abandoned its religious teachings. In 1823, after living the life of a "card-playing infidel" he reunited with the church and abandoned medicine in favor of theology. As a student of the Rev. Robert Glenn he was licensed to preach in Kingsport (1825) and ordained a year later at Rogersville, Tenn. At the death of a brother in 1827 he succeeded to his pulpit in Danville, Ky. In 1830 he moved to Marion County, Mo., where he established a manual-labor college at Greenfields and served as its president for five years. In 1836 he became embroiled in the slavery issue so violently that he had to find residence in a free state. He took refuge across the river in Quincy, Ill., where he founded a similar college. Early in his career he had been involved in a publishing venture when he aided two other ministers in the publication of *The Calvinistic Magazine*. In 1837 he published *Cause and Cure of Infidelity*, which the American Tract Society republished in 1841.

Nelson's hymn, "My Days Are Gliding Swiftly By" (q.v.), written in 1835, became very popular. Two of his hymns appeared in James Gallagher's *Selection,* published in 1835 as a supplement to an edition of Isaac Watts's *Psalms and Hymns.*

Alice Nevin, organist and choir director; b. Pittsburgh, Pa., Aug. 1, 1837; d. Lancaster, Pa., Nov. 19, 1925.

Alice Nevin was long active as organist and choir leader in the chapel of Franklin and Marshall College and also, for a time, in the First Reformed Church in Lancaster, Pa. She aided in the establishment of St. Luke's Reformed Church which she served in many ways. She published *Hymns and Carols for Church and Sunday School* in 1879. It included five original tunes: RESURRECTION ("He Hides Within the Lily") (q.v.), CECIL, and ELSIE, with two others to which she gave no titles.

Edwin H. Nevin, minister; b. Shippensburg, Pa., May 9, 1814; d. June 2, 1889.

Edwin H. Nevin graduated from Jefferson College in 1833 and from Princeton Seminary in 1836. From 1836 to 1857 he served churches as a Presbyterian minister and, from the latter date until 1868, held a pastorate in the Congregational Church. Illness then forced him to recuperate for a period of six years. When he recovered he filled pulpits of Reformed churches at Lancaster and Philadelphia, Pa.

Nevin wrote several hymns, all of them but "Live on the Field of Battle" appearing in Charles Dexter Cleveland's *Lyra Sacra Americana,* published in 1868. Three were included in Elias Nason's *Congregational Hymn Book* (1857). See "Oh! 'Tis Glorious" and "Happy, Saviour, Would I Be."

John Jacob Niles, folk singer and arranger; b. Louisville, Ky., *April* 28, 1892; d. March 1, 1980.

John Jacob Niles was educated at the Cincinnati Conservatory of Music and the Schola Cantorum in Paris. He studied with A. Bimboni and Edgar Stillman Kelly at the former institution and with Vincent d'Indy at the latter. He was also a student at the Conservatory of Music in the University of Lyons.

Singing countertenor and accompanying himself on dulcimers of his own design, he toured this country, England, and continental Europe presenting Anglo-American folk songs and ballads on the concert stage. An authority on the music of the Southern Appalachians, where he did extensive field research among the hill folk of Kentucky, Virginia, Tennessee, North Carolina, and Georgia, he collected ballads, carols, and folk songs.

A frequent contributor to periodicals, Niles is the author of *Singing Soldiers* and *Songs My Mother Never Taught Me.* His music publications include *Seven Kentucky Mountain Songs, Seven Negro Exaltations, Songs of the Hill-Folk, Ten Christmas Carols from the Southern Appalachian Mountains, Ballads and Tragic Legends.*

On June 2, 1949, Niles received the honorary degree of Mus.D. from the Cincinnati Conservatory of Music. See his "In All the Magic of Christmas-Tide," composed for *American Hymns,* for which he wrote both words and music.

Nathaniel Niles, local leader and author; b. South Kingston, R.I., April 3, 1741; d. Oct. 31, 1828.

After illness forced him to drop out of Harvard at the end of a year, Nathaniel Niles entered the College of New Jersey (now Princeton) from which he later graduated. He studied, successively, medicine, law, and theology. Although he was never ordained, he occasionally preached. Shortly before the Revolutionary War he settled in Norwich, Conn., and married. Toward the end of the war he bought a large tract of land in Orange County, Vt., and in 1782 or 1783 he and several friends went there to live, the first settlers in what became West Fairlee township.

From 1784 until Niles retired to his farm at the age of seventy-one, he held many local offices—sometimes two at once. He was a vigorous thinker and, a rarity in Vermont, a Jeffersonian Democrat who fought slavery and banks. Although his political activities were frequently stormy, he was logical and forceful enough to be listened to if not always agreed with. In 1793 Dartmouth College made Niles a trustee, a position he held until 1820.

Niles was known as an inventor and as the author of theological articles and sermons. His one venture in the writing of poetry was "Why Should Vain Mortals Tremble" (q.v.), for which Andrew Law wrote the music.

Anna Nitschmann, Moravian hymn writer; b. 1715; d. Herrn-hut, Saxony, May 22, 1760.

Anna Nitschmann was the sister of Bishop David Nitschmann who founded the Moravian Church in America. On June 27, 1757, she became the second wife of Count von Zinzendorf (q.v.). The mar-riage was kept secret because the count did not wish to tell his mother that he was marrying a peasant and because Anna had un-finished duties with the Single Sisters' choir. The Count announced the marriage from Zeist with a lengthy letter of explanation to the churches on November 10, 1758.

After their marriage they continued their rounds of the Moravian congregations, much as they had done before in their separate capacities. They made a tour of Western Germany and Switzerland in 1757, and in 1758 left Herrnhut again for Holland, Greenland, America, the West Indies, Surinam, Tranquebar, Abyssinia, and the Near East. On Christmas Eve, 1759, they returned once again to Herrnhut amid scenes of great rejoicing. They both fell ill the fol-lowing spring. Zinzendorf died on May 9, 1760, and Anna survived him by thirteen days. They were buried at Herrnhut. See "Die kleine Heerde zeugen."

Paul Nordoff, composer, pianist, and teacher; b. Philadelphia, Pa., June 4, 1909; d. Herdecke, West Germany, Jan. 18, 1977.

Paul Nordoff was educated at the Philadelphia Conservatory of Music (B.M., 1928; M.M., 1930), and at the Juilliard Graduate School (1928–33). He studied piano with Hendrik Ezerman and Olga Samaroff and composition with Rubin Goldmark. In spite of a rule forbidding the award of full fellowships in more than one major subject, Nordoff was permitted to hold simultaneous fellowships in piano and composition while at Juilliard. Within a few months of his graduation cum laude, Nordoff won the Columbia University Bearns Prize. That same year he was awarded a Guggenheim Fel-lowship, which was renewed in 1935.

In 1933 John Erskine, the president of the Juilliard Foundation, invited Nordoff to make some modern settings of Stephen Foster melodies. During a subsequent trip abroad these, along with other Nordoff compositions, were published by B. Schott and Company of Mainz. In 1934 Nordoff played his first piano concerto with the Groningen Orchestra in the Netherlands. In the same year Eugene Ormandy performed his *Secular Mass for Chorus and Orchestra* with the Minneapolis Symphony Orchestra, which Ormandy then directed. A Pulitzer prize was awarded Nordoff in 1940 for his *Quintet for*

Piano and String Quartet. He wrote incidental music for Katharine Cornell's *Romeo and Juliet* in 1936; a dance for Martha Graham, *Every Soul Is a Circus,* in 1939; and *Tallyho* for Agnes de Mille in 1944. He has composed two operas, *The Masterpiece* and *The Sea-Change,* and has composed works commissioned by the League of Composers, the Little Orchestra Society, Eugene List and Carroll Glenn, the Louisville Philharmonic Orchestra, and Columbia University. Nordoff devoted his last years to music therapy, working especially with brain-damaged and retarded children. See his settings for "From Countless Hearts" and "Heaven, Heaven, Heaven Is the Place," both composed for *American Hymns.*

John W. Norris, Episcopal minister; b. Sioux City, Iowa, Dec. 8, 1893.

John W. Norris worked on the *Sioux City Journal* for a number of years before going on to college. After graduation from the University of Pennsylvania, he studied at the Philadelphia Divinity School (S.T.B., 1925). He spent four years as an assistant at St. Peter's Church, Philadelphia, and twelve at Bustleton, Pa., in the Memorial Church of St. Luke. After serving as an instructor in church music at the Philadelphia Divinity School (1937– 41), he was appointed superintendent of Lawrence Hall, a church school for boys in Chicago (1941–45). He was rector of St. John's Parish, Poultney, Vt. (1945–48), and from 1948 rector of St. Michael's Church in Brattleboro. From 1937 he served as a member of both the Joint Commission on Church Music and the Joint Commission on the Revision of the Hymnal for the Protestant Episcopal Church. See his "Give Peace, O God, the Nations Cry."

Frank Mason North, Methodist minister and executive; b. New York City, Dec. 3, 1850; d. Madison, N.J., Dec. 17, 1935.

During a busy life Frank Mason North found time to write a small group of hymns, and in particular "Where Cross the Crowded Ways of Life" (q.v.). After attending private schools in New York City North went to Wesleyan University (A.B. 1872). After working for his father during the ensuing year he returned to the university to prepare himself for the Methodist ministry. Then followed a period (1873–92) in which he was active as a pastor in Florida, New York, and Connecticut.

In 1892 he became corresponding secretary of the New York

Church Extension and Missionary Society, in 1912 corresponding secretary of the Methodist Episcopal Church, and in 1916 president of the Federal Council of Churches of Christ in America, an organization formed largely because of his own initiatives.

Recognition came to North in the form of honorary degrees from Wesleyan University (D.D. and L.L.D.). In addition to serving as trustee for his alma mater (from 1899) and of Drew Theological Seminary (from 1907), he was a member of the executive board of universities in China and Japan.

Andrews Norton, scholar, educator, and hymn writer; b. Hingham, Mass., Dec. 31, 1786; d. Newport, R.I., Sept. 18, 1853.

Andrews Norton was perhaps better known as a scholar and teacher. His hymns, which had appeared in various periodicals, were collected and published only after his death.

After attending Derby Academy in Hingham, Norton entered Harvard, where he graduated in 1804. He was a tutor at Bowdoin and later at Harvard, where in 1813 he became librarian and later followed Dr. Channing as lecturer in biblical criticism. As Dexter Professor of Sacred Literature (from 1819) he taught in the newly formed Harvard theological school until 1830. Though he edited the *General Repository and Review,* his most important work was *The Genuineness of the Gospels,* the fourth volume of which, as well as his translation of the gospels, was published after his death. See "My God, I Thank Thee."

George Oates, American tune writer; fl. early 19th cent.

George Oates was a contemporary of Lowell Mason and his tune ATLANTIC, in the seventh edition of Lowell Mason's *Boston Handel and Haydn Society Collection* (1829), is his best-known composition. It was widely sung for a considerable period. See his PRESCOTT ("I Am Weary of Straying") which, as Lowell Mason notes, was "composed and presented to the Editor for the *Choir* by Geo. Oates."

Samson Occom, Mohegan Indian, preacher, and missionary; b. Mohegan, near New London, Conn., 1723; d. July 14, 1792.

At the age of sixteen Samson Occom (Occum) was much influenced by Rev. James Davenport, an evangelist of the Great Awakening. From 1743 to 1747 he was a pupil of Rev. Eleazer Wheelock of Lebanon, Conn. In 1749 he became a schoolmaster and minister to the Montauk tribe of Long Island. After his success among the Indians had attracted attention he was ordained by the Long Island Presbytery in 1759.

From 1761 to 1763 he made two trips as a missionary to the Oneida tribe in New York, and in 1765 he accompanied Rev. Nathaniel Whitaker of Norwich, Conn., on a journey to England for the purpose of raising funds for Wheelock's Indian Charity School. Occom created a sensation in Britain. In two years he preached more than three hundred times, usually to crowded houses. Financially the trip was a great success. During their stay in England and Scotland Occom and Whitaker collected nearly £9,500. The whole amount was deposited with Lord Dartmouth, chairman of the committee, and later applied to the building of a college in New Hampshire, to which the name Dartmouth was given by way of compliment.

In 1768 Occom returned to his own people at Mohegan as their pastor and adviser, championing their rights and resisting white encroachments on their lands. He moved to the Brotherton Tract, Oneida County, N.Y., in 1786 with a group of Indians from Long Island and New England. He was regarded as a great orator in his own language. Occom himself issued a *Choice Collection of Hymns and Spiritual Songs* in 1774 at New London, Conn. See his "Waked by the Gospel's Powerful Sound."

Arne Oldberg, composer; b. Youngstown, Ohio, July 12, 1871; d. 1962.

Arne Oldberg was educated in the public schools of Ohio and Illinois. He studied piano with August Hyllested, counterpoint, composition, and orchestration with Adolf Koelling, Frederick Grant Gleason, and Wilhelm Middelschulte at Chicago, piano with Theodor Leschetizsky at Vienna (1893–95), and composition with Josef Rheinberger at Munich (1898). In 1899 Oldberg joined the faculty of Northwestern University, where he was professor of piano and composition and director of the piano and graduate departments until his retirement in 1941. He also taught summer classes at the University of Southern California for five years.

Oldberg's orchestral works consist of seven symphonies, two overtures (*Paola and Francesca*, 1908; *Festival*, 1909), a rhapsody (*Rhapsody*, 1915), a fantasy (*At Night*, 1916), a symphonic poem (*The Sea*, 1936), a set of twelve *Variations* for organ and orchestra, a concerto for horn, a concerto for organ, and two concertos for piano and orchestra. His chamber works include a string quartet, two quintets for piano and strings, a quintet for piano and woodwinds. He also composed a piano sonata, and many smaller works. His *St. Francis of Assisi* (for baritone and orchestra) dates from 1953.

Oldberg's *Second Piano Concerto* was awarded a first prize of $1,000 in the Hollywood Bowl competition of 1931; it had its premiere in the Bowl under Frederick Stock a year later. His compositions were chiefly introduced by the Chicago, Philadelphia, and Minneapolis symphony orchestras, often at the North Shore Festivals. See his GILDER ("To Thee, Eternal Soul, Be Praise").

Henry Kemble Oliver, musician, teacher, and public official; b. Beverly, Mass., Nov. 24, 1800; d. Salem, Mass., Aug. 12, 1885.

It was appropriate that Henry Kemble Oliver, as a man of seventy-two years, should have been asked to conduct his tune FEDERAL STREET at the mammoth Peace Jubilee in Boston (1872). They realized as we do now that he would be remembered by this tune. His mother was musical, and it was from her that he learned tunes by Billings and Holden, New England's music of an earlier day. At ten years of age he sang as a boy soprano in the Park Street Church, Boston and later was the organist there. He prepared for college at the Boston Latin School and Phillips Andover. After two years at Harvard he transferred to Dartmouth (A.B. 1818).

For nearly a quarter century he taught school in his native Salem (1818–42), also playing the organ first at St. Peter's Church and later at the North Church. From 1848 to 1858 he was the superintendant of the Atlantic Cotton Mills, Lawrence, Mass., where he was organist at the Unitarian Church. His services to his state included a period as adjutant general. He organized and was the first director of the Massachusetts Bureau of Statistics of Labor, and was state treasurer during the troubled days of the Civil War. On his return to Salem he was elected mayor for four years.

It was Oliver who was chiefly responsible for two musical organizations in Salem, the Mozart Association and the Salem Glee Club. His collection of *Original Hymn Tunes* was dedicated to the Salem Oratorical Society (1875). He also published a *Collection of Church Music* (1860) and, with Samuel P. Tuckerman and Silas A. Bancroft, *The National Lyre* (1848). See SYDNEY ("As Shadows Cast by Cloud and Sun"), WYEFORD ("A King Shall Reign in Righteousness"), FEDERAL STREET ("Lord of All Being, Throned Afar"), CATON ("Mysterious Presence! Source of All"), CROWN POINT ("O Love Divine, That Stooped to Share"), CHADWICK ("O Thou Who Didst Ordain the

Word"), LEVERETT ("Sovereign and Transforming Grace"), CLONBERNE ("Thou One in All, Thou All in One"), and VINCROVE ("Wilt Thou Not Visit Me?").

Thomas Olivers, Methodist preacher; b. near Newtown, Montgomeryshire, England, 1725; d. March 1799.

Thomas Olivers early became an orphan and was brought up by various relatives. Apprenticed to a shoemaker, he spent a youthful period of immorality which forced him to leave his birthplace and go to Shrewsbury and Bristol. In the latter city he heard George White-field preach a sermon which made him an ardent convert to Christianity. Discouraged from joining Whitefield's followers he subsequently became a member of the Methodist Society at Bradford-on-Avon. There he met John Wesley (q.v.), who engaged him as a preacher. He went at once as an evangelist to Cornwall (October 1, 1753), where he spent the rest of his life. For some time he was co-editor with John Wesley of the *Arminian Magazine.* He composed the tune HELMSLEY ("Jesus, Master, O Discover") (q.v.) and wrote several hymns: "The God of Abraham Praise," "Come Immortal King of Glory," and "O Thou God of My Salvation" as well as an elegy on the death of John Wesley.

Timothy Olmstead, military musician and church composer; b. Phoenix, N.Y., Nov. 12, 1759; d. Aug. 15, 1848.

As a boy of sixteen Timothy Olmstead responded to the call for troops after the engagement at Lexington and joined the East Hartford company, which was ordered to Boston. During the Revolutionary War he enlisted and was a musician in two Connecticut regiments, the Seventh and the Ninth. His second cousin, Alice Olmstead, who became his wife on May 2, 1783, bore him thirteen children. Olmstead was in Hartford, Conn., in 1785. From there he went to Whitestone, N.Y., and in 1811 we find him in Rome, N.Y., where Alice Olmstead died on February 5. In 1814 he aided in the defense of New London as a member of the Connecticut First Militia Regiment.

A number of his compositions were included in Andrew Law's *Art of Singing* (1794). His own collection was *The Musical Olio* (Northampton, Mass., 1805) and he added to their number in the second edition published in New London in 1811. He avoided the use of shape notes, which had been employed earlier by Andrew Law (q.v.)

in his *Music Primer* (4th ed., Cambridge, Mass., 1803). "I have thought best to print in characters universally made use of, having not as yet been made to perceive the utility of the simplifications and new inventions, which are so frequently presented us for our improvement." In the matter of arrangements he sought to please all tastes. "I have inserted some tunes in three parts and some in four, some with counters and some with second trebles. Part of the airs are placed for the tenor voice and part for the female voice . . ." Olmstead's experience as an army musician was refleccted in his *Martial Music: A Collection of Marches Harmonized for Field Bands . . .* (Boston, 1807). See LOUDON ("Blessed Comforter Divine") and WASHINGTON ("Shall Man, O God of Light").

Ernst W. Olson, translator, editor, and poet; b. Finja Parish, Sweden, March 16, 1870; d. Chicago, Ill., Oct. 6, 1958.

Ernst W. Olson was an editor of Swedish periodicals before he came to this country. Here he became office editor and secretary of literature for the Augustana Book Concern in Minneapolis (1911–49). He was chief translator of Swedish hymns for the 1925 edition of the Augustana Lutheran hymnal, published in Rock Island, Ill. He wrote the Swedish text for the New Sweden Tercentenary Hymn (1638–1938), called "Hymn for the Pioneers." *The History of the Augustana Book Concern: Publishers to the Augustana Synod,* which appeared in 1933, was prepared by Olson. A second book, *Olaf Olsson, the Man, His Work, His Thought,* came out in 1941.

Olson died shortly after the publication of the Lutheran *Service Book and Hymnal* in 1958. He had been a member of the joint commission responsible for the volume. It included four of his translations from the Swedish and his paraphrase of Psalm 121. See "God of Peace, in Peace Preserve Us."

Henry Ustic Onderdonk, bishop of the Protestant Episcopal Church, hymn writer, and compiler, b. New York City, March 16, 1789; d. Dec. 6, 1858.

Henry Ustic Onderdonk attended Columbia College (B.A., 1805; M.A., 1808; D.D., 1827). He pursued medical studies in London and at the University of Edinburgh (M.D., 1810). On his return to this country in 1815 he began to practice, but within the year gave up medicine for the ministry. After studying theology with Bishop Hobart, he was ordained in the Protestant Episcopal Church and was missionary at Canandaigua, N.Y. (1818), rector of St. Anne's in Brooklyn, and bishop, succeeding Bishop White of Philadelphia (1836). Suspended in 1844 for intemperance, he spent several years in retirement, but was reinstated in 1856. Both Onderdonk and William Augustus Muhlenberg (q.v.) worked on the committee which produced the *Prayer Book Collection* (1826) and nine of Onderdonk's own hymns were included. This volume, which introduced hymns and indeed American hymns in addition to psalm paraphrases, marked an important change in Episcopalian practice. Onderdonk was associated with Muhlenberg in compiling *Plain Music for the Book of Common Prayer* (1854). See "On Zion and on Lebanon," "The Spirit in Our Hearts," and "Though I Should Seek."

Josiah Osgood, composer and compiler of church music; fl. mid-19th cent.

Josiah Osgood was associate editor, with S. Hill, of Artemas N. Johnson's *Bay State Collection* (Boston, 1849). With Johnson he assisted Benjamin F. Baker in compiling the *Melodia Sacra* (1852). Osgood was also a principal contributor to Johnson's *The Handel Collection of Church Music* (1854). Johnson, in his *Empire Collection* (1862), refers to Osgood as of Chelsea, Mass. See BERLIN ("Day of God, Thou Blessed Day") and EDEN ("Heaven Is Here").

Heinrich Otto, Pennsylvania poet; fl. 18th cent.

Heinrich Otto's German poem "Haus Segen" ("A Blessing on the House") first appeared as a broadside and was later selected by John Joseph Stoudt for inclusion in his *Pennsylvania German Poetry, 1685–1830*. See "Guter Gott! Dir ich befehle."

Oscar R. Overby, music director and educator; b. Griggs Co., S.D., Sept. 29, 1892.

Oscar Overby received his chief training at Concordia College in Moorhead, Minn., Northwestern Conservatory of Music, Minneapolis, New England Conservatory of Music, Boston, St. Olaf College, Northfield, Minn., and Columbia University. He received a B.M. from St. Olaf and a Mus.D. from Augustana College, Sioux Falls, S.D.

He was executive director and musical director of the International Choral Union of the Evangelical Lutheran Church of America from the time of its establishment in 1949. From 1921 to 1950 he was professor of music, instructor in theory, music history, music education, instrumentation, composition, and choral conducting at St. Olaf College. In 1948–49 he was guest instructor and choral director of Shimer College, Mt. Carroll, Ill. For shorter periods before 1920 he held positions as music instructor and director at Park Region College, Fergus Falls, and at Concordia College, Moorhead, Minn.

The Choral Union, of which Overby was musical director, is a church-wide organization of all the choirs and musicians of the Evangelical Lutheran Church. In this work he succeeded his life-long colleague, the late F. Melius Christiansen, and held the position from 1941 to 1950. The new office of Church Music founded in 1949, of which he was executive director, has as its mission the promotion of a church-wide ministry of music. See OUR CHRIST ("I Know Not How That Bethlehem's Babe") and PRECIOUS CHILD (same).

John Paddon, vocalist; d. 1846.

John Paddon must be distinguished from James Padden (1768–1835), who was organist of Exeter Cathedral. Unfortunately our information about John is sketchy. *The Columbian Sentinel* reported a "Concert of Vocal Music" given in August 1823, in which he appeared as a singer with three Miss Gillinghams from New York. Paddon's tune QUEBEC CHAPEL ("On Zion and On Lebanon") (q.v.) appeared in Jonathan Mayhew Wainwright's *Music of the Church* (1828) and was repeated in the same editor's *Psalmodia Evangelica* of 1830.

Philip Pain, poet; d. 1668?

Philip Pain's book of poetry, *Daily Meditations*, was, according to the title page, begun on July 19, 1666. It was printed by Marmaduke Johnson in Cambridge, Mass., in 1668, and reissued by Johnson and Samuel Green in 1670. The book was considered "lost" until a copy was discovered in 1923. Oscar Wegelin thought it "the earliest known specimen of original American verse printed in the English Colonies" (*Early American Poetry*, p. 60). However, there is no positive proof that Pain was an American. He refers to himself in the postscript as a "Pilot young," and the title page tells us that he "lately suffering shipwreck was drowned." All else is speculation. According to

Leon Howard, "We may assume that he was reared in an environment which enabled him to become acquainted with some of the best of contemporary English poetry and that his education, although deeply religious, was in the liberal piety of George Herbert" (Huntington Library facsimile ed. of Pain, San Marino, Calif.). See "Whilst in This World I Stay."

David Paine, organist and music teacher; fl. early 19th cent.

David Paine, uncle of the American composer John Knowles Paine, was active in Portland, Maine, in the 1830s and '40s. He was the organist for the first performance of Haydn's *Creation* in Portland (April 24, 1837). In addition to teaching music, he was the proprietor of a music store located on Middle Street (1838) and later over the store of his brother, Jacob S. Paine (1840). His *Portland Sacred Music Society's Collection of Church Music* (Portland, 1839) includes original tunes by the compiler. The Portland First Parish Church had a local reputation for its fine music. Paine was organist there in 1840–41. See HOLINESS ("Hither We Come, Our Dearest Lord").

John Knowles Paine, composer; b. Portland, Maine, Jan. 9, 1839; d. Cambridge, Mass., April 25, 1906.

John Knowles Paine founded the music department at Harvard University. His HARVARD HYMN is a fine example of the Victorian processional hymn. Paine studied with a German-born music teacher, Hermann Kotzschmar, then went to Germany to continue his education. He toured there as a concert organist and conducted his *Mass in D* in Berlin. He was the first American composer to have a work in large form performed in Europe.

On his return in 1862 Paine was appointed organist and instructor of music at Harvard. A voluntary and unpaid series of lectures on musical form met with increased success under President Eliot. To the series Paine added harmony and counterpoint. Not only did this mark the beginning of the Harvard music department, it also established a pattern gradually imitated elsewhere in the United States. Paine was promoted to assistant professor and, in 1875, to professor.

His major creative effort was directed toward orchestral compositions in the larger forms. His two symphonies, the second subtitled *Spring,* were published in full score. He also wrote symphonic poems on Shakespearean themes, *The Tempest* and *As You Like It,* and two sea pieces, *Ocean Fantasy* and *Island Fantasy*. He wrote incidental music for *Oedipus Tyrannus* for a Cambridge performance. He was a music editor of *Hymns and Songs of Praise* (1874) for which he wrote six tunes: KINGDOM, LINCOLN, CONSOLATION, DEVOTION, FIRST FRUITS, and DIES IRAE. See DEVOTION ("Behold the Shade of Night Is Now Receding") and CENTENNIAL HYMN ("Today Beneath Benignant Skies").

Ray Palmer, Congregational minister and hymn writer; b. Little Compton, R.I., Nov. 12, 1808; d. Newark, N.J., March 29, 1887.

After attending Phillips Academy, Andover, Mass., Ray Palmer entered Yale, receiving his A.B. in 1830. He went to Bath, Me., in 1835 as pastor of the Central Congregational Church there. From 1850 to 1865 he was pastor of the First Congregational Church at Albany, N.Y. In the latter year he went to New York City as secretary of the American Congregational Union. After he resigned the secretaryship he moved to Newark, N.J. where he remained until 1887.

Best known of Palmer's hymns is "My Faith Looks Up to Thee" (q.v.), first published in *Spiritual Songs for Social Worship* by Thomas Hastings and Lowell Mason in 1832. In 1858 *The Sabbath Hymn Book* by Professors Edwards A. Park and Austin Phelps of Andover Theological Seminary included hymns by Palmer which established his reputation as one of the foremost hymn writers of his time. Four of his hymns included in that work were free translations from the Latin (old Latin hymnody had hitherto been little known to American Protestants, although the *Plymouth Collection* of 1855 had introduced a number of translations) and three were original hymns: "Jesus, These Eyes Have Never Seen" (q.v.), "Lord, My Weak Thought in Vain Would Climb" (q.v.), and a third, which has dropped out of common use.

A gifted speaker and writer he contributed often to periodicals and was the author of several books: *Memoirs and Select Remains of Charles Pond* (1829), *The Spirit's Life, A Poem* (1837), *How to Live* (1839), *Doctrinal Text Book* (1839), *Spiritual Improvement* (1839; repub., 1851, as *Closet Hours*), *What Is Truth?* (1860), *Remember Me* (1865), *Hymns and Holy Hours* (1873). A complete edition of his *Poetical Works* was issued in 1875. See also "Behold, The Shade of Night Is Now Receding."

Roswell Park, educator and minister; b. Lebanon, Conn.,
Oct. 1, 1807; d. Chicago, Ill., July 16, 1869.

Roswell Park was twelve when his family moved to Otsego County,
N.Y. In his sophomore year at Hamilton College he received an appointment to West Point, which he accepted, graduating as highest-
ranking man in the class of 1831. After serving at army engineering
posts in Newport and Boston he resigned from the army in 1836
and for the next six years served as a professor of chemistry at the
University of Pennsylvania. During his professorial period he decided to enter the ministry of the Protestant Episcopal Church.

In Burlington, Vt., he prepared for holy orders under the direction of Bishop George Washington Doane (q.v.); in 1843 he became
a deacon, in 1844 a priest. Appointed rector of Christ Church, Pom-
fret, Conn., he served in that capacity from 1845 to 1852, at the
same time conducting the Christ Church Hall preparatory school
there. As headmaster of that school he became well known throughout New England.

After declining the presidency of Norwich University in 1850, he
traveled to Europe in 1852. Upon his return he became the first
president of Racine College in Wisconsin. Opening the institution in
November 1852, he remained its president until 1863, acting as rector of St. Luke's Church in Racine at the same time.

In 1863 he withdrew from both positions to move to Chicago,
where he founded Immanuel Hall, a classical and scientific school
which he directed until his death. His publications included: *Selections of Juvenile and Miscellaneous Poems* (1836, revised in 1856 and
published as *Jerusalem and Other Poems*), *A Sketch of the History and To-
pography of West Point* (1840), *Pantology: or a Systematic Survey of
Human Knowledge,* and *Handbook for American Travelers in Europe*
(1853). An original member of the American Association for the Advancement of Science, he was affiliated with many other scientific
and literary societies. See "Jesus Spreads His Banner O'er Us."

Edwin Pond Parker, Congregational minister and hymn
writer; b. Castine, Maine, Jan. 13, 1836; d. Hartford, Conn.,
May 28, 1925.

For a half century Edwin Pond Parker served as minister of the
Second or South Congregational Church of Hartford, Conn. The
Christmas Eve services which he introduced there were the first in a
nonliturgical church in New England. *Song Flowers* (1866), which he
edited, contains many hymns for which he wrote both words and
music. Parker was editor of the *Book of Praise* (1868) and contributed

original hymns to this volume and to the *Christian Hymnal* of 1877. See "Master, No Offering," which dates from 1888. His MERCY ("Holy Spirit, Truth Divine") (q.v.), an arrangement of Louis Moreau Gottschalk's "Last Hope," has been widely sung.

Horatio Parker, composer, organist, and educator; b. Auburndale, Mass., Sept. 15, 1863; d. Cedarhurst, N.Y., Dec. 18, 1919.

Horatio Parker's father was an architect, his mother the village organist. At the age of fourteen the son, who had previously disliked music, began to study the piano and to compose. Two years later he was organist at Dedham, Mass., and wrote hymn tunes and choral music for the service there. After studying music in Boston (composition with George W. Chadwick), Parker went to Munich in 1882 where he studied organ and composition with Josef Rheinberger.

In 1885 Parker concluded his studies in Germany, then settled in New York. He was influenced by Antonin Dvořák, then director of the National Conservatory of Music where Parker taught counterpoint. His most widely acclaimed score, the *Hora Novissima,* was the first American work to be performed at the Three Choirs Festival in England. In 1893 he became organist of Trinity Church, Boston, and in 1894, professor of music at Yale. In addition to teaching, he organized and conducted the New Haven Symphony, continued as organist of Trinity Church and later of St. Nicholas, New York City, and directed choral groups in Derby and New Haven, Conn., and in Philadelphia.

His prize-winning opera *Mona* was produced by the Metropolitan Opera in 1912. *Fairyland,* his second opera, won a prize offered by the National Federation of Music Clubs and was performed in Los Angeles. Parker's hymn tunes appeared chiefly in *The Hymnal Revised and Enlarged* (1903) which he edited. See CLOVELLY ("From Heart to Heart"), PRO PATRIA ("God of the Nations" and "Heralds of Christ"), MOUNT SION ("O Master Workman of the Race"), PIXHAM ("O Thou Whose Gracious Presence Shone" and "We Praise Thee, God, for Harvests Earned"), KING OF GLORY ("Our Father, by Whose Name"), and MISSION ("The Voice of God Is Calling").

Leonard Parker, composer; fl. early 20th cent.

The PANOPLY OF LIGHT (q.v.), by Leonard Parker, was associated with and named for Theodore Chickering Williams' "Hast Thou

Heard It, O My Brother" in the *Hymnal for American Youth* (1926). It had appeared earlier under the name FESTAL DAY in a Sunday-School book entitled *Heart and Voice* (1908). It was reprinted in 1924 in *The Beacon Hymnal for Sunday Schools.* FESTAL DAY, another tune by Parker, appeared in the *Methodist Sunday School Hymnal* in 1911.

Parmenter, composer; fl. 18th cent.

Parmenter is remembered as the composer of COMPLAINT ("Spare Us, O Lord, Aloud We Pray") (q.v.). Harriet Beecher Stowe describes the tune in a remarkable passage in "The Pearl of Orr's Island." It first appeared in Timothy Swan's *Federal Harmony* (1790) as "never before published" and with the name of the composer not given. The tune was reprinted in Oliver Holden's *Union Harmony* (1793) and is there attributed to Parmenter.

Robert William Parsons, singer and composer; b. Exeter, England; d. by drowning, Newark-upon-Trent, Jan. 25, 1569/70.

Sworn gentleman of the Chapel Royal in 1563, Robert William Parsons is erroneously said to have been organist at Westminster Abbey. He wrote much church music remarkable for its ingenious part-writing and original effects of harmony. In Barnard's 1641 collection, *Selected Church Music,* there is a service in four, five, six, and seven parts, and a full anthem in six. Low's *Directions* (1664) included Parsons' *Burial Service.* His settings of the "In Nomine" melody were much praised by Butler in his *Principles of Music,* and one of his songs, "Enforced by Love or Feare," was praised by Burney and printed as an example of Parsons' rich and curious harmony. Parsons also contributed THE LAMENTATION ("O Lord, Turn Not Away Thy Face") (q.v.) to Ravenscroft's *The Whole Booke of Psalmes* (1621).

Francis Daniel Pastorius, scholar and writer; b. Sommerhausen, Germany, Sept. 26, 1651; d. Jan. 2, 1720.

Francis Daniel Pastorius entered the University of Altdorf at seventeen. For his law studies he went to Strassburg, Basle, and Jena. In 1676 he received the degree of doctor of laws at Nuremberg, and in 1679 he was lecturing on law in Frankfurt. In 1680–81 he traveled through France, England, Ireland, and Italy. On his return to

Frankfurt he learned that a group of his friends had bought land in Pennsylvania from William Penn. They insisted that he go to America as their agent to survey the land and establish a town. He reached Pennsylvania in 1683 with some twenty Lutheran and Reformed families and they settled Germantown.

In 1688 Pastorius married Annecke, daughter of Dr. Heinrich Klostermanns of Milheim. He served as justice of the peace, county judge, and member of the Pennsylvania assembly. He turned from pietism to become a Quaker and headmaster of the Friends' School in Philadelphia (1697) and Germantown (1702–c.1708). He presented to the Society of Friends the first formal indictment of slavery made in the United States. Pastorius wrote devotional verse in both English and German. See "Great God, Preserver of All Things" and "Ob ich deiner schon vergiss."

John Peck, farmer, teacher, and poet; b. Rehoboth, Mass., 1735; d. Montpelier, Vt., March 4, 1812.

John Peck's birthplace, the Rehoboth of the early proprietors, included not only the present town, but also Seekonk, Mass., and Pawtucket, R.I. John's father was Henry Peck. John went to Royalston, Mass., in about 1775. He was long a town officer there. He married Mary Brown and in 1806 moved to Montpelier, Vt., where he remained until his death. The family genealogy reports dubiously that he was "quite a poet." Three publications have been attributed to him (although the first two have also been considered the work of a later John whose dates are 1780–1849). They are: *A short poem, containing a descant of the universal plan* . . . (Boston, 1818), *A descant on Universalism* . . . , and *A Description of the Last Judgment* (Boston, 1773). Two hymns selected from the latter volume appear in William Billings' *Continental Harmony* (1794). Billings calls both tunes WEST SUDBURY, but, in a note at the foot of the index, corrects that to "What If the Saint Must Die" (q.v.) to SUDBURY. This confusion is repeated in later books, about half still calling it WEST SUDBURY. The hymn, "Here Is a Song" (q.v.), was also set by Elisha West in his *Musical Concert* (1802).

William A. Percy, poet; b. Greenville, Miss., May 14, 1885; d. there Jan. 21, 1942.

William A. Percy was educated at the University of the South (B.A., 1904) and Harvard (LL.B., 1908). After practicing law in his father's office, he was active in Belgian Relief (1916–17). In 1918 he became a captain in the 37th Division and received the Croix de Guerre. After World War I he lived near Greenville, Miss., where he was in charge of relief operations during the flood of 1927. In 1924 he published *Enzio's Kingdom and Other Poems* and, in 1941, his autobiography, *Lanterns on the Levee: Recollections of a Planter's Son.* A collection of his poems was published after his death. See "They Cast Their Nets in Galilee."

Emily Swan Perkins, hymn composer; b. Chicago, Ill., Oct. 19, 1866; d. Riverdale, N.Y., June 27, 1941.

Emily Swan Perkins was the daughter of a father active in Christian work. Before she was ten years old she was playing the piano for services in a large Sunday School where he was superintendent. Her high-school years were spent in Cleveland, where she graduated in 1885. In that city, too, she was active in school and church activities. A brief residence in Denver followed where Miss Perkins gained experience as an accompanist.

Early in 1900 Miss Perkins moved with her family to Riverdale, N.Y. Active in the Red Cross, she devoted her home to war work during World War I, and about the same time began to write hymns. She was a member of the National Board of the YWCA from 1933 to 1938.

In 1921 Miss Perkins published *Stonehurst Hymn Tunes.* In 1922 she and a small group of friends interested in hymnology began the meetings which led to the formation of the Hymn Society of America. *Riverdale Hymn Tunes,* her second volume of published hymns, appeared in 1938.

After almost twenty years' service as corresponding secretary to the Hymn Society of America, Emily Perkins resigned in January 1941. She died the following June. See BURG, with her text "Thou Art, O God, the God of Might," and LAUFER ("O Day of Light and Gladness").

William Oscar Perkins, teacher, conductor, and compiler;
b. Stockbridge, Vt., May 23, 1831; d. Boston, Mass.,
Jan. 13, 1902.

William Oscar Perkins was the oldest of the three musical Perkins brothers. The other two were Julius Edson Perkins and Henry Southwick Perkins. William studied music in London with Wetherbee and in Milan with G. Perini. He then settled in Boston and in 1871 established an academy, where he taught. At the same time he was active as conductor and composer. In 1879 he received the degree of Doctor of Music from Hamilton College. He published some forty books of songs, sacred and secular. See DANVERS ("Fear Not, Poor Weary One").

Vincent Persichetti, composer, pianist, and teacher; b. Philadelphia, Pa., June 6, 1915.

Vincent Persichetti began to study piano at age five, harmony at eight, counterpoint at nine. Educated at the Combs College of Music (B.M., 1936), at the Curtis Institute of Music (1939), and the Philadelphia Conservatory of Music (M.M., 1941), he benefited from such teachers as Russell King Miller (1926–36), Olga Samaroff (1939–42), Paul Nordoff (1939–41), Fritz Reiner (1939–41), and Roy Harris (1943). Organist and choir director of the Arch Street Presbyterian Church for sixteen years (1932–48), he was head of the Composition Department at Combs from 1936 to 1942. He has been on the faculty of the Philadelphia Conservatory since 1942 and at the Juilliard School in New York City since 1948. Music editor of the Elkan Vogel Company, he occasionally writes articles about music.

Persichetti's *Dance Overture* won the Juilliard Publication Award in 1943; his *Third Piano Sonata* won first prize at the Colorado College Fine Arts Festival in 1943, and his *Second String Quartet* won the Blue Network Prize for Chamber Music in 1945. He has also won prizes given by the American Federation of Music Clubs and the American Guild of Organists. Persichetti was granted the honorary Mus.D. degree by the Philadelphia Conservatory of Music in 1945 and was recipient of a grant from the National Institute of Letters in 1948.

Persichetti has composed six symphonies; *The Hollow Men* (for trumpet and string orchestra), 1944; *Concertino for Piano and Orchestra,* 1941; two string quartets; nine piano sonatas; and a *Quintet for Piano and Strings,* 1956. He responded to a request for an original hymn tune for *American Hymns* by producing a collection which was published in 1956 as *Hymns and Responses for the Church Year.* STAR ("purer than purest pure") is one of the compositions from that collection.

Sylvanus D. Phelps, Baptist minister and author; b. Suffield, Conn., May 15, 1816; d. New Haven, Conn., Nov. 23, 1895.

Sylvanus D. Phelps was educated at the Connecticut Literary Institute, at Brown University, and at Yale Theological Seminary. Early called to the ministry he settled in New Haven, Conn., where he was pastor of the First Baptist Church for twenty-eight years beginning in 1846. At one time editor of the *Christian Secretary* at Hartford, Phelps published several books of poetry and prose. There were nine editions of his *Holy Land.*

Phelps began writing hymns during his college days. Some of his first efforts were songs for children. Of the many which he wrote, "Saviour, Thy Dying Love" (q.v.) is best known. His son, William Lyon Phelps, for many years professor of English literature at Yale, once wrote of him: "He was always deeply gratified by the success of one of his hymns, 'Saviour, Thy Dying Love,' and he wished that 'author of the hymn' be put on his grave-stone in the New Haven cemetery. It was."

Harriett C. Phillips, Sunday School teacher and hymn writer; b. Sharon, Conn., 1806; d. 1884.

Harriett C. Phillips lived in New York City, where she wrote verses and devoted herself to the Sunday School movement. Her best-remembered hymn, "We Bring No Glittering Treasures," was written for a Sunday School festival and first published in the Methodist Episcopal *Hymns* (1849). Five of her hymns appeared in W. C. Hoyt's *Family and Social Melodies* (1853). She often wrote verses which were published in *The Christian Advocate* under an assumed name. Of them she once said, "I usually wrote to please a friend or to beguile a weary hour, not thinking that they would be read in coming years."

Philip Phillips, singing evangelist; b. Chautauqua Co., near Jamestown, N.Y., 1834; d. Delaware, Ohio, June 25, 1895.

As soon as he was old enough Philip Phillips worked on the farm. He was naturally musical and made his first appearance as a singer when he was only five. At the age of nineteen he became a singing master. Two years later he was on the road, singing his own songs to melodeon accompaniment wherever he was received, and selling copies of the songs which he had published. He shared in the popularity which gospel hymns aroused, and his publishing ventures thrived. He toured widely as the "Singing Pilgrim," singing the simple songs which he composed and accompanying himself on the reed organ. His account of his world journey may be read in his *The Song Pilgrimage Around and Throughout the World* (1880). His hymn "I Have Heard of a Saviour's Love" appeared in Ira D. Sankey's *Songs and Solos.* Among the collections which Phillips published were *The Singing Pilgrim* (cop. 1866), a set of hymns based on John Bunyan's *Pilgrim's Progress,* and *The New Hymn and Tune Book* (New York, 1867). See the tunes to "In Some Way or Other, the Lord Will Provide" and "One Sweetly Solemn Thought" (NEARER HOME).

Daniel Pinkham, composer and teacher; b. Lynn, Mass., June 5, 1923.

Daniel Pinkham was educated at Phillips Academy, Andover, Mass., and at Harvard University (A.B., 1943; M.A., 1944), where he studied with Walter Piston. He also worked with Nadia Boulanger (1940–41), Aaron Copland (1946), Arthur Honegger (1947), and Samuel Barber (1947). Pinkham, now teaching at the Boston Conservatory of Music, has taught at Boston University and, in 1950, was appointed harpsichordist to the Boston Symphony. He was a Visiting Lecturer on Music at Harvard (1957–58). He has composed a ballet (*Narragansett Bay*). His orchestral works in addition to two symphonies include *Catacoustical Measures* and *Signs of the Zodiac.* Among his choral works is *St. Mark's Passion.* See his setting of "Bow Down, Mountain," by Norma Farber, composed especially for *American Hymns.*

Constantine Pise, Catholic priest, educator, and author; b. Annapolis, Md., Nov. 22, 1801; d. Brooklyn, N.Y., May 26, 1866.

Constantine Pise studied at Georgetown College, Washington, D.C., became a member of the Society of Jesus, and went to Rome. On his return to the United States he prepared for the priesthood and taught at Mount St. Mary's. Ordained on March 19, 1825, he was in Baltimore from 1827 to 1832, then at St. Patrick's, Washington, D.C., where he became the first Catholic priest to serve as chaplain of the Senate (1832–33). After a period at St. Patrick's Cathedral, New York City, he founded the church of St. Charles Borromeo in Brooklyn (1850), where he stayed for the rest of his life. Pise, widely known and esteemed as both teacher and preacher, was an effective defender of his faith at a time when it was under attack in this country. See "Let the Deep Organ Swell."

William Piutti, music teacher and hymn tune composer; fl. late 19th cent.

We know only that William Piutti was a brother of Max Piutti, who was born in Saxony in 1852, emigrated to the United States in 1874, and taught music at Wells College until 1883. Both Max and William contributed tunes to Melancthon W. Stryker's *Christian Chorals* (1885) and *College Hymnal* (1896). See William Piutti's ITHACA ("God of Our Fathers").

John Playford, English music publisher; b. Norfolk, England, 1623; d. London, Nov. 1686.

John Playford, a friend of Pepys the diarist, was called "Honest John Playford." His first publication, *The English Dancing-Master,* which appeared in 1650, is both an important collection of folk melodies and a pioneer document for the English country dance. From that time until the end of his life he dominated the field of music publishing in England. Among the publications relevant to our field of interest is the *Breefe Introduction to the Skill of Musicke* (1654), a concise and popular handbook which included simple settings of familiar psalm tunes. Playford also published *Psalms and Hymns in Solemn Musick of four parts on the Common Tunes to the Psalms in Metre: used in Parish Churches* (1671), *The Whole Book of Psalms: With the Usual Hymns and Spiritual Songs* (London, 1677; 20th ed., 1757), and *Six Hymns for 1 Voice to the Organ* (1671). In 1684 Playford, who had begun to feel the effects of age and illness, turned his business over to his son Henry. He died two years later. Although he was primarily a publisher, John Playford included compositions of his own in *Cantica Sacra* (1674) and elsewhere. Unlike Thomas Ravenscroft he did not enlist the services of contemporary composers, and the psalm arrangements he published were his own. Indeed, in the preface to *The Whole Book of Psalms* he says, "I have composed all the Musical Tunes into Three Parts." The psalm settings by Playford had an important influence on psalm singing in the colonies. The thirteen psalm tunes with their basses included in the 1698 edition of the *Bay Psalm Book* were copies from Playford's *Breefe Introduction to the Skill of Musicke.* John Tufts derived thirty-one of the thirty-seven tunes in *A Plain Introduction to Singing Psalm Tunes* (5th ed., 1726) either directly from Playford's *Whole Book of Psalms* or indirectly through the similar publication of Thomas Walter, and these were by no means the only American borrowings. WORCESTER ("Eternal God, How They're Increased"), PSALM 69 ("I to the Lord from My Distress"), NUNC DIMITTIS ("O Lord, Almighty God"), and

VENI CREATOR ("Once More, O God, Vouchsafe to Shine") come from the 1671 psalter, and CANTERBURY ("For Lo! My Jonah, How He Slumped"), ST. DAVID ("How Glorious Are the Morning Stars"), CAMBRIDGE ("My Heart, How Very Hard It's Grown"), PSALM 41 ("When the Seed of Thy Word Is Cast"), and HYMN ON THE DIVINE USE OF MUSIC ("With Christ and All His Shining Train") from that of 1677.

Sylvanus Billings Pond, piano manufacturer, publisher, and musician; b. near Worcester, Mass., April 5, 1792; d. New York City, c.1871.

In 1820, Sylvanus Billings Pond, a successful piano manufacturer of Albany, N.Y., became a partner in the publishing firm of Machan & Pond. In 1832 the business was transferred to New York where it was called Firth and Hall. In 1848, Firth, Pond & Company became the publisher of much of Stephen Foster's music. When Sylvanus Pond retired in 1850 his son William succeeded him and eventually bought the business, which became William A. Pond & Company.

Sylvanus Pond's name appeared in the October 2, 1838, issue of the *New York Commercial Advertiser* as "Vocal Leader" of the forthcoming public performance by the New York Academy of Sacred Music. He was also a conductor of the New York Sacred Music Society. The *United States Psalmody* was compiled and published by Pond in 1841, and in 1866 he was the musical editor of *The Book of Praise* for the Reformed Church of America. Five of Pond's tunes enjoyed considerable popularity: MADISON, HENRY, SIBERIA, FIRTH ("O For the Happy Hour") (q.v.), and ARMENIA ("O Thou Whose Own Vast Temple Stands") (q.v.).

Hugh Porter, organist and educator; b. Heron Lake, Minn., Sept. 18, 1897; d. New York City, Sept. 22, 1960.

A graduate of the Evanston, Ill., Township High School (1918), Hugh Porter was educated at the American Conservatory of Music in Chicago (B.Mus., 1920), Northwestern University (B.A., 1924), and the School of Sacred Music, Union Theological Seminary (S.M.M., 1930; D.S.M., 1944). He became a fellow of the American Guild of Organists in 1932. Porter studied piano with Howard Wells (1918–20), organ with Wilhelm Middelschulte (1918–20), Lynnwood Farnam (1924–27), and T. Tertius Noble (1924–27), theory with Rosario Scalero (1923–24), piano and coaching with Frank LaForge (1924–25), and coaching in organ with Nadia Boulanger (1939).

He gave recitals in Chicago at Kimball Hall (1923), in New York at Town Hall (1926), in Boston at Trinity Church (1933), and in Washington at the Library of Congress (1934). In 1944 he made a transcontinental concert tour. Organist of the New First Congregational Church in Chicago (1920–23), he later held similar posts in New York at the Calvary Episcopal Church (1924–27), the Church of the Heavenly Rest (1930), the Second Presbyterian Church (1931–35), and the Collegiate Church of St. Nicholas (1936–47). He also served as organist for the Chautauqua Institution (1925–31), and the Oratorio Society of New York.

A former member of the faculty of the American Conservatory of Music in Chicago (1920–23), of New York University (1925–28), the David Mannes Music School (1927–28), and Juilliard Summer School (1932–45), he joined the staff of the School of Sacred Music, Union Theological Seminary, in 1931, becoming the Helen and Clarence Dickinson Professor and Director of the school in 1945. Among Porter's compositions are the anthems "Fruit of the Spirit" (1932) and "O Master Let Me Walk" (1933), and the choral prelude "Es ist ein Ros." See RENASCENCE ("O God, I Cried, No Dark Disguise"). Porter and his wife, Ethel F. Porter, were the music editors of the *Pilgrim Hymnal* of 1958.

Quincy Porter, composer and educator; b. New Haven, Conn., Feb. 7, 1897; d. Nov. 12, 1966.

A descendant of Jonathan Edwards, Quincy Porter graduated from Yale in 1919, then entered the Yale School of Music, where he studied with Horatio Parker and David Stanley Smith, won two prizes in composition, and graduated in 1921. After study in Paris with Vincent D'Indy and Lucien Capet, he returned to New York in 1922. With Roger Sessions he studied with Ernest Bloch, following him to Cleveland when Bloch accepted a position there. Porter played viola in the Ribaupierre Quartet during his stay in Cleveland.

A Guggenheim Fellowship enabled him to return to Paris in 1928 for a two-year stay. He taught at the Cleveland Institute in 1931–32 and in late 1932 joined the faculty of Vassar College as professor of music and conductor of the orchestra. He resigned in 1938 to become Dean of the New England Conservatory of Music and in 1942 Director. In 1946 he accepted a professorship of composition at the Yale School of Music.

Awarded the Coolidge medal in 1943, an honorary doctorate from the University of Rochester in 1944, an M.A. (privatim) from Yale in 1946, he received a Pulitzer prize in 1953, and was a member of the National Institute of Arts and Letters. Perhaps best known for his sensitive chamber music (Quartet 8, 1950, has been recorded) he has also written for orchestra. His *Concerto Concertante for Two Pianos* (1953) and two symphonies (1934 and 1961–62) are important. The latter was a Louisville commission. His tune for "I Stood within the Heart of God" was composed for *American Hymns*, as was the setting for "Eternal God, Whose Power Upholds."

Walter Porter, English composer; b. 1595?; d. Nov. 1659.

Walter Porter was the son of Henry Porter, who in 1600 gradu-ated B.Mus. at Oxford and in 1603 was a performer on the sackbut at the court of James I. Walter Porter was sworn gentleman of the Chapel Royal in 1616 while awaiting a vacancy among the tenor singers. In February 1617 he succeeded Peter Wright. In 1639, when Richard Portman was organist at Westminster Abbey, Porter was appointed master of the choristers there. Among his patrons were Lord Digby, first Earl of Bristol, and Sir Edward Spencer. Porter was relieved of his post during the Commonwealth. He was buried at St. Margaret's Church, Westminster, on November 30, 1659.

Porter's printed works include *Madrigales and Ayres of two, three, foure, and five voyces* (1632); *Ayres and Madrigals . . . with a thorough-bass for the Organ or Theorbo-lute in the Italian way* (1639); *Psalms and Anthems for two voices to the organ, first set* (1639) (Playford adver-tisement); *Mottets of Two Voyces for Treble or Tenor and Bass. With the continued Bass or Score: To be performed to an Organ, Harpsycon, Lute or Bass-Viol* (1657), the words of some of these taken from George Sandys' *Paraphrase; Divine Hymns,* advertised by John Playford (q.v.) (1664); and *Psalms of Sir George Sandys,* set to music for two voices by Walter Porter, and advertised in 1671.

The British Museum possesses texts for anthems by Porter, includ-ing full anthems ("Brethren," "Consider Mine Enemies"); single an-thems ("O Praise the Lord," "Ponder My Words," "O Give Thanks," "O Lord, Thou Hast Searched"). See his setting of George Sandys' "O Blest Estate, Blest from Above."

Waldo S. Pratt, educator, musicologist, and organist; b. Philadelphia, Pa., Nov. 10, 1857; d. Hartford, Conn., July 29, 1939.

Waldo S. Pratt's major contributions were in the fields of psal-mody and American music. His study on Ainsworth's psalter (*The*

Music of the Pilgrims, 1921) and that on the psalter of Clement Marot and Théodore de Bèze (*The Music of the French Psalter: 1562,* Columbia University Press, 1939) as well as the *American Supplement* to Grove's *Dictionary of Music and Musicians* (1920; enl. 1928) were important works. His *History of Music* (1907; enl. eds. 1927, 1935) was written to serve his needs as a teacher.

Pratt (Williams College A.B. 1878) did graduate work at Johns Hopkins University in the fields of archeology and esthetics, not music. This led to an appointment as assistant director of the Metropolitan Museum of Art. He may almost be said to have developed his musical gifts by himself, although he did study with B.C. Blodgett of Pittsfield, Mass.

He had a long association with the Hartford Theological Seminary from 1882, teaching his speciality, hymnology (from 1889), but later the broader area of public worship (from 1917). He played the organ and directed choirs not only at the seminary (1882–85), but also at North Adams, Mass. (St. John's Protestant Episcopal Church, 1873–76), Williams College (1876–78), and Hartford (Asylum Hill Congregational Church, 1882–90). Pratt lectured on the history of music at Smith College (1895–1908), at Mt. Holyoke College (1896–99), and at the Institute of Musical Art, New York City (1905–20).

In his *Musical Ministries in the Church* (1901) Pratt expressed his views on the role of music in the church service. His tune NORTH ADAMS appeared in *In Excelsis* (1897), his GREYLOCK ("O Lord of Life") (q.v.) as a broadside.

Elizabeth Payson Prentiss, writer of essays, poems, and books for children; b. Portland, Maine, Oct. 26, 1818; d. Dorset, Vt., Aug. 13, 1878.

The first piece by Elizabeth Payson appeared in the *Youth's Companion* in 1834. When she was twenty-five she went to teach in a girls' school in Richmond, Va. Five years later, after her return to Portland, she married Rev. George Lewis Prentiss, who had just been ordained as the minister of the South Trinitarian Church in New Bedford, Mass. In 1851 he was called to the Mercer Street Presbyterian Church in New York City. There Mrs. Prentiss became a friend of Susan and Anna Warner (q.v.) and spent part of the summer of 1853 at the Warner home on Constitution Island opposite West Point, where all three ladies worked at books for children. The *Susy Books* by Mrs. Prentiss became popular. Dr. Prentiss resigned his pastorate in 1854 because of poor health and, helped by his congregation and by other friends, he and Mrs. Prentiss were able to go abroad for two years. When they returned to New York they established the Church of the Covenant, dedicated in 1865. Mrs. Prentiss' *Stepping Heavenward* (1869), written during a period of illness, was widely read. It was followed by a collection of religious poems, *Golden Hours* (1874). See her best-known hymn, "More Love to Thee, O Christ."

F. Price, fl. early 19th cent.

In *Southern Harmony* the name of F. Price is associated with SOLEMN THOUGHT (q.v.), sung to the text beginning "Remember, sinful youth, you must die." George P. Jackson, in his *Spiritual Folk-Songs of Early America* (p. 113) noted that other Southern books have associated the same song with several other authors as an indication of its folk character.

Thomas Prince, minister; b. Sandwich, Mass., May 15, 1687; d. Boston, Mass., Oct. 22, 1758.

Thomas Prince received an A.B. from Harvard in 1707. After his graduation he spent several years in England, but returned to Boston in 1717, where he became minister of the Old South Church (1717–58). While he occupied that pulpit he brought out *The Psalms, Hymns, and Spiritual Songs of the Old and New Testaments Faithfully translated into English metre: Being the New-England Psalm-Book Revised and Improved* (Boston, 1758), Prince had revised the *Bay Psalm Book* to such an extent that this version may be considered his own. Prince died just as his volume came from the press, and the book was used for the first time at the Old South Church the Sunday after his death. The church used it until 1786. See "Give Ear, O God, to My Loud Cry," "O Lord, Bow Down Thine Ear," and "With Christ and All His Shining Train."

E. K. Prouty, singing master; b. Charleston, N.H., 1801; d. Newbury, Vt., Sept. 26, 1869.

While E. K. Prouty was still a child the family moved to Waterford, Vt., where his father died. The boy loved music, but had no means of getting instruction in it. When he was grown and making a living as a traveling cloth salesman, he took every opportunity to join singing groups. After he had achieved the status of merchant he always found time, on his buying trips to Boston, to consult with Lowell Mason (q.v.). Eventually Prouty became well known as a singing master in Vermont and was the first there to use a syllable for each step of the scale, instead of relying on fa, sol, and la only, as did the earlier American singing masters. When he was thirty-two he gave up business to devote all his time to music. In 1837 he was the leading vocal teacher in Burlington, Plattsburg, and St. Albans, Vt. In 1840 he directed a Vermont Musical Convention in Montpelier. He taught music in Newbury Seminary for a period beginning in 1851 and in Thetford Academy in 1854. Although he did not publish a collection of his own, a number of his tunes, including COMP-TON ("Hail to the Sabbath Day") (q.v.), appeared in music books of the period.

Daniel Purcell, organist and composer; b. London c.1660; d. there Dec. 12, 1717.

Daniel Purcell has been overshadowed by his celebrated brother Henry, whom he replaced as a composer of stage music on the latter's death in 1695. He was organist of Magdalen College, Oxford (1688-95), and later of St. Andrew's of Holborn (1713-17). He composed anthems, songs, and odes, including several to St. Cecilia and a funeral ode on the death of his brother Henry. Of special interest to us is his *The Psalm Tunes set full for the Organ or Harpsichord* (1718) which shows how an organist might play them during a service. See ST. DAVID ("Lord, Who's the Happy Man").

Henry Purcell, Anglican clergyman and musician; b. Herefordshire, England, 1742; d. Charleston, S.C., March 24, 1802.

At seventeen Henry Purcell matriculated at Oxford University, where he took his A.B. in 1764 and later his D.D. In 1768 he was ordained by the Bishop of London. As a chaplain in the British army, he came to America in 1770.

For five years Purcell was rector of St. George's parish in Dorchester, S.C. After serving a year in Christ Church, Berkeley, S.C., he became chaplain of a South Carolina regiment in 1776. Appointed Deputy Judge Advocate General for that state in 1778, Purcell then became rector of St. Michael's Church in Charleston (1783-1802).

Although we know nothing of his musical training, he wrote psalm tunes of good quality which are preserved in the Eckhard Manuscript. See HEREFORD ("Arise, My Soul! With Rapture Rise!"). He should be distinguished from the earlier Henry Purcell (c.1659–1695), the greatest English composer of his period.

Johann C. Pyrlaeus, linguist and educator; b. Pansa, Germany, April 25, 1713; d. Herrnhut, Saxony, 1785.

Johann C. Pyrlaeus was educated at Leipzig. When he was twenty-seven he came to Pennsylvania and there married Suzanne Benezet of Philadelphia. His skill as a linguist and his interest in the new country led him to study Indian speech. He acquired fluency particularly in the Mohawk and Mohican dialects. He was a trained musician and also a pedagogue, directing a school for missionaries at Bethlehem, Pa. In 1751 he returned to Germany to spend the remaining years of his life. See his "Jesu, komm herein."

Beatrice Quickenden, writer and teacher; b. Garden Grove, Iowa, Jan. 17, 1902; d. San Francisco, Nov. 24, 1967.

Beatrice Quickenden spent her youth in Montana. Educated at the University of California and Occidental College in Los Angeles (B.A., 1922) she married John St. Edmunds (q.v.). During their years together in San Francisco (1948–54) she acted as publicity director for the Campion Society, which he founded and directed. Mrs. Edmunds wrote articles and verse for periodicals and was an organist, pianist, and teacher of music. See "Hail, Oh Hail to the King," which was set to music by John St. Edmunds for *American Hymns.*

Jeremiah E. Rankin, Congregational minister and hymn writer; b. Thornton, N.H., Jan. 2, 1828; d. Cleveland, Ohio, Nov. 28, 1904.

Jeremiah E. Rankin is best remembered for his hymn of parting, "God Be With You Till We Meet Again" (q.v.) although it is interesting to note that John Julian, writing at an earlier period, stated that "Laboring and Heavy Laden" was his best known hymn.

After attending Middlebury College, Vt., as an undergraduate, Rankin went to Andover Theological Seminary. He graduated there in 1854, was ordained in the following year, and acted as pastor to churches in New York, Vermont, and Massachusetts. For fifteen years he was the minister of the First Congregational Church, Washington, D.C. (from 1869), and he served the Valley Congregational Church for another fifteen-year period (from 1874). In 1889 he went to Washington, D.C., to become president of Howard University.

Rankin contributed original hymns to *Songs of the New Life* (1869) by Darius E. Jones, edited *Gospel Temperance Hymns* (1878), and was one of the editors of *Gospel Bells* (1883). The latter included many of his own hymns, six to his own melodies.

Thomas Ravenscroft, English composer, editor, and arranger; b. c.1590; d. c.1633.

Thomas Ravenscroft was trained in the choir of St. Paul's Cathedral. He graduated from Cambridge with the degree of B. Mus. in 1607 and was later in charge of the music at Christ's Hospital (1618–22). Ravenscroft edited two important collections of rounds, *Pammelia* and *Deuteromelia,* both of which appeared in 1609. "Three Blind Mice" appeared in the latter for the first time, as well as the catch "Hold Thy Peace, Knave," sung in Shakespeare's *Twelfth Night.* A collection of songs entitled *Melismata, Musical Phansies, Fitting the Court, Citie, and Country Humours* was published in 1611. In theoretical matters Ravenscroft was a conservative. *A Briefe Discourse* (1614) was a vain attempt to revive the notation of the previous century. Most important from our point of view was *The Whole Booke of Psalmes* (1621), which presented the psalm tunes in common use in four-part settings by Ravenscroft himself and by contemporary English composers. See DA PACEM ("Give Peace in These Our Days, O Lord"), DUMFERMERLING ("If Birds That Neither Sow Nor Reap"), TE DEUM ("Lord, Many Times Thou Pleased Art"), OLD 113TH ("Not to Us, Not Unto Us Lord"), FRENCH TUNE or DUNDEE C.M. ("Thou Lord, Hast Been Our Sure Defense"), LANDAFFE ("When Sun Doth Rise"), and DUKE'S TUNE ("Wherein Consists the High Estate").

Daniel Read, composer and compiler; b. Rehoboth, Mass., Nov. 16, 1757; d. New Haven, Conn., Dec. 4, 1836.

Daniel Read, a worker in ivory and a comb-maker, was active as a singing master, publisher, and compiler. His publications include:

American Singing Book (New Haven, Conn., 1875), *American Musical Magazine*, Vol. I (New Haven, 1786–87), *Introduction to Psalmody* (New Haven, 1790), *Columbian Harmonist* (No. 1, New Haven, 1793; No. 2, 1794; No. 3, 1795; and No. 4, 1810), *American Musical Miscellany* (Northampton, Mass., 1798), and *New Haven Collection* (Dedham, Mass., 1818). Another collection, his last, survives only in manuscript. See WINDHAM ("Broad Is the Road") and RUSSIA ("God from His Throne with Piercing Eye"). LISBON was also widely sung.

Gardner Read, composer and educator; b. Evanston, Ill., Jan. 2, 1913.

Gardner Read studied at the Eastman School of Music (B.M., 1936; M.M., 1937) under Bernard Rogers and Howard Hanson. Later, more advanced work abroad followed with Ildebrando Pizzetti and Jean Sibelius, and at the Berkshire Music Center with Aaron Copland (1941). He has held posts at the St. Louis Institute of Music (1941), the Conservatory of Music of Kansas City (1943), and the Cleveland Institute of Music (1945), before going to the College of Music of Boston University, where he has been chairman since 1950. Read's success as a composer has been recognized by a series of awards: Juilliard publication prizes in 1938 and 1941 for *Sketches of the City* and *Prelude and Toccata;* Paderewski Fund, first prize, for *Symphony No. 2* in 1943; and Composers Press publication prize for *First Overture* in 1948. His *Night Flight,* Opus 44 (1944), and his *Toccata Giocosa,* Opus 94 (1953), have been recorded. Read's *Eight Preludes on Old Southern Hymns* for organ dates from 1931. His hymn tune NEW DAY was composed for *American Hymns* in 1955 to a text ("This New Day") by his wife, Vail Read.

Vail Read; b. Terre Haute, Ind., July 14, 1909.

Vail Read, née Margaret Vail Payne, was educated at Indiana State Teachers College (B.A., 1931). She did graduate work at the University of Chicago and the Bread Loaf School of English. She taught music in schools in Indiana and Akron, Ohio, until her marriage to Gardner Read in 1940. From 1936 to 1940 she served during summers on the staff of the National Music Camp at Interlochen, Mich.

Until 1947 Mrs. Read collaborated in concerts of her husband's works. Since that date she has confined her professional work to proofreading and occasional writing. Her poem "This New Day" was set to music by her husband for *American Hymns.*

Lewis H. Redner, organist; b. Philadelphia, Pa., 1831; d. Atlantic City, N.J., 1908.

After attending public school, Lewis Redner was employed by a real estate firm and showed such aptitude for the business that he was taken into the firm at the age of twenty-one. He later went into business for himself and continued to prosper.

In addition he was active as a church musician and played the organ in several churches in his native city, most notably at Holy Trinity when Phillips Brooks was the rector, Redner also was superintendant of the Sunday School there for a period of nineteen years during which there was a remarkable increase in attendance. See his St. Louis, which was composed for "O Little Town of Bethlehem" (q.v.) by Phillips Brooks.

Luther Reed, pastor, educator, and administrator; b. North Wales, Pa., March 21, 1873; d. April 5, 1972.

After attending Franklin and Marshall College, Luther Reed went to the Lutheran Theological Seminary in Mt. Airy (now Philadelphia). He graduated in 1895 and went to the University of Leipzig, graduating in 1902. He held pastorates in Allegheny (1895–1903) and Jeannette, Pa. (1903–04). In 1906 he became director of the Krauth Memorial Library at the Lutheran Theological Seminary and, in 1911, professor of liturgics and church art, a post he held for thirty-four years. From 1938 to 1948 he was president of the seminary.

With Harry E. Archer he edited a number of musical service books, and he was chairman of the joint commission that published the *Service Book and Hymnal* of 1958, the first hymnal adopted by eight of the Lutheran synods. See his Sursum Corda ("Lord Jesus Christ, We Humbly Pray"). Note that Alfred Marion Smith chose the same name for an original tune also included in *American Hymns* ("Peace Is the Mind's Old Wilderness").

H. S. Reese; b. Jasper Co., Ga., 1828; d. date unknown.

H. S. Reese served as pastor of the Missionary Baptist Church for fifty-five years. The *Sacred Harp* of 1859, which contains his version of Sweet morning ("The Happy Day Will Soon Appear") (q.v.), states that he then resided in Turin, Ga.

George Richards, Universalist minister; b. near Newport, R.I., c. 1755; d. Philadelphia, Pa., March 1, 1814.

After the Revolution George Richards became a schoolmaster and occasional preacher in Boston. Between 1793 and 1809 he was pastor of a Universalist Church in Portsmouth, N.H. Later he accepted a call to preach in Philadelphia, where he established the *Freemason's Magazine and General Miscellany,* which he edited for two years.

The author of a number of odes and Masonic orations, Richards wrote *An Historical Discourse on the Death of General Washington* (Portsmouth, N.H., 1800). Many of his patriotic poems about the Revolution were published in the *Massachusetts Magazine* (1789–92). His *A Collection of Hymns designed for the use of the Universal Churches* (Dover, N.H., 2d ed., 1806) contains a number of his own hymns. He had previously edited and contributed fifty-two hymns to *Psalms, Hymns and Spiritual Songs: Selected and Original: Designed for the use of the Church Universal, in public and private devotion* (Boston, 1792). See "Long as the Darkening Cloud Abode" and "Th' Almighty Spake, and Gabriel Sped."

C. F. Richter, b. 1676; d. 1711.

C. F. Richter was a physician who cared for the children in the orphanage and other institutions established by August Hermann Francke at Halle. He also wrote religious verse in the Pietist manner for which he composed his own melodies. Although he published no collection of his own, his works may be found in the *Darmstadt Songbook* of 1698 and in the collections of Johann Balthasar König (q.v.) and Johann Anastasius Freylinghausen (q.v.). Richter wrote the German hymn translated by John Wesley as "My Soul Before Thee Prostrate Lies" (q.v.).

Howard Chandler Robbins, Dean of the Cathedral of St. John the Divine; b. Philadelphia, Pa., Dec. 11, 1876; d. March 21, 1952.

Howard Chandler Robbins received his B.A. from Yale in 1899 and in 1903 his B.D. from the Episcopal Theological Seminary. In 1903 he was ordained deacon, in 1904 priest. After a period in which he was curate at St. Peter's, Morristown, N.J., he became the rector of St. Paul's in Englewood, N.J. (1905–11), then of the Church of the Incarnation, New York City (1911–17). Robbins was dean of

St. John the Divine in New York from 1917 to 1929. He resigned to teach pastoral theology in the General Theological Seminary and retired in 1941. A member of the Joint Commission on the Revision of *The Hymnal,* he was represented in *The Hymnal 1940* by one translation and five original hymns. Of these "The Sabbath Day Was By," "And Have the Bright Immensities," and "Put Forth, O God, Thy Spirit's Might" are included here, the last with CHELSEA SQUARE, the tune of which is by Robbins, the harmonies by Ray Francis Brown.

Daniel C. Roberts, Episcopal clergyman and educator; b. Bridgehampton, N.Y., Nov. 5, 1841; d. Concord, N.H., Oct. 31, 1907.

Vicar of St. Paul's Episcopal Church, Concord, N.H., for almost thirty years, Daniel C. Roberts had previously held similar posts in Montpelier, Vt. (Christ Church), Lowell, Mass. (St. John's), and Brandon, Vt. (St. Thomas). After attending Kenyon College (from 1857) his career was interrupted by service as a private in the 84th Ohio Volunteers (from 1862). A civilian once more, Roberts prepared himself for the ministry and was ordained deacon and priest in successive years (1865 and 1866). A veteran himself, he was chaplain of the Grand Army of the Republic in New Hampshire. He was active in the New Hampshire State Historical Society and was the president for several years. In 1885 Norwich University granted him the degree of D.D. See his familiar national hymn, "God of Our Fathers, Whose Almighty Hand."

Gurdon Robins, Baptist minister and author; b. Hartford, Conn., Nov. 7, 1813; d. there May 23, 1883.

Although Gurdon Robins had no more than a public school education he read widely and contributed both verse and prose to the newspapers. His principal occupation was as a book dealer. During the Civil War he was a first lieutenant and quartermaster in the Sixteenth Connecticut Volunteer Infantry, was captured, imprisoned, and eventually released in broken health. After the war he lived in Hartford where he became city clerk. See his "There is a Land Mine Eye Hath Seen" and "When Thickly Beats the Storms of Life," both of which were published in the *Psalmist* (1843) as anonymous. A third hymn "No Night Shall Be in Heaven" was included in the *Baptist Hymn and Tune Book* (1871).

George Rogers, Universalist pastor; b. 1805; d. Cincinnati, Ohio, July 6, 1846.

George Rogers edited a *Universalist Hymn Book* that was published in 1845. Four of the twenty-six original hymns that appeared in this volume were reprinted in *Church Harmonies: New and Old* (1895). See "As Gentle Dews Distill."

Robert Rogerson, physician, tenor, and composer; b. 1757; d. 1806.

Dr. Robert Rogerson was tenor soloist in a performance of *The Oratorio of Jonah* presented in Stone Chapel, Boston, October 27, 1789, in the presence of George Washington, who was then on his inaugural tour. In 1793 an *Anthem to the Memory of John Hancock, Late Governor and Commander in Chief of Massachusetts* was attributed to Dr. Rogerson. The title "Doctor," the dates, and the locale seem to fit Dr. Robert Rogerson, a doctor of medicine who resided in 1787 on what was then Ship Street, now Commerce Street, Boston. It is necessary to distinguish between Dr. Robert Rogerson and his son Robert, who was also musical, a member of the Handel and Haydn Society, and its president for the year 1823. It was the son who owned the Ebenezer Goodrich pipe organ, built about 1812, which was played in his home on Beacon Hill (then Somerset Place, now Alston Street). See BRANDYWINE ("Sinners, Will You Scorn the Message?").

George F. Root, music educator and composer; b. Sheffield, Mass., Aug. 30, 1820; d. Bailey's Island, Maine, Aug. 8, 1899.

After studying with local teachers George Root moved to Boston, where he met Lowell Mason and became his assistant in teaching music in the Boston public schools and in classes for teachers at the Boston Academy. In 1844 Root went to New York to become music teacher at Abbot's Institute for Young Lad:es and later at the New York Institution for the Blind, where Fanny J. Crosby (q.v.) was one of his students. He formed a vocal quartet which became popular. In 1850 he went to Europe for further study. In 1853 he helped to organize the New York Musical Institute. In 1859 Root moved to Chicago, where his brother was a partner in the music firm of Root and Cady. Their entire stock was destroyed in the great fire of 1871, but they were able to surmount this disaster.

Root obtained his first successes with such popular songs as "Hazel

Dell," with text by Fanny Crosby, but was best known for his Civil War songs "Just before the Battle, Mother" and "Tramp, Tramp, Tramp, the Boys Are Marching." An industrious and successful composer and compiler of sacred music, his *The Shawm* (edited with William Batchelder Bradbury, 1853) and the *Diapason* (1860) were widely used. See Shining Shore ("My Days Are Gliding Swiftly By" and "Wayfarers in the Wilderness"), Cottage ("Our Father, God"), Trust ("Happy, Saviour, Would I Be"), and The Beauteous Day ("We Are Watching, We Are Waiting"). He also pioneered in editing Sunday-School music books: *The Prize, The Glory,* and *The Triumph* (1868).

Ned Rorem, American composer; b. Spring Grove, Ind., Oct. 23, 1923.

Ned Rorem received his early education at the University of Chicago Elementary and High Schools while studying harmony and counterpoint with Leo Sowerby (q.v.). Professional training included a stint at Northwestern Music School (1940–42), Curtis Institute of Music (1943), and the Juilliard School of Music (B.Mus.,1946; M.Mus., 1948).

Rorem's awards include two fellowships at Tanglewood (1946, 1947), the Gershwin Memorial award (1948), the Lili Boulanger award (1950), Prix de Biarritz (1951), a Fulbright fellowship (1951–52), the Eurydice Choral award (1954), a Louisville Symphony Orchestra commission (1955), La Jolla Symphony grant (1956), American Woodwind Ensemble grant (1957), and Guggenheim fellowship (1957–58).

His works include music in every medium: chamber music (*Violin Sonata, Mountain Song for Flute and Piano, Sinfonia for Fifteen Wind Instruments*); two string quartets; choruses (*Four Madrigals, From an Unknown Past, Five Prayers for the Young, The Poets' Requiem*); piano music (three sonatas, two concertos, and two pieces for two pianos); opera (*A Childhood Miracle, The Robbers*); orchestral compositions (two symphonies, *Lento for Strings, Six Songs* for high voice and orchestra, *Six Irish Poems* for voice and orchestra, *Design for Orchestra*); and over two hundred songs.

After living in France and Morocco for several years, Ned Rorem returned to the United States in 1956. See the setting of "Sing My Soul," which he composed for *American Hymns*.

Carl Olof Rosenius, Swedish preacher and hymn writer; b.
Nysatra, Vasterbotten, 1816; d. 1868.

Carl Olof Rosenius had intended to become a pastor of the Lutheran Church like his father, but as a student he was much influenced by George Scott, an English Methodist then in Sweden. Although never ordained, he became an influential Lutheran
preacher. He wrote extensively for *The Pietist,* which he edited from
1842 to 1862. His hymns, were very popular, partly through the efforts of Oskar Ahnfelt (q.v.), who sang them and provided them
with tunes. See "Med Gud och hans Vanscap."

Francis Rous, author of a metric paraphrase of the Psalms; b.
Dittischan, Devon, 1579; d. Acton, Middlesex, England,
Jan. 7, 1658/59.

Francis Rous was educated at Oxford (B.A. 1596/97), and at the
University of Leyden from which he graduated in February
1598/99. For several years he lived in seclusion in Cornwall, occupying himself with theological studies and writing books. Entering Parliament in 1625 as a member from Truro, Rous continued to represent that or some neighboring constituency in such Parliaments as
were summoned. Rous held many offices under the Commonwealth.
At first a Presbyterian, he later joined the Independents. In 1637
Cromwell made him a member of his council of state, and in 1657 a
peer of the realm.

Although he wrote much, chiefly on religious subjects, he is best
remembered for his *Psalms of David in English Meeter.* During the al-
tercations concerning the version of the psalter made by King James,
Rous had been working on his own. He had it printed without his
name in Rotterdam, brought over to England, and distributed
among members of Parliament. In 1641 he published a second edition with his name on the title page. By April 1643, the House of
Commons had approved his version and the book was printed for
general use. In a drastically revised form it was the foundation upon
which the Scottish psalter of 1650 was based. This version was sung
in the colonies by Presbyterians of Scottish origin. See "Help, Lord,
Because the Godly Man," "I to the Hills Will Lift Mine Eyes," and
"The Lord's My Shepherd, I'll Not Want."

Andrew Rudman, Lutheran pastor; d. 1708.

Andrew Rudman studied with Jasper Svedberg at the University
of Uppsala. In 1697 he came to America, where he preached at Wi-

caco, a hamlet near Philadelphia, where he built the Gloria Dei Church and served as its pastor. As provost he was the spiritual leader of the other Swedish churches on the Delaware. His diary refers to a little spinet that he carried with him. He published two pamphlets containing hymns (Philadelphia, c.1700), which are the first Swedish imprints in this country. His diary mentions other hymns of his, but they have not survived. He moved to New York as pastor of the Dutch Lutheran congregation there, and in 1703, in the Gloria Dei Church, he presided at the first Lutheran ordination in this county. He was also pastor of English churches in Frankfort and Oxford. See "When Shall My Pilgrimage, Jesus My Saviour, Be Ended?"

Kenneth E. Runkel, organist and composer; b. Lisbon, Iowa, June 10, 1882; d. ?

A student at Cornell College, Mt. Vernon, Iowa (1898–1900), Kenneth E. Runkel received the B.Mus. in 1927 from MacPhail College of Music, Minneapolis, became a licentiate in composition at the Conservatory of McGill University in 1931, and a licentiate and fellow of Trinity College of Music, London, in 1937. A fellow of the American Guild of Organists and an associate of the Canadian College of Organists, he was active both as professor of music and as organist and choirmaster. His academic associations were with Mt. Union College in Ohio (1909–11), and with Leander Clark College (1917–18), Baylor University (1923–27), and Lon Morris College in Texas (1929–33). As an organist he held posts at Christ Episcopal Church (1904–06) and House of Hope Presbyterian Church (1906–09) in St. Paul, Minn., and as organist-director at Grace Methodist Church in Waterloo, Iowa, at the First Methodist Church in Russell, Ky. (1943–58), and at the Flagler Memorial Presbyterian Church in St. Augustine, Fla. (from 1958).

Runkel was especially interested in compositions for several choirs. He published ninety-five anthems of which twenty-four were composed for three-choir groups. He also wrote two cantatas: *The Good Samaritan* (1928) and *The Promise Fulfilled* (1940). His instrumental works include compositions for organ, and for piano and organ, which are still in manuscript. See his ETERNAL LIGHT ("Not Only Where God's Free Winds Blow").

Ernest Edwin Ryden, pastor, author, and hymnologist; b. Kansas City, Mo., Sept. 12, 1886; d. ?

Ernest Edwin Ryden was the son of Swedish pioneers who settled on the prairies in 1870–71. After attending the schools of Kansas City, he worked as a newspaper reporter, then entered Augustana College, graduating in 1910. He was Associated Press editor of the Moline *Dispatch* for a year before enrolling in the Augustana Theological Seminary. After his ordination he was the pastor of Lutheran churches in Jamestown, N.Y., and St. Paul, Minn. In 1934 and for twenty-seven years thereafter he edited *The Lutheran Companion,* the official organ of the Augustana Lutheran Church. From 1938 to 1942 Ryden was president of the American Lutheran Conference. He was a member of the committee responsible for the Augustana hymnal of 1925 and was secretary for the commission which produced the *Service Book and Hymnal* of 1958. He wrote two books in the field of hymnology: *The Story of Our Hymns* (1925) and *The Story of Christian Hymnody* (1959). In addition to translations from the Swedish and Finnish, he wrote original hymns, among which is "The Twilight Shadows Round Me Fall." He translated "When Shall My Pilgrimage, Jesus My Saviour, Be Ended?" from the Swedish for *American Hymns.*

John St. Edmunds, composer and arranger; b. San Francisco, Calif., June 10, 1913.

John St. Edmunds was educated at the University of California (B.A., 1940) and Columbia University (M.S., 1954). He also studied at the Curtis Institute of Music (1939–40). A winner of the Bearns Prize from Columbia University in 1937, he received the Seidl Traveling Fellowship from the same institution in 1940. He spent 1950–51 as a Fulbright Fellow in England doing arrangements of the Purcell songs and was the recipient of a grant from the Italian government (1954–56) for work on seventeenth-century solo music, chiefly that of Alessandro Scarlatti and Benedetto Marcello.

He was assistant professor of theory and song literature at Syracuse University in 1946–47. From 1948 to 1954 he was active as the founder and director of the Campion Society in San Francisco, producing eight festivals of little-known early and contemporary music. In 1952–53 he was connected with the San Francisco Public Library. In 1958 he became the curator of the Americana Collection in the Music Division of the New York Public Library. He was a lecturer in music at the University of California in Berkeley (1965–66). In 1967 he became a fellow of the Folger Shakespeare Library. He resided in England as Senior Fulbright Fellow (1968–69) and Guggenheim Fellow (1969–70), working on an edition of Purcell songs and on composition. See STEVENSON ("Hail, Oh Hail to the King"), which was especially composed for *American Hymns.*

Robert L. Sanders, composer and teacher; b. Chicago, Ill., July 2, 1906; d. Delray Beach, Fla., Dec. 26, 1974.

Robert L. Sanders attended the Bush Conservatory in Chicago. Later, as a fellow of the American Academy in Rome, he studied with Ottorino Respighi, Alfredo Bustini, and Luigi Dobici. In Paris he studied with Guy de Lincourt and Paul Brand. From 1933 he was active in Chicago as organist and conductor. In 1938 he became dean of the School of Music at Indiana University and in 1954 he joined the Music Department of Brooklyn College.

Among his compositions are three "Little Symphonies": in G Major (1939), in B Flat Major (1953), and in D Major (1966). There is a *Symphony for Concert Band,* composed for the Goldman Band, and a *Symphony in A Major* for orchestra. He has also written compositions for brass: sonatas for trombone and for horn with piano and a *Scherzo and Dirge* for four trombones. A member of the committee that produced the last two Unitarian-Universalist hymnals (*Hymns of the Spirit,* 1937, and *Hymns for the Celebration of Life,* 1964), he contributed original hymns and arrangements to both. A thematic index of hymn tunes planned to reveal similarities in melodic contour exists as a card file. See WOODLAWN ("When Thy Heart with Joy O'erflowing").

Edwin Sandys, member of Parliament and treasurer of the Virginia Company; b. Worcester, England, Dec. 9, 1561; d. Northborne, Kent, Oct. 1629.

Edwin Sandys, older brother of George Sandys (q.v.), attended the Merchant Taylor's School and then went to Oxford. For seven years Sandys held the prebend of Wetwang in York, given him by his father, the archbishop, but he never took orders. Since a prebend involved income received from an ecclesiastical establishment in return for service there, it seems probable that Sandys intended to do this. During those years he studied in the Middle Temple and traveled on the continent. Upon his return to England he resigned the prebend and gave all his time to politics.

He went to Scotland to enter the service of King James, and when James ascended the English throne in 1603 Sandys came with him and was knighted. From that date he was active and prominent in government affairs. In 1605 his *Relation of the State of Religion in the Western Parts of the World* was published; later that year his books were ordered to be burned in St. Paul's Churchyard by the High Commissioner. In 1607 on his motion the journals of the House of Commons were for the first time ordered to be kept regularly. He collaborated with Sir Francis Bacon in drawing up a remonstrance against the king's conduct towards parliament in the session of 1604–11.

In 1617 Sandys began to take part in the affairs of the Virginia Company, and as long as he lived his influence in its affairs continued. He succeeded Sir Thomas Smythe as treasurer in 1619, in which capacity he drafted two new charters giving it representative government. In 1621 Sandys and a man named Sedden were imprisoned. Because he had persuaded the Archbishop of Canterbury to allow Brownists and Separatists to go to Virginia, it was feared he meant to make it a "free popular state" and go there himself to head it. He wrote the texts for Robert Tailour's *Fifti Select Psalms* (1615) including "In Pilgrim Life Our Rest" (q.v.).

George Sandys, poet, brother of Edwin Sandys (q.v.); b. Bishopthorpe, Yorkshire, England, March 21, 1577/78; d. Bexley Abbey, Kent, March 1644.

On December 5, 1589, George Sandys and his brother Henry matriculated at St. Mary Hall, Oxford, but George apparently never took a degree there. In 1610, after his mother's death, he left England on an extended tour of France, Italy, Cyprus, Turkey, Egypt, and Palestine.

In 1621 Sandys became colonial treasurer of the Virginia Company and sailed for Virginia with Sir Francis Wyatt, the new governor, who had married Sandys's niece. When Virginia became a crown colony, he was a member of the council (1624, '26, and '28). He acquired a plantation and worked at developing it, but apparently quarreled with his neighbors and with the council as well. On March 4, 1627/28 Governor Francis West and the colonial council informed the privy council that Sandys had defied the rights of other settlers. When a special commission was appointed in 1631, Sandys petitioned for the post of secretary and was refused. He apparently left Virginia soon after. Upon his return to London he was appointed a gentleman of the privy council of Charles I. An attempt by Sandys to restore the old Virginia Company was rejected by the House and by the king.

Aside from translations of Ovid and Vergil, Sandys's interest for us lies in his paraphrases of the Psalms (1636), the *Divine Poems* (1638), and the *Song of Solomon* (1641). The psalm paraphrases were republished in 1637 with new tunes by Henry Lawes. A selection with music by Henry and William Lawes was published as *Choice Psalmes put into Musicke for Three Voices* (1648). See "The Bounty of Jehovah Praise," "Judah in Exile Wanders," and "O Blest Estate, Blest from Above."

Sister M. Cherubim Schaefer, O.S.F., educator and composer; b. 1886.

After studying music with John Singenberger Sister M. Cherubim Schaefer organized and long administered the School of Music, Alverno College, Milwaukee. The excellence of her work in the field of church music was recognized by the award, which she received in 1938, from the American Cecilian Society. The *Alverno Hymnal,* issued in three volumes (1941–54), contains her original hymn tunes as well as her arrangements of traditional material. She also composed motets, masses, and two volumes of organ music. See "Rejoice, Let Alleluias Ring," for which she wrote the text as well as the music.

J. G. Schmauk, organist; fl. mid-19th cent.

J. G. Schmauk, compiler of a chorale collection entitled *Deutsche Harmonie oder Mehrstimmige Gesange für deutsche Singschulen und Kirchen,* was an organist, music master, and teacher at the Frankischen Akademie associated with St. Michael's and Zion's Congregation in Philadelphia. See his arrangement of ACH GOTT UND HERR ("Yoke Soft and Dear").

Balthasar Schmid, fl. c.1750.

Balthasar Schmid was the compiler of *Nürnbergische Kirchen-Lieder,* a collection of chorales, which appeared in 1748. See ALLEIN GOTT IN DER HÖHE ("Gebenedeyt Sey Allzeit"), NUN FREUT EUCH, LIEBEN CHRISTEN GMEIN ("Jehovah, Herr und Majestät"), HÖR LIEBE SEELE ("Ein Lämmlein Geht"), and LOBT GOTT IHR CHRISTEN ALLZUGLEICH. ("Nun Schlaff du Liebes Kindelein").

William Schuman, composer and executive; b. New York City, Aug. 4, 1910.

William Schuman attended Columbia University, where he received the B.S. in 1935 and the M.A. in 1937. He attended the Juilliard School of Music and, in addition, studied harmony with Max Persin, counterpoint with Charles Haubiel, composition with Roy Harris, and conducting at the Salzburg Mozarteum. He was a member of the arts faculty at Sarah Lawrence College (1935–45), president of the Juilliard School of Music (1945–62), and president of Lincoln Center (1962–69). He has been a special consultant on publications for G. Schirmer, Inc., from 1945.

Awarded a Guggenheim fellowship in composition in 1939–40 and another in 1940–41, Schuman was also the winner of the first Town Hall League of Composers award for his *String Quartet No. 3* (1942), and received the first annual award of the New York Critics Circle in the same year (Third Symphony). In 1943 he won the first Pulitzer prize ever awarded for music ("A Free Song"). His compositions include eight symphonies, four string quartets, the ballets *Judith* (1950) and *Undertow* (1945), the *New England Triptych* (1956) for orchestra and his *Chester* (1946) for band based on themes by William Billings, and the *Song of Orpheus* (1963) for cello and orchestra. See his "The Lord Has a Child," composed for *American Hymns* to a text by Langston Hughes.

Heinrich Schütz, German composer; b. Köstritz, Saxony, Germany, Oct. 8, 1585; d. Dresden, Nov. 6, 1672.

Heinrich Schütz became a choirboy in the court chapel of Cassel in 1599. His legal studies at Marburg University (1607), begun in compliance with the plans of his parents, were interrupted when Landgrave Moritz of Hesse-Cassel recognized his musical talents and sent him to Venice to study with Giovanni Gabrieli (1609–12). There he became familiar with the music for two or more vocal or instrumental choirs as performed in St. Mark's and with the dramatic monodic style of the early opera composers. He was able to absorb and fuse these influences with the German polyphonic style which was his heritage.

On his return to Germany he first became court organist at Cassel (1613), then temporary (1615) and finally permanent (1617) conductor at Dresden. During the Thirty Years' War Schütz spent three periods in Copenhagen as conductor of court music in that city, but when conditions in Dresden were more favorable he resettled there (from 1645). Aside from the lost opera *Daphne* (1627), the first to be performed in Germany, and the lost ballet *Orpheus and Euridice* (1638), his distinctive contribution is to be found in his sacred works in dramatic style using the solo voice in recitative with obbligato instruments, but retaining the chorus both as a dramatic and as a musical element. The four Passions (1665–66) are noteworthy. The point at which Schütz came closest to the chorale was in his settings for voice of the Psalms as rendered in German verse by Cornelius Becker (1628). See PSALM 4 ("Ich Bin ein Herr").

Elizabeth Scott, hymn writer; b. Norwich, England, c.1708; d. Wethersfield, Conn., June 13, 1776.

Elizabeth Scott was born into a devout and literate English family. Her father was an Independent minister of Norwich and her brother Thomas a minister and writer of hymns and poetry. In 1749 she met Colonel Elisha Williams of Connecticut, who had been president of Yale College for thirteen years. He had traveled to England on colonial business (he was making an attempt to secure back payment for the troops) and during the two years of his stay his wife died and he married Elizabeth Scott. After a narrow escape from shipwreck on the Atlantic they arrived in Connecticut and made their home in Wethersfield. Colonel Williams died there in 1755. Six years later his widow married Hon. William Smith of New York City and was again widowed in 1769. She then returned to Wethersfield where she spent the rest of her life. All of her hymns were written before 1750, but a number were printed from manuscript copies.

Several of her hymns had appeared in *The Christian Magazine* in 1763 and 1764. Twenty-one were published in the Bristol Baptist *Collection* (1769) of John Ash and Caleb Evans, others in J. Dobell's *New Selections* (1806), including one of her best: "See How the Rising Sun" (q.v.). A manuscript collection of her hymns is preserved at Yale University. See also her "Now Let Our Hearts Their Glory Wake."

Robert B. Y. Scott, pastor of the United Church of Canada and educator; b. Toronto, Ont., July 16, 1899.

After completing his undergraduate studies at Knox College, Robert B. Y. Scott earned his Ph.D. at the University of Toronto, then spent a year in Europe. Ordained as a minister of the United Church of Canada (1926) Scott went to Long Branch, Ontario, as minister, but after two years there became professor of the Old Testament at Union College, Vancouver. In 1931 he accepted a similar position at McGill University in Montreal. Still later he became Danforth Professor of Religion at Princeton University.

Among his publications are *The Original Language of the Apocalypse* and *The Relevance of the Prophets. Towards the Christian Revolution* was written with Gregory Vlastos as co-author. Scott's hymns express his aspirations toward a society which should embody Christian ideals, an ideal which he also sought through an organization called the "Fellowship for a Christian Social Order." See "O Day of God, Draw Nigh."

Eliza Scudder, poet; b. Boston, Mass., Nov. 14, 1821; d. Weston, Mass., Sept. 27, 1896.

Eliza Scudder's parents were Barnstable people who later became residents of Boston, where her father was in business. He died when she was a baby. When she was in her early twenties she lived with an older sister in Salem. That companionship was particularly precious to the younger girl because of the handicap of lifelong eye trouble. Of a deeply religious nature, she joined the Congregational Church in girlhood. Later she became a convert to Unitarian doctrine, but was influenced by the preaching of Phillips Brooks (q.v.). She joined the Episcopal church toward the end of her life and was an associate of the Sisterhood of Saint Margaret.

Two of her hymns were published in *Hymns of the Spirit* (Samuel Longfellow and Samuel Johnson, 1864) and others in publications of her uncle, Edward H. Sears (q.v.). Her own *Hymns and Sonnets* appeared in 1880. In her last years her frailty compelled her to move from North to South and back as the seasons changed; to be thus separated from her sister for long periods caused her much distress. She died on the same day as her sister, just a few hours later. They were buried side by side in Weston, Mass. See "Thou Grace Divine, Encircling All" and "Thou Long Disowned, Reviled, Oppressed."

Artis Seagrave, hymn writer; fl. late 18th cent.

Artis Seagrave was admitted by baptism to the Pittsgrove Baptist Church in New Jersey on September 26, 1773, and his wife Sarah was admitted by baptism on the same date. Sarah died on April 8, 1787, and Seagrave subsequently married Priscilla Thirston, October 26, 1779, and Elizabeth Shinn, December 10, 1782. He appears to have become a Universalist after the latter date, since he contributed twenty-one hymns to *Evangelical Psalms, Hymns, and Spiritual Songs,* the work of a committee authorized by the second Universalist meeting in Philadelphia, May 25, 1791. In 1797 and again in 1799 he was elected a member of the General Free Assembly of New Jersey. His will, dated December 22, 1806, was proved on November 17, 1808. See "Let All Created Things."

Edmund Hamilton Sears, Unitarian minister and author; b. Sandisfield, Mass., April 6, 1810; d. Weston, Mass., Jan. 16, 1876.

After studying a short time at Westfield Academy, Edmund Hamilton Sears entered Union College, Schenectady, N.Y. (B.A., 1834). He studied law briefly, then theology, while he held a position on the faculty of the Academy at Brattleboro, Vt. He graduated from Harvard Divinity School in 1837. Ordained to the ministry of the Unitarian Church in 1839, he became pastor of the church at Wayland, Mass. He moved to Lancaster, Mass., to accept the pastorate there and remained there until 1847, when he was forced to resign because of ill health. When the Wayland pulpit again became vacant in 1848, he returned to his old charge for sixteen years. In 1866 he accepted a post at Weston, Mass., where he died eleven years later. Union College gave him the degree of D.D. in 1871. The dates given here follow those in Henry Wilder Foote, *American Unitarian Hymn Writers and Hymns.* They differ at several points from those given by F. M. Bird in Julian's *Dictionary of Hymnology.*

Sears's *Regeneration* (1854) was written at the request of the American Unitarian Association. His *Athenasis; or, Foregleams of Immortality* (1858) was praised by Elizabeth Barrett Browning. He published *The Fourth Gospel the Heart of Christ* in 1872 and, in 1875, *Sermons and Songs of the Christian Life.* Sears is remembered for two Christmas carols of lasting merit: see "Calm, on the Listening Ear of Night" and "It Came upon the Midnight Clear."

William Selby, organist and composer; b. England, 1738; d. after 1804.

The first item concerning the arrival of William Selby in this country is in the records of Trinity Church, Newport, R.I.:

December 20, 1773: Whereas Mr. William Selby is arrived in town from London, in consequence of an application made to him by the Wardens of the Church, and now offers himself as an organist . . . it is therefore voted:

that he be received as organist of the Church, and that he be paid at the rate of £ 30 sterling per annum . . . and that the wardens be requested to collect by subscription ten guineas or more for him, towards paying his passage to America.

He also advertised that he will "teach the violin, flute, harpsichord and other instruments in use." In 1744 he was reelected as organist and "a new stop for the organ" was to be obtained from London "agreeably to Mr. Selby's selection."

Perhaps because of the British occupation of Newport, Selby moved to Boston. An entry in the records of Trinity Church there, dated Easter Monday, 1777, notes that "Mr. Wm Selby having acted as organist for the greatest part of the Year past—a public Collection for his benefit ordered." In 1782 he played at King's Chapel, where he remained until 1804. See his St. Sepulchre ("Far from Our Friends"), Dunbarton ("My God, I Thank Thee"), and Alhallows Tune ("Thus Spoke the Saviour").

George R. Seltzer, Lutheran pastor, liturgist, and hymnologist; b. Lebanon, Pa., March 15, 1902; d. 1974.

George R. Seltzer was educated at Muhlenberg College (A.B., 1925), the Lutheran Theological Seminary (S.T.M., 1934), and the Hartford Seminary Foundation (Ph.D., 1936), where he served as a librarian and pastor. He was actively associated with the publication of the Lutheran *Service Book and Hymnal* (1958), serving as a member of the Commission on the Common Liturgy and the Commission on the Common Hymnal (1945–58). In that work he acted as chairman of the joint editorial committee, of the text committee, and of the committee on occasional services. He was also a continuing member of the Commission on the Liturgy and Hymnal and a contributor to various publications and liturgical collections from 1930. Seltzer was professor of liturgics and church art at the Lutheran Theological Seminary in Philadelphia until his retirement in 1950. See "Come, All Ye People."

Henricus Selyns, first Dutch Reformed clergyman in America; b. Amsterdam, 1636; d. 1701.

Educated at the University of Leyden, Henricus Selyns was probably the most cultured of the Dutch preachers who came to New Netherlands, and it is thought that the Amsterdam Classis chose him from among three candidates partly because of his knowledge of English. He was ordained February 16, 1660, and reached New Amsterdam on June 11 of that year.

The congregation of 134 persons at Breuckelen (Brooklyn) could not pay a salary of more than 300 guilders in grain, so Governor Stuyvesant added 250 guilders on condition that Selyns preach every Sunday evening in the chapel on his plantation, or bouwerie.

Selyns, who had signed a contract for four years, returned to Holland in 1664, where he accepted a call to Waverveen. Twice he refused offers that would have taken him back to America, but in 1681 was prevailed upon to accept a third call to the colony, which had in the meantime become New York. Landing on August 6, 1682, he was received with joy and affection by the congregation of St. Nicholas at the fort; Bergen and Haarlem also had pulpits which he filled occasionally. Thanks to Selyns' persistent efforts, the Dutch Reformed Church in 1696 obtained the first charter granted in the colony.

A tolerant man in ecclesiastical matters, Selyns allowed both French and English clergymen to use his church for their services. Labadists were often to be found in his audiences, and he was on terms of friendship with both William Penn (although he condemned the principles of the Quakers) and the English ministers in Boston. He wrote a long Latin poem which was prefixed to Cotton Mather's *Magnalia Christi Americana* (1702).

As official Latin Secretary for New Amsterdam, he handled learned and cultural matters for Governor Stuyvesant. He wrote occasional verse including "O Kersnacht" ("O Christmas Night") (q.v.).

Samuel Sewall, diarist; b. Bishopstoke, England, March 28, 1652; d. Boston, Mass., Jan. 1, 1730.

Samuel Sewall came to New England with his father in 1661. After graduating from Harvard in 1671 he was chosen resident fellow there in 1673. Made a freeman April 29, 1679, he became a deputy to the General Court (1683) and from 1684 to 1686 was a member of the Council. While traveling in England on business (1688–89) he appeared before the king and the Governor's Council and assisted Increase Mather in his efforts to recover the Massachusetts charter. On his return he resumed his seat on the Council and in 1691 was named a councilor in the new charter which the colony was forced to accept. This post he held until 1725 when he declined reelection.

One of the special commissioners appointed by Governor William Phips, Samuel Sewall participated in the decision condemning nineteen people to death for witchcraft in Salem in August 1692, but was the only member of that group to confess his error publicly. Sewall showed concern for the Indians and his *The Selling of Joseph* (1700) was an early tract against slavery. In 1715 he became judge of probate for Suffolk County and, in 1718, chief justice of the superior court of judicature, an office he held for ten years. See his "Once More, Our God, Vouchsafe to Shine."

Oliver Shaw, blind organist, teacher, and composer; b. Middleboro, Mass., March 13, 1779; d. Providence, R.I., Dec. 31, 1848.

As a child Oliver Shaw lost the sight of one eye when playing with a penknife. His father, a mariner, later took his son to sea with him for several years. Shaw is supposed to have lost the sight in his other eye by taking an observation of the sun soon after he had yellow fever.

He then turned to music, studying for two years with John Berkenhead, blind organist of Trinity Church, Newport, R.I., and for two more years with Gottlieb Graupner of Boston. Thomas Granger taught him to play wind instruments. Shaw first taught music at Dedham, Mass., and it was probably there that he met the youthful Lowell Mason and encouraged him to pursue his musical career. Shaw moved to Providence in 1807, where he played the organ in the First Congregational Church and furnished musicians for the commencement exercises at Brown University. His tenure at the church was marked by threats of resignation on his part and by upward adjustments of his salary by the church fathers. He joined the Second Baptist Church in 1834.

Shaw was much in demand as a teacher. His house was a veritable conservatory and as many as ten students lived there with him. Each room could serve as a practice room and was provided with a piano, while in the large room downstairs there was an organ and three pianos. Religious exercises at which he officiated at the organ were mandatory in his household. He was one of the conductors and president of the Psallonian Society (1816–32), which was devoted to the improvement of sacred music. The Society gave many concerts during the years of its existence. Nathaniel Gould (q.v.) claimed that Shaw was the first to import the works of Haydn to this country. He remembered Shaw as an old man tottering from house to house to give lessons. Shaw's interest in wind music bore fruit in *For the Gentlemen: A Favorite selection of instrumental music* . . . (Dedham, Mass., 1807), optionally for two clarinets, flute, and bassoon, or two violins, flute, and violoncello.

The *Columbian Sacred Harmony* (1808) was issued jointly by Shaw, Albee, and Mann. Later collections by Shaw alone were the *Provi-*

dence Selection (1815), *Melodia Sacra* (1819), and the *Social and Sacred Melodist* (1835). A number of his hymn tunes were named for neighboring towns (TAUNTON, DIGHTON) or for streets in Providence (WEYBOSSET, MEETING, PLEASANT). His sacred songs, which were sentimental settings of devotional verse in ballad style, had a considerable success in his own day. "Mary's Tears" was sung in Boston at a Handel and Haydn Society performance in 1817 in the presence of President James Monroe. Shaw received $1,500 for "There's Nothing True but Heaven." An arrangement of this song, called GENTLENESS, was included in *The Baptist Hymnal* of 1883. See BENEVOLENT Street ("Come, Holy Spirit, Dove Divine").

Franklin L. Sheppard, Presbyterian and amateur musician; b. Philadelphia, Pa., Aug. 7, 1852; d. Germantown, Pa., Feb. 15, 1930.

Franklin Sheppard was educated at the Classical School of William Pewsmith and the University of Pennsylvania (B.A., 1872). He graduated at the head of his class and was a charter member of the university's chapter of Phi Beta Kappa. In 1875 he went to Baltimore to supervise his father's foundry. Although he had been confirmed an Episcopalian, Sheppard became an active member of the Second Presbyterian Church and served as Sunday-School teacher and director of music. He was often sent to the General Assembly as a lay delegate and eventually became president of the Board of Publications and Sabbath School work. Editor of *Alleluia* (1915), a Sunday School hymnal that sold over a half million copies, Sheppard was also a lay member of the editorial committee for the Presbyterian *Hymnal* of 1911. See his TERRA BEATA ("This Is My Father's World"), an arrangement of an English folk song, which was called TERRA PATRIS by the editors of *The Hymnal* (Presbyterian) of 1933.

William Fiske Sherwin, voice teacher and conductor; b. Buckland, Mass., March 14, 1826; d. April 14, 1888.

At the age of ten William Fiske Sherwin sang alto in the church choir. Two years later he learned to play the cello. Because both his parents were invalids, Sherwin contributed to their support at an early age. He became a schoolteacher in New York State and sent his wages home, reserving three dollars a week for himself. At the age of fifteen he studied with Lowell Mason in Boston. Later he taught voice at the New England Conservatory of Music and was a music editor for Bigelow and Main. When Bishop John Vincent was seeking a capable organizer and director for the chorus at Chautauqua he selected Sherwin, who had a talent for making large groups sing. See his BREAD OF LIFE ("Break Thou the Bread of Life"), CHAUTAUQUA ("Day Is Dying in the West"), and ASSURANCE ("God of the Prophets! Bless the Prophets' Sons").

Ernest W. Shurtleff, clergyman and author; b. Boston, Mass., April 4, 1862; d. Paris, Aug. 29, 1917.

Ernest W. Shurtleff prepared for college at the Boston Latin School, attended Harvard, and then the Andover Theological Seminary (graduated 1883). Contemporaries at Andover remembered that he played the organ on Sundays at Stone Chapel. Ordained in 1889, he went successively to churches at Ventura, Calif. (1889–90); Plymouth, Mass. (1891–98); and to the First Church in Minneapolis, Minn. (1898–1905) as Congregational minister. At the end of his term in Minneapolis, Ripon College gave him an honorary D.D. degree, and in the same year he went to Germany to organize the American Church in Frankfurt. Remaining abroad, he was put in charge of student activities of the Academy Vitti, in the Latin Quarter of Paris, where he worked from 1906 until his death eleven years later. During World War I both he and his wife were relief workers.

Shurtleff's first published book was *Poems* (1883). It was followed by *New Year's Peace* (1885), *Song of Hope* (1886), *Shadow of the Angel* (1886), and *Song of the Waters* (1913). He is remembered for the hymn of consecration which he wrote in 1887 for the graduation of his class at Andover, "Lead On, O King Eternal" (q.v.).

Lydia H. Sigourney, poet and author; b. Norwich, Conn., Sept. 1, 1791; d. Hartford, Conn., June 10, 1865.

Lydia Sigourney was a precocious child who learned to read at three and was writing verses by the time she was seven. Since teaching was the only career open to the young women of her time, she opened a girls' school in Norwich in 1811. In this enterprise she was associated with Nancy Maria Hyde. In 1814 she opened a select school for young ladies in Hartford, which she operated successfully until the year of her marriage with Charles Sigourney, a merchant of Huguenot descent.

Moral Pieces, her first volume of poems, appeared in 1815, but her husband objected to her literary activities, and the early years of her marriage were devoted to her children, her home, and her social and religious duties. In a lifetime that stretched from Washington's second term in office through the death of Lincoln she maintained a wide acquaintance with famous people both at home and abroad. By 1827 she was publishing anonymously poems and articles in books and magazines. By 1830 more than twenty periodicals were accepting them regularly. In 1833 *Letters to Young Ladies* was issued under her own name, and her fame was established. Literature became her trade and she gloried in it.

During her career as America's leading woman poet she wrote not less than fifty-six volumes, besides contributing more than 2,000 articles to nearly 300 different periodicals. Hymns by Mrs. Sigourney appeared in Asahel Nettleton's *Village Hymns* (1824), James M. Winchell's *Additional Hymns* (1832), Leonard Bacon's *Psalms and Hymns for Christian Use and Worship* (1845), and John G. Adams and Edwin H. Chapin's *Hymns for Christian Devotion* (1846). Among the nine hymns contributed to *Select Hymns* (Hartford, 1836) by James H. Linsley and Gustavus Davis was "Labourers of Christ! Arise" (q.v.), her best-known hymn. See also "Blest Comforter Divine," "Onward, Onward, Men of Heaven!", and "We Praise Thee, If One Rescued Soul."

Nicasius de Sillè, poet; b. Arnhem, Holland, Sept. 23, 1610; d. place and date unknown.

Nicasius de Sillè was a descendant of a Belgian diplomat who fled to Holland in the sixteenth century because of religious persecution. Young Nicasius was trained in military science and law. Appointed by the Dutch West India Company to be second in command to Stuyvesant, de Sillè sailed for New Amsterdam on August 23, 1654, with his five motherless children. Arriving at their destination on the third of November he recorded in writing a description of the welcome he received. For two years the governor was suspicious of his new first councilor, but in 1656, after a dreadful Indian massacre which elicited a petition from the citizens of New Amsterdam to the West India Company for a new governor, Stuyvesant suddenly became conscious of de Sillè's true worth and appointed him church warden and city *schout* (sheriff). The company made him *schout-fiscal* (attorney-general) of the whole province, successor to Van Tienhoven.

De Sillè became one of the proprietors of New Utrecht on Long Island, where in 1657 he built the first house erected in that town. His greatest happiness seems to have been derived from quiet enjoyment of his life there. A trilogy written out of his experiences and observations became his chief poetic work, from the third part of which came his "Song in the Manner of the 116th Psalm" ("God Stelt Ons Hier") (q.v.).

Jacob Singer, rabbi and composer; b. Kruspils (Kreuzburg), Latvia, 1883; d. Chicago, Ill., Aug. 4, 1964.

Jacob Singer was brought to the United States at the age of nine. Educated at the University of Cincinnati (A.B., 1907; A.M., 1908), he was ordained at Hebrew Union College (1908). After doing postgraduate work at Johns Hopkins University (1910–12) he studied music at Baltimore's Peabody Conservatory (1916), and received the Ph.D. degree from the University of Nebraska.

Singer served as a rabbi of Congregation Beth Israel at York, Pa. (1909–12), B'nai Jeshurun, Lincoln, Neb. (1912–13), and Temple Mizpah, Chicago (from 1923). He was associate professor of the history and theory of music at the University of Nebraska (1916–23) and lecturer on liturgical music at Northwestern University in Evanston, Ill. (from 1931).

During World War I Singer was a chaplain at Camp Funston and Fort Riley, Kans. (1917–18). He founded B'nai B'rith Hillel Foundation at Northwestern University and served as its director (1933–34). He was president of the Chicago Rabbinical Association (1939–41). A member of the Board of Governors of the Hebrew Union College, he was elected president of its alumni association in 1942.

Singer's writings include *Taboo in the Hebrew Scriptures* (Chicago and London, 1928) and articles in such publications as *Central Conference of American Rabbis, Year Book,* the year book of the Music Teachers National Association, and the *Universal Jewish Encyclopedia.* He composed *A Sunny Morning Spring,* a children's operetta; six liturgical numbers; and hymns for the *Union Hymnal* (1932), of which he was a co-editor. See his settings for "Kindle the Taper" and "Let There Be Light."

William W. Sleeper, Congregational minister; b. Worcester, Mass., Feb. 12, 1855; d. Wellesley, Mass., March 27, 1927.

After William Sleeper graduated from Phillips Exeter Academy in 1875, he went to Bowdoin College for a year, then graduated from Amherst in 1878. He studied for the ministry in the Hartford Theological Seminary and went to Bulgaria as a missionary from 1852 to 1887. Before settling in Wellesley as pastor of the Congregational

Church he served in Webster, Worcester, and Stoneham, Mass., as well as in Beloit, Mich., East Boston, Mass., and Rutland, Vt. He organized outings and picnics on the grounds of Wellesley College for the poor children of Boston during the period 1912 to 1918. His tune AMERICA THE BEAUTIFUL ("Though Fatherland Be Vast") (q.v.) was originally composed for the familiar lines of Katherine Lee Bates. "America the Beautiful," however, is generally sung to another American tune, MATERNA, by Samuel A. Ward, although this tune was named for and originally set to "O Mother Dear, Jerusalem."

Alfred Morton Smith, Episcopal clergyman and composer; b. Jenkintown, Pa.; d. Feb. 26, 1971.

After Alfred Morton Smith graduated from the University of Pennsylvania with a B.S. in 1901, he attended the Philadelphia Divinity School (B.D., 1905; S.T.B., 1911). In 1905 he was ordained a deacon; in 1906, a priest. After serving in Philadelphia and Long Beach, Calif., he went to the Church of St. Matthias in Los Angeles, where he remained from 1906 to 1916. From 1916 to 1918 he worked with the City Mission of Los Angeles. During World War I he was an army chaplain, serving in France and, with the Army of Occupation, in Germany. In 1919 he returned to Philadelphia, where he worked in the City Mission and served as chaplain at the Eastern State Penitentiary, Sleighton Farm School, and in the city hospitals. He was associate priest at St. Elisabeth's Church, 1930–33. His musical compositions include two masses and three hymn tunes published in *The Hymnal 1940*. See SURSUM CORDA ("Peace Is the Mind's Old Wilderness"). Note that there are two different tunes in *American Hymns* with this name. The other is by Luther Reed ("Lord Jesus Christ, We Humbly Pray").

Caroline Sprague Smith; b. Salem, Mass., 1827; d. 1886.

Caroline S. Smith was married to Charles Smith, pastor of the South Church of Andover, Mass. Mrs. Smith, inspired by hearing a sermon by H. M. Dexter on "The Adaptedness of Religion to the Wants of the Aged," wrote "Tarry with Me, O My Saviour" (q.v.) in the summer of 1852.

David S. Smith, music educator and composer; b. Toledo, Ohio, July 6, 1877; d. New Haven, Conn., Dec. 17, 1949.

David Smith was educated at Yale (B.A., 1900; B.Mus., 1903; M.A., 1916). He remained there as instructor of music (1903–09), assistant professor (1909–16), professor (1916–25), dean of the School of Music (1920–40), and Battell Professor of Music (1925–46). Given honorary degrees by Northwestern University (Mus.D., 1918) and the Cincinnati Conservatory of Music (Mus.D., 1927), he was a member of the Council of the American Academy in Rome, a Fellow of the American Guild of Organists, and a member of the National Institute of Arts and Letters and of the American Academy of Arts and Sciences.

Conductor for twenty-six years of the New Haven Symphony and the Horatio Parker Choir, Smith on occasion was invited to conduct the New York Philharmonic, the Boston, Cleveland, and Detroit symphony orchestras. Four times he received awards from the Society for the Publication of American Music (*Sonata Pastorale,* 1918; *Sonata, Opus 51,* 1921; *String Quartet in C Major, Opus 46,* 1921; *String Quartet, C Major, Opus 71,* 1934).

Smith's *First Symphony* was performed by the Chicago Symphony Orchestra under Frederick Stock at the North Shore Festival (1912); his *Second* was heard at the Norfolk Festival in 1918; a *Third* dates from 1928; a *Fourth,* written in 1937, was first performed by the Boston Symphony Orchestra in April 1939; and a *Fifth* appeared before his death. In all, he wrote eight string quartets (the eighth was heard at the Coolidge Festival in the Library of Congress, April 14, 1940). Smith also composed two large choral works, *The Rhapsody of St. Bernard* (1915) and *The Vision of Isaiah* (1927), and an opera, *Merrymount.* See FORTITUDE ("Be Strong! We Are Not Here to Play").

Eunice Smith, author; fl. end of 18th cent.

Eunice Smith is known by two books: the first was printed in Boston in 1792 by E. Russell for Thomas Bassett in Dunbarton. Its title read: *Some arguments against worldly-mindedness, and needless care and trouble. With some other useful instructions. Represented in a dialogue or discourse between two, called by the names of Mary and Martha.*

The second book, printed "for the proprietor" at Greenfield, Mass. (1798), was called: *Some motives to engage those who have professed the name of the Lord Jesus, to depart from all iniquity and study a close walk with God. To which are affixed a number of songs.* See "Dear Brethren, Are Your Harps in Tune?" and "Dear Happy Souls."

Samuel Francis Smith, linguist, minister, and author; b. Boston, Mass., Oct. 21, 1808; d. Newton Center, Mass., Nov. 16, 1895.

Samuel Francis Smith was educated at the Boston Latin School (1825), Harvard College, where he was in the same class as Oliver Wendell Holmes, and Andover Theological Seminary (1832). His first church was in Waterville, Maine (1834–42), where he also taught modern languages at Colby College. He acquired a knowledge of fifteen languages and, at the age of eighty-six, was eagerly seeking an appropriate textbook so that he could start the study of Russian. From 1842 to 1854 he was pastor of the Baptist Church at Newton, Mass., a post which he relinquished to become secretary of the American Baptist Missionary Union.

The earliest of his hymns were written while he was still a divinity student, as was his famous "My Country, 'Tis of Thee." He, with Baron Stow, edited *The Psalmist: A New Collection of Hymns* (1843), the most important Baptist hymnal of its period. In 1844 he published the *Social Psalmist* and *Lyric Gems*. See "As Flows the Rapid River," "Down to the Sacred Wave," "The Morning Light Is Breaking," and "Softly Fades the Twilight Ray."

Samuel J. Smith, Quaker farmer; b. near Burlington, N.J., 1771; d. there Nov. 14, 1835.

The forebears of Samuel J. Smith were among the early settlers of New Jersey and his grandfather was treasurer of the province and author of a *History of New Jersey* (1765). Samuel J. Smith was unusually retiring, even as a child, and his education was limited to what he could learn at the local school since he resisted attempts to send him away to complete his education. He was, however, an assiduous and intelligent reader throughout his life. An excellent farmer, he was a benevolent and charitable man, with a natural inclination toward poetic expression, which led him to write verse. He became known as the "Bard of Hickory Grove." Some of his poems were printed in a local publication called *The Rural Visitor* and a collection, *Miscellaneous Writings of the late Samuel J. Smith*, was published in 1836. "Arise, My Soul! With Rapture Rise!" (q.v.), which Julian notes as in the Episcopal *Prayer Book Collection* of 1826, had appeared earlier in *A Selection of Psalms, with Occasional Hymns* (Charleston, 1792).

Eliza R. Snow, Mormon poet; b. Becket, Mass., Jan. 21 1804; d. Salt Lake City, Utah, Dec. 5, 1887.

Eliza R. Snow was quite young when her family moved West and settled in Mantua, Ohio. In 1835 she was in Kirtland, Ohio, where she taught in a "select school for young ladies" and wrote poems which appeared in the local press. There she joined the Latter-Day Saints and married Joseph Smith. Her important *Collection of Sacred Hymns for the Church of Jesus Christ of Latter-day Saints* was first published in Kirtland. Another edition, in which she used the name Emma Smith, appeared in Nauvoo, Ill., in 1841. She joined in the migration to Missouri and then to Illinois. After Joseph Smith was murdered in Nauvoo on June 27, 1844, Eliza Snow joined the group led by Brigham Young. She was the driver of an ox team on the long journey which ended in Utah. Both her mother and her father died on the way. In October 1847, she arrived in Salt Lake Valley, Utah. In 1849 she became one of the wives of Brigham Young and lived in the "Lion's House" for the remainder of her life. Zealous in church affairs, she was a prolific writer of hymns and occasional verse. Her best-known hymn, originally sung to the tune of Stephen Foster's "Gentle Annie," was "O My Father, Thou that Dwellest." Her *Poems, Historical and Political* were published in two volumes (1856 and 1877). See "Think Not When You Gather to Zion."

Leo Sowerby, organist, choirmaster, and composer; b. Grand Rapids, Mich., May 1, 1895; d. Port Clinton, Ohio, July 7, 1968.

Leo Sowerby moved to Chicago at the age of fourteen and studied piano with Calvin Lampert and Percy Grainger and composition with Arthur Olaf Andersen. From 1917 to 1919 Sowerby served in the army here and in France. He became the regimental bandmaster with the 332d Field Artillery. Granted a Master of Music degree in 1918 from the American Conservatory in Chicago, Sowerby later received an honorary Mus.D. from the University of Rochester (1934). In 1921 he became the first fellow of the American Academy in Rome. He returned to the United States in 1924 to resume his duties as teacher of composition at the American Conservatory, becoming head of the department when his former teacher Arthur Olaf Andersen moved to Arizona. In May 1927, Sowerby became organist and choirmaster at St. James Church in Chicago. His special interest in lively folk dances is shown by compositions based on the *Irish Washerwoman* (1916) and *Money Musk* (1924). He composed the concert overture *Comes Autumn Time* (1916) and a symphonic poem

Prairie (1929) after Carl Sandberg's poem. His *Canticle of the Sun* won a Pulitzer prize in 1946. His hymn tune THE SHEPHERDS ("As I Went Down to David's Town") was composed for *American Hymns.*

Ishmael Spicer, music teacher; fl. mid-18th cent.

Ishmael Spicer, active in Philadelphia, taught a singing school "for the improvement of church musicke" in the Court House in 1789. His class had made sufficient progress in six months to give a concert at the Protestant Episcopal church there. Apparently Spicer had a share in the revision of Andrew Adgate's *The Philadelphia Harmony,* which first appeared in 1788, since the edition of 1790 listed him as coeditor. See NEW JERSEY ("Blest Is the Man Whose Tender Breast").

Johann M. Spiess, organist, composer, and compiler; b. Switzerland, 1696; d. Bern, 1772.

Johann M. Spiess was active in Bergzabern and later in Heidelberg, where he was preceptor in the Gymnasium and music director at St. Peter's Church. In July 1746, he was appointed cathedral organist in Bern, where he served until his death. He published *Davids Harpffen-Spiel* (1751), Geistliche Arien (1761), and *Musikalische Bibel-Andachten* (1762). See LOBT GOTT IHR CHRISTEN ALLZUGLEICH ("A Joyful Sound It Is") and NUN RUHEN ALLE WÄLDER ("Lamm Gottes Abgeschlachtet").

William Staughton, poet and minister; b. England, Jan. 4, 1770; d. Dec. 12, 1829.

With training as a silversmith and minister, William Staughton came to the United States in 1793 and was first settled in Georgetown, S.C., as minister of the Baptist church. In 1795 he moved to New York and then to Bordentown, N.J., to head a school. In Burlington, N.J., where he went in 1798 he was again the head of a school, but managed to preach and was chiefly responsible for the organization of a Baptist church. He moved to Philadelphia in 1805 where he was the minister of the First Baptist Church, remaining until 1811 when a group of his parishioners who had decided to establish a new church, the Sansom Street Church, called him as their pastor.

In addition to his ministerial duties Staughton taught candidates
for the ministry in his own home and when the Baptist Board of
Missions was organized he became their first corresponding secretary.

He was chosen as president of Columbian College, Washington,
D.C., in 1821, but moved back to Philadelphia in 1829. He was offered the post of president of a college in Georgetown, Ky., but died
on the way there.

Staughton, who had written verse from the age of twelve, published *Juvenile Poems,* in which his hymn "Pardoning Love" appeared.
See "Tell Us, Ye Servants of the Lord."

G. Waring Stebbins, organist and composer; b. Albion, N.Y., June 16, 1869; d. New York City, Feb. 21, 1930.

George Waring Stebbins was the son of the well-known evangelist
George C. Stebbins. He studied in New York and Paris. After 1893,
he held various positions as church organist in Brooklyn and New
York.

Two Compositions for Organ: Wedding Song and Scherzando by G.
Waring Stebbins was copyrighted by G. Schirmer in 1907. Two of
Stebbins' hymn tunes have appeared in American hymnals: EASTER
FLOWERS in the Boston edition of *The Hymnal 1916* and MANCHESTER
("The Gray Hills Taught Me Patience") (q.v.) in two hymnals edited
by H. Augustine Smith, *The American Student Hymnal* (1928) and the
New Hymnal for American Youth (1930).

Jacob Steendam, poet, merchant, and trader; b. Enkhuizen, Holland, 1616; d. Batavia, c.1672.

As an employee of the Dutch East India Company, Jacob Steendam visited coastal Guinea and the African Gold Coast, where he
witnessed the capture of Fort Axen from the Portuguese in February 1641. His collection of poems *Den Distelfink (The Goldfinch)* was
published (1650) when he returned to Amsterdam. Steendam then
sailed to New Netherlands, where in 1652 he bought a farm at
Amersfort (Flatbush) and in 1653 a house and lot on Pearl Street,
another on Broadway, and a farm at Maspeth. He was active in the
civic and commercial affairs of New Amsterdam from 1652 to 1661.
In an effort to call attention to the neglect of that colony, he became
the first New York poet, publishing *The Complaint of New Amsterdam
to Her Mother* (1659). A second poem, *The Praise of New Netherland,*
was published in 1661 after Steendam returned to Holland.

He did not return to New Netherlands, which the British took in 1664. In 1666 Steendam became "orphan master" and "comforter of sick" in Batavia. His *Moral Songs for the Batavian Youth* appeared in 1671. See his "Als ik des Herren Werk" and "Laet ons den Herre singen."

William Steffe, composer; fl. mid-19th cent.

In *The Story of the Hymns and Tunes,* Theron Brown and Hezekiah Butterworth call him John William Steffe of Richmond, Va., composer of Sunday School tunes. He may have composed or adapted the tune for "Say, brothers, will you meet us," which was later adapted to Julia Ward Howe's "Battle Hymn of the Republic." It first appeared without attribution in Charles Dunbar's *Union Harp* (1858). Only later was it attributed to Steffe. See THE BATTLE HYMN OF THE REPUBLIC ("Mine Eyes Have Seen the Glory").

Thomas Sternhold, co-author of the "Old Version"; b. at Southampton or Awre on the Severn, England, c.1500; d. Aug. 23, 1549.

Authorities cannot agree on the exact place of Thomas Sternhold's birth, but a record does exist which states that he lived on an estate called "The Hayfield" in the parish of Awre, with John Hopkins as a near neighbor—"from Awre first sounded out the Psalms of David by Thomas Sternhold and John Hopkins." The fact that Hopkins was concerned in the posthumous edition of Sternhold's psalms and was apparently responsible for adding three others of Sternhold's translations to the version in 1561 makes the story in the register possible.

There is some reason to believe that Sternhold entered Christ Church, Oxford, but did not take a degree. He became one of the grooms of the robes of Henry VIII and was evidently a favorite, since a legacy of a hundred marks was left him by the king's will. His earliest metrical versions of the Psalms may have been composed during Henry's reign. They won the ear of Edward VI, and the only edition which Sternhold lived to publish, *Certayne Psalmes Chosē out of the Psalter of David and drawē into English Metre by Thomas Sternhold, grome of ye Kynges Maiesties Roobes,* was dedicated to Edward and printed by Edward Whitchurch, probably early in 1549.

See his "I Lift My Heart to Thee," "The Lord Descended from Above," and "My Shepherd Is the Living Lord."

Jervis Henry Stevens, organist; b. London, June 26, 1750; d. Charleston, S.C., July 21, 1828.

The family of Jervis Henry Stevens came to this country, moving from Georgia to Charleston, S.C., where his father became the organist of St. Michael's. When his father died the son applied for the position, but it went to Mrs. Ann Windsor. He did succeed his father as deputy postmaster at Charleston, acting also as secretary to the deputy postmaster general. During the Revolution he served in the cavalry.

In 1783 he acted as temporary organist at St. Michael's where Henry Purcell, who was also a musician, was rector. At this time Stevens composed CHURCH STREET ("O Gracious Jesus, Blessed Lord!") (q.v.) and HACKNEY. In 1775 Stevens married Elizabeth Davis, whose father was rector of St. Mark's Parish.

In 1790 he became the organist of St. Philip's where he remained for twenty-five years. The church records tell that he was ordered by the vestry to conform to the rubrics of the prayer book, that he ordered twelve prayer books and twelve hymnbooks for the choir, and that he asked that a window be made in the choir loft. He was coroner for the Charleston District, 1801–22. From his second marriage to Susannah Sullivan in 1828 he had one daughter, Mary Anne Jane.

Joseph Steward, editor; b. 1752; d. 1822.

Joseph Steward's importance to hymnology lies in the fact that he, with Abel Flint and Rev. Nathan Strong (q.v.), was one of the editors of *The Hartford Selection* of 1799. *The Hartford Selection* was widely used as a revival songbook. The extent of Steward's original contributions is uncertain. Asahel Nettleton, in the preface to his *Village Hymns* (1824), noted that he had included "a few of the originals from *The Hartford Selection*. These, though already familiar to many, will yet be consulted with feelings of new interest when associated with the names of *Strong* and *Steward*." In this way four hymns by Steward, including "God from His Throne with Piercing Eye" (q.v.) and "My Soul Would Fain Indulge a Hope" (q.v.), have been identified.

George Craig Stewart, Episcopal bishop; b. Saginaw, Mich., Aug. 18, 1879; d. Chicago, Ill., May 6, 1940.

George Craig Stewart went to Chicago as a boy of fourteen and worked his way through high school and Northwestern University.

From the latter institution, where he was a distinguished debater, he received his B.A. degree in 1902. Soon afterwards he entered the ministry of the Methodist Church, and his first assignment was at Calumet Heights.

The following year he decided to enter the Episcopal ministry. After serving as lay assistant at St. Peter's Church in Chicago he was ordained to the priesthood in 1903 and called to the pulpit at St. Elizabeth's Church in Glencoe, Ill. In 1904 he became rector of St. Luke's Church, Evanston, where he remained until his consecration as bishop coadjutor of the Diocese of Chicago in 1930. The following November he automatically became bishop of the diocese upon the death of Bishop Griswold.

During World War I he served as chaplain in an evacuation hospital of the A.E.F. In 1927 he was a delegate to the Lausanne Conference on Faith and Order, and in 1937 to a similar conference in Edinburgh. A member of the National Council of the Episcopal Church for fifteen years, he was also one of four American members of the base committee of the Utrecht Conference on Church Unity in 1938.

During the twenty-five years that Stewart was rector of St. Luke's that parish grew to become one of the outstanding parishes in the United States with a membership of more than 3,000. A distinguished preacher, he was a writer of note, and the author of several books. See "As I Went Down to David's Town."

William Grant Still, composer, arranger, and conductor; b. Woodville, Miss., May 11, 1895; d. Los Angeles, Calif. Dec. 3, 1978.

William Grant Still was educated in the public schools of Little Rock, Ark., where his mother taught literature in the high school. He attended Wilberforce University (1911–15), the Oberlin Conservatory of Music, and the New England Conservatory, and studied privately with George W. Chadwick and Edgard Varèse. He learned to orchestrate by playing in professional orchestras and by arranging music for W. C. Handy, Donald Voorhees, Sophie Tucker, Paul Whiteman, Willard Robison, and Artie Shaw. For several years he arranged and conducted the Deep River Hour over CBS and WOR.

Still became the first black to conduct a major orchestra in the United States when, in 1936, he directed the Los Angeles Philharmonic in his own compositions in the Hollywood Bowl. He was the recipient of a Guggenheim Fellowship (1934), a Rosenwald Fellowship (1939), and the second Harmon Award for the year's greatest contribution to American Negro culture (1927). Wilberforce University awarded him the honorary Master of Music in 1936; Howard University, the honorary doctorate in 1941; and Oberlin, the same degree in 1947.

Among his compositions are the ballets *La Guiablesse* (1927), *Sahdji* (1930); and *Lenox Avenue* (1937); the *Afro-American Symphony* (1931); the opera *Troubled Island* (1938), to a text by Langston Hughes; and the *Festive Overture* (1944), composed for the fiftieth anniversary of the Cincinnati Symphony. See his setting of "All That I Am," composed for *American Hymns*.

Edgar P. Stites, fl. late 19th cent.

Little is known of Edgar P. Stites beyond the fact that he was a native of New Jersey, a ship builder, and a cousin of Eliza E. Hewitt, a hymn writer. About 1875, while attending a Methodist camp meeting at Ocean Grove, N.J., he wrote a poem beginning "I've reached the land of corn and wine" (q.v.), based on Isaiah 35:10. The camp-meeting leader, John Sweney, liked it and composed music for it.

Jay T. Stocking, clergyman and educator; b. Lisbon, N.Y., April 19, 1870; d. Newton Centre, Mass., Jan. 27, 1936.

Although most of his publications were stories for children, Jay T. Stocking wrote one notable hymn: "O Master Workman of the Race" (q.v.). Educated at Amherst (A.B. 1895), he taught from 1895 to 1898 at a preparatory school in Lawrenceville, N.J. before he continued his education at Yale where he received the B.D. in 1901 and was ordained as a Congregational minister. In 1902–03 he continued his studies in the University of Berlin. He became assistant pastor of the Church of the Redeemer (New Haven, Conn.) after which he held pastorates at the First Church, Bellows Falls, Vt. (1903–05), the Central Church, Newtonville, Mass. (1905–14), the Firat Church, Washington, D.C. (1914–15), Union Congregational Church, Upper Montclair, N.J. (1915–27), Pilgrim Congregational Church, St. Louis, Mo. (1927–35), and the Congregational Church, Newton Centre, Mass. (1935–36).

A trustee of Oberlin College and of other educational institutions, he served his own denomination as trustee for the Congregational Conference of Missouri and the Congregational Annuity Fund. The National Council of the Congregational Christian Churches chose him as moderator in 1934–35 and he was a member of the Commission on International Justice and Good Will of the Federal Council of Churches. His publications included: *The City That Never Was Reached* (1911), *The Golden Goblet* (1914), *Queery Queer* (1926), *Mr. Friend O'Man* (1920), and *Stocking Tales* (1937).

John H. Stockton, Methodist evangelist, pastor, and hymn writer; b. New Hope, Pa., April 19, 1813; d. Philadelphia, Pa., March 25, 1877.

John H. Stockton was converted at a Methodist camp meeting in Paulsboro, N.J., in 1832. After becoming a member of the Methodist Episcopal Church in 1838 he was licensed to exhort in 1844 and to preach in 1846. The New Jersey Methodist Conference received him on trial in 1853 and into full relationship in 1857. Although the decision to become an itinerant was a difficult one for him to make, he finally said, "Here am I, send me."

After many years spent in pastoral and evangelistic work, Stockton retired in 1874 and, before his death, published two hymnals: *Salvation Melodies* (1874) and *Precious Songs* (1875). Moody and Sankey considered him a valuable assistant in their revival meetings in Philadelphia. Ira D. Sankey once wrote him: "I thank my Heavenly Father for enabling you to write so much sweet music, as well as words; and I hope you may long be spared to bless the world with your 'precious songs.' I wish you to accept our regards for one whose songs have been blessed to tens of thousands in the lands beyond the seas." See "Come, Every Soul" and its tune STOCKTON.

Henry J. Storer, teacher of the theory of music and composer; b. Cambridge, Mass., Aug. 28, 1860; d. Belmont, Mass., May 1, 1935.

Henry J. Storer was best remembered as a composer of hymn tunes. He had little formal training in music beyond what he learned from his parents. He first taught harmony and composition in Albany, later in Boston where he also read manuscript for the Oliver Ditson Company and wrote articles for *The Musician*. He composed anthems, songs, and organ works. His *Three Processional Hymns* (1891) is the source of PATMOS (O'er Continent and Ocean"). See also PACIFIC ("Hills of God, Break Forth in Singing") and O SION HASTE ("O Sion Haste, Thy Mission High Fulfilling").

Harriet Beecher Stowe, author; b. Litchfield, Conn., June 14, 1811; d. Hartford, Conn., July 1, 1896.

Harriet Beecher Stowe, daughter of Lyman Beecher, Congregational minister, and sister of Charles and Henry Ward Beecher, was four years old when her mother died. When Harriet was thirteen she was sent to Hartford to attend a school for girls. In 1832 the family moved to Cincinnati, where her father became head of Lane Theological Seminary and her sister Catherine established the Western Female Institute. Employed as a teacher in Catherine's school, Harriet apparently liked the new environment. She wrote sketches for the *Western Monthly Magazine* and won a $50 prize for a story subsequently reprinted in *The Mayflower*.

In 1836 she married Calvin Ellis Stowe, professor of biblical literature at Lane Seminary. He encouraged her to continue her writing. Altogether Mrs. Stowe spent eighteen years in Cincinnati. There six of her seven children were born. In 1850 Stowe accepted a professorship at Bowdoin College, Brunswick, Maine. After the birth of her seventh child, Mrs. Stowe started *Uncle Tom's Cabin*. First published as a serial (June 1851–April 1852) it appeared as a book in March 1852. Ten thousand copies were sold in less than a week and thirty thousand within the year. For nearly thirty years Mrs. Stowe wrote on the average a book a year, some of the best dealing with the New England of her girlhood. Her most widely used hymns appeared in the *Plymouth Collection* (1855). See "Abide in Me, O Lord, and I in Thee," "Still, Still with Thee," and "When Winds Are Raging."

George Strebeck, Lutheran, later Episcopal pastor; fl. late 18th cent.

George Strebeck became the assistant of Dr. John F. Kunze (q.v.) in preparing an English translation of the catechism and of the liturgy of the psalms. He contributed hymns to Kunze's *Hymn and Prayer Book For the Use of such Lutheran Churches as use the English Language* (1795). His contributions were marked by the letter "S." His pastoral career was marked by shifting associations. He had been a Methodist itinerant preacher before his ordination as a Lutheran pastor. During his association with Dr. Kunze he preached doctrines inconsistent with Lutheran belief to a congregation he had organized and he was subject to expulsion by the Synod. In 1800, having made confession of wrongdoing, he was restored to membership. In 1804 he was ordained an Episcopalian and organized St. Stephen's Church in New York. See "A Joyful Sound It Is."

Sebastian Streeter, Universalist minister and hymn writer; fl. early 19th cent.

Sebastian Streeter and his brother Russell Streeter edited *The New Hymn Book, Designed for Universalist Societies* (Boston, 1829), to which Sebastian contributed a number of hymns. The success of their efforts is indicated by the fact that the book reached a thirty-fifth edition in 1845. Sebastian Streeter delivered an address at the last service (1838) held in the old meeting house of the First Universalist Church in Boston. See "A King Shall Reign in Righteousness" and "Lo, What Enraptured Songs of Praise."

Nathan Strong, Congregational minister; b. Coventry, Conn., Oct. 16, 1748; d. Dec. 28, 1816.

Nathan Strong received his early education from his father, a minister. In 1765 he entered Yale University, from which he graduated with highest honors. Timothy Dwight, who was his classmate and his equal in scholarship, was rated second in the class because he was younger. President Ezra Stiles called Strong "the most universal scholar" he ever knew. After graduation Strong studied law, but shortly decided upon the ministry. He had been appointed a tutor at Yale in 1772, a post which he gave up the next year to become the pastor of the First Congregational Church of Hartford, Conn. Ordained in January of the following year, he remained pastor of that church as long as he lived, absenting himself for a short time to serve as chaplain in the army during the Revolution. After the war he held memorable revival services.

Strong's most celebrated work, *The Doctrine of Eternal Misery Reconcilable with the Infinite Benevolence of God,* was published in 1796. He published two volumes of sermons (1798 and 1800) and was the principal editor, with Abel Flint and Joseph Steward, of a volume intended for revival services, *The Hartford Selection of Hymns* (1799). This widely used collection included original hymns by Americans without naming the authors. However, Asahel Nettleton's *Village Hymns* (1824) reprints and identifies eight of Strong's hymns. See "Almighty Sovereign of the Skies!" "The Summer Harvest Spreads the Fields," and "Swell the Anthem, Raise the Song."

Melanchthon W. Stryker, minister, educator, and hymn
writer; b. Vernon, N.Y., Jan. 7, 1851; d. Clinton, N.Y., Dec. 6,
1929.

Melanchthon W. Stryker was educated at Hamilton College and
Auburn Theological Seminary. Ordained to the Presbyterian ministry in 1876, he held pastorates in Auburn and Ithaca, N.Y., Holyoke, Mass., and Chicago. Stryker became president of Hamilton
College in 1892 after a ministry of seven years at the Fourth Presbyterian Church in Chicago. He retired from the presidency of Hamilton in 1917. Hamilton, Lafayette, and Wesleyan honored him with
degrees.

His published works include: *A Song of Miriam* (1888), *Church Song*
(1889), *Dies Irae* (1893), *Lattermath* (1896), *English Bible Versions and
Their Origins* (1915), *Complete Versing of the Psalms of Israel* (1915),
Faculae Annorus (1917), *Vesper Bells* (1919), *Christian Praise* (1920),
Ethics in Outline (1923). Several of his own hymns were included in
the hymnals which he edited. See his "Almighty Lord, with One Accord" and "God of Our Fathers."

Simeon Stubbs, English composer; fl. 17th cent.

Some of the anthems of Simeon Stubbs are preserved in manuscript. He was among those who composed psalm tune settings for
Thomas Ravenscroft's *The Whole Booke of Psalmes* (1621). See his version of MARTYRS ("If Thou Wilt Hear").

Thomas O. Summers, Methodist pastor and educator; b. near
Corfe Castle, Dorsetshire, England, Oct. 11, 1812; d. May 6,
1882.

When Thomas O. Summers came to the United States in 1835, he
was accepted as a member of the Baltimore Conference of the
Methodist Church South. At first he served as a missionary in Texas
(1840–43). After a period in Tuscaloosa, Ala. (1844), he became
the conference secretary (1845). The next year he went to Charleston, S.C., where he became pastor and professor of theology at
Vanderbilt University. Although he served as chairman of the hymn
book committee and edited *Songs of Zion* (1851) and the *Wesleyan
Psalter* (1855), he was best remembered for a morning hymn, "The
Morning Bright with Rosy Light" (q.v.), written for his first child,
and an evening hymn, "The Daylight Fades," intended for the second.

Leonard Swain, Congregational minister; b. Concord, N.H.,
Feb. 26, 1821; d. Providence, R.I., July 14, 1869.

Leonard Swain received his education at Dartmouth College and
Andover Theological Seminary. In 1847 he accepted the pastorate
of the Congregational Church at Nashua, N.H., and five years later
was called to be the minister of the Central Church of Providence,
R.I. Brown University honored him with the degree of D.D. in 1857.
See his "My Soul, Weigh Not Thy Life."

Timothy Swan, singing master, composer, and compiler; b.
Worcester, Mass., July 23, 1758; d. Northfield, Mass., July 23,
1842.

Timothy Swan was the eighth of thirteen children. Upon his father's death he went to Boston. When he was sixteen he moved to
Groton, Mass., and lived with a brother. There he received his only
formal musical education—three weeks' attendance at a singing
school, which set him to composing, naturally in a rather rough fashion. He enlisted in the American forces at Cambridge, and having
acquired a fife learned to play it with the help of an English musician. Back home after his military service, he was apprenticed to a
brother-in-law in Northfield, Mass., to learn hat-making. While there
he chanced upon an article in an encyclopedia on the science of
music which made him take up tune-making again.

MONTAGUE and POLAND came first. After them he wrote many
other tunes which circulated in manuscript throughout New England. One musician who heard POLAND for the first time could not
believe that a boy of eighteen had written it. Swan's way of working
was first to write the melody and then, note by note, each of the supporting parts.

His apprenticeship finished, he moved in 1779 to the town of Suffield, Conn., and there, in 1783, he married Mary Gay, a musical
daughter of the minister of the First Congregational Church. Both
of them were excellent singers. During the twenty-eight years of his
life in Suffield, Swan taught singing schools. His pupils were a credit
to him, his concerts were popular, and his rendition of certain songs
became locally famous.

Of Swan's church tunes his own favorite was CHINA ("Why Do We
Mourn Departing Friends?") (q.v.). Although a contemporary critic
called it one of the most unscientific tunes ever published, ordinary
folk liked it best. For a century it was sung at funerals. Among his
other tunes were QUINCY, OCEAN, LONDON, SPRING, POWNAL, and
RAINBOW.

A book of tunes not signed by Swan but believed to be his was called *The Federal Harmony*. First published in 1785 it had several subsequent editions. Metcalf states that *The Songster's Assistant* (c.1800) contains songs by Swan. He is represented in Mason's *The Complete Pocket Song Book* (1802) and in *The Songster's Museum* (1803). Swan may have been the compiler of the latter book.

From 1807 Swan lived in Northfield, where he became the local librarian. Occasionally he turned out a poem, sometimes in Scottish dialect, which found its way into a newspaper. He was described as a prepossessing gentleman of quick mind and genial disposition, who loved lilacs and delighted in the colony of blackbirds established in the Lombardy poplars planted around his house. His neighbors called him "poor, proud, and indolent," because his habit of reading into the night made him a late riser. "He passed his last night in this manner," an early biographer says, "and died in his bed."

Joseph Emerson Sweetser, organist and compiler; b. 1825; d. 1873.

Joseph Emerson Sweetser came to this country as a young man, at a time when the influence of Lowell Mason (q.v.) and Thomas Hastings (q.v.) was at its height. Sweetser became the organist of the Church of the Puritans, Broadway and 15th Street, New York City, where George B. Cheever was pastor.

In 1849 Sweetser and George F. Root published *A Collection of Church Music,* later more popularly known as the Root and Sweetser Collection. In 1851 Sweetser and Cheever published *Christian Melodies.* See ST. LOUIS ("Blest Be the Wondrous Grace") and ROSEHILL ("O Life That Maketh All Things New"). Note that Lewis H. Redner's familiar setting of "O Little Town of Bethlehem" is also called ST. LOUIS.

John R. Sweney, composer and editor of gospel hymnbooks; b. West Chester, Pa., Dec. 31, 1837; d. April 10, 1899.

During the Civil War John R. Sweney was leader of a military band. When the war ended he took up the study of the violin and piano. Well-known as a choral conductor, he taught music in the Pennsylvania Military Academy for more than twenty-five years. A spiritual crisis in his life caused him to devote himself completely to religious work. Well-known as a gospel song composer, he was in great demand as music director for camp meetings and conventions.

In his later years he joined William J. Kirkpatrick in editing and publishing more than sixty gospel hymnals. See BEULAH LAND ("I've Reached the Land of Corn and Wine").

J. T., composer; fl. late 19th cent.

J. T. is the only clue given to the identity of the composer who wrote the setting of Henry Wadsworth Longfellow's "I Heard the Bells on Christmas Day," published in *Heart and Voice* (1910), edited by the Rev. Charles W. Wendté.

Robert Tailour, English composer and teacher; fl. 17th cent.

Robert Tailour published *Sacred Hymns: Consisting of Fifti Select Psalms of David and Others* in London in 1615. This paraphrase of the Psalms was by Sir Edwin Sandys (q.v.). Tailour was music master to the family of King James I, for whose daughter Elizabeth this volume may have been compiled. The music was "set to be sung in five parts, as also to the Viole, and Lute or Orpharion." See "In Pilgrim Life Our Rest."

William Tans'ur, wandering English psalmodist; b. Dunchurch, Warwickshire, England, 1706; d. St. Neot's, Oct. 7, 1783.

With an interest in music and a propensity to rove, William Tans'ur traveled about, holding classes wherever he paused. He is known to have been in Barnes, Ewell, Cambridge, Stamford, Boston, Leicester, and Saint Neot's, where he also sold books. His first collection which probably contains original tunes was *A Compleat Melody; or, The Harmony of Sion* (1734), later called *The Royal Melody Compleat; or, The New Harmony of Sion*. According to Tans'ur's own description it was "the most curiosest book that ever was published." His *New Musical Grammar,* in which he called himself "Musico Theorico," had appeared in 1746. Later publications were *The Psalm Singer's Jewel* (1760) and *The Elements of Musick Display'd,* issued in London in 1772.

Since his *Royal Melody Compleat; or, The New Harmony of Sion* was printed in this country by Daniel Bayley as early as 1767, Tans'ur must be regarded as an important influence on our own psalmodists. See ST. MARTIN's ("Awake, My Soul, Betimes Awake").

William B. Tappan, clockmaker, teacher, minister, and poet; b. Beverly, Mass., Oct. 24, 1794; d. West Needham, Mass., June 18, 1849.

After serving his apprenticeship as a clockmaker, William Tappan traveled to Philadelphia in 1815 and worked there at his trade. He left Philadelphia in 1818 to go to Somerville, N.J., where he devoted his time to study. He then returned to Philadelphia and became a teacher. In 1819 he published *New England and Other Poems,* in 1820 his *Songs of Judah,* and in 1822 his *Lyrics.*

In 1826 he accepted a position with the American Sunday School Union. In this capacity he spent a period of time in Cincinnati (1829–34) and another in Philadelphia (1834–38), before he moved to Boston in 1838. In 1841 he obtained a license to preach from the Congregational Association. He died in 1849, a victim of an epidemic of cholera.

During his lifetime he published ten volumes of verse; several were revised and republished during his years in Massachusetts, including *Poetry of the Heart* (1845), *Sacred and Miscellaneous Poems* (1846), *Poetry of Life* (1847), *The Sunday-School and Other Poems* (1848), and *Late and Early Poems* (1849). See "The Ransomed Spirit to Her Home," "There Is an Hour of Peaceful Rest," " 'Tis Midnight and on Olive's Brow," and "Wake, Isles of the South."

Nahum Tate, poet; b. Dublin, 1652; d. London, Aug. 12, 1715.

After attending Trinity College, Dublin, Nahum Tate became a member of Dryden's circle and wrote Part Two of *Absalom and Achitophel* under Dryden's guidance. He succeeded Thomas Shadwell as poet laureate in 1692. Tate and Nicholas Brady wrote the metrical psalter, known as the "New Version" (1696). It is not clear how the task of paraphrasing the Psalms was divided between them, but it was Tate who responded to hostile criticism with his *Essay on Psalmody* (1710). See their version of Psalm 15: "Lord, Who's the Happy Man."

Caleb J. Taylor, teacher, Methodist preacher, and frontier hymnist; b. St. Mary's Parish, Md., June 20, 1763; d. Kenton Co., Ohio, near Cincinnati, 1817.

Caleb J. Taylor grew up on the farm of his Irish, Roman Catholic parents and became a schoolteacher at the age of eighteen. He was converted to Methodism while employed as a teacher in Virginia and Pennsylvania and began to preach. In 1792 he lived in the vicinity of Maysville, Ky. In 1810 he became an itinerant of the Western Conference, but two years later accepted a call and became a settled pastor.

Speaking of both Taylor and John A. Granade, Thomas S. Hinde, whose *Pilgrim Songster* (1814) contained eleven hymns by Taylor, said that "these two poets composed their songs during the great revivals of religion in the states of Kentucky and Tennessee about the years 1802, 3, and 4." He went on to comment on "the peculiar turn of these two interesting poets," stating that Granade "has gone to receive his reward, and the latter nearly ready for it." Taylor's death did not come until three years later, in 1817. He is said to have been profoundly depressed in his last years. See "O Jesus, My Saviour, I Know Thou Art Mine."

Edward Taylor, poet and minister; b. Sketchly, Leicestershire, England, 1642; d. Westfield, Mass., June 29, 1729.

Edward Taylor left England to avoid the discrimination against nonconformists there, arriving in Massachusetts in 1668. In 1671 he graduated from Harvard and in December of that year was in Westfield, Mass., where he had accepted a call to be the first minister. Because of the troubled state of what was then a frontier town and because of the smallness of the congregation, the church was not formally organized until August 27, 1679. Once installed Taylor remained until his death, also serving for much of the period as a physician. During this time he composed a long series of versified meditations which he regarded as a form of worship. In their intensity and in the richness and variety of imagery they reveal the poet in a man whose outward life was not different from that of many other pioneer preachers. Especially striking is Taylor's use of musical imagery, although the inventory of his library does not suggest that he was a practicing musician. For this aspect of Taylor's verse see "The Angels Sung a Carol" and its note. See also "In Heaven Soaring Up" and "Thou Art the Tree of Life." For the latter Henry Cowell composed a setting which is published in *American Hymns* for the first time.

Raynor Taylor, composer and organist; b. England, c.1747; d. Philadelphia, Pa., Aug. 17, 1825.

Raynor Taylor, a choirboy in the Chapel Royal in England, attended the last rites for Handel and let his hat fall into the grave. A friend remarked, "Never mind, he left you some of his brains in return." At eighteen he was organist at Chelmsford, near London. He had a flair for ballad writing and a liking for the stage that made him successful as music director for the Sadler's Wells Theatre in London from 1765. He left England in 1792.

Taylor gave concerts in Baltimore and later in Annapolis, where he was organist at St. Anne's Church. He then moved to Philadelphia, where he remained as organist of St. Peter's Church for almost thirty years. He wrote several plays and the incidental music for others. A monody on the death of Washington composed by Taylor and Alexander Reinagle was much admired. The Musical Fund Society was founded in 1820 by Taylor, Benjamin Carr, John G. Schetky, Thomas Loud, and Charles F. Hupfield. Samuel Holyoke's *Harmonia Americana* (1802) contains five tunes by Taylor: BADDOW, MAHON, STEPNEY, CHESTERBROOK, and TIGRIS ("Hail Our Incarnate God!") (q.v.).

Virgil Corydon Taylor, organist and compiler; b. Barkhamstead, Conn., April 2, 1817; d. Des Moines, Iowa, Jan. 30, 1891.

Virgil Corydon Taylor resided for a time in Hartford, Conn. From 1851 he was successively organist of the Central Baptist Church and the First Dutch Reformed Church of Poughkeepsie. After serving as organist and choir director of a Baptist church in Brooklyn, he went to Niagara Falls, N.Y., and then to Des Moines, Iowa, where he was associated with St. Paul's Episcopal Church until his death.

Taylor was active as a voice teacher and conductor and in the period 1850–77 as an organizer of musical conventions. His industry as composer and compiler is evidenced by a series of publications, among which were his *Sacred Minstrel or American Church Music Book* (New York, 1846) and *Choral Anthems* (Boston, 1850). In the former appeared his LOUVAN ("Lord, My Weak Thought in Vain Would Climb") (q.v.), which has remained in use from that time to the present.

Alexander R. Thompson, pastor and hymnbook editor; b. New York City, Oct. 22, 1812; d. Brooklyn, N.Y., Feb. 8, 1895.

Alexander R. Thompson graduated from New York University in 1842 and then studied theology at Princeton where he graduated in

1845. During that year he was licensed by the Second Presbytery of New York and served as assistant pastor at the Central Reformed Dutch Church in Brooklyn, then at the Presbyterian Church at Eighth Street, Astor Place, New York City. In 1846 Thompson became the pastor of the First Presbyterian Church of Morristown, N.J. Other pastorates included a church at Bedford, East Brooklyn (1848), the Reformed Dutch Church of Tomkinsville, Staten Island (1848–51), and the Reformed Dutch Church of Stapleton, Staten Island. In 1862 he went to St. Paul's Reformed Dutch Church in New York City as associate pastor, replacing the pastor George W. Bethune later in the same year. His last pastorate was at the North Reformed Church, Brooklyn (from 1874). An honorary D.D. was conferred on him in 1873. Joint editor of the Reformed Dutch *Hymns of the Church* (1869) and the *Hymns of Prayer and Praise* (1871), he contributed hymns and translations from the Latin to these and to other collections. See "Wayfarers in the Wilderness."

Mary A. Thomson, poet; b. London, Dec. 5, 1834; d. Philadelphia, Pa., March 11, 1923.

Mary A. Faulkner, who came to this country as a young girl, married John Thomson, librarian of the Free Library in Philadelphia. She was the author of several poems and hymns, eight of which appeared in *The Churchman* (New York) and thirty-four in *The Living Church* (Chicago). Four were published in *The Hymnal Revised and Enlarged* (1892): "Now the Blessed Dayspring," "O King of Saints, We Give Thee Praise and Glory" (q.v.), "O Sion, Haste, Thy Mission High Fulfilling" (q.v.), and "Saviour, for the Little One."

Virgil Thomson, composer and music critic; b. Kansas City, Mo., Nov. 25, 1896.

Virgil Thomson was a church organist and choirmaster before he served as an aviator in World War I. He then went to Harvard and graduated in 1922. He was organist and choirmaster of King's Chapel in Boston for a year and then for two years assistant instructor in music at Harvard and director of the glee club. He spent eight years, 1924 to 1932, in Paris where he studied with Nadia Boulanger and became a member of the Gertrude Stein circle.

From 1934 to 1937 he was director of "The Friends and Enemies of Modern Music" in Hartford, Conn. During 1936 he was music director for several of the federal theaters in New York. He was appointed chief music critic of the *New York Herald Tribune* in 1940 until he retired in 1954.

Thomson's critical views are reflected in *The State of Music* (1939), *The Musical Scene* (1945), *The Art of Judging Music* (1948), and *Music Right and Left* (1951). His music often has an American flavor based on the use of hymn tunes and folk melodies, but he also writes in a dissonant neoclassic manner. He is best known for his operas based on texts by Gertrude Stein: *Four Saints in Three Acts* (1934) and *The Mother of Us All* (1947). The music for the films *The Plow That Broke the Plains* (1936), *The River* (1937), and *Louisiana Story* (1948) were arranged as orchestral suites by the composer. His ballet *Filling Station* dates from 1938. He wrote musical portraits of friends for various media. More closely related to our field are *Symphony on a Hymn Tune* (1928), *Four Sets of Variations and Fugues on Gospel Hymns* for organ, and *Sacred Choral Hymns from the Old South* for mixed chorus a capella. His musical settings for "It Seems That God Bestowed Somehow" and "Praise Him Who Makes Us Happy" were composed for *American Hymns*.

Stephen Tilden, author; b. 1690; d. 1766.

Stephen Tilden's one publication, *Miscellaneous Poems* ([New London?], 1756), began with an apology to the reader: "It may justly seem a matter of great surprise, that a Man near 70 years of Age, should attempt to be an Author: It may justly be deem'd by you or any other *Gentlemen,* to be the product of Superannuation . . . I tho't at this critical Juncture it might be of some service to the Public, to attempt to animate, and stir up the martial spirits of our Soldiery, which is the utmost I can do under my present Circumstances." See "O Heaven Indulge."

Thomas Tillam, religious leader; fl. 17th cent.

Thomas Tillam came to this country in 1638 and wrote a poem "Upon the first sight of New England June 29, 1638" (see "Hail, Holy Land"). Apparently a man of learning concerned with religion, he associated himself first with the Seventh Day Adventists, then founded a sect of his own. He eventually left New England for Heidelberg, then under the rule of a liberal Elector who presumably would not look askance on unorthodox beliefs.

In the preface to a book published in London in 1667 is a quotation from a work by Thomas Tillam. That book, *Declaration of a Fu-*

ture Glorious State, was written by Samuel Hutchinson, brother-in-law of Anne Hutchinson, who stirred up both interest and opposition in Boston by her leadership of a religious group called the Antinomians. That Tillam and Samuel Hutchinson were acquainted seems likely.

Henry Timrod, poet of the Confederacy; b. Charleston, S.C., Dec. 8, 1826; d. Columbia, S.C., Oct. 6, 1867.

Educated in the Charleston schools and at Franklin College (later the University of Georgia), Henry Timrod became a friend of the Southern poet Paul Hamilton Hayne. Ill health and a lack of money forced him to withdraw from college at the end of two years. He found employment as a tutor on a Carolina plantation where he stayed ten years. During his vacations he returned to Charleston where he joined the literary group around William Gilmore Simms and *Russell's Magazine* (1837–61), to which Timrod contributed poems and prose articles.

In 1860 Ticknor and Fields published a small collection of Timrod's poems, which was favorably reviewed in both North and South. The stress of events soon obscured his success, and his disappointment was displaced by his own emotions at the approach of war. In 1861 he wrote his ode *Ethnogenesis,* which was followed by impassioned and fervent war poems that stirred the South. In March 1862, Timrod enlisted in a South Carolina regiment; after Shiloh he served as a correspondent of the *Charleston Mercury.* In December he was discharged with incipient tuberculosis. In 1864 he moved to Columbia to become editor and part proprietor of the *South Carolinian* and married Kate Goodwin, an English girl whom he had loved for a long time. A year later Columbia was burned and Timrod reduced to abject poverty. *The Poems of Henry Timrod,* edited by his friend Paul Hamilton Hayne, appeared in 1873. See his "Faint Falls the Gentle Voice" and "Sleep Sweetly."

William G. Tomer, teacher and musician; b. 1832; d. 1896.

After serving in the Union army William G. Tomer became successively a clerk in Washington, D.C., and a teacher in the public schools of New Jersey. He was in charge of the music of the Grace Methodist Episcopal Church of Washington when, in response to a request by Rev. Jeremiah Rankin, he wrote the familiar tune to Rankin's "God Be with You Till We Meet Again."

F. Bland Tucker, Episcopal priest; b. Norfolk, Va., Jan. 6, 1895.

After graduating from the University of Virginia (A.B., 1914), F. Bland Tucker served as a private in Evacuation Hospital No. 15 of the A.E.F. He then attended the Virginia Theological Seminary and in 1918 was ordained as a deacon and in 1920, as a priest. From 1920 to 1925 he served in a church in Brunswick County, Va., then until 1945 at St. John's, Georgetown, Washington, D.C. In 1951 he became rector of the Old Christ Church in Savannah, Ga. As a member of the Joint Commission on the Revision of the Hymnal he helped in the preparation of *The Hymnal 1940.* See his "All Praise to Thee" and "Our Father, by Whose Name."

William Tuckey, organist and composer; b. Somersetshire, England, 1708; d. Philadelphia, Pa., Sept. 14, 1781.

William Tuckey came to New York before 1753, fortified with the prestige attained as vicar-choral and parish clerk at Bristol Cathedral. In 1757 he offered his services in an advertisement "to amend the singing in publick congregations" and "to set to music any piece on any subject." After a discouraging period during which he planned to return to England at the end of a year, he changed his mind and remained in this country, eventually establishing himself as a leading figure in New York's musical life. Both he and his fellow countryman William Selby contributed much to the development of public taste.

Tuckey became organist at Trinity Church and taught singing in its charity school two evenings a week. He was paid fifteen pounds for providing the music at the dedication of St. Paul's Chapel. He composed and rehearsed a Thanksgiving anthem which was performed in the presence of General Amherst to celebrate the latter's conquest of Canada. In October 1766, Tuckey gave a concert of church music in Mr. Burns's New Assembly Room for voices and instruments. Early in the month he had advertised for "gentlemen who play on any instrument to lend assistance," and advance notices promised a group of forty performers. A later concert in January 1770, was noteworthy as the first public performance of Handel's *Messiah* in America, although it was given in abbreviated form.

Of Tuckey's own compositions an anthem entitled *Jehovah Reigns,* based on the 97th Psalm, and his tune LIVERPOOL were well known and liked. In 1771 he solicited subscriptions for a number of works he planned to publish. See his PSALM 97 ("Almighty Sovereign of the Skies!"), which was extracted from the anthem.

John Tufts, Congregational minister; b. Medford, Mass.,
Feb. 26, 1688; d. Amesbury, Mass., Aug. 17, 1752.

After graduation from Harvard College (1708), John Tufts was
ordained a minister of the Second Church of Christ in West Newbury (1714). His *A Very Plain and Easy Introduction to the Art of Singing
Psalm Tunes; with the Cantus or Trebles of Twenty-eight Psalm Tunes, Con-
trived in Such a Manner As that the Learner May Attain the Skill of Singing Them with the Greatest Ease and Speed Imaginable* was published in
1714/15. No copy of the first edition is extant. Tufts used letters on
the staff instead of notes. His publication was violently opposed by
those who believed that psalm tunes should be learned by rote
rather than by reading music notation. In spite of all objections
Tufts's book had wide circulation, reaching an eleventh edition. It
was sometimes bound with the *Bay Psalm Book.*
    The end of Tufts's life was clouded. On February 26, 1738, a
council was called to consider "The distressed state and condition of
ye Second Church of Christ in Newbury by reason of their reverend
pastor Mr. John Tufts being charged by a woman or women of his
indecent carriage and also of his abusive and unchristian behavior to
them." Tufts neither responded to the charges nor attempted to defend himself but finally asked for a dismissal. The demand was
granted two months later and his church refused to recommend him
for further employment as a minister. See HACKNEY ("Give Ear, O
God, to My Loud Cry"), STANDISH ("God of My Life!"), and 100TH
PSALM TUNE NEW ("Thrice Blest the Man").

John Tullidge, Mormon musician and music critic; b. England; d. Salt Lake City, Utah, Jan. 1874.

John Tullidge was apparently a successful musician in Great Britain, where he led the choir of St. Mary's Cathedral Church, Newport, South Wales, and served as one of the conductors of the York
Harmonic Society. In 1843 he organized the Newport Harmonic Society. The first member of his family to become a Mormon convert,
in about 1851, was his son Edward. Tullidge himself came to the
United States and traveled west with his son John, and his son's wife
and child. In September 1863, they reached their destination, but
the child died on the way. A year later John Tullidge joined the
Mormon Church. He gave the first concert in Salt Lake City in September 1864, and became the first music critic in Utah. When the
orchestra at the Salt Lake theater needed music, it was Tullidge who
made the arrangements for them. In 1857 a collection of thirty-eight
easy anthems by Tullidge was published in England. In 1869 he

published a choral song, "Hail! Young, Beautiful Spring," said to be the first music printed in the Rocky Mountain region. See the tune which he composed for Eliza Snow's "Think Not When You Gather to Zion."

Henry Hallam Tweedy, Congregational minister, educator, and hymnologist; b. Binghamton, N.Y., Aug. 5, 1868; d. Sept. 11, 1953.

After attending Phillips Andover Academy, Henry Hallam Tweedy pursued undergraduate studies at Yale, then went to the Union Theological Seminary and the University of Berlin for more advanced studies. After his ordination as a Congregational minister he went to Utica, N.Y., where he served as the minister of the Plymouth Church (1898–1902), then to the South Church, Bridgeport, Conn. (1902–09). In 1909 he received the M.A. at Yale and was appointed professor of practical theology at the Yale Divinity School, a post which he held until 1937. Tweedy was a frequent visiting preacher at preparatory schools and his sermons at Battell Chapel were memorable. His interest in church music led him to write *The Minister and His Hymnal* and to compile *Christian Worship and Praise.* See two settings of "Eternal God, Whose Power Upholds" and "O Gracious Father of Mankind."

Royall Tyler, wit, playwright, novelist, and jurist; b. Boston, Mass., July 18, 1757; d. Brattleboro, Vt., Aug. 26, 1826.

Royall Tyler graduated from Harvard in 1776. As major of the Independent Company of Boston he took part in the attempt to capture Newport in 1778. Tyler had studied law in Boston and was admitted to the bar in Falmouth (now Portland), Maine. He was in military service again during Shays's Rebellion. A trip to New York gave Tyler the opportunity to see Sheridan's *School for Scandal,* which gave him the idea of writing *The Contrast,* the second play by an American to be put on by a professional troupe. Produced April 16, 1787, it was well received. His novel *The Algerine Captive* was published in 1797. He moved from Boston to Guilford, Vt., in 1790, and was chief justice of the Vermont supreme court, 1807–13. Among Tyler's occasional verse is a Christmas carol "Hail to the Joyous Day" (q.v.).

Thomas Cogswell Upham, Congregational minister; b. Deerfield, N.H., Jan. 30, 1799; d. New York City, April 2, 1872.

After attending Dartmouth College and Andover Seminary,
Thomas Cogswell Upham was ordained as a Congregational minister. He then went to Bowdoin College as professor of mental and
moral philosophy, a post he held for forty-two years. *Mental
Philosophy,* a textbook in his chosen field, was highly regarded in its
time. His biography of Mme. Jeanne Guyon with translations of her
hymns dates from 1847; a volume of Upham's poems appeared in
1852. See "Fear Not, Poor Weary One," which, with four other
hymns, appeared in *Hymns and Songs of Praise* (1874).

Adrianus Valerius, Dutch notary; b. Middelburg, Holland,
1575; d. Veere, Holland, Jan. 27, 1620.

Adrianus Valerius is chiefly remembered for his *Nederlandtsche
Gedenkclanck . . .* (Haarlem, 1626), which contained a notable collec-
tion of popular tunes: English, German, Italian, and French, with
accompaniments in tablature for lute or cittern. See the English
Fortune My Foe ("Als Ik Des Herren Werk") and Ferretti's Sei
Tanto Gratiosa ("Laat Ons Den Herre Singen").

Peter Valton, organist and composer; b. England, date unknown; d. Feb. 10, 1784.

Before coming to this country Peter Valton had served as organist
at King's Chapel, Westminster Abbey, and at St. George's, Hanover
Square, and had composed catches and a glee. He came here to play
at St. Philip's Church in Charleston, S.C. (1764–81). He also engaged
in various musical activities, selling spinets and harpsichords, teaching, and giving concerts. British troops occupied Charleston in
1780–81. In the latter year St. Michael's, which had been closed, was
reopened by a rector with loyalist convictions. Valton volunteered to
play the organ and probably remained there two years. In addition
to occasional works Valton composed six sonatas for harpsichord or
organ and contributed eleven tunes to Jacob Eckhard's choirmaster's
book. See St. Michael's ("At Length the Busy Day Is Done").

Mark Van Doren, writer, critic, and educator; b. Hope, Ill., June 13, 1894; d. Torrington, Conn., Dec. 10, 1972.

Mark Van Doren was educated at the University of Illinois (A.B., 1914; A.M., 1915) and at Columbia University (Ph.D., 1920). He served as an instructor in the English department at Columbia (1920–24), an assistant professor (1924–35), an associate professor (1935–42), and a professor (1942–59). He was a lecturer at St. John's College, Annapolis, from 1937 and was a member of its board of visitors and governors from 1943 to 1953. From 1924 to 1928 he was literary editor of *The Nation* and, from 1935 to 1938, its motion picture critic. In 1944 Bowdoin College conferred on Van Doren an honorary Litt.D. He was a member of the American Academy of Arts and Letters and was chairman of the National Book and Author War Bond Committee (1943–45).

Van Doren wrote critical studies of Thoreau (1916), Dryden (1920), Edwin Arlington Robinson (1927), Shakespeare (1939), and Nathaniel Hawthorne (1949). *Private Reader* (1942) is a collection of critical prose and *Noble Voice* (1946) is a study of ten great poems. He also wrote several novels, including *The Transients* (1935), *Windless Cabins* (1940), *Tilda* (1943), and a book of stories, *Nobody Say a Word* (1953). His poetry included *Spring Thunder* (1924), *Jonathan Gentry* (1931), *Collected Poems* (1939), which won a 1940 Pulitzer prize, *The Mayfield Deer* (1941), *Our Lady Peace* (1942), *Seven Sleepers* (1944), *Country New Year* (1946), *Introduction to Poetry* (1951), *Spring Birth and Other Poems* (1953), and *Selected Poems* (1954). See his "Praise Him Who Makes Us Happy" and "Why, Lord?"

Henry Van Dyke, clergyman, essayist, and diplomat; b. Germantown, Pa., Nov. 10, 1852; d. Princeton, N.J., April 10, 1933.

Henry Van Dyke grew up in Brooklyn where he graduated from the Polytechnic Institute. He entered Princeton (A.B., 1873; A.M., 1876) and then the Princeton Theological Seminary from which he graduated in 1877. After a year's travel abroad he was ordained in 1879 to begin his career as pastor of the United Congregational Church in Newport, Rhode Island. At the Brick Presbyterian Church in New York City (1883–1900) he became widely known as a preacher of courage and distinction.

Van Dyke accepted the Murray professorship of English literature at Princeton at the turn of the century, succeeding James O. Murray there as well as at the Brick Church. At Princeton he became a friend of Woodrow Wilson, who later appointed him minister to the Netherlands and Luxembourg (1913–17).

In 1902–03 Van Dyke served as moderator of the Presbyterian Church in the United States. In 1908–09 he was American lecturer at the Sorbonne. Leaving his diplomatic post in 1917, he returned to this country to volunteer for active service in the U.S. Navy and was made a lieutenant commander in the Chaplain Corps. One of the original advocates of the League to Enforce Peace, he worked indefatigably in its cause. In 1923 Van Dyke retired to devote himself to literary work, much of it concerned with the revision of *The Book of Common Prayer* (adopted 1931). See "Jesus, Thou Divine Companion," and "O Lord Our God, Thy Mighty Hand."

Jones Very, author; b. Salem, Mass., Aug. 28, 1813; d. there May 8, 1880.

Son of a sea captain, Jones Very accompanied his father on the last two voyages (1823 and 1824) the latter made to Europe. Graduated with second honors from Harvard (1836) he remained there as Greek tutor for the following two years. He was Unitarian in belief, but never held a permanent pastorate, although he often appeared as a preacher.

Most of Very's life was spent in Salem where he devoted himself to writing. His *Essays and Poems* appeared in 1839, and after that date he contributed numerous articles to the *Salem Gazette,* the *Salem Observer,* the *Christian Register,* and the *Monthly Magazine.* Some of Very's poems appeared in the *Book of Hymns* (1846) by Samuel Longfellow and Samuel Johnson and in their later *Hymns of the Spirit* (1864). See "Wilt Thou Not Visit Me."

William M. Vories, missionary; b. Leavenworth, Kan., Oct. 28, 1880.

William M. Vories was educated at Colorado College, where he became a student volunteer for foreign missions. He stipulated that, if he did become a missionary, he should be sent to a neglected field where no missionary work had been done before and should not be paid a salary. He wanted to earn his own living and work under the auspices of no denomination.

Six months after he received his Ph.D. from Colorado College (1905), the International YMCA secured a teaching position for him at Omi-Hachiman, Japan. It was there that he established the Omi Mission. In spite of violent opposition and personal persecution, Vories developed it into a large enterprise divided into seventeen departments of work, each administered by a competent staff.

Because he was convinced that Christianity would not appeal to the Japanese unless it reached them in a practical way, he returned to the United States to study architecture in order to teach the Japanese how to build more substantially and economically. Manned by a staff of forty, the architecture department of the Omi Mission has never been able to meet all the demands for its services. During the first eighteen years of its activity, the department drew up building plans for 114 churches and YMCA buildings, 118 school buildings, 164 residences, and 24 business houses.

As described in Vories' book *A Mustard Seed in Japan,* the Omi Mission specialized in women's work, kindergarten activities, a playground program, general evangelization, newspaper evangelism, the publication of tracts and books, the student YMCA, and the treatment of tuberculosis patients. Its hospital for tuberculars was the most complete in all Japan.

Vories' parents joined him in 1914 to help in his work. His father became the general treasurer of the organization and held that position until his death in 1925. In 1919 Vories, who had married a woman of the Japanese nobility, took out naturalization papers and adopted his wife's name. In 1930 he delivered the baccalaureate sermon at Colorado College, at which time the honorary LL.D. was awarded him. The author of a number of articles and books, he published the English-language monthly, *The Omi Mustard Seed,* which was distributed to interested supporters of his organization. See "Let There Be Light."

Jonathan Mayhew Wainwright, Episcopal clergyman; b. Liverpool, England, Feb. 24, 1792; d. New York City, Sept. 21, 1854.

Born to an American family living in England, Jonathan Mayhew Wainwright came to the United States with them in 1803. He graduated from Harvard in 1812 and, while an undergraduate, he was organist of Christ Church in Boston. From 1815 to 1817 he tutored at Harvard and prepared for the Episcopal ministry. In 1818 he was appointed rector of Christ Church, Hartford, Conn. As a member of a literary club there, he saw a good deal of Peter Parley (pseud. of Samuel G. Goodrich) and William Stone. He settled in New York acting as assistant at Trinity Church (1819–21) before becoming the rector of Grace Church (1821–34). Rector of Boston's Trinity Church from 1834, he returned to New York again as rector of St. John's Chapel (1837–54), becoming provisional bishop of New York in 1852.

In 1819 he compiled a set of chants adapted to the hymns used in morning and evening prayer. *Music of the Church* was published in

1828 and *Psalmodia Evangelica* in 1830. See HARTFORD ("While O'er
the Deep Thy Servants Sail").

Samuel Wakefield, composer and compiler; b. 1799; d. 1895.

Samuel Wakefield, described by Silas W. Leonard and A. D. Fillmore in the *Christian Psalmist* (1851) as a "distinguished composer of
Pittsburgh, Pennsylvania," was the grandfather of the American
composer Charles Wakefield Cadman. An autodidact, he composed
hymns and hymn tunes and wrote on music, grammar, and theology. He must have been an expert craftsman if he built the first pipe
organ west of the Alleghenies as has been claimed. Editor and compiler of *Ecclesiastical Harmony,* the *American Repository of Sacred Music,*
and the *Christian Harp,* he joined William Hunter in editing the *Minstrel of Zion* (1854). See THE DYING BACKSLIDER (" 'Go, Bring Me,'
Said the Dying Fair") and THE ITINERANT'S DEATH ("The Music of
His Steps").

David Walker, fl. mid-19th cent.

The setting of THE HEBREW CHILDREN ("Where Are the Hebrew
Children") (q.v.) which appeared in the 1854 edition of *Southern
Harmony* was credited to David Walker, a brother of the compiler
William Walker. A footnote stated that "This tune was set to music
by David Walker in 1841: also the last two verses of the song are his
composition." "Set to music" is to be understood in the sense of
"arranged," since the tune and text were probably sung before they
appeared in the Southern tune books.

William Walker, singing master and compiler; b. near Cross Keys, S.C., May 6, 1809; d. Spartanburg, S.C., Sept. 24, 1875.

William Walker's family moved to a new location near Cedar
Spring in the Spartanburg area when he was eighteen. After a period of schooling which was limited to the rudiments, he became a
member of the Baptist church and began to teach in singing schools.
Known as Singin' Billy Walker, to distinguish him from two other
Spartanburg men with the same name, he was associated with his
brother-in-law Benjamin Franklin White (q.v.) (they were married to

the Golightly sisters Amy and Thurza). There is evidence that they worked together in compiling *The Southern Harmony,* but only Walker's name appeared on the title page when it came out in 1835, thus causing a rift between Walker and White. The latter moved to Georgia and published his own book, *The Sacred Harp,* in 1844. Both books, *The Southern Harmony* and *The Sacred Harp,* became household words in the rural South, for they included hymns that had been handed down for generations. Before the Civil War the collections were so popular that they were stocked in general stores along with grits and tobacco. In 1845 Walker published the *Southern and Western Harmonist* and in 1866 *Christian Harmony.* In *The Southern Harmony* Walker had used a four-shape notation with symbols for mi, fa, sol, and la, but in his later publications he followed the trend toward the seven-shape notation with a distinctive note pattern for each note of the scale. *Fruits and Flowers,* a small Sunday School book, appeared in 1869. Walker's gravestone in Magnolia Cemetery records his forty-five years as a singing master. See FRENCH BROAD ("High O'er the Hills"), SAINTS BOUND FOR HEAVEN ("Our Bondage It Shall End"), and HICKS' FAREWELL ("The Time Is Swiftly Rolling On").

William H. Walter, organist and composer; b. Newark, N.J., July 1, 1825; d. New York City, 1893.

At an early age William H. Walter was organist in a Presbyterian Church and at Grace Episcopal Church in Newark, N.J. From 1842 he was in New York as organist successively of the Church of the Epiphany, St. John's Chapel, St. Paul's Chapel, and Trinity Chapel. Columbia University gave him the D.Mus. degree in 1864, and he became university organist the following year. His tune called FESTAL SONG has remained in use and was included in *The Hymnal 1940.* His original compositions in larger form included masses, services, and anthems. Other publications were: *Manual of Church Music* (1860), *Chorale and Hymns, Hymnal with Tunes Old and New, Selections of Psalms with Chants* (1857), *The Common Prayer, with Ritual Song* (1868). See WITNESSES ("O King of Saints, We Give Thee Praise and Glory") and FESTAL SONG ("Rise Up, O Men of God").

Clarence A. Walworth, Catholic priest, missionary, and author; b. Plattsburg, N.Y., May 30, 1820; d. Albany, N.Y., Sept. 19, 1900.

After graduating from Union College, Schenectady, N.Y. (1838), Clarence A. Walworth became a lawyer but preferred religious studies. While at the General Theological Seminary in New York City he was influenced by the Tractarian movement, became a Roman Catholic, and was ordained in 1848 in Holland. After a period of missionary work he went to St. Peter's Church, Troy, N.Y. In 1861 he rejoined his former associates, now organized as the Paulist Fathers, but in 1865 was unable to continue because of poor health. Walworth then became pastor of St. Mary's Church in Albany. He advocated basic reforms including temperance and a more enlightened policy toward the St. Regis Indians. He also spoke against the evils of the expanding industrial complex and the misuse of political power. His paraphrase of the "Te Deum," "Holy God, We Praise Thy Name" (q.v.), became one of the foremost lyrics of English-speaking Catholics.

Henry Ware Jr., Unitarian minister and educator; b. Hingham, Mass., April 21, 1794; d. Framingham, Mass., Sept. 25, 1843.

After graduating from Harvard, Henry Ware Jr. became minister of the Second Church in Boston at the age of twenty-three. He served there for twelve years. In his first year his Easter hymn, "Lift Your Glad Voices in Triumph on High" (q.v.), was published. In 1819 he wrote a hymn, "Great God, the Followers of Thy Son" (q.v.), to be sung at the ordination of Jared Sparks in Baltimore on May 5, 1819. On this occasion William Ellery Channing preached a sermon that became famous because it raised the banner of Unitarianism against the more conservative and orthodox forms of Congregationalism. When Ware wished to resign in 1828 because of his precarious state of health, Ralph Waldo Emerson was engaged to assist him as associate pastor. From 1829 to 1842 he was professor of pulpit eloquence and pastoral care in Harvard Divinity School and, for a time, edited *The Christian Disciple*, later *The Christian Examiner*. "All Nature's Works His Praise Declare" was written for the dedication of a church organ.

Anna B. Warner, writer; b. New York City, Aug. 31, 1827; d. Constitution Island, N.Y., Jan 23, 1915.

The Warner sisters, Anna and Susan, spent their early years in New York City. Their father, a prosperous lawyer, bought Constitution Island, in the Hudson opposite West Point, as a summer home, but he lost so heavily in the panic of 1837 that the old house on the island became the family home. The sisters, eager to do something to earn money, turned to writing. Susan's *Wide, Wide World* was a great success and her second novel, *Queechy,* nearly equaled it. Anna's *Dollars and Sense* and her other stories for young people sold moderately well over a long period.

For more than fifty years the sisters devoted their Sunday afternoons to conducting a Bible class for cadets from West Point. Their man of all work, Buckner, would row the flat-bottomed boat to the dock where the holders of permits waited to be ferried. After the lesson, followed by tea and gingerbread, he would row them back. Susan was the teacher until her death in 1885, when Anna took her place. Anna was the compiler of *Hymns of the Church Militant* (1858). See her children's hymn "Jesus Loves Me, This I know," "One More Day's Work for Jesus," and "We Would See Jesus."

George W. Warren, organist, choirmaster, and composer; b. Albany, N.Y., Aug. 17, 1828; d. New York City, March 17, 1902.

A self-taught musician, George W. Warren was educated at Racine College in Wisconsin. He became organist at St. Peter's Church in Albany (1846–58), then served at St. Paul's in the same city until 1860, when he moved to Brooklyn to act in a similar capacity at Holy Trinity Church (1860–70). His appointment there was followed by thirty years as organist and choirmaster at St. Thomas' Church in New York City.

Warren's alma mater bestowed the Mus.D. degree on him. He composed a substantial amount of church music and edited and published a hymnal, *Warren's Hymns and Tunes, as Sung at St. Thomas' Church,* in 1888. See HOSPITAL SUNDAY HYMN ("Father, Who Mak'st The Suff'ring Sons"), NATIONAL HYMN ("God of Our Fathers, Whose Almighty Hand"), and LOG COLLEGE ("O Thou Whose Feet Have Climbed Life's Hill").

Samuel Prowse Warren, organist; b. Montreal, Canada, Feb. 18, 1841; d. New York City, Oct. 7, 1915.

The son of an organ builder, Samuel Prowse Warren studied organ at an early age and gave a public recital at the age of twelve. For eight years he served as organist of the American Presbyterian Church in Montreal. Later he went to Germany where he studied organ with Karl A. Haupt and piano with Gustav Schumann. On his return he settled in New York City. He was organist at All Souls

Unitarian Church, where he remained from 1866 to 1868, at Grace Church, 1868–74, and again 1876–94. During the period 1874–76 he was at Trinity Church. He became widely known as a concert organist. He ended his career as organist of the First Presbyterian Church, East Orange, N.J. Warren was one of the organizers of the American Guild of Organists. See his HALLELUJAH ("Hallelujah! Praise the Lord").

William F. Warren, Methodist minister and educator, b. Williamsburg, Mass., March 13, 1833; d. Brookline, Mass., Dec. 6, 1929.

After his graduation from Wesleyan University, William F. Warren was active as a preacher and teacher. In 1861 he became a professor in Bremen, Germany, where he remained until 1866. He then became dean of the Theological School of Boston University and in 1873 president of Boston University, "a position which he held with distinction for thirty years." See "I Worship Thee, O Holy Ghost."

Henry S. Washburn, insurance executive and legislator; b. Providence, R.I., June 10, 1813; d. 1903.

Henry S. Washburn spent his early years in Kingston, Mass. After finishing grammar school he went to work in a Boston bookstore. When he decided that he wanted to go to college, he entered Worcester Academy, and in 1836 matriculated at Brown University but because of health problems he was unable to complete his studies. After serving as director of publications for the New England Sabbath School Union he was active as a businessman in Worcester and Boston, and then joined the Union Mutual Life Insurance Company as its President. In 1876 he went abroad on an assignment to make a survey of life insurance work in Great Britain, France, and Germany.

Washburn was active, too, in public service. He was on the Boston School Board for nine years, was state representative for Massachusetts (1871 and 1872) and state senator in 1873.

On the death of a member of the Fifteenth Massachusetts Volunteers in the Civil War, he wrote *The Vacant Chair*. A number of his hymns and poems were composed for special occasions. See "Almighty God, Thy Constant Care."

Japhet Combs Washburn, composer and compiler; fl. early 19th cent.

Japhet (Japhaeth) Coombs Washburn edited two tune books: *The Parish Harmony; or, Fairfax Collection* (1813) and *The Temple Harmony*, published by E. Goodale of Hallowell, Maine, in 1818 (3d ed., 1821), where he is described as "of China, Maine." One of his tunes, NEW MILFORD ("Sing to the Lord Most High") (q.v.), antedated his own collections since it was included in Abraham Maxim's *Northern Harmony* (c.1804).

Jared B. Waterbury, Congregational minister; b. New York City, Aug. 11, 1799; d. Brooklyn, N.Y., Dec. 31, 1876.

Jared B. Waterbury graduated from Yale College in 1822. After serving as pastor of the Congregational Church at Hudson, N.Y., he went to the Bowdoin Street Congregational Church in Boston. Among his publications were *Advice to A Young Christian* and *The Officer on Duty*.

Most of his hymn writing was done in his early years. Several of his hymns were published in Joshua Leavitt's *The Christian Lyre* (1831). See "I Have Fought the Good Fight" and "Sinner, Is Thy Heart at Rest?"

Lawrence W. Watson, organist and botanist; b. Charlottetown, Prince Edward Island, Canada, May 2, 1860; d. there, July 17, 1925.

After studying music at a local Roman Catholic convent, Lawrence Watson became, at eighteen, the organist for St. Peter's Episcopal Cathedral of Charlottetown. After a short stay at the University of Edinburgh, where he studied medicine, he again took up his musical profession and continued it until five years before his death in Charlottetown. His son wrote of his father as a man of many interests— oil painting, botany, research for the government in the flora and fauna of the island. A species of violet which he discovered was named for him.

On Prince Edward Island there was no manufacturing or any related means of making a living, so the young people were often forced to migrate to other parts of Canada. Home was then always referred to as "the Island." In collaboration with another Islander, L. M. Montgomery, who wrote the popular *Anne of Green Gables,*

Watson wrote "The Island Hymn." See SALVE DOMINE ("O Beautiful My Country").

Catherine H. Watterman, poet; b. Philadelphia, Pa., April 12, 1812; d. 1897.

Catherine H. Watterman wrote and published her early poems under her maiden name. In 1840 she married Captain George J. Esling of the Merchant Marine and lived in Rio de Janeiro until her husband's death four years later. She continued writing after she returned to Philadelphia. In 1850 her poems were collected and published under the title *The Broken Bracelet and Other Poems.* She is remembered for a cento "Come unto Me, When Shadows Darkly Gather."

Isaac Watts, writer of hymns and psalm paraphrases; b. Southampton, England, July 17, 1674; d. Abney Park, England, Nov. 25, 1748.

Isaac Watts treated his subject matter with more freedom than most of his predecessors, who had sought above all else a literal rendering. Although some opposed his verses, they were eventually regarded in many quarters as almost the equivalent of Holy Writ. The son of a clothier turned schoolmaster, Watts began to learn Latin at age five and to write at seven, producing first some devotional pieces to please his mother. His father was thrown into jail as a nonconformist, but he held to his beliefs which his son shared as he grew up. As a nonconformist Watts was unable to enter either Oxford or Cambridge, but at sixteen he attended an academy at Stoke Newington. At twenty-two he became a tutor in the family of Sir John Hertopp of Stoke Newington. At twenty-four he was appointed assistant to the pastor of an Independent congregation in Mark Lane, London, and after four years became its pastor. Never strong, he was obliged to give up his church after several busy years. In 1712 he went to live with Sir Thomas Abney of Abney Park, where in his last years he preached occasionally but gave most of his time to writing.

He began to write hymns at age sixteen. Many are still in use. His verses for children were classics of a special kind. The psalm paraphrases were first published in this country by Benjamin Franklin (Philadelphia, 1729). The earliest appearance of the hymns was in 1739 in Boston. The former were generally welcomed, but they were subjected to a variety of editorial treatments that may be followed in part by reading the accounts of John Mycall, Joel Barlow, and Timothy Dwight. Finally it was decided that the needs of congregations would be best served by a selection such as those published by Samuel Worcester and by James M. Winchell (better known as "Worcester's Watts" and "Winchell's Watts"). Though the hymns were immediately welcomed as religious literature, the exclusive devotion of many congregations to psalmody delayed their use in the church service. However, the Wesleys and George Whitefield used them in this country in revival meetings from 1735 and 1739. See "Broad Is the Road," "Spare Us, O Lord, Aloud We Pray," "Where Nothing Dwelt But Beasts of Prey," and "Why Do We Mourn Departing Friends."

George J. Webb, conductor, organist, and compiler; b. Rushmore Lodge, Wiltshire, England, June 24, 1803; d. Orange, N.J., Oct. 7, 1887.

George J. Webb studied music with Alexander Lucas of Salisbury and became organist at Falmouth, but resigned at the age of twenty-seven to emigrate to the United States where he settled in Boston. Soon after his arrival he became organist at the Old South Church. Lowell Mason (q.v.) and he became fast friends; Webb helped Mason found the Boston Academy of Music and assisted him in establishing conventions for the instruction of music teachers. They collaborated in the editing and publishing of the *Odeon* (1837), *The Psaltery* (1845), *The National Psalmist* (1848), and *Cantica Laudis* (1850).

A member of the faculty of the Academy, Webb was professor of secular music; he also served as choral conductor and leader of orchestral music. Appointed to arrange the musical service of the Swedenborgian Church, of which he was a member, he composed a number of anthems and hymn tunes. He was president of the Handel and Haydn Society in 1840. His publications include *Scripture and Worship* (1834), the *Massachusetts Collection of Psalmody* (1840), and *The American Glee Book* (1841). Two periodicals listed him as editor: *The Musical Library* (1835–36) and *The Musical Cabinet* (1837–40).

From 1870 Webb made his home in Orange, N.J., teaching in New York until 1885 when he retired. See WEBB ("The Morning Light Is Breaking" and "Stand Up, Stand Up, for Jesus").

J. P. Webster, violinist, music teacher, and composer; b. Elkhorn, Wis., 1819; d. 1875.

A resident of Elkhorn, Wis., J. P. Webster collaborated with S. Fillmore Bennett in composing and publishing songs and in compiling *The Signet Ring,* in which his music to "There's a Land That Is Fairer Than Day" (q.v.) appeared.

Jacob Weinberg, pianist and composer; b. Odessa, Russia, July 5, 1879; d. New York City, Nov. 2, 1956.

Jacob Weinberg studied at the Moscow Conservatory and in 1910 went to Vienna to study with Theodor Leschetizky. On his return to Odessa, he taught piano at the conservatory (1915–21). He then spent five years in Jerusalem where he was influenced by Palestinian folk music. In 1926 he came to the United States where he taught piano at Hunter College in New York City and at the New York College of Music.

Weinberg's compositions included the prize-winning folk opera *The Pioneers* (1926); the oratorios *Isaiah* and *The Life of Moses;* a setting of the *Gettysburg Address,* an ode for chorus and orchestra; and various instrumental pieces. He also wrote essays on Russian music for *The Musical Quarterly.* A contributor of original hymn tunes to the *Union Hymnal,* he also published *30 Hymns and Songs for Congregation-School-Home,* which contained original settings as well as arrangements. See the tune set to "Hail the Glorious Golden City" and that to "How Goodly Is Thy House."

Conrad Weiser, Lutheran layman; b. Wurtenberg, Germany, 1696; d. near Womelsdorf, Pa., 1760.

Conrad Weiser came to the United States as a boy. In 1710 he was living in Schoharie, N.Y.; the Tulpehocken region of Pennsylvania was his later home. At the time of his death he had settled near Womelsdorf. Always an influential man in his area, he became distinguished as a justice and an Indian interpreter. His daughter, Anna Maria, married Henry Melchior Mühlenberg, an early Pennsylvania Lutheran leader. See "Jehovah, Herr und Majestät."

Marcus Morris Wells, farmer and Baptist layman; b. Otsego, N.Y., Oct. 2, 1815; d. Hartwick, N.Y., July 17, 1895.

Marcus Morris Wells was converted in a Buffalo mission church. He later lived in Cooperstown and Hartwick, N.Y., where he owned a farm and made farm implements. After his death a memorial window was placed in the Baptist church of Hartwick. The one hymn for which he is known is "Holy Spirit, Faithful Guide" (q.v.).

Charles Wesley, evangelist, preacher, and hymn writer; b. Epworth, Lincolnshire, England, Dec. 18, 1707; d. London, March 29, 1788.

Charles Wesley, son of Samuel and Susanna Wesley, was a younger brother of John Wesley (q.v.), famed Methodist religious leader. Educated at Westminster School and Christ Church, Oxford, where he graduated in 1729 (and where he and a group of friends were first dubbed "Methodists"), he remained at Oxford as a college tutor until 1735, when he accompanied his brother John on a four months' trip to Georgia. They arrived in Savannah in February 1736. Charles was secretary to General Oglethorpe until December of that year, when he returned to England because of ill health. The Wesley brothers became acquainted with the Moravian leader Nicolaus L. Zinzendorf (q.v.) and were influenced by him and by Peter Bohler, another Moravian. After Charles Wesley's "conversion" on Whitsunday, May 21, 1738, he became a zealous preacher. Although he was not the organizer that John was, he joined his brother as an itinerant evangelist for several years. In 1756 he settled in Bristol and, in 1771, moved to London where he died in 1788. Always strongly opposed to his brother's ordinations, he refused to be buried in the unconsecrated ground at City Road and was buried instead at Marylebone Old Church.

Although he did not start to write hymns until his twenty-seventh year, Charles Wesley was a prolific poet. It is estimated that he wrote at least 6,500 hymns during his lifetime. Although their early works were jointly issued, it is generally assumed that the original hymns were written by Charles and the translations were made by John. As poet of the Evangelical Revival in England, Charles wrote verse constantly and spontaneously. His last lines were dictated to his wife as he lay dying.

Hymns and Sacred Poems by John and Charles Wesley, published in London in 1739, was brought to the colonies in the same year by the celebrated evangelist George Whitefield. An American edition appeared in Philadelphia in 1740. In spite of this early start Charles

Wesley's hymns were little sung for a considerable period, largely because the Methodists themselves were not organized in the colonies before 1766. See "Ah! Lovely Appearance of Death!"

John Wesley, founder of Methodism; b. Epworth Rectory, Lincolnshire, England, June 17, 1703; d. London, March 2, 1791.

John Wesley's direct contributions to American hymnody are limited to five translations from the German which were included in the historic *Collection of Psalms and Hymns* (Charleston, S.C., 1737), the first collection containing hymns (as distinct from metrical paraphrases of biblical passages) published in North America. On October 14, 1735, John and Charles Wesley, with Charles Delamotte and Benjamin Ingham, sailed for Georgia as missionaries sent by the Society for the Propagation of the Gospel. On board ship were twenty-six German Moravians led by David Nitschmann (1696–1772), their newly made bishop. The Wesley brothers were greatly impressed by the hymn singing which the Moravians so enjoyed, and John Wesley set about learning German at once. Reaching Savannah on February 6, 1736, they were met by James Oglethorpe, who introduced them to Gottlieb Spangenberg (1704–92), afterwards Moravian bishop, who gave Wesley a new view of the importance of evangelical doctrine. For a month John Wesley lodged with Spangenberg and his friends. His first letter to Nicolaus L. Zinzendorf (q.v.) was written in March of that year. Wesley's Georgia mission lasted less than two years. He left Georgia for England in December 1737, explaining the reasons for his resignation to the Oglethorpe trustees upon his arrival. See "Jesu, To Thee My Heart I Bow," and "My Soul Before Thee Prostrate Lies."

Robert A. West, editor and author; b. Thetford, England, 1809; d. Georgetown, Washington, D.C., Feb. 1, 1865.

Robert A. West came to the United States in 1843. A year later he became the official reporter of the General Conference of the Methodist Episcopal Church. In 1848 he was one of a committee which was formed to compile a new hymn book. *Hymns for the Use of the Methodist Episcopal Church*, which was published in the next year contained two hymns by West, "Come Let Us Tune Our Loftiest Song" (q.v.) and "Now, Lord, Fulfill Thy Faithful Word."

Benjamin Franklin White, singing master and editor; b. Spartanburg, S.C., Sept. 20, 1800; d. Atlanta, Ga., Dec. 5, 1879.

Benjamin Franklin White was an editor of *The Sacred Harp,* a singing book which, in successive editions from 1844 to 1936, preserved and made available to Southern singers the New England compositions and traditional folk hymns which formed their repertory.

White had little schooling and learned music without formal lessons. In about 1840 he was the editor of a newspaper in Harris County, Ga., called *The Organ,* and a clerk of the superior court. His real vocation, however, was that of singing master. He became president of the Southern Musical Convention (organized 1845), which brought the Sacred Harp Singers together for their annual "singings." Although White belonged to the Missionary Baptists, he attended the services of many other denominations in the course of his work in a spirit of tolerance rare in any period. He was esteemed as a man as well as a musician. "He was gentle in his nature, loveable in disposition, and treated everyone with universal kindness." He is credited with the arrangement of MORNING TRUMPET ("Oh, When Shall I See Jesus?") (q.v.).

George L. White, teacher and organizer of the Fisk Jubilee Singers; b. Cadiz, N.Y., 1838; d. date unknown.

George L. White, the son of a blacksmith, left school at age fourteen to become a teacher. Both father and son were musical. Although the son was untrained in music, he got his pupils to sing so well that they attracted much attention. After army service in the Civil War, White worked for the Freedman's Bureau. He became treasurer of Fisk University and taught singing there. His first concert, in 1870, was followed by many others. Their success suggested a fund-raising tour in 1871 by the group, which became known as the Jubilee Singers. They toured not only in this country but abroad (England, Scotland, Germany). The tours were of great financial importance to Fisk and they also made the spirituals known to wider audiences. See "Didn't My Lord Deliver Daniel?" and "Go Down Moses."

T. B. White, composer; fl. mid-19th cent.

T. B. White contributed tunes to two collections edited by E. L. White: *The Modern Harp* (1846) and *White's Church Melodist* (1851).

The tune called WHITE ("Father, in Thy Mysterious Presence Kneeling") (q.v.) in the Unitarian *Hymn and Tune Book* of 1846 had previously appeared in *The Modern Harp* as "Go to the Grave."

Walt Whitman, poet; b. Huntington, N.Y., May 31, 1819; d. Camden, N.J., March 26, 1892.

Walt Whitman wrote no hymns. It was not his contemporaries but rather editors and composers of the twentieth century who were attracted by the buoyant idealism and the vigor of certain passages. It was natural that the English composer Vaughan Williams, who based his Sea Symphony on passages from Whitman, should also set his "Away My Soul" as a hymn (1920). Although another English composer, Martin Shaw, appears to have been the first to set "All the Past We Leave Behind" as a hymn (1925), his example was followed in the United States by William B. Olds (1937), Irving Lowens (1955), and Philip James (PAUMONOK, 1964) (q.v.).

Thomas Whittemore, clergyman, author, and composer; b. Boston, Mass., Jan. 1, 1800; d. Cambridge, Mass., March 21, 1861.

Thomas Whittemore had some public school education, but his family was too poor to allow him to complete his course. Three times he was apprenticed to a trade. Twice he ran away. In 1820 he came under the influence of Rev. Hosea Ballou II (q.v.), a Universalist minister, who steadied him. Given a chance to preach, Whittemore did so well that his mentor took him into the Ballou family and helped him prepare for ordination, which took place in 1821. After becoming an influential pastor in Cambridgeport, Mass., he bought and edited a magazine, *Trumpet and Universalist,* which was profitable for thirty-three years. He wrote many books and pamphlets, composed music, and compiled a series of hymnbooks, including *Songs of Zion* (1837) and *The Gospel Harmonist* (1841). In his later years Whittemore wrote a life of Hosea Ballou and his own autobiography.

Whittemore also displayed marked ability in other fields. In 1830 he was elected to the state legislature where he served several years. From 1835 to 1845 he lectured on temperance. In 1840 he successfully reorganized the Cambridge bank. In 1849 he was chosen president of the Vermont and Massachusetts Railroad and proved himself able to solve its financial difficulties. Whittemore died in Cambridge while working on the revision of his *Modern History of*

Universalism. See his tunes AGAWAM ("Cast Thy Bread upon the Waters"), WATKIN ("As Gentle Dews Distill"), PERSIA ("Lo, What Enraptured Songs of Praise"), HOLDEN ("Send Forth, O God, Thy Light and Truth"), and SPRING STREET ("Ye Realms Below the Skies").

John Greenleaf Whittier, poet and reformer; b. Haverhill, Mass., Dec. 17, 1807; d. Hampton Falls, N.H., Sept. 7, 1892.

John Greenleaf Whittier was a Quaker, a group which did not then practice hymn singing, and he considered himself unmusical. In spite of this he must be regarded as one of the most important American hymn writers. Some of his hymns were written for particular occasions, but more were formed as centos from his longer poems. The Unitarians were largely instrumental in bringing his hymns into use, notably through the collections issued by Samuel Longfellow and Samuel Johnson.

With little formal education Whittier was profoundly influenced by his religion and by such poets as Burns. One of his earliest poems, sent to the Newburyport *Free Press* by his sister Mary, was published in William Lloyd Garrison's paper, and with Garrison's aid Whittier got an editorial position on a Boston paper (1829). His first book, *Legends of New England in Prose and Verse* (1831), showed his interest in regional themes.

Whittier became an ardent Abolitionist, a delegate to the antislavery convention in Philadelphia, and a member of the Massachusetts legislature (1835). He was one of the first to suggest the formation of the Republican Party and always considered himself one of its founders. After the Civil War Whittier wrote his winter idyl *Snow-Bound* (1866) which is considered his greatest work. See "Dear Lord and Father of Mankind," "Immortal Love, Forever Full," and "O Thou! Whose Presence Went Before."

William Whittingham, Protestant leader and writer of metrical psalm paraphrases; b. Chester, England, 1524; d. June 10, 1579.

Educated at Oxford, William Whittingham interrupted his work on the M.A. to travel and to study in French universities. On his return in 1553 he found that the accession of Queen Mary made England dangerous for him and he managed to escape to France after pleading for the release of Peter Martyr.

He joined the English Protestants in Frankfurt (June 27, 1554) and after a controversy developed on the revision of the Prayer Book went to Geneva, where in 1559 he succeeded Calvin as minister. After Mary's death he remained in Geneva to complete the translation of the Bible known as the Geneva or "Breeches" Bible. It was also at Geneva that he wrote his psalm paraphrases and the metrical versions of the *Song of Simeon* and the *Lord's Prayer*.

Whittingham took leave of the council in Geneva on May 30, 1560, and returned to England. In 1561 he became dean at Durham Cathedral, where he diligently supervised the grammar and singing schools, "himselfe being skillfull in musicke." His extreme Protestant views—he objected to the surplice and cope as "popish apparel"—made him enemies and two commissions were appointed to hear charges against him, the first inactive and the second ineffectual because Whittingham died before they could report. See his "Now Israel May Say and That Truly."

Michael Wigglesworth, minister and poet; b. England, Oct. 18, 1631; d. Malden, Mass., May 27, 1705.

Michael Wigglesworth graduated from Harvard in 1651, then stayed on for a time as tutor. He was later ordained in Malden, Mass., and served a church there. A tiny, frail person, he was constantly subject to illness and, when unable to preach, would write. *Day of Doom,* produced in this way, is a long narrative poem based on the biblical account of the Last Judgment. *Meat Out of the Eater; or, Meditations concerning the necessity, and usefulness of Afflictions unto God's Children; all tending to prepare them for, and comfort them under the Cross,* a poem divided into sections of ten- or twelve-line stanzas, is a meditation on the usefulness of affliction. Both books went through several editions. See "For Just Men Light Is Sown" and "Welcome, Sweet Rest."

John Henry Wilcox, organist; b. Savannah, Ga., Oct. 6, 1827; d. Boston, June 29, 1875.

John Henry Wilcox graduated from Trinity College, in Hartford, Conn., in 1849, and the year afterward became organist at St. Paul's Episcopal Church in Boston. An expert in organ construction, he was also a talented performer. When a large organ was installed in the Church of the Immaculate Conception he took charge of it and remained as organist there until July 1874. He wrote a considerable amount of music for the Roman Catholic church service, and in 1864 Georgetown College conferred upon him the honorary Doctor of Music. See FABEN ("Saviour, Sprinkle Many Nations").

Aaron Williams, English engraver, publisher, and composer; b. London, 1731; d. there 1776.

Aaron Williams was the clerk in the Scottish church in London. His collection *Universal Psalmodist* came out in 1763. It was reprinted here in 1771 by Daniel Bayley and bound with William Tans'ur's *Royal Melody Complete*. His name appeared on the programs of some of the first concerts given in this country. "An Anthem from the 122d Psalm" was played at the Grand Concert given in Philadelphia in May 1786. His anthem "O Lord God of Israel" was sung at the First Uranian Concert in Philadelphia later in the same year, both concerts a result of Andrew Adgate's activity in that city. On the day before the Uranian concert, another was given in Boston, where William Selby (q.v.) was the city's musical leader, and that program carried the names of Williams, William Billings (q.v.), and others. See ST. THOMAS ("I Love Thy Kingdom, Lord").

David McK. Williams, organist, choirmaster, and composer; b. Carnarvonshire, Wales, Feb. 20, 1887.

Organist and choirmaster David Mck. Williams devoted his career to the musical service of the Episcopal Church. He was brought to Denver, Colo., by his parents, where he became a choir boy at the Cathedral of St. John in the Wilderness. When only thirteen he played the organ and directed the choir at St. Peter's Church there. He accepted a position at Grace Church Chapel, New York City in 1908, but in 1911 went abroad for advanced study. He attended the Schola Cantorum in Paris, where his teachers included Vincent D'Indy, Charles Marie Widor, and Louis Vierne. In New York again, he was organist of the Church of the Holy Communion, returning to this post after a period of service with the Canadian Artillery (1914–16). His next and last post as organist and choir director was at St. Bartholomew's Church, New York City, where he remained from 1920 to 1947. He then taught both at the Juilliard School and the Union Theological Seminary. He served on the joint Commission on the Revision of the Hymnal and contributed six tunes including GEORGETOWN (q.v.) to the *Hymnal 1940*.

Roger Williams, founder of Rhode Island; b. London, c.1603; d. Providence, R.I., 1682/83.

Although Roger Williams wrote no hymns, he did include short, moralizing poems in his study of the speech of the Narragansett Indians, *A Key into the Language of America* (1643), in which he frequently contrasts Indian virtues with the shortcomings of the white settlers.

Educated at Cambridge, he attended a meeting (1629) of the founders of the Massachusetts Bay Colony and, on December 1, 1630, set sail for America with his bride. Once in the New World, he found himself in conflict with the established authorities which reached a climax in the decision to banish him in 1635. He escaped arrest, reached what is now Rhode Island, and settled Providence in 1636. In 1644 he succeeded in obtaining a charter for Providence Plantations. Under his rule the Jews came to Rhode Island and later the Quakers, who were persecuted everywhere else in New England. Williams' later years were troubled by a controversy with George Fox, the Quaker leader, and by King Philip's War, where as a man of over seventy he found himself captain of the troops of Providence Plantations and a witness to the failure of his attempts to deal justly with the Indians. See his "If Birds That Neither Sow nor Reap" and "When Sun Doth Rise."

Theodore Chickering Williams, Unitarian minister and educator; b. Brookline, Mass., July 2, 1855; d. Boston, Mass., May 6, 1915.

Educated at Harvard (A.B., 1876) and the Harvard Divinity School (B.D., 1882), Theodore Chickering Williams received the Litt.D. from Western Reserve University in 1911. After serving as the minister of the Unitarian Church in Winchester, Mass. (1882) he became the pastor of All Souls' Church in New York City (1883–96). He was the first headmaster of the Hackley School at Tarrytown, N.Y. (1899–1905), and was later headmaster of the Roxbury Latin School (1907–09).

A classical scholar, he wrote *Character Building* (1894) and *Poems of Belief* (1910) and published translations of *The Elegies of Tibullus,* from Virgil's *Aeneid* (1917) as well as Virgil's *Georgics and Eclogues* (1915). Williams was also a hymn writer of distinction. See "Hast Thou Heard It, O My Brother," "My Country, to Thy Shore," and "When Thy Heart with Joy O'erflowing."

Love Maria Willis, editor and author; b. Hancock, N.H., June 9, 1824; d. Elmira, N.Y., Nov. 26, 1908.

The marriage of Love Maria Willis and Dr. Frederick L. H. Willis, a physician, of Boston, took place in 1858. For several years she was one of the editors of *The Banner of Light* published in Boston. Later she served in the same capacity on *Tiffany's Monthly Magazine.* To both she was a frequent contributor. She also wrote hymns. One of them, "Father, Hear the Prayer I Offer," was published in the latter periodical in 1859. In 1864 it reappeared in Samuel Longfellow and Samuel Johnson's *Hymns of the Spirit* in rewritten form, its title changed to "Father, Hear the Prayer We Offer" (q.v.). It was listed as anonymous. Almost all Unitarian hymnbooks since 1864 have included it.

Richard S. Willis, critic, editor, and composer; b. Boston, Mass., Feb. 10, 1819; d. Detroit, Mich., May 7, 1900.

The father of Richard S. Willis was Deacon Nathaniel Willis, who established the *Youth's Companion.* The son attended Yale (B.A. 1841) where he found an outlet for his musical talents by composing and arranging music for student performances and by serving as the president of the Beethoven Society. It was his interest in music which prevailed, for instead of going on to graduate school Willis pursued advanced musical studies in Germany, first in Frankfort with Schnyder von Wartensee, then in Leipzig with Moritz Hauptmann and Mendelssohn, who took a friendly interest in his compositions and revised several of them.

In 1847 Willis was at Yale again, as a teacher of German. He then turned to music criticism and journalism in response to advice given him by Charles A. Dana and was on the staff of the *New York Tribune, The Albion,* and *The Musical Times.* He became the editor of several magazines dealing with music, *The Musical Times, The Musical World,* and *Once a Month. Our Church Music* (1856) deals with its subject both in a practical way and from the point of view of aesthetics. *Church Chorals* (1850) was a collection of choir music. His poems appeared in *Pen and Lute* and *Miscellaneous Lyrics.* See CAROL ("It Came Upon the Midnight Clear").

Edwin H. Wilson, Unitarian minister; b. Woodhaven, N.Y., Aug. 23, 1898.

Edwin H. Wilson was educated at Boston University (B.A., 1922), Meadville Theological School (B.D., 1926; D.D., 1949), and the

University of Chicago (A.M., 1928). He was ordained to the ministry of the Unitarian Church in 1928 and held pastorates in First Church, Dayton, Ohio (1928–32); Third Church, Chicago (1932–44); All Souls Church, Schenectady, N.Y. (1941–46); and First Society, Salt Lake City, Utah (1946–49). During his Salt Lake City residence he was a lecturer in philosophy at the University of Utah (1946–48). From 1935 to 1949 he was executive secretary of the American Humanist Association and executive director in 1949.

Wilson served two terms as president of the Unitarian Fellowship for Social Justice (1936–37 and 1950–51) and was a member of the business committee of the commission on adult education for the American Unitarian Association. A member of the advisory council for Protestants and Other Americans United to Maintain Separation of Church and State, he was also a member of the organizing committee of the International Humanist and Ethical Union in 1952. See "Where Is Our Holy Church?"

John Wilson, pastor and poet; b. England, c.1591; d. Boston, Mass., Aug. 7, 1667.

Son of a chaplain and canon of Windsor, John Wilson was educated at Eton and King's College, Cambridge, where he held both a scholarship and a fellowship. He received the B.A. degree in 1610 and the M.A. in 1613. Admitted to the Inner Temple in 1610 after reading law for a year or two, he began preaching. Despite suspensions for nonconformity Wilson was lecturer at Sudbury in Suffolk from 1618 to 1630, when he sailed for Boston and became preacher at the First Church when it was organized at Charlestown. There he remained, although he made trips to England in 1631, 1634, and 1635, and shared the pulpit with John Cotton from 1633 to 1652, the year of Cotton's death.

Wilson's *Song of Deliverance* was published in 1626 in England. He continued to write verse in this country. Two elegiac poems in the form of anagrams on the name of their subject, William Tompson, were preserved in the manuscript journal of William's son Joseph, of Billerica, Mass. Wilson has also been considered the author of *The day-breaking, if not the sun-rising of the gospels with the Indians in New England* (London, 1647), although it has sometimes been attributed to John Elliott, the apostle to the Indians. A lecture or sermon, *A Seasonable Watch-Word Unto Christians against the Dreams & Dreamers of this Generation* (Cambridge, 1677), which Wilson delivered in 1665, describes him as "sometime Pastor of the Church of Christ in Boston in New England . . ." After Wilson's death his *Song of Deliverance* was reprinted in Boston in 1680 as a memorial to him. See

"Confess We All, Before the Lord," "For Lo! My Jonah How He Slumped," and "Whoso Would See This Song of Heavenly Choice."

Caleb T. Winchester, educator; b. Montville, Conn., Jan. 18, 1847; d. Middletown, Conn., March 24, 1920.

Caleb T. Winchester graduated from Wesleyan University, Middletown, Conn., in 1869 and four years later was appointed to its faculty as professor of English literature. Middletown remained his home as long as he lived. In 1871 he wrote "The Lord Our God Alone Is Strong" (q.v.) for the dedication of the Orange Judd Hall of Natural Science at Wesleyan. It was first published in *The Hymn and Tune Book* of the Methodist Episcopal Church (1878).

Winchester wrote several books: *William Wordsworth: How to Know Him; Some Principles of Literary Criticism; Essays; Life of John Wesley;* and *Five Short Courses of Reading in English Literature.* In 1892 Dickinson College conferred on him the degree of Litt.D.

Elhanan Winchester, Universalist preacher, theologian, and poet; b. Brookline, Mass., Sept. 30, 1751; d. Hartford, Conn., April 18, 1797.

Elhanan Winchester had a remarkably retentive memory, which made learning easy for him, in spite of the fact that his formal schooling was limited. In 1770 he began to preach as a Baptist. From the beginning he attracted large congregations. In Philadelphia his convictions were altered in the direction of Universalism. His church divided and the majority left with him.

In 1787 Winchester left America for England. There he preached and published a number of religious works. He returned abruptly to America, although his work in England was increasingly successful. He contracted four marriages, each terminated by the death of a wife, and was advised by friends not to marry again. In spite of this he took a fifth wife who was so subject to sudden and uncontrollable outbursts that at one point he considered providing for her in America and returning to England himself. Winchester's *Thirteen Hymns Suited to the Present Times* (2d ed., Baltimore, 1776) contains patriotic hymns, including "Behold with Joy" (q.v.). The opening stanza of Winchester's fifth hymn beginning "Let tyrants shake their iron rod" is the same as the opening stanza of the famous patriotic hymn by William Billings published in 1770 in his *New England Psalm Singer.*

Isaac M. Wise, rabbi, administrator, author, and editor; b. Steingrub, Bohemia, March 29, 1819; d. Cincinnati, Ohio, Nov. 26, 1900.

Isaac M. Wise (originally Weis) attended his father's private Hebrew day school until he was nine. He then went to live with his paternal grandfather, a physician. Dr. Weis's death when the boy was twelve threw him on his own resources, for his parents were too poor to help him. He had already decided to become a rabbi, so he went to Prague and attended schools there. In 1835 he entered the most famous rabbinical school in Bohemia at Jenikau. After further study at the University of Prague and at the University of Vienna he was made a rabbi at the age of twenty-three. In 1846 he and his young wife migrated to the United States where he adopted the cause of liberal Judaism from the start. He headed synagogues in Albany and Cincinnati, remaining at the latter until his death. After a few months in Cincinnati he began publishing a weekly newspaper, the *Israelite* (later the *American Israelite*).

Rabbi Wise worked unceasingly and successfully to perfect the organization of Jewish congregations in the United States. As a liberal he "combined the spirit of Judaism with the free spirit of America." His three outstanding achievements were: the organizing of the American Hebrew Congregations (1873); the founding of Hebrew Union College (1875), of which he served as president for twenty-five years; and the forming of the Central Conference of American Rabbis (1889), of which he was president for eleven years.

A prolific writer, Wise published, besides his editorials in the *Israelite*, books and pamphlets including his *History of the Israelitish Nation from Abraham to the Present Time* (1854), *The Cosmic God* (1876), *History of the Hebrew's Second Commonwealth* (1880), *Pronaos to Holy Writ* (1891), and *Reminiscences* (1901). See "In Mercy, Lord, Incline Thine Ear."

Joseph Wise, youth counselor, teacher, and lecturer; b. Louisville, Ky., 1940.

Joseph Wise received the A.B. and St.B. from St. Mary's in Baltimore, Md. At Catholic University, Washington, D.C., he specialized in counseling and guidance (M.Ed.) and Religious Education (M.A.) He has published and recorded *Gonna Sing My Lord, Hand in Hand, A New Day,* and *Watch with Me,* and is the author of two books, *Songprints* and *The Body at Liturgy.* See his "Glory."

George Wither, English poet and satirist; b. Bentworth, Hampshire, England, June 11, 1588; d. London, May 2, 1667.

George Wither spent two years at Magdalen College, Oxford (1604–06), and settled in London in about 1610. After studying law he joined a minor inn of the court and was entered at Lincoln's Inn in 1615. His real interest, however, was in writing. His earlier works consisted of satires, like his *Abuses Stript and Whipt* (1613), which was widely read but which brought Wither a period of imprisonment, and pastoral poems, including *The Shepherd's Hunting* (1615), *Fidelia* (1616), and *Faire-Virtue, the Mistresse of Phil'Arete* (1622).

The Hymns and Songs of the Church, with tunes supplied by Orlando Gibbons, appeared in 1623. Wither not only secured a copyright but a direction that it should be inserted in every copy of the authorized *Psalm-book in Meeter* which the Stationer's Company printed under earlier patents. They refused either to include it or to sell any copies. Wither's *Psalms of David* (1632) was copyrighted and required to be bound with all Bibles, but met with similar opposition. Some of Wither's best hymns were included in the later *Halleluiah: or Britain's Second Remembrancer* (1641).

Although Wither had earlier served as captain under Charles I, he sided with Parliament in the Civil War. He was captured by the Royalists, but his life was saved by Sir John Denham, who said that while Wither lived he, Denham, could not be called the worst poet in England. See "Lord, Many Times Thou Pleased Art."

Leonard Withington, Congregational minister; b. Dorchester, Mass., 1789; d. Newburyport, Mass., April 22, 1885.

Leonard Withington attended Yale, graduating in 1814. Two years later he was called to the First Congregational Church of Newburyport as pastor. See "O Saviour of a World Undone."

Samuel Wolcott, Congregational clergyman; b. South Windsor, Conn., July 2, 1813; d. Longmeadow, Mass., Feb. 24, 1886.

After attending Yale (A.B., 1833) and Andover Theological Seminary, Samuel Wolcott went to Syria but was forced to leave in 1842 because of health problems. He then served as minister in Belchertown, Mass., Providence, R.I., Chicago, Ill., and Cleveland, Ohio. While there he also served as secretary of the Ohio Home Missionary Society. A prolific hymn writer in later life, Wolcott was fifty-six when he completed the first one. See "Christ for the World! We Sing" and "Father! I Own Thy Voice."

Aaron R. Wolfe, educator; b. Mendham, N.J., Sept. 6, 1821; d. Oct. 6, 1902.

Aaron R. Wolfe was a graduate of Williams College (1844) and Union Theological Seminary (1851). The Third Presbytery of New York granted him a license April 9, 1851. After serving as the principal of a girls' school in Tallahassee, Fla. (1852–55), he went to Montclair, N.J., where in 1859 he founded the Hillside Seminary for Young Ladies. He retired in 1872 because of poor health. Seven of his hymns appeared in Thomas Hastings' *Church Melodies* (1859) under his initials, "A. R. W." See "Complete in Thee, No Work of Mine" and "A Parting Hymn We Sing."

Isaac B. Woodbury, teacher, compiler, and composer; b. Beverly, Mass., Oct. 23, 1819; d. Columbia, S.C., Oct. 26, 1858.

Isaac B. Woodbury was early apprenticed to a blacksmith, but his musical gifts made him choose a different calling. He sought musical instruction in Boston at the age of thirteen. He had a splendid tenor voice and went to Europe at the age of nineteen to prepare for grand opera. After he had achieved some success as a ballad singer, he returned to the United States to conduct concerts and teach. For six years he taught in Boston, where he sang with the Bay State Glee Club. Later, when he moved to Bellows Falls, Vt., he founded and conducted the New Hampshire and Vermont Musical Association.

He went to New York in 1849, where he directed the music of the Rutgers Street Church until 1851 when the precarious state of his health made it impossible for him to continue. Soon afterwards he became editor of the *New York Musical Review* and returned to Europe gathering news items and acquiring music for his collections.

Woodbury published several tune books, of which his *Dulcimer; or, New York Collection of Sacred Music* (1850 and later) was very successful. His *Elements of Musical Composition,* which had been published in 1844, was reissued as the *Self-Instructor in Musical Composition.* His *New Lute of Zion,* which incorporated a great deal of material gathered from his European trip, appeared in 1856 and became popular. Other titles published by him were: *Liber Musicus* (1851), and *Cythara* (1854). *The Day Spring* (1859), was compiled after his death by Sylvester Main. See the tune for "Mother Dear, O! Pray for

Me" and SELENA ("Again, as Evening's Shadow Falls"), TALMAR ("At the Door of Mercy Sighing"), TAMAR ("The Chosen Three, on Mountain Height"), LAKE ENON ("Jesus, I Live to Thee"), and TRUMPET ("Lift Your Glad Voices in Triumph on High").

Jonathan C. Woodman, choir director and teacher; b. Newburyport, Mass., July 12, 1813; d. Brooklyn, N.Y., Feb. 5, 1894.

When Lowell Mason began teaching music in the public schools of Boston, Jonathan C. Woodman was his first assistant. He appeared as soloist at early concerts of the Boston Academy of Music. George F. Root (q.v.), another assistant of Lowell Mason, married Woodman's sister, Mary Olive Woodman. When Mason and Root conducted their first Normal Institute in New York in 1853, Woodman again assisted them. He settled in Brooklyn where he was organist at the First Presbyterian Church and at Packer Collegiate Institute. Frank J. Metcalf, in *American Writers and Compilers of Sacred Music,* remarks that he was "a fairly good organist for those early days" but concedes that he was a fine choir director. His son Raymond Huntington Woodman was to succeed him in both posts. The father compiled *The Musical Casket* in 1858. It contains CALL (after his middle and his mother's maiden name) and his most famous tune, STATE STREET ("And Canst Thou, Sinner, Slight") (q.v.).

John W. Work, arranger, composer, and teacher; b. Tullahosa, Tenn., June 15, 1901.

John W. Work was educated at Fisk University (B.A.) and Yale (B.Mus.). He held a two-year fellowship from the Julius Rosenwald Foundation. From 1927 to 1931 he conducted the Men's Glee Club at Fisk and later became professor of music theory. Work arranged many Negro melodies and composed piano suites (*Appalachia, Scuppernong, Sassafras*), and larger works, such as *The Singers* for chorus and orchestra, *Taliafer, Nocturne, From the Deep South,* and *Golgotha Is a Mountain* for solo, chorus, and orchestra. In 1940 Work published *American Negro Songs,* a comprehensive collection of 230 Negro folk songs, both religious and secular. See his arrangements of "Calvary," "I'm Agoing To Lay Down My Sword," and "O Mary, Don't You Weep, Don't You Mourn."

Denis Wortman, clergyman; b. Hopewell, N.Y., April 30, 1835; d. 1922.

Denis Wortman attended Amherst College, graduating with an A.B. in 1857. He then went to the New Brunswick Theological Seminary from which he graduated in 1860. He served churches in Brooklyn, N.Y., Philadelphia, Pa., and Schenectady N.Y. Later he was secretary of ministerial relief and president of the General Synod of the Dutch Reformed Church in 1901. For the centennial celebration of the New Brunswick Theological Seminary in 1884 he wrote the hymn "God of the Prophets! Bless the Prophets' Sons" (q.v.). See also "Today Beneath Benignant Skies."

C. M. Wyman; fl. 19th cent.

C. M. Wyman was the compiler of *The Psalm,* a collection of sacred music for chorus, singing schools, and conventions, published in Chicago by Root and Cady in 1870. See IMPERIAL ("God, to Thee We Humbly Bow").

Don Yoder, educator and authority on Pennsylvania Dutch folk song and on folk life; b. Altoona, Pa., Aug. 27, 1921.

After studying at Franklin and Marshall College (B.A. 1942) and the University of Chicago (B.D., 1945, Ph. D., 1947) he taught at the Union Theological Seminary and at Franklin and Marshall College. In 1956 he went to the University of Pennsylvania as associate professor, and in 1975 became professor of folklife studies and adjunct professor of religious thought. Yoder was joint editor of a collection of Pennsylvania Dutch folk songs entitled *Songs along the Mahantongo* (1951). His significance for hymnology lies in his discovery and publication of gospel hymns in Pennsylvania Dutch. See "O seid im Arnscht," which is taken from his *Pennsylvania Spirituals* (1961). Yoder was a founder of the Pennsylvania Folklife Society (1949). He was associate editor of *The Pennsylvania Dutchman* (1949–56) and of *Pennsylvania Folklife* (1956–62), becoming editor of the latter publication in 1962. His *American Folklife* appeared in 1976.

Sarah E. York; fl. early 19th cent.; b. 1819, d. 1851

Sarah E. York, born Sarah Waldo, wrote the hymn beginning "I am weary of straying" (q.v.), which appeared in the Reformed Dutch

Psalms and Hymns published in 1847. *A Memoir of Sarah Emily York, formerly S. E. Waldo, Missionary in Greece,* by Rebecca B. Medberry, was published in Boston in 1853.

Alfred Young, priest and musician; fl. late 19th cent.

Father Alfred Young was the editor of the *Catholic Hymnal* (New York, 1888), compiled for use at the Church of St. Paul the Apostle. All the hymn tunes were of his composition. He was also the editor of *New Carols*. See his setting for "Holy God, We Praise Thy Name."

Charles Zeuner, organist, composer, and compiler; b. Eisleben, Saxony, Sept. 20, 1795; d. Philadelphia, Pa., Nov. 7, 1857.

Charles (Heinrich Christopher) Zeuner grew up in the musical tradition of the Lutheran church of Saxony. When he came to the United States in 1824 he changed his given name to Charles and was active in Boston. Since he had been a court musician in Germany, Boston welcomed him as a man of superior ability and training. He played the organ at the Park Street Congregational Church and at St. Paul's Church and for the Handel and Haydn Society (1830–37). Elected president of that society in 1838, he found himself at odds with the singers and had to resign.

In 1854 he abandoned Boston for Philadelphia and served as the organist of two churches there, St. Anne's Episcopal Church and the Arch Street Presbyterian Church. Despondent in these last years, he died a suicide.

Zeuner, in addition to contributing tunes to contemporary collections, compiled several of his own: *Church Music* (a collection of anthems, 1831), *The American Harp* (his most important publication, 1832), *The New Village Harmony for Sabbath Schools* (1834), and *The Ancient Lyre* (1834). He composed one oratorio, *The Feast of Tabernacles,* performed for eight evenings at the Odeon Theatre, Boston, incurring a substantial deficit. See IRA ("By Vows of Love Together Bound"), KNOWLTON ("Lord, at This Closing Hour"), TAPPAN ("Lord, Deliver, Thou Canst Save"), UTICA ("The Spirit in Our Hearts"), and MISSIONARY CHANT ("Thou Lord of Hosts, Whose Guiding Hand") his most widely used tune.

Charles L. Ziegler, businessman and editor; b. Roxbury, Mass., July 11, 1864; d. Waban (Newton), Mass., Sept. 1960.

Charles L. Ziegler's father had established a silk manufacturing plant in Boston, and Charles, as the oldest son, was taken into the business after graduation from the Roxbury high school. He later directed and expanded this enterprise. His musical training appears to have been slight. His son states that "he took piano lessons, but probably few. His piano playing like his organ playing (on a good Mason-Hamlin reed organ . . .) always seemed to me quite unorthodox . . . For many years as Sunday School Superintendent in Highland Church, Roxbury, he accompanied the children on a piano with great gusto." Charles L. Ziegler was a zealous Congregationalist and served as treasurer of the Board of Ministerial Aid. With Charles L. Noyes he edited the *Pilgrim Hymnal* of 1904, to which he contributed tunes including GRACE ("As Tranquil Streams"), REX AETERNUS ("Lead On, O King Eternal"), and GLADDEN ("O Master, Let Us Walk with Thee").

Nicolaus L. Zinzendorf, Moravian bishop and hymn writer; b. Dresden, Germany, May 26, 1700; d. Herrnhut, Germany, May 9, 1760.

Nicolaus Zinzendorf was educated at Halle (1710–16) where he came under Pietist influences. He later studied law at the University of Wittenberg (1716–19) and became a counselor at the Court of Saxony. His rejection by his cousin Theodora turned Zinzendorf's thoughts to religion, and he sought to establish a free association of Christians without connection with the structure of government. Zinzendorf built the village of Herrnhut as a place of refuge for persecuted Moravians.

Our chief concern is with the brief period Count Zinzendorf spent in America. Induced to visit the Penns by the letters of Spangenberg and Whitefield, he landed with his daughter Benigna and a party of five at New York on December 2, 1741, and proceeded to Philadelphia. His chief aim was to unite all the Pennsylvania German Protestants in an association to be known as the "Congregation of God in the Spirit." He issued seven calls for "union synods" or free conferences, but his vision of Christian union could not be realized among people so addicted to separatism. In June 1742, he abandoned his plan. During the latter half of that year Zinzendorf made three missionary journeys among the Indians and aided in establishing Moravian congregations at Bethlehem (which owes its name to him), Nazareth, Philadelphia, Hebron, Heidelberg, Lancaster, and York in

BIBLIOGRAPHY

Allen, William F., Charles P. Ware, and Lucy M. Garrison. *Slave Songs of the United States.* New York: Peter Smith, 1929.

Anderson, John. *A Discourse on the Divine Ordinance of Singing Psalms.* Philadelphia: William Young, 1791.

Andrews, Edward D. *The Gift To Be Simple.* New York: Dover, 1962.

Atkins, Charles L. "American Congregationalists and Their Hymnals," *Bulletin of the American Congregational Association,* 2 (January 1951), 3–18.

Barbour, James M. *The Church Music of William Billings.* East Lansing: Michigan State University Press, 1960.

—— "The Texts of Billings' Church Music," *Criticism* 1 (Winter 1959), 49–61.

The Bay Psalm Book. Facsimile of the first edition of 1640. With a companion volume: *The Enigma of the Bay Psalm Book,* by Zoltan Haraszti. Chicago: University of Chicago Press, 1956.

Benson, Louis F. *The English Hymn.* Philadelphia: Presbyterian Board of Publication, 1915.

—— *Studies of Familiar Hymns.* Series 2. Philadelphia: Westminster Press, 1923.

Bentley, William. *The Diary of William Bentley D.D.* (Pastor of the East Church, Salem, Mass.) 4 vols. Salem: Essex Institute, 1904–14.

Bio-Bibliographical Index of Musicians in the United States of America Since Colonial Times. 2d ed. Washington, D.C.: Pan American Union, Music Section, 1956.

Blair, Samuel. "A Discourse on Psalmody, Delivered by the Rev. Samuel Blair, in the Presbyterian Church in Neshaminy, at a public concert given by Mr. Spicer." Philadelphia: John M'Culloch, 1789.

Britton, Allen P. "Theoretical Introductions in American Tunebooks to 1800." Diss., University of Michigan, 1949.

Brooks, Henry M. *Olden-Time Music: A Compilation from Newspapers and Books.* Boston: Ticknor, 1888.

Brown, Hugh. "Discourse on Scripture Psalmody in Praising God"; and "Against Instrumental Music in Public Worship." North White Creek, N.Y.: R. K. Crocker, 1859.

Brown, Robert B. and Frank X. Braun. "The Tunebook of Conrad Doll," *Papers of the Bibliographical Society of America,* 42 (3d quarter 1948), 3–12.

Brown, Theron and Hezekiah Butterworth. *The Story of the Hymns and Tunes.* New York: George H. Doran, 1906.

Burrage, Henry. *Baptist Hymn Writers.* Portland, Me.: Brown, Thurston, 1888.

614 *Bibliography*

Cartwright, Peter. *Autobiography of Peter Cartwright, the Backwoods Preacher.* New York: Carleton and Porter, 1857.

Champions of Freedom. The Huguenot Memorial Society of Oxford (Mass.). Worcester, Mass.: Asa Bartlett Press, 1958.

Cheney, Simeon P. *The American Singing Book.* Boston: White Smith, 1879. (Contains biographies of American tune writers.)

Church Music and Musical Life in Pennsylvania. Philadelphia: National Society of the Colonial Dames of America, 1926–47.

Companion to the Hymnal: A Handbook to the 1964 Methodist Hymnal. New York and Nashville: Abingdon Press, 1970.

Cornwall, J. Spencer. *Stories of Our Mormon Hymns.* Salt Lake City: Deseret Book Co., 1963.

Cotton, John. *Singing of Psalms a Gospel Ordinance: A Treatise Wherein Are Handled These Foure Particulars: 1. Touching the Duty Itself; 2. Touching the Matter To Be Sung; 3. Touching the Singers; 4. Touching the Manner of Singing.* London: printed by M. S. for H. Allen and J. Rothwell, 1647.

Covert, William C. and Calvin W. Laufer. *Handbook to the Hymnal.* Philadelphia: Presbyterian Board of Christian Education, 1935.

Crawford, Robert A. *Andrew Law, American Psalmodist.* Evanston, Ill.: Northwestern University Press, 1968.

Curwen, John S. *"Music in Worship" and Other Papers on People's Psalmody.* London: Tonic Sol-Fa Agency, 1880.

—— *Studies in Worship Music.* London: J. Curwen, 1st Series, 1865; 2d Series, 1880.

Dearmer, Percy and Archibald Jacob. *Songs of Praise Discussed.* London: Oxford University Press, 1933.

Diehl, Katherine S. *Hymns and Tunes: An Index.* New York: Scarecrow Press, 1966.

Douen (Orentin). *Clément Marot et le Psautier Huguenot.* 2 vols. Paris: Imprimerie National, 1878.

Duffield, Samuel W. *English Hymns: Their Authors and History.* New York: Funk & Wagnalls, 1886.

Earle, Alice M. *The Sabbath in Puritan New England.* 7th ed. New York: Scribner, 1893.

Edwards, George T. *Music and Musicians of Maine.* Portland: Southworth Press, 1928.

Ellinwood, Leonard. "Problems and Opportunities in Modern Hymnology," *Journal of the American Musicological Society,* 1 (Summer 1948), 41–47.

—— *Religious Music in America.* Princeton, N.J.: Princeton University Press, 1961.

Evanson, Jacob A. and George Swetnam, eds. *Early Western Pennsylvania Hymns and Hymn-Tunes, 1816–1846.* Coraopolis, Pa.: Yahres Publications, 1958. (Contains biographies.)

Fenner, Thomas P. *Hampton and Its Students*. New York: Putnam, 1874.

Fisher, William A. *Notes on Music in Old Boston*. Boston: Oliver Ditson, 1918.

—— *Ye Olde New-England Psalm-Tunes*. Boston: Oliver Ditson, 1930.

Foote, Arthur, 2d. *Henry Wilder Foote: Hymnologist*. Papers of the Hymn Society, No. 26. New York: Hymn Society of America, 1968.

Foote, Henry Wilder. *American Unitarian Hymn Writers and Hymns*. Cambridge, Mass.: Hymn Society of America, 1959.

——*American Universalist Hymn Writers and Hymns*. Cambridge, Mass.: Hymn Society of America, 1959.

——*Three Centuries of American Hymnody*. Cambridge, Mass.: Harvard University Press, 1940.

Frost, Maurice. *English and Scottish Psalm and Hymn Tunes, c.1543–1677*. London and New York: Oxford University Press, 1953.

——ed. *Historical Companion to "Hymns Ancient and Modern."* London: William Clowes, 1962.

Gilman, Samuel. *Memoirs of a New England Village Choir with Occasional Reflections. By a Member. . . .* Boston: S. G. Goodrich, 1829.

Gold, Charles E. "The Gospel Song, Contemporary Opinion," *The Hymn*, 9 (July 1958), 69–73.

Goldman, Richard F. and Roger Smith, eds. *Landmarks of Early American Music*. New York: G. Schirmer, 1943.

Goodenough, Caroline L. *High Lights on Hymnists and Their Hymns*. Rochester, Mass.: published by the author, 1931.

Gould, Nathaniel D. *History of Church Music in America*. Boston: A. N. Johnson, 1853.

Greenway, John. *American Folk Songs of Protest*. Philadelphia: University of Pennsylvania Press, 1953.

Grove's Dictionary of Music and Musicians, American Supplement (Vol. VI). Waldo S. Pratt, ed. New York: Macmillan, 1920.

Haeussler, Armin. *The Story of Our Hymns: The Handbook to the Hymnal of the Evangelical and Reformed Church*. St. Louis: Eden, 1952.

Hall, Jacob H. *Biography of Gospel Song and Hymn Writers*. New York: Fleming H. Revell, 1914.

Hamilton, Kenneth G. "The Bethlehem Christmas Hymn," *Transactions of the Moravian Historical Society*, Bethlehem, Pa., 14, Pts. 1 and 2 (1947), 11–23.

Hatfield, Edwin F. *The Poets of the Church*. New York: A. D. F. Randolph, 1884.

Hedge, Lemuel. *The Duty and Manner of Singing in Christian Churches, Considered and Illustrated: "A Sermon Preached at a Singing Lecture in Warwick, January 29, 1772."* Boston: R. Draper, 1772.

Henry, H. T. "A Philadelphia Choir Book of 1787," *The Catholic Choirmaster*. 25 (September 1939), 107–16.

Hess, Albert G. "Observations on *The Lamenting Voice of the Hidden Love*." *Journal of the American Musicological Society*, 5 (Fall 1952), 211–23.

Hewins, James M. *Hints Concerning Church Music*. Boston: Ide & Dutton, 1856.

History of the Handel and Haydn Society of Boston, Massachusetts. 2 vols. in 3. Boston: A. Mudge, 1883–1934.

Hodges, Faustina H. *Edward Hodges*. New York and London: Putnam, 1896.

Homes, Nathaniel. *Gospel Musick:* "The Singing of Davids Psalms etc. in the Publick Congregations, or Private families Asserted, and Vindicated, Against a Printed Pamphlet." London: H. Overton, 1644.

Hood, George. *History of Music in New England*. Boston: Wilkins, Carter, 1846.

Horn, Dorothy D. *Sing to Me of Heaven*. Gainesville: University of Florida Press, 1970.

Hostetler, Lester. *Handbook to the Mennonite Hymnary*. Newton, Kan.: Board of Publications of the General Conference of the Mennonite Church of North America, 1940.

A Hundred Years of Music in America. W. S. B. Mathews, asst. ed. Chicago: G. L. Howe, 1889.

The Hymnal: 1940 Companion. New York: The Church Pension Fund, 1949.

The Hymns of Frank Mason North. New York: Hymn Society of America, 1970.

Jackson, George P. *Another Sheaf of White Spirituals*. Gainesville: University of Florida Press, 1952.

——*Down-East Spirituals and Others*. Locust Valley, N.Y.: J. J. Augustin, 1939.

——*Spiritual Folk-Songs of Early America*. Locust Valley, N.Y.: J. J. Augustin, 1937.

——*White and Negro Spirituals*. Locust Valley, N.Y.: J. J. Augustin, 1943.

——*White Spirituals in the Southern Uplands*. Hatboro, Pa.: Folklore Associates, 1964.

Jantz, Harold S. "The First Century of New England Verse," *Proceedings of the American Antiquarian Society*, 53 (1944), 219–523.

Johnson, H. Earle. *Musical Interludes in Boston, 1795–1830*. New York: Columbia University Press, 1943.

Jones, F. O. *A Handbook of American Music and Musicians*. Buffalo, N.Y.: C. W. Moulton, 1887.

Julian, John. *A Dictionary of Hymnology*, 2 vols. 1st ed. 1892; rpt. New York: Dover, 1957.

Kerr, Phil. *Music in Evangelism.* Glendale, Calif.: Gospel Music Publishers, 1939.

Knauff, Christopher W. *Doctor Tucker; Priest-Musician.* New York: A. D. F. Randolph, 1897.

Kouwenhoven, John A. "Some Unfamiliar Aspects of Singing in New England," *New England Quarterly,* 6 (September 1933), 567–88.

Liemohn, Edwin. *The Chorale through Four Hundred Years of Musical Development as a Congregational Hymn.* Philadelphia: Muhlenberg Press, 1953.

Lightwood, James T. *Hymn Tunes and Their Story.* London: Epworth Press, 1923.

——*The Music of the Methodist Hymn-Book.* London: Epworth Press, 1935.

Livingston, Neil, ed. *The Scottish Metrical Psalter of A.D. 1635, Reprinted in Full from the Original Work: Dissertations, Notes, and Facsimiles.* Glasgow: Maclure and Macdonald, 1864.

Lowens, Irving. "The Bay Psalm Book in 17th-Century New England," *Journal of the American Musicological Society,* 8 (Spring 1955), 22–29.

——"Daniel Read's World," *Music Library Association Notes* (March 1952), pp. 233–48.

——*Music and Musicians in Early America.* New York: Norton, 1964.

——"The Origins of the American Fuguing Tune," *Journal of the American Musicological Society,* 6 (Spring 1953), 43–52.

Lowens, Irving and Allen P. Britton. "The Easy Instructor (1798–1831): A History and Bibliography of the First Shape Note Tune Book," *Journal of Research in Music Education* (Spring 1953), pp. 30–55.

McConnell, Cecilio. *La historia del himno en Castellano.* El Paso, Texas: Casa Bautista de Publicaciones, 1963.

McCutchan, Robert G. "American Church Composers of the Early Nineteenth Century," *Church History* (September 1933).

McCutchan, Robert G. *Hymn Tune Names.* New York and Nashville: Abingdon Press, 1957.

—— *Our Hymnody: A Manual of the Methodist Hymnal.* New York: Methodist Book Concern, 1937.

MacDougal, Hamilton C. *Early New England Psalmody: An Historical Appreciation.* Brattleboro, Vt.: Stephen Day Press, 1940.

McKissick, Marvin. "The Function of Music in American Revivalism since 1875." *The Hymn,* 9 (October 1958), 107–17.

Mainzer, Joseph. *Gaelic Psalm Tunes of Ross-shire and the Neghboring Counties.* Edinburgh: J. Johnstone, 1844.

Mangler, Joyce E. "Andrew Law, Class of 1775: The Contribution of a Musical Reformer." *Books at Brown,* 18 (January 1957), 60–67, 77.

Mangler, Joyce E. "Andrew Law: Musical Reformer." M.A. thesis, Brown University, 1956.

—— "Early Music in Rhode Island Churches." I. "Music in the First Congregational Church, Providence, 1770–1850." *Rhode Island History*, 17 (January 1958), 1–9.

Marsh, J. B. T. *The Story of the Jubilee Singers*. Boston: Houghton, Osgood, 1880.

Mason, Henry L. *Hymn-Tunes of Lowell Mason: A Bibliography*. Cambridge, Mass.: Harvard University Press, 1944.

Mayhew, Experience. "Narratives of the Lives of Pious Indian Children." Boston: printed for Samuel Gerrish, bookseller, 1787.

Messiter, Arthur H. *A History of the Choir and Music of Trinity Church, New York*. New York: E. S. Gorham, 1906.

Metcalf, Frank J. *American Psalmody; or, Titles of Books Containing Tunes Printed in America from 1721 to 1820*. New York: Da Capo Press, 1968.

—— *American Writers and Compilers of Sacred Music*. New York: Russell & Russell, 1967.

—— *Stories of Hymn Tunes*. New York and Nashville: Abingdon Press, 1928.

Middleton, J. E. *The First Canadian Christmas Carol, by Father Jean de Brebeuf*. Toronto, 1927.

Murphy, Henry C. *Anthology of New Netherlands*, 1865.

Nelson, Carl L. "The Sacred Music of the Swedish Immigrants." In *The Swedish Immigrant Community in Transition: Essays in Honor of Dr. Conrad Bergendoff*. Rock Island, Ill.: Augustana Historical Society, 1963.

Ninde, Edward S. *The Story of the American Hymn*. New York and Cincinnati: Abingdon Press, 1921.

Nutter, Charles S. and Wilbur F. Tillett. *The Hymns and Hymn Writers of the Church*. New York and Cincinnati: Methodist Book Concern, 1911.

Otis, Philo A. *The Hymns You Ought To Know*. Chicago: Clayton F. Summy, 1928.

Patrick, Millar. *Four Centuries of Scottish Psalmody*. London: Oxford University Press, 1949.

Phillips, Philip. *Around the World, Richly Illustrating a Tour throughout Twenty Countries with Philip Phillips*. New York: Phillips, 1887.

Pichieri, Louis. *Music in New Hampshire, 1623–1800*. New York: Columbia University Press, 1960.

Pierce, Edwin H. "The Rise and Fall of the 'Fugue-Tune," *Musical Quarterly*, 16 (1930), 214.

Pierik, Marie. *When the People Sang*. Boston: McLaughlin & Reilly, 1949.

Place, Charles A. *The Early Forms of Worship in North America*. Worcester, Mass.: American Antiquarian Society, 1930.

Polack, W. G. *Handbook to the Lutheran Hymnal.* St. Louis: Concordia, 1942.

Pratt, Waldo S. *The Music of the French Psalter of 1562.* New York: Columbia University Press, 1939.

—— *The Music of the Pilgrims.* Boston: Oliver Ditson, 1921.

Price, Carl F. *The Music and Hymnody of the Methodist Hymnal.* New York and Cincinnati: Methodist Book Concern, 1911.

Putnam, Alfred P. *Singers and Songs of the Liberal Faith.* Boston: Roberts, 1875.

Renstrom, A. G. "The Earliest Swedish Imprints in the United States," *Papers of the Bibliographic Society of America,* 39 (1945), 181–91.

Reynolds, William J. *Hymns of Our Faith: A Handbook for the Baptist Hymnal.* Nashville: Broadman Press, 1964.

—— *A Survey of Christian Hymnody.* New York: Holt, Rinehart and Winston, 1963.

Rich, Arthur L. *Lowell Mason.* Chapel Hill: University of North Carolina Press, 1946.

Ritter, Frederic L. *Music in America.* New York: Scribner, 1883.

Robinson, Charles S. *Annotations upon Popular Hymns.* New York: Hunt Eaton, 1893.

Rodeheaver, Homer. *Hymnal and Handbook for Standard Hymns and Gospel Songs.* Chicago and Philadelphia: Rodeheaver, 1931.

Rogers, Kirby. *An Index to Maurice Frost's English and Scottish Psalm and Hymn Tunes.* (MLA Index Series, No. 8.) Ann Arbor, Mich.: Edwards, 1967.

Ronander, Albert C., and Ethel K. Porter. *Guide to the Pilgrim Hymnal.* Philadelphia: United Church Press, 1966.

Routley, Erik. *The Church and Music.* Rev. ed. London: Gerald Duckworth, 1967.

Ryden, Ernest E. *The Story of Christian Hymnody.* Rock Island, Ill.: Augustana, 1961.

—— *The Story of Our Hymns.* Rock Island, Ill.: Augustana, 1930.

Sachse, Julius F. *The Music of the Ephrata Cloister.* Lancaster, Pa.: author, 1903.

Sankey, Ira D. *My Life and the Story of the Gospel Hymns.* New York: Harper, 1907.

Schalk, Carl. *The Roots of Hymnody in the Lutheran Church—Missouri Synod.* Church Music Pamphlet Series: Hymnology, No. 2. St. Louis: Concordia, 1965.

Scholes, Percy A. *The Puritans and Music in England and New England.* London: Oxford University Press, 1934.

—— "The Truth about the New England Puritans and Music," *Musical Quarterly,* 19 (1933), 1.

Seeger, Charles. "Contrapuntal Style in the Three-Voice Shape-Note Hymns," *Musical Quarterly,* 24 (1940), 483–93.

Seipt, Allen Anders. *Schwenkfelder Hymnology and the Sources of the First Schwenkfelder Hymn-Book Printed in America.* Philadelphia: Americana Germanica Press, 1909.

Sewall, Samuel. *Diary.* 3 vols. Boston: Massachusetts Historical Society, 1879–82.

Simions, M. Laird, ed. *Evenings with Moody and Sankey.* Philadelphia: Porter and Coates, 1877.

Sonneck, O. G. *Francis Hopkinson: The First American Poet-Composer (1737–1791)* and *James Lyon: Patriot, Preacher, Psalmodist (1735–1794).* Washington, D.C.: printed for the author, 1905.

Standish, L. W. *The Old Stoughton Musical Society: An Historical and Informative Record of the Oldest Choral Society in America.* Stoughton, Mass.: Stoughton, 1929.

Statler, Ruth B. *Handbook on Brethren Hymns.* Elgin, Ill.: Brethren Press, 1959.

Stebbins, George C. *Reminiscences and Gospel Hymn Stories.* New York: George H. Doran, 1924.

Stevenson, Arthur L. *The Story of Southern Hymnology.* Roanoke, Va.: Stone, 1931.

Stoudt, John J. *Pennsylvania German Poetry.* Allentown: Pennsylvania German Folklore Society, 1956.

Symmes, Thomas. "The Reasonableness of Regular Singing, or, Singing by Note; in an Essay, To Revive the True and Ancient Mode of Singing Psalm-Tunes According to the Pattern in Our New England Psalm-Books; the Knowledge and Practice of which Is Greatly Decay'd in Most Congregations." Boston: printed by B. Green for Samuel Gerrish and sold at his shop, 1720.

Taylor, Erich A. O'D. "Music in Newport, 1733," *New American Church Monthly,* 45 (January 1939), 26–31.

Terry, Richard, ed. *Calvin's First Psalter.* London: Ernest Benn, 1932.

Terry, Richard. *A Forgotten Psalter and Other Essays.* London: Oxford University Press, 1929. (See the opening essay on the Scottish psalter of 1635.)

—— *On Music's Borders.* London: T. Fisher Unwin, 1927. (See ch. 36: "The Obsession of the Hymn-Tune.")

Thacher, Peter. "An Essay Preached by Several Ministers of the Gospel, for the Satisfaction of Their Pious And Conscientious Brethren, as to Sundry Questions and Cases of Conscience, Concerning the Singing of Psalms." Boston: printed by S. Kneeland for Samuel Gerrish and sold at his shop, 1723.

Wheelwright, D. Sterling. "The Role of Hymnody in the Development of the Mormon Movement." Diss., University of Maryland, 1943.

Whitlock, Virginia M. "Music in the Mormon Church during the Sojourn in Nauvoo." M.A. thesis, University of Iowa, 1940.

Williams, George W. "Charleston Church Music, 1652–1833," *Journal of the American Musicological Society,* 7 (Spring 1954), 35–40.

—— "Eighteenth-Century Organists of St. Michael's, Charleston," *South Carolina Historical Magazine,* 53 (July 1952), 146–54; 212–22.

Williams, Henry L. "The Development of the Moravian Hymnal," *Transactions of the Moravian Historical Society.* Nazareth, Pa., 18, Pt. 2 (1962).

Willis, Richard Storrs. *Our Church Music.* New York: Dana, 1856.

Winslow, Ola E. "Victory in the 'Singing Seats,' " *New England Galaxy,* 3 (Spring 1962), 3–14.

Yoder, Don. *Pennsylvania Spirituals.* Lancaster: Pennsylvania Folklife Society, 1961.

—— "Spirituals from the Pennsylvania Dutch Country," *Pennsylvania Dutchman,* 8 (Fall/Winter 1956/57), 22–33.

Zahn, Johannes. *Die Melodien der deutschen evangelischen Kirchenlieder.* 6 vols. Hildesheim: G. Olms, 1963.